THE Which? Guide to Country Pubs

THE Which? Guide to Country Pubs

EDITED BY **DAVID MABEY**

CONSUMERS' ASSOCIATION

Which? Books are commissioned and researched by
Consumers' Association and published by
Which? Ltd, 2 Marylebone Road,
London NW1 4DF

Distributed by The Penguin Group:
Penguin Books Ltd, 27 Wrights Lane,
London W8 5TZ

British Library Cataloguing in Publication Data
A catalogue record for this book is
available from the British Library

ISBN 0 85202 650 1

For a full list of Which? books, please write to:
Which? Books, Castlemead, Gascoyne Way,
Hertford X, SG14 1LH

Cover photograph by John Parker
Cover and typographic design by Paul Saunders

Typeset by Saxon Graphics Ltd, Derby
Printed and bound in England by Clays Ltd, St Ives plc

CONTENTS

How to use the *Guide* p 7
The top-rated pubs p 10
Beer awards p 12
Wine awards p 14
Introduction p 17

ENGLAND p 23

SCOTLAND p 435

WALES p 467

ISLE OF MAN p 505

OUT AND ABOUT p 509

Index of main entries p 567
Report forms pp 585 and 617
Maps p 593

How to use the *Guide*

The *Guide* is divided into two parts. At the front (from page 23) is the main section, which lists country pubs throughout Britain selected for the quality of their food, drink and atmosphere; the selections are based on reports from the general public backed up by independent inspections. Towards the back you will find 'Out and about', which features more than 300 additional pubs that are well worth a visit.

Layout
Both parts of the *Guide* are further divided into the following sections: England, Scotland, Wales and the Isle of Man. Pubs are listed alphabetically by location; they are put in their true *geographical* location, rather than at their postal address.

If a pub is difficult to find, directions are given (under the address and telephone number). It is always worth checking by telephone if you are unsure about the exact location of an out-of-the-way pub.

How to find a pub in a particular area
Go to the full-colour maps at the back at the book and choose the general area that you want. Towns and villages where pubs in the Guide are located are marked with a tankard symbol; turn to that location in the appropriate section of the book, where you will find details of the pub (or pubs) there.

Awards
denotes a pub where the quality of the bar food is comparable to that of a 'serious' restaurant – i.e. ingredients are consistently first-class and imagination and style are hallmarks of the kitchen. See page 10 for list of top-rated pubs.

signifies that the pub offers superior bar food backed up by all-round excellence in areas such as service, cleanliness and atmosphere. See pages 10–11 for list.

denotes a pub serving exceptional draught beers. See pages 12–13 for list.

indicates a pub serving better-than-average wines. See pages 14–15 for list.

◆ in the 'Out and about' section singles out pubs that are considered a cut above the rest.

Other symbols in entries
▲ indicates a main-entry pub which offers accommodation.

'Flashes' **VIEWS**

These highlight a particular point of interest in selected main entries, such as 'puddings', 'views' or 'haunted'.

Sample dishes
These are listed at the end of each main entry and are examples of typical dishes from the menu. Prices are based on figures provided by the pub licensee; in most cases, prices have been rounded up to the nearest 25 pence. Note that items listed may not always be available (particularly if they are 'specials').

Food and drink
Details of bar food mentioned in the entries are based on official inspection reports, notes from readers and information provided by the licensees. Many pubs vary their menus from day to day, so specific items may no longer be in the kitchen's repertoire. Dishes on separate restaurant menus – if not available in the bar – are not described in the entries.

Similarly, the range of draught beers may differ from time to time, especially if a pub has guest brews.

Information about wine is geared to what is generally available in the bar, rather than in a separate restaurant if there is one. House wines, 'wines of the month' and bin ends can vary from time to time.

Opening hours and other details
The information given in the italics section at the end of each entry has been supplied by the pub and may be subject to change. If you are making a special journey, it is always worth while phoning beforehand to check opening and bar food times, and any other details that are important to you, such as restrictions on children or dogs, wheelchair access, etc.

- 'Open' times: these are the pub's full licensing hours. Opening times may vary, especially in pubs that rely heavily on seasonal trade; many places also have different opening hours over Christmas and bank holidays.
- Bar food (and restaurant) times: these denote when food is served in the bar (and restaurant, if there is one – although, as noted above, details of bar food only are given in the entries). L and D are sometimes used to indicated lunch and dinner, to avoid confusion.

- Children: if children are welcome inside the pub, this is stated; any restrictions on children are noted.
- Car park: if a pub has its own car park, this is listed. If parking is a problem or there are any unusual circumstances, this is normally mentioned in the text.
- Wheelchair access: this means that the proprietor has confirmed that the entrance to the bar/dining-room is at least 80cm wide and passages at least 120cm across – the Royal Association for Disability and Rehabilitation (RADAR) recommendations. If 'also WC' is given, it means that the proprietor has told us that the toilet facilities are suitable for disabled people.
- Garden/patio: details are based on information provided by the licensee. If a pub has a children's play area or any other interesting feature – e.g. a boules pitch – this is mentioned in the text.
- Smoking: restrictions on smoking or special areas designated for non-smokers are noted.
- Music: if background or live music is ever played, or if a pub has a jukebox, this is stated; otherwise 'no music' is noted.
- Dogs: any restrictions on dogs *inside* the pub are listed. Most pubs will allow dogs in their gardens. Guide dogs are normally exempt from restrictions, although it is best to check beforehand if you have special requirements.
- Cards: major credit cards, Delta and Switch are listed if a pub accepts these as a means of payment. If a pub does not accept cards, we note this.
- Accommodation: if a pub offers overnight accommodation, the number of bedrooms and a range of B&B prices – from the lowest you can expect to pay for a single room (or single occupancy of a twin/double) to the most you are likely to pay for a twin/double – are listed. Pub bedrooms have not been officially inspected for this guide. Additional accommodation – e.g. in a self-catering cottage – is normally mentioned in the text.

Report forms

At the back of the book are report forms which you may use to recount your experiences in the pubs already featured in this *Guide*, or in other pubs which you think should be included. The address is freepost, so no stamp is necessary (full details on the report forms). Because *The Which? Guide to Country Pubs*, like its sister publication *The Good Food Guide*, relies to a great extent on unsolicited feedback from readers, your comments are invaluable to us and will form a major part of our research when we prepare future editions.

The top-rated pubs

✿✿ indicates a pub where the quality of the bar food is comparable to that of a 'serious' restaurant – i.e. ingredients are consistently first-class and imagination and style are hallmarks of the kitchen.

ENGLAND
Cambridgeshire
Three Horseshoes, Madingley
Cumbria
Punch Bowl Inn, Crosthwaite
Devon
Drewe Arms, Broadhembury
Essex
White Hart, Great Yeldham
Greater Manchester
White Hart, Lydgate
Hereford & Worcester
Riverside Inn, Aymestrey
Roebuck, Brimfield
North Yorkshire
Angel Inn, Hetton
Blue Lion, East Witton
Crab & Lobster, Asenby
Plough Inn, Saxton
Oxfordshire
Bear & Ragged Staff, Cumnor
Clanfield Tavern, Clanfield
Sir Charles Napier Inn, Chinnor
Suffolk
Angel Inn, Stoke-by-Nayland
White Hart, Nayland
West Sussex
Crabtree, Lower Beeding
Wiltshire
George & Dragon, Rowde

WALES
Powys
Nantyffin Cider Mill Inn, Crickhowell

✿ indicates a pub offering superior bar food backed up by all-round excellence in areas such as service, cleanliness and atmosphere.

ENGLAND
Berkshire
Dundas Arms, Kintbury
Royal Oak, Yattendon
Water Rat, Marsh Benham
Buckinghamshire
Angel Inn, Long Crendon
Five Arrows Hotel, Waddesdon
Rising Sun, Little Hampden
Walnut Tree, Fawley
Cambridgeshire
Anchor Inn, Sutton Gault
Pheasant Inn, Keyston
Cheshire
Alvanley Arms, Cotebrook
Co Durham
Rose and Crown, Romaldkirk
Cornwall
Springer Spaniel, Treburley
Trengilly Wartha Inn, Nancenoy
Cumbria
Bay Horse Inn, Ulverston
Snooty Fox, Kirkby Lonsdale
Derbyshire
Waltzing Weasel, Birch Vale
Devon
Arundell Arms, Lifton
Cott Inn, Dartington
Cridford Inn, Trusham
Jack in the Green, Rockbeare
Nobody Inn, Doddiscombsleigh
Dorset
Fox Inn, Corscombe
Three Horseshoes, Powerstock
East Sussex
Griffin Inn, Fletching
Essex
Bell Inn, Horndon on the Hill
Bull Inn, Blackmore End

Gloucestershire
Fox Inn, Lower Oddington
New Inn, Coln St Aldwyns
Greater Manchester
Devonshire Arms, Mellor
Hampshire
Red House, Whitchurch
Hereford & Worcester
Sun Inn, Winforton
Talbot Hotel, Knightwick
Kent
Harrow Inn, Ightham
Plough, Stalisfield Green
Lancashire
Bushell's Arms, Goosnargh
Leicestershire
Peacock Inn, Redmile
Lincolnshire
Chequers, Gedney Dyke
Norfolk
Hoste Arms, Burnham Market
Wildebeest Arms, Stoke Holy Cross
Northamptonshire
Bell, Little Addington
Northumberland
Cook and Barker Inn, Newton-on-the-Moor
Manor House Inn, Carterway Heads
North Yorkshire
Black Bull Inn, Moulton
Foresters Arms, Carlton
Sportsman's Arms, Wath-in-Nidderdale
Star Inn, Harome
Wombwell Arms, Wass
Nottinghamshire
Martins Arms, Colston Bassett
Oxfordshire
Blewbury Inn, Blewbury
Boar's Head, Ardington
Crooked Billet, Stoke Row
George Hotel, Dorchester-on-Thames
Lamb Inn, Buckland
Merry Miller, Cothill
Vine Inn, Cumnor
Shropshire
Feathers, Brockton
Hundred House Hotel, Norton
Somerset
Crown Hotel, Exford
Woolpack, Beckington
Suffolk
Beehive, Horringer
Crown Inn, Snape
Star Inn, Lidgate
West Sussex
White Horse Inn, Chilgrove
West Yorkshire
Butchers Arms, Hepworth
Olive Branch, Marsden
Wiltshire
Three Crowns, Brinkworth

SCOTLAND
Argyll & Bute
Kilberry Inn, Kilberry
Borders
Wheatsheaf Hotel, Swinton
Dumfries & Galloway
Riverside Inn, Canonbie

WALES
Cardiff
Caesar's Arms, Creigiau
Conwy
Queen's Head, Glanwydden
Gwynedd
Penhelig Arms Hotel, Aberdovey
Monmouthshire
Clytha Arms, Clytha
Pembrokeshire
Tafarn Newydd, Rosebush
Powys
Bear Hotel, Crickhowell
Griffin Inn, Llyswen
Red Lion Inn, LLanfihangel nant Melan

Pubs serving exceptional draught beers

Most pubs in the *Guide* serve acceptable real ales. This list includes establishments which are making a special effort in that direction. In all of them the quality of draught beers is exceptional, and this is backed up by knowledgeable cellar work. We have also taken into account the range of styles and strengths available. Pubs that support independent local and regional country breweries have been given preference.

ENGLAND
Bath & N. E. Somerset
Hope & Anchor Inn, Midford
Bedfordshire
Three Cranes, Turvey
Berkshire
Bell Inn, Aldworth
Pot Kiln, Frilsham
Buckinghamshire
Five Arrows Hotel, Waddesdon
Red Lion, Chenies
Cambridgeshire
The Kings, Reach
Cheshire
Leather's Smithy, Langley
Cornwall
Halzephron Inn, Gunwalloe
Rising Sun, Gunnislake
Royal Oak, Lostwithiel
Trengilly Wartha Inn, Nancenoy
Cumbria
Abbey Bridge, Lanercost
Bay Horse Inn, Ulverston
Drunken Duck Inn, Ambleside
Masons Arms, Cartmel Fell
Punch Bowl Inn, Crosthwaite
Royal Oak Inn, Appleby
Shepherds Inn, Melmerby
Queens Head Hotel, Troutbeck
White Horse Inn, Scales
Derbyshire
Three Stags Heads, Wardlow Mires
White Horse Inn, Woolley Moor
Devon
Church House Inn, Holne
Cridford Inn, Trusham
Drewe Arms, Broadhembury
Masons Arms, Branscombe
Masons Arms Inn, Knowstone
New Inn, Coleford
Nobody Inn, Doddiscombsleigh
Peter Tavy Inn, Peter Tavy
Tally Ho, Hatherleigh
Tower Inn, Slapton
Waterman's Arms, Ashprington
Dorset
Fox Inn, Corscombe
Langton Arms, Tarrant Monkton
Roebuck, Sixpenny Handley
East Sussex
Griffin Inn, Fletching
Ram Inn, Firle
Ypres Inn, Rye
Essex
Cap & Feathers, Tillingham
Cricketers Arms, Rickling Green
Queens Head Inn, Littlebury
Gloucestershire
Crown Inn, Blockley
Farmer's Arms, Apperley
Fox Inn, Lower Oddington
Kings Head, Bledington
Ostrich Inn, Newland
Greater Manchester
Navigation Inn, Dobcross
Hampshire
Coach and Horses, Rotherwick
Five Bells, Buriton
Flower Pots Inn, Cheriton
George Inn, St Mary Bourne
Old Beams Inn, Ibsley
Peat Spade Inn, Longstock
Red House, Whitchurch
Sun, Bentworth
White Horse Inn, Priors Dean
Yew Tree Inn, Lower Wield
Hereford & Worcester
Pandy Inn, Dorstone
Riverside Inn, Aymestrey
Sun Inn, Winforton
Hertfordshire
Fox & Hounds, Barley
Lytton Arms, Knebworth
Kent
Bell, Smarden
Black Bull, Cliffe
Cliffe Tavern, St Margaret's at Cliffe
Dering Arms, Pluckley
Little Brown Jug, Chiddingstone Causeway
Ringlestone Inn, Harrietsham
Three Chimneys, Biddenden
Leicestershire
Black Horse, Walcote
Crown Inn, Old Dalby
Old Barn Inn, Glooston
Norfolk
Fishermans Return, Winterton-on-Sea
Red Lion, Stiffkey
Three Horseshoes, Warham All Saints
Northamptonshire
Falcon Inn, Fotheringhay

Olde Coach House Inn, Ashby St Ledgers
Queens Head, Sutton Bassett
Snooty Fox, Lowick
Northumberland
Dipton Mill, Hexham
Manor House Inn, Carterway Heads
North Yorkshire
Malt Shovel, Brearton
Old Bridge Inn, Ripponden
Plough Inn, Saxton
Wombwell Arms, Wass
Nottinghamshire
Cross Keys, Upton
Martins Arms, Colston Bassett
Oxfordshire
Plough, Finstock
Roebuck Inn, North Newington
Shropshire
Crown, Munslow
George & Dragon, Much Wenlock
Hundred House Hotel, Norton
Red Lion, Llanfair Waterdine
Somerset
Crossways Inn, West Huntspill
Fitzhead Inn, Fitzhead
Greyhound Inn, Staple Fitzpaine
Horse & Groom, East Woodlands
Royal Oak of Luxborough, Luxborough
Westbury Inn, Westbury-sub-Mendip
White Horse, Stogumber
Suffolk
Angel, Lavenham
Crown, Westleton
White Hart, Boxford
Surrey
Plough Inn, Coldharbour
Warwickshire
Blue Boar, Temple Grafton
Fox & Hounds Inn, Great Wolford
West Sussex
Cricketers, Duncton
Elsted Inn, Elsted Marsh
George and Dragon, Burpham
Halfway Bridge Inn, Halfway Bridge
Hare & Hounds, Stoughton
Three Horseshoes, Elsted
West Yorkshire
Old Bridge Inn, Ripponden
Wiltshire
Harrow Inn, Little Bedwyn
Horse and Groom, Charlton
White Hart, Ford

SCOTLAND
Borders
Craw Inn, Auchencrow
Traquair Arms, Innerleithen
Dumfries & Galloway
Riverside Inn, Canonbie
East Lothian
Waterside, Haddington
Fife
Ship Inn, Limekilns
Perthshire & Kinross
Tormaukin Hotel, Glendevon
Stirling
Clachan Inn, Drymen
Lade Inn, Kilmahog

WALES
Gwynedd
Cwellyn Arms, Rhyd-ddu
Grapes Hotel, Maentwrog
Harp Inn, Llandwrog
Monmouthshire
Boat Inn, Penallt
Carpenters Arms, Shirenewton
Clytha Arms, Clytha
Red Hart, Llanvapley
Pembrokeshire
Armstrong Arms, Stackpole
Carew Inn, Carew
Tafarn Newydd, Rosebush
Powys
Bell Inn, Llanyre
Nantyffin Cider Mill Inn, Crickhowell
Neath Port Talbot
Butchers Arms, Alltwen
Vale of Glamorgan
Blue Anchor Inn, East Aberthaw
Wrexham
Boat Inn, Erbistock

ISLE OF MAN
Creek Inn, Peel

Pubs serving better-than-average wine 🍇

This award goes to pubs offering better-than-average wines – especially in the bar. In particular, we have looked at the quality of house wines, the range and selection of different bottles available, how they are kept and served, and the price. We also have taken into account the make-up of the full wine list, as well as the choice of suppliers and merchants.

ENGLAND
Bath & N. E. Somerset
Carpenters Arms, Stanton Wick
Bedfordshire
Knife & Cleaver, Houghton Conquest
Berkshire
Bird in Hand, Knowl Hill
Dundas Arms, Kintbury
Fish, Bray
Royal Oak, Yattendon
Buckinghamshire
Angel Inn, Long Crendon
Annie Bailey's, Cuddington
Five Arrows Hotel, Waddesdon
Pheasant, Ballinger Common
Rising Sun, Little Hampden
Walnut Tree, Fawley
Cambridgeshire
Anchor Inn, Sutton Gault
Chequers, Fowlmere
Red Lion, Kirtling
Pheasant Inn, Keyston
Queen's Head, Kirtling
Three Horseshoes, Madingley
Cheshire
Cholmondeley Arms, Cholmondeley
Co Durham
Duke of York, Fir Tree
Fox and Hounds, Cotherstone
Morritt Arms, Greta Bridge
Rose and Crown, Romaldkirk
Cornwall
Halzephron Inn, Gunwalloe
Pandora Inn, Mylor Bridge
Trengilly Wartha Inn, Nancenoy
Cumbria
Bay Horse Inn, Ulverston
Punch Bowl Inn, Crosthwaite
Queens Head Hotel, Troutbeck
Royal Oak Inn, Appleby
Snooty Fox, Kirkby Lonsdale
Derbyshire
Waltzing Weasel, Birch Vale
White Horse Inn, Woolley Moor
Devon
Arundell Arms, Lifton
Cott Inn, Dartington
Cridford Inn, Trusham
Drewe Arms, Broadhembury
Half Moon Inn, Sheepwash
Jack in the Green, Rockbeare
Kings Arms Inn, Stockland
Masons Arms, Branscombe
Masons Arms Inn, Knowstone
New Inn, Coleford
Nobody Inn, Doddiscombsleigh
Old Rydon Inn, Kingsteignton
Dorset
Fox Inn, Corscombe
Manor Hotel, West Bexington
Three Horseshoes, Powerstock
East Sussex
Griffin Inn, Fletching
Essex
Bell Inn, Horndon on the Hill
Bull Inn, Blackmore End
Cricketers Arms, Rickling Green
White Hart, Great Yeldham
Greater Manchester
White Hart, Lydgate
Gloucestershire
Crown Inn, Blockley
Fox Inn, Lower Oddington
Kings Head, Bledington
New Inn, Coln St Aldwyns
Ostrich Inn, Newland
Wyndham Arms, Clearwell
Hampshire
Fox Inn, Bramdean
Fox Inn, Tangley
George Inn, St Mary Bourne
Peat Spade Inn, Longstock
Red House, Whitchurch
Rose & Thistle, Rockbourne
Hereford & Worcester
Rhydspence Inn, Whitney
Roebuck, Brimfield
Sun Inn, Winforton
Talbot Hotel, Knightwick
Ye Olde Salutation Inn, Weobley
Hertfordshire
George & Dragon, Watton-at-Stone
Isle of Wight
Seaview Hotel, Seaview
Kent
Bottle House Inn, Smart's Hill
Castle Inn, Chiddingstone
Hare, Langton Green
Plough, Stalisfield Green
Lancashire
Bushell's Arms, Goosnargh
Hark to Bounty, Slaidburn
Inn at Whitewell, Whitewell
New Inn, Yealand Conyers
Leicestershire
Blue Ball Inn, Braunston

Old Barn Inn, Glooston
Peacock Inn, Redmile
Lincolnshire
Chequers, Gedney Dyke
Norfolk
Hoste Arms, Burnham Market
Ratcatchers Inn, Eastgate
Rose & Crown, Snettisham
Saracen's Head, Wolterton
White Horse Hotel, Blakeney
Wildebeest Arms, Stoke Holy Cross
Northamptonshire
Bell, Little Addington
Falcon Inn, Fotheringhay
Olde Coach House Inn, Ashby St Ledgers
Queens Head, Sutton Bassett
Northumberland
General Havelock Inn, Haydon Bridge
Manor House Inn, Carterway Heads
North Yorkshire
Angel Inn, Hetton
Black Bull Inn, Moulton
Blue Lion, East Witton
Crab & Lobster, Asenby
Fauconberg Arms, Coxwold
Foresters Arms, Carlton
General Tarleton, Ferrensby
Nags Head, Pickhill
Old Bridge Inn, Ripponden
Plough Inn, Saxton
Sportsman's Arms, Wath-in-Nidderdale
Star Inn, Harome
Three Hares, Bilbrough
White Swan, Pickering
Wombwell Arms, Wass
Nottinghamshire
Martins Arms, Colston Bassett
Oxfordshire
Abingdon Arms, Beckley
Bear & Ragged Staff, Cumnor
Blewbury Inn, Blewbury
Blue Boar Inn, Longworth
Clanfield Tavern, Clanfield
George Hotel, Dorchester-on-Thames
Lamb Inn, Buckland
Merry Miller, Cothill
Perch & Pike Inn, South Stoke
Red Lion, Steeple Aston
Roebuck Inn, North Newington
Sir Charles Napier Inn, Chinnor
Tite Inn, Chadlington
Vine Inn, Cumnor
Shropshire
Bradford Arms, Llanymynech
Crown Inn, Hopton Wafers
Hundred House Hotel, Norton
Somerset
Bell Inn, Buckland Dinham
Crown Hotel, Exford
Kings Arms Inn, Montacute
Rising Sun, Knapp
Suffolk
Angel, Lavenham
Angel Inn, Stoke-by-Nayland
Beehive, Horringer
Crown, Westleton
Crown Inn, Snape
Ship Inn, Dunwich
Six Bells, Bardwell
White Hart, Nayland
Surrey
Brickmakers Arms, Windlesham
Warwickshire
Blue Boar, Temple Grafton
Red Lion, Little Compton
West Sussex
Crabtree, Lower Beeding
George and Dragon, Burpham
Horse Guards Inn, Tillington
White Horse Inn, Chilgrove
West Yorkshire
Kaye Arms, Grange Moor
Old Bridge Inn, Ripponden
Olive Branch, Marsden
Wiltshire
Bell, Ramsbury
George & Dragon, Rowde
Harrow Inn, Little Bedwyn
Silver Plough, Pitton
Three Crowns, Brinkworth
White Hart, Ford

SCOTLAND
Aberdeenshire
Lairhillock, Netherley
Argyll & Bute
Isle of Colonsay Hotel, Colonsay
Borders
Burts Hotel, Melrose
Craw Inn, Auchencrow
Wheatsheaf Hotel, Swinton
Dumfries & Galloway
Creebridge House Hotel, Minnigaff,
Riverside Inn, Canonbie
Perthshire & Kinross
Deil's Cauldron, Comrie
Tormaukin Hotel, Glendevon

WALES
Conwy
Queen's Head, Glanwydden
Gwynedd
Penhelig Arms Hotel, Aberdovey
Isle of Anglesey
Ye Olde Bulls Head Inn, Beaumaris
Monmouthshire
Clytha Arms, Clytha
Pembrokeshire
Tafarn Newydd, Rosebush
Powys
Bear Hotel, Crickhowell
Griffin Inn, Llyswen
Nantyffin Cider Mill Inn, Crickhowell
Vale of Glamorgan
Bush Inn, St Hilary

The Editor

David Mabey, a food writer, journalist and broadcaster with a special interest in British food and drink, is a regular contributor to Which? publications. He has written more than 12 books, including *Thorson's Organic Consumer Guide* and *Everything in the Larder* (BBC Books), and was co-editor of *The Budget Good Food Guide* and *The Good Food Directory* (Consumers' Association). He has been Editor of *The Which? Guide to Country Pubs* since the first edition appeared in 1993.

***Which? Guide to Country Pubs* stickers**

Owing to a change of policy at Consumers' Association, pubs that feature in the 1997 edition of the *Guide* as main entries have been provided with free stickers which they may use for display purposes. The stickers will be valid until March 1999. For the first time, too, pubs will be allowed to state the fact that they are in the current *Guide* in their advertising and promotional material. By issuing our own official stickers, we shall be bringing the achievement of the selected establishments to the notice of a wider audience. If, however, you find a pub advertising it is in the *Guide* when it is not, we would be grateful to hear from you.

Introduction

This completely new edition – the third – of *The Which? Guide to Country Pubs* recommends close to 1,000 establishments in England, Scotland, Wales and the Isle of Man. What we have sought out is the pub that is worth a special trip, not just because the beers it serves are well kept and the atmosphere is welcoming, but also because it offers something extra: an interesting selection of wines or local ciders, perhaps, or (in Scotland, maybe) specialist malt whiskies, and, above all, good food – a trend no doubt encouraged by the drink/driving laws.

Pub food is big business these days. A Mintel survey published in 1996 revealed that we spend more than £4 billion each year eating in Britain's hostelries. That is on a par with expenditure in restaurants, although it is, not surprisingly, less than we spend in fast-food outlets. 'Country' pubs make a huge contribution to the £4 billion and it is easy to see why. Pub food has improved by leaps and bounds in recent years: the combination of good quality, value for money and a refreshing lack of pretentiousness has proved a real winner with the clientele.

With the help of pub-goers, readers and inspectors (many of whom have earned their gastronomic stripes appraising restaurants for *The Good Food Guide*), we have been able to put together a selection of the very best pubs in Britain. Some of those among the main entries serve food that is often on a par with that of a 'serious' restaurant, although we are also concerned with the quality of the drink, atmosphere and the general facilities on offer. At its best, the country pub offers an irresistible experience.

Research and inspections for this edition of the *Guide* have highlighted a definite shift in the centres of regional excellence. The West Country, for so long the heartland of good country pubs serving good food, has been blighted by over-exposure, too much reliance on seasonal trade and a hefty dose of 'resting on laurels'. By contrast, other areas are waxing strongly: East Anglia, the Midland shires, Yorkshire and Lancashire, for example, have all yielded some splendid discoveries, and this is reflected not only in the number of entries included for each area, but also in the number of 'rosette' winners (see page 10 for a list of the 'Top-rated pubs').

Identity crisis?

As pub food becomes more ambitious and more sophisticated, with 'chefs' beginning to take over from 'cooks' in a number of country-pub kitchens, the debate over just what constitutes a pub gets ever more heated. One lobby believes fervently that pubs should be pubs, not restaurants in disguise. The *Guide* favours a more open-minded approach. Great country pubs thrive on diversity and their ability to adapt to the mood of the times. That is surely one key to their long-term survival. Of course, there is still a place for the local watering-hole where food is purely incidental: some of these splendid places are listed in the *Guide*'s 'Out and about' section starting on page 509; in this edition we have highlighted (with a diamond symbol) 'Out and about' establishments that are, for one reason or another, especially worth a visit. They represent something uniquely British: places where a spirited sense of local identity defines the mood, where the beer is good and the welcome is friendly.

As for many other places, change and consolidation continue. From our research, it is clear that Britain's country pubs are not about to be pigeonholed. Some of the new breed may seem perilously close to bar/brasseries, but most cling on doggedly to their public-house roots. A few have moved far beyond their origins; to be sure, they may serve draught beer, but their *modus operandi* and style mean that the term 'country pub' no longer describes them. Three come to mind: the Crown in Southwold, Suffolk; the Three Lions, Stuckton, Hampshire and the Fish at Sutton Courtenay, Oxfordshire don't feature in this edition of the *Guide*. This is no disparagement of the quality of the food they offer: it is just that they are no longer – in the real sense – genuine pubs; they have made the transition to fully-fledged restaurant.

Now that food is moving ever upwards on the agenda, there are also signs of modest empire-building. Some pub owners/landlords are doing what restaurateurs have been doing for a long time: they are opening sister establishments. This trend may not be on the scale of the restaurant 'empires' established by Sir Terence Conran or Antony Worrall-Thompson, but it is a significant one. Denis Watkins of the Angel Inn, Hetton, North Yorkshire recently acquired the General Tarleton at Ferrensby, while the owners of the Beehive, Horringer, Suffolk now have a second pub in Kirtling in Cambridgeshire. In East Anglia there is also the Huntsbridge Group – three pubs and a hotel under one umbrella with a distinct 'house style' but independently run by talented chefs who call most of the shots.

Links in the chain

The national brewery conglomerates are past masters at 'theming' and levelling; their formulaic food pubs and eating houses are everywhere. All that is fine if that is the sort of thing that you want, although pubs of that description do not feature in this guide.

But a new development has started to have a damaging effect on the country pub scene. A number of entrepreneurs are buying up some of England's most attractive pubs, especially those with an established reputation for good food. We looked at a number of these pubs in detail since their change of ownership and, without exception, all of them were found wanting. In some cases, the quality of the food on offer had gone perceptibly downhill since our last assessment in the previous *Guide*; in others, standards had slipped to such an extent that food was dire. Typically, troubleshooting managers move into these pubs for a few weeks, then minions take their place and the kitchens are often staffed by 'chefs' who often have no right to the name. Menus might seem promising, but the results on the plate generally tell a very different story. Pubs that once had rock-solid stature now seem to be in a permanent state of flux.

Along with the regimented food and management formula comes the interior design. What was uniquely cosy or quirkily eccentric is often quickly replaced by ever-so-neat-and-tidy furnishings and clutter culled from the pub-fitter's collective curiosity shop. It is a character-stifling exercise and one guaranteed to rip the heart and soul out of any decent hostelry.

Spilling the beans

The *Guide* continues to champion the cause of honest pub cooking and we are heartened by places that use fresh ingredients, preferably from local sources. In this edition we have highlighted pubs that are working closely with local suppliers with a 'local produce' flash. The other side of the coin is, of course, an increasingly sophisticated repertoire of ready-made dishes from the large catering and freezer companies. But alongside that trend, there is also now an ever-growing band of small cottage caterers who are beginning to make a highly persuasive specialist inroad into the catering-in-pubs trend, offering anything from balti curries to old-fashioned nursery puddings.

Even when a pub kitchen is making a laudable attempt at home-cooking with its main dishes and 'specials', too often the starters (tiger prawns in filo pastry, deep-fried Brie and so on) have been ordered from a catalogue. The appearance of a delivery lorry in the pub car park confirms the practice; otherwise, occasionally, the landlord spills the beans: 'Sorry, toad-in-the-hole isn't on, because the delivery van hasn't been yet.' At the other end of the menu, there are puddings, gâteaux and so on, many of which are produced with a certain degree of domestic finesse by up-and-coming catering outfits. Thankfully, more landlords are aware of the need to distinguish between what is home-made and bought-in, and they are prepared to own up on that score.

Vegetarians are rightly aggrieved that non-meat dishes still tend to play second fiddle even if a pub kitchen is making proper savoury pies and casseroles for carnivores. Too often a few token meatless offerings are put on as an afterthought and too often these are chosen from caterers' catalogues. How many times have you seen vegetable lasagne, mushroom and nut fettucine, or wheat and walnut casserole on a menu? (Although in some cases, these dishes will be *bona fide* home-made offerings, in too many others they are the sorts of things that arrive on the caterer's van.) The justification is usually that there is little demand for these items, and it's not worth the kitchen's time and effort to produce the real thing. However, a few pubs do make the effort to provide home-made vegetarian dishes – for example, the Bell Inn in Llanyre, Wales and the Pear Tree in Hildersham, Cambridgeshire – and when that happens the results can be a real eye-opener and a pleasure for the palate.

Children's nightmares

In the previous edition, we looked forward with a degree of hopeful anticipation to the improvements that the 'children's certificate' scheme might bring to pubs in England and Wales. The idea has proved its worth in Scotland and, judging by recent reports, it pleases both licensees and customers there. Since the scheme for England and Wales became law in February 1995, it has been a very different story south of the border.

The idea seemed simple: if a pub was deemed to have a suitable 'family atmosphere' and adequate facilities, it would be granted a certificate which would allow the landlord to cater for children under 14 if accompanied by adults – with certain provisos. In practice, however, every licensing board and local authority has had its own views and criteria on the subject. Inconsistency has been rife, and there has been an ludicrous lack of consensus across the board. No wonder many pubs haven't even bothered to apply for the certificate. Some have been content to improvise or dream up their own rules (children restricted to the 'blue-carpeted' areas, for example); others display apologetic signs pleading for good behaviour and parental restraint. The situation is shambolic. What was billed as an almost revolutionary, forward-looking scheme has been all but scuppered by inept and prohibitive bureaucracy. Consistency across licensing boards and magistrates is what is needed: flexible but well-defined rules should be put forward, and uniformly agreed to, by all bodies concerned so that pubs – and consumers – know exactly what having a children's certificate means.

Last orders

Country pubs continue to change and evolve. New issues surface, new threats to their livelihood come and go. Two major changes, one affecting the way pubs are 'tied' to breweries, the other concerning potential changes to the rules that apply to the sale of guest ales (something that European breweries have been campaigning for), are currently on hold – although sooner or later they will be up for debate. At grass-roots level, tenancies and ownerships change; companies large and small try to grab a piece of the action; chefs are head-hunted and move around. At the *Guide* we are able to monitor the big picture, but we need feedback from you, the customers, who spend money in Britain's country pubs. We are hungry for comments, hot tips, praise or damnation – all are equally valuable. If you have used the *Guide* and visited any of the pubs it recommends, do please write to tell us about your experience, good or bad. It will cost you nothing. Use one of the forms at the back of the book or simply write a letter (FREEPOST to *The Which? Guide to Country Pubs*, 2 Marylebone Road, London NW1 1YN). Every report adds to our knowledge, helps fill out the broader picture and lays the basis for the next *Guide*.

Meanwhile, many thanks to all of you who have contributed to this edition. We look forward to hearing from you again soon.

David Mabey

ENGLAND

ALCISTON East Sussex map 3

Rose Cottage

LOCAL PRODUCE

Alciston TEL: (01323) 870377
off A27, between Lewes and Polegate

A devotion to fresh local produce singles out this aptly named village pub, which has been run by the Lewis family since 1959. Landlord Ian shoots pheasants at nearby Firle and his brother-in-law brings in venison, which is braised with port and Guinness. The pub's own chickens provide eggs, while many vegetables are grown organically a few hundred yards away. In the bar you can choose from a menu that brings together old favourites such as ploughman's, honey-roast ham, and rump steak as well as wild rabbit in cream and mustard sauce, pork fillet in cider and honey, and chargrilled chicken on a skewer with toasted sweetcorn salsa. Fish specials vary from day to day, and Sunday lunches might include lamb marinated in red wine, rosemary and garlic. Real ales and wines of the month supplement Harveys Best Bitter, Merrydown bottled cider, and sparkling apple juice. At the time of writing, part of the paddock is being converted into a family room ('*no* bouncy castle or climbing frame,' insists Mr Lewis). SAMPLE DISHES: warm salad of mushrooms; bacon and avocado £3.50; Thai-style chicken curry £6; sticky toffee pudding £3.

Open *11.30 to 2.30, 6.30 to 11, Sun 12 to 2.30, 7 to 10.30; bar food 12 to 2, 7 to 10; restaurant Mon to Sat 7 to 9*
Details *Children welcome in eating areas (no children under 6 evenings) Car park Wheelchair access Garden and patio No smoking in restaurant Background music Dogs welcome Access, Delta, Switch, Visa*

ALDBURY Hertfordshire map 3

Valiant Trooper

Aldbury TEL: (01442) 851203
from A41 at Tring take right turn to Aldbury

'Backpackers with walking sticks and muddy boots tread the streets with camera-wielding sightseers,' noted one visitor to this premier-league photogenic village in excellent rambling country just off the ancient Ridgeway Path. The pub was once called the Royal Oak – it changed its name in 1803, possibly because the Duke of Wellington reputedly met his troops here to discuss tactics. There's nothing fancy about the modest bar menu, but ingredients are well chosen, and the dishes are genuinely home-made. Beyond open sandwiches, salads and omelettes you might find a high-protein mixed grill, cottage pie, Kashmir chicken and a fresh fish of the day. Desserts are redoubtable offerings like bread-and-butter pudding. A slightly more ambitious menu is served in Troopers Eating House – a converted stable block that once served as Boy Scouts' hut and local bikers' club. Two guest beers supplement regulars such as Fuller's London Pride, Bass and John Smith's; wines are sold by the glass. SAMPLE DISHES: three-cheese ploughman's £3.50; liver, bacon and onion casserole £5; fruit crumble £2.

Open *11.30 to 11, Sun 12 to 10.30; bar food all week L 12 to 2 (2.30 Sun), Mon to Sat D 6.30 to 9.15; restaurant Tue to Sun L 12 to 2, Tue to Sat D 7.30 to 10*
Details *Children welcome in eating areas Car park Wheelchair access Garden and patio No smoking in 1 bar L only No music Dogs welcome on a lead Access, Visa*

ALDERMINSTER Warwickshire **map 5**

Bell

Shipston Road, Alderminster TEL: (01789) 450414
on A3400, S of Stratford-upon-Avon

Formerly a coaching-inn on the main London to Birmingham road, the Bell now functions as an up-market bistro-cum-bar with high aspirations and eager young staff. Eat in one of the pleasantly furnished, civilised dining-rooms or in the conservatory with its views over the Stour Valley. The blackboard menu, which changes monthly, is bolstered by specials including fresh fish in the shape of, say, grilled brochette of scallops with hollandaise. Other typical offerings might run to avocado salad with Stilton dressing, crispy topped lamb casserole, and Normandy pork chops cooked with apple, spring onion and cider sauce. Reporters have also enthused about the two-course business lunches (served every weekday). Special events and theme nights are a feature of the place; otherwise Charlecote Park (National Trust) and Hidcote Manor Gardens may provide pleasant distraction. The wine list is worth exploring and guest beers such as Hook Norton Best Bitter and Wadworth 6X are put on in rotation. SAMPLE DISHES: cream of onion soup £2.75; chicken suprême with orange, honey and ginger sauce £8.75; sticky figgy pudding £3.50.

Open *12 to 3, 7 to 11 (10.30 Sun); bar food 12 to 2 (1.45 Sun), 7 to 9.30; closed evenings 24 to 27 Dec, 1 Jan*
Details *Children welcome Car park Wheelchair access (also WC) Garden No smoking in eating area Live music Dogs welcome Access, Switch, Visa*

ALDERTON **Gloucestershire** **map 5**

Gardeners Arms

Beckford Road, Alderton TEL: (01242) 620257
off A438, 7m E of Tewkesbury

A 'beautifully finished' thatch is the first thing you notice when you reach this well-tended 400-year-old pub. Inside, it is almost domestic, with sofas to sit on and attractive drawings and prints on the walls. The place seems geared up for food, and at lunch-time there's a short menu built around regular supplies of good-quality ingredients. Casseroles and salads supplement regular items like spicy Indonesian smoked mackerel, or ham off the bone with fried egg and sauté potatoes. The memory of steak, kidney and mushroom pie with crumbly shortcrust pastry led one reporter to remark that 'we shall never knowingly pass such a pie again'. Others have been delighted by 'excellent' grilled Portuguese sardines with butter, dill and lemon juice, not to mention damson and sloe ice-cream (made locally, but 'one of the absolute best ice-creams I've ever had!'). In the evening the menu is geared to the restaurant, and the repertoire is filled out with more substantial dishes such as rack of lamb with garlic and rosemary, and whole baby chicken stuffed with sweet peppers and grapes. Draught beers are well-known names like Wadworth 6X and Theakston XB, and there are some interesting wines on the blackboard list. Alderton is within striking distance of Hidcote Manor Gardens and the Silk Mill at Beckford. SAMPLE DISHES: chicken and vegetable broth £2.50; grilled whole Brixham plaice £7.50; blackcurrant and apple crumble £3.

Open *11 to 2.30, 6.30 to 11, Sun 12 to 3, 7 to 10.30; bar food Tue to Sun L 12 to 2, Tue to Sat D 7 to 9; restaurant Sun L 12 to 2.30 (booking essential), Mon to Sat D 7 to 9*
Details *Children welcome in eating areas Car park Wheelchair access (also WC) Garden and patio No music Dogs welcome in 1 bar Access, Switch, Visa*

ALDWORTH **Berkshire** **map 2**

Bell Inn

Aldworth TEL: (01635) 578272
on B4009, 3m W of Streatley

'A unique country pub,' and long may it remain so, is the popular view about this superlative hostelry opposite the old village well. Ian Macaulay has been in residence since 1974, but the place has been in the family for over 200 years, and it is not about to change. The building was originally a medieval hall, and inside it has 'tremendous character', with stone flagged floors, panelled walls and sturdy benches. Mine host presides over the glass-panelled serving hatch, local drinkers crowd the hallway, and there are a few candlelit nooks and crannies to squeeze into. It always seems to be 'full of happy people', with plenty of conversation flowing, but no music or mobile phones. A stupendous selection of real ales is one reason why this place is so treasured: Old Tyler from the West Berkshire Brewery lines up beside Arkell's 3B and Kingsdown Ale, Morrells Oxford Mild and Oxford Bitter. Hot crusty rolls filled with everything from Stilton to Devon crab are the staples on the food front, and 'very good' they are too. You might also get a 'big basket' of salad, not to mention hot soup in the winter months. Bread and cheese, ice-creams and the occasional hot pudding complete a simple, but perfectly appropriate, picture. One reporter also noted that 'morning coffee comes on a tray with a jug of milk, sugar bowl and a tiny basket with a chocolate mint – all for 60p!' The area is great walking country, with the Ridgeway Path and the Berkshire Downs close by. SAMPLE DISHES: Brie roll £1; spicy prawns £1.50; hot sticky toffee pudding £2.

Open *Tue to Sat 11 to 3, 6 to 11, Sun 12 to 3, 7 to 10.30 (open bank hol Mons); bar food Tue to Sat 11 to 2.45, 6 to 10.45, Sun 12 to 3, 7 to 10.30; closed 25 Dec*
Details *Children welcome in 1 room Car park Garden No music Dogs welcome on a lead No cards*

AMBLESIDE Cumbria **map 8**

▲ *Drunken Duck Inn*

Barngates, Ambleside TEL: (01539) 436347
off B5286, between Ambleside and Hawkshead, 3m S of Ambleside

Benches on the verandah at the front of this 400-year-old isolated pub have magnificent views over Windermere and the surrounding fells. Inside is a series of rooms with original beams, open log fires, a delightful mixture of wooden furniture, and walls filled with tasteful prints and watercolours – in addition to a painted board that explains how the pub acquired its rather curious name (a rather frenetic tale involving spilt beer, worse-for-wear ducks and premature plucking). Rolls and ploughman's are served only at lunch-time, but at all times you can expect the blackboard to announce dishes like beef and vegetables in Drunken Duck Ale, Cumberland sausage casserole, deep-fried half a Gressingham duck, or lamb provençale. Vegetarians are particularly well catered for: courgette, pepper and mozzarella bake, and aubergine, coconut and pepper curry with rice were two options on a typical menu. A choice of custard, yoghurt or whipped cream is offered with puddings such as jam roly-poly or fruit crumble. Theakston Old Peculier, Boddingtons Bitter and Mitchell's Lancaster Bomber are among the real ales on draught. Drunken Duck Bitter is the house beer, and the pub's own-label wines are sold by the glass. Ambleside is at the heart of Lakeland and can get packed, so arrive early. SAMPLE DISHES: plaice goujons with curried mayonnaise dip £4; pork and apples in cider £6.50; hot chocolate fudge cake £3.

Open *11.30 to 3, 6 to 11; bar food 12 to 2, 6.30 to 9; closed 25 Dec*
Details *Children welcome Car park Wheelchair access (also WC) Garden No smoking in 1 dining-room Live music Dogs welcome Access, Amex, Delta, Switch, Visa Accommodation: 9 rooms, B&B £44 to £79*

AMERSHAM Buckinghamshire **map 3**

Kings Arms

30 High Street, Old Amersham TEL: (01494) 726333

The Kings Arms is a country-town inn of antiquity and pedigree. It began life around 1450 as two separate timber-framed houses and was extended in the eighteenth century to include a Georgian front with sash windows. Through an archway and between the two halves is a flower-filled courtyard; inside – in the bar – are ancient timbers, beams, oak floors, nooks and crannies, 'with no concession to modernity'. A fire often burns in the open hearth. The bar menu promises plain, honest, no-frills food along the lines of filled baguettes and sandwiches, chicken liver pâté, spiced lamb and salad in pitta bread, and 'first-class' turkey, ham and leek pie packed with chunks of meat. In addition, there are specials such as rabbit casserole and seafood risotto, and you could finish off stylishly with crême brûlée, served in a coffee cup with a brandy snap. More elaborate dishes are served in the beamed dining room. Ind Coope Burton Ale is kept in top condition, along with Benskins Bitter, Marlow Rebellion IPA and guests such as Scanlon's Middlesex Gold. A handful of wines from the full restaurant list are offered in the bar. SAMPLE DISHES: tomato soup £2.50; pasta carbonara £5; chocolate torte £2.50.

Open *11 to 11, Sun 12 to 3, 7 to 10.30; bar food 12 to 2.30, 6 to 9; restaurant Tue to Sun L 12 to 2, Tue to Sat D 7 to 9.30 (10 Sat)*
Details *Children welcome in 1 area of bar Car park Wheelchair access Garden No-smoking area until 7pm No music Dogs welcome on a lead Access, Amex, Delta, Diners, Switch, Visa*

AMPLEFORTH **North Yorkshire** **map 9**

White Swan

Ampleforth TEL: (01439) 788239
off A170 or B1257, 10m E of Thirsk

This comfortably modernised stone inn lies at the heart of Ampleforth, an attractive village on the edge of the Hambleton Hills and a short distance from the famous college. Food brings in the crowds, and the long printed menu has something for every taste, from plain smoked salmon with brown bread and butter, through grilled Whitby haddock with parsley sauce, to fillet steak Rossini. A blackboard lists the specials of the day, and the kitchen uses a lot of game in season: rabbit pie, roast mallard, and pan-fried pheasant with port and redcurrants, for instance. Desserts may be equally seasonal, with plum slice, and raspberry pavlova, although there could also be tiramisù and sticky toffee pudding. John Smith's and Tetley Bitter are on draught, and wines are sold by the glass, with the full list running to around 25 bottles. Sutton Bank, nearby, is popular for its walks and views. SAMPLE DISHES: cream of vegetable soup £2; steak pie £6; apple pie £2.50.

Open *11.30 to 2.30, 6 to 11, Sun 12 to 3, 7 to 10.30; bar food and restaurant 11.45 to 2, 7 to 9.30 (6.30 to 9.30 in summer)*
Details *Children welcome in bar eating area Car park Wheelchair access Garden and patio No smoking in dining-room Background music No dogs Access, Switch, Visa*

APPERLEY **Gloucestershire** **map 5**

Farmer's Arms 

Ledbury Road, Lower Apperley TEL: (01452) 780307
on B4213, SW of Tewkesbury

Mayhem's Brewery has its home in a building beside this half-timbered pub. As one reporter noted, 'serious work' obviously goes on in here, judging by the abundance of vats, pipes and water-ducts on view: there's a special gallery where visitors can watch the process, and tours and tastings can be arranged. The end-products include Odda's Light ('something one would not easily tire of') and, in contrast, dark, strong-tasting Sundown 'for sipping in the evening'. Handpumps in the open-plan bar, with its polished wood, sepia prints and bed-warming pans, also dispense Wadworth 6X and guest beers. Daily deliveries of fresh fish form the mainstay of the menu: you can order 'regular' or 'mega' portions with piles of big chips, or try something like trout or lightly poached salmon with hollandaise sauce. Steaks and pies please those with carnivorous appetites, and there's a biggish choice of gâteaux and desserts to choose from. Outside, in the grounds, are all manner of attractions including waterfalls, an adventure playground and a Wendy house; the countryside nearby is well worth a trip. SAMPLE DISHES: chicken liver pâté £3.25; fish mixed grill £8.75; bread-and-butter pudding £2.

Open *11 to 2.30, 6 to 11, Sun 12 to 3, 7 to 10.30; bar food 11 to 2, 6 to 10; restaurant 12 to 2, 7 to 10*
Details *Children welcome Car park Wheelchair access Patio Background and live music Guide dogs only Access, Delta, Switch, Visa*

APPLEBY Cumbria map 10

▲ *Royal Oak Inn*

Bongate, Appleby TEL: (01768) 351463
just off A66 at S edge of Appleby, 12m SE of Penrith

This long, whitewashed inn is just to the south of the pretty little town of Appleby, set in the Eden Valley. The area is well worth exploring either on foot or via the scenic Carlisle to Settle Railway, which stops here. Inside is a civilised lounge bar, with chintz-cushioned chairs, beams and panelling, an open fire, gleaming brass and copper, and prints on the walls; the taproom also has an open fire and panelling. One menu covers both bars and separate dining-rooms. This takes in a broad range of dishes: crab, prawn and cheese pancake, smoked haddock fish-cakes, Bongate lamb pudding, and chicken, apple and leek sausage as well as the traditional Cumberland version. Blackboards announce an equally impressive choice: to start, there might be twice-baked cheese and spinach soufflé, or potted pork, followed by half a roast Goosnargh duck with apple sauce, beef in beer pie, or ham shank with steamed potatoes; fish specials could include roast salmon, and Manx lobster cooked in various ways. Real ales constantly change; brews such as Theakston Best Bitter, Yates Bitter and Bongate Special Pale Ale are typical. More than 80 bottles from around the world feature on the wine list, with several sold by the glass. SAMPLE DISHES: Stilton, port and smoked bacon pâté £2.75; chicken breast in lemon, cream and tarragon sauce £10; Belgian chocolate truffle cake £3.

Open *11.30 to 3, 6 to 11, Sun 12 to 3, 6.30 to 11; bar food and restaurant 12 to 2, 6.30 to 9; no food 25 Dec*
Details *Children welcome in bar eating area Car park Wheelchair access Patio No smoking in 1 dining-room No music No dogs Access, Amex, Delta, Diners, Switch, Visa Accommodation: 9 rooms, B&B £29 to £39*

APPLEY **Somerset** **map 2**

Globe Inn

Appley TEL: (01823) 672327
off A38, 4m W of Wellington

A network of lanes through peaceful, spreading countryside leads to this real country pub. All three bars have open fires for cold days, and well-spaced tables set ready for customers. On the wide-ranging menu you can expect things like garlic king prawns, fish soup or mushrooms cooked in cream, garlic and horseradish, followed by main courses along the lines of lamb curry, garlic-battered chicken, steaks, and beef Stroganov. Specials, such as lemon sole, or chicken in white wine sauce, are listed separately, as are puddings, which range from the traditional – Black Forest gâteau – to the more exotic – banana pancake with rum and caramel sauce. At Sunday lunch-time roasts take centre stage. Cotleigh Tawny and a guest ale are on draught, with Lane's Farmhouse cider in summer, and the wine list runs to about 25 bottles, with house wines sold by the glass. SAMPLE DISHES: celery soup £2.25; roast duckling with chilli, plum and spring onion sauce £10.25; 'Scotch Mist' (double cream, honey, whisky and crushed meringue) £3.50.

Open *11 to 3, 6.30 to 11, Sun 12 to 3, 7 to 11; bar food Tue to Sun L 12 to 2, all week D 7 to 9.30; restaurant Sun L 12 to 2, Tue to Sat D 7 to 9.30*
Details *Children welcome in eating areas Car park Garden No smoking in dining-room No music No dogs Access, Switch, Visa*

ARDELEY **Hertfordshire** **map 3**

Jolly Waggoner

Ardeley TEL: (01438) 861350
off B1037 at Cromer, 5m E of Stevenage

'Like the reverse of the Tardis,' observed a reporter. What she meant was that this pink rambling pub looks huge from the outside, but isn't large at all once you step into the bar. Beams and exposed timbers set the tone, and lots of dried flowers, paintings of the pub and knick-knacks are dotted around. It's all very homely and cosy. The bar menu has plenty of variety, taking in smoked salmon and warm goats'-cheese croûton, unusual salads (including one with stir-fried chicken and cashew nuts), and a good creamy version of omelette Arnold Bennett, as well ploughman's, home-made burgers and locally made sausages. Added to this are blackboard specials – anything from a full English breakfast fry-up to stuffed peppers –

while puddings are mostly things like chocolate truffle tart and fruit crème brûlée. A more expensive evening menu and Sunday lunch are offered in the restaurant. This is a Greene King pub, with IPA and Abbot Ale on draught; around two dozen wines provide a fair choice. SAMPLE DISHES: French onion soup £2.75; steak, kidney and oyster mushroom pie £7.25; sticky toffee pudding £3.25

Open *12 to 2, 6.30 to 11, Sun 12 to 3, 7 to 10.30; bar food Tue to Sun 12 to 2, Tue to Sat 6.45 to 9; restaurant Sun L 12 to 2, Tue to Sat D 6.45 to 9*
Details *Children over 7 welcome Car park Garden and patio No music No dogs Access, Delta, Visa*

ARDINGTON Oxfordshire **map 2**

Boar's Head

Ardington TEL: (01235) 833254
off A417, 2m E of Wantage

Right next to the church in an intriguing and picturesque 'estate village', the Boar's Head is one of that rare breed – a genuine country pub serving food of star quality without the mannered approach or high-flown posturing adopted by some other establishments. Duncan and Elizabeth Basterfield have worked wonders since they arrived towards the end of 1993. They have even found time to set up a little cottage industry producing oils, vinaigrettes and dressings as a sideline.

Inside the pub are two dining-rooms with a drinkers' enclave at one end. Low-key prints and mirrors hang on the sandy-coloured walls; the furniture is sturdy. Service is kindness and politeness personified. This is the sort of pub that seems eager to cater for families and groups – and there's not a kid's 'chip menu' in sight. Instead it offers a sensibly short blackboard of dishes intended to jazz up the palate. Salads are given a prominent billing: red mullet is paired with wild mushrooms, brilliant smoked beef is served with French beans and chopped 'hen's egg', while chunks of spicy merguez sauce surround a cylinder of potato salad topped with home-made chutney ('an excellent contrast'). King scallops might be steamed with clams, cockles and lime or cooked as a casserole with sliced new potatoes (a witty visual pun), flat mushrooms and whole cherry tomatoes. Vegetables are often inspired: roast partridge with fresh apricots was accompanied on one occasion by 'out-of-this-world cubes of swede' poached in stock with curry spices. There's no letting up towards the finish, with pistachio mousse, mascarpone and home-made truffles as well as black cherry tart and banoffi pie. All the incidentals – such as the great home-made breads and unsalted butter which arrive automatically – are in tune. A dozen or so wines are tilted towards the southern hemisphere, while those wanting a pint could order Morland Original or Fuller's London Pride. 'After lunch we walked a footpath by Ardington House and felt we'd had a near-perfect outing,' concluded one contented soul. SAMPLE DISHES: smoked chicken with mango and jalapeños £5.25; chump of lamb with a honey and mint glaze £10.75; chocolate muffins with lemon curd and chocolate sauce £4.

Open *11.30 to 2.30, 6 to 11, Sun 12 to 3, 7 to 10.30; bar food Tue to Sun L 12 to 2, Tue to Sat D 7 to 9.30; 25 Dec drinks only 12 to 2, 26 Dec drinks only 12 to 4*
Details *Children welcome Car park Wheelchair access (also WC) Garden Background music Guide dogs only Access, Delta, Switch, Visa*

ARKESDEN Essex **map 3**

Axe and Compasses

Arkesden TEL: (01799) 550272
off B1038, 1m N of Clavering

The setting is a rural backwater on the border of Hertfordshire and Essex, and this partly thatched pub is very much the life and soul of the village. Modern extensions have made the interior surprisingly spacious, with fireplaces at both ends and walls adorned with horse brasses. The bar menu changes monthly and it provides a fair selection of sound dishes along the lines of oven-baked trout with prawns and capers, and Barnsley chop with mint gravy, as well as a few more ambitious offerings that may include roast pheasant with rösti and Madeira sauce, and monkfish with roasted red pepper sauce. Home-made sweets range from raspberry and hazelnut meringue to chocolate Malakoff. A full restaurant menu is also available. This is a Greene King pub, with IPA and Abbot Ale on handpump; around 30 familiar wines provide good-value drinking. SAMPLE DISHES: beef casserole with dumplings £6; stir-fried vegetables in puff pastry with mustard sauce £7.50; apple pie £2.50.

Open *11.30 to 3, 6 to 11, Sun 12 to 3, 7 to 10.30; bar food and restaurant 12 to 2 (3 Sun), 6.30 to 9*
Details *Children welcome in dining-room Car park Patio No music No dogs Access, Visa*

Prices quoted in an entry are based on information supplied by the pub, rounded up to the nearest 25 pence. These prices may have changed since publication and are meant only as a guide.

ARLINGTON East Sussex map 3

Old Oak Inn

Arlington TEL: (01323) 482072
off A22, 4m SW of Hailsham outside village of Arlington

Outside the village in an area of woods and fields with the South Downs a few miles away, this 300-year-old pub draws plenty of trade from outdoor types walking or riding in the neighbourhood. The food here is 'rather good' noted one reporter: the menu is sensibly short, and the accent is plain English. Expect such things as ploughman's, steak and kidney pudding, fish pie, curries and casseroles, plus fruit tarts, warm lemon meringue pie and other familiar puddings. Sunday lunch is a roast, and full evening meals are served in the restaurant. Harveys Sussex Best, Hall & Woodhouse Dorset Best and a guest ale are drawn direct from the cask, so 'do not be alarmed by the absence of levers at the bar'. SAMPLE DISHES: grilled mussels in garlic £3.50; beef Wellington £8; banoffi pie £2.25.

Open *Mon to Sat 11 to 3, 6 to 11, Sun 12 to 3, 7 to 10.30; bar food all week L 12 to 2, Mon to Sat D 7 to 9; restaurant all week D only 7 to 10.30*
Details *Children welcome in dining-room Car park Garden Smoking discouraged in restaurant Background music Dogs welcome in bar only Access, Switch, Visa*

ARMATHWAITE Cumbria map 10

▲ *Dukes Head*

Armathwaite TEL: (01697) 472226
off A6, between Carlisle and Penrith

'A bit off the beaten track,' concluded one reporter, but 'worth the diversion.' This white-washed inn at the centre of the tiny village of Armathwaite in the Eden Valley provides welcome refreshment for ramblers, birdwatchers and sightseers alike. In addition, according to the proprietors, anglers can find 'some of the finest trout and salmon fishing in the north of England' at nearby Eden Gorge. The lounge bar is 'homely' and comfortable with chintz-cushioned chairs and settees; there is also a small bar with a pool table, and a separate, bookable dining-room. One menu operates throughout, and offers promising dishes such as hot buttered shrimps, pork and venison pâté, local trout with almonds and pistachios, along with sandwiches, omelettes and children's meals. Blackboard specials might include salmon with lemon butter, prawns in filo pastry with garlic dip, baked avocado filled with ham, and mussels in cider. Beers available on handpump are Castle Eden, Boddingtons and a guest ale. House wines are served by the glass, and there's an interesting list of 18 bins from around the world. SAMPLE DISHES: egg, prawn and asparagus mayonnaise £3.75; breaded fillet of pork with apple sauce £7; meringues with toffee ice and toffee sauce £2.75.

Open *11 to 3, 5.30 to 11, Sun 12 to 3, 7 to 10.30; bar food and restaurant 12 to 2, 6.30 to 9*
Details *Children welcome Car park Wheelchair access (also WC) Garden Background music; jukebox Dogs welcome Access, Delta, Visa Accommodation: 5 rooms, B&B £25 to £48*

ASENBY North Yorkshire **map 9**

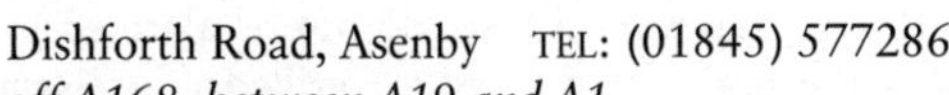

Dishforth Road, Asenby TEL: (01845) 577286
off A168, between A19 and A1

The owners 'must spend their lives looking round the auctions', concluded one reporter after a visit to this 'quirky' pub/restaurant just off the A1. Inside is 'a minefield of bric-a-brac' – crab and lobster pots appropriately hang from the ceilings, along with a clutter of wicker baskets, drums, jockey caps, fishing rods and more besides. Old fairground slot machines are dotted around the place, and the gent's toilet is lined with ancient sheet music. It's always packed and it's great fun: you can even sit at the bar, sip a glass of champagne and nibble at curried sausages before ordering.

True to the spirit of the place, the brasserie menu served in the bar dazzles with delights of every description; fish steals the limelight although the choice ranges far beyond the fruits of the sea. What impresses is the sheer imagination and daring of it all. On the fish front you might find potted prawns with tomato butter and Parmesan toast, a chunk of cod with artichoke mash and onion sauce, and deep-fried red mullet with lemon grass, chilli and ginger. Meat and game also receive the treatment: choose Thai beef pancakes, or black pudding with sage potatoes and toffee apples, as a starter, then follow on with Indonesian clay-baked chicken with bananas, five-spice quail with pineapple salsa, or a plate of roast pork with bacon, onions and sausages. A vegetarian reporter raved about 'really excellent' fully ripe goats' cheese with hazelnuts in filo pastry with sweet 'honeycomb' salad. Rounding things off there are such exotica as lavender crème brûlée with shortbread, and pear and prune tarte Tatin; otherwise have British cheese with ginger oatmeal biscuits. At lunch-time it's also possible to get club sandwiches. The restaurant menu follows the same theme, although prices are somewhat higher. Barbecues are held in the garden on Sunday lunch-times in summer. Black Sheep Bitter, Timothy Taylor Landlord and Theakston XB remind you that this is still a pub, although most interest centres on the 120-strong wine list, which includes 14 by the glass. SAMPLE DISHES: terrine of pork, ham and bacon with apples and prunes £4; lemon sole with spinach and wholegrain mustard £11.50; pannacotta with poached fruits £4.25.

Open *all week 11.30 (12 Sun) to 3, Mon to Sat 6.30 to 11; bar food and restaurant all week L 12 to 2.30, Mon to Sat D 6.30 to 9.30 (10 Sat), summer Sun barbecue 12 to 3*
Details *Children welcome Car park Wheelchair access Garden and patio No smoking in dining-room Background and live music No dogs Access, Amex, Switch, Visa Accommodation: 7 rooms, B&B £55 to £75*

ASHBY ST LEDGERS Northamptonshire map 5

▲ *Olde Coach House Inn*

Ashby St Ledgers TEL: (01788) 890349
off A361, 4m N of Daventry

Behind the ivy-clad exterior of this former farmhouse lies a series of rooms: a lounge, a pool room, and an open-plan approach to the others. One has an open fire, another an old museum-piece of a stove set up with black cooking-pots; up a few steps is a dining area, where tables can be booked. A chilled cabinet is stacked with enticements in the form of pies from which wedges are cut, and salads with, say, home-cooked ham or rare roast beef. Hot food is ordered here too: deep-fried scampi, various steaks and pastas, escalope of turkey grilled with Brie, or seafood crumble. Fruit pies and tarts are prominent among the desserts, and you may find summer pudding in season. Drinks are taken very seriously, with four guest ales backing up Everards Old Original, St Leger Ale, Jennings Cumberland Ale and Flowers Original. Around 12 wines are served by the glass from a list numbering 35. Children can colour in the illustration on the front of their menu, and they also have an adventure garden to play in. Ashby St Ledgers gained fame in times gone by, when Guy Fawkes and his accomplices used the village manor house to hatch their explosive plans. SAMPLE DISHES: vegetable soup £2.25; chargrilled chicken breast marinated in lemon and garlic £8.25; cassis St Honoré £3.

Open *12 to 2.30, 6 to 11, Sun 12 to 2.30, 7 to 10.30; bar food 12 to 2 (3 Sat and Sun), 6 to 9.30; closed 25 Dec*
Details *Children welcome Car park Wheelchair access (also WC) Garden No smoking in dining-room Background music Dogs welcome Access, Amex, Delta, Diners, Switch, Visa Accommodation: 6 rooms, B&B £46 to £75*

ASHPRINGTON Devon map 1

▲ *Durant Arms*

Ashprington TEL: (01803) 732240
off A381 Totnes to Kingsbridge road, 2m SE of Totnes

'An excellent welcome to us as holiday-makers,' begins a report from a couple away from their home base in Gloucestershire. This 200-year-old inn, not far from the River Dart, is a well-maintained, civilised venue with a generally sound reputation for food. No-frills dishes such as home-cooked ham, egg and chips, steak and kidney pie, and seafood bake could be followed by, say, raspberry pavlova or bread-and-butter pudding. Supper-time brings a few more ambitious dishes like chicken with asparagus, and 'excellent' pork with Stilton sauce. Wadworth 6X and Flowers Original are on draught, and there's a useful list of 14 wines by the glass (note the Sharpham Reserve from the local vineyard). Morning coffee and cream teas are served outside licensing hours. There's a self-catering cottage in the grounds as well as in-house accommodation. SAMPLE DISHES: leek and Stilton soup £2.25; pan-fried plaice fillets £6; blackberry and apple pie £2.75.

Open *11.30 to 2.30, 6 to 11, Sun 12 to 2.30, 7 to 10.30; bar food 12.15 to 2, 6.45 to 9.45*
Details *Children welcome in dining-room Car park Wheelchair access (also WC) Patio Background and live music Dogs welcome Access, Delta, Switch, Visa Accommodation: 2 rooms, B&B £20*

▲ *Waterman's Arms*

Bow Bridge, Ashprington TEL: (01803) 732214
off A381 Totnes to Kingsbridge road, 2m SE of Totnes

'What an idyllic setting,' commented one reporter. The Waterman's Arms sits on a quiet country road right beside the River Harbourne complete with its ducks, horse chestnut trees and an ancient hump-back bridge. The stone-built inn has had a number of former lives; once a smithy, a brewery and even a prison, it has now been much extended to provide a welcoming warren of small rooms decorated with brass, copper, dried hops and boating pictures. Service is polite, and there is plenty of room for eating. The printed menu offers a range of starters from chicken liver and green peppercorn pâté to honeydew melon, while main courses take in spicy Mexican nachos, chickpea and lime pasanda, steak and kidney pie, and pastas; also look for the seafood platter loaded with Brixham crab, fresh salmon, prawns, smoked salmon and smoked trout. Specials are chalked up on a board and could include huntsman's pie (mixed meats in a spicy tomato sauce), or grilled lemon sole. Draught beers are also listed on a board – among them Palmers IPA, Dartmoor Best, Bass and Boddingtons. Cider buffs can choose from Flownes Neck and potent Old Pig Squeel, and two dozen wines are available. If you fancy a trip out, you can set a course for historic Totnes where an Elizabethan market is held each week from March to October. SAMPLE DISHES: crab cocktail £5; mixed-meat platter £7; chocolate and Grand Marnier mousse £3.

Open *11.30 to 3, 6 to 11, Sun 12 to 3, 7 to 10.30; bar food 12 to 2.30, 6.30 to 9.30; restaurant Sun L 12 to 2.30, all week D 7 to 9.30*
Details *Children welcome in bar eating area Car park Wheelchair access (also WC) Garden and patio No smoking in restaurant Background and live music Dogs welcome Access, Amex, Delta, Switch, Visa Accommodation: 15 rooms, B&B £32 to £70*

ASKERSWELL Dorset map 2

Spyway Inn

Askerswell TEL: (01308) 485250
off A35, 4m E of Bridport

Deep in Thomas Hardy's 'Wessex', but only a short detour off the Dorchester to Bridport road, the Spyway still feels 'far from the madding crowd' and has the rusticity to prove it. Old settles and agricultural implements set the tone. The printed menu consists largely of variations on the ploughman's theme (the 'Woodman's' version comes with hot sausages and tomato pickle), along with salads, omelettes and seafood. Grills are added in the evening. There are also specials in the shape of home-made pies, winter casseroles and vegetarian bakes. Sweets are mostly ice-creams and sundaes. Ruddles County, Ushers Best and Adnams Bitter are on draught, and 40 whiskies are on show. Two dozen good-value wines are available by the glass or bottle, and the pub stocks 'country' fruit wines aplenty. SAMPLE DISHES: Stilton ploughman's £4; steak and onion pie £4.50; butterscotch nut sundae £2.

Open *Tue to Sat 11 to 3, 6 to 11, Sun 12 to 3, 7 to 10.30; bar food Tue to Sun 12 to 2, 6.45 (7 Sun) to 9.15*
Details *No children Car park Wheelchair access Garden and patio No smoking in 1 dining-room No music No dogs Amex, Diners*

Licensing hours and bar food times are based on information supplied by each establishment and are correct at the time of going to press.

ASKRIGG **North Yorkshire** **map 8**

▲ *King's Arms Hotel*

Askrigg TEL: (01969) 650258
off A684 Sedburgh to Bedale road, ½m N of Bainbridge

Set in the ancient Yorkshire Dales village of Askrigg – which means 'ash trees in the nook' – this civilised stone inn-cum-hotel was built in 1760 for John Pratt to house his famous racing stable. Fifty years later it became a well-known coaching-inn and is now famous as being the Drovers Arms in the TV series *All Creatures Great and Small*. In fact, the back parlour is called the Drovers Bar and houses a display of photographs from the series. There are two other bars, as well as the Clubroom Restaurant, which serves five-course meals, and the Silks Grill, where steaks, chops and grilled fish dominate the menu. Otherwise you'll find local produce on offer in the bars, with the emphasis on lamb, game in season, and Yorkshire specialities. Look out for Feather Fowlie (a hearty local soup made from vegetables, pearl barley and chicken), Peat Bog Pie (shepherd's pie with black pudding and oatmeal), and Singed Panacalty (a potato pancake with bacon, onions, poached eggs and melted cheese). Several of the wines on the global list are available by the glass and a handful in half-bottles. You can also choose from a range of malt whiskies. Beers include Theakston XB, Dent Bitter and Younger No. 3. Nearby are Aysgarth Falls, Castle Bolton and Hardraw Force. SAMPLE DISHES: lambs' liver pâté with Cumberland sauce £3; suprême of chicken forestière £6.25; bread-and-butter pudding with vanilla custard £2.75.

Open *11 to 3 (5 Sat), 6.30 to 11, Sun 11 to 3, 7 to 10.30; bar food and restaurants 12 to 2, 6.30 to 9, Sun 12 to 2, 7 to 8.30*
Details *Children welcome Car park Wheelchair access (also WC) Patio No smoking in restaurants Live music and jukebox Dogs welcome in bars Access, Amex, Switch, Visa Accommodation: 11 rooms, B&B £50 to £108*

ASWARBY **Lincolnshire** **map 6**

▲ *Tally Ho Inn*

Aswarby, nr Sleaford TEL: (01529) 455205
on A15 Peterborough to Lincoln road

The Tally Ho was built over 300 years ago as a farmhouse for the Aswarby country estate and today it stands alone among fields on the edge of the village. The bar has the feel of a traditional country pub, with beams, old bricks, a log fire, prints on the walls and newspapers laid out. The printed menu is supported by regularly changing specials written on blackboards at each end of the bar. Salmon and spinach fish-cakes are popular, as are Lincolnshire sausages, and generous ploughman's with home-made chutney. Specials might embrace starters like warm salad of marinated chicken leg with Chinese spices, and main courses such as beef bourguignon, pork and pepper kebabs, and aubergine stuffed with mushrooms, onion and celery served with a herby tomato sauce. There are always four puddings: plums from the garden poached in brandy syrup with cinnamon, or vanilla ice-cream with a red fruit sauce, for example. The restaurant to the rear has its own longer menu. Bass, Bateman XB and a guest ale are well kept, and a handful of wines from an interesting list are sold by the glass. Bedrooms are in what was the farmhouse dairy and barn. SAMPLE DISHES: smoked mackerel pâté £3.25; rabbit and mustard pie £6; banana cheesecake with hot butterscotch sauce £2.50.

Open *12 to 3, 6 to 11, Sun 12 to 3, 7 to 10.30; bar food 12 to 2.30, 6.30 (7 Sun) to 10; restaurant Sun L 12 to 2.30, Mon to Sat D 7 to 10*
Details *Children welcome in eating areas Car park Garden No pipes or cigars in restaurant Background music Dogs welcome Access, Delta, Visa Accommodation: 6 rooms, B&B £30 to £45*

AWRE Gloucestershire **map 2**

Red Hart Inn

Awre, nr Newnham-on-Severn TEL: (01594) 510220
off A48 Newnham to Chepstow road, 2m S of Newnham

A hodgepodge of quaint items decorates the main bar area at this old pub at the end of a promontory sticking out into the Severn Estuary: copper, stuffed birds, paintings, rifles and fishing tools. Beams covered with hop-bines, an old fireplace, lantern wall-lights and old wooden tables and chairs with worn leather-clad seats complete the picture. The kitchen produces plainly cooked food but the quality is high. You can expect the likes of fried whitebait, home-baked ham in a ploughman's or with egg and chips, salmon mayonnaise, steaks, and mushroom and nut fettuccine. Desserts may include sticky toffee pudding, and chocolate marquise with Grand Marnier and brandy. The separate restaurant has its own, longer menu. Dorothy Goodbody's from the Wye Valley Brewery is on draught, and there's a rudimentary wine list. The setting is a delight; Awre consists of a few cottages and a church, with farms nearby, looking over mud flats to the estuary. SAMPLE DISHES: fan-tail prawns with garlic dip £5.25; mixed grill £8.25; fruit crème brûlée £2.75.

Open *Tue to Sun 11 to 2.30, 7 to 11, Sun 12 to 3, 7 to 10.30; bar food and restaurant Tue to Sun L 12 to 2, Tue to Sat D 7 to 9.30*

Details *Children welcome Car park Wheelchair access (also WC) Garden No smoking in dining-room Background music No dogs Access, Switch, Visa*

AXFORD Wiltshire **map 2**

▲ *Red Lion*

Axford (01672) 520271
off A4, 3m E of Marlborough, between Mildenhall and Ramsbury

The historic townscapes of Marlborough and the natural delights of Savernake Forest – not to mention the Kennet & Avon Canal – make this 300-year-old flint pub a useful base-camp for enthusiasts of all kinds. Devotees of fresh fish are also likely be seen in the pine-panelled bar or the modest dining-room. The blackboard lists an excellent range of piscine offerings – ultra-fresh sardines, lemon sole, sea bass, and brill – which are grilled or poached to order and served on the bone. Bivalves and crustacea are not neglected either: clams, oysters, mussels, lobster, and a mixed platter pan-fried in garlic, all appear when available. Seasonal game is a good match for the fish, and the kitchen produces dishes such as pigeon breasts in madeira, partridge with chestnuts and tarragon, casseroled wild duck with blueberries and sage, as well as making use of wild boar, goose and kangaroo. The standard menu covers more familiar ground, from roast beef salad to lamb rogan josh, while desserts are displayed on the 'refrigerated trolley'. Around nine wines are served by the glass and the list is tailored to meet the needs of restaurant customers. Wadworth 6X, Hook Norton Best and a guest ale are on draught. SAMPLE DISHES: goats' cheese in filo pastry £3.50; salmon steak grilled in butter and fennel £9.50; spotted dick £3.

Open *Mon to Sat 11 to 3, 6.30 to 11, Sun 12 to 3.30, 7 to 10.30; bar food and restaurant all week 12 to 2.15, 7 to 10.30*
Details *Children welcome Car park Wheelchair access (also WC) Garden and patio No smoking in restaurant Background music No dogs Access, Delta, Switch, Visa Accommodation: 4 rooms, B&B £30 to £45*

AYMESTREY **Hereford & Worcester** **map 5**

▲ *Riverside Inn* ✿✿ 🍺

Aymestrey TEL: (01568) 708440
on A4110, 6m NW of Leominster

As the name suggests, this massive sixteenth-century half-timbered building stands by the banks of a river – the Lugg, to be precise – with a steep, wooded hillside looming up towards the back. Inside is a heavily beamed warren of rooms, although the most striking feature is the barn-like dining area on a lower level than the rest of the pub, with views of the water through its glass walls. The whole pub is congenial and laid-back, and talkative landlord Steve Bowen happily accommodates all comers from, according to one reporter, 'local Hardy-esque types to a couple of Frenchmen in short sleeves'. You can drink at the bar, eat where you like, and there's no obligation to have a full meal.

If all this makes the Riverside Inn sound like any typical country pub, you are in for a surprise. When the Bowens took over in 1994, they brought in chef Steve Reynolds, fresh from toning up his culinary muscles with Albert Roux at Le Gavroche. From Mayfair to the Marches is quite a leap, but there's little doubt that what he delivers is pub cooking of the highest order. Dishes may have restaurant overtones, but the context, the informality and the prices tell a different story. Menus change each month, the kitchen follows the seasons and there's a keenness to make use of local produce. Hereford rump steak is chargrilled, saddle of Welsh lamb is served with juniper sauce, and wild venison might be paired with a compote of damsons or with pink pepper sauce. Duck (in this case French) is perfectly roasted and served with a silky, buttery sauce containing whole elderberries. This is food that makes you sit up and take notice – largely because it is based on impeccable raw materials. Something as simple as smoked chicken salad with crispy bacon and croûtons is lifted to new heights, and the kitchen also takes on board everything from seared salmon with avocado salsa and sauce vièrge, to steak and kidney pie, and mushroom Stroganov, not to mention filled baguettes. Some desserts are made personally by local lady Liz Merriman, ice-creams are produced on the premises, and cheeses are totally British (Skirrid, Pencarreg and St Illtyd, for example).

The output of local breweries shows up splendidly in Marches Priory Ale and Woodhampton Kingfisher Ale; you can also drink beers from the Otter brewery in Devon. Local ciders such as Weston's Stowford Press are on tap. The interesting list of around 30 wines – from a local importer in Kington – is perfectly tailored to the needs of an inn rather than a restaurant; look for the house white from Bodenham Manor Estate. The Riverside Inn is right on the recently opened Mortimer Trail, a 25-mile route between Ludlow and Kington. Also nearby are Croft Castle and Berrington Hall (both National Trust). SAMPLE DISHES: baby squid pan-fried with garlic and parsley £5; roast guinea-fowl on a bed of grilled polenta £10; sticky toffee pudding £2.75.

Open *12 to 3, 6.30 to 11, Sun 12 to 3, 7 to 10.30; bar food and restaurant 12 to 2, 7 to 10*
Details *Children welcome in dining-room Car park Garden and patio Smoking discouraged in restaurant No music Dogs welcome Access, Delta, Switch, Visa Accommodation: 6 rooms, B&B £20 to £60*

BADBY Northamptonshire **map 5**

▲ *Windmill*

Main Street, Badby TEL: (01327) 702363
on A361 Daventry to Banbury road, 2m S of Daventry

Tables and chairs outside this brown-stone thatched pub, with a profusion of flowers in hanging baskets, are ideal for al fresco eating and drinking in summer. The inside does not betray the confidence shown by the exterior; it's all flagstones and beams, a large inglenook and comfortable furnishings. The printed menu consists mainly of traditional pub fare, from sandwiches, fried whitebait, and popcorn prawns, to main courses of lasagne, 'pile of pasta' with vegetables and cheese sauce, and steaks. Look at the blackboard for more enterprising daily specials and puddings, among which might be green-lipped mussels with garlic and cream sauce, duck breast with summer fruit sauce, and Belgian apple flan. Real ales include Wadworth 6X, Boddingtons and Flowers Original. Speciality evenings, featuring folk and jazz music are held regularly. Nearby attractions include Silverstone motor-racing circuit and Towcester race-course; for walkers there are the Knightley and Nene Ways, as well as Badby Woods and Fawsley Park, all easily accessible by foot. SAMPLE DISHES: Bury black pudding with mustard sauce £4; poached salmon suprême with dill mayonnaise £8.25; Key lime cheesecake £2.50.

Open *11.30 to 3, 5.30 to 11, Sun 12 to 3, 7 to 10.30; bar food and restaurant 12 to 2 (2.30 Sun), 7 to 9.30*
Details *Children welcome in eating areas Car park Wheelchair access (also WC) Garden and patio Background and live music Dogs welcome Access, Amex, Visa Accommodation: 8 rooms, B&B £40 to £65*

Assessments of wine in pubs is based largely on what is available in the bar. Many pubs also have full restaurant wine lists.

BAINBRIDGE **North Yorkshire** **map 8**

▲ *Rose & Crown Hotel*

Bainbridge TEL: (01969) 650225
on A684, between Hawes and Leyburn, 4m E of Hawes

Dating from 1445, the Rose & Crown lays claim to being one of the most venerable of all Yorkshire inns. It stands opposite Bainbridge village green (complete with stocks), with grounds running down to the banks of the River Ure, where anglers can flex their rods. Remnants of the past can be seen in the beams, panelling and open fires, and the 'local's bar' is dedicated to the pursuit of pub games. The bar menu offers homespun stuff such as Dales cheeses with pickles and chutney, country soup with 'sippets', and Bainbridge rarebit with kidneys and mushrooms, as well as a few more trendy dishes including a warm salad of bacon and scampi, and pan-fried duck breast with blackcurrant sauce. Desserts are listed on a blackboard and might take in sticky toffee pudding and bread-and-butter pudding. Sandwiches are also available every lunch-time. Dinner and full Sunday lunch are served in the restaurant (although you can eat a single-course meal from the latter's menu in the bar or on the terraces, 'space permitting'). John Smith's and Webster's Yorkshire Bitter are on handpump; the short wine list makes familiar reading. The pub is also home of the Wensleydale Forest Horn, which is blown each evening from Holy Rood (September 27) to Shrovetide – a reminder of the time when it was an aural beacon used to guide travellers through Wensleydale forest to the sanctuary of Bainbridge itself. SAMPLE DISHES: terrine of duck with home-made chutney £3.25; poached salmon with prawn and tarragon sauce £7.75; brandy-snap basket with passion-fruit sorbet £3.

Open *11am to 11pm, Sun 12 to 10.30; bar food 12 to 2, 6 to 9, Sun 12 to 2.30, 6 to 9; restaurant Sun L 12 to 2.30, all week D 7 to 9.30*
Details *Children welcome in bar eating area Car park Wheelchair access (also WC) Patio Background music; jukebox Dogs welcome in 1 bar only Access, Delta, Visa Accommodation: 11 rooms, B&B £24 to £60*

BALLINGER COMMON **Buckinghamshire** **map 3**

Pheasant 🍇

Ballinger Common TEL: (01494) 837236
off A413 at Great Missenden, 3m W of Chesham

The sign saying 'Pheasant Inn – Eating House' should leave you in no doubt as to the prime purpose in life of this village pub overlooking the common and the cricket pitch. Outside there are flowers on the patio, inside are exposed beams aplenty, plus the obligatory quota of china, prints and brassware; a bright conservatory done out in pastel shades is used for overspill and private parties. The printed menu is a long trek through ploughman's and 'Ballinger burgers' to warm calf's liver and bacon salad, and salmon en croûte, but those in the know tend to head straight for the specials board. Avocado and crab bake, and sliced chicken breast in hot pepper sauce have both been heartily endorsed, but the range extends to tapas of smoked fish, rack of lamb with herb crust, and beef fillet with port and wild mushroom sauce. A slice of home-made summer pudding makes a pleasing finish (even at the beginning of October); otherwise you might choose chocolate fudge cheesecake, or blackcurrant sorbet. The list of around two dozen wines is 'dated, sourced and sensibly priced' and the range is broad. For those drinking beer in this free house, there is a choice of Wadworth 6X and Greene King Abbot Ale. SAMPLE DISHES: Portuguese sardines in garlic butter £3.75; pork fillet with apricot sauce £10.75; hazelnut meringue £3.25.

Open *all week 12 to 3, Mon to Sat 6.30 to 11; bar food all week 12 to 2, Mon to Sat 6.45 to 9.30*
Details *Children over 8 welcome in conservatory and dining-room Car park Wheelchair access (also WC) Patio No smoking in conservatory Background music No dogs Access, Amex, Delta, Switch, Visa*

BANTHAM Devon **map 1**

▲ *Sloop Inn*

Bantham TEL: (01548) 560489 and 560215
off A379, 4m W of Kingsbridge

Not surprisingly for a pub just a couple of hundred yards from the sea, various nautical memorabilia are found in the front bar, with its beams and flagstones; to the side is an area with an open fire, comfortable chairs and exposed stone walls, while to the rear is a plainly furnished dining-area with sloping panelling made to look like a ship's cabin. Sandwiches, salads and ploughman's feature on the printed menu, along with locally smoked salmon with prawns, local lamb steak, grills, and pasties. More interest lies in the long blackboard list, which makes full use of the connections with the sea: grilled sardines, moules marinière, skate wings, chargrilled monkfish, sea bass with Pernod and pink peppercorn sauce, and so on. Meat eaters may be more satisfied by duckling breast with cranberry gravy, roast pheasant, or loin of pork with cider and mustard sauce, for example. On draught are Ushers Best, Blackawton Bitter and Bass, and around ten wines are served by the glass from a list of over fifty. You can work up an appetite by walking over the dunes to the sea or taking the South Devon Coast Path, which runs past the pub, or go fishing, sailing – or even windsurfing. SAMPLE DISHES: laverbread with ham and cockles £3.75; fillets of turbot with tomato and basil sauce £10; blackcurrant sorbet £2.25.

Open *11 to 2.30, 6 to 11, Sun 12 to 2.30, 7 to 10.30; bar food and restaurant 12 to 2, 7 to 10*
Details *Children welcome in eating areas Car park Patio No cigars or pipes Background music Dogs welcome Delta, Switch Accommodation: 5 rooms, B&B £29 to £59*

BARDWELL Suffolk map 6

▲ *Six Bells* 🍇

The Green, Bardwell TEL: (01359) 250820
off A143/A1088, 2m N of Ixworth

Pubs these days are hard to pigeonhole. Owners Richard and Carol Salmon describe their sixteenth-century listed building as a 'country inn'; others feel that it is perhaps more of a hotel with a restaurant for non-residents. One blackboard menu is served in the bar, the dining-room and now also in the conservatory, and the cooking shows plenty of flair and imagination. There's a homespun flavour to potted shrimps, steak and kidney casserole, and roast loin of new season's lamb with bubble and squeak, while other dishes move with the times. Black pudding is served with chargrilled potato, caramelised apple and red onion marmalade; chicken comes on a bed of courgettes with a honey and mustard sauce dotted with pine kernels; while pan-fried fillet of halibut sits on a mixture of potatoes, artichoke hearts and bacon with a warm olive oil, lemon and parsley dressing. At lunch-time you can also get sandwiches and things like Suffolk sausages and mash, or prawn and pesto pasta. Desserts range from chilled blackcurrant syllabub to 'luxury' bread-and-butter pudding. Cheeses – and biscuits – are from Neals Yard. Wine is taken seriously: weekly promotions are a regular feature and the list is a substantial tome peppered with interesting names; five wines are generally sold by the glass and oodles of mulled wine is dished out in winter. Adnams Bitter, Wadworth 6X and Theakston XB are on handpump, and it's worth looking out for the bottled beer of the month (Berg Quell from Germany, for example). SAMPLE DISHES: tomato and orange soup £2.75; fillet of smoked haddock rarebit on potato pancake £8; banana vacherin £3.50.

Open *12 to 2.30, 6.30 to 11 (10.30 winter), Sun 12 to 2.30, 7 to 10.30 (10 winter); bar food and restaurant 12 to 1.30 (1.45 Sat and Sun), 7 to 9.30*
Details *Children welcome Car park Garden and patio No smoking in conservatory Occasional live music No dogs Access, Delta, Visa Accommodation: 8 rooms, B&B £40 to £70*

BARHAM **Suffolk** **map 6**

The Sorrel Horse

Barham, nr Claydon TEL: (01473) 830327
off A14 at Claydon, 5m N of Ipswich

'A pleasant old inn' is how one reporter describes this large pub a few miles from Ipswich opposite Shrublands Park health farm. Inside is now one large bar done out in modern country style with a few alcoves and 'imitation' oak beams. The whole place is spotless, the atmosphere is respectable, staff are friendly. Three menus effectively run in tandem: first a standard line-up built around things with 'very good' chips; then a 'round the world' menu concentrating on different national cuisines from the West Indies to Germany; finally, a promising list of specials that may include 'delicious' lamb casserole, jugged hare, roast goose, sausage and onion pie and so forth. Soups – including 'thick and flavoursome' leek and potato, and tomato and basil – have been praised, along with assorted salads. Desserts range from apple and cherry pie to death by chocolate. Tolly Cobbold Bitter and Ind Coope Burton Ale are on handpump, and a few wines are chalked on a board. SAMPLE DISHES: crab cocktail with chilli sauce £3; rabbit casserole £5; chocolate and rum mousse £2.50.

Open *11 to 3, 5 to 11, Sun 12 to 3.30, 7 to 10.30; bar food 11 to 2, 6.30 to 10 (9.30 Sun)*
Details *Children welcome Car park Wheelchair access Garden Background music Dogs welcome Access, Delta, Switch, Visa*

BARLEY **Hertfordshire** **map 3**

Fox & Hounds

Barley TEL: (01763) 848459
off B1039, 3m SE of Royston

Game and sports are an energetic feature of this rambling seventeenth-century pub: in the rabbit warren of little rooms clustered around a huge log fire, customers play chess and chequers, bar billiards, darts and skittles. Trophies also testify to the prowess of the local cricket team. Apart from winning and 'taking part', the main attraction at the Fox and Hounds is beer. Licensees Rita and Michael Nicholson brew their own, and you can see the little brewhouse just off the bar. Flame Thrower is their standard tipple, but up to ten handpumps also dispense Adnams Bitter, Broadside and many more; Crones is on tap for cider drinkers, and the pub has a decent wine list – also courtesy of Adnams. Pies and casseroles laced with real ale show up on the bar menu, which caters for just about every taste. Expect anything from mussels, swordfish, and mixed seafood in champagne sauce, to spare ribs, paella and curries. The blackboard is colour co-ordinated so that vegetarians and vegans can see what is on offer for them: it might be a parcel of vegetables with tomato and tarragon sauce, or barley and vegetable casserole with dumplings. In the garden is a great children's play area, and it's worth taking a serious look at the extraordinary pub 'gallows' sign that stretches across the road. SAMPLE DISHES: battered mushrooms stuffed with Stilton £3.25; lamb, tomato and aubergine casserole £7; raspberry pavlova £2.50.

Open *12 to 2.30, 6 to 11, Sun 12 to 2.30, 7 to 10.30; bar food and restaurant 12.15 to 2, 6.30 to 9.30*
Details *Children welcome in dining-room and games room Car park Wheelchair access (also WC) No-smoking area in dining-room Occasional live music No dogs in dining-room Access, Amex, Delta, Switch, Visa*

BARNARD GATE Oxfordshire map 2

Boot Inn

Barnard Gate, nr Eynsham TEL: (01865) 881231
just off A40, between Witney and Oxford

The Boot is a friendly, unpretentious place, with a quarry-tiled bar and two eating areas off it. Log fires burn in cool weather, adding an even more welcoming feel. Food doesn't disappoint, either, and the kitchen comes up with some interesting ideas: terrine of pork, pigeon and quail with cranberry sauce, and smoked wild goose breast are among the starters, with crab and salmon rösti fish-cakes, and a vegetarian pasta, among what the menu calls 'light dishes'. Fish specials are listed on a board – the pub's signature dish is grilled king prawns with garlic mayonnaise. Meaty offerings might include such things as a brochette of chargrilled chicken breast with mint and yoghurt dip, crispy roast duck with orange and cognac sauce, and minute steak with pepper sauce and string chips. Sticky toffee pudding heads the list of desserts. Fuller's London Pride, Boddingtons and Hook Norton Best Bitter are on draught; wines are sold by the glass, and the list has been chosen with care. SAMPLE DISHES: gravlax with creamed horseradish £6; steak and kidney pudding £9.25; steamed syrup sponge with custard £3.50.

Open *11am to 11pm, Sun 12 to 3, 7 to 10.30; bar food 12 to 2 (3 Sun), 7 to 10*
Details *Children welcome Car park Wheelchair access Garden and patio No-smoking area Background and live music Dogs welcome in bar only Access, Visa*

BARNOLDBY LE BECK **N.E. Lincolnshire** **map 9**

Ship Inn

Barnoldby le Beck TEL: (01472) 822308
off A18, 4m SW of Grimsby

In a village near Grimsby and not far from the Lincolnshire Wolds, the Ship is reckoned to be a 'truly delightful little place' bursting with charm. Much attention centres on the output of the kitchen. Chef Kevin Blakesman formerly 'cooked meals for the Royal Family', states the brochure; now he offers the populace such dishes as garlic mushrooms, steak and kidney pie with shortcrust pastry, and beef bourguignon. Fish from Grimsby Docks appears in the guise of croustade of seafood Mornay, battered haddock, and halibut steak with prawns and herb and garlic butter. In addition, the pub also has a 'brasserie menu' (which can be ordered at the bar): expect typically up-beat dishes such as spiced crab-cakes with mustard and coriander, calf's liver with olive mash, and Indonesian clay-baked chicken. Theakston Best, Younger No. 3 Ale and Courage Directors are on handpump and the wine list is bolstered by regularly changing 'house specials'. SAMPLE DISHES: seafood crêpe £4; rustic lamb with Madeira sauce £10; hot chocolate and brandy fudge cake £2.50.

Open *11 to 3, 6.30 to 11, Sun 12 to 3, 7 to 10.30; bar food and restaurant 12 to 2, 7 to 9.30*
Details *Children welcome Car park Wheelchair access Garden and patio Background music Guide dogs only Access, Switch, Visa*

BARNSTON **Merseyside** **map 7**

Fox & Hounds

Barnston Road, Barnston TEL: (0151) 648 7685
off A551, 1¼m N of Heswall

The Fox & Hounds 'has friendliness, honesty and integrity', notes a reporter, although you won't find much in the way of the usual beams and bucolic paraphenalia. This is a vintage '30s Merseyside pub and it's extremely well maintained. Old photographs of the district line the walls, and flowers appear in profusion. Staff dressed 'in their own clothes' provide first-class service, while licensee and cook Helen Leech works industriously in the kitchen. Here is a pub that wears its culinary heart on its sleeve: 'we do not serve chips, burgers, pizzas, etc. or children's meals' says a note on the menu. The blackboard menu changes daily 'depending on the weather, supplies and the creative mood of the cook' – as a result, you might find such things as 'flavoursome' fish pie, 'extremely good' lasagne, lamb hotpot, and baked salmon coated with wholegrain mustard and honey. Home-made puddings, including chocolate fudge cake and lemon meringue pie, are served with cream, ice-cream or custard. A separate printed menu offers ploughman's, sandwiches and filled jacket potatoes. Courage Directors, Ruddles, Websters and John Smiths are augmented by a guest brew; 50 whiskies are on display, and house wine comes by the glass. SAMPLE DISHES: prawn cocktail £2.50; Somerset pork chop in cider sauce £5.50; carrot cake £2.25.

Open *Mon to Thur 11.30 to 3, 5.30 to 11, Fri to Sun 11.30 to 11; bar food all week L only 12 to 2*
Details *Children welcome in dining-room Car park Wheelchair access Garden and patio No music Dogs welcome exc. in eating areas*

BASSENTHWAITE LAKE Cumbria map 10

▲ *Pheasant Inn*

Bassenthwaite Lake TEL: (01768) 776234
off A66, at NW end of lake, 7m NW of Keswick

Only a minor road separates the Pheasant, with its beautiful flower garden that slopes down into woods, from the edge of Bassenthwaite Lake. The long, low inn was built 400 years ago as a farmhouse, and one of the two airy, comfortably furnished lounges was once the original kitchen. In this genteel atmosphere visitors congregate for some excellent regional food. Local Herdwick lamb with orange segments and Cumberland sauce, potted Silloth shrimps, and Cumberland sausage platter feature alongside smoked chicken, or leek, Stilton and walnut cheesecake, and salads. Bar food is served only at lunch-time and, apart from soup and some puddings, is confined to cold dishes. The separate snug bar with its tobacco-brown walls and a ceiling varnished to a high gloss is 'where the real atmosphere' is, according to one reporter, and on handpump you will find Morland Old Speckled Hen, Bass and Theakston Best. A comprehensive list of over 50 wines include many by the half-bottle; otherwise try a glass of elderflower wine. Full set-price meals are available in the dining-room. Before you leave, look at the framed collection of cigarette cards of famous inns in the hall: the Pheasant is there among them. SAMPLE DISHES: lentil and tomato soup £2.25; devilled crab pot £5; steamed sponge pudding £3.

Open *11.30 to 2.30 (3 Sun), 5.30 to 10.30 (11 Fri and Sat), Sun 12 to 2.30, 7 to 10.30; bar food L only 12 to 2; restaurant Sat and Sun L 12.30 to 1.30, all week D 7 to 8.30*
Details *Children welcome in dining-room Car park Wheelchair access (also WC) Garden No smoking in restaurant No music Dogs welcome Access, Switch, Visa Accommodation: 20 rooms, B&B £50 to £100*

BATCOMBE Somerset map 2

Batcombe Inn

Batcombe TEL: (01749) 850359
off A359 between Bruton and Frome, 3m N of Bruton

'Find the church' is Claire and Derek Blezard's advice to anyone trying to locate their exceedingly remote country inn deep in the Batcombe Vale. This is reckoned to be the family pub *par excellence*, with every conceivable amenity and facility for children – from toys and games to an adventure playground in the garden. Children also have their own mini-menu, while grown-ups can take their pick from big burgers, plates of 'real' sausages, enterprising salads (duck and sun-dried tomato, for example) and Thai curries. Fish shows up in the shape of, say, grilled red mullet sprinkled with goats' cheese, or poached smoked haddock with prawn and mushroom sauce, while vegetarians could opt for artichoke and asparagus bake, or lettuce, basil and cheese roulade. Mendip Magic cider is an alternative tipple to Butcombe Bitter or Wadworth 6X, and the pub stocks an international list of around 70 wines. SAMPLE DISHES: deep-fried Brie with kiwi and pineapple dip £3.75; chicken, ham and asparagus pie £6; lime and pecan slice £2.75.

Open *12 to 2.30, 7 to 11 (10.30 Sun); bar food and restaurant 12 to 2, 7 to 10 (9.30 Sun); closed Mon Oct to Mar*
Details *Children welcome Car park Wheelchair access (also WC) Garden and patio No smoking in dining-room No music No dogs Access, Delta, Switch, Visa*

BECKINGTON Somerset map 2

▲ *Woolpack* ✿

Beckington TEL: (01373) 831244
off A36 and A381, 3m NE of Frome

The Woolpack is the kind of pub that is likely to be 'bursting at the seams' by seven o'clock on a Thursday evening. For the most part, popularity is generated by what happens in the kitchen. The place itself is divided up into several areas: those with an aversion to cigarette smoke head for the lounge and one of the dining-rooms, which are kitted out in true pub fashion with assorted prints, portraits, 'naive art' and so forth; others make use of an attractive, light area with cane furniture dotted around. Whatever the setting, one menu is the order of the day.

Excellent raw materials are the inspiration for a repertoire that allows for plenty of flexibility: a goodly number of dishes can be eaten as either starters or main courses. Sandwiches are available at lunch-time, although the thrust of the cooking is a good deal more ambitious than that. To begin, there might be warm salad of calf's liver and black pudding topped with a poached egg or potted rabbit terrine with date chutney, while centrepiece dishes could range from sauté monkfish with shiitake mushrooms, noodles and oyster sauce to breast of guinea fowl with artichokes, pancetta and thyme. Simpler offerings have also been applauded – avocado salad with Cornish crab mayonnaise, 'huge' fish-cakes, and a vegetarian dish of leeks and mushrooms in puff pastry, for example. Desserts range from the refined (white and dark chocolate terrine wrapped in amaretto-soaked sponge with coffee sauce) to the home-spun (fruits of the forest crumble with clotted cream). A constantly changing selection of real ales might include Greene King IPA, Butcombe Bitter and Nethergate Old Growler; the wine list runs to about 50 bins, with a fair showing of halves and several available by the glass. SAMPLE DISHES: grilled goats' cheese on a ciabatta croûte with pesto £5; venison casserole with poached pears and red wine £4.50; iced drambuie parfait with raspberry coulis £5.

Open *Mon to Sat 12 to 3, 6 to 11, Sun 12 to 3, 7 to 10.30; bar food and restaurant all week 12 to 2, 7 to 10 (9 Sun)*
Details *Children welcome in eating areas Car park Patio No smoking in dining-room and lounge No music Dogs welcome Access, Amex, Delta, Switch, Visa Accommodation: 12 rooms, B&B £55 to £85*

BECKLEY Oxfordshire **map 2**

Abingdon Arms 🍇

High Street, Beckley TEL: (01865) 351311
off B4027, 5m NE of Oxford

The Greatbatches have had their name over the door of this Oxfordshire stone pub since 1970, and their innkeeping philosophy is not about to be knocked off course. As regards food, they take their cue from the seasons: winter brings bouillabaisse, chicken and mushroom curry, baked ham with mustard sauce and other appropriate offerings; in summer there are salads, fresh crab with ginger dressing, and smoked chicken with yoghurt and mint sauce. A few items – like marinated anchovies with potato salad, pork and goose rillettes, and apple and almond tart – run throughout the year, and an assortment of British and Continental cheeses is ever-present. The wine list runs to around 40 bins, chosen with an eye for quality and value for money; beer drinkers have a choice of Hook Norton Best or Adnams Bitter. Children aren't allowed inside the pub, but the well-equipped garden is suitable. Beckley is well placed for a trip to Waterperry Gardens or Studley Priory, and Oxford is a short drive away. SAMPLE DISHES: fish soup with mussels and prawns £4; tagliolini with sun-dried tomato and wild mushroom sauce £6.25; rich chocolate torte £2.50.

Open *11.30 to 2.30, 6.30 to 11, Sun 12 to 2.30, 8 to 10.30; bar food all week L 12.15 to 1.45, Mon to Sat D 7.15 to 9*
Details *No children Car park Patio No music Dogs welcome on a lead No cards*

BEER Devon **map 2**

▲ *Anchor Inn*

Beer TEL: (01297) 20386
off A3052, between Seaton and Sidmouth

'A great position by the harbour' and a clifftop garden overlooking the beach make this a great summer-time seaside rendezvous, as well as an all-year-round retreat. Inside, the Anchor is 'determinedly old-fashioned', with serried rows of tables and chairs in the eating area and waitresses 'in nylon uniforms'. It is all very clean and respectable. The great scoring point here is fish, which is as fresh as can be: if you want to know what you are about to eat, take a look at the identification posters on the walls. Blackboards spell out the catches and dishes of the day: medallions of monkfish might come with a wine sauce and roasted red peppers, while 'wonderful' grilled fillet of brill holds its own with an unlikely topping of banana and a pool of mango chutney. Salmon and beef fillet are smoked on the premises, soups sound intriguing, and you can also get snacks ranging from crab sandwiches and spicy chicken baguettes to ploughman's served with 'a jar of special chutney' (Somerset Brie with fig and apricot, for example). Desserts and gâteaux are served with clotted cream. Otter Ale and Bitter, plus Wadworth 6X and Jack Ratt cider are on tap, and the well-spread wine list generally includes around six by the glass. The pub makes a good base-camp for energetic walks along the cliff or trips to explore the Roman quarry workings or model railway exhibitions nearby. SAMPLE DISHES: cauliflower and red pepper soup £2; grilled fillet of sea bass with lime, apple and red pepper £11; bread-and-butter pudding £2.75.

Open *11am to 11pm, Sun 12 to 10.30; bar food 12 to 2, 7 to 9.30; restaurant all week 12 to 2, 7.30 to 9.30*
Details *Children welcome in bar eating area Garden Smoking discouraged in restaurant Background and live music; jukebox Dogs welcome in public bar Access, Delta, Switch, Visa Accommodation: 8 rooms, B&B £37 to £64*

BELLINGDON Buckinghamshire map 3

Bull

Bellingdon TEL: (01494) 758163
off A416, 3m NW of Chesham

Dine at the Bull and the chances are you'll find 'spotted Richard and custard' on the menu, for this is a dining-pub with slightly formal 'restaurant' aspirations. Don't expect much in the way of pub snacks; instead, you're likely to encounter starters such as prawn and asparagus brochette with a hoisin sauce, deep-fried Normandy Brie, or melon and sorbet, alongside a selection of main courses like lamb cobbler, or 'well-timed' tuna steak with olive oil and garlic. Also note the chef's renowned lager-battered plaice with mushy peas and chips. Beers on draught include Ind Coope Burton Ale and Benskins Bitter, with Addlestones cask cider also available. The wine list features around 20 well-known names. In the bar are plenty of exposed beams and old pictures of bulls on the partly timbered walls, as well as a large inglenook fireplace. Outside, a large and attractive garden is laid out at the front of this old brick-and-tile-hung building, which is set in popular walking country. SAMPLE DISHES: coarse pork pâté £4.50; wild mushroom crêpe with plum sauce £9; apple and gooseberry crumble £3.

Open *11 to 3, 6 to 11, Sun 12 to 3, 7 to 10.30; bar food and restaurant all week L 12 to 2, Mon to Sat D 7 to 9*
Details *Children welcome Car park Wheelchair access (also WC) Garden No music Dogs welcome Access, Switch, Visa*

BENTWORTH Hampshire map 2

Sun

Sun Hill, Bentworth TEL: (01420) 562338
off A339 Alton to Basingstoke, 3m W of Alton

The Sun is in the centre of the village; it's small and cottagey-looking, with white walls and a slate roof, and tables outside that are ideal for summer eating and drinking. The interior is cosy, with a small dining-room to each side of the wooden-floored bar: low ceilings, dark beams hung with mugs, log fires burning in winter, and plants on the tables all contribute to a civilised atmosphere. A printed menu lists snacks like sandwiches, pasta and a few pub staples, while a blackboard announces the daily specials: a soup starts things off, and to follow there could be salmon fish-cakes with crab sauce, sweet-and-sour chicken, lamb casseroled with port and redcurrants, beef in ale, and spinach and ricotta pancakes. A reporter describes the chocolate truffle cake as 'heaven', and among the other puddings may be date crumble slice, and banana ice-cream. A good choice of real ales on draught includes locally brewed Cheriton Pots Ale, Worldham Old Dray Bitter and Marston's Pedigree. House wines are sold by the glass. Bentworth is in a lovely area of rolling fields, gently undulating hills, woods and hedges; Jane Austen's house is in nearby Chawton. SAMPLE DISHES: chicken soup £2.20; mixed seafood in lobster sauce £7.50; chocolate roulade £2.50.

Open *12 to 3, 6 to 11, Sun 12 to 3, 7 to 10.30; bar food 12 to 2, 7 to 9.30 (9 Sun summer); closed Sun evening Nov to Easter*
Details *Children welcome in dining-room Car park Wheelchair access Patio No music Dogs welcome on a lead No cards*

BERROW Hereford & Worcester **map 5**

Duke of York

Berrow TEL: (01684) 833449
off A438 midway between Ledbury and Tewkesbury

Food is the main concern in this cosy, fifteenth-century pub just south of the Malvern Hills. Tables are laid out for eating in both bars, or you could opt for the more formal restaurant. The same menu of 'traditional bar meals' is available in either, offering plenty of choice at each course: starters tread the 'soup, prawn cocktail, and pâté' path, taking in green-lip mussels in garlic butter, and deep-fried Brie with cranberry sauce along the way. Main courses include the likes of Barnsley chop, and giant Yorkshire pudding with beef, a selection of fish and vegetarian dishes such as salmon hollandaise, and broccoli and cream cheese bake, plus a range of speciality steaks. For those with a sweet tooth – and enough room – there are always about 20 desserts available, from bread-and-butter pudding to toffee crunch pie. Boddingtons and Marston's Pedigree are on draught; the short wine list includes a selection by the glass. SAMPLE DISHES: savoury mushrooms £3; rack of lamb £8.75; steamed ginger pudding £2.40.

Open *11 to 3, 6.30 (7 winter) to 11, Sun 12 to 3, 7 to 10.30; bar food and restaurant 12 to 2, 7 to 10*
Details *Children welcome Car park Wheelchair access Garden and patio No smoking area Background music Dogs welcome in bar only Access, Delta, Switch, Visa*

Recommendations for good country pubs will be very welcome.

BERWICK East Sussex map 3

Cricketers Arms

Berwick Village TEL: (01323) 870469
just off A27 Lewes to Polegate road

Visitors to this 'lovely' little brick pub are bowled over by its enchanting prettiness. Out front is one cottagey garden, out back is another, liberally sprinkled with picnic tables: 'we had the added excitement of being joined by a grass snake for part of the meal,' observed one couple who called in for lunch. This is a popular local eating place with a limited printed menu backed up by a handful of specials. Steak sandwiches with 'really crispy golden chips' are highly popular, but you can also get soup such as leek and tomato, chicken goujons, ploughman's and jacket potatoes. Specials could include 'excellent-quality' lamb steak with redcurrant and mint gravy, sea bass with parsley butter, or broccoli, pepper and pasta bake for vegetarians. Home-made treacle tart, and bread-and-butter pudding make wholesome finales. Harveys Best Bitter, Sussex Pale Ale and Old Ale (in season) are drawn direct from casks in the tap room, and the pub advertises 'wines of the month'. SAMPLE DISHES: creamy garlic mushrooms £3.75; Berwick ham, egg and chips £4; chocolate pudding with chocolate sauce £2.50.

Open *11 to 3, 6 to 11, Sun 12 to 3, 6.30 to 10.30; bar food 12 to 2.15, 6.30 to 9 (9.30 Fri and Sat)*
Details *Children welcome in bar eating area Car park Wheelchair access (also WC) Garden No music Dogs welcome on a lead No cards*

BEST BEECH East Sussex map 3

▲ *Best Beech Inn*

Mayfield Lane, Best Beech TEL: (01892) 782046
on B2100, midway between Mark Cross and Wadhurst

One visitor found a 'genuinely nice feel' emanating from this popular pub set in the shadows of overhanging trees at a crossroads near the smart village of Wadhurst. The building looks Victorian, though parts of it date back to 1680, and inside all is gleaming copper, patterns, plates and prints. Two large blackboards in the entrance hall announce the dishes of the day: perhaps soft roes on toast as a starter, and then pan-fried trout fillet with prawns and almonds. Or consult the printed menu and you'll find it full of old favourites such as avocado and prawns, deep-fried mushrooms, sirloin steak, and salads. Puddings are recited by a waitress. Real ale drinkers have a choice of Fremlins, Harveys and Fuller's London Pride, and those who prefer wine will find the mainly French list running to around 20 bins, with a number available by the half-bottle. Bodiam, Sissinghurst Castle and Chartwell are short drives away. SAMPLE DISHES: deep-fried whitebait £3.25; Best Beech Chicken (chicken breast stuffed with cream cheese, garlic, onions and bacon, and served with a cream sauce) £6.25; apple pie with home-made ice-cream £2.50.

Open *Tue to Fri 11.30 to 2.30, Mon to Sat 6 to 11, Sun 12 to 2.30, 7 to 10.30; bar food Tue to Sun L 12 to 2, Mon to Sat 7 to 9.30; restaurant Tue to Sat D only 7 to 9.30*
Details *Children welcome in eating areas Car park Wheelchair access Patio No smoking in restaurant Background music Dogs welcome on a lead Access, Switch, Visa Accommodation: 7 rooms, B&B £25 to £45*

BIDDENDEN Kent **map 3**

Three Chimneys

Biddenden, nr Ashford TEL: (01580) 291472
on A262, 2m W of Biddenden

The Three Chimneys is every tourist's dream of an English country pub: a cottage-like building surrounded by brick paths and pretty gardens. It even has a large oasthouse (now converted) opposite, as if to emphasise that this is the Garden of England. The interior is equally attractive, adorned with dried flowers, hop-bines, country artefacts and pictures; old oak furniture is comfortably arranged in the three linked rooms that make up the main bar. The principal eating area, the Garden Room, is in a very successfully executed modern extension. Blackboards proclaim the menu of around four dishes per course, and the landlord tells us that 'two or three vegetarian dishes are always available on request'. You could start with mussel soup, smoked mackerel pâté, or spinach and ham mousse; go on to lamb and rosemary casserole, steak and mushroom pie, turkey fricassee, or prawn and mushroom quiche; and end with date and walnut pudding, pear tart, or nutty treacle tart – desserts are accompanied by unpasteurised cream. Around seven real ales are tapped from casks behind the bar, among them Morland Old Speckled Hen, Wadworth 6X and Harveys Best. Own-label wines are served by the glass, and the full list of 40 bottles, plus 15 halves, includes one from a local vineyard. SAMPLE DISHES: pear and Stilton tartlet £3; steak and oyster pie £6.75; gooseberry and almond tart £3.

Open *11 to 2.30, 6 to 11, Sun 12 to 2.30, 7 to 10.30; bar food and restaurant 12 to 2, 7 to 10; closed 25 and 26 Dec*
Details *Children welcome in dining-room Car park Wheelchair access Garden No music Dogs welcome No cards*

BILBROUGH **North Yorkshire** **map 9**

▲ *Three Hares*

Main Street, Bilbrough TEL: (01937) 832128
off A64, between Tadcaster and York

Readers heap praise on the quality of the cooking at this former coaching-inn, now known more as a restaurant than as a pub. 'We had dinner one night last week: it was so excellent we went back the next night and it was just as good,' said one confirmed fan. The carpeted and wallpapered bar, with bits and pieces in copper and brass, has its own extensive menu (a separate restaurant is in a former smithy). Vegetable tempura with sweet-and-sour sauce has been described as 'tasty and fresh', and among other starters might be ham and oxtail terrine, or smoked haddock brandade. The kitchen illustrates its flair and imagination in main courses such as poached salmon with cucumber noodles, or spicy lamb sausages, and an Oriental influence shows in salmon and prawn croquette with a coconut and lemon grass sauce. Much use is made of local produce and game: venison liver with lardons, and wild boar sausages with spiced couscous and marsala sauce may crop up on the blackboard. Ice-creams are made in-house, and other puddings maintain the high standards: marmalade sponge, or baked chocolate tart with candied orange, for example. Real ales change regularly, and could include Fuller's London Pride and Marston's Pedigree. Eight wines come by the glass, with wines of the week listed on a board. SAMPLE DISHES: bresaola with pickled vegetables £4.25; casseroled saddle of rabbit with shallots and herbs £7; iced meringue gâteau with fruit coulis £3.25.

Open *Tue to Sat and bank hol Mon 12 to 2.30, 7 (6.30 Fri and Sat) to 11, Sun 12 to 3, 7 to 10.30; bar food Tue to Sun 12 to 2, 7 (6.30 Fri and Sat) to 9.30 (9 Sun); restaurant Tue to Sat D only 7 to 9.30*
Details *Children welcome in bar eating area Car park Wheelchair access (also WC) Patio No smoking in 1 dining-room No music No dogs Access, Delta, Switch, Visa*

BIRCHOVER **Derbyshire** **map 5**

Druid Inn

Main Street, Birchover TEL: (01629) 650302
from A6 nr Haddon Hall take B5056; Birchover signposted on left after 2m

Haddon Hall, Riber Castle Wildlife Park and Matlock are all within striking distance of this Peak District pub in good walking country.

Even closer are the two rocking stones on Row Tor, high above the eighteenth-century ivy-covered building; the stones were thought to have connections with the Druids – hence the inn's name. In the rather plain, rambling interior there isn't much elbow room for a casual drink, for the place rapidly fills up with famished sightseers and others seeking solid sustenance. Dip into the vast menu and you'll find influences from far and near: chicken tikka, bobotie, moussaka, Turkish lamb casserole, Dorset jugged steak in port with sausage dumplings, bouillabaisse, and local pheasant and venison casserole give an indication of the range of main courses, while starters include the likes of Buxton Blue cheese deep-fried and served with apricot dip, Szechuan spare ribs, and New Zealand mussels. Puddings tend to be patriotic British old-timers such as sherry and fruit trifle. Greene King Abbot Ale, Morland Old Speckled Hen and Mansfield Bitter are among the real ales on draught, and own-label wines come by the glass. A front terrace overlooking fields is a pleasant spot in summer. SAMPLE DISHES: Stilton and port pâté £4; marinated rack of lamb with redcurrant and gooseberry sauce £12; summer pudding £2.50.

Open *12 to 3, 7 to 11; bar food 12 to 2, 7 to 9.30 (9 Sun and winter)*
Details *Children welcome in dining-room until 8.15 Car park Wheelchair access Patio No smoking in 2 rooms Background music No dogs Access, Amex, Delta, Diners, Switch, Visa*

BIRCH VALE Derbyshire map 8

▲ *Waltzing Weasel*

New Mills Road, Birch Vale TEL: (01663) 743402
on A6015, ½m W of Hayfield

A citizen of Cheshire who has been visiting this stone-built roadside inn for the last 30 years has noticed many changes, but confirms that the place still holds sway as a genuine country pub. Owners Michael and Linda Atkinson have up-graded the interior, but the mood remains convivial. Lunch revolves around a highly regarded hot and cold buffet served in both the bar and the dining-room (which has the added attraction of dramatic views of Kinder Scout through its mullioned windows). You might start with soup, smoked tuna, or game pâté before moving on to lobster salad, Barnsley chops, or steak and kidney pie. Puddings tend to be old favourites such as treacle tart, fruit crumble and chocolate mousse.

Evening meals are served in the restaurant, although one reporter was happily accommodated in the bar, where he feasted on pigeon pie with cherries accompanied by accurately timed vegetables (including 'proper' roast potatoes and 'excellent home-grown cabbage'). Other options might be braised rabbit, beef in whisky, or grilled halibut in lemon butter. Beer drinkers are well served with the likes of Marston's Bitter and Pedigree and, occasionally, Whim Hartington Bitter and Hoskins Churchill's Pride. The list of 45 wines has been chosen with an eye for quality and value for money. Outside is an impressive garden 'complete with visiting rabbit which is tolerated sympathetically'; Haddon Hall, Bakewell, and Buxton with its Opera House are within striking distance if you aren't in the mood for perambulating the Peaks. SAMPLE DISHES: marinated anchovies £4.50; summer chicken £9.50; bread-and-butter pudding £3.

Open *11 to 3, 5.30 to 11, Sun 12 to 3, 7 to 10.30; bar food 12 to 2, 7 to 9.30; restaurant D only 7 to 9*
Details *Children welcome in dining-room Car park Wheelchair access (also WC) Garden No music Dogs by arrangement Access, Delta, Switch, Visa Accommodation: 8 rooms, B&B £45 to £95*

BLACKBOYS **East Sussex** **map 3**

Blackboys Inn

Lewes Road, Blackboys TEL: (01825) 890283
on B2192, 3m E of Uckfield

The Blackboys is 'a superb place to come and eat outside in summer', according to a reporter, and shielding the pretty building from the road is a lawn with benches, tables and a duck-pond. Inside is a series of small rooms with low beams, lots of panelling and traditional furnishings. Standard pub fare – ploughman's, home-smoked ham or sausage with eggs and chips, for instance – is on offer as well as dishes like mushrooms baked with port and Stilton, and coq au vin. Fish is a strong point, with anything from battered cod, and seafood pancake, to crab salad, and Spanish fish stew available. A good selection of desserts features crème brûlée and nursery treats like marmalade pudding with custard. Harveys Sussex Best Bitter, IPA and Armada Ale are on draught, and wines are chosen from a board. Service has been described as 'good and helpful'. SAMPLE DISHES: chicken and prawn galette £7; fish curry with brown rice £5; treacle tart £2.75.

Open *11 to 3, 6 to 11; bar food 12 to 2, 6.30 to 10*
Details *Children welcome Car park Garden and patio Jukebox Dogs welcome Access, Switch, Visa*

Use the maps and index at the back of the Guide *to plan your trip.*

BLACKBROOK Surrey map 3

Plough

Blackbrook TEL: (01306) 886603
off A24, 1½m SE of Dorking

A pleasant atmosphere permeates throughout this Surrey pub: there are several eating areas based around a central bar, ornamented with collections of old bottles and framed memorabilia on the walls. A printed menu offers simple dishes such as ploughman's and sandwiches, while blackboards list more exciting options along the lines of seafood and mushroom casserole loaded with mussels, clams, prawns and large chunks of salmon under a lid of puff pastry, or an 'enormous portion' of whole baby chicken cacciatora with a herby stuffing and a selection of vegetables from the market. Puddings include profiteroles, Dutch apple tart, rhubarb and ginger crumble, and blueberry pancakes. King & Barnes Sussex, Festive and Broadwood are on draught, joined by a seasonal guest – Christmas Ale or Corn Beer, perhaps. A wide choice of wines is available by the glass, and specials are listed on boards. You can sit outside and enjoy the impressive floral display in summer, and for children there's a Swiss playhouse. SAMPLE DISHES: deep-fried onion rings £2.50; vegetable curry with nan bread £6; Bakewell tart £2.75.

Open *11 to 2.30, 6 to 11, Sat 11 to 3, 6 to 11, Sun 12 to 3, 6 to 11; bar food all week L 12 to 2, Tue to Sat D 7 to 9.30*
Details *Children over 14 welcome if eating Car park Garden and patio No-smoking area No music Dogs welcome No cards*

BLACKMORE END Essex map 3

Bull Inn

Blackmore End TEL: (01371) 851037
between A1017 and B1053, 6m N of Braintree

The Bull is every inch a family business. Christopher and Mary Bruce are emphatically in charge, and since taking up residence have turned the place into one of the best pub/restaurants in Essex. Dining areas are tacked on to either end of the pleasant beamed bar, and you can eat anywhere you like. Service is at its sharpest when Mary Bruce is keeping an eye on things, but it is never less than 'satisfactory'.

Reporters who know the place reckon that Christopher Bruce's cooking is getting better and better. If you are looking for a snack, the familiar trio of sandwiches, ploughman's and jacket potatoes is backed up by a few things with chips, but the serious stuff is to be found on the blackboard. The repertoire changes every two weeks and it reads well. Starters such as fresh figs with San Danielle Parma ham, warm tiger prawns in lemon beurre blanc with Chinese noodles, or sliced pigeon breast with red onion compote and seared courgettes would make an ideal one-course meal. Otherwise the list of dishes yo-yos convincingly between the classic (breadcrumbed escalope of veal topped with fried egg, capers and anchovies) and the modern (roast fillet of cod with herb and Parmesan crust with a white wine, tomato and chive cream sauce). Ostrich and kangaroo even leap into the limelight – perhaps in company with glazed shallots, pink peppercorns and armagnac sauce. Bavarian bread pudding, crème brûlée and hot banana and toffee pancake are best-selling sweets; otherwise the range extends to honey syllabub in a brandy snap-basket with orange segments, and baked Catalan cream with raspberries and blueberries. Set lunches (including on Sunday) provide decent value. The tip-top wine list is prefaced by some vintage gems, and the collection of 60 bins is reliable across the range; house wines are sold by the glass. Up to five handpumps dispense brews such as Adnams Bitter, Greene King IPA and Mauldons White Adder, plus weekly guests. SAMPLE DISHES: sweet-cured herrings with apple and gherkin salad £4; duck breast with damsons and red wine sauce £11; hot apple and summer fruit strudel £3.50.

Open *12 to 3, 6.30 to 11, Sun 12 to 3, 7 to 10.30; bar food Tue to Sun 12 to 2, 7 to 10 (9 Sun); restaurant Tue to Sun 12 to 1.45, 7 to 9.45 (9 Sun); open Mon bank hols*
Details *Children welcome in dining-room Car park No cigars/pipes in restaurant No music No dogs Access, Delta, Switch, Visa*

BLACKO Lancashire **map 8**

▲ *Moorcock Inn*

Gisburn Road, Blacko TEL: (01282) 614186
on A682, 2m N of Nelson

Once a farmhouse on the high expanses of Pendleside's open moorland, with the Pendle walk passing the door, the Moorcock Inn was renovated using local stone to keep faith with its past. Much of the interior is laid out for dining and it's best to focus on the blackboard of daily specials: here you might encounter lemon sole filled with crabmeat, chicken breast in wine and mushroom sauce, and schnitzel with tomato and onion salad. The short printed menu is familiar stuff: open sandwiches, lasagne, macaroni cheese and so on. A decent list of home-made hot and cold puddings, from raspberry pavlova to apple crumble, rounds things off. This is a Thwaites tied house, with Bitter and Mild on draught; a handful of wines are also on show. If you are feeling energetic, set off across the moors to look at the famous Black Tower, a striking circular monument about a mile from the pub. SAMPLE DISHES: garlic prawns £3.50; pork fillet in pepper sauce £6; toffee nut tart £2.50.

Open *Mon to Fri 12 to 2, 7 to 11.30, Sat and Sun 12 to 10.30; bar food Mon to Fri 12 to 2.30, 6.45 to 10, Sat and Sun 12 to 10*
Details *Children welcome Car park Wheelchair access (also WC) Garden Background music Dogs welcome Access, Amex, Delta, Diners, Switch, Visa Accommodation: 3 rooms, B&B £15 to £40*

BLAKENEY Norfolk map 6

▲ *White Horse Hotel* 🍇

4 High Street, Blakeney TEL: (01263) 740574
on A149, 5m W of Holt

This seventeenth-century coaching-inn set round a courtyard became Blakeney's first hotel in the early 1900s – although it's best remembered by incomers and locals as a seminal North Norfolk coastal boozer. In recent years it has been substantially revamped, but the long main bar still resounds with bustle and chat. The printed bar menu is straightforward stuff, ranging from cockle chowder, and fisherman's pie, to pâté, steaks and salads; while daily specials provide variety in the shape of bacon and bean soup, grilled sea trout with asparagus sauce, and aubergine, tomato and Mozzarella bake. Puddings are comforting staples such as spotted dick, and sticky date and walnut pudding. In the converted stables is a separate restaurant (with its own chef) which is open for evening meals. Around 40 keenly selected wines from Adnams are supplemented by blackboard specials by the glass or bottle. Adnams Bitter is on handpump, beside Boddingtons and Flowers Original. It's worth taking a walk down the high street to the quayside, where boat trips go out along the cut to the National Trust Reserve at Blakeney Point, renowned for its seal colonies. SAMPLE DISHES: deep-fried soft herring roes on toast £3.50; steak and kidney pudding £5.50; treacle tart £2.50.

Open *11 to 3, 6 to 11, Sun 12 to 3, 7 to 10.30, Aug all week 11am to 11pm; bar food 12 to 2.30, 6 to 9 (9.30 July and Aug); restaurant Tue to Sat D only 7 to 9.30*
Details *Children welcome in dining-room Car park Wheelchair access Garden No-smoking area No music No dogs Access, Amex, Delta, Switch, Visa Accommodation: 9 rooms, B&B £30 to £70*

🍇 *indicates a pub serving better-than-average wine.*

BLEDINGTON Gloucestershire map 5

▲ *Kings Head*

The Green, Bledington, nr Kingham TEL: (01608) 658365
on B4450 Chipping Norton to Stow-on-the-Wold road

This creeper-clad, fifteenth-century Cotswold stone pub is charmingly unspoilt and efficiently run. It has a welcoming air and pulls the crowds, many of whom are there for the food: on a Sunday lunch-time you may have to share a table, but the staff cope admirably with the hordes. The regularly changing bar menu supplements pub staples with fish dishes like chargrilled swordfish steak, and baked fillets of brill with tarragon and grapes, and game such as local rabbit with cider and mustard. Sandwiches are on ciabatta or granary, and children have their own menu. Reporters have praised pink rack of lamb served in 'a nicely balanced, unthickened plum sauce', while the bread pudding is a splendidly rich confection. The separate dining-room serves a longer à la carte menu in the evening, but at lunch-time it's used as a family eating area. On tap are Hook Norton and Wadworth 6X, backed up by monthly-changing guests such as Uley Pigs Ear, Wild's Wild Oats, and Stanway Old Eccentric. Up to 40 different malt whiskies are on show, and the wine list is above average for a pub, running to 60 bins with seven decent tipples available by the glass, a classic selection and a wide choice from France and the New World. The village green serves as the pub garden and Morris Dancers can be seen performing there in the summer months. The traditional game of Aunt Sally is played on the private patio at the back of the pub. SAMPLE DISHES: braised kidneys Bledington £5; monkfish with steamed chives and mint £9; chocolate and brandy mousse £2.25.

Open *11 to 2.30, 6 to 11, Sun 12 to 2, 7 to 10.30; bar food and restaurant 12 to 2 (1.45 Sun), 7 to 9.45; closed 24 and 25 Dec*
Details *Children welcome in dining-room Car park Wheelchair access Garden and patio No-smoking area Background and live music No dogs Access, Delta, Switch, Visa Accommodation: 14 rooms, B&B £35 to £75*

BLEDLOW Buckinghamshire map 3

Lions of Bledlow

Church End, Bledlow TEL: (01844) 343345
off B4009, 2m SW of Princes Risborough; take West Lane, not Bledlow Ridge turning

A former sixteenth-century coaching-inn, the Lions is an ideal place to begin and end a country stroll: it sits at the edge of the village and is surrounded by footpaths – one even leads from the pub door into the Chiltern beechwoods. With its unspoilt character, warming winter fires and good summer al fresco facilities, it's a favourite pit-stop throughout the year. The exterior is low and white-painted, while inside there's a series of low interconnecting beamed rooms around a central bar. The specials board could include lamb cutlets, fish-cakes, or poached salmon with herb butter. If you are feeling in the mood for something spicy, dip into the printed menu, which offers chicken tikka masala, a Mexican combination of chicken burrito and chilli con carne, as well as seafood pancakes. A good range of real ales on handpump includes Ruddles County, Wadworth 6X, Courage Best, John Smiths and local brew Wychert Ale from Vale Brewery. Nearby is Hughenden Manor and West Wycombe Park. SAMPLE DISHES: leek and artichoke soup £2; steak and Guinness pie £5.50; banoffi pie £2.50.

Open *11.30 to 3, 6 to 11, Sun 12 to 3, 7 to 10.30; bar food and restaurant 12 to 2, 7 to 9.30 (10 Fri and Sat); no food Sun D winter*
Details *Children welcome in eating areas Car park Wheelchair access Garden and patio No music Dogs welcome in bar Access, Amex, Delta, Diners, Switch, Visa*

BLEWBURY Oxfordshire map 2

▲ *Blewbury Inn*

Blewbury TEL: (01235) 850496
just off A417 Wantage to Streatley road, 3m S of Didcot

The Blewbury Inn is the kind of place that celebrates 'the diversity of pubs', concluded one report about this re-vitalised hostelry in a South Oxfordshire village. It is also a place that is unusual in its ambitions – aiming skywards as far as food is concerned, while maintaining service with a smile and a refreshing lack of pretence. Eat in the bar or in the six-table dining-room with its understated décor and stencils on mustard-coloured walls. At lunch you can call in for a one-dish meal – anything from shredded chicken and cumin salad, or confit of duck with gooseberry chutney, to kidneys in mustard sauce, or even an omelette. Home-baked bread and butter come with all dishes, whether they be starters or main courses.

Evening brings a more structured, restaurant-style *carte* with four choices at each stage, although it mines the same culinary vein. High points from one excellent supper included a warm salad of pink, gamey pigeon and bacon with unusual leaves, and perfectly cooked succulent rib-eye steak in a thin gravy darkened with black beans and soy, while a substantial tranche of salmon draped over a heap of fresh crab in a pink sauce was 'much appreciated by a Norfolk woman who knows her crabs'. Other possibilities range from stir-fried grey mullet and pheasant eggs poached in red wine, to pan-fried chicken breast with creamed leeks, and whole roast Dover sole with parsley salsa. Among the desserts might be chocolate mousse with cherry sauce, or elderflower sorbet with poached pear. Morells Oxford Mild and beers from the Hook Norton brewery are supplemented by a guest bitter; the wine list (from Christopher Piper of Ottery St Mary) has been upgraded and it manages to offer quality at prices that will not offend; four house wines are served by the glass. SAMPLE DISHES: avocado and chorizo £4; fricassee of rabbit £10; caramelised bananas with banana ice-cream £4.

Open *11 to 2.30 (3 Sat), 6 to 11, Sun 12 to 3, 7 to 10.30; bar food and restaurant Tue to Sun L 12 to 2, Tue to Sat D 7 to 9 (9.30 Sat)*
Details *Children welcome Car park Wheelchair access (also WC) No smoking in restaurant Background music Dogs welcome Access, Delta, Switch, Visa Accommodation: 3 rooms, B&B £32 to £50*

BLOCKLEY Gloucestershire **map 5**

▲ *Crown Inn*

High Street, Blockley TEL: (01386) 700245
on B4479, 3m NW of Moreton-in-Marsh

This is 'a BIG operation', warns a reporter. The Crown stands right in the centre of the village on a steeply sloping hillside and has developed far beyond the realms of local watering-hole into a fully fledged 21-bedroom hotel complete with a restaurant and a brasserie majoring in seafood. To discover the pubby roots of the place you need to descend a full-sized stairway from the side entrance of the building and head for the tiny bar. Sandwiches and baguettes are supplemented by things like salad niçoise, chicken satay with chips, and three kinds of sausage with home-made chutney. There are also fish specials along the lines of lemon sole with lemon and parsley butter, fresh sardines, and calamari with tartare sauce. In addition, the midweek fixed-price lunch menu is reckoned to be fair value for up-market dishes such as fanned melon with cassis sorbet, and fresh tuna with light tomato sauce. As if to emphasise that this is still a pub, there's a fine stock of real ales, including Hook Norton Bitter, Butcombe and Goffs Jouster among others. The wine list also has some first-rate stuff, although prices are by no means cheap; eleven, including a 'wonderful' South African Pinotage, are served by the glass. Blockley is within easy reach of Batsford Park arboretum and falconry centre. SAMPLE DISHES: spinach, oregano and feta cheese pie £6; cod in beer and chive batter £7; crème brûlée £4.

Open *11am to midnight, Sun 12 to 2.30, 6.30 to 11; bar food and restaurant all week 12 to 2 (2.30 Sun), 7 to 10*

Details *Children welcome in bar eating area Car park Patio No music Dogs welcome Access, Amex, Delta, Diners, Visa Accommodation: 21 rooms, B&B £60 to £120*

BLYFORD Suffolk **map 6**

▲ *Queen's Head Inn*

Southwold Road, Blyford TEL: (01502) 478404
on B1123, 3m E of Halesworth

'Way back in 1970 I had my very first pint of Adnams here,' reflects one of Suffolk's adopted sons. A lot of ale has been pulled through the pipes since then, but the Queen's Head still maintains its reputation as a fine place to sample the full range of local brews (including seasonal Barley Mow, Tally Ho and Mayday Ale). Although the cream-painted building dates back to the fifteenth century, the roof was re-thatched a few years ago after a devastating fire. The interior is all oak beams, nooks and crannies, with a wonderful jumble of brassware, kettles and so forth festooned around the fireplace. Hearty country cooking is the order of the day and dishes are chalked up on a blackboard: Lowestoft cod ('fresh from the quay at 7.30,' says the menu) is done in 'beautifully light' crisp batter, pheasant is served with burgundy sauce and 'gigantic' roast potatoes, rabbit is casseroled, home-cooked ham is accompanied by fried free-range eggs. Roasts are a fixture. Puddings are often given a boozy flourish: fruit trifle is laced with Adnams sherry, bread-and-butter pudding with rum. A comprehensive wine list is also available. The pub stands in five acres of grassland with a large, safe garden. A secret passage runs from the cellar to the church across the road (worth a look for its medieval 'Doom' painting). SAMPLE DISHES: cheese, broccoli and apple soup £2.75; braised venison with redcurrants, pears and mushrooms £7.50; apple and sultana sponge pudding £2.75.

Open *11 to 3, 6.30 to 11, Sun 12 to 3, 7 to 10.30; bar food and restaurant 12 to 2, 7 to 9*
Details *Children welcome in eating areas Car park Wheelchair access (also WC) Garden and patio No smoking in dining-rooms No music Guide dogs only No cards Accommodation: 2 rooms, B&B £40 to £50*

BOLTER END Buckinghamshire map 3

Peacock

Bolter End, Lane End TEL: (01494) 881417
on B482 Marlow to Stokenchurch road

A cheerful atmosphere pervades in this roadside Chilterns inn with its beams, low ceilings and lots of snug little nooks and crannies. The menu endorses a reporter's view that food is 'out of the ordinary without being flagrantly exotic'. Items could include half a roast shoulder of lamb, chicken balti, tiger prawns in filo, battered cod, and steaks; while the three daily specials listed on a blackboard may take in salmon stuffed with prawns, Cajun chicken, or Sicilian mushrooms. Sunday lunch sees roast Aberdeen Angus. Baked Bramley apple with mincemeat may be on the board around Christmas, with pannacotta, and orange and brandy pancakes among the puddings on the printed menu. Brakspear, Adnams and Tetley Bitter are on draught, while chalkboards list reasonably priced, regularly changing wines, plus bottles of the month; house wines come by the glass. SAMPLE DISHES: cod and prawn Mornay with rice £7; Lincolnshire pork sausages £5.50; strawberry sherry trifle £2.50.

Open *11.45 to 2.30, 6 to 11, Sun 12 to 3; bar food all week L 12 to 2, Mon to Sat D 7 to 9.45*
Details *No children under 14 Car park Wheelchair access Garden No smoking in 1 bar No music Dogs welcome Access, Amex, Delta, Diners, Switch, Visa*

BONCHURCH Isle of Wight map 2

▲ *Bonchurch Inn*

The Shute, Bonchurch TEL: (01983) 852611
off A3055, just NE of Ventnor

This is not a 'typical resort pub', notes one reporter. Licensees Ulisse and Aline Besozzi are Italian, and you can expect a Mediterranean welcome at their unassuming village local beneath the steep rock slope of Bonchurch Shute. Inside, it seems very Victorian and unspoilt, with a 'motley mix' of wooden furniture and a few bright paintings and prints adding a dash of colour; bar billiards and other pub games can be played in the family room. A scattering of typical trattoria dishes appear on the bar menu, including pizza napolitana, canneloni with spinach and risotto milanese; otherwise it's back home for ploughman's, things with chips, or steak and grilled halibut steak. The restaurant menu has an even stronger Continental accent. Courage Directors and Best, plus Morland Old Speckled Hen, are on draught, and a few Italian wines show up on the list. If you fancy sightseeing, Shanklin Chine and Appuldurcombe House are within easy reach. SAMPLE DISHES: minestrone £2; king prawns provençale £5.50; zabaglione £3.50.

Open *11 to 3, 6.30 to 11, Sun 12 to 3, 7 to 10.30; bar food 11 to 2.30, 6.30 to 9; restaurant all week D only 6.30 to 8.45 (bookings only)*
Details *Children welcome in eating areas and family room Car park Garden and patio Background music Dogs welcome exc. in family room Access, Delta, Visa Accommodation: 3 rooms, B&B £18 to £35*

BOOTHSDALE Cheshire **map 7**

Boot Inn

Boothsdale, Willington TEL: (01829) 751375
just S of A54 Chester to Winsford road at turning signposted Kelsall

The Boot is close to a 'picturesque' area known locally as Little Switzerland, and Oulton Park motor-racing circuit is a short distance away. The main bar of the pub features a wood-burning stove, and there is a separate restaurant with Windsor chairs and tables set for eating. Sandwiches and baguettes are sold in the bars, full meals in the restaurant. Available throughout are dishes such as steaks, warm smoked trout, or Cumberland sausage, plus daily specials from the blackboard: perhaps a starter of Stilton and bacon salad, followed by chicken breast with sun-dried tomatoes, and Bakewell tart. Greenalls, Worthington E and a guest ale of the week are on tap, and the wine list includes about two dozen reasonably priced bottles. SAMPLE DISHES: kidneys in a red wine, mushroom and onion sauce £4; pan-fried beef with asparagus and mushrooms £13.50; coffee and walnut cheesecake £3.

Open *11 to 3, 6 to 11, Sun 12 to 3, 7 to 10.30; bar food 11 to 2.30, 6 to 9.30, sandwiches available Sat and Sun 2.30 to 6; closed 25 Dec evening*
Details *Children welcome in bar eating area Car park Wheelchair access Garden and patio No-smoking area No music No dogs Access, Switch, Visa*

BORASTON Shropshire **map 5**

▲ *Peacock*

Worcester Road, Boraston TEL: (01584) 810506
off A456, 1½m E of Tenbury Wells

The Peacock, a rambling white-painted building dating from the fourteenth century, is well placed for Croft Castle and Berrington

Hall (both National Trust) and the lovely town of Ludlow. The charming oak-panelled lounge has an inglenook, a comfortable mixture of old tables and chairs, pew settles and a heavily beamed ceiling strewn with hops; a vaulted-ceilinged room at the rear acts as a dining area, and there's a separate bar. Fish is a speciality of the keen and talented team in the kitchen, who produce 'beautifully presented' dishes using top-quality ingredients: on offer might be fillet of cod on olive mash with deep-fried leeks, chargrilled tuna on a bed of tagliatelle with saffron sauce, or sea bass with gazpacho sauce. Other options could include breast of duck with spicy plum sauce, roast pheasant on sweet potato with prunes and chestnuts, and chargrilled venison with wild mushrooms and a sauce of sage in white wine. Lemon tart – 'tangy, with good, light pastry' – gets the thumbs-up. Tetley, Bass and Ind Coope Burton Ale are on draught, with around half a dozen wines by the glass. SAMPLE DISHES: smoked haddock rarebit £5; fillet of salmon with basil salsa and white wine sauce £10; sticky toffee pudding with pecan sauce £4.

Open *11.30 to 3, 6 to 11, Sun 12 to 3, 7 to 10.30; bar food 12 to 2.15, 7 to 9.30*
Details *Children welcome Car park Wheelchair access Garden and patio No smoking in lounge Occasional background music No dogs Access, Switch, Visa Accommodation: 3 rooms, room only £40 to £65*

BOROUGHBRIDGE **North Yorkshire** **map 8**

▲ *Black Bull*

6 St James Square, Boroughbridge TEL: (01423) 322413

Sitting pretty on the corner of St James Square, this seven-centuries-old white-painted pub is very much the hub of historic Boroughbridge. Landlady Margaret Crystal runs a tight ship here, and the mood is one of busy efficiency. The main reason why the crowds swell 'in numbers in the front rooms' is, quite simply, the food on offer. Bar snacks are not the usual predictable offerings: instead the menu ranges far and wide for onion and blue-cheese tartlet, Cajun chicken with a 'pasta rösti', and stir-fried beef with Thai spices and sweet soy sauce. Added to that are even more jazzy fish specials, such as chargrilled sea bass with roasted Mediterranean vegetables and black olive sauce, and roast salmon with tomato and onion compote. Desserts are in the same mould – warm apricot rice pudding with banana ice-cream and vanilla sauce, for example. More ambitious meals are served in the restaurant. Up to ten wines by the glass are advertised on a blackboard, and the full list is a global selection. Black Sheep Best and Special are on draught alongside John Smiths. Boroughbridge is within reach of the cathedral town of

Ripon and the Roman site at Aldborough. SAMPLE DISHES: chicken-liver parfait with toasted brioche and piccalilli £3.50; beef stew cooked in stout £5.25; glazed lemon tart with orange cream sauce £3.

Open *11am to 11pm, Sun 12 to 10.30; bar food and restaurant 12 to 2.30, 7 to 9.30 (10 Fri and Sat)*
Details *Children welcome in eating areas Wheelchair access (also WC) Patio No music No dogs Access, Amex, Delta, Switch, Visa Accommodation: 4 rooms, B&B £32 to £45*

BOXFORD Suffolk **map 6**

White Hart

Broad Street, Boxford TEL: (01787) 211071
on A1071 between Sudbury and Hadleigh

Real ales are a strong suit at this main-street village pub: two to three weekly-changing guest beers join regulars Greene King IPA and Adnams Extra and Broadside. The landlord also hosts a weekend-long beer festival each August where people can sample some interesting ales from breweries around the country: Thunderstorm from Wiltshire's Hop Back Brewery, and Ramsbottom from Dent Brewery in Cumbria, for instance. The long menu offers 'a full range of authentic curries', the landlord tells us, and a wide choice of fish dishes – a mixed salad of ordinary, butterfly and smoked prawns and crevettes, for example. Other options could include chicken tikka sausages or French onion soup, and main courses of gammon with leek and Stilton sauce, braised liver and bacon, or 'Hartbreaker' (escalope of chicken breast with a poached egg, spinach and a mini-portion of spaghetti bolognese). Cheesecakes, fruit crumbles and alcoholic bread-and-butter pudding are offered for dessert. Lay & Wheeler from nearby Colchester supplies the wines on the reasonably priced list. Gainsborough's birthplace is just down the road in Sudbury, while Flatford Mill is south of East Bergholt in the opposite direction. SAMPLE DISHES: goujons of plaice with curry dip £3; grilled lamb chops with Cumberland sauce £6; banana fritters with hot toffee sauce £2.50.

Open *12 to 3, 6 to 11, Sun 12 to 3, 7 to 10.30; bar food 12 to 2.30, 6.30 to 9.30, Sun 7 to 9*
Details *Children welcome Car park Wheelchair access Garden and patio No smoking in dining-room Background music Dogs welcome Access, Delta, Switch, Visa*

The details under the text are taken from questionnaires sent to all pubs that feature in the book.

BRAMDEAN Hampshire map 2

Fox Inn

Bramdean TEL: (01962) 771363
on A272 Winchester to Petersfield road, 3m SE of New Alresford

'On a sunny autumnal day, the drive to [this] pub was bliss,' remarked one traveller after cruising through glorious Hampshire countryside. The Fox is a well-maintained, neat and tidy hostelry, with low beams, cushioned benches, tidy log baskets by the fire and several staff serving with a degree of pleasant correctness. The whole place is devoted to food, and fish is the main strength. On the blackboard you might find Orkney marinated herrings and locally smoked trout as well as fresh offerings such as grilled sea bass, halibut Mornay, and whole boned plaice stuffed with prawns and crab. Alternatives to seafood might be avocado with smoked chicken and mayonnaise, braised beef in red wine, and pan-fried lamb's liver with bacon. A few more-expensive, restaurant-style dishes, such as breast of guinea-fowl Normandy, and monkfish with tarragon and cream sauce, appear in the evening. Marston's Pedigree is on handpump and there's a well-rounded list of about three dozen wines, including a couple of wines of the month. SAMPLE DISHES: baked mushrooms with dolcelatte £4.50; fillet of beef Stroganov with rice £9; lemon tart £2.50.

Open *10.30 to 3, 6 to 11, Sun 12 to 3, 7 to 10.30; bar food 12 to 2, 7 to 9; closed 25 Dec*
Details *No children Car park Wheelchair access (also WC) Garden and patio No-smoking area Background music Dogs welcome by arrangement Access, Amex, Delta, Switch, Visa*

BRANSCOMBE Devon map 2

▲ *Masons Arms*

Branscombe TEL: (01297) 680300
off A3052, 5m E of Sidmouth

Nestling in a hollow down long twisting lanes, this fourteenth-century ivy-clad inn is a welcome sight to hungry drivers who might have thought they'd missed the pub down some side turning. Inside there's a slate floor, a large log-burning fireplace, lots of tables and assorted chairs in a series of semi-open rooms complete with beams and standing timbers. Food is imaginative both on the menu and specials board, though prices tend towards restaurant rather than pub. The blackboard majors in fresh fish: Dover sole, salmon, lobster and trout, for example. And for meat eaters the choice could be steak, spicy meatballs, grilled gammon with sweet-and-sour sauce, or the spit roast of the day. The printed menu has class, too: starters include smoked salmon and crab mousse, and venison and pistachio nut terrine, while main courses range from chicken peperonata to noisette of lamb. Local mussels with pasta have been 'excellent', and steamed fruit pudding with a classic white sauce was a fine way to end for one reporter. A separate restaurant opens in the evenings and Sunday lunch-time. On handpump there's a strong selection of real ales, including Otter Ale and Dartmoor Best, as well as two guest beers. Fourteen wines feature on the list, all available by the glass. The beach of Branscombe Mouth with its stunning cliffs is well worth the walk through fields and woodland. SAMPLE DISHES: tempura mushrooms £3.50; pork and haricot bean casserole £9.25; oranges in Cointreau £3.

Open *Mon to Fri 11 to 3, 6 to 11, Sat 11am to 11pm, Sun 12 to 10.30; bar food 12 to 2 (2.30 summer), 7 to 9 (9.30 summer); restaurant Sun L 12 to 2, all week D 7 to 9*
Details *Children welcome Car park Wheelchair access Patio Live music Dogs welcome on a lead Access, Delta, Switch, Visa Accommodation: 20 rooms, B&B £24 to £96*

BRASSINGTON Derbyshire **map 5**

Ye Olde Gate Inn

HAUNTED

Well Street, Brassington TEL: (01629) 540448
just off B3035 Ashbourne to Wirksworth road, 4m W of Wirksworth

'What we really liked about this place was that it felt like a real pub – a cosy, attractive place to come with friends,' write a couple of visitors who found their way to Ye Olde Gate. The sight of a well-worn terracotta-tiled floor, a range with an open fire, and tankards hanging from ceiling-beams no doubt reinforced that feeling. Barbecues are held in summer in the back garden, and at other times you can expect main courses along the lines of roast loin of lamb, Cajun chicken, cheesy leek and potato bake, steaks, and cod and prawn crumble. Baguettes added at lunch-times make decision-making more difficult: one filled with Dovedale Blue cheese has been described as 'excellent'. Puddings tend towards the sweet and stodgy: death by chocolate, and pecan pie, for instance. Marston's Pedigree is on draught, with Owd Rodger in winter, and house wines come by the glass. Rumour has it that one room of the pub is haunted by a spirit from the days when the place doubled as a 'hospital' during the Civil War. SAMPLE DISHES: salad of baby mixed greens with mango £4; 'creamy' chicken on garlic and mushroom tagliatelle £7.50; warm ginger bread with rum butter £2.50.

Open *Tue to Sat 12 to 2.30, Mon to Sat 6 to 11, Sun 12 to 3, 7 to 10.30; bar food Tue to Sun L 12 to 1.45 (2 Fri to Sun), Tue to Sat (and Sun summer) D 7 to 9*
Details *No children under 10 Car park Wheelchair access (also WC) Garden No smoking in dining-room No music Dogs welcome No cards*

BRAUNSTON **Leicestershire** **map 5**

Blue Ball Inn 🍇

6 Cedar Street, Braunston TEL: (01572) 722135
2m SW of Oakham off A6003

Having been meticulously and splendidly refurbished by its previous owners Celia and Colin Crawford (see Peacock Inn, Redmile), this 300-year-old stone and thatched inn was acquired by the Old English Pub Company in the summer of 1996. The interior still has a 'tasteful simplicity', with beams everywhere, comfortable alcoves to relax in and sturdy stripped wood tables to sit at. For those wishing to eat, it is civilised yet informal. A short menu of bar snacks such as cumin-flavoured fish-cakes with chutney, braised spare ribs, and stir-fried vegetable curry is augmented by slightly more imaginative blackboard specials; 'succulent' guinea-fowl stuffed with garlic mousse and served with port and honey sauce is one of the more interesting ideas. Fixed-price menus, written in French with English explanations, are available in the no-smoking restaurant. Around eight wines are offered by the glass and the full list runs to 40 bins drawn from sound sources; prices are very fair. Beers on handpump include Theakston XB, Marston's Pedigree and Ruddles County among others. Braunston is a short drive from the myriad attractions of Rutland Water. SAMPLE DISHES: Caesar leaf salad £5; rack of lamb £12.50; profiteroles £3.25.

Open *12 to 3, 6 to 11, Sun 12 to 10.30; bar food and restaurant 12 to 2, 7 to 10*
Details *Children welcome in eating areas Car park Patio No smoking in restaurant and 1 area of bar Background music No dogs Access, Amex, Delta, Switch, Visa*

BRAY **Berkshire** **map 3**

Fish 🍇

Old Mill Lane, Bray TEL: (01628) 781111

This white-painted Georgian brick pub, originally known as the Albion, re-opened after major renovation and refurbishment as the Fish. There's a good pubby bar at the front, with locals popping in for a pint and a chat around the fire. To the rear is a dining-room with soft lighting, candles, tasteful fish pictures and a warm décor; and beyond that is a conservatory dining-area. As the pub's new name suggests, fish is the thing here, although something like chicken breast with bacon and Gruyère sauce may be among the small choice of meaty alternatives on the monthly-changing printed menu. Mussel and bacon chowder, smoked haddock and spinach fish-cakes, and anchovy and chilli crostini are among the starters, while a blackboard proclaims the daily-changing main courses: grilled mullet on caper and parsley mash, pan-fried king scallops with black pasta and saffron and red pepper sauce, and seared tuna with avocado and tomato salsa are the sort of modern dishes you can expect. Plum bread-and-butter pudding is an interesting variation, and there may also be pecan fudge pie and lemon tart. Brakspear Special and Adnams Bitter are dispensed at the bar, and around seven wines are sold by the glass from a list of almost exclusively Australian and French bottles. SAMPLE DISHES: seafood soup with garlic rouille and croûtons £4; grilled plaice with pesto mash and lemon beurre blanc £10.50; steamed chocolate pudding £3.50.

Open *11 to 3, 6 to 11, Sun 12 to 3; bar food all week L 12 to 2, Mon to Sat D 7 to 9.30*
Details *Children welcome in bar eating area Car park Garden No cigars or pipes; no smoking in conservatory No music Dogs welcome in bar only Access, Delta, Switch, Visa*

BREARTON **North Yorkshire** **map 9**

Malt Shovel 🍺

Brearton TEL: (01423) 862929
off A61 and B6165, 2m E of Ripley

'The tiny bar is jam-packed with drinks,' noted one reporter. On handpump are no fewer than five real ales, usually including Daleside Nightjar from nearby Harrogate, Old Mill Bitter (an East Yorkshire brew) and Theakston Best from Ripon, plus two guest beers such as Innkeeper's Special Reserve from Coach House Breweries in Warrington. Added to that are 25 malt whiskies as well as – in season – real cider from Pipkin. Or turn to the wine list of about 16 bins, with a small selection sold by the glass. Inside, the sixteenth-century pub has a rustic feel with its beams and brasses, old wood panels and low ceilings. Service is down-to-earth, friendly and helpful. Bar food is chalked up on blackboards and runs to about 20 frequently changing main courses that might take in home-baked ham with a grain mustard and honey sauce, steak and ale pie, char-grilled vegetables, and seafood like Cajun fish or poached salmon. Finish with lemon flan, steamed ginger pudding, or apple and cinnamon pie, and 'excellent and strong' coffee. In summer the Malt Shovel is a haunt of Morris dancers. SAMPLE DISHES: goats' cheese and leek tart £4; lamb shanks £5.50; chocolate bread-and-butter pudding £2.50.

Open *Tue to Sun 12 to 3, 6.45 to 11, Sun 12 to 3, 7 to 10.30; bar food Tue to Sun L 12 to 2, Tue to Sat D 7 to 9*
Details *Children welcome Car park Wheelchair access Garden and patio No music Dogs welcome No cards*

BRIMFIELD Hereford & Worcester map 5

▲ *Roebuck*

LOCAL PRODUCE

Brimfield TEL: (01584) 711230
just off A49 Leominster to Ludlow road, 4m W of Tenbury Wells

Since 1983 Carole Evans has sought to re-define the notion of pub food in Britain. The Roebuck is her hostelry, the kitchen is her adopted home. Three very different areas are the setting for bar food which takes its cue from raw materials that are true to the region. Grafted on to this is a culinary talent that is equally at home with back-to-the-roots domestic cooking and fine-tuned cuisine – although this is thankfully free from dodgy ideas or flim-flam. Carole's commitment to local produce is mightily impressive: she buys Trelough ducks from Barry Clark's 'kind' enterprise in Wormbridge; a village postman often delivers partridges and pigeons; salmon could be the wild kind from the Wye; while the Herefordshire countryside provides everything from hop shoots to ceps (which might be roasted whole as a starter). Supporting the local cause is a serious devotion to domestic enterprise: here is a kitchen that is forever making mustards, pickles, chutneys, marmalade and sausages – not to mention an array of breads, including a pumpkin version ('dyed' green with viscous oil and textured with crunchy seeds).

The seasonal bar menu makes for deceptively simple reading: crab pots with Melba toast, baked queen scallops with mushrooms and garlic butter, steak and kidney pie, Berkshire loin chop with apple sauce. But beyond that are signs of experimentation. Huge mussels come with spinach and pesto; belly pork (a relatively new addition to the larder) is served with its skin crisped up on a bed of tomatoes, onions and beans; individual suet puddings might be filled with smoked chicken, bacon, leeks and a dash of Dunkertons perry. Desserts go the whole way, with baked apples stuffed with marinated fruits, visually stunning 'ice bowls' embedded with flowers and leaves and filled with seasonal sorbets, not to mention an equally dazzling caramel pyramid encasing a couple of dollops of brown-bread ice-cream. As an alternative, there's also a cheese list that brims over with superb regional specimens, from Stinking Bishop to Hereford Hop. In addition to the bar menu, you can also eat a fixed-price lunch in the bar or in the premier-league Poppies Restaurant, where food of a higher order is available

The Roebuck wine list is a lengthy, well-considered tome, with splendid stuff from classy French sources, an intriguing batch of New World bottles and much more besides. House wines change regularly, depending on the cellar. Beer drinkers have Morland Old Speckled Hen, Crown Buckley Reverend James and 'local sporting ales' to choose from. SAMPLE DISHES: mushroom and herb risotto £6; beef in beer with herb dumplings £8; marmalade steamed pudding with whisky custard £5.50

Open *Tue to Sun 12 to 3, all week 7 to 11 (10 Sun); bar food and restaurant Tue to Sat 12 to 2, 7 to 10*
Details *Children welcome Car park Patio No music Dogs welcome Access, Delta, Switch, Visa Accommodation: 3 rooms, B&B £45 to £60*

BRINKWORTH **Wiltshire** **map 2**

Three Crowns

Brinkworth TEL: (01666) 510366
on B4042 Malmesbury to Wootton Bassett road

At first glance you might think this was the archetypal village pub – a conglomeration of buildings (some ivy-clad) by the church and the green. Inside it maintains a certain bucolic image, with a 'mix and match' assortment of old and new pine, pews, captain's chairs, barrels and tubs dotted around the bustling bar. This is where drinkers come to quaff local brews such as Wadworth 6X and Archers Village IPA in addition to Bass and Castle Eden Ale. If a snack is required to go with the pint, the kitchen can offer jacket potatoes, ploughman's, and double-decker cottage rolls (including versions with smoked chicken).

In the conservatory dining-room overlooking the garden it's a very different story. Chef/landlord Anthony Windle 'has the right ideas about ingredients', according to one Welsh correspondent, and it shows in his ambitious restaurant-style menu. There are no starters, just a lengthy list of main courses and puddings with an underlying richness derived from plenty of cream and alcohol. Home-made pies (ranging from 'very eatable' steak and kidney to pork and venison) are a speciality, and a few new-wave sources of protein surface in the shape of crocodile, kangaroo, ostrich and wild boar. In between is a 'wonderful choice' of fresh fish: suprême of tuna cooked Creole-style and garnished with seared scallops, poached cod fillet with Cheddar cheese and chive sauce, and baked whole sea bass with apple and apricot stuffing, for example. The platter of mixed seafood also greatly impressed one reporter – particularly steamed mussels of unmatchable freshness. Balancing all these are griddled Scotch steaks, which are offered with all manner of sauces, from café de Paris to green peppercorn and brandy. A harvest festival of six spot-on vegetables comes on a large tray. Desserts range from deep-fried orange ice-cream to kiwi and gin sorbet. Wine is enthusiastically promoted: five house wines are well chosen, and the list of around 50 bins is a global slate tilted towards what is affordable. SAMPLE DISHES: Wiltshire ham double-decker £3; medallions of venison with wild mushrooms and a damson and redcurrant sauce £14; rum-and-raisin cheesecake £3.75.

Open *10 to 3, 6 to 11, Sun 12 to 3, 6 to 10.30; bar food 12 to 2, 6.30 to 9.30*

Details *Children welcome in bar eating area Car park Wheelchair access (also WC) Garden and patio No smoking in conservatory eating area Background music Dogs welcome in bar only Access, Amex, Delta, Diners, Switch, Visa*

BRISLEY Norfolk map 6

Brisley Bell

The Green, Brisley TEL: (01362) 668686
on B1145, 6m NW of East Dereham

This 400-year-old brick and flint pub overlooks the largest area of common land in Norfolk, making it a popular haunt of walkers and birdwatchers. The business of the day – relaxation, refreshment and chat – is conducted in a split-level bar with lots of exposed brick-work, beams and a large fireplace. Landlord Les Philp goes to Lowestoft market regularly to hand-pick fish for the kitchen, and his list of blackboard specials is the main attraction on the food side of things. Otherwise the menu plays safe with breaded mushrooms, a daily roast, and homely puddings along the lines of apple pie and treacle tart. More showy dishes – lobster thermidor, steak au poivre and so on – are served in the separate restaurant. Greene King IPA is on handpump. Brisley is within striking distance of Gressenhall Museum and Pensthorpe Waterfowl Park, and Fakenham Racecourse isn't far away if you fancy a flutter. SAMPLE DISHES: French onion soup £2; salmon with hollandaise sauce £5; lemon meringue pie £2.

Open *Mon to Sat 11 to 3, 6 to 11, Sun 12 to 3, 7 to 10.30; bar food and restaurant 12 to 2.30, 7 to 9.30*
Details *Children welcome Car park Wheelchair access (also WC) Garden and patio Background music Dogs welcome Access, Visa*

BROADHEMBURY Devon map 2

Drewe Arms

Broadhembury TEL: (01404) 841267
off A373, between Cullompton and Honiton

'If only there were more pubs like this,' mused one reporter clearly realising that this is one of the few hostelries in the land where traditional virtues really do count for a great deal. The setting couldn't be more seductive: a seven-centuries-old thatched cottage, warmed by a large log fire and emblematically decorated with carved walking sticks, farming implements, even an eel-catcher's basket hung from the ceiling. This is Kerstin and Nigel Burge's domain and they run it like a dream. It is, quite simply, 'a lovely place'.

Few would argue that freshness is one of the keys to good pub food, and the kitchen of the Drewe Arms is right at the top of the league table. Fish is its focus. In the bar you can indulge in the 'Gang Plank' – a huge plate laden with thickly buttered fresh bread, smoked salmon, gravlax, prawns, ripe Brie in good condition, and a tiny, well-dressed salad. Otherwise there are open sandwiches, marinated herrings, and a list of specials that could include roasted cod with anchovies, salmon fish-cakes with tomato and dill sauce, and grilled loin of tuna with pesto (a rare concession to fashion). If something meaty is required, look for BLTs and sirloin steak. Reporters have also eulogised in detail about the 'really excellent' pea and ham soup, based on a rich meaty stock derived from simmered bones and loaded with tiny pieces of ham and whole peas. Moving on to desserts, there are further temptations in the form of sticky toffee, chocolate and banana pudding or crème brûlée. In case you fancy testing the repertoire to its limit, a more extensive three-course fixed-price menu is served in the restaurant.

The Drewe Arms is a pub that has never lost sight of its roots or its locality: real ales are from the Otter Brewery at Luppitt, about five miles from Broadhembury, and you can sample Otter Bitter, Ale, Bright and Head in the bar, along with draughts of Bollhayes cider. Devon merchant Christopher Piper is the pub's wine supplier and the list is a high-class selection that gives equal prominence to red and whites, provides plenty in the way of half-bottles and includes five house wines by the glass. SAMPLE DISHES: smoked salmon soup £3; hot chicken and bacon salad £7.50; spiced apple crumble £3.75.

Open *11 to 3, 6 to 11, Sun 12 to 3, 7 to 10.30; bar food and restaurant 12 to 2, 7 to 10*
Details *Children welcome in eating areas Car park Wheelchair access (also WC) Garden No music Dogs welcome No cards*

BROCKTON Shropshire map 5

Feathers ✿

Brockton TEL: (01746) 785202
on B4378, 5m SW of Much Wenlock

Martin and Andrea Hayward moved into this roadside pub in 1990 and since then have transformed it into a remarkably designed venue with wine bar and bistro overtones. Once you have got over the culture shock, you should be reassured by the sight of handpumps offering Banks's Bitter and Morells Varsity in the bar. Food is given a high priority, and the menu features the kind of dishes you might find in a country restaurant with aspirations. To begin, there might be crostini, mushrooms filled with pâté in garlic butter, or crispy bacon and Stilton salad. Main courses display influences from far and wide: duck might be marinated teriyaki-style in wine, herbs, soy and garlic, or crisply roasted in a light gravy. Fillets of white fish are gilded with a lemon and chive crust, chicken breast is baked in a skillet with spicy chilli, garlic and tomato sauce. Vegetarians are likely to be offered things like penne pasta baked with spinach, tomato and pumpkin seeds, or puff pastry 'bouchées' of toasted vegetables with cream and tarragon sauce. Sweets, including steamed toffee pudding with fudge sauce, are on a blackboard. The wine list is a shortish list of two dozen bins covering a lot of territory, from Mexico to South Africa; house wines are served by the glass. SAMPLE DISHES: mussels sauté in white wine £4; herb-stuffed lamb fillet baked in red wine and redcurrant sauce £9.75; steamed toffee pudding with fudge sauce £3.25.

Open *Tue to Fri 6.30 to 11, Sat and Sun 12 to 3, 7 to 10.30; bar food Sat and Sun L 12 to 1.45, Tue to Sat D 6.30 to 9.30, Sun D 7 to 9*
Details *Children welcome Car park Wheelchair access Patio Background music No dogs Delta, Switch*

✿ *indicates a pub serving outstanding bar food, backed up by all-round excellence in other departments, such as service, atmosphere and cleanliness.*

BROOME **Shropshire** **map 5**

Engine & Tender

Broome TEL: (01588) 660275
turn off A49 at Craven Arms, take B4368 signposted Clun, then B4367 and turn right at crossroads after 1m

'Very, very English,' writes a reporter of this pub by a railway line, 'and very odd,' referring to the railway memorabilia and the hodge-podge of other items on display, including a grandfather clock and a lampshade depicting a half-timbered mansion, with the light shining through its windows. Mugs hang from the beams and even the arches between rooms, and the theme is continued into the dining-area. There's nothing odd about the food on offer, and most dishes are tried and tested pub favourites: toasted sandwiches, omelettes, home-made pâté, steak and kidney pie, and grilled salmon, with a couple of specials – perhaps braised liver with onions – providing variety. A big choice of desserts includes the likes of apple pie, treacle tart, and bread-and-butter pudding. The pub's very own ale, Engine & 10der (made by local brewery Wood), is among the beers on draught, and wines are served by the glass. Broome seems to be in the middle of nowhere; a camping and caravan site next door must appeal to those wanting to get away from it all. Stokesay Castle, nearby, is well worth seeing. SAMPLE DISHES: seafood platter £3.25; deep-fried battered cod £5; sherry trifle £2.50.

Open *Tue to Sun 12 to 3, all week 7 to 11.30 (10.30 Sun); bar food and restaurant Tue to Sun and bank hols L 12 to 2, Tue to Sat and bank hols D 7 to 9.30*
Details *Children welcome Car park Wheelchair access (also WC) Garden Background and occasional live music; jukebox No dogs No cards*

BUCKDEN **North Yorkshire** **map 8**

▲ *Buck Inn*

Buckden TEL: (01756) 760228 and 760416
on B6160, between Kettleworth and West Burton

Buckden is a popular centre for walkers, with plenty of lanes and paths crisscrossing the area hereabouts. The pub looks over the village green towards the River Wharfe; behind it, Buckden Pike soars to over 2,000 feet. The comfortable lounge bar features an open fire and a high shelf displaying a number of decorative plates. The blackboard menu changes at each session, and might offer green-lip mussels marinière, poached chicken breast on spinach and potato mash, or grilled halibut glazed with capers, followed by

Bailey's cheesecake. One reporter praised the lunchtime ploughman's – a generous portion of three cheeses, plus 'proper crusty bread', pickles, celery and apple – and the 'cheery and friendly' staff. Hand-pulled real ales include three from Theakston, as well as Black Sheep and Morland Old Speckled Hen. In the separate restaurant the wine list runs to more than 70 bins. 'All in all an excellent hostelry,' concluded one satisfied customer. SAMPLE DISHES: crab tartlet £3.75; chargrilled wild boar steak with coarse-grain mustard sauce and black pudding risotto £9; orange and Cointreau tart £3.25.

Open *11am to 11pm, Sun 12 to 3, 7 to 10.30; bar food and restaurant 12 to 2 (12 to 8.30 Sun during Aug), 6.30 to 9 (9.30 weekends)*
Details *Children welcome Car park Wheelchair access (also WC) Patio No smoking in restaurant Background music Dogs welcome Access, Delta, Switch, Visa Accommodation: 14 rooms, B&B £34 to £82*

BUCKLAND Oxfordshire **map 2**

▲ *Lamb Inn*

Lamb Lane, Buckland TEL: (01367) 870484
off A420, midway between Faringdon and Kingston Bagpuize

Paul Barnard is 'trying to be all things to all men' at this 200-year-old stone inn, and by all accounts he is succeeding. Not only has he turned it into one of the foremost dining pubs in the area, he also finds time to make and sell jams, chutneys, sauces and vinegars, not to mention offering a outside catering service for weddings, conferences and the like. And if you turn up with the family on a sunny Sunday evening in summer, you might find a barbecue in full swing.

Like many new-breed pubs of its kind, the Lamb has a single blackboard menu that serves both the hop-garlanded bar and the dining-room. What the kitchen offers is a cross-Channel selection of dishes based around judiciously chosen raw materials. Salmon and prawn kedgeree, rump steak and grouse pie, boiled beef and carrots, and roast saddle of hare couldn't be more patriotically British, while confit de canard, globe artichoke and seafood bourride, and daube of lamb bang the drum emphatically for France. But inspiration doesn't end there: from the Mediterranean come peperonata soufflé, and a warm salad of grilled fresh tuna and anchovies; from the Far East appears chicken, almond and coconut curry. The same diversity applies to desserts, which range from greengage compote, junket, and Norfolk treacle tart, to mango and ginger brûlée, and coconut and pineapple mousse. Adnams Broadside and Morland Original are on draught, but most drinkers head straight for the top-class wine list; a total of sixteen (including five excellent house wines) are offered by the glass from a selection that covers most style and grape varieties. The village of Buckland is home to descendants of the Duke of Wellington, and it's a lovely tranquil spot, with spectacular views across the Thames flood plain. SAMPLE DISHES: rabbit and guinea-fowl terrine £4.25; fillet of salmon with lime sauce £10.25; orange and cardamom tart £3.75.

Open *11 to 3, 5.30 to 11, Sun 12 to 3, 7 to 10.30; bar food and restaurant 12 to 2, 6.30 to 9.30*
Details *Children welcome Car park Garden and patio No smoking in restaurant Background and live music No dogs Access, Amex, Delta, Switch, Visa Accommodation: 4 rooms, B&B £35 to £45*

BUCKLAND DINHAM Somerset map 2

Bell Inn

High Street, Buckland Dinham TEL: (01373) 462956
on A362 Frome to Radstock road, 1½m NW of Frome

Wine buffs take note: the Bell Inn will do you proud with a vast list of 87 bins plus a further nine house wines, each carefully described. House and dessert wines are available by the glass, as are four non-vintage ports (and if you are keen on the vintage stuff, landlord Paul Hartley-Nadhar would appreciate two days' notice so he can decant a bottle). Ivy-clad and at the top of a steep hill, the Bell retains its original oak beams, flagstone floor and fireplace despite being modernised and refurbished to accommodate an enlarged restaurant. The smiles from the staff are genuine, service is prompt, and food is 'generous and good value', in the view of one visitor. The bar menu lists jackets and baguettes along with pies, pastas, salads, all-day breakfast and ploughman's lunch. The restaurant menu is more ambitious, extending to such delights as ostrich in red wine and cranberry gravy, and grilled tuna loin; Sunday lunch is taken very seriously. Draught beers include Courage Best, Theakston XB and Ruddles County. Outside is a large walled garden with a play area and barbecue, and next door to the pub is a two-acre paddock where they hold special events and picnics. The local countryside is peppered with plenty of good walks. SAMPLE DISHES: baguette filled with tuna mayonnaise £3; turkey and venison pie with chips and salad £5; treacle tart £3.

Open *11 to 3, 5.30 to 11, Sun 12 to 3, 6 to 10.30; bar food and restaurant 12 to 2.45, 6.30 to 10*
Details *Children welcome in bar eating area Car park Wheelchair access Garden and patio No-smoking area in restaurant Background music Dogs welcome on a lead Access, Amex, Delta, Diners, Switch, Visa*

BURFORD **Oxfordshire** **map 5**

▲ *Lamb Inn*

Sheep Street, Burford TEL: (01993) 823155

This venerable Cotswold hostelry looks as pretty as a picture, with vines and roses creeping over the façade and a cottagey walled garden at the back. Inside, it is all beams and flagged floors that bear their history well. Lunch in the bar is a civilised affair, with no Muzak to disturb the peace. The menu blends old and new, traditional and trendy, which means that steak and kidney pie, lamb curry, and venison and mushroom casserole sit alongside terrine of salmon, sole and king prawns, or warm salad of smoked duck and sun-dried tomatoes. Ploughman's and baguettes are also available, while puddings have included an 'excellent' crème de menthe cheesecake. Dinners and Sunday lunch are served in the pillared restaurant. Wadworth IPA, 6X and Old Timer are on handpump, along with Hook Norton Best Bitter, and the wine list is a comprehensive slate of over 70 bins. The Lamb has a car park for residents, although one reporter recommended leaving the car in the public car park and walking to the inn. SAMPLE DISHES: smoked salmon fritters on chervil mustard cream £5; roast saddle of lamb with a port *jus* £7; summer pudding £2.50.

Open *11 to 2.30, 6 to 11, Sun 12 to 2.30, 7 to 10.30; bar food Mon to Sat L 12 to 2; restaurant Sun L 12 to 2.45, all week D 7 to 9*
Details *Children welcome Garden No smoking in dining-room No music Dogs welcome Access, Switch, Visa Accommodation: 15 rooms, B&B £57.50 to £100*

BURHAM **Kent** **map 3**

Golden Eagle

80 Church Street, Burham TEL: (01634) 668975
off A229, between Maidstone and Rochester

The setting – a little Kentish village with views of the Medway – may seem quintessentially English, but there's something rather unexpected about this simple little pub. The interior is typically traditional, but the menu jets straight to the Far East for inspiration. Around two dozen dishes show influences from China, Malaysia, Singapore and Thailand: sweet-and-sour crispy pork, mee goreng, king prawns with tomatoes and garlic, and coconut beef are examples. There's also a goodly array of vegetarian options, mostly based around stir-fried vegetables with different sauces. A few stalwart

English pub dishes such as scampi, gammon, or sausages, served with chips or jacket potato, provide sustenance for those with less spicily inclined palates. Real ales, including Marston's Pedigree and Wadworth 6X, are emphatically patriotic, and the pub sells a handful of workaday wines. SAMPLE DISHES: spare ribs £5.50; crispy lemon chicken £7.25; mixed vegetables in garlic and onion sauce £7.

Open *11 to 2.30, 6.15 to 11, Sun 12 to 3, 7 to 10.30; bar food 12 to 2, 7 to 10; closed 25 and 26 Dec*
Details *No children Car park Wheelchair access Patio No-smoking area Background music No dogs Access, Delta, Switch, Visa*

BURITON Hampshire **map 2**

Five Bells

High Street, Buriton TEL: (01730) 263584
off A3, 1m S of Petersfield

Named after the five bells of Buriton church, this pub can trace its records back to 1639. The part of the building now housing the restaurant was once a farrier's serving the horses and carts of traders on the market-run between Chichester and Petersfield. At one time it was also the village morgue; a small lady in grey peasant clothes is said to haunt the building – sightings generally occur in the morning. The main part of the pub is taken up with a rambling series of rooms with rustic furniture, rugs strewn over woodblock floors and no fewer than four open fires and woodburning stoves. Live folk-music and jazz are regular attractions. Blackboard menus are hung on heavy beams in one bar, and the list of dishes is an ever-changing slate with the emphasis on hearty country cooking. Jugged hare, steak and pheasant casserole, wild rabbit with prunes and calvados, and beef in beer are red-blooded fillers; otherwise you can expect anything from smoked-chicken salad, and three-cheese and asparagus charlotte, to sardines in garlic butter, and grilled red snapper. To finish, there are roulades, crumbles and fruit pies. A first-rate stock of real ales includes Ballard's Best, Friary Meux Bitter, Ind Coope Burton Ale and a trio from the Ringwood Brewery. House wines are served by the glass and the short list is quite affordable. Buriton is ideal for walkers trekking the South Downs Way, and is within reach of Butser Ancient Farm and Uppark (National Trust). The pub offers self-catering accommodation. SAMPLE DISHES: devilled whitebait £3.75; pork, leek and Stilton crumble £7; caramel and walnut torte £2.75.

Open *11 to 2.30 (3 Fri and Sat), 5.30 to 11, Sun 12 to 3, 7 to 10.30; bar food and restaurant all week 12 to 2, 6.30 to 10*
Details *Children welcome in dining-room and 1 bar Car park Wheelchair access Garden and patio Background and live music Dogs welcome in public bar only Access, Amex, Delta, Switch, Visa*

BURNHAM MARKET Norfolk map 6

▲ *Hoste Arms* 🏵 🍇

The Green, Burnham Market TEL: (01328) 738777
on B1155, 5m W of Wells

'Probably the biggest building in Burnham Market,' reckoned one correspondent after a visit to this substantial inn overlooking the Georgian village green. The place needs to be large, because there's so much happening. Monthly art exhibitions and traditional jazz evenings are just the beginning; the pub serves breakfast, morning coffee and afternoon teas, and there's even a walled garden terrace for al fresco dining. Owner Paul Whittome and his staff deserve full marks for coping with crowds of all ages without ever seeming to lose their cool; youngsters are given colouring sheets to amuse them when they arrive.

Flexbility is the key to eating at the Hoste: you could feast on foie gras in the bar or tuck into game sausages and bubble and squeak in the restaurant. Fish – much of it local – is the star attraction. Burnham Norton oysters get top billing, but the kitchen gets straight to the heart of eclectic '90s cooking with carpaccio of tuna, and seared scallops on black pasta and champagne sauce. The skill and deftness show in slices of marinated salmon smothered in a zingy, 'incredibly moreish' citrus and chive beurre blanc, and 'startlingly fresh' roasted plaice with home-made fettucine and slivers of juicy roasted red pepper. Meat and game receive similar treatment: sauté chicken livers with a beetroot and rocket salad produced an ecstatic response one Sunday lunch-time, as did roast leg of lamb on a mound of cabbage with a rosemary gravy. Elsewhere on the menu you can expect anything from braised ham hock with root vegetables and grain mustard to stir-fried Szechuan beef. Puddings, such as mango mousse, pecan pie, and unexpectedly 'light and refreshing' poached pear with rice pudding, end proceedings on a high note. A mini-list of interesting wines by the glass provides fine drinking, and the full list of 70 bins is well worth investigating. Woodforde's Wherry Bitter, Greene King IPA and Abbot Ale are kept in decent condition. SAMPLE DISHES: salad of smoked chicken with mango dressing £5.25; baked cod fillet with lime, spring onion and tamarind oil £8.50; lemon torte with apricot coulis £3.25.

Open *11am to 11pm, Sun 12 to 3, 7 to 10.30; bar food and restaurant 12 to 2, 7 to 9*

Details *Children welcome Car park Wheelchair access (also WC) Garden and patio No-smoking area Live music Dogs welcome Access, Amex, Delta, Switch, Visa Accommodation: 21 rooms, B&B £42 to £60*

🍇 *indicates a pub serving better-than-average wine.*

BURPHAM West Sussex map 3

George and Dragon

Burpham TEL: (01903) 883131

2½m up single track, no-through road signposted Warningcamp off A27, 1m E of Arundel

Facing Burpham House in the heart of a small Downland village, the George and Dragon is an old pub with modern additions. The result is what one reporter called 'a harmonious jumble'. James Rose and Kate Holle have built up a solid reputation here and the intentions of the place are clear from the blackboards listing not only food, but beer as well. The kitchen believes in 'decently firm English cookery' and the style shows up emphatically in specials such as creamy celery soup ('as good as anything you could hope for'), braised lamb shanks, and whole local pigeon with bacon and red wine sauce. Fish is excellent, whether it be cod with parsley butter and an ample helping of new potatoes, or medallions of monkfish with saffron sauce. Standard pub snacks are on the printed menu, while desserts such as 'deeply flavoured' dark-chocolate mousse and stem-ginger sponge pudding are listed on a separate board behind the bar. Evening meals and Sunday lunch are also served in the restaurant. Real ale is given proper attention, and among the well-kept brews you might find local Arundel Bitter and Harveys Best or, from further afield, Woodforde's and Cotleigh Bitter. Sixty wines from around the world provide a decent choice by the bottle or glass. The scenery around Burpham is stunning, with views across the Arun valley towards Arundel Castle. SAMPLE DISHES: smoked mackerel pâté £3; turkey escalopes with asparagus sauce £7.50; crème brûlée £3.

Open *11 to 2.30, 6 to 11, Sun 12 to 3, 7 to 10.30; bar food 12 to 2, 7 to 9.45; restaurant Sun L 12 to 2, all week D 7.15 to 9.30; closed Sun eve Oct to Apr*

Details *No children under 10 Car park Wheelchair access (also WC) Patio Background music No dogs Access, Switch, Visa*

BUTLEY Suffolk map 6

Oyster Inn

Butley TEL: (01394) 450790

on B1084, 4m W of Orford

Diminutive, unspoilt and four centuries old, the Oyster Inn is a thoroughly likeable village local with plenty going for it. There are no machines or Muzak in the bar (although folk musicians play live on Sunday evenings). Swathes of hops hang from the beams, watercolours adorn the walls and there's often a real fire. The blackboard menu is a lengthy affair, but there is plenty that is genuinely home-cooked. A generous bowlful of tender moules marinière is the kind of dish 'definitely worth a detour', noted one happy recipient; otherwise the choice takes in everything from duck with apple, lemon and mint sauce, and civet of venison to lamb kleftiko, chicken tikka balti, and kebab of langoustines and 'crevettes' with garlic butter. Puddings could be plum pie or chestnut, apricot and orange crumble. The Oyster is an Adnams pub with its full range of draught beers, as well as a list of a dozen wines from the prestigious Southwold cellar. A guide to local walks is on sale in the pub, which is within trekking distance of Tunstall Forest. Also nearby are some prime natural history sites, notably the ancient deer park at Staverton Thicks – an area of woodland that has some of the largest rowan trees and hollies in England as well as pollarded oaks. SAMPLE DISHES: crispy potato skins with dip £2; salmon, cod and mushroom pie £6.25; ginger pudding £2.25.

Open *Mon to Fri 11 to 3, 6 to 11, Sat 11am to 11pm, Sun 12 to 4, 7 to 10.30; bar food all week L 12 to 2, Mon to Sat D 7 to 9.30*
Details *Children welcome in eating areas Car park Wheelchair access Background and live music Dogs welcome in bar and snug only Access, Delta, Diners, Switch, Visa*

BUTTERMERE Cumbria map 10

▲ *Bridge Hotel*

Buttermere TEL: (01768) 770252
on B5289, 1m E of Crummock Water

Enter the rustic bar at the Bridge Hotel and chances are it will be packed with Lakeland walkers slaking their thirst. The stone-built inn, first licensed in 1735, overlooks lakes and fells affording breathtaking views, and sensibly opens at 9am to serve breakfast to those energetic types during the summer. Specials from the blackboard include dishes such as local favourite 'tattie ash' (a beef casserole with pickled beetroot), or braised local guinea-fowl. Otherwise, you might try Cumberland hotpot from the printed menu. One reporter vows to 'starve myself to do justice to the size of the meals' next time he returns. For those wishing to eat less, a 'snack corner' offers ploughman's and the like. Starters and sweets are available only if a main course is ordered. For fine weather, there is a patio with tables looking across the lake, and the residents' restaurant is open to the public in the evenings. At the busy bar well-kept beers include Tetley Imperial, Calder's Best Scotch Ale and Theakston Old Peculier on handpump as well as Addlestone's cider. The wine list features over

50 bins, with house wines available by the glass. SAMPLE DISHES: deep-fried brie £3; grilled Borrowdale trout £6; forest fruit crumble £2.50.

Open *11am to 11pm, Sun 12 to 10.30; bar food 12 to 2.30, 6 to 9.30; restaurant all week D only 7 to 8.30*
Details *Children welcome Car park Wheelchair access Patio No music No dogs Access, Delta, Switch, Visa Accommodation: 22 rooms, B&B £34 to £39*

BUTTERTON Staffordshire **map 5**

▲ *Black Lion Inn*

Butterton TEL: (01538) 304232
just off B5053, 6m E of Leek

Built in 1782, the solid, stone Black Lion contains a series of rooms and alcoves with beams hung with pots and jugs, many open fires, and china, pictures and brass on the walls. Le Bistro is a separate restaurant with its own menu, but bar food is served throughout the rest of the pub. The repertoire ranges from pâté, and breaded prawns, through grills, and vegetable Stroganov, to apple pie, all backed up by dishes of the day, along the lines of beef in red wine, lamb casserole, gammon in Madeira or Lincolnshire sausage casserole. The pub has a wide range of real ales, among them Morland Old Speckled Hen, Theakston Black Bull Bitter and Ridleys ESX Best, and house wines are served by the glass. Butterton is a picturesque village with good views over the Peak District. Nearby attractions include Alton Towers and Chatsworth House. SAMPLE DISHES: smoked mackerel £3; chicken provençale £5.50; blackcurrant cheesecake £2.

Open *12 to 3, 7 to 11 (10.30 Sun); bar food Thu to Tue L 12 to 2, all week D 7 to 9.30; restaurant Sun L 12 to 2, Fri and Sat D 7 to 9.30*
Details *Children welcome Car park Wheelchair access (also WC) Garden and patio Background and live music Dogs welcome Access, Amex, Delta, Switch, Visa Accommodation: 3 rooms, B&B £35 to £50*

BYLAND ABBEY North Yorkshire **map 9**

Abbey Inn

Byland Abbey TEL: (01347) 868204
off A170, between Thirsk and Helmsley, 2m W of Ampleforth

'I just adore the way the interior has been decorated, creating a warm and comfortable atmosphere,' writes an enthusiast. Indeed, there's much to catch the eye: a motley collection of high-backed chairs, scatter-cushioned settles and tables, rugs on the flagstones, tall candlesticks, rural artefacts and dried flowers. With all that, and the ruins of Byland Abbey directly opposite, it's no wonder the place gets busy. People are attracted by the enterprising food as much as anything else, and booking is advisable. What are listed as light dishes at lunch-times become starters in the evening: how about stuffed lemon sole with lobster and mushroom sauce? For a main course, rolled, boned chicken is stuffed with ham, apricots and redcurrants, and rump of pork comes with apple and bacon sauce; there may also be Stilton and leek pie, lamb rogan josh, and medallions of venison with Cumberland sauce. Pudding-lovers have a choice of, say, raspberry bombe, chocolate profiteroles or treacle sponge. Black Sheep and Theakston Best are on draught, a handful of wines come by the glass, and there's a good showing of half-bottles. SAMPLE DISHES: pear, Silton and bacon salad £4; lamb shank with mint and mushroom gravy £8.25; chocolate and rum slice £3.

Open *Tue to Sat 11 to 2.30, 6.30 to 11, Sun 11 to 2.30; bar food 12 to 1.45, 6.30 to 9.30*
Details *Children welcome Car park Wheelchair access (also WC) Garden and patio Background music No dogs Access, Switch, Visa*

BYTHORN Cambridgeshire **map 6**

White Hart

Bythorn TEL: (01832) 710226
just off A14 Thrapston to Newmarket road

This whitewashed pub on the main road (if it can be so called) through the village was being refurbished as the *Guide* went to press and an extension being added, although the internal arrangement of three or four rooms is unlikely to change. From the bar menu you could choose minestrone soup, Thai-style chicken, seafood pasta, or rump steak with mushroom sauce, say. The restaurant menu, which is also available in the bar, is altogether more indulgent, featuring scallop mousse ('trific,' writes an inspector), smoked duck with figs, and pear and Roquefort salad, and main courses such as Gressingham duck with pickled cabbage, pork fillet with apple chutney and calvados sauce, and pan-fried veal kidneys with green peppercorn sauce. Fruity puddings preponderate over the pastry and sponge varieties: cherry soup, pears poached in cardamom syrup, or blackcurrant meringue, for example. Greene King IPA and Abbot are on draught, and good-quality house wines are poured by the glass. SAMPLE DISHES: seafood aspic

£4.50; roast loin of pork with orange sauce £7.50; brandy-snap basket with rum cream and butterscotch ice-cream £4.

Open *Tue to Sun 11 to 3, Tue to Sat 6 to 11; bar food and restaurant Tue to Sat L 11.45 to 1.45, Tue to Fri D 7 to 9.45*
Details *Children welcome Car park Wheelchair access Patio No smoking in restaurant No music No dogs Access, Delta, Switch, Visa*

CALVER Derbyshire map 8

▲ *Chequers Inn*

Froggatt Edge, nr Calver TEL: (01433) 630231
on B6054, off A623 6m N of Bakewell

Calver is ideally placed for walkers, with paths along the River Derwent and up to the gritstone rocks of Froggatt Edge and Curbar Edge. Calver Mill was built by Richard Arkwright in 1805, but the Chequers is even older than that. Inside the comfortable L-shaped bar, blackboards proclaim the specials of the day; pumpkin soup, lamb's liver and onions, and apple pie could be among them. Otherwise select from the printed menu, which offers such things as kipper and whisky pâté, spinach and wild mushroom roulade, kidneys in red wine, or lamb, aubergine and mushroom masala. Understandably, Bakewell pudding figures among the desserts (you can buy one boxed to take home), together with summer pudding, or chocolate flan. Ward's Best is the regular draught beer, and guest real ales might include Smiles Best or Moonlight Mouse; the separate restaurant has a full wine list. Chatsworth House is just a few miles away. SAMPLE DISHES: potted crab with black olives £2.50; spicy lamb sausage with butter-beans £5; apricot and mincemeat jalousie £2.

Open *11 to 3, 5.30 to 11, Sun 12 to 10.30; bar food Mon to Sat 12 to 2, 6 to 9.30, Sun 12 to 9.30; restaurant all week 12 to 2, 7 to 9*
Details *Children welcome in dining-room Car park Wheelchair access Garden and patio No music No dogs Access, Delta, Switch, Visa Accommodation: 6 rooms, B&B £42 to £64*

CARLTON North Yorkshire map 8

▲ *Foresters Arms*

Carlton in Coverdale TEL: (01969) 640272
off A684, 5m SW of Leyburn

The sight of people sitting in the bar of a Yorkshire Dales pub, eating chicken liver parfait, or Toulouse sausages, might seem incongruous, but that's exactly what happens in the Foresters Arms. The revamped seventeenth-century building stands by the narrow winding road between Leyburn and Kettlewell, and inside, it is all you might expect, with its stone floors, settles and oak beams. If you fancy no more than a light lunch, there's a menu of straightforward single-dish meals ranging from Spanish omelette, and bookmaker steak sandwich, to king prawn and smoked bacon salad, or ragoût of woodland mushrooms with tagliatelle.

The kitchen also steps boldly into the world of chargrilled lamb steak with garlic mash for its full repertoire. There is often a lot happening on the plate, but reporters generally agree that the results are cohesive and adventurous. Here you might find baked crab and asparagus gâteau, or a strudel of leeks and blue cheese accompanied by breast of wood pigeon and black pudding – and that's just for starters. The menu then progresses to a duo of boneless quail with bean cassoulet and polenta croûtons, fillet of cod with Welsh rarebit and saffron risotto, as well as calf's liver with onion marmalade, and chicken breast with ratatouille. Hot mango soufflé is a typically up-beat dessert; otherwise there might be summer pudding, or a terrine of bitter chocolate. A range of coffees, teas and infusions come with home-made sweetmeats. The wine list deals in sound drinking, although the real bargains are the 18 house selections. Theakston Best, John Smith's and Tetley Bitter are on handpump. Middleham Castle and Aysgarth Falls are not far away, and there is good walking all around. SAMPLE DISHES: terrine of ham, garlic and pork £3.75; chargrilled tuna with pesto salad £9; baked treacle tart with ginger ice-cream £4.

Open *Tue to Sat 12 to 3, Mon to Sat 6.30 to 11, Sun 12 to 3, 7 to 10.30; bar food Tue to Sun L 12 to 2, Tue to Sat D 7 to 9; restaurant Sun L 12 to 2, Tue to Sun D 7 to 9.30*
Details *Children welcome in bar eating area Car park Wheelchair access Patio No-smoking area Background music Dogs welcome Access, Delta, Switch, Visa Accommodation: 3 rooms, B&B £40 to £60*

CARTERWAY HEADS Northumberland map 10

▲ *Manor House Inn*

Carterway Heads, Shotley Bridge TEL: (01207) 255268
on A68, 3m W of Consett

The dark stone exterior may seem rather 'forbidding in the dank, misty evening', observed one visitor to this remote moorland pub, but once over the threshold the welcome and atmosphere are invitingly warm. One menu is served throughout, whether you choose to eat in the bar or the little dining-room with its pinkwashed stone walls, flowers and candles on the tables. A blackboard lists the day's offerings – plus specials – and the choice is reckoned to be exceedingly 'generous'.

A fistful of dishes have received endorsements, from marinated juniper herrings, and Cumberland sausages and mash with mustard sauce, to salmon with asparagus and beurre blanc, braised pigeon breasts with wild mushrooms (including jew's-ears and trompettes de mort), and chicken with ginger and chilli ('with some hot pockets of flavour' in it). There are also items with a cosmopolitan accent – warm salad of smoked bacon and mange-tout, or wild salmon with Puy lentils and baby spinach, for example. Sticky toffee pudding seems to be the people's choice from the dessert list, but you might also order fruit compote with meringues, raspberry and gooseberry Betty, or one of the unusual home-made ice-creams such as cherry and Amaretto. Cheeses, such as Beamish, are characterful, flavoursome and local. All of this comes at prices that are astonishingly reasonable: 'I queried the bill, thinking they had undercharged us,' admitted one reporter incredulously.

The pub has a splendid line-up of real ales that include Butterknowle Bitter and Big Lamp Bitter plus two guest brews; Weston's Vintage cider is also on tap and there are 'real' apple juices for those who need to take the wheel. The short wine list packs a lot of interest into a small space, and additional racks and bottles are tucked away in various parts of the building. From the pub you can take a pleasant walk down to Derwent Reservoir. SAMPLE DISHES: roast aubergine and pepper moussaka £3; pork casserole with tomato and mustard £7; pineapple upside-down pudding £3.

Open *11 to 3, 6 to 11, Sun 12 to 3, 7 to 10.30; bar food and restaurant 12 to 2.30, 7 to 9.30 (9 Sun); closed 25 Dec*
Details *Children welcome in eating areas Car park Wheelchair access Garden No smoking in restaurant No music No dogs Access, Amex, Delta, Switch, Visa Accommodation: 4 rooms, B&B £23 to £40*

CARTHORPE North Yorkshire map 9

Fox and Hounds

Carthorpe TEL: (01845) 567433
off A1, 4m SE of Bedale

Business is brisk in this converted smithy in the heart of the Dales. If the partly panelled lounge area is full, the adjacent dining-area is the place to head for. The same menu applies throughout the place. Expect to find such dishes as duck liver pâté in port jelly, vegetable soup, chicken breast stuffed with Coverdale cheese, rack of lamb, and grilled Dover sole. Fish generally dominates the blackboard specials, depending on what the markets can provide: salmon fishcakes, queen scallop and prawn Mornay, or mussels in cheese sauce to start, followed by perhaps poached halibut with mustard sauce, or roast cod. 'The sweet course is always a picture,' writes a reporter; try iced raspberry and blackcurrant soufflé, or chocolate and pear tart with vanilla ice-cream. On draught are Theakston Bitter and John Smith's; house wines, plus at least four others, come by the glass. The cathedral at Ripon, just to the south, is worth seeing; its crypt is a rare survivor from Saxon times. SAMPLE DISHES: smoked haddock and leek soup £2.50; salmon and prawns in rolled lemon sole with white wine sauce £9; tipsy trifle £3.

Open *Tue to Sat 12 to 2.30, 7 to 11, Sun 12 to 3, 7 to 10.30; bar food and restaurant Tue to Sun 12 to 2, 7 to 9.30*
Details *Children welcome Car park Wheelchair access (also WC) No smoking in dining-room Background music No dogs Access, Delta, Switch, Visa*

CARTMEL FELL Cumbria map 8

Masons Arms

Strawberry Bank, Cartmel Fell TEL: (01539) 568486
off A5074, turn left at sign for Bowland Bridge, 1m up hill

Renowned for its array of bottled beers (over 100 at the last count) and 20 different wheat beers, the Masons Arms is also a well-established micro-brewery, producing three real ales with names taken from the works of local author Arthur Ransome – Amazon, Great Northern and Big Six. Also on draught is a Belgian guest beer, plus Liefman's Kriek, Frambozen, Bitburger, Dortmunder and Budvar, with other specialist brews from top European sources. Inside, three cosy rooms with their beams, panelling and stone floors reflect the age of the pub; outside, a terrace overlooks Winster Valley and the fells beyond. The printed menu trots through down-to-earth fare with a noticeable vegetarian presence: stuffed vine leaves, hazelnut and lentil pâté, and burritos, for example, as well as French-style fish soup, a pile of ribs, and rogan josh. Daily specials 'play an Oscar-winning supporting role', according to the owners, and might include creamy curried mushrooms, spiced aubergine crêpes, chicken and Stilton strudel, or salmon, whiting and scallop pie with Parmesan pastry. Salads and sandwiches feature too, and puddings come with cream, custard or yoghurt. The short but witty wine list offers a few by the glass. SAMPLE DISHES: Morecambe Bay potted shrimps £4.75; minted lamb lasagne £7; ginger and lemon sponge £3.

Open *Mon to Thur 11.30 to 3, 6 to 11, Fri and Sat 11.30 to 11, Sun 12 to 10.30; bar food 12 to 2, 6 to 8.45; closed 25 Dec and evening 26 Dec, limited food L 26 Dec*
Details *Children welcome Car park Patio No smoking in 1 room (subject to availability) No music No dogs Access, Amex, Delta, Switch, Visa*

CASTERTON Cumbria map 8

▲ *Pheasant Inn*

Casterton, nr Kirkby Lonsdale TEL: (01524) 271230
on A683, 1m N of junction with A65

'Our favourite dining venue,' writes a reporter. 'My wife and I now travel approximately 30 miles each way to eat at the Pheasant.' The attraction is the imaginative menu served throughout the bar with its comfortable settles, wooden tables and a log fire in winter. Dishes range from sandwiches and omelettes, Cumberland gammon and sausages, and chargrilled Aberdeen Angus steaks, to desserts such as 'superb' sticky toffee pudding. The specials menu encompasses things like seafood salad, noisettes of lamb, or coconut-battered king prawns, and puddings like gooseberry crumble. Cask-conditioned real ales include Marston's Pedigree, Theakston Best, and Charles Wells Bombardier, and the wine list features more than 30 bottles of good quality; there is also a wide selection of malt whiskies. The pub's situation in the attractive Lune Valley makes it perfect for both the Lake District and the Yorkshire Dales. SAMPLE DISHES: feta, celery, tomato and olive salad £4.50; baked Scottish red bream £13; lemon posset £3.

Open *all week 11 to 3, Tue to Sat 6 to 11 (10.30 Sun); bar food 12 to 2, 6.30 to 9 (Fri and Sat 9.30); restaurant Tue to Sun D only 7 to 9 (restaurant closed Sun Oct to end March)*
Details *Children welcome Car park Wheelchair access (also WC) Garden and patio No smoking in dining-room Background and live music; jukebox Dogs welcome Access, Delta, Diners, Switch, Visa Accommodation: 9 rooms, B&B £35 to £64*

CASTLE HEDINGHAM Essex map 3

Bell

10 James Street, Castle Hedingham TEL: (01787) 460350
off B1058, 4m NW of Halstead

For three decades, landlady Sandra Ferguson has allowed this admirably unimproved village pub to run along in its own way. As a result, its genuine old-fashioned atmosphere remains intact. A reporter describes the food as 'tasty pub fare' without frills. The menu nips along briskly, taking in the likes of smoked prawns with garlic dip, lamb burgers, steak and Guinness pie, balti chicken, and treacle tart, as well as ploughman's and pizzas. Also look for huffers (two sausages in a bap). The Bell has no cellar but Greene King

Abbot Ale and IPA, Shepherd Neame Masterbrew and a guest ale are drawn direct from casks behind the bar. Families enjoy the prospect of sitting shaded by trees in the garden. SAMPLE DISHES: smoked mackerel pâté with toast £3.50; Thai chicken curry £5.50; bread pudding with cream £2.25.

Open *11.30 to 3, 6 to 11, Sun 12 to 3, 7 to 10.30; bar food all week L 12 to 2 (2.30 Sat and Sun), Tue to Sun and bank hol Mon D 7 to 10 (9.30 Sun)*
Details *Children welcome Car park Wheelchair access Garden and patio No smoking in 1 room Background and live music Dogs by prior arrangement only No cards*

CHADLINGTON Oxfordshire **map 5**

Tite Inn

Mill End, Chadlington TEL: (01608) 676475
off A361, 2½m S of Chipping Norton

The Tite is on a steep hillside, so it has excellent views over rolling Cotswolds countryside, with a big garden making the most of them. Inside is open-plan, with centuries-old ceiling-beams and rough stone walls, and all is kept neat and tidy. The garden room – notice the grapevine (with plastic parrots!) covering its ceiling – is the place for those who want to avoid cigarette smoke. Drinks are very good on all fronts. Four real ales are dispensed, including Brakspear Special and – not for the faint-hearted – The Dog's Bollocks from Wychwood, and Inch's cider is on draught. A lot of thought has gone into the wine list, which has a strong bias towards the New World; up to ten wines are sold by the glass. 'Fresh, tasty, simple' and 'very good raw materials' said an inspector of the bar food. On the blackboard may be around ten starters, including gazpacho, chicken liver pâté, and Stilton pears, while among main courses may be bobotie, lambs' kidneys braised in port, baked gammon with parsley sauce, and lamb curry. Meringue glacé and a fruit crumble could be among the puddings. 'Very nice atmosphere, very civilised,' concludes a report. SAMPLE DISHES: carrot soup £2.50; chicken breast in cider and honey sauce £7; banana cheesecake with toffee sauce £3.

Open *Tue to Sat and bank hol Mons 12 to 2.30 (3 in summer), 6.30 to 11, Sun 12 to 3 (3.30 in summer), 7 to 10.30; bar food and restaurant Tue to Sun L 12 to 2, Tue to Sat D 7 to 9*
Details *Children welcome Car park Wheelchair access (also WC) Garden No smoking in 1 room Background music Dogs welcome No cards*

All details are as accurate as possible at the time of going to press, but pubs often change hands, and it is wise to check beforehand by telephone anything that is particularly important to you.

CHALE Isle of Wight map 2

▲ *Wight Mouse Inn*

Chale TEL: (01983) 730431
on B3399, 5m W of Ventnor

This comfortable inn adjoining the Clarendon Hotel is in a superb position overlooking Chale Bay and beyond to Tennyson Down and the Needles. The spacious interior, with open fires, and various interesting artefacts decorating the walls, can be packed with holidaymakers during the summer, although there's plenty of room for eating. The wide choice of fish dishes is appropriate for a seaside setting, among them deep-fried clams, crab and prawn Mornay, battered cod, and a fisherman's platter. Meat eaters could go for anything from ham, egg and chips to wiener schnitzel, and steaks. Salads, sandwiches, pizzas and vegetarian dishes make up the rest of the menu; gâteaux, locally produced ice-creams, and knickerbocker glory round it off. About six real ales are dispensed, including Morland Old Speckled Hen, Wadworth 6X and Marston's Pedigree; local wines appear on the list, and you could come here every day of the year and never have the same whisky twice. There is live music every night, and children have their own entertainments in the extensive gardens, including rides on Arthur the Shetland pony. SAMPLE DISHES: garlic-battered mushrooms £3; pan-fried lemon sole £7.50; apple tart £2.

Open *11am to midnight, Sun 12 to 10.30; bar food and restaurant 12 to 10 (9.30 Sun)*
Details *Children welcome Car park Wheelchair access (also WC) Garden and patio No-smoking area Background and live music; jukebox Dogs welcome in bar only Access, Delta, Switch, Visa Accommodation: 15 rooms, B&B £25 to £70*

CHAPEL AMBLE Cornwall map 1

Maltsters Arms

Chapel Amble TEL: (01208) 812473
off A39, 2m N of Wadebridge

This grey-slated, white-painted pub, with a crown of thatch over its porch, is reached along narrow country lanes (liable to flood in heavy rain). The main bar has been opened up, and refurbishment was under way as the *Guide* went to press, although the rough stone walls, large fireplace, a slate floor, carpeted areas and beams will no doubt remain. The standard menu lists basic pub food: pâté, breaded plaice and chips, and 'sizzle' dishes (chicken with ginger, beef with oyster sauce, for instance), plus, at lunch-times, a good choice of interesting fillings for jacket potatoes and sandwiches. The highlight is the daily-changing blackboard of fish specials – anything from sardines pan-fried with garlic, through megrim glazed with flambé strawberries and brown sugar, to turbot thermidor. Another board offers butterfly prawns with chilli dip, steak and ale pie, and lamb and pumpkin curry. Pumpkin pie may turn up among the desserts, and the creditable cheeseboard is entirely West Country farmhouse. The pub dispenses its own Maltster's real ale plus Cornish Coaster from local Sharp's Brewery, and there's also Fuller's London Pride and a guest beer; plenty of wines are sold by the glass from an enterprising list. SAMPLE DISHES: stir-fried duck breast £5; fillets of red mullet with sweet-and-sour sauce £8; chocolate and whisky mousse £3.

Open *10.30 to 2.30, 6 to 11, Sun 12 to 2.30, 7 to 10.30; bar food and restaurant 12 to 1.45 (2 summer), 6.15 to 9 (9.30 summer)*
Details *Children welcome in dining-room Car park Wheelchair access Patio No smoking in restaurant Background music Guide dogs only Access, Switch, Visa*

CHARLTON Wiltshire **map 2**

▲ *Horse and Groom*

The Street, Charlton TEL: (01666) 823904
on B4040 Malmesbury to Cricklade road, 2m E of Malmesbury

This civilised former coaching-inn, set back from the road on the edge of the village, seems smarter than ever. The sixteenth-century building has a neat stone exterior, while inside there are two charming bars with prints and paintings hanging on the walls, and dried flower arrangements throughout. For a light meal or a snack, head for the bar, complete with rustic pine furnishings on a woodblock floor, stone walls and an open log fire. The blackboard menu offers various filled rolls and jacket potatoes alongside other more substantial dishes such as fish and chips, Wiltshire ham, egg and chips, cottage pie, and lamb Madras. A more elaborate restaurant menu is served in the adjacent lounge and in the neatly laid dining-room, where hops adorn the beams and the atmosphere is relaxed. Beers on draught are a good selection of quality names from local breweries – Uley Old Spot Prize Ale, Wadworth 6X, Archers Village Bitter and Wickwar Old Merryford Ale; and wines from around the world are available by the glass. SAMPLE DISHES: leek and potato soup £2.75; seafood provençale £10.50; date and walnut treacle pudding with hot toffee sauce £2.75.

Open *winter all week 12 to 3, 7 to 11 (10.30 Sun), summer Mon to Fri 12 to 3, 6 to 11, Sat and Sun 12 to 11; bar food 12 to 2, 7 to 10 (9.30 Sun)*

Details *Children welcome Car park Wheelchair access (also WC) Garden Background music Dogs welcome in bar Access, Amex, Delta, Switch, Visa Accommodation: 3 rooms, B&B £55 to £75*

CHELSWORTH **Suffolk** **map 6**

▲ *Peacock Inn*

The Street, Chelsworth TEL: (01449) 740758
on B1115 between Monks Eleigh and Bildeston

Dating back to the fourteenth century, and one of the oldest buildings in the village, the Peacock breathes attractive rusticity. There's a pretty view of the River Brett from the front windows, and the bar is a mass of old beams, brasses and pictures. On Sundays, the inglenook fireplace is used for spit-roasting. The pub was in a state of flux and a new management team had just moved in when our inspector visited, but it is hoped that any teething troubles will be sorted out quickly. At present, the chalked-up menu promises such things as smoked salmon and trout terrine, ragoût of rabbit on a bed of noodles, and baked fillets of red mullet with ratatouille and sauce tapénade. Pies (pork, apple and cider, for example), jacket potatoes and 'light bites' appear in winter, salads and wholemeal 'hoagies' in summer. Puddings are recited at the table: treacle sponge with syrup sauce and ice-cream was 'a schoolboy treat' for one reporter well beyond his short-trousered days. Weekly guest ales supplement regulars such as Adnams Bitter, Theakston XB and Greene King IPA; around 40 wines cover a lot of territory and 'wines of the month' are offered by the bottle or glass. SAMPLE DISHES: fresh figs, ham and mozzarella salad £4; poached salmon steak with herb butter £9; orange and brandy pudding £3.50.

Open *11.30 to 3, 6.30 to 11, Sun 12 to 3, 7 to 10.30; bar food and restaurant 12 to 2.30, 7 to 9.15 (12 to 9.15 Sat and Sun summer)*
Details *Children welcome Car park Wheelchair access (also WC) Garden and patio No smoking in restaurant Background and live music Dogs welcome Access, Amex, Delta, Switch, Visa Accommodation: 3 rooms, B&B £35 to £45*

CHENIES Buckinghamshire map 3

Red Lion

Chenies TEL: (01923) 282722
off A404, between Chorleywood and Little Chalfont

'A good stopover to avoid terminal frustration on the M25,' noted one relieved traveller; another was equally pleased to relax for lunch in this popular pub 'after trudging five miles through the Chess Valley'. The tiny four-table dining area may seem 'claustrophobic' – it's better to camp in the general bar at the front. The food is reckoned to be 'good pub stuff', particularly the speciality of the house, billed as 'The Internationally Acclaimed Famous Original Chenies' lamb pie, whose reputation is now spread via the Internet. The menu also takes in various pastas and everything from toad-in-the-hole to vegetable risotto. If you want a snack there are things like 'chunky' vegetable chilli in pitta bread, and French bread sticks with enterprising fillings. Otherwise, for a more ambitious plateful, try roast baby chicken stuffed with cream cheese and almonds, or shark steak. Landlord Mike Norris keeps a fine selection of real ales: Lion Pride is brewed for the pub by the Rebellion Beer Company in Marlow, or you might choose Vale's Notley Ale, Wadworth 6X or Benskins Best. The wine list is a short, reasonably priced selection. Chenies Manor is nearby. SAMPLE DISHES: baked avocado with tomato sauce and cheese topping £3.50; turkey and spinach lasagne £5.50; chocolate roulade £2.50.

Open *11 to 3, 5.30 to 11, Sun 12 to 3, 6.30 to 10.30; bar food 12 to 2, 7 to 10 (9.30 Sun)*
Details *No children Car park Wheelchair access (also WC) No music Dogs welcome Access, Amex, Delta, Switch, Visa*

CHERITON Hampshire map 2

▲ *Flower Pots Inn*

Cheriton TEL: (01962) 771318
on B3046, 4m S of New Alresford

A sweet, hoppy smell fills the air at the Flower Pots: across the car park of this solid-looking, red-brick pub is the converted wooden barn where the pub's own ales are brewed. Cheriton Best Bitter and Diggers Gold, well-known in the area, are tapped from casks behind the bar. 'I went for the lighter Pots Ale, which was superb,' writes a reporter, who added: 'I am not a beer drinker, but it tasted natural, smooth and well balanced.' Inside, the L-shaped public bar is all quarry-tiled floors, with a log-burning fire, solid tables and chairs, and a glassed-over well; the lounge is more intimate, thanks to a sofa, and carpets covering bare boards. A small family room is equipped for children, with a television, games, paper and colouring pencils, and books. In keeping with the pub's style, the menu is simple and short: baps come with good ham, prawns and so on, sandwiches are plain or toasted, and there are such things as jacket potatoes, chilli – described by a reporter as 'excellent' – and perhaps a curry. 'Shame they don't do puddings,' writes the same reporter, who nevertheless thought the inn a 'bench-mark for many village pubs'. SAMPLE DISHES: lamb and apricot hotpot £4.25; beef stew £4.25.

Open *12 to 2.30, 6 to 11, Sun 12 to 3, 7 to 10.30; bar food all week L 12 to 2, Mon to Sat D 7 to 9; no food 25 Dec and some bank hol evenings*
Details *Car park Wheelchair access Garden No music Dogs welcome No cards Accommodation: 5 rooms, B&B £26 to £45*

CHERITON BISHOP Devon map 1

▲ *Old Thatch Inn*

Cheriton Bishop TEL: (01647) 24204
off A30, between Exeter and Okehampton, 6m SW of Crediton

'When I arrived at 1.45 on a Friday, they had been so busy that the menu was reduced to soup and sandwiches.' So if you want a meal, either get here early or book a table: reservations are taken for all areas of the bar. The menu ranges from salads and ploughman's to devilled mushrooms, spare ribs, battered fish, and a mixed grill. A blackboard lists the daily specials: locally smoked mackerel, vegetable curry, pork with prunes, and lentil and mushroom gratin, for example. Puddings are mostly fruit tarts, trifles and cheesecakes. There's plenty of room for eating in the long, beamed bar, split in two by a striking open log fire, with – predictably for a thatched pub – thatching implements lining the walls. Hall & Woodhouse Tanglefoot, Wadworth 6X and Cotleigh Tawny are on draught, and six house wines are sold by the half-carafe from a decent list. Handy for travellers on the A30, the pub stands on the fringe of Dartmoor. SAMPLE DISHES: curried vegetable soup £1.75; baked lemon sole stuffed with mushrooms and prawns £8.75; meringue with vanilla ice-cream coated with coffee and brandy sauce £2.75.

Open *12 (11.30 Sat summer) to 3, 7 (6.30 Fri and Sat, and 6 Mon to Sat summer) to 11 (10.30 Sun); bar food 12 to 2.15, 7 (6.30 June to Oct) to 9.15*
Details *No children Car park Wheelchair access Background music Dogs on leads only Access, Visa Accommodation: 3 rooms, B&B £34 to £46*

CHESHAM Buckinghamshire map 3

Black Horse Inn

Chesham Vale, Chesham TEL: (01494) 784656
take Hawridge road, off A416 to Berkhamsted road, 1½m N of Chesham

Pies and sausages are the main attractions on the menu at this centuries-old listed pub set in good walking country. Chicken, leek and walnut; wild rabbit, tarragon and mustard; and game, cider and wild mushrooms are just some of the tantalising combinations of ingredients that go into the former. The selection of sausages includes wild boar, apple and red wine; beef, dill and mustard; and venison. Other dishes range from salads and ploughman's to smoked trout, grilled swordfish, and chicken breast with asparagus sauce and steaks. There are no puddings: 'you should see how tiny the kitchen is,' explained a waitress. A feeling of comfort pervades the large, L-shaped interior, broken up by pillars, with cream-painted brick walls, beams and an inglenook. Marston's Pedigree, Adnams Bitter and Benskins Bitter are among the well-kept ales on draught, and wines are served by the glass from a modest and reasonably priced list. Plenty of picnic tables in the huge garden allow for al fresco eating and drinking in the summer. SAMPLE DISHES: garlic mushrooms £3.25; grilled halibut with parsley butter £7; steak and kidney pie with Burton ale £6.25.

Open *11.30 to 2.30, 6 to 11, Sun 12 to 3, 7 to 10.30; bar food 12 to 2, 6 (7 Sun) to 9.30*
Details *Children welcome in bar eating area Car park Wheelchair access Garden and patio Background music Dogs welcome No cards*

CHICKSGROVE Wiltshire map 2

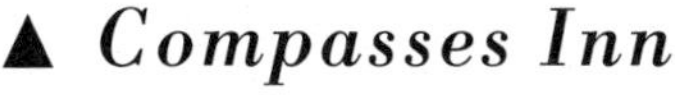

▲ *Compasses Inn*

Chicksgrove TEL: (01722) 714318
1m NW of A30 between Swallowcliffe and Fovant

Entering this 600-year-old pub is, according to one visitor, almost like stepping back in time, as the thatched, rough-stone cottage somehow keeps an air of an earlier century'. A fire burns in the huge inglenook, beams are low, and the booth seating gives the bar the look of a stable, especially with the old farming implements on the walls. Tiny windows mean it's dark, even during the day. Food, advertised on a blackboard, changes weekly and is a cut above normal pub grub. The imaginative menu could include tiger prawn salad with a chilli vinaigrette, or home-made chicken liver pâté as starters; duck breast in a pink peppercorn sauce, grilled red mullet, steak and Guinness pie, or lasagne as main dishes; and a tempting array of puddings such as chocolate torte, summer pudding or raspberry meringue. Adnams, Bass and Wadworth 6X, as well as Old Wardour from the local Tisbury brewery, are on handpump; a small selection of wines includes a handful by the glass. Nearby are Old Wardour Castle, Fovant Badges and Wilton House. SAMPLE DISHES: mozzarella and tomato salad £3.50; salmon fillet with garlic and herb butter £7; cinnamon brûlée £2.75.

Open *Tue to Sun 11 to 3, 6.30 to 11; bar food Tue to Sun 12 to 2, 7 to 9 (9.30 Fri and Sat)*
Details *Children welcome Car park Wheelchair access Garden No music Dogs welcome Access, Delta, Switch, Visa Accommodation: 5 rooms, B&B £25 to £45*

CHIDDINGLY East Sussex **map 3**

Six Bells

Chiddingly TEL: (01825) 872227
off A22 Uckfield to Eastbourne road at Golden Cross service station

'A genuine village pub frequented by locals and lots of visitors, and serving cheap but very good-quality home-made food,' runs an endorsement from a reporter. The village in question is attractive, and the Six Bells itself is old, with low ceilings, brick floors, beams, and an ornately carved bar counter. The long menu is chalked on a board, and the food has been described as 'genuine home-cooking with no frills'. In reality, this means dishes like onion soup, ever-popular steak and kidney pie, honey-roast ham, spare ribs, and vegetable lasagne. Puddings are traditional: banana split, raspberry pavlova, and banoffi pie 'with lots of gooey caramel on top'. Harveys Best and Courage Directors are on draught, along with a guest ale. Boules, a pergola and a fish-pond are features of the garden. SAMPLE DISHES: garlic prawns £4; chicken and mushroom pie £2.50; chocolate nut sundae £2.50.

Open *10.30 to 3, 6 to 11 (12 Tue, Fri and Sat), Sun 12 to 3, 7 to 10.30; bar food 11 to 2.30, 6 to 11*
Details *Children welcome in family room Car park Garden Live music Dogs welcome on a lead No cards*

CHIDDINGSTONE Kent map 3

Castle Inn

Chiddingstone TEL: (01892) 870247
off B2027, 4m E of Edenbridge

The row of timbered cottages known today as Chiddingstone first received a mention in AD 814, licensee Nigel Lucas tells us, and the first reference to the premises that now form the Castle Inn was in 1420. These days it is under the wing of the National Trust and is a heavyweight tourist hot spot. The printed menu on offer in the two atmosphere-laden bars includes bowls of soup, pasta, salads and so on, plus a handful of 'ice-cream specialities' from Spain; there is also a list of specials such as skate with black butter, and beef and ale pie. In addition, a good-value fixed-price 'fireside menu' is available every session except Sunday lunch-time. The impressive and carefully selected list of about 150 wines includes representatives of just about everywhere from Corsica to Chile, as well as a handful from Kentish vineyards. Southern England also supplies real ales in the shape of Larkins Traditional Bitter and Harveys Best. A short drive will take you to Chiddingstone Castle, Hever Castle and Penshurst Place. SAMPLE DISHES: home-made pâté £3.75; roast rack of lamb £7.50; autumn hedgerow fruit pudding £2.75.

Open *weekdays 11 to 3, 6 to 11, Sat 11am to 11pm, Sun 11 to 10.30; bar food weekdays 12 to 2.45, 6 to 10.45, Sat and Sun all day; restaurant 12 to 2, 7.30 to 9.30*
Details *Children welcome in eating areas Garden and patio No music Dogs welcome Access, Amex, Delta, Diners, Switch, Visa*

CHIDDINGSTONE CAUSEWAY Kent map 3

▲ *Little Brown Jug*

Chiddingstone Causeway TEL: (01892) 870318
on B2027 Edenbridge to Tonbridge road

The Little Brown Jug is an extensively modernised and enlarged Victorian building immediately opposite Penshurst Station. Penshurst Place, where Sir Philip Sidney – soldier, poet and diplomat – was born in 1554, is a short distance away and is worth visiting for its great hall alone. The pub is carpeted and spacious, with dark wooden furniture and open fires, and has a large garden with plenty of seating to take any overspill at busy periods. The daily-changing menu caters admirably for all tastes and palates. Fish dishes on offer may encompass crab thermidor, salmon fish-cakes, skate wing with capers, and tuna in a red wine and horseradish sauce, while meat eaters might enjoy lamb fillet braised in redcurrant jelly with orange, mint and rosemary, steak and Guinness pie, chicken suprême, or venison sausages. More than a nod is paid to vegetarians – how about mushroom, parsnip and cashew-nut roast in filo pastry with sherry sauce? Children have a section of the menu, and a decent choice of ploughman's and steaks is always available. Real ales might include Gale's HSB, Ringwood Old Thumper and Hop Back Summer Lightning, and wines are sold by the glass. SAMPLE DISHES: goujons of plaice £3.50; rabbit in rum and mixed berry sauce £7; chocolate and Amaretto slice £3.

Open *11.30 to 3, 6 to 11, Sun 12 to 3, 7 to 10.30; bar food 12 to 2 (2.30 Sat and Sun), 6.30 to 9.30 (9.15 Sun)*
Details *Children welcome in bar eating area Car park Wheelchair access Garden and patio No-smoking area No music Dogs on leads welcome Access, Delta, Switch, Visa Accommodation: 7 rooms, B&B £28 to £38*

CHILGROVE West Sussex map 3

▲ *White Horse Inn* 🏵 🍇

Chilgrove TEL: (01243) 535219
on B2141, between Chichester and Petersfield

'It was my birthday, and I wanted to spend it with a good friend – Barry Phillips' wine list,' wrote a city-dweller in festive mood. Over the last two decades the owner of this civilised country pub has devoutly assembled one of the most extraordinary cellars in Britain; he continues to buy and sell with dedication and enthusiasm, and is always ready to educate and advise when customers begin perusing the mighty tome. Here are magnificent clarets of serious pedigree, a superb German selection, heavenly dessert wines and much more. If you haven't time to browse, head straight for the mini-list of 16 splendid wines by the glass, and if wine really isn't your tipple, you could settle for a pint of Ballard's Trotton Bitter.

On the food side of things there are no-nonsense bar lunches of sandwiches and salads, backed up by plates of Whitstable oysters, braised oxtail, grilled gammon and a couple of vegetarian offerings like red and sweet pepper omelette, and ratatouille bake. Bar suppers revolve around an equally forthright fixed-price menu, along the lines of grilled collop of salmon with creamed leeks, suprême of chicken with mushroom sauce, and pan-fried apples with Kahlua served with banana sorbet. Fixed-price lunches and dinners (with supplements) are served in the restaurant. Note that children are not allowed inside the pub, although there's green space outside for a run around. Accommodation is in nearby Forge Cottage, owned by chef and co-proprietor Neil Rushbridger. The White Horse makes a handy staging post for Goodwood Races and the open-air museum at West Dean. SAMPLE DISHES: steak butty £5; crab salad £8.50; bread-and-butter pudding £3.50.

Open *all week 11 to 3, Tue to Sat 6 to 11; bar food Tue to Sun L 12 to 2, Tue to Sat D 6 to 10; restaurant Tue to Sat 12 to 2, 7 to 10*
Details *No children Car park Wheelchair access Garden No music Dogs in bar only Access, Delta, Diners, Switch, Visa Accommodation: 5 rooms, B&B £35*

CHINNOR Oxfordshire map 2

Sir Charles Napier Inn

Sprigg's Alley, nr Chinnor TEL: (01494) 483011
off B4009, turn right at Chinnor roundabout, carry on 2m up hill to Sprigg's Alley

At first glance the 'Napier' might seem like just another Chiltern farmhouse, high up on the road towards Bledlow Ridge. Drive round the back – into the car park – and it's a very different story. All around are sculptures – voluptuous nude torsos, black polished pigs, a rhino here, a gorilla there. It's an ever-changing show of the latest creations from local artist Michael Cooper. But that is just the beginning. Walk past the terrace, with its luxuriantly tangled vine and seriously wonky chairs and tables, and make your way inside. The bar is an eccentric's dream, stuffed with all manner of weatherbeaten armchairs, curios, effigies and yet more sculptures. There's no escape in the dining-room either, where antique prints, and a hotchpotch of table and chairs set the tone.

Julie Griffiths and family run this place with 'easy going' coolness and good humour. Chef Batiste Tolu defines what arrives on the plate. This is not conventional pub cooking as we know it, although its heart and soul are in the right place. Fish is reckoned to be the star of the show: chargrilled squid with red pepper salsa and 'three long leaves of rocket' was described as 'visual clarity and understatement at its best'; linguine might be served with 'spectacular' fresh clams in the shell and a sauce fired up with chilli and basil, moist sea bass could appear on a pile of marsh samphire with an 'impeccable' hollandaise, while baked lobster is a 'mighty beast'. Away from the sea, you might also encounter wild mushroom risotto, roast grey-leg partridge with braised red cabbage, and chargrilled calf's liver with caramelised onions and mash. Desserts are fine enough (crunchy raspberry brûlée, for example), but it would be a sin to miss out on the cheeseboard, reckoned by one reporter to offer a 'brilliant' selection: 'buttery' Bonchester, 'excellent' Cotherstone, 'first-rate'

Wanboidy, plus St Davids, Skirrid and more. The wine list is out of the top drawer: the range is spectacular, and includes champagnes by the glass to start, and *eaux-de-vie*, chilli vodka and much more to finish. There are also draught beers such as Wadworth 6X. SAMPLE DISHES: baked black pudding with sweet potatoes and fennel £6; roast saddle of lamb with cumin, coriander and dauphinois potatoes £13.50; sticky date pudding with toffee sauce £5.50

Open *12 to 3, 6.30 to 11, Sun 12 to 3, 7 to 10.30; bar food Tue to Fri L 12.30 to 2.30; restaurant Tue to Sun L 12.30 to 2.30 (3.30 Sun), Tue to Sat D 7 to 10*
Details *Children welcome at lunch-time Car park Wheelchair access Garden and patio No-smoking areas Background music No dogs Access, Amex, Delta, Switch, Visa*

CHOLMONDELEY Cheshire map 5

▲ *Cholmondeley Arms* 🍇

Cholmondeley TEL: (01829) 720300
on A49, 5½m N of Whitchurch, nr entrance to Cholmondeley Castle and Gardens

The food at this pub/brasserie in the unusual setting of a converted school goes from strength to strength. Best bets are the interesting dishes on the daily-changing specials board: vol-au-vent of mussels and leeks, or sweetbread and bacon terrine, followed perhaps by rabbit braised with wine, mustard and thyme, or rack of lamb with mint hollandaise ('one of the finest dishes my husband has eaten this year – lean, tender, sweet-tasting meat and lots of it'). Puddings run to rhubarb and ginger crumble, Bakewell tart, and an iced Grand Marnier soufflé that turned out to be 'a winner all the way' for one reporter. The printed menu sticks largely to the tried and tested: sandwiches, starters like garlic mushrooms with bacon, or hot crab pâté, and main courses such as omelettes, deep-fried plaice and steaks. The wine list offers a decent choice of more than 60 bins, with four whites and two reds sold by the glass. Marston's Pedigree and Best and Boddingtons are on draught. SAMPLE DISHES: goats'-cheese soufflé £4.25; pork escalope grilled with Gruyère and tomatoes £8.25; hot fudged bananas £3.50.

Open *11 to 3, 7 to 11; bar food 12 to 2.15 (2.30 Sun), 7 (6.30 Sat) to 10; closed 25 Dec*
Details *Children welcome Car park Wheelchair access Garden and patio No music Dogs welcome Access, Delta, Switch, Visa Accommodation: 6 rooms, B&B £40 to £54*

CHUDLEIGH KNIGHTON Devon map 1

Claycutters Arms

Chudleigh Knighton TEL: (01626) 853345
on B3344, 4m N of Newton Abbot

'A genuine hostelry, serving the community,' is how one reporter described this partly thatched 300-year-old pub overlooking Dartmoor. The beamed interior has been much modernised, the atmosphere may be smoky, and there are no airs and graces. Service is youthful and friendly. The kitchen has serious aspirations and the menu served in the bar and dining-room shows plenty of ambition. Fish is a strong suit: 'carefully cooked' fillet of sea bass is served with a prawn, mustard and dill sauce; brochettes of salmon and sole come with a sweet salsa; while roast medallions of monkfish are enlivened with coriander and crab sauce. Meat and game dishes are in similar vein: warm duck salad with redcurrant glaze, for example, or steamed breast of chicken filled with spinach and orange and served with apple and calvados sauce. Among the list of desserts you might find warm blueberry and apple tart, and strawberry charlotte. Beer drinkers are offered Bass, Flowers Original and guest ales such as Eldridge Pope Royal Oak; the pub also has a short but serviceable wine list. SAMPLE DISHES: trio of deep-fried cheeses with passion-fruit and cherry sauce £3.50; braised guinea-fowl with white wine and brandy sauce £6; brandy-snap basket with fresh fruit topped with sorbet £2.25.

Open *11 to 3, 6 to 11, Sun 12 to 3, 7 to 10.30; bar food and restaurant 12 to 2.30, 6.45 (7 Sun) to 9.30*
Details *Children welcome in eating areas Car park Wheelchair access Patio Background and live music Dogs welcome Access, Delta, Diners, Switch, Visa*

CHURCHINFORD Somerset map 2

▲ *York Inn*

Honiton Road, Churchinford TEL: (01823) 601333
off B3170, 8m S of Taunton

Churchinford stands in an area of outstanding natural beauty and the village is also designated 'environmentally sensitive'. The York Inn – parts of which date back to the sixteenth century – fits in perfectly, with its well-preserved oak beams and open fireplace. Visitors have been impressed by the quality of the food: 'Presentation and taste were of an exceptionally high standard,' concluded one reporter. Bar snacks such as soups, moussaka, savoury flans and things with chips are always on offer, but it pays to consult the printed menu of more up-market dishes. Here you can expect smoked salmon with crème fraiche, confit of duck, herb-crusted rack of lamb, fettucine with roasted vegetables and so forth. Prices of most dishes are reduced at lunch-time. Puddings range from crêpes suzette to 'unusual' ice-creams. Wadworth 6X and locally brewed Otter Ale are bolstered by regular guest beers and scrumpy is also on tap. The wine list is wide-ranging and it is also worth delving into the list of bin ends. There is a riding school just outside the village, and anglers can dip their rods at Fishponds and Otterhead lakes. SAMPLE DISHES: rarebit with red onion relish £4; chicken dijonnaise £9; apple and raspberry tart £3.

Open *12 to 3, 6 to 11, Sun 12 to 3.30, 7 to 10.30; bar food and restaurant 12 to 2, 7 to 9.30; Oct to April closed Mon L, no food Sun evenings*
Details *Children welcome Car park Wheelchair access Patio Background and live music; jukebox Dogs welcome on a lead Access, Amex, Delta, Visa Accommodation: 4 rooms, B&B £29.50 to £35*

CHURCH KNOWLE Dorset map 2

New Inn

Church Knowle TEL: (01929) 480357
off A351, 4m S of Wareham

You'd never know it, but the 400-year-old New Inn was devastated by fire in February 1996. However, sympathetic rebuilding, painstakingly carried out, has ensured that thatch and beams are just as they were before the disaster. The pub, which has its own camp site, is set on the quiet main road through this charming grey-stone village not far from Corfe Castle. Panoramic views from the big back garden look out over the Dorset hills. The large menu shows enterprise, with dishes for every taste and appetite. Choose from half a pint of prawns, New Forest game pie, grilled salmon steak, bangers and mash, and a roast, to name but a few. Blackboard specials include lots of fresh fish such as Brixham plaice, Dover sole, or moules marinière. Royal Wessex Bitter, Flowers Original and Eden Bitter are on draught. Sixteen good-value wines are available by the glass. SAMPLE DISHES: Dorset Blue Vinney cheese soup £2.25; roast leg of Dorset lamb 'in mint condition' £5.50; summer pudding with clotted cream £3.

Open *11 to 3, 6 (7 winter) to 11; bar food 12 to 2.30, 6 (7 winter) to 9.30; closed Mon Jan to Mar*
Details *Children welcome in bar eating-area Car park Wheelchair access (also WC) Garden and patio No-smoking area Background and live music No dogs Access, Delta, Switch, Visa*

CLANFIELD Oxfordshire map 2

Clanfield Tavern

Clanfield TEL: (01367) 810223
on A4095 Witney to Farringdon road

Don't be fooled by the history-laden exterior or the rabbit warren of bare-stoned, beamed rooms that make up the bar area. The conservatory, which forms the main dining-area of the pub, is an absolutely stunning piece of modern creative design, with no expense spared. A huge barn-like space, crowned with an exotically tented canopy, is illuminated by spotlights on rails strung across the width of the room and a convoluted floor-standing candelabra; most extraordinary of all, however, is a giant tree stretching horizontally over the ceiling, with copper pipes twisting around the trunk and every branch ending in a bare lit bulb. Even some of the ladies' loos are fabulously done out in zebra stripes or leopard spots. Beyond the glass French doors is a tiny walled courtyard taken up almost entirely by a tiered fountain encircled with potted plants.

The décor suggests a tavern of two halves, and so does the menu (although you can eat anywhere you like). On the one hand is a printed slate of dishes that are wholeheartedly in the traditional mould of Brie parcels, deep-fried chicken goujons, steak sandwiches, and trout with almonds, plus a few lunchtime 'light bites'. By contrast, the specials board is shot through with exciting modern ideas with restaurant overtones. Sesame-seed crab-cakes are served with 'salsa piquante', steamed Cornish cod comes with a spiced *beurre blanc*, while vegetarians might be offered a medley of tortilla, stuffed tomato and a Savoy cabbage parcel. A prosaic-sounding terrine of smoked fish is – in reality – an 'incredibly fresh, wonderfully colourful' kaleidoscope of components, textures and flavours involving a vivid roulade including spinach, whole fillets of numerous fish, a mousse of smoked cod's roe and much more, complemented by a lemon dressing tinged with Pernod. Almost on a par – at one meal – was a gutsy haunch of venison steak with a sauce of black peppercorns and numerous wild mushrooms. Puddings keep up the momentum with lemon tart (attributed to a certain 'Gary'), home-made plum ice-cream, and poached pear with a calvados sabayon.

Several good house wines come by the glass, and the short list of around two dozen well-chosen bins shouldn't put much strain on the wallet. Hook Norton Best Bitter, Flowers Original and Boddingtons are the regulars on handpump. To the south-west of Clanfield is Buscot Park (an eighteenth-century house with pleasure gardens) and the Iron Age hill fort at Badbury Hill. SAMPLE DISHES: Cheddar and onion soup £2.25; braised leg of lamb steak in herb *jus* £9; chocolate bavarois with orange cream £2.75.

Open *11.30 to 2.30, 6 to 11, Sun 12 to 3, 7 to 10.30; bar food and restaurant 11.30 to 2, 6 to 10, Sun 12 to 2, 7 to 10*
Details *Children welcome Car park Wheelchair access (also WC) No-smoking areas No music No dogs Access, Diners, Switch, Visa*

CLAVERING Essex map 3

▲ *Cricketers*

Clavering TEL: (01799) 550442
on B1038, off M11, between Saffron Walden and Bishop's Stortford

Wooden ceiling-beams and pillars bear witness to the sixteenth-century origins of this village pub; warming-pans and horse brasses hang on the timbers and dried-flower arrangements add colour. Comfort is provided by button-back upholstered benches and stools. The seasonally changing menu might include seafood tortellini, rack of lamb with garlic and oregano sauce, and tuna baked with olives. Tuesday is fish night, when you can expect starters such as sauté scallops and scampi, and main courses like grilled fillets of hake. A pudding club is held on Wednesday serving 'steaming, sticky, old-fashioned' savoury and sweet puddings such as steak and kidney, Yorkshire with roast beef, and heartwarming concoctions with custard. A separate restaurant has its own menu. Adnams Bitter, and Flowers Original and IPA are on handpump; about 50 wines feature on the list, of which six are sold by the glass. Audley End House, with grounds landscaped by Capability Brown, is on the edge of Saffron Walden, and the town itself is well worth a visit too. SAMPLE DISHES: crab and avocado salad £4.25; fillet of pork with calvados and walnut sauce £9.25; mango pavlova £3.

Open *11 to 3, 6 to 11, Sun 12 to 4, 7 to 10.30; bar food and restaurant 12 to 2, 7 to 10*
Details *Children welcome in bar eating area Car park Wheelchair access Garden and patio No-smoking area Background music No dogs Access, Amex, Switch, Visa Accommodation: 6 rooms, room only £50 to £60*

CLEARWELL Gloucestershire map 2

▲ *Wyndham Arms*

Clearwell TEL: (01594) 833666
on B4231, 2m S of Coleford

John and Rosemary Stanford bought the Wyndham Arms in 1973 because they wanted a reason to live in this enchanting piece of countryside on the edge of the Royal Forest of Dean. Their son recently joined them, after completing his hotel training in Switzerland. The pub is etched with 600 years of history, although the owners have brought it firmly into the twentieth century with hotel and conference facilities. Salmon from the Severn and the Wye makes its seasonal appearance on the bar menu – cold in open sandwiches and salads or hot with a velouté sauce. Locally caught wild fish also appear in their 'smoked' state. Variety is provided by Stilton stuffed pears, the 'Cowboy's Breakfast', vegetable curry, and grilled lamb cutlets. More formal meals can also be taken in the restaurant. The wine list features the full range from the Wyndham Estate in Australia's Hunter Valley, which has the same family origins as the pub; there is also a tip-top selection of house wines. Beer drinkers will find solace in draught Bass, cider buffs in Weston's Vintage. Clearwell is close to numerous attractions: Symond's Yat Rock, Tintern Abbey, Slimbridge Wildfowl Sanctuary and the Roman and Anglo-Saxon iron mines at Clearwell Caves, to name but four. SAMPLE DISHES: deep-fried soft herring roes £6; pan-fried lamb's liver with grilled bacon £8.50; knickerbocker glory £3.

Open *11am to 11pm, Sun 12 to 3, 7 to 10.30; bar food and restaurant 12 to 2, 6 to 9.30 (9 Sun)*
Details *Children welcome Car park Wheelchair access (also WC) Garden and patio No smoking in restaurant No music Dogs welcome Access, Amex, Delta, Diners, Switch, Visa Accommodation: 15 rooms, B&B £30.50 to £52.50*

CLEY NEXT THE SEA Norfolk map 6

▲ *George & Dragon Hotel*

High Street, Cley next the Sea, nr Holt
TEL: (01263) 740652
on A149, E of Blakeney

'The building is a remarkable piece of architecture, with a terracotta George & Dragon over the main entrance,' observed a visitor casting his eye over this imposing edifice, erected in 1897. '*The* Doctor Long' founded the Norfolk Naturalists Trust here in 1926, and devotees believe that this is a fitting monument to his foresightedness. Without doubt it is now the most renowned birdwatchers' pub in England. The 'bird bible', recording rare sightings, has pride of place on a lectern in the bar; there's also a hide actually inside the lounge and a specially built 'scrape' (shallow lake, to entice feathered visitors). The kitchen takes its cue from what the region can produce: fish is out of the North Sea; kippers, cider-pickled herrings and other cured delicacies are provided by the Cley Smokehouse down the street; local asparagus finds its way into a pie topped with herb pastry; mushrooms grown in the area go into a tart. The list of specials also extends to jugged hare, Norfolk lamb and lentil casserole, Thai curried chicken with noodles, not to mention pan-fried dabs, slip soles, and 'lined' cod in prawn, cream and wine sauce. To finish off, there are locally made ice-creams and sorbets, as well as cheesecakes and crumbles. A dozen kinds of calvados are on show; otherwise look for the English wines on the workmanlike list, or try a pint of Wolf from the brewery in Attleborough if it's on. There are great walks along the nearby Norfolk coastal paths, or you can join the hordes who point their camera lenses at the famous local windmill. SAMPLE DISHES: country pâté with salad and brown toast £3; steak, kidney and mushroom pie £6; toffee cream tart £2.50.

Open *11 to 2.30, 6 to 11, Sun 12 to 3, 7 to 10.30; bar food and restaurant 12 to 2, 7 to 8.45*
Details *Children welcome in dining-room Car park Wheelchair access (also WC) Garden Background music Dogs welcome Accommodation: 8 rooms, B&B £30 to £65*

CLIFFE Kent **map 3**

Black Bull

186 Church Street, Cliffe TEL: (01634) 220893
off B2000, 5m N of Rochester

The village of Cliffe is strung out along the marshy Hoo Peninsula, a flat Kentish backwater where the prison hulks of Victorian days used to lie. It's a different story now – especially in summer, when birdwatchers have their binoculars focused and the local pubs are busy. From the outside, the Black Bull looks like any one of hundreds of solid Victorian watering-holes. What singles it out is the food. 'The smell draws you through' the high-ceilinged interior, with its dark wooden tables and gold coloured banquettes. Soh Pek Berry offers an unexpected taste of the Far East, with a menu that is both accessible and slightly intriguing. From China come spring rolls, sweet and sour pork, and lohan chai Buddhist vegetables; Thailand contributes satays and delicately flavoured curries, but the strongest influence is Malaysia. Here you'll find mutabak (deep-fried bread stuffed with spiced beef, served with red pickled onions), as well as nasi goreng, beef rendang, fried hokkein mee (noodles with meat, fish and vegetables) and special braised pork with Chinese mushrooms and chestnuts. Sunday brunch is an immensely popular and good-value 'tiffin' (children eat for half price) and there's an 'ethnic buffet' the first Wednesday of each month. A more extensive evening menu is also available in the basement restaurant called Tapestries.

Imported bottled beers such as Tiger, Kirin and Tsing Tao suit the food, and the pub has a well-deserved reputation for traditional British ales: up to six are regularly on handpump, including Wadworth 6X, Thwaites Bitter, Courage Directors and so on. Sake features on the serviceable wine list, and there are also some Chinese spirits, which the landlord admits 'are better smelt than slurped'. SAMPLE DISHES: spare ribs £4; stir-fried beef with peppers, bamboo shoots and black bean sauce £7; mango sorbet £2.75.

Open *12 to 2.30, 7 to 11, Sun 12 to 2.30, 7 to 10.30; bar food and restaurant all week L 12 to 2, Tue to Sat D 7 to 9 (10 Sat)*
Details *Children welcome in eating areas Car park Wheelchair access (also WC) Patio No smoking in dining-room Background and live music; jukebox Dogs welcome in bar only Access, Switch, Visa*

CLIFTON HAMPDEN Oxfordshire map 2

▲ *Plough Inn*

Abingdon Road, Clifton Hampden TEL: (01865) 407811
S of A415 Clifton Hampden to Dorchester road

'A wonderful thatched pub' set in a village of similar properties near the River Thames, according to a reporter who was also impressed by the 'enthusiastic and very hospitable' landlord. The food served in the small, stylish oak-beamed dining-room is equally pleasing. Oak-smoked chicken salad with pesto dressing, steak and beer pie, and – not surprisingly – Turkish baklava, are the sort of dishes to expect on the menu. Draught beers include Courage Best, Webster's Yorkshire Bitter and Ruddles County. House wines are served by the glass, and there's a smattering of half-bottles – plus vintage champagne – among the 50 bins on the wine list. SAMPLE DISHES: tomato and mozzarella salad £6; smoked salmon italienne £7; chocolate mousse £3.25.

Open *all week 11am to midnight; bar food and restaurant 11am to midnight*
Details *Children welcome Car park Wheelchair access (also WC) Garden and patio No smoking throughout pub No music Guide dogs only Access, Switch, Visa Accommodation: 8 rooms, B&B £50 to £75*

COLDHARBOUR Surrey map 3

▲ *Plough Inn*

Coldharbour Lane, Coldharbour TEL: (01306) 711793
3½m SW of Dorking, signposted Leith Hill and Coldharbour

The road winds gently uphill, through 'stunning' countryside with gently sloping hills, vast fields and woods all around; this is great walking territory. At the top, in a simple hamlet of scattered houses, is the black-and-white Plough Inn. You might think you had tripped back to the nineteenth century when you enter the pub, with its beams, well-worn brown furnishings, copper kettles and a few vicious-looking animal traps on the walls. This is the real-ale pub *par excellence*. The owners recently set up their own Leith Hill Brewery on the premises and you can sample the fruits of their endeavours in the shape of Crooked Furrow. Otherwise a 'brilliant' selection brings the faithful to the bar for pints of Adnams Broadside, Ringwood Old Thumper, Hall & Woodhouse Badger Bitter, Hop Garden Gold from the Hogs Back Brewery, and many more; Biddenden cider and Gales country fruit wines are suitable alcoholic alternatives. Almost everything – including bread – is made on the premises, according to the owners, and the menu has a homespun drift. The mainstays are dishes like steak and onion pudding, lamb and mint hotpot, pork with apple and sage dumplings, and steamed syrup sponge. There are also a few more exotic items such as Thai chicken, and pan-fried hake with garlic butter and dill sauce. SAMPLE DISHES: cream of winter vegetable soup £3; spicy sausage and mixed bean casserole £5; chocolate roulade £3.

Open *Mon to Fri 11.30 to 3, 6.30 (7 winter) to 11, Sat and Sun 11.30 to 11 (10.30 Sun); bar food and restaurant 12 to 2 (2.30 weekends), 7.30 to 9.30 (9 Sun)*
Details *Children welcome in bar eating area Wheelchair access Garden No smoking in restaurant Background music Dogs welcome No cards Accommodation: 3 rooms, B&B £25 to £50*

COLEFORD Devon map 1

▲ *New Inn*

LOCAL PRODUCE

Coleford TEL: (01363) 84242
off A377 Exeter to Barnstaple road, 4m W of Crediton

The New Inn is actually very old. It was built in the thirteenth century and, like many of its neighbours in this Devon backwater, it's fashioned from cob stone and topped with a thatched roof. Tankards and horse brasses hang from the beams, a log fire crackles in winter. The kitchen draws upon abundant supplies of local produce: fish from Brixham might appear in the shape of seafood provençale, or fillet of brill with cream, lemon and butter sauce; eggs are free-range; additive-free sausages are made by the firm of Bangers; ice-creams are produced at Langage Farm. And, of course, ploughman's features cheeses from the region. Elsewhere, the menu tips its hat to fashion, serving warm pigeon breast and smoked bacon salad with orange vinaigrette, and delves into the ethnic repertoire for rogan josh with poppadum and sambal. Among the desserts look for Wembworthy cream – blackcurrants with a yoghurt and cream topping. Drinks also have a noticeable West Country accent: well-kept real ales include Otter Ale and Hall & Woodhouse Badger Bitter, as well as Wadworth 6X and Fuller's London Pride. The wine list is a good slate from Christopher Piper Wines of Ottery St Mary, with nine quality house wines topping the bill. In warm weather it's pleasant to sit outside at tables by the stream. SAMPLE DISHES: grilled goat's cheese and walnut salad £4.25; chicken Stroganov £8.50; chocolate layered mousse £2.75.

Open *11.30 to 2.30, 6 to 11, Sun 12 to 2.30, 7 to 10.30; bar food 12 to 2, 7 to 10, Sun D 7 to 9.30; closed 25 and 26 Dec*
Details *Children welcome in eating areas Car park Wheelchair access Garden Background music Dogs welcome by arrangement Access, Amex, Delta, Diners, Switch, Visa Accommodation: 5 rooms, B&B £38 to £60*

COLESHILL Buckinghamshire **map 3**

Red Lion

Village Road, Coleshill TEL: (01494) 727020
off A355 Amersham to Beaconsfield road

This unpretentious Chiltern pub is tucked away down narrow lanes, and the village pond is just across the road. A bustling, convivial atmosphere prevails. The small bar menu offers a selection of snacks such as filled jacket potatoes, ploughman's, salads and nibbles like creamed sardines on toast, but if you are hungry the blackboard is the place to look. There's nothing too fancy, but the food is well cooked and the portions are large. On a typical day the choice might include baked ham in parsley sauce, grilled lamb cutlets, or salmon Mornay, while desserts could range from treacle and walnut tart to lemon meringue pie. Sunday lunch is a roast with all the trimmings. Service is relaxed and friendly and the chatty landlord's presence adds to the welcoming ambience. Beers include Flowers IPA, Tetley and Fuller's London Pride, and wine is sold by the glass. In warm weather you can sit outside under the parasols and enjoy the leafy countryside. SAMPLE DISHES: jacket potato with prawn mayonnaise

£4.25; chicken in bacon, mushroom and peppercorn sauce £6.25; chocolate trifle £2.25.

Open *weekdays 11 to 3, 5.30 to 11, Sat 11am to 11pm, Sun 12 to 4, 7 to 10.30; bar food 12 to 2.15, 7 to 9*
Details *Children welcome Car park Wheelchair access (also WC) Garden No music Dogs welcome No cards*

COLNE BRIDGE West Yorkshire map 8

Royal & Ancient

19 Dalton Bank Road, Colne Bridge TEL: (01484) 425461
on B6118, 2m SE of M62 junction 25

Named after the famous Scottish golf course, this sandstone pub emphasises the sporting theme with appropriate cartoons on the walls. Bar food is advertised on two blackboards. One features baguettes – salmon and cucumber mayonnaise, beef and horseradish, and hot pork with mint sauce, for example – which are served with salad and chips. The other blackboard concentrates on dishes such as beef and Guinness pie, pan-fried cutlets of lamb, chilli, and Yorkshire hog roast. The separate restaurant – renamed Mr Skeffington's since the new owners took over in 1996 – has been extended; if you order a main meal in the bar and the restaurant isn't full, you will be offered a table there. Beers on draught in this free-house include Tetley Bitter, Black Sheep Special and Timothy Taylor Landlord, plus a guest brew every two weeks. The small wine list extends to Switzerland, and 'quite acceptable' house wine is for sale by the glass. SAMPLE DISHES: mozzarella wrapped in bacon, bread-crumbed and deep fried £2.25; venison steak with lavender swede £9; fruit bavarois with citrus sauce £3.

Open *11am to 11pm; bar food and restaurant 11am to 10pm*
Details *Children welcome Car park Wheelchair access Patio No cigars in restaurant Background music Dogs welcome Access, Delta, Diners, Switch, Visa*

COLN ST ALDWYNS Gloucestershire map 2

▲ *New Inn* ✿ 🍇

Coln St Aldwyns TEL: (01285) 750651
off B4425, Cirencester to Burford road, 2m SW of Bibury

Brian and Sandra-Anne Evans have worked hard to make this one of the most 'impeccably kept' inns in the Cotswolds, and it creates an immediate impression of civilised antiquity. The building itself is Elizabethan, creeper-clad and bedecked with flower baskets in the summer; inside, it is 'mercifully unchanged', although creature comforts abound. Dried hops dangle from the ceiling, old oil paintings hang on the exposed stone walls, a stuffed buzzard gazes down on the well-heeled clientele.

Chef Stephen Morey made the move from country-house hotel to country pub in 1996 and his style is ambitious – although he is quite prepared to offer bar customers a menu peppered with stalwarts such as soup with home-baked breads, fish and chips with baked beans, and gammon with chips and fried egg. This is all good, honest stuff, but other dishes suggest that the kitchen pitches most of its efforts further up the culinary ladder. Onion tart is served on a rich, strong gravy with lentils, pieces of sauté chicken liver and mushrooms; pithiviers of goats' cheese comes with tomatoes and basil; and vegetarians might also opt for wild mushroom and Parmesan risotto with garden herbs. Tiger prawns are spiked with Thai spices, other fish might be grilled and jazzed up with salsa verde. Desserts take in homespun favourites such as Bakewell tart and rice-pudding with jam, as well as warm pecan pie with toffee sauce and coconut ice-cream, or white chocolate and Amaretto cheesecake with passion-fruit. A more up-market menu is served in the restaurant. The wine list is deemed 'better than average' for a pub, with four decent house selections by the glass and a good spread elsewhere. A quartet of real ales includes Hook Norton Best, Wadworth 6X, Morland Original and Theakston Best. SAMPLE DISHES: Welsh rarebit glazed with basil pesto £4.25; braised oxtail with mustard and herb dumplings £8.50; prune and armagnac ice-cream with baked hazelnut meringue £4.

Open *11 to 3, 5.30 to 11, Sun 12 to 3, 7 to 10.30 (Sat 11am to 11pm); bar food and restaurant 12 to 2 (2.30 Sun), 7 to 9.30*
Details *Children welcome in bar eating area Car park Wheelchair access (also WC) Patio No smoking in dining-room No music Dogs on leads welcome in bar Access, Amex, Delta, Switch, Visa Accommodation: 14 rooms, B&B £55 to £95*

COLSTON BASSETT Nottinghamshire map 5

Martins Arms

School Lane, Colston Bassett TEL: (01949) 81361
off A46 Leicester to Newark road, 4m S of Bingham

'We are shortly opening our antiques and interiors business in the stables and will be opening for morning coffee and afternoon tea,' write the owners of the ever-expanding Martins Arms. Built as the squire's residence on Colston Bassett estate around 1690, it is now one of the most highly regarded country pub/restaurants in the Vale of Belvoir. A sedate mood prevails in the bar, where dapper staff serve and a pianist plays from time to time. Order one of the speciality sandwiches and you will get open-textured Italian-style bread with fillings such as salmon cured with jasmine tea and demerara sugar, or a butterfly of Toulouse sausage topped with sauté onions and flat mushrooms. The rest of the menu is equally challenging and full of invention: brochette of marinated king prawns is served with a sweet pepper and pineapple salsa, a gâteau of lamb layered with chicken and herb mousse comes with a rosemary and redcurrant *jus*, while chargrilled medallions of pork are 'entwined' with oak-smoked salmon then finished with a creamy champagne sauce studded with morels. Even the ploughman's is a dressed-up version, while desserts range from sweetened goats'-cheese terrine to apple charlotte. Similar offerings are served in the dining-room, with a touch more elaboration.

The wine list is a choice selection of around 30 bins supplied by Lay & Wheeler with a good spread and very fair prices. Real ale buffs can choose from Bateman's XB, XXXB and Dark Mild, or opt for Adnams, Marston's Pedigree or Fuller's London Pride. Children under 14 are not allowed inside the pub, but there is a big garden, complete with a croquet lawn, and pleasant views and walks all around. SAMPLE DISHES: Colston Bassett Caesar salad £7; Cajun chicken breast with Louisiana sweet potato gumbo £11.50; warm strawberry mille-feuille £3.50.

Open *12 to 3, 6 to 11, Sun 12 to 3, 7 to 10.30; bar food all week L 12 to 2, Mon to Sat D 6 to 10; restaurant all week D only 7 to 9.30*
Details *Children over 14 welcome Car park Wheelchair access (also WC) Garden Live music No dogs Access, Switch, Visa*

COMBE HAY Bath and N.E. Somerset map 2

▲ *Wheatsheaf*

Combe Hay TEL: (01225) 833504
off A367, 3m S of Bath

On a good day you may see buzzards wheeling in the sky from the three-tiered terraced gardens of this low, whitewashed pub. The views over the woods and fields are stunning, especially in summer. Crowds are also enticed by the food. Menus are chalked on blackboards and the list is a long one. The line-up changes from week to week, and the kitchen aims high with pan-fried chicken livers with smoked bacon in tarragon sauce served on a warm croissant, or honey-roast marinated duck breast with a ginger and mushroom sauce. Home-made pies and ploughman's strike a less fancy note, while vegetarians could be tempted by, say, baked marrow stuffed with spicy ratatouille. Desserts are familiar items including banoffi pie and bread-and-butter pudding. Butcombe Bitter is kept in very good order, along with Wadworth 6X and Courage Best; the wine list runs to 20 bins. SAMPLE DISHES: mushroom and courgette soup £2.75; whole grilled local trout topped with a caper, pepper and tomato salsa £7; treacle sponge £3.

Open *11 to 2.30, 6.30 to 10.30 (11 Fri and Sat), Sun 12 to 3, 7 to 10.30; bar food and restaurant 12 to 2, 6.30 to 9.30, Sun 12 to 2, 7 to 9.30*
Details *Children welcome in eating areas Car park Wheelchair access Garden and patio No music Dogs welcome on a lead Access, Switch, Visa Accommodation: 3 rooms, B&B £45 to £70*

COMPTON Surrey — map 3

▲ *Harrow Inn*

The Street, Compton TEL: (01483) 810379
on B3000, signposted Compton, off A3

Every part of this village-centre pub is used for eating, and there are plenty of tables in the traditionally furnished small rooms, with their brightly patterned carpets, cream walls, dark woodwork and low ceilings. The printed menu carries tried-and-tested pub fare – sandwiches, salads, and dishes like battered cod. More enterprising items are chalked on a board, where you might find terrine of chicken, pork and pistachios, monkfish with bacon, beef Stroganov, and cous-cous with chunky vegetables; Sunday sees the addition of a traditional roast. Among the puddings are likely to be chocolate ice-cream, and crème brûlée. Breakfast is served every morning, and the restaurant is open for dinner. Harveys Sussex Best Bitter, Greene King IPA and Ind Coope Burton Ale are on draught, and house wines are sold by the glass. Loseley House, the sixteenth-century mansion famous for its herd of Jerseys, is nearby; you can also tour the dairy. SAMPLE DISHES: mussels in cream and tarragon sauce £5.75; chicken fillet with avocado, bacon and cheese £8.25; treacle tart £3.25.

Open *11 to 3, 5.30 to 11, Sun 11 to 4, 7 to 10.30; bar food 12 to 3, 6 to 10; restaurant D only 6 to 10; closed Sun evening in winter*
Details *Children welcome Car park Wheelchair access Garden and patio Background music Dogs welcome Access, Amex, Delta, Switch, Visa Accommodation: 4 rooms, room only £35*

Use the maps and index at the back of the Guide *to plan your trip.*

COMPTON MARTIN Bath and N.E. Somerset map 2

Ring O'Bells

Main Street, Compton Martin TEL: (01761) 221284
on A368, between Weston-super-Mare and Bath

Families are admirably accommodated in this village pub under the the north ridge of the Mendip Hills: a high chair in the lounge bar, climbing frame and swings in the safe garden, as well as a toy-laden games room are just some of its child-friendly attributes. The printed menu is a familiar stroll through pan-fried sardines with tomato and herb sauce, chilli, lasagne and the like, backed up by snacks such as steak sandwiches, omelettes and BLTs. It's also worth consulting the blackboard, which might span anything from Somerset pork to Chinese chicken, as well as assorted steaks and grills. Butcombe Bitter is the resident beer, but you will also find Wadworth 6X, Wilmot's Premium Ale, Courage Best and a guest brew on draught; the short wine list includes four house wines by the glass. Chew Valley and Blagdon Lake are nearby. SAMPLE DISHES: Stilton mushrooms in puff pastry £3; Barnsley lamb chops £6.25; bread-and-butter pudding £2.25.

Open *11.30 to 3, 6.30 to 11, Sun 12 to 3, 7 to 10.30; bar food and restaurant 12 to 2, 7 (7.30 Sun) to 9.30 (10 Fri and Sat)*
Details *Children welcome in eating areas Car park Wheelchair access (also WC) Garden No smoking in family room No music Guide dogs only Access, Delta, Switch, Visa*

COOKHAM DEAN Berkshire map 3

▲ *Inn on the Green*

The Green, Cookham Dean TEL: (01628) 482638
off A404, S of M40 junction 4

From the outside, this village pub looks typically mock-Tudor, but the interior is full of real character. Several dining areas are arranged around the main bar, where the décor is all stripped beams and sturdy pine furniture, with two open fires. This is a 'good family destination', noted one reporter, especially in summer, when children can cavort in the one-acre garden (complete with play equipment and a five-a-side pitch). Bar food is limited to lunch-times, but the menu manages to pack plenty of interest into a small space. Soup comes with Continental breads, röstis are topped with spicy chilli, or tomato sauce and roasted vegetables. Meat and game dominate the show: warm salad of black pudding with sauté potatoes, game terrine with preserved oranges, and wild boar and venison sausages from the Denham Estate, for example. Alternatively, you could choose anything from an open sandwich topped with smoked salmon and sour cream to grilled chicken breast with noodles and pesto. Brakspear Bitter, Fuller's London Pride and Bishop's Tipple are on draught. Three house wines are served by the glass, while the full list is tailored to the needs of customers taking dinner in the restaurant, where fondues are a novel attraction. SAMPLE DISHES: open roast beef and salad sandwich £4; calf's liver and bacon with mash and onion gravy £6.50; sticky toffee pudding £3.50.

Open *12 to 3, 6 to 11, Sun 12 to 3, 7 to 10.30; bar food Mon to Sat L only 12.30 to 3; restaurant all week 12 to 2.30, 7.30 to 10*
Details *Children welcome in bar eating area Car park Garden and patio No music Dogs welcome Access, Amex, Delta, Switch, Visa Accommodation: 6 rooms, B&B £45 to £85*

Jolly Farmer

Church Road, Cookham Dean TEL: (01628) 482905
off A404, S of M40 junction 4

A village consortium bought this 200-year-old pub opposite the parish church during the 1980s and the place continues to be well supported by the local community. A chatty atmosphere prevails in the two simply furnished bars. The varied lunchtime blackboard takes in such things as a warm salad of smoked chicken, bacon and avocado based on good fresh ingredients, and pies with shortcrust pastry lids 'baked on', as well as moules marinière, beef Stroganov, and pasta with spicy tomato, basil and olive sauce, followed by blackberry crumble, treacle tart and the like. A few more imaginative ideas show up on the evening menu. Courage Best is regularly on handpump, but it's worth checking the list of guest brews, which might include Brakspear Bitter, Gale's HSB, Titanic Lifeboat Ale and, occasionally, something from the Marlow Brewery. SAMPLE DISHES: deep-fried potato skins with dip £4; calf's liver with bacon and onions £9; banoffi pie £2.75.

Open *11.30 to 3, 5.30 (6 Sat) to 11, Sun 12 to 3, 7 to 10.30; bar food and restaurant all week L 12 to 2.30 (2 Sunday), Tue to Sat D 7.30 to 9.30*
Details *Children welcome Car park Wheelchair access Garden and patio No music Dogs welcome Access, Delta, Switch, Visa*

If you visit any pubs that you think should appear in the Guide, *write to tell us –* The Which? Guide to Country Pubs, *FREEPOST, 2 Marylebone Road, London NW1 1YN.*

Report forms are at the back of the book; write a letter if you prefer.

CORBRIDGE **Northumberland** **map 10**

▲ *Angel Inn*

Main Street, Corbridge TEL: (01434) 632119
on A68/A69, 4m E of Hexham

Originally known as the Head Inn, this seventeenth-century hostelry lays claim to being the oldest in Corbridge; it used to be the staging-post for the mail coach and legend has it that the landlord was duty-bound to read out the news from the Newcastle papers to his local clientele. Times change, but the Angel – as it is now known – is still a popular venue for eating and drinking. The bar menu is a daily selection of dishes with plenty of robust gutsiness and an eye for the produce of the region: game casserole is laced with Theakston ale, fillet of Tyne salmon and dressed Craster crab are both served with salad. Otherwise you can expect anything from fillet of turbot with mussels and white wine to a special mixed grill, and broccoli and Stilton bake. Most main courses are available in half-portions, and more extensive menus are offered in the restaurant. Theakston Best and Younger No. 3 Ale are on draught and the pub has a broadly based wine list. Hadrian's Wall is within easy reach, along with the historic Abbey of St Wilfred in Hexham and the Roman town of Corstopitum. SAMPLE DISHES: smoked salmon and taramasalata £3.25; stir-fried lemon and garlic chicken with rice £6; caramel pavlova £2.50.

Open *11am to 11pm, Sun 12 to 3, 7 to 10.30; bar food and restaurant 12 to 2.15, 6 (7 restaurant) to 9.15*
Details *Children welcome in eating areas Car park Wheelchair access (also WC) Garden No smoking in dining-room No music Dogs by arrangement Access, Amex, Delta, Diners, Switch, Visa Accommodation: 7 rooms, B&B £42 to £64*

CORSCOMBE **Dorset** **map 2**

▲ *Fox Inn*

Corscombe TEL: (01935) 891330
off A356, 6m SE of Crewkerne

Descend lanes of ever-decreasing size to reach this pub outside the village. The setting comprises 'woods, fields, bird song, a stream', and the seventeenth-century thatched building fits in perfectly. 'Martyn Lee is a terrific landlord, genuinely friendly, chatty and solicitious,' according to one fan of the place. He has left the interior untouched – the stone floors are bare, there is pine everywhere, log fires burn, and fox-hunting scenes line the walls. The only music will be from an occasional live pianist. There's also a new conservatory full of flowers with a communal oak table that can seat more than 20 people.

The pub is not only the centre of village gossip, but a purveyor of excellent food and drink to boot. Chef Will Longman came here from the Three Horseshoes, Powerstock (see entry), so it isn't surprising that the ambitious specials board majors in fish. Grilled turbot with chanterelle sauce, brill with endive sauce, and succulent pan-seared scallops with a 'rich, winey' sauce and stir-fried vegetables are typical of his light, confident style. Those who don't fancy seafood could go for 'excellent' aubergine fritters with tomato sauce, grilled goats' cheese with lots of 'peppery' rocket and salad leaves, marinated lamb steak with mash, or even cottage pie. 'No chips or microwaves' is the kitchen's clarion call. Plaudits have also been heaped on the desserts, especially glorious home-made meringues with clotted cream. Shepherd Neame Spitfire, Exmoor Ale and Fuller's London Pride will please the real ale lobby, while the pub also serves home-made sloe gin, damson vodka and something called 'Long Fox's Brush Wobbler'. The short list of two dozen wines does a commendable job by keeping prices realistically pegged. SAMPLE DISHES: cuttlefish braised in provençale sauce £4; local venison casserole £8; caramelised pear tart £3.

Open *weekdays 12 to 3, 7 to 11, Sat 12 to 11, Sun 12 to 10.30; bar food 12 to 2, 7 to 9 (9.30 Fri and Sat)*
Details *Children welcome in bar eating area Car park Wheelchair access Garden and patio Live music No dogs Access, Switch, Visa Accommodation: 6 rooms, B&B £45 to £65*

COTEBROOK Cheshire map 7

▲ *Alvanley Arms* ✿

Forest Road, Cotebrook TEL: (01829) 760200
on A49, 3m NE of Tarporley

Delamere Forest, where nature-lovers might see kestrels, sparrowhawks, foxes and badgers, is not far from this converted farmhouse. The beamed bar, decorated with brass and copper artefacts, and furnished with comfortable captain's chairs and stools, is likely to be full of diners tucking in to a substantial meal, rather than those dropping in for a pint. A long menu offers anything from sandwiches or ploughman's to the pub's signature dishes of steak pie served with 'first-class' vegetables, or cod and chips with mushy peas. There might also be honey-glazed lamb chops, or blackboard specials such as shrimp tart in butter vinaigrette, Welsh rarebit, suprême of tuna, or roast duck breast in apple and calvados sauce. Home-made apple pie satisfied one reporter's longing for a genuine, old-style sweet. The pub is tied to Robinson's Brewery with Bitter and Hatters Mild on handpumps at the bar. House wines are served by the carafe and half-carafe as well as by the glass. Thirteenth-century Beeston Castle is just the other side of Tarporley, sitting atop a hump rising sheer on one side from the Cheshire Plain: it's worth the long climb for the views alone. SAMPLE DISHES: leek, potato and tarragon soup £2.25; sauté guinea-fowl with mustard sauce £7.50; meringue nest with raspberries £2.50.

Open *11 to 3, 5.30 to 11, Sun 12 to 3, 7 to 10.30; bar food 12 to 2, 6 to 9.30 (9 Sun to Tue)*
Details *Children welcome in dining-room Car park Wheelchair access (also WC) Garden Background music Guide dogs only Access, Delta, Switch, Visa Accommodation: 3 rooms, B&B £25 to £30*

COTHERSTONE Co Durham map 10

▲ *Fox and Hounds* 🍇

Cotherstone TEL: (01833) 650241
on B6277, 3m NW of Barnard Castle

A coaching-inn for over 200 years, the Fox and Hounds is, according to landlord Michael Carlisle, situated on the 'quiet route to Scotland', and overlooks the two village greens. Inside, the bar is heavily beamed and simply furnished; log fires blaze in winter. A printed menu is available throughout the pub, and features snacks such as gammon steak sandwiches, chicken curry, and ploughman's with more substantial dishes – grilled Dover sole, breast of chicken wrapped in bacon and served in an Irish whiskey sauce, and rack of Teesdale lamb with mint gravy, for example. Real ales include Ruddles County, but also look out for the local White Boar Bitter, Hambleton Best and Goldfield. The wine list runs to 38 bins, with half a dozen from the New World, and ten half-bottles. The pub is well placed for exploring beautiful Upper Teesdale and is surrounded by a wealth of walking routes. Raby Castle, Barnard Castle and Rokeby Park are all nearby. SAMPLE DISHES: Craster smoked salmon £5.50; escalope of pork in a calvados sauce £10; apple pie with cream £2.75.

Open *11.30 to 3, 6 to 11, Sun 12 to 2.30, 7 to 10.30; bar food and restaurant 11.30 to 2.30, 6.30 to 9.30; closed 25 Dec*
Details *Children welcome Car park Wheelchair access (also WC) Patio No smoking in 1 dining-room Background music No dogs Access, Visa Accommodation: 3 rooms, B&B £38 to £50*

🍇 *indicates a pub serving better-than-average wine.*

COTHILL Oxfordshire map 2

Merry Miller

Cothill TEL: (01865) 390390
from A34 Abingdon interchange take A415 towards Witney, take first right then second right

Built as a granary during the seventeenth century, the Merry Miller has been impressively refurbished and 'beautifully restored' by its current owners. Old and new blend tastefully in the bar and dining areas: original beams, flagstones and a log fire in the grate sit comfortably with panelling, modern pine tables and pictures for sale from Sunningwell School of Art on the walls. A pianist plays most Tuesday evenings and Sunday lunch-time. To all intents and purposes the whole place operates as a pub/restaurant.

A short menu of bar snacks at lunch-time takes in warm quiche, kipper and whisky pâté, and bubble and squeak with beer gravy, plus sandwiches and even a chip butty with malt vinegar and parsley. But the kitchen shows its serious intentions with blackboard specials, including baked fillet of sea bream with a well-judged grain mustard sauce and thinly shredded deep-fried leeks. Chef James Tea was head-hunted from the kitchens of Le Manoir aux Quat' Saisons, and evidence of finely tuned technique shows in the more extensive *carte* that can also be plundered at lunch-time. Crab timbale is artfully presented with a garnish of roasted red peppers and concentric circles of sauce and herbs; home-smoked wild boar comes with baby artichokes; chargrilled chicken is served with parsnip purée and roast garlic *jus*. Desserts tread a similar path: bread-and-butter pudding appears as a mound of white bread circles interleaved with lots of sultanas with syrup on a pool of crème anglaise; otherwise there might be honey-glazed pears with white chocolate ice-cream and caramel sauce, or Bramley apple charlotte with apple crisps. In the evening you can order only from this menu.

The list of around 30 wines is thoughtfully assembled, with some interesting modern names and several – including house bubbly – by the glass. Merry Miller Best Bitter is the house beer, but you can also sample Theakston, Hook Norton Best and Wychert Bitter on draught. SAMPLE DISHES: celery, apple and Stilton soup £2; breast of duck with jasmine tea and lime sauce £9; passion-fruit delice with mango coulis £4.

Open *Mon to Thu 11 to 2.30, 6 to 10.30, Fri and Sat 11 to 2.30, 6 to 11, Sun 12 to 3, 7 to 10.30; bar food 12 to 2, 6.45 to 9.45; restaurant 12 to 2, 7 to 10.30 (9.30 Sun)*
Details *Children welcome in eating areas Car park Wheelchair access (also WC) Garden and patio No smoking in restaurant Background and live music No dogs Access, Delta, Switch, Visa*

COTTERED Hertfordshire **map 3**

Bull

Cottered TEL: (01763) 281243
on A507, between Buntingford and Baldock

Cottered is a very pretty village with a green and charming cottages; on certain days of the year you may even see Morris Men or sword-dancers. Inside the pub are two bars; the public bar is done out in dark green, the lounge is salmon-pink, while the tiny dining-room is in navy. The kitchen makes good use of the chargrill for dishes such as fillet of salmon, steaks, and chicken breast stuffed with bacon and served with herb and garlic butter. Staff bring a blackboard of daily specials to the tables, and customers can order, say, mussels in garlic butter, calf's liver, or fillet of plaice. Lunches tend to be more restricted, and there is a traditional roast or two on Sundays. Puddings are also chalked up on boards: among them may be chocolate and almond mousse, and crème brûlée. Greene King IPA and Abbot Ale are on draught, and there's a short wine list. SAMPLE DISHES: vegetable soup £2.75; rack of smoked pork ribs £10.50; bread and brandy pudding £2.75.

Open *12 to 3, 6.30 to 11, Sun 12 to 3, 7 to 10.30; bar food and restaurant 12 to 2, 7 to 9.30*
Details *No children under 7 Car park Wheelchair access (also WC) Garden and patio Background music No dogs Access, Delta, Visa*

COWBEECH East Sussex **map 3**

Merrie Harriers

Cowbeech TEL: (01323) 833108
off A271, 4m NE of Hailsham

'This is where we started and now finish,' pronounced one couple enigmatically. They have been coming to the Merrie Harriers since 1962 and what they value about the place is summed up by the epithets 'Real country. Real log fires. Real pretty dressed waitresses.' The pub is a white 'lapped boarded' building with a big garden at the back providing sweeping views across the Weald. Inside there's a comfortable, if 'slightly detached', bar with a separate area down a few steps at the back, which reminded one reporter of 'a teashop'. The menu is long, taking in everything from mozzarella, leek and pasta bake to mixed grills, and breast of duck with Morello cherry sauce. Prices may seem 'a touch high' but there's also the option of a good-value two-course lunch which offers, say, grilled breast of chicken with a buttery orange and tarragon sauce followed by light-textured bread pudding. Harveys Best and Flowers IPA are on draught. SAMPLE DISHES: onion and cheese soup £2.50; rainbow trout with mushroom and almond sauce £9; summer pudding £3.

Open *11 to 2.30, 6 to 11, Sun 12 to 3, 7 to 10.30; bar food and restaurant 12 to 2, 6.30 to 9*
Details *Children welcome in restaurant Car park Wheelchair access (also WC) Garden and patio No smoking in restaurant Background music No dogs Access, Delta, Switch, Visa*

COXWOLD North Yorkshire **map 9**

▲ *Fauconberg Arms*

Main Street, Coxwold TEL: (01347) 868214

Named after the Earl of Fauconberg, who lived at Newburgh Priory and married Oliver Cromwell's daughter, this is a country inn of substance. From the locals' bar at the back there are views of Byland Abbey and Sutton Bank, while the 'fine' old lounge bar is sturdily furnished, with antique settles, rugs strewn over stone floors and a splendid stone fireplace. One wide-ranging menu is served throughout the place, and the kitchen seems to be at home with battered Whitby cod, fillet of trout in breadcrumbs, and chicken curry, as well as deep-fried pastry 'envelopes' of Stilton and celery pâté served with spiced peach mayonnaise, duckling with jasmine and orange sauce, and pan-fried loin of lamb with 'thick minty gravy'. Desserts range from bread-and-butter pudding to chocolate cappuccino cup with coffee mousse. Twenty wines from around the world, many available by the glass, appear on the printed list, while bin-ends are advertised on a blackboard. Draught beers include John Smith's, Tetley Bitter and Theakston Best. Novelist Laurence Sterne (author of *Tristram Shandy*) was vicar of the local church during the 1760s, and the parsonage – called Shandy Hall – is open to the public; Newburgh Priory is also close by. SAMPLE DISHES: leek mousse layered with smoked salmon £3.75; steak pie with Theakston Old Peculier Ale £6; butterscotch pudding with home-made custard £3.

Open *11 to 3, 6 (7 Nov to Mar, Mon to Fri) to 11, Sun 12 to 3, 7 to 10.30; bar food and restaurant all week 12 to 1.45, 7 to 8.45; closed Monday D winter*
Details *Children welcome Car park Patio No music No dogs in eating areas Visa Accommodation: 4 rooms, B&B £24 to £45*

SAMPLE DISHES: *listed in the main text of an entry indicate three typical dishes from the menu to give some idea of the style of cooking and prices.*

CRANMORE **Somerset** **map 2**

Strode Arms

Cranmore TEL: (01749) 880450
just S of A361, 4m E of Shepton Mallet

Beams in the low ceilings, a huge inglenook and exposed-brick walls all add to the cosy, relaxed atmosphere at this ancient converted farmhouse. To the front, a terrace looks across to the village pond; behind is a beer garden and car park. The menu offers the likes of egg mayonnaise, smoked trout, escalope of veal, fillet of sole, and steaks, but it's worth casting an eye over the list of blackboard specials, which could include timbale of smoked salmon and smoked salmon mousse, lamb hotpot, venison and bacon pie, and wild mushroom risotto. To finish, there's spotted dick, perhaps, or marshmallow cheesecake. On draught are Flowers IPA, Fuller's London Pride and Marston's Pedigree. House wines are served by the glass, and the full list features a local white and a sweet Muscat of Samos. Moated Nunney Castle is worth a diversion, and the famous house and gardens of Stourhead are not too far if you want to make a day of it. SAMPLE DISHES: smoked fish terrine £3.75; ballottine of honey-roasted duck £8.50; strawberry mille-feuille £2.75.

Open *11.30 to 2.30, 6.30 to 11, Sun 12 to 3, 7 to 10.30; bar food and restaurant 12 to 2, 7 to 9.30 (10 Fri and Sat)*
Details *Children welcome in dining-room Car park Wheelchair access (also WC) Garden and patio No music Dogs welcome in bar area only Access, Visa*

CRAZIES HILL **Berkshire** **map 3**

Horns

Crazies Hill, nr Wargrave TEL: (01734) 401416
off A4 at Kiln Green, 3m N of Twyford

In Tudor times, this was a hunting lodge; 200 years later, a barn was added and, luckily, further sympathetic restorations have diluted none of the pub's attractiveness. It is all timber and whitewashed brick outside, while three inter-connecting bars within have natural pine tables, exposed beams and open fires. During most lunch-times you'll find ploughman's and filled baguettes as well as a specials board, which could include roast pheasant, smoked chicken and courgette pancakes, or beef and ale pie. Otherwise the printed menu offers a choice of pastas, steaks, and items such as warm salad of bacon, avocado and Stilton. In the evenings the choice extends to roast partridge with apple and calvados, or monkfish and king prawn kebabs. This is a Brakspear pub, with Bitter, Special, Old and OBJ on handpump. The wine list runs to 24 bins and a couple of half-bottles. Close by is the Shire Horse Centre. SAMPLE DISHES: aubergine pâté with toasted pitta bread £4.25; breast of duck with a plum sauce £11; banoffi pie £3.25.

Open *11 to 2.30, 6 to 11, Sun 12 to 3, 7 to 10.30; bar food and restaurant all week L 12 to 2 (reduced menu Sun and Mon), Mon to Sat D 7 to 9.30 (9 Mon); closed 25 and 26 Dec, and eve 1 Jan*
Details *Children welcome in dining-room L only Car park Wheelchair access (also WC) Garden No music Dogs welcome L only Access, Delta, Switch, Visa*

CRONDALL Hampshire map 3

Plume of Feathers

The Borough, Crondall TEL: (01252) 850245
just S of A287 Odiham to Farnham road

A relaxing old-world charm defines the mood of this ancient oak-framed pub, with its beams, exposed-brick walls, open fires, and tapestry-covered stools. Chalkboards proclaim the dishes of the day, which could be avocado and bacon salad, steak and mushroom pie, vegetarian stir-fry, fish-cakes with parsley sauce, or Goan chicken curry. Game appears in season: venison steak in red wine sauce, perhaps, or roast breast of pheasant. Puddings are seasonal too, with hot winter fruit salad, and a crumble sharing the bill with traditional sherry trifle, or chocolate fudge cake. 'No background music, no jukebox, no fruit machine, no chips,' writes the landlord: music to the ears of traditionalists. Booking a table is advisable in the restaurant. Morland Old Speckled Hen is among the ales on draught, and there's a full wine list. SAMPLE DISHES: mussels in garlic and cream £6; lambs' liver with bacon and onions £6; sticky toffee pudding £2.75.

Open *11 to 3, 6.30 to 11, Sun 12 to 3, 7 to 10.30; bar food and restaurant all week L 12 to 2, Mon to Sat D 7 to 9.30*
Details *Children welcome Car park Wheelchair access Garden and patio No-smoking area No music Dogs welcome on a lead Access, Amex, Delta, Visa*

Many pubs have separate restaurants, with very different menus. These have not been inspected. A recommendation for the pub/bar food does not necessarily imply that the restaurant is also recommended.

CROSLAND HILL **West Yorkshire** **map 8**

Sands House

Blackmoorfoot Road, Crosland Hill TEL: (01484) 654478
off A62, 2m SW of Huddersfield town centre

The eponymous 'Sands' is a reference to the Yorkshire sandstone quarry not far from this moorland pub. The building itself is – naturally – made of the local stone, and inside, it is a veritable horologist's treasure house, with clocks of every size, shape and description dotted around the three connecting rooms. The daily-changing menu, listed on blackboards, usually offers around half a dozen starters and puddings and double that number of main courses, plus what the pub calls 'big soups', and sandwiches – Brie and bacon, for example; also look for 'Po-Boy' (roast beef, mustard and onions in French bread). Cajun salmon on stir-fried vegetables may be among the main courses, along with a vegetarian dish like broccoli, nut and cream-cheese roulade, with a dessert such as treacle sponge bringing up the rear. Boddingtons, Ruddles Best, John Smith's and Courage Directors are on draught, and house wines come by the glass. SAMPLE DISHES: cod, leek, bacon and potato rösti with rarebit topping £4; pork fillet in pepper and wine sauce £7; apricot brandy meringue £2.50.

Open *11am to 11pm, Sun 12 to 10.30; bar food 11.30 to 2.30, 5 to 9.30*
Details *Children welcome in eating areas Car park Wheelchair access (also WC) Garden Background music No dogs Access, Amex, Delta, Switch, Visa*

CROSTHWAITE **Cumbria** **map 8**

▲ *Punch Bowl Inn*

Crosthwaite TEL: (01539) 568237
off A5074, 3m S of Windermere

'Easy to find (if you know the way!)' advises a correspondent: this revitalised village pub stands on an unclassified road between Kendal and Windermere. Inside, there seems to be an 'endless number of rooms' including a balcony, with wall-to-wall carpeting adding a touch of luxury to what might seem rather 'spartan' surroundings. Framed and signed menus from some of Europe's top chefs suggest that something gastronomically serious is going on here. In fact, chef/proprietor Steven Doherty earned his stripes at Le Gavroche and his cooking has echoes of what one reporter dubbed 'the new breed of smart London restaurants'. The difference is in the price and in the refreshing lack of stuffed-shirt formality. Everyone comments on the easy-going atmosphere of the place and the friendliness of Marjorie Doherty and her staff.

The cooking is 'peasant rustic' and surprisingly sophisticated by turns, and it is all done with a sure touch. Doherty isn't afraid to dust off venerable classics such as garbure béarnaise, cod bonne femme and chicken schnitzel; he even produces émincés of chicken Albert – no doubt in homage to his famous mentor, M. Roux. His output bristles with unexpected touches: hot goats'-cheese salad comes with roasted beetroot and button onions, while roasted tuna steak is cooked in sesame oil with a soy and ginger sauce accompanied by wholewheat noodles. The juice from local damsons goes into the sauce for confit of duck, while the whole fruit – served hot – accompanies vanilla and white chocolate sponge pudding. Other desserts range from tarte Tatin to expertly crafted floating islands, which one recipient thought would be 'popular with children and those with a sweet tooth'. On Sunday there's a special lunch menu which is reckoned to be outstanding value for two or three courses. Real ales are treated with the respect they deserve, and they are likely to be good North Country names such as Theakston Best, Jennings Snecklifter and Black Sheep Special Bitter. The short list of around 20 wines is as reasonably priced as the food; the range is catholic and several are offered by the glass. The area around Crosthwaite is delightful: 'the Lyth Valley is particularly beautiful during damson blossom time,' according to one traveller. SAMPLE DISHES: grilled game salad with hazelnut dressing £4; seared fillet of salmon antiboise £7; pear and raspberry crème brûlée £2.50.

Open *12 to 3, 6 to 11, Sun 12 to 2.30, 6 to 10.30; bar food 12 to 2, 6 to 9*
Details *Children welcome Car park Wheelchair access Patio No-smoking area No music Dogs in bar and snug only Access, Delta, Switch, Visa Accommodation: 3 rooms, B&B £23 to £30*

CUDDINGTON Buckinghamshire map 2

Annie Bailey's 🍇

Upper Church Street, Cuddington TEL: (01844) 291215
off A418, 4½m W of Aylesbury

Annie Bailey? Who she? An erstwhile local landlady, by all accounts. Much has changed since she was born in 1794, though she might recognise the brick inglenook. Most of the pub is given over to eating, including a large dining-room to the rear, so the bar area is small. Old photographs on the walls, the stripped wooden floor and quirky ornaments (including an accordion and a pair of ice skates) give style and character to the place, and candles create a soft glow.

'Staff talk enthusiastically about how good the food is,' writes a reporter, 'and it is!' Interesting breads kick things off – ciabatta, tomato, and Milwaukee rye, for example. One reporter was impressed by a starter of seafood-platter (gravlax, tartare of smoked haddock, smoked salmon and dressed crab); you could also try AB's fish-cake, or smoked duck breast with oranges. Fish and seasonal game also form the backbone of main courses: loin of venison in red wine and black treacle sauce, guinea-fowl on Puy lentils, or seared peppered salmon with crème fraîche and cucumber sauce, for example, although there may also be such dishes as chicken suprême with tarragon sauce. Apple and raspberry pie with 'meltingly good' pastry, or pear frangipane, makes an impressive finale. Don't expect a wide choice of real ales (Brakspear Bitter is the only draught beer), but some big names can be found on the wine list. House wines (including AB's champagne) are served by the glass, and there's a good selection of bottles for less than £10. Fortnightly wine-tasting sessions are well supported. SAMPLE DISHES: Scottish black pudding on red cabbage £4.50; breast of Lunesdale duck on rösti £12; treacle sponge pudding with custard £3.50.

Open *Tue to Fri 12 to 2.45, 6.30 to 11, Sat 6 to 11, Sun 12 to 4; bar food and restaurant Tue to Fri and Sun L 12 to 2.45, Tue to Sat D 6.30 to 10*
Details *Children welcome Car park Wheelchair access Garden and patio Background and live music No dogs Access, Amex, Delta, Diners, Visa*

CUMNOR Oxfordshire **map 2**

Bear & Ragged Staff

Appleton Road, Cumnor TEL: (01865) 862329
off A420, 4m W of Oxford

Bruce and Kay Buchan moved to this 400-year-old village pub past the duck pond, having made a name for themselves at the Fish at Sutton Courtenay. In a very English setting of flagstones, bare stone walls and beamed ceilings, Bruce is delivering food that commands serious attention. Fish remains the main theme. Cornish squid comes with sauce gribiche and sun-dried peppers, roast monkfish is served with chickpeas and toasted ratatouille, sea bass is paired with clam provençale. Flavours are true and natural; ideas are perfectly attuned to the gastronomic mood of the '90s. Meat and game are given equally vivid treatment: roasted beetroots are the rosy-red accompaniment for rare breast of duck, while sweet-and-sour onions set off fillet of Aberdeen Angus in puff pastry.

In the Bear Bar, for a smaller outlay, you can also get less-heavyweight dishes along the lines of baked avocado with Welsh rarebit, salmon with lyonnaise potatoes and chilli pickle, and roast shoulder of lamb with tomato and olive chutney. The pudding menu gets to grips with gratin of pink grapefruit with passion-fruit sorbet, and white chocolate quenelles with dark chocolate sauce; otherwise there are English farmhouse cheeses to finish. The atmosphere both in the bar and in the long, picture-filled dining-room is 'great' and service is 'pleasantly informal'. This is a Morrells pub, with Oxford Ale, Varsity and Graduate on handpump. The wine list offers a good spread with six decent house wines offered by the glass. SAMPLE DISHES: gâteau of aubergines, cracked wheat and mozzarella £6.75; tranche of cod with duxelle, herb crust and chive gratin £12.50; warm prune and almond tart with vanilla ice-cream £5.

Open *11 to 3, 5.30 to 11, Sun 12 to 3, 7 to 10.30; bar food and restaurant 12 to 2.15, 7 to 9.30 (10 Fri and Sat)*
Details *Children welcome in eating areas Car park Wheelchair access (also WC) Garden No smoking in 1 bar; no cigars in restaurant Background music Guide dogs only Access, Amex, Delta, Switch, Visa*

▲ *Vine Inn*

11 Abingdon Road, Cumnor TEL: (01865) 862567

A 'real-life' vine is trained across the front of this whitewashed village pub, whose core dates back to 1743. The present owners are from Whites Restaurant and Wine Shop in Oxford, so aspirations are high and most of the floor space in the maze of interconnecting rooms is given over to tables for diners. The whole place is run with cheerful efficiency and it attracts an affluent young crowd. The blackboard menu is shot through with fashionable themes and ideas: warm salads, such as pigeon breast with sun-dried tomato, or duck with hoisin dressing, dominate the starters, although you can also get pasta – mushroom ravioli, for example. Stir-fries and steaks have their own mini-section and main courses could range from Thai beef curry, and fish-cakes, to escalope of salmon with strawberry sauce, or curious-sounding kangaroo with blueberry caramel. Incidentals are up to the mark, and they know how to cook chips here. Desserts might include 'excellent' fruit tarts and bread-and-butter pudding 'showered with nutmeg'. Fresh baguettes are always available for those wanting a quick snack.

The short, reasonably priced wine list – chalked on a board above the bar – is full of good things: half-bottles are much in evidence and half a dozen wines are sold by the glass. For beer drinkers, Adnams, Wadworth 6X and Hampshire Arthur Pendragon are on draught. There's a large beer garden at the back of the pub with tables, chairs and a children's play area; games of Aunt Sally are played from time to time. SAMPLE DISHES: warm chicken liver and croûton salad £4.25; escalope of chicken with mustard sauce £8; summer pudding £3.

Open *11 to 2.30, 6 to 11, Sun 12 to 3, 7 to 10.30; bar food and restaurant 12.30 to 2.15, 6.30 to 9.15*
Details *Children welcome in eating areas Car park Wheelchair access (also WC) Garden and patio No smoking in conservatory Background music Dogs welcome on a lead Access, Delta, Switch, Visa Accommodation: 1 room, B&B £35 to £50*

DALWOOD Devon map 2

Tuckers Arms

Dalwood TEL: (01404) 881342
1m N of A35, between Honiton and Axminster

Dalwood is an uplifting kind of place with wonderful highbanked lanes and rolling countryside all around. No wonder it is much favoured by walkers and birdwatchers – the heritage Coastal Path (with its dramatic sea views) and the marshes of the Axe estuary are close by. At the heart of the village is the Tuckers Arms, a thirteenth-century thatched longhouse with views up to Dalwood Hill from its garden. Inside, it is welcoming and stoically traditional, and 'nothing is too much trouble' for the staff, noted one reporter. A skittle alley adds a touch of extra interest. Fish specials are notable features of the long menu, which takes in such things as avocado and seafood salad, crab and sesame toasts with green salad and plum sauce, and sauté king scallops with tarragon cider, mustard and cream, as well as fillet steak with pâté and sherry, and venison steak with port and Stilton. Desserts range from traditional treacle and walnut tart with clotted cream, and upside-down pineapple sponge with custard, to chocolate and orange pavlova. Two- and three-course special deals are also good value, while Sunday night is curry night. The pub dispenses Otter Ale and Flowers Original and there's an extensive wine list with plenty of choice from around the world. SAMPLE DISHES: smoked haddock with cream cheese and mushrooms £3.50; pan-fried sea bass with garlic, lemon and prawns £8.25; autumn fruit meringue £3.

Open *11 to 3, 6 to 11, Sun 12 to 3, 7 to 10.30 (12 to 3, 7 to 11 Mon to Fri Winter); bar food and restaurant 12 to 2, 7 to 10*
Details *Children welcome in bar eating area Car park Wheelchair access Garden and patio Background music No dogs Access, Amex, Delta, Switch, Visa Accommodation: 5 rooms, B&B £25 to £40*

DANEHILL East Sussex map 3

Coach & Horses

School Lane, Danehill TEL: (01825) 740369
on A275, 8m S of East Grinstead, 1m down School Lane signposted Chelwood

The garden, with its large lawn, flower-beds and white furniture, is the attraction here in summer, and the fenced-off children's play area has been described as 'quite excellent'. The saloon bar is half-panelled, with a boarded ceiling, blue-upholstered benches, and plenty of flowers. Snacks like sandwiches, burgers, and sausage with egg and chips are always available. Otherwise for lunch you can look to minted pea soup, grilled field mushrooms and bacon, deep-fried cod, gammon, or liver and bacon. Sunday brings the addition of traditional roasts. In the evening the menu broadens out to take in scallops grilled with bacon, turkey enchilada with chilli and onion salsa, fish stew with parsley dumplings, or chicken breast stuffed with mascarpone and rosemary. Vegetarians are always well catered for (the pub grows its own vegetables too). Bread-and-butter pudding and chocolate fudge cake are the sorts of desserts to expect. Harveys Sussex Best Bitter and one or two guest ales are on draught, and house wines come by the glass. SAMPLE DISHES: lentil soup £2.25; trout fillets with tarragon sauce £7.25; blackberry and apple crumble £2.50.

Open *11 to 2.30, 6 to 11, Sun 12 to 3, 7 to 10.30; bar food all week L 12 to 2, Mon to Sat D 7 to 9*
Details *Children welcome in bar eating area Car park Wheelchair access Garden No smoking in eating area Live music No dogs in eating area Access, Delta, Switch, Visa*

DARTINGTON Devon map 1

▲ *Cott Inn*

Dartington TEL: (01803) 863777
S of A385, 2m NW of Totnes

Way back when the A385 was the old Ashburton to Totnes turnpike road, the Cott Inn was at the real centre of things. The key player in those days was a wealthy Dutch burgher named Johannes Cott who obtained a licence for the premises in 1320 so that local packhorse drivers and travellers could rest up and wet their whistles on their journeys. Today the inn is the amalgamation of a whole row of cottages, with reputedly one of the longest thatched roofs in Britain. A huge log fire oftens burns at each end of the bar, and standing timbers, 'thick, thick walls', carved pews and tiny-paned windows set the tone. 'What a wonderful place,' exclaimed an inspector.

Lunch is a hot and cold buffet of great renown, but the kitchen's reputation hinges on what happens in the evening. Two blackboard menus are dominated by fresh fish from Brixham and Plymouth as well as supplies of seasonal game. Imagination abounds. Superb sweet mussels come in a garlicky tomato sauce 'really pungent with basil', crab-cakes are served with sweet ginger and lime dip, and monkfish is pan-fried with hazelnuts in a blue cheese sauce. Simple, effective presentation and clear flavours also shine through in spicy pork with ginger, roasted red peppers and good al dente tagliatelle, tagine of lamb, or breast of guinea-fowl stuffed with chicken liver pâté served with bramble jelly sauce. Desserts such as sticky pear and ginger pudding, or apricot and banana mascarpone tart, come with clotted cream. Eleven tip-top wines are served by the glass and the full list of around 40 bins offers the prospect of affordable, high-quality drinking. Bass and Butcombe Bitter are on draught and you can also get Inch's Harvest Scrumpy. The nearby Dartington Craft Centre is a must and it's also worth taking a look at Dartington Hall and the Totnes to Buckfastleigh steam railway. SAMPLE DISHES: grilled goats' cheese with cranberry dressing £4.25; venison casserole with red wine and juniper berries £9.75; ratafia Bakewell tart £3.25.

Open *11 to 2.30, 5.30 to 11, Sun 12 to 3, 7 to 10.30; bar food 12 to 2.15 (2.30 Sun), 6 to 9.30; closed evening 25 Dec*
Details *Children welcome in dining-room Car park Garden and patio No smoking in restaurant; no-smoking area in bar Live music Dogs welcome Access, Amex, Delta, Switch, Visa Accommodation: 6 rooms, B&B £41 to £55*

DENSHAW Greater Manchester **map 8**

Rams Head Inn

Denshaw TEL: (01457) 874802
on A672, 3m S of M62 Jct 22

Set high on the top of Saddleworth Moor – yet only 3 miles from the M62 and the city lights of Oldham – the Rams Head continues to serve the public just as it did in the days when its was an ale house on the old pack-horse route from Rochdale to Huddersfield. You can call in for just a coffee and a baguette or choose something light from the starters on the blackboard – minestrone soup, fish-cakes with home-made chips, or braised butter-beans topped with melted cheese, for example. Main dishes are often given a modern twist, as in warm smoked salmon with lime and green peppercorn marinade, salad of black pudding and potatoes with warm cider vinaigrette, roast duck with Puy lentils, and venison steak with celeriac purée. Desserts include some inventive ideas such as steamed chocolate pudding with citrus salad and Grand Marnier cream, or white chocolate cheesecake with black cherries poached in kirsch. On Fridays extra fish dishes are added to the normal repertoire (fillet of sea bass on basil-flavoured mash, chargrilled tuna with tomato and olive sauce, for instance). The two-course set-menu is also recommended (leek and potato soup followed by goujons of cod in tempura batter with vegetables is typical). Well-kept Tetley Bitter and Timothy Taylor Landlord are on draught, and the wine list is supplemented with a blackboard list. SAMPLE DISHES: smoked Finnan haddock with garlic mayonnaise £4; sauté lamb's kidneys with grain mustard sauce £8; pecan pie with Chantilly cream £3

Open *Tue to Sat 12 to 3, 6 to 11, Sun 12 to 10.30; bar food and restaurant Tue to Sat 12 to 2, 6 to 10, Sun and bank hols 12 to 8.30*
Details *Children welcome in eating areas Car park Wheelchair access Garden and patio No-smoking areas Background music No dogs Access, Amex, Delta, Switch, Visa*

DOBCROSS Greater Manchester **map 8**

Navigation Inn

Wool Road, Dobcross TEL: (01457) 872418
off A6052, 4m NE of Oldham

After a visit to the increasingly popular tourist village of Uppermill, you can walk to the relative calm of the stone-built Navigation Inn. This is a no-nonsense rendezvous where locals and visitors chat happily together, and service is affable. The menu is a straight run through garlic mushrooms, lasagne, curries and the like, bolstered by a few more ambitious specials; expect dishes such as chicken suprême in leek and Stilton sauce, or rolled fillet of sole stuffed with scallops and crabmeat. Puddings return to the tried-and-tested theme of fruit pies, gâteaux and so on. The Navigation has a good cellar, with Banks's Bitter, Hanson's Mild and Morrels Varsity kept in decent condition; wines come by the glass. SAMPLE DISHES: mushroom soup £1.75; fillet of salmon in dill sauce £6; chocolate fudge cake £2.

Open *weekdays 11.30 to 3, 5 to 11, Sat and Sun 11.30 to 11; bar food all week L 12 to 2, Mon to Sat D 5 to 8.30 (7.30 Mon and Tue)*
Details *Children welcome Car park Wheelchair access (also WC) Patio Background music No dogs No cards*

DOCKING **Norfolk** **map 6**

Hare Arms

Station Road, Docking TEL: (01485) 518402
on B1153, 11m W of Fakenham

Terence Mickelbrough has done a grand job in refurbishing this 400-year-old village pub. The building was once a courthouse and the various interconnecting rooms have names like Witness Room and Gallery; the cellar is – of course – the Dungeons. Colour schemes are pale blues and terracotta red, with rural bric-à-brac on the beams and some cosy alcoves, especially in the dining-room. All of this makes an attractive setting for ambitious and stylish cooking. The landlord's son is at the stove and he is capable of producing quite complex dishes such as pan-fried halibut with tomato coulis and spicy fried oysters, and lamb cutlets with port wine and prune marmalade, as well as dabbling with ostrich and kangaroo. Vegetables are well thought of; desserts include banoffi pie, and white and milk chocolate lasagne. Every other Thursday evening is a fish and live jazz night; on alternate weeks you can expect gastronomic events featuring an international cuisine. Adnams Bitter, Benskins, Flowers Original and Wadworth 6X are among a useful selection of real ales, and wines are reckoned to be 'far above the normal quality'. A camp site and barbecue were under construction as we went to press, and accommodation is promised for summer 1997. SAMPLE DISHES: leek and potato soup £2.75; chilli chicken stir-fry with noodles and oyster sauce £8; sticky toffee pudding £2.75.

Open *summer 11m to 11pm, winter 11 to 3, 6 to 11, Sun all year 11 to 3, 6 to 10.30; bar food and restaurant 12 to 2.30, 6 to 10*
Details *Children welcome in dining-room Car park Wheelchair access (also WC) Patio No smoking in 1 room Occasional background and live music No dogs in eating areas No cards*

DODDISCOMBSLEIGH **Devon** **map 1**

▲ *Nobody Inn*

Doddiscombsleigh TEL: (01647) 252394
3m W of A38, Haldon racecourse exit

'My idea of what a country pub should be like,' enthused one roving reporter. Here's how she described the wonderfully atmospheric interior of this splendid inn: 'The overall effect is darkness and shadow – enhanced by heavy carved benches and chairs, solid tables and intimate window seats. Low lamp light deepens the shadows, between the beams the ceiling is "stained ox-blood" – walls, too, are dark.' The whole place is kept in pristine condition, service cannot be faulted, and the welcome from landlord Nicholas Borst-Smith is exactly right.

The reason for coming here is first and foremost the spectacular selection of West Country cheeses from the cream of the region's farmhouse producers. Up to 40 are available at any time, but it is an ever-changing list with 'a constant ebb and flow of varieties'. You get six on a plate with biscuits or bread (they might have names like Sharpham, Belstone, Vergin and Jerganthal). The uncompromising commitment to real food and local produce shows in everything from the ingredients that go into the renowned Nobody soup, and the sausages and mash with Roman Nut mustard, to organic honeycomb toffee ice-cream, and the clotted cream served with the equally famous spiced bread pudding. In the bar you can also get BLTs, stuffed pitta bread, and blackboard specials such as heartwarmingly nourishing butter-bean casserole, or Arabian lamb cooked in turmeric, cinnamon and prune sauce served with couscous. Slightly more ambitious evening meals are available in the restaurant.

The Nobody Inn wine list is a truly remarkable tome documenting around 800 bins (including at least 20 by the glass); the pub is also a wine merchant's with a shop for off-sales. Nobody's (brewed by the Branscombe Brewery) is the house tipple, but you might also find Bass, PG Steam and a guest ale, often tapped direct from the cask. As if that isn't enough, there are 230 whiskies, and ciders from Grays and Luscomb produced to the pub's own specification and 'lightly gassed'. SAMPLE DISHES: Nobody pâté £3.25; duck pie with salad £4; warm treacle tart £2.50.

Open *12 to 2.30, 6 (7 winter) to 11, Sun 12 to 3, 7 to 10.30; bar food all week L 12 to 2, Tue to Sat D 7 to 10; restaurant D only Tue to Sat 7 to 10*
Details *No children Car park Wheelchair access Patio No smoking in dining-room No music No dogs Access, Delta, Switch, Visa Accommodation: 7 rooms, B&B £35 to £59*

DOLTON Devon map 1

▲ *Union Inn*

Dolton TEL: (01805) 804633
on B3217, 7m S of Great Torrington

Originally built as a traditional Devon longhouse, the Union has been a hostelry for nearly 200 years. Inside there are two, quite small, low-beamed bars filled with settles and benches. Country prints adorn the walls, log fires blaze in winter and service is friendly. Landlord Ian Fisher, who took over here in early 1996, doubles as chef, and the blackboard menu shows a serious approach to food. There's praise for Japanese-style deep-fried king prawns and sea bass is reckoned to be 'outstanding'. Otherwise you might find braised oxtail with red wine, or fillet of red bream with spicy tomato sauce. The printed menu consists mainly of grills, but has three vegetarian dishes. Beers include Dartmoor Best and the local Hicks Special with the occasional guest ale. Inches Stonehouse cider is available too, and the wine list runs to 20 bins. Dolton village is on the Tarka Trail and the Halsdon nature reserve is nearby. SAMPLE DISHES: moules marinière with home-baked bread £4; pan-fried leg of lamb steak £7; orange brandy pudding £2.50.

Open *12 to 2.30 (exc Wed), 6 to 11, Sun 12 to 3, 7 to 10.30; bar food and restaurant Thur to Tue L 12 to 2, all week D 7 to 9.30*
Details *Children welcome in eating areas Car park Garden No-smoking area No music No dogs in restaurant Access, Visa Accommodation: 3 rooms, £22.50 to £45*

DORCHESTER-ON-THAMES Oxfordshire map 2

▲ *George Hotel*

High Street, Dorchester-on-Thames TEL: (01865) 340404
on A423, 4m NW of Wallingford

The eighteenth-century carriage outside this coaching-inn is a reminder of the days when Dorchester was on the main Bristol to London road – although the timber-framed building itself was in business some three centuries before that. Drinking and bar snacking take place in an attractive converted barn with old photographs, swathes of dried flowers and fruit hung on the walls, and bottles of oils and vinegars laid out on display. A tapestry of St George hangs over the fireplace. Cottage-loaf 'sandwiches' filled with steak are renowned, but the menu has a modern edge and caters well for vegetarians: meatless pâté comes with toasted home-made brioche, a layered gâteau of roasted vegetables is topped with mozzarella and served with provençale sauce, while a 'filo pastry roulade' of oyster mushrooms, creamed spinach and pine-nuts presented with warm mayonnaise pleased one lunchtime reporter. Flesh-eaters could settle for escalope of chicken rolled in oats with a mild whisky and wild mushroom sauce, roast rack of lamb, or fillet of cod with caper, lemon and parsley sauce. Desserts such as a trio of ice-creams and pavlova have been crowd-pleasers. More ambitious food is served in the restaurant. Brakspear Bitter and a guest ale are on draught, but the wine list is what attracts most imbibers: the classy collection of 150 bins globe trots in search of quality – even as far as Russia; house wines are praiseworthy and there are plenty of halves to boot.

Dorchester Abbey, across the road from the inn, is well worth a look before you leave the village. SAMPLE DISHES: fish mousse in warm parsley sauce £4; grilled lamb sausages with minted gravy £8; blackberry bavarois £3.50.

Open *11 to 3, 6 to 11, Sun 12 to 3, 7 to 10.30; bar food and restaurant 12 to 2, 7 to 9.30*
Details *Children welcome in dining-room Car park Garden Background music No dogs Access, Amex, Delta, Diners, Switch, Visa Accommodation: 18 rooms, B&B £52.50 to £75*

DORSTONE Hereford & Worcester map 5

Pandy Inn

Dorstone TEL: (01981) 550273
off B4348 Hay-on-Wye to Hereford road, 5m E of Hay-on-Wye

Chris and Margaret Burtonwood's boast is that they run 'the oldest inn in Herefordshire'. Their whitewashed stone pub was – so the story goes – built in 1185 by Richard de Brico to house his workers constructing Dorstone Church; it was his way of atoning for his part in the murder of Thomas à Becket. Today, the Pandy (the word means 'fulling mill') is at the centre of an interesting little village in the heart of the enchanting Golden Valley. It's a friendly, inviting place with exposed stone walls adorned with coaching lamps, and low beams garlanded with green hops. The lady of the house cooks, the landlord runs the bar. Vegetarians are offered plenty of choice, with dishes such as garlic, mushroom and spinach crêpes, and butter-bean and broccoli crumble, as well as soups like celery and Stilton. The kitchen also delivers home-made pies (wild rabbit, for example), oxtail stew, and hock of lamb with pearl barley, as well as a few more fashionable items, including warm salad of chicken livers with balsamic dressing. Wales contributes lavercakes wrapped in bacon, Asia yields spicy garlic chicken with fenugreek and poppy seeds. Ploughman's and the cheeseboard include cheeses made in the village, and desserts might feature ewe's-milk ice-cream. Otherwise finish with a fruit crumble or carrot cake. Dorothy Goodbody's Springtime Bitter from the local Wye Valley Brewery is regularly on draught, along with Bass and regular guest brews in rotation. Seventeen wines are mostly from Tanners of Shrewsbury. SAMPLE DISHES: country-style pâté with juniper and onion marmalade £3.75; salmon fish-cakes with tomato and basil coulis £6.25; lemon brûlée £3.

Open *12 to 3, 7 to 11 (10.30 Sun); bar food 12 to 2, 7 to 10; closed Mon and Tue Nov to Easter*
Details *Children welcome Car park Wheelchair access (also WC) Garden No-smoking area Live music Fri evening in summer No dogs No cards*

DOWNHAM **Lancashire** **map 8**

Assheton Arms

Downham TEL: (01200) 441227
off A59, 3m NE of Clitheroe

From Downham, paths lead up to the brooding presence of Pendle Hill, which gave its name to the Witches of Pendle, tried for sorcery in the seventeenth century. The witches could even have drunk here, for the stone-built pub dates from the sixteenth century, and the village stocks are nearby. The interior is comfortable, with a large stone fireplace, and spindle-backed chairs and high settles around wooden tables. Bar food ranges from sandwiches and starters like prawns piri-piri, or Morecambe Bay shrimps, to steaks, chicken and mushroom pie, or turkey cordon bleu, backed up by a choice of vegetarian and fish dishes: mushroom tagliatelle, and grilled sea bream with capers, for instance. Flowers Original, Castle Eden Ale and Boddingtons Bitter are on draught, and three house wines from a list of more than 20 are sold by the glass. SAMPLE DISHES: ham and vegetable broth £2.25; venison, bacon and cranberry casserole £8; spotted dick £2.50.

Open *12 to 3, 7 to 11 (10.30 Sun); bar food 12 to 2 (2.30 Sun), 7 to 10*
Details *Children welcome Car park Wheelchair access (also WC) Patio No-smoking area Background music Dogs welcome Access, Amex, Delta, Switch, Visa*

DUNCTON **West Sussex** **map 3**

Cricketers

Duncton TEL: (01798) 342473
on A285, 3m S of Petworth

Standing on a quiet green patch before one of the more dramatic ascents on the South Downs, this two-storey farmhouse seems to be 'a living part' of its surroundings. At the front is a tarred shed housing a skittle alley, at the back a well-established garden that has been laid out with some degree of thought. Photographs of the pub – past and present – are hung around the bar, and a fine inglenook and log fire command one end of the room. Landlord and staff seem to maintain the balance between relaxed chumminess and skilled professionalism. Fine real ales, including Archers Golden, Woodforde's Wherry, Young's and Friary Meux are ordered at the bar. If you want food, you need to go to the hatch, where menus are displayed on blackboards. The kitchen handles good ingredients simply and there's a refreshing lack of pretence about the style: whole plaice ('a fat fish in fine condition') grilled without adornments, perfectly timed roast partridge with 'a decent, light gravy', and chunky apple pie with custard. Otherwise the range embraces everything from garlic mushrooms, and ham and egg with home-made chips to Duncton Mill trout with sun-dried tomato sauce. About 30 wines feature on the list, including four by the glass. SAMPLE DISHES: carrot and tarragon soup £2.50; crispy duck with stir-fried vegetables £9; ginger sponge £2.75.

Open *Mon to Sat 11 to 2.30, 6 to 11, Sun 12 to 3.30; bar food all week L 12 to 2, Tue to Sat D 6.30 to 9.30*
Details *Children welcome in dining-area only Car park Wheelchair access (also WC) Garden Live music Dogs welcome Access, Visa*

DUNSFOLD Surrey **map 3**

Sun Inn

The Common, Dunsfold TEL: (01483) 200242
off B2130, 4m SW of Cranleigh

A pretty setting adds to the charm of this white-painted Georgian house which stands on the common directly opposite the village pond – no wonder the crowds descend on sunny days. Expect queues at the bar in the high season and during holidays. A printed menu advertises the usual sandwiches and ploughman's, but the blackboard of specials moves beyond home-made steak and kidney pie into the likes of pork dijonnaise and venison sausages in red wine. Puddings – listed on a separate board – are also the home-made kind. The wine list includes a decent spread from around the world, including some organics. Beer drinkers should be happy with King & Barnes Sussex Bitter, Friary Meux Bitter and Marston's Pedigree. SAMPLE DISHES: vegetable samosas £4; chargrilled trout £8; hazelnut and raspberry roulade £2.75.

Open *11 to 3, 6 to 11, Sun 12 to 3, 7 to 10.30; bar food 12 to 2.15, 7 to 10 (9.30 Sun)*
Details *Children welcome in dining-room Wheelchair access Garden Live music Dogs welcome Access, Amex*

DUNWICH Suffolk map 6

▲ *Ship Inn*

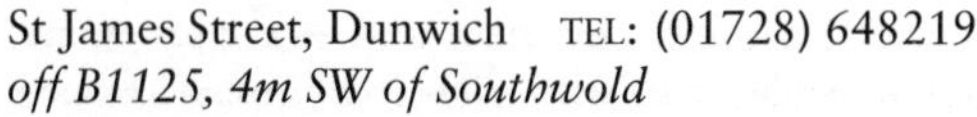

St James Street, Dunwich TEL: (01728) 648219
off B1125, 4m SW of Southwold

Once a great medieval port, Dunwich has been falling into the sea over the centuries; the cliffs continue to tumble and erode. You can sometimes buy fish from the local boats moored on the shingle beach; otherwise head for the Ship Inn, where the catch is cooked and served in pleasantly convivial surroundings. A fire often blazes in the bar, some of the seats are fashioned from old wooden casks, and all kinds of memorabilia are dotted around; there's also a light, airy conservatory for relaxation. Lunch is a simple affair – soup, fish and chips with home-made tartare sauce, ploughman's, pies, salads and so on. In the evening you can expect something a little more elaborate in the shape of crispy Camembert parcels with Suffolk jelly, fish crumble, and roast chicken with lemon sauce. Puddings and ice-creams are home-made, cheeses come with biscuits or Suffolk rusks. Adnams and Greene King beers are on draught and the pub has a very serviceable list of around two dozen wines gleaned from the affordable reaches of Adnams cellars. Outside is a sprawling garden dominated by the canopy of a resplendent fig tree. There are some great walks nearby, while Dunwich Heath National Nature Reserve and Minsmere Bird Reserve are wildlife hot-spots within striking distance. SAMPLE DISHES: fried black pudding with apples £4; steak and mushroom pie £7.50; chocolate and Cointreau cheesecake £3.

Open *11 to 3, 6 to 11, Sun 12 to 3, 7 to 10.30; bar food 12 to 2, 7 to 9.30 (9 winter); closed 25 Dec evening*
Details *Children welcome in dining-room Car park Wheelchair access Garden and patio No music Dogs welcome Access, Switch, Visa Accommodation: 3 rooms, B&B £35 to £56*

EASEBOURNE West Sussex map 3

White Horse

Easebourne Street, Easebourne TEL: (01730) 813521
off A272, 1m NE of Midhurst

Visitors are attracted to Easebourne for many reasons: seventeenth-century Petworth house, with gardens landscaped by Capability Brown, is just down the road; walkers come for the setting on the South Downs; and there's polo at nearby Cowdray Park. The food at this pub opposite the village church is 'highly recommended' by one couple who also praise the pleasant staff and homely atmosphere. Ploughman's, salads and other pub staples are listed on the menu alongside casseroles and home-made pies (filled with chicken and mushroom, or steak and Guinness, for example). A range of fish dishes might include, say, grilled fillet of plaice stuffed with prawns, depending on the day's catch. Otherwise there's game in season – roast pheasant in wine sauce – or a choice of vegetarian dishes, such as leek and mushroom crumble. Traditional puddings – maybe spotted dick, and fruit crumble – are served with custard or ice-cream. Greene King IPA and Abbot Ale are on draught. SAMPLE DISHES: prawn cocktail £2.50; half a shoulder of lamb £6.25; treacle tart £2.75.

Open *11am to 11pm, Sun 12 to 10.30; bar food and restaurant 12 to 2, 7 to 9.30*
Details *Children welcome Car park Garden and patio Background music Dogs welcome Access, Amex, Switch, Visa*

EASINGTON Buckinghamshire **map 2**

Mole & Chicken

Easington TEL: (01844) 208387
off B4011, 1m N of Long Crendon on Chilton road

In Victorian times this intriguingly named hostelry was the village watering-hole and shop rolled into one. Now it is a place where food comes first and has the crowds to prove it. The menu is a wide-ranging affair embracing everything from satays to seared salmon fillet with oatmeal, lime and garlic crust. In between you will also find various pasta dishes, warm salad of crispy duck and bacon with plum and red wine sauce, half a shoulder of lamb cooked with honey, garlic and rosemary, a whole rack of barbecued ribs, and chargrilled Barnsley chop served on a bed of Mediterranean vegetables. Fish specials and desserts are listed on blackboards. Tanner's Jack and Old Speckled Hen from the Morland brewery and Hook Norton Bitter are on draught, and the pub has a list of 25 French and New World wines. The views from the terraced garden are among the most spectacular in this part of the Chilterns, taking in some of the area's finest villages. SAMPLE DISHES: mushrooms à la grecque £4.50; lamb korma £7.50; steamed jam sponge £4.

Open *11 to 3.30, 6 to 12, Sun 12 to 11; bar food Mon to Sat 12 to 2, 7 to 10, Sun 12 to 9.30; closed 25 Dec*
Details *Children welcome Car park Wheelchair access Garden and patio Background music No dogs Access, Amex, Delta, Switch, Visa*

EAST DEAN **East Sussex** **map 3**

Tiger Inn

The Green, East Dean TEL: (01323) 423209
off A269 Seaford to Eastbourne road, 4m W of Eastbourne

Morris dancers and other performers may be seen doing their stuff on the village green that fronts this white-painted inn. Part of the building still exhibits what the landlord calls 'rickety eleventh-century architecture', and there is plenty of atmosphere in the low-ceilinged bars. South-coast fish shows up on the bar menu, along with simple things like home-made steak and kidney pie, and Captain Morgan's bread-and-butter pudding (laced with the eponymous dark rum). Morland Old Speckled Hen, Flowers Original and Wadworth 6X are on handpump beside Harveys Best; the wine list also provides plenty of variety. East Dean is within reach of Birling Gap (a notable tourist spot) and the seaside is a short drive away. SAMPLE DISHES: melted Stilton and tomato macaroni cheese with garlic bread £5; game casserole £6; chocolate 'fridge' cake £2.50.

Open *July to Sept 11am to 11pm, Sun 12 to 10.30, Oct to June 11 to 3, 6 to 11, Sun 12 to 3, 7 to 10.30; bar food 12 to 2, 6.30 to 9 (9.30 Fri and Sat)*
Details *Children welcome in family room Car park Wheelchair access Garden and patio No smoking in family room No music Dogs welcome No cards*

EASTGATE **Norfolk** **map 6**

Ratcatchers Inn

Eastgate TEL: (01603) 871430
10m NW of Norwich off B1149 Holt road, 1m SE of Cawston

This extremely popular freehouse, built in 1861, stands at a remote crossroads just outside Cawston. Despite its 'very rural' location, the Ratcatchers attracts a loyal following and it's advisable to book if you intend to eat, especially at weekends. The beamed L-shaped bar has an open fire and is comfortably furnished. It's mainly geared to dining, with just a small area for drinkers, and there is an adjacent restaurant which offers dishes from the same 'mighty tome of a menu'. Starters are named after local villages – Wells Whitebait, Brockdish Buttons (Norfolk garlic mushrooms) and Cawston Cups (bacon, mushrooms and cambazola cheese under a puff pastry lid). There's a wide selection of pies, and meat dishes named after film stars – 'Heston's Massive Rump', for example, is a 20oz steak. Daily specials might feature pan-fried calf's liver with smoked bacon and onions, or duck breast with juniper and port sauce, while a 'catch of the day' board lists fish from the Norfolk coast and Billingsgate market: Cromer crab baked with cheddar, mustard and cream, served with salad and pickled samphire, or sauté monkfish flamed in vodka with pink peppercorns and cream, for example. Puddings get their names from the world of Charles Dickens: Mrs Peggoty's Bowl (spiced pear on a meringue nest), and Mr Pickwick's Parcel (brandy-snap basket filled with iced chocolate and rum mousse). Beers on draught include Adnams Extra, Hancocks and Bass. The interesting wine list runs to 40 bins, with a good selection of house wines available by the glass and a handful by the half-bottle. Nearby are the Bure Valley Railway at Aylsham, Blickling Hall and Mannington Hall Gardens. SAMPLE DISHES: Mundesley mackerel (smoked mackerel with hot horseradish sauce) £4.75; Peppard's peppered chicken £10; Mr Micawber's cake (white Belgian chocolate cheesecake) £5.

Open *11.45 to 3, 6 to 11, Sun 12 to 3, 7 to 10.30; bar food and restaurant 12 to 2, 6 to 10, Sun 12 to 2, 7 to 9.45; closed 25 and 26 Dec*
Details *Children welcome in bar eating area Car park Wheelchair access (also WC) Garden No smoking in restaurant Background music Guide dogs only No cards*

EAST HADDON Northamptonshire map 5

▲ *Red Lion Hotel*

Main Street, East Haddon TEL: (01604) 770223
off A248, 8m NW of Northampton

'Gourmet bar food was the draw' for a couple of visitors to what they describe as a 'serious eating pub', adding 'this wasn't a holiday, but there was quite a wait for a table'. Inside the thatched, stone-built pub are green-painted wood-panelled walls, with plates along picture rails, brass ornaments, and open fires. Sandwiches and ploughman's are found on the daily-changing bar menu, along with items like goats'-cheese toasties on a bed of leaves, or vegetable pasta bake. Starters could include avocado with feta cheese, or smoked trout, while traditional roasts, beef bourguignon in Yorkshire pudding, home-made faggots, and pork chop with orange and apricot sauce, could show up among the meat main courses. Piscine alternatives might include fish-cakes with tomato and basil sauce, and salmon, cod and haddock pie. Desserts are the old-fashioned kind – sponge pudding with syrup and fruit, crumbles, and so on. A good choice of real ales includes not only Bombardier and Eagle IPA from the Charles Wells brewery (to which the pub is tied) but also Young's Special, Morland Old Speckled Hen and Marston's Pedigree. Two nearby places of interest are Althorp House (home of the Spencer family) and Guilsborough Grange Wildlife Park. SAMPLE DISHES: winter vegetable soup £3; grilled fillet of plaice £9; bread-and-butter pudding £3.50.

Open *11 to 2.30, 6 to 11, Sun 12 to 2.30; bar food and restaurant all week L 12.15 to 2, Mon to Sat D 7 to 9.30*
Details *Children welcome in eating areas Car park Wheelchair access (also WC) Garden and patio Background music No dogs Access, Amex, Delta, Diners, Switch, Visa Accommodation: 5 rooms, B&B £50 to £65*

EAST HENDRED Oxfordshire **map 2**

Plough

Orchard Lane, East Hendred TEL: (01235) 833213
off A417 Wantage to Streatley road, 4m E of Wantage

Green-fingered Bill and Carmel Sheehan continue to win prizes for their horticultural prowess, and visitors to their village pub can admire the effort and skill that has gone into their cottage garden. In summer, when the crowds descend, it must be like a flower show in full swing. Away from the blooms, scents and bright colours, there's plenty to catch the eye in the bar. Farming implements adorn the walls, and the blackboard menu is also worth a look. Salads, such as smoked chicken and mango with hazelnut dressing, or mixed seafood with Caesar dressing make appetising starters, while main courses range from suprême of chicken with creamy Creole sauce to grilled rump steak. At lunch-time you can also get sandwiches, jacket potatoes, pies and other run-of-the-mill bar snacks. Flowers Original and Morland Beechnut are on handpump and wines are also available. SAMPLE DISHES: mussels in tomato and basil sauce £3.25; medallions of pork with dijonnaise sauce £8.75; toffee and apple cheesecake £3.

Open *11 to 3, 6 to 11, Sun 12 to 10.30; bar food 11.30 to 2.30, 6.30 to 9.30*
Details *Children welcome Car park Wheelchair access (also WC) Garden Background music No-smoking area No dogs Access, Amex, Delta, Diners, Switch, Visa*

EASTON Suffolk **map 6**

White Horse

Easton TEL: (01728) 746456
off B1078, 2m N of Wickham Market

Four centuries old and still going strong, this pinkwashed Suffolk inn is everything you would expect from a genuine country pub that wears its heart on its sleeve. Walk past the bird box to reach the door. The handwritten menu plays safe with pork liver pâté, ploughman's, baguettes, and chilli, but it's worth looking out for the home-made pies (chicken and leek, for example) as well as livelier offerings such as avocado, prawn and crispy bacon salad, stir-fried chicken with hoisin sauce, and crab and prawn thermidor. Sunday lunch is a roast, with reduced prices for children. Flowers Original and IPA are supplemented by a guest brew, and the pub has a fair list of reasonably priced wines. Families with children should note that there is a play area in the garden. SAMPLE DISHES: garlic mushrooms £3.50; chicken breast with leek and Stilton sauce £8; raspberry and butterscotch tart £2.75.

Open *11.30 to 2.30, 6.30 to 11, Sun 12 to 3, 7 to 10.30; bar food and restaurant 11.30 to 2.30, 6.30 to 9.45*
Details *Children welcome Car park Wheelchair access Garden and patio No smoking in restaurant Live music Dogs welcome Access, Delta, Switch, Visa*

EAST WITTON North Yorkshire **map 8**

▲ *Blue Lion* ✿✿ 🍇

East Witton TEL: (01969) 624273
on A6108 Masham to Leyburn road, 2m SE of Middleham

A couple who ate dinner in the dimly lit flagstoned bar in front of a roaring log fire reckoned this was a near-heavenly bolt-hole on a snowy February night. The Blue Lion began life as a coaching-inn towards the end of the eighteenth century, pulling in travellers and drovers on their journeys through Wensleydale. Since 1990, landlord Paul Klein has transformed it into one of the serious contenders for pub food in the Dales. The bar menu is a real firecracker, fizzing with ideas that were once the sole province of big-city brasseries. How about a warm terrine of black and white pudding with caramelised apples and grain mustard sauce? Or confit of lamb shoulder baked in filo pastry with a pearl barley, tomato and onion gravy? Or even chargrilled sardines with gratinated fennel and lemon oil dressng? If that sounds too daring, you could choose from rillettes of wild boar, Welsh rarebit, and steak and kidney pudding. As a finale you might try treacle sponge, tarte Tatin, or a 'princely' variation on queen of puddings. Such fashionable juggling with ingredients can too often fall flat, but chef Chris Clarke knows his way around the contemporary larder, and the kitchen succeeds in delivering high-quality modern food without pretence. A separate restaurant is open most evenings for dinners in a similar vein, as well as Sunday lunch.

The wine list is extensive, well described and soundly priced, with selections from all regions and a handy number available by the glass. Beer drinkers have a choice of Theakston and Black Sheep Bitter. East Witton is at the gateway to Wensleydale and Coverdale, and is within striking distance of Jervaulx Abbey. SAMPLE DISHES: Tuscan salad of chargrilled vegetables with anchovies and black olives £4; pan-fried fillet of red mullet with balsamic sauce scented with walnut oil and oranges £9.50; bread-and-butter pudding with custard £3.25.

Open *11 to 11, Sun 11 to 10.30; bar food 12 to 2.15, 7 to 9.30; restaurant Sun L 12 to 2.15, Tue to Sat D 7 to 9.30*
Details *Children welcome Car park Garden and patio No music Dogs welcome Access, Delta, Switch, Visa Accommodation: 12 rooms, B&B £45 to £75*

EAST WOODLANDS Somerset map 2

Horse & Groom

East Woodlands TEL: (01373) 462802
off A361, 2m S of Frome

The Marquess of Bath owns this cheerful, efficiently run white-washed stone inn – appropriately, since Longleat House is nearby. East Woodlands is a tiny farm hamlet on the eastern edge of the Mendips. Good country walks abound in this area, so be prepared for ramblers in the bar and the lounge, where you can flop into an armchair and soak up the heat of the inglenook. Reasonably priced baguettes, ploughman's and salads kick off the menu, which continues with such dishes as chicken and cider bake, king prawn satay, ribeye steak with a sauce of red wine and button mushrooms, and plaice, prawn and crab roulade. One reporter was highly enthusiastic about 'exquisite' banana and butterscotch mille-feuille as the finale to a pleasurable meal. Wadworth 6X, Bateman XB, Greene King IPA and Butcombe Bitter are on draught, and a blackboard lists the wines sold by the glass. Other local attractions include Nunney Castle, and Stourhead, an eighteenth-century Palladian house with breath-taking landscaped gardens. SAMPLE DISHES: broccoli, tomato and hazelnut bake £2.75; smoked haddock and prawn casserole £6.50; syrup sponge pudding £3.

Open *11.30 to 2.30, 6.30 to 11, Sun 12 to 3, 7 to 10.30; bar food and restaurant Tue to Sun L 12 to 1.45, Tue to Sat D 6.30 to 9*
Details *Children welcome in bar eating area Car park Wheelchair access Garden No smoking in dining-room No music Dogs on leads welcome in public bar Access, Delta, Visa*

EFFINGHAM Surrey map 3

Plough

Orestan Lane, Effingham TEL: (01372) 458121
½m N of A246 Guildford to Leatherhead road, signposted Effingham junction

A couple who ventured into Derek and Lynn Sutherland's music-free village pub one bank holiday Monday were so bowled over by everything they experienced that they vowed to return on a cold winter's night because 'it is such a warm place to eat and they look after you well'. Scampi and chips, and poached salmon in dill sauce with new potatoes have both been excellent, and the menu also includes such robust specialities as cod and prawn mornay, bacon and mushroom au gratin, and roasted vegetable bake. Home-made sweets might range from sticky toffee pudding to strawberry palmiers. The full line-up of Young's beers – including Winter Warmer and Dirty Dick Oatmeal Stout – is available in season, and decent house wine comes in large glasses. Effingham is not far from Polesden Lacey (National Trust). SAMPLE DISHES: beef and Stilton pie £4.50; chicken and asparagus crêpe £4.50; chocolate cheesecake £2.50.

Open *11 to 3, 6 to 11, Sun 12 to 3, 7 to 10.30; bar food 11.45 to 2, 6.45 to 9.30*
Details *Children over 14 welcome in bar eating area Car park Wheelchair access Garden and patio No-smoking area No music Guide dogs only No cards*

EGLOSHAYLE Cornwall map 1

Earl of St Vincent

Egloshayle TEL: (01208) 814807
on A389, just E of Wadebridge

This terrific little pub, tucked away up a tiny, narrow lane, originally housed masons working on the village church. The white-painted slate-roofed building is adorned with many hanging baskets in summer. Inside, amid the heavy old beams and timbers, the atmosphere is 'tremendous'; you'll hear the therapeutic sound of the collection of working clocks, from an old grandfather to Westminster chimes. Every surface not covered by a timepiece is instead adorned with prints, watercolours, ornamental plates, pottery pieces and statues. The place has the air of being lovingly maintained, and the welcome couldn't be warmer – one visitor arriving in a wild hail storm was 'ordered' to sit by the fire while her drink was brought over. Food is straightforward and uncomplicated. As well as the usual jacket potatoes, sandwiches and salads, the menu features fresh fish from nearby Padstow in dishes such as grilled Dover sole. Chef's specials, listed separately, include the likes of beef Stroganov and roast duckling, and Sunday lunch is a traditional roast. The pudding menu lists the kinds of dishes that weightwatchers dread: coffee cream and walnut gâteau, treacle tart, and sticky toffee and hazelnut meringue. This is a St Austell-tied house with Tinners and Trelawny's Pride on handpump; and the wine list is decent and inexpensive. SAMPLE DISHES: seafood platter £4.25; tournedos Rossini £12; apricot and almond roulade £2.

Open *11 to 3, 6.30 to 11, Sun 12 to 3, 7 to 10.30; bar food all week L 12 to 2, Mon to Sat D 7 to 9*
Details *Children welcome in bar eating area Car park Wheelchair access (also WC) Garden and patio Background music No dogs Access, Delta, Switch, Visa*

ELKESLEY Nottinghamshire map 9

Robin Hood Inn

Elkesley TEL: (01777) 838259
on A1, 4m S of Retford

This unassuming pub is a popular destination for walkers, who congregate in the public bar for plates of sandwiches. Otherwise, hungry travellers making their way along the A1 will find this an excellent stop-off point for a more substantial lunch. The landlord is an enthusiastic cook who presents a blackboard of above-average pub fare: you might be offered cauliflower soup flavoured with rosemary, pan-fried suprême of pheasant on a bed of braised red cabbage and apple, or the much-praised red sea bream on olive and caper mash with salsa dressing. Among the seasonal recommendations are pan-fried lamb's liver with onions and sage, and grilled fillet of salmon with stewed leeks and mushrooms in a white-wine sauce, or you may opt for the snacks, steaks or grills. There's also a special three-course set menu and a good choice of extravagant desserts.

Real ales include Boddingtons, Flowers Original and Castle Eden Ale, while wine drinkers can choose from a range of six, all served by the glass. Nearby are Sherwood Forest, Clumber Park, the Dukeries and the Robin Hood Visitor Centre. SAMPLE DISHES: herring fillets marinated in a sweet dill sauce £3.75; Provence-style chicken breast £8; grilled honey-apples with toffee cream £3.

Open *Mon to Fri 11.30 to 3, 6.30 to 11, Sat 11.30 to 11, Sun 12 to 3, 7 to 10.30; bar food all week L 12 to 2, Mon to Sat D 7 to 9*
Details *Children welcome Car park Garden Background music Dogs welcome in public bar only Access, Delta, Switch, Visa*

ELSLACK North Yorkshire map 8

▲ *Tempest Arms*

Elslack TEL: (01282) 842450
off A56/A59, 4m W of Skipton

Although the Tempest is at the side of the A56 – from the windows you can see cars whizzing along – bushes and other foliage block the noise, and the countryside surrounding the pub is quite spectacular (Elslack is on the fringe of the Yorkshire Dales National Park). 'Comfortable but unspoilt' sums up the interior of the place, with its plain stone walls, horse brasses, log fires and local pictures depicting the past, all in keeping with the inn's 200-year history. A daily blackboard – offering perhaps leek and potato soup, or sardines in garlic butter, followed by halibut with lemon cream sauce, then bread-and-butter pudding – supplements the interesting-looking printed menu. Items on this could range from filo parcels of fish, or goats'-cheese salad, to shoulder of lamb with redcurrant and mint gravy, or 'ale and hearty pie' (beef and mushrooms casseroled in ale with a flaky pastry topping). This is a Jennings pub, with a guest beer – Black Sheep, perhaps – joining the brewery's full range. There's also a good selection of reasonably priced wines, with several by the glass. SAMPLE DISHES: smoked haddock chowder £3; corn-fed chicken braised in white wine with tarragon sauce £7; sherry trifle £2.50.

Open *11 to 11, Sun 12 to 10.30; bar food and restaurant Mon to Fri 12 to 2.30, 6 to 10 (9.30 restaurant); Sat and Sun 12 to 10 (9.30 restaurant)*
Details *Children welcome in eating areas Car park Wheelchair access Garden and patio Background music No dogs Access, Amex, Delta, Switch, Visa Accommodation: 10 rooms, B&B £47 to £54*

If you disagree with any assessment made in the Guide, *write to tell us why* – The Which? Guide to Country Pubs, *FREEPOST, 2 Marylebone Road, London NW1 1YN.*

ELSTEAD **Surrey** **map 3**

Woolpack

The Green, Elstead TEL: (01252) 703106
on B3001 Milford to Farnham road, 4m W of Godalming

The Woolpack, much modernised over the years, is effectively divided into two large bars. Both have log-burning fires, but one is more atmospheric with a low ceiling and beams, while the other is lighter, brighter and feels more modern. Wool memorabilia are dotted about (fleeces were stored here before it became a pub), along with old bottles, copper and other bric-à-brac. The walls are decorated with Victorian engravings and country prints. A chill-cabinet is full of cold dishes like roast ham and lots of salads, while a blackboard lists the specials: baked goats' cheese with mango, garlic and chives, and mushroom Stroganov, followed by Thai beef, turkey escalope in vermouth, tarragon and mushroom sauce, and duck casseroled in sherry, coriander and pineapple. The pub prides itself on its large selection of home-made desserts of pavlovas, pies, roulades and so on. Regularly changing real ales, tapped from jacketed casks behind the bar, may include Greene King Abbot Ale, and a good selection of wines is available by the glass. SAMPLE DISHES: celery, Stilton and almond soup £2.50; calf's liver in red Martini, orange and sage butter £9; chocolate mousse £3.

Open *11 to 2.30, 6 to 11, Sun 12 to 3, 7 to 10.30; bar food and restaurant 12 to 2, 7 to 9.45 (9 Sun); closed 25 Dec evening and 26 Dec*
Details *Children welcome in dining-room Car park Wheelchair access Garden No music Dogs welcome Access, Delta, Switch, Visa*

ELSTED **West Sussex** **map 3**

Three Horseshoes

Elsted TEL: (01730) 825746
off A271, 3m W of Midhurst

On a bank high above the road, the Three Horseshoes is 'the sort of pub every village should have', observed one correspondent. Its attractions are many. Some relish the peaceful setting and the unpretentiousness of the two low-ceilinged bars with their standing timbers, well-worn tiled floors, pitch-pine panelling and sturdy tables. Others are here for the beer: in this case Cheriton Pots Ale from the Flower Pots Inn, Cheriton (see entry), Ballards Best and Ringwood Fortyniner are the main contenders. Food in this 'easy-going place' is fulsomely in the country tradition: robust soups, chunky bread, mashed potatoes 'with real lumps', no-frills puddings such as treacle tart; the blackboard also advertises such things as broccoli and Brie lasagne, and braised lamb with apples and apricots in a 'tomato chutney sauce' and, perhaps, ploughman's with locally produced cheese from Gospel Green. SAMPLE DISHES: parsnip and ginger soup £3.50; steak, kidney and Murphy's stout pie £8.50; baked chocolate cheesecake £3.50.

Open *11 to 2.30, 6 to 11, Sun 12 to 3, 7 to 10.30; bar food all week L 12 to 2, Mon to Sat D 7 to 9.30; closed Sun evening October to Easter*
Details *Children welcome Car park Garden No music Dogs welcome in bar only Access, Delta, Switch, Visa*

ELSTED MARSH West Sussex map 3

▲ *Elsted Inn*

LOCAL PRODUCE

Elsted Marsh TEL: (01730) 813662
off A272, 3m W of Midhurst and 1m N of Elsted

Built to serve the railway in the steam age, when there was a station next door, this plain white-painted Victorian pub is still a neighbourhood watering-hole, although its emphasis has now shifted to food. Old railway photographs share the wall space in the bare-boarded bars with blackboards advertising the day's menus. 'Granny cooking' is how Tweazle Jones and Barry Horton describe what they do; more accurately, they turn out 'copious quantities of plain English food' without frills. The strength of this 'slick' set-up is its dedication to the produce of the region. Sausages and raised pies are produced by local enthusiast Ron Puttock, bread is from the National Trust bakery at Sindon, and mutton comes courtesy of a relative's herd of Jacob sheep. Added to this are free-range chickens and ducks, 'field-raised' veal, not to mention plentiful supplies of game. Durleighmarsh asparagus appears in summer, while steak and kidney pudding is a winter-time best-seller. Other favoured dishes might be macaroni cheese, salmon fish-cakes, Irish stew, and Sussex cassoulet. Homespun puddings, such as plum crumble, come with Jersey cream from a nearby farm. Two-course weekday lunches are excellent value. Ballards beer was originally brewed here and the pub still serves the full range, as well as Fuller's London Pride and two guests, usually from small independents; also look for Gospel Green 'méthode champenoise' cider, which is brewed in the area. The seasonally changing wine list has some fair-value wines by the glass. Outside is a big garden with a floodlit boules pitch and a terrace for barbecues. SAMPLE DISHES: aubergine with home-made pesto and tomato sauce £3.50; rabbit in mustard sauce £7.50; treacle tart £3.

Open *11.30 to 3, 6 to 11.30, Sun 12 to 3, 7 to 10.30; bar food and restaurant 12 to 2, 7 to 9 (9.30 summer, 10 Fri and Sat all year); sandwiches 12 to 2.30*

Details *Children welcome in dining-room Car park Wheelchair access Garden and patio Occasional live music Dogs welcome Access, Delta, Switch, Visa Accommodation: 4 rooms, B&B £25 to £45*

ELTERWATER Cumbria **map 8**

▲ *Britannia Inn*

Elterwater TEL: (01539) 437210
off A593, 3m W of Ambleside

The Britannia is a long, low, whitewashed building overlooking the village green at this cluster of cottages that constitutes Elterwater. Plenty of tables and chairs on the terraced forecourt accommodate some of the crowds that descend on both village and pub in season. Inside, go through the hall, with its rocking-chair, and to the right you find the small, cosy bar, where there are settles, an open fire, and pictures of SS *Britannia*. Place your food order at the bar and sit wherever you can. The menu is backed up by daily specials; on offer may be broccoli and asparagus soup, filled jacket potatoes, Langdale farmhouse pie (chicken, lamb and ham), pork chop baked in cider with onions and apples, and roast leg of Shrewsbury lamb with red wine sauce. Bakewell tart, and baked apple stuffed with mincemeat, may be among the puddings. Portions tend towards the hearty – no doubt adding to the appeal of the place for the many walkers who come here. Two guest ales are on draught as well as Jennings Bitter and Cumberland Ale, and Boddingtons; three house wines come by the glass. SAMPLE DISHES: lentil and mushroom cannelloni £2.50; monkfish with tomato and garlic sauce £6.50; sticky toffee pudding £2.50.

Open *11am to 11pm, Sun 12 to 10.30; bar food 12 to 2, 6.30 to 9.30; afternoon snacks 2 to 5.30; closed 25 Dec*
Details *Children welcome Patio No smoking in dining-room No music Dogs welcome Access, Amex, Delta, Switch, Visa Accommodation: 13 rooms, B&B £18 to £60*

EMPINGHAM Leicestershire map 6

▲ *White Horse*

2 Main Street, Empingham TEL: (01780) 460221
off A606 Oakham to Stamford road, 5m W of Stamford

If you fancy working up an appetite, there's a pleasant stroll across the dam of Rutland Water and along the lanes to this pub at the higher end of a pretty village. Originally a court house, it has grown and evolved over the years into a well-run inn with up-to-the-minute comforts. The bar menu is a sound selection of cold and hot dishes ranging from leek and Stilton pâté, and an 'ample' Rutland platter featuring Melton Mowbray pork pie, home-baked ham and Rutland cheese, to chicken breast coated in grain mustard and baked in a lattice of pastry. For vegetarians there might be giant Rutland mushrooms topped with vegetable provençale, and there's always a 'catch of the day'. Desserts are such things as sherry trifle and treacle sponge, plus a sweet of the day at a reduced price. Full evening meals, plus Saturday and Sunday lunch, are also served in the restaurant. Beer buffs should look for locally brewed Oakham and Grainstore beers, alongside Ruddles, Courage Directors and Morland Old Speckled Hen; the wine list runs to 40 bins. SAMPLE DISHES: filo tiger prawns with teriyaki sauce £4.25; steak, kidney and Guinness pie £6.75; gipsy whisky cake £2.75.

Open *11am to 11pm, Sun 11 to 3, 7 to 10.30; bar food 12 to 2.15, 7 to 9.30; restaurant Sat and Sun L 12 to 2.15, all week D 7 to 9.30*
Details *Children welcome Car park Wheelchair access (also WC) Garden No smoking in restaurant Background music No dogs Access, Amex, Delta, Diners, Switch, Visa Accommodation: 14 rooms, B&B £35 to £58*

EXFORD Somerset map 1

▲ *Crown Hotel* ✿ 🍇

Exford TEL: (01643) 831554
on B3224, 9m SW of Minehead

'Food within the classic pub idiom, but so rarely seen,' enthused one visitor after a meal at this seventeenth-century coaching-inn set in the heart of Exmoor National Park. The building, which stands opposite the village green, has been imaginatively styled: to one side is 'a quiet country hotel', to the other a simpler rustic bar with guns and stuffed pheasants mounted on the walls and tables fashioned from large water butts. Service is polite and correct, and it's all very civilised.

A printed bar menu is available, but the real excitement is in the list of blackboard specials. This is serious stuff, and the kitchen delivers. One dish sums up the style precisely: a slow-cooked stew of English lamb loaded with chunks of meat 'tender enough to be cut with a fork' served in a plain stock of cooking juices with root vegetables and dumplings. 'No cream, no wine, no mucking about – perfect,' concluded one reporter. Otherwise the list of possibilities runs to pan-fried fish sausage with creamed leeks and dill, smoked chicken and king prawn salad with sesame dressing, braised oxtail, and roast aubergine stuffed with ratatouille. Crème brûlée 'flecked with tiny black dots of vanilla' is a spot-on example of the genre in every detail; alternatively, you could finish with lemon posset with 'oyster biscuit', or pecan and coconut pie. More ambitious dinners and Sunday lunch are served in the restaurant. Thirteen wines are available by the glass and the full list is a good slate with plenty of half-bottles to choose from. Real ale fans should find satisfaction in Wadworth 6X, Boddingtons and Parish Poachers. SAMPLE DISHES: mushroom risotto with Parmesan cheese £3.50; roast salmon with parsley potatoes and hollandaise sauce £7.50; treacle sponge pudding with vanilla custard £3.

Open *11 to 3, 6 to 11, Sun 12 to 3, 7 to 11; bar food 12 to 2, 6.30 to 9.30; restaurant Sun L 12 to 2, all week D 7 to 9.30*
Details *Children welcome in eating areas Car park Wheelchair access Garden No music Dogs welcome in bar only Access, Amex, Delta, Switch, Visa Accommodation: 17 rooms, B&B £40 to £94*

EXLADE STREET Oxfordshire map 2

▲ *Highwayman*

Exlade Street TEL: (01491) 682020
off A4074, between Reading and Wallingford, 4m NE of Pangbourne

The Highwayman is a big, sprawling, white-painted building set into a hill, with steps leading up to a terraced garden that tends to get very full in summer. It can get busy inside too, and you may find yourself sharing a table and perhaps sitting in one of the chairs made from old beer barrels. Food and drink bring in the crowds. Among a good choice of the latter are Fuller's London Pride, Gibbs Mew The Bishop's Tipple and Boddingtons, while a wide-ranging menu encompasses braised mussels in curry and coriander, chicken liver parfait, avocado with crab and pink grapefruit, and main courses of venison sausages with mash, rack of lamb with roasted beetroot, and ribeye steak with garlic butter. Fish options may include Dover sole, a warm salad of red mullet, and crispy-skinned salmon with ginger and cucumber sauce. Wines by the glass include champagne, and there's a good choice of malt whiskies and brandies. SAMPLE DISHES: garlic mushrooms with bacon £5; lobster linguini £9; crème brûlée £4.

Open *11 to 3, 6 to 11, Sun 12 to 3, 7 to 10.30; bar food and restaurant 11.30 to 2.30, 6 to 10.30*
Details *No children Car park Garden and patio Background music Dogs welcome in bar only Access, Delta, Switch, Visa Accommodation: 5 rooms, B&B £45 to £60*

EYAM Derbyshire **map 8**

▲ *Miners Arms*

Water Lane, Eyam TEL: (01433) 630853
off B6521, 5m N of Bakewell

The pub's name reflects the importance of Eyam as a centre of lead-mining, which started in Roman times and continued for nearly two thousand years. Today, the village is better known for its position in the Peak District National Park, and both Chatsworth House and Haddon Hall, a medieval manor-house, are within driving distance. Given the fact that the pub was built in 1630, it isn't surprising that it is – apparently – inhabited by at least one ghost. Thankfully, the atmosphere in the beamed bar is relaxed and friendly; this is where lunch is served, while dinner is available only in the restaurant. The bar menu might offer a choice from Cumberland sausages in onion gravy, crispy roast duck, cod Mornay, and salmon and broccoli quiche; home-made soup, a roast, ploughman's and sandwiches are regular fixtures. Bakewell pudding with custard, fresh fruit pavlova, and sherry trifle may be among the dessert options. Tetley and Stones Bitter are on draught. SAMPLE DISHES: carrot and lentil soup £2; poached salmon in white wine sauce £5.75; chocolate and Grand Marnier mousse £2.

Open *Tue to Sun 12 to 3, Mon to Sat 7 to 11; bar food Tue to Sat L only 12 to 2; restaurant Sun L 12 to 1.30, Tue to Sat D 7 to 9*
Details *Children welcome Car park Wheelchair access (also WC) Garden No music No dogs during food serving times Access, Delta, Visa Accommodation: 7 rooms, B&B £25 to £50*

EYNSFORD Kent map 3

Malt Shovel

Station Road, Eynsford TEL: (01322) 862164
on A225, 2m SE of Swanley

From the south, the A225 runs through a pretty valley in a wooded and unspoilt area surrounded on all sides by motorways. The timbered Malt Shovel is right in the centre of the village. A cheerful, buzzy atmosphere prevails within, and a fish tank proclaims that seafood is the kitchen's forte: baked potato stuffed with prawns and crabmeat; tagliatelle with scallops, ham and mushrooms; red mullet pan-fried with thyme and mushrooms; and a duo of turbot and Dover sole braised in beer are the sort of dishes to expect. Chicago ribs, steaks, lasagne, or cottage pie may have more appeal to meat-eaters. Puddings are a roll-call of the traditional – crème brûlée and treacle tart among them. A good choice of around six real ales includes Marston's Pedigree, Morland Old Speckled Hen and Fuller's London Pride, and a broad range of wines is offered by the glass, including several whites to go with the fish. SAMPLE DISHES: moules marinière £6; lobster thermidor £13; chocolate and nut torte £2.50.

Open *11 to 3, 7 (6 Sat) to 11, Sun 11 to 4, 7 to 10; bar food and restaurant 12 to 2.30 (3 Sun), 7 to 10*
Details *Children welcome in eating areas Car park Patio No-smoking area Background music Guide dogs only Access, Amex, Delta, Switch, Visa*

FARNHAM Dorset map 2

▲ *Museum Hotel*

Farnham TEL: (01725) 516261
off A354, 9m NE of Blandford Forum

Once the museum for the local estate, this sturdy edifice now serves the needs of locals and visitors in search of refreshment. The Woodland Bar is for darts and drinkers (Wadworth 6X, Brakspear and Smiles Best are among the real ales on handpump), while eaters head for the Coopers Bar, with its inglenook and bread oven, low beams and green-cushioned seats; a conservatory extension acts as a dining-room. You could order a sandwich or try something more substantial, like salmon fish-cakes with spicy tomato sauce, beef Stroganov, or mussels with bacon and leeks – described by a reporter as 'excellent' – and finish with strawberry meringue or a fruit crumble. The wine list is a decent selection, though some prices can be a bit on the high side. Shaftesbury is worth visiting while you're in the locality. SAMPLE DISHES: crab and monkfish bisque £3.50; grilled Dover sole £13; strawberry pancakes £3.50.

Open *11 to 3, 6 to 11, Sun 12 to 3, 7 to 10.30; bar food and restaurant 12 to 2, 7 to 9.30; closed 25 December*
Details *Children welcome in dining-room Car park Wheelchair access (also WC) Garden and patio Background and live music Guide dogs only Access, Delta, Switch, Visa Accommodation: 4 rooms, B&B £40 to £55*

FAVERSHAM Kent — map 3

Albion

Front Brents, Faversham TEL: (01795) 591411
on Faversham Creek, near town centre

Front Brents is a pleasant riverside row of pretty cottages fronted by a towpath lined with weeping willows. The Albion – small, well-maintained and clapboarded – is in the middle of all this, with picnic tables beside the path. Within there's just one long room, divided in the middle by the bar, decorated in eau-de-Nil, with some pitch-pine panelling, nautical prints, dried flowers and plain wooden tables and chairs. Light streams in through big picture windows. The choice of dishes on the blackboard is an imaginative amalgam of traditional pub food with restaurant flourishes. Rabbit and plum casserole, pot-roast partridge with blackberry and apple sauce, 'excellent' beef, mushroom and ale pie, and dressed local crab are typical of the kitchen's style. Starters range from fish soup or grilled sardines to pan-fried sweetbreads with white wine, mushrooms and cream. Vegetables are 'carefully cooked', while decent custard is served with desserts like 'wonderful' steamed date and apple pudding. Shepherd Neame Master Brew Bitter, Bishops Finger and Spitfire are on draught, and wines are a sound assortment, with some by the glass chalked up on a board. SAMPLE DISHES: cassoulet of seafood £4; stuffed saddle of lamb with rosemary, garlic and red wine £9.75; black cherry clafoutis £3.25.

Open *11 to 3, 6.30 (6 Fri and Sat) to 11, Sun 12 to 3, 7 to 10.30; bar food 12 to 2, 7 to 9.30 (10 Fri and Sat), Sun 6 (7 winter) to 9*
Details *Children welcome in bar eating area Car park Wheelchair access (also WC) Garden and patio Background music Dogs in bar only Access, Delta, Diners, Switch, Visa*

After the main section of the Guide *is the 'Out and about' section listing additional pubs that are well worth a visit. Reports on these entries are most welcome.*

FAWLEY **Buckinghamshire** **map 2**

▲ *Walnut Tree*

Fawley TEL: (01491) 638360
off A4155 Henley to Marlow road, 4m N of Henley

The road is a tortuous one – through Chiltern lanes, up a hill, past Fawley's village green then on a further 300 yards – but eventually you will reach the Walnut Tree. At first glance it looks more like a 1950s private residence, with its neat brick walls festooned with creepers, rectangular chimneys and tiled roofs on two levels; but a tiny logo above the door tells you where you are. Tables with parasols are laid out on the patio, and more rustic benches are under the trees in the garden.

Meals are served in the bar and the smoke-free conservatory, from a menu that is sound rather than frivolous in its intentions. Home-made burgers, a daily curry, baked ham with parsley sauce, and ploughman's represent the 'pubby' aspect of the place. Other dishes have distinct 'restaurant' overtones: expect the likes of warm smoked chicken salad flamed in honey and coriander vinaigrette, roast guinea-fowl with a creamed leek and mustard sauce, and king scallops and tiger prawns served Chinese-style with vegetable chow mein and lemon soy sauce. To finish, there's an impressive choice of ice-creams and sorbets, as well as desserts ranging from hot treacle tart to praline and caramel cheesecake. The Walnut Tree is a Brakspear pub, with Bitter and Special on draught; it also boasts a serious wine list with five house wines by the glass and a catholic range at realistic prices. SAMPLE DISHES: baked Brie stuffed with celery and walnuts in filo pastry £4; beef Stroganov £10; caramelised lemon tart £2.75.

Open *12 to 3, 6 to 11, Sun 12 to 3, 7 to 10.30; bar food and restaurant all week L 12 to 2.15, Mon to Sat D 7 to 9.45*
Details *Children welcome in dining-room Car park Wheelchair access Garden and patio No smoking in conservatory Background music Dogs in bar only Access, Delta, Switch, Visa Accommodation: 2 rooms, B&B £40 to £55*

FELSHAM **Suffolk** **map 6**

Six Bells

Church Road, Felsham TEL: (01449) 736268
off A14, 7m SE of Bury St Edmunds

'This is what a real pub should be,' said one visitor who persevered along what seemed innumerable un-numbered country lanes to find this hostelry right 'out in the sticks'. The atmosphere inside is friendly, and passers-by are made to feel very welcome in the large oak-beamed bar where darts players rub shoulders with diners. Food of the down-to-earth variety is advertised on various blackboards round the bar, and might include items like garlic mushrooms, feta cheese and tomato salad, lasagne, and cottage pie. One reporter tucked into a steak and kidney pie that 'made a lovely warming winter meal' and said he would definitely be returning for another visit. Vegetarians are well catered for, with perhaps mixed-bean casserole, mushroom and cashew pilaff. Old-fashioned puddings include spicy apple crumble, Bakewell tart, and chocolate fudge cake; the banoffi pie was considered by one customer to be 'one of the best I've ever had'. This is a Greene King pub, and the full range of IPA, Dark Mild and Abbot Ale as well as seasonal brews on draught. The wine list is an ever-changing slate, and several are available by the glass. SAMPLE DISHES: leek and sweetcorn soup £2.50; steak and Abbot ale pie £5.25; bread-and-butter pudding £2.50.

Open *Mon 6 to 11, Tue to Fri 12 to 2.30, 6 to 11, Sat and Sun 12 to 3, 7 to 11 (10.30 Sun); bar food and restaurant Tue to Sun L 12 to 1.45, all week D 7 to 9*

Details *Children welcome Car park Wheelchair access (also WC) Garden No smoking in restaurant Background music Dogs welcome No cards*

FENSTANTON Cambridgeshire **map 6**

King William IV

Fenstanton TEL: (01480) 462467
off A604, 5m SE of Huntingdon

Originally a trio of seventeenth-century cottages, this is now a popular village pub with a thriving trade from both travellers taking a breather from the A14 and locals. Drinking is the main business in the lively bar; other areas, including the plant-filled Garden Room, are laid-up for dining. The printed menu has plenty of standards (including a decent home-made lasagne), but best options are the more imaginative blackboard specials. Typical dishes might include suprême of halibut with dill and cream sauce, roast loin of rabbit with wild mushroom and port sauce, and breast of woodpigeon with caramelised cucumber and shallots – not to mention steak and kidney pudding with a suet crust. Desserts tend to be straightforward – profiteroles or treacle and walnut tart, for example. This is a Greene King tied house with IPA, Abbot Ale and Rayments Special Bitter on draught. Landscaper Capability Brown is buried in Fenstanton churchyard, and Houghton Mill (National Trust) and Bourn Windmill at Caxton, are within driving distance. SAMPLE

DISHES: artichoke hearts in garlic butter £3.50; turkey and asparagus crêpes with Stilton sauce £7; bread-and-butter pudding £2.50.

Open *Mon to Sat 11 to 3.30, 6 to 11, Sun 12 to 10.30; bar food Sun L 12 to 3.30, Mon to Sat D 12 to 2.15, 7 to 10*
Details *Children welcome Car park Wheelchair access Patio No-smoking area Background and live music Dogs welcome Access, Amex, Delta, Switch, Visa*

FERRENSBY North Yorkshire map 9

▲ *General Tarleton* 🍇

Boroughbridge Road, Ferrensby TEL: (01423) 340284
off A6065, 3m N of Knaresborough

Having established the Angel Inn at Hetton (see entry) as one of the classiest pubs in all of Britain, Denis Watkins and John Topham recently branched out and acquired this modest 200-year-old coaching-inn between Harrogate and the A1. What was once a 'drinkers'' haunt attached to the hotel is now a bar/brasserie – although the cosiness, beams and open fire have been retained. Order your food at the bar, and wait to be served by on-the-ball young staff.

Chef James O'Connor began his career at Hetton, and echoes of the old place can be found in the 'little moneybags' of seafood with lobster sauce, the open 'AWT' sandwich of cream cheese, smoked salmon, bacon, and mango chutney, and the 'beautifully presented' Tuscan terrine of roasted vegetables and pesto served with a Parmesan biscuit and tapénade crostini. More substantial offerings come in the shape of perfectly timed calf's liver on a bed of creamy mash and spinach with onion marmalade, confit of duck with braised cabbage, and poached smoked haddock served 'brunch-style' with bubble and squeak, poached egg, black pudding and grain-mustard sauce. Puddings include a well-executed French apple tart with caramel ice-cream, Eton mess, and lemon-cream pot with shortbread biscuits. A full menu is also served in the main dining-room (a converted granary) every evening, except Sunday. It was early days and the repertoire was still evolving when our inspector looked in, but great things are expected.

Real ales on handpump include Tetley Bitter as well as Black Sheep Bitter and Special. The wine list runs to around 50 well chosen bins spanning vintage clarets to some vigorous youthful wines from the New World; 12 wines by the glass are chalked on a blackboard. The inn is named after a certain Sir Banastre Tarleton, soldier and vote-winning politician, whose portrait by Joshua Reynolds hangs in the bar. SAMPLE DISHES: rustic fish soup with rouille and

Gruyère £4.25; pot-roast shoulder of lamb with olive mash and salsa verde £8.75; chocolate marquise £4.

Open *all week 12 to 3, 5.45 to 11; bar food 12 to 2, 6 to 10 (9.30 Sun); restaurant Mon to Sat D only 6 to 9.30*
Details *Children welcome Car park Wheelchair access (also WC) Garden and patio No smoking in restaurant Background music Dogs welcome in hotel only Access, Visa Accommodation: 15 rooms, room only £48 to £63*

FINGEST Buckinghamshire map 3

Chequers Inn

Fingest TEL: (01491) 638335
3½m SE of M40 Jct. 5

Five centuries old and still in business, the Chequers remains one of those pubs with a creditable all-round reputation. The interior has what one reporter called 'a pleasing charm' about it, with a personalised array of china plates, copper churns, old firearms and blow lamps dotted around the bar. The menu is thoroughly traditional, with a daily roast, a regular cold buffet at lunch-time and other dishes ranging from ploughman's to chicken and ham pie, curried prawns and lasagne, plus desserts along the lines of oranges in caramel sauce, and jam roly-poly with custard. A separate dining-room is used for more elaborate restaurant-style meals. The Chequers is a Brakspear-tied house, with Special, Pale and Old Ale on handpump; the wine list runs to about 40 bins and house wine is sold by the glass. From the massive pub garden you should be able to glimpse Fingest's Norman church with its ancient tower and twin-pitched roof. SAMPLE DISHES: potted shrimps on toast £4; steak, kidney and mushroom pie £6.50; fresh fruit trifle £2.75.

Open *11 to 3, 6.30 to 11, Sun 12 to 3, 7 to 10.30; bar food and restaurant all week L 11.30 to 2.30, Mon to Sat D 7 to 10*
Details *Children welcome Car park Wheelchair access (also WC) Garden No smoking in 1 room No music No dogs Access, Amex, Diners, Visa*

FINSTOCK Oxfordshire map 5

▲ *Plough*

The Bottom, Finstock TEL: (01993) 868333
just off B4022, between Charlbury and Witney

An impressive range of real ales is pulled at the bar of this thatched stone inn in a quiet village: Hook Norton Old Hooky, Adnams Broadside, Morland Old Speckled Hen, Ringwood Fortyniner, Gales and Archers Golden Bitter. The bar, with a cheery fire and brightened by fresh flowers, is described as very friendly, and there's plenty of room in the dining-area. The menu is pretty much a list of pub staples – from pâté to steaks – though crevettes and snails add a touch of glamour, and the soups of the day are interesting. Specials of the week, listed on boards, may have more excitement, with John Dory, or blue-nose shark with a wild berry purée, among the fish, and steak, Stilton and stout pie, or fillet of beef with whisky and black pepper sauce aimed at meat eaters. Bringing up the rear are puddings such as strawberry and rhubarb crumble. Baps, snacks and ploughman's are served at every session, and house wines are sold by the glass. SAMPLE DISHES: hare and walnut pâté £4.75; fish au gratin £8; raisin and marmalade pancake £3.25.

Open *Mon to Sat 11 to 3, 7 to 11, Sun 12 to 3, 7 to 10.30; bar food and restaurant 12 to 2 (2.30 Sun), 7 to 9.30; closed evening 25 and 26 Dec*
Details *Children welcome in dining-room Car park Wheelchair access Garden Background music Dogs welcome Access, Amex, Delta, Diners, Switch, Visa Accommodation: 1 room, B&B £45 to £55*

FIRLE East Sussex map 3

▲ *Ram Inn*

LOCAL PRODUCE

Firle TEL: (01273) 858222
off A27 Lewes to Eastbourne road, 4m SE of Lewes

The setting is a tranquil estate village handy for walks on the South Downs, but the Ram still feels like a genuine neighbourhood watering-hole. You need to look hard to find any signs of designer 'improvement' in the refreshingly unpretentious bar, with its uncarpeted floors and functional furniture: don't expect much in the way of formalities or standing on ceremony, warn several reporters. This is a family business. Landlord Michael Wooller's son Keith runs the bar and cellar, keeping top-drawer real ales such as Otter Bitter, Hop Back Summer Lightning and a cluster from nearby Harveys of Lewes (including Armada Ale and seasonal Old Ale) in prime condition.

Another son, Paul, does most of the cooking and bases his repertoire resolutely on what the local region can produce. Fish is from the coast, ham comes from free-range pigs, home-grown apples turn up in pork and cider pie as well as a version of Bakewell sponge, while Willets Farm supplies genuine ice-creams. At lunch-time you can also get a range of ploughman's built around the new breed of Sussex farmhouse cheeses: organic Ashdown Foresters, Duddleswell soft ewe's milk cheese and several from Myrtle Grove Farm (including a smoked version) are the stars. Soups come with a choice of three breads, barbecued ribs are marinated in red wine, black treacle and cumin, and vegetarians might be offered leek, mushroom and macaroni bake. Three white wines from Sussex vineyards appear on the short list and house wines are served by the glass. SAMPLE DISHES: cream of cauliflower soup with garlic bread £3.75; grilled mackerel with new potatoes £6; banana and toffee pie £3.

Open *11.30 to 3, 7 to 11, Sun 12 to 3, 7 to 10.30; bar food 12 to 2, 7 to 9; closed 25 Dec eve*
Details *Children welcome in 1 bar Car park Wheelchair access (also WC) Garden No smoking in 1 bar Live music Dogs welcome Access, Delta, Visa Accommodation: 5 rooms, B&B £25 to £65*

FIR TREE Co Durham map 10

▲ *Duke of York*

Fir Tree TEL: (01388) 762848
on A68, 4m S of Tow Law

A godsend for travellers on the main A68 between York and Edinburgh, this greatly extended eighteenth-century country inn stands in more than five acres of grounds complete with a landscaped beer garden. Sit outside if the weather allows; otherwise retreat to the comfort of the bar with its African spears and hunting rifles, exhibits of Stone Age flints and traditional oak furniture fashioned by famous craftsman 'Mouseman' Thompson (his trade mark was a carved rodent). The daily blackboard lists a range of familiar pub dishes ranging from home-made steak and kidney pie, and fresh Aberdeen cod, to sauced specialities along the lines of lamb in hot pepper sauce, and beef bourguignon. Steaks and salads are also available, and half a dozen sweets might include apple and blackberry tart. Sunday lunch is a roast and full meals are served in the restaurant. Bass and a guest ale are on handpump, and the pub has an impressive wine list courtesy of Bibendum with a strong New World contingent and three house wines by the glass. SAMPLE DISHES: hot roast beef in a bun £3.50; chicken Marengo £8.50; ginger ice-cream £3.

Open *all week 11am to 11pm; bar food and restaurant 12 to 2, 6.30 to 9.30*
Details *Children welcome Car park Wheelchair access Garden Background music No dogs Access, Diners, Switch, Visa Accommodation: 4 rooms, B&B £48 to £65*

FITZHEAD Somerset map 2

Fitzhead Inn

Fitzhead TEL: (01823) 400667
off B3227, 2m N of Milverton

Patrick Groves and Sally Harvey seem to be ticking over quite happily in their cosy little pub off the beaten track. They now have two cats, while chickens and ducks roam in the garden. The skittle alley is an all-year attraction, and there are barbecues in summer. Food could be as simple as a ploughman's or a bowl of home-made soup; otherwise order something more ambitious, such as pigeon breast wrapped in bacon with glazed shallots and mushroom and wine sauce, or fillet steak flambé in brandy with wild mushroom and garlic sauce. Seasonal seafood is also worth noting – paupiettes of Dover and lemon sole filled with spinach, with creamy watercress sauce, or grilled fillets of red mullet and John Dory with prawn, coconut and coriander sauce, for example. Desserts are things like rich chocolate torte, and banana, Malibu and praline cheesecake. Real ales, varying from week to week, might include Cotleigh Tawny and Otter Ale, and Bellhayes cider is on tap. The wine list features over 170 bins, many of them available by the glass. SAMPLE DISHES: smoked trout and mackerel pâté with chive cream sauce £2.75; pan-roast loin of venison with glazed walnuts and figs and liquorice scented sauce £11; rum truffle ganache £2.50.

Open *12 to 3, 7 to 11 (10.30 Sun); bar food 12 to 2, 7 to 10*
Details *Children welcome Wheelchair access Garden Background music Dogs welcome No cards*

FLETCHING East Sussex map 3

▲ *Griffin Inn*

VIEWS

Fletching TEL: (01825) 722890
off A272, between Maresfield and Newick, 3m NW of Uckfield

Fletching's Norman church can be seen for miles around and it shares the village limelight with the Griffin. The pub is a classic English 'brick and tile', built in the sixteenth century and still going strong. Much of its success and allure is due to the efforts of its owners, the Pullan family, and their staff: everyone comments on the tip-top hospitality and service 'with a smile' that is such a feature of the place. The cosy beamed bar gets packed even on a February lunch-time, the menu is chalked on a blackboard and the repertoire is changed twice daily. You can expect a cosmopolitan line-up of dishes ranging from home-made hand-raised pork pie, Fletching sausages with mash and mustard gravy, and fish pie, to sizzling stuffed mussels, Moroccan-style braised lamb shank with couscous, and Thai prawn curry. The Mediterranean also has its say with hot ciabatta sandwiches, crespolini, and polpette (veal and herb meatballs) with tagliatelle. Desserts range from tarte Tatin to prune and Armagnac ice-cream, and you can also get savouries such as 'devils on horseback'. Fish nights are a popular attraction and a full *carte* is available in the traditionally furnished restaurant.

Nigel Pullan keeps a first-rate cellar with brews such as Harveys Best, TEA from the Hogs Back Brewery and Hall & Woodhouse Tanglefoot regularly on handpump. The wine list is equally impressive, including a good selection by the glass and plenty of high-quality drinking, particularly from Italy and the New World. From the splendid tiered garden there are glorious views of the Ouse Valley and Sheffield Park. Culture vultures should note that Glyndebourne and Bateman's (home of Rudyard Kipling) are within driving distance. SAMPLE DISHES: Caesar salad £4.25; chicken florentine £7.25; raspberry meringue roulade £3.50.

Open *12 to 3, 6 to 11, Sun 12 to 3, 7 to 10.30; bar food 12 to 2.15 (2.30 Sat and Sun), 7 to 9.30; restaurant 12 (12.30 Sun) to 2.15, 7 (7.30 Sun) to 9.30; closed 25 Dec*

Details *Children welcome Car park Wheelchair access (also WC) Garden and patio Live music; jukebox Dogs welcome Access, Amex, Delta, Switch, Visa Accommodation: 4 rooms, B&B £50 to £75*

FORD Buckinghamshire **map 3**

Dinton Hermit

Water Lane, Ford TEL: (01296) 748379
off A418, 4m SW of Aylesbury

This particular Hermit resides not in Dinton, but in the village of Ford itself. The pub is named after a certain John Bigg, a recluse who died in 1696 (a print of the man hangs on the wall). Service in the small bar and dining-room is friendly and casual, and the menu is full of pub staples such as scampi, lasagne, chilli, jacket potatoes and salads, with a sprinkling of more ambitious fare like Stilton and asparagus pancake, and kidneys in cognac sauce. It is all simple, but skilfully executed. The evening menu is slightly larger, extending to halibut steak in dill and caper cream sauce, and turkey breast in celery sauce with prawn and rice pyramids. Real ales on draught are Wadworth 6X, ABC bitter and Adnams. House wine is sold by the glass. SAMPLE DISHES: petite smokies £4.50; chicken florentine £10; stem ginger with ice-cream and chocolate sauce £3.25.

Open *11 to 2.30, 6 to 11, Sun 12 to 2, 7 to 10.30; bar food Tue to Sat 12 to 2, 7 to 9*
Details *Children welcome in bar eating area Car park Wheelchair access (also WC) Garden No music No dogs No cards*

FORD Gloucestershire **map 5**

▲ *Plough Inn*

Ford TEL: (01386) 584215
on B4077, 4m E of Winchcombe

The Plough is a solid Cotswold-stone pub on a sharp bend in the road, overlooking attractive countryside. Inside, an equine theme prevails, with photographs of racing scenes and personalities in the tiny black-panelled bar, and hunting-horns, horse brasses and even more photographs in the slate-roofed bar. Fresh flowers on the big old-fashioned tables add some colour, and the entire place is bright and attractive. A blackboard at the entrance lists a wide variety of dishes, and you could even make use of the long seat while you decide on what to have. The range could include chicken liver pâté, deep-fried baby Camembert, and garlic mushrooms to start, followed by curries, steak and kidney pie, Cornish plaice, and chicken stuffed with apricots and herbs. Sandwiches and jacket potatoes are also available, and desserts could run to fruit crumbles, sticky toffee pudding, or treacle tart. The pub is tied to Donnington, with the brewery's beers well kept on draught. House wines are offered by the glass from the short list. Note the pub's long opening hours: breakfast is served from 9am. Sudeley Castle isn't far for those wanting a day out. SAMPLE DISHES: chicken and mushroom soup £2.75; braised rabbit £7; chocolate and nut crunch £3.

Open *9am to 11pm, Sun 9am to 10.30pm; bar food 9 to 2.30, 6 to 9.30 (9 Sun)*
Details *Children welcome Car park Wheelchair access (also WC) Garden Background music Dogs welcome Access, Switch, Visa Accommodation: 4 rooms, B&B £35 to £50*

Licensing hours and bar food times are based on information supplied by each establishment and are correct at the time of going to press.

FORD **Wiltshire** **map 2**

▲ *White Hart*

Ford TEL: (01249) 782213
on A420, 5m W of Chippenham

First licensed in 1553, this 'old inn by the trout stream' is still a great crowd-pleaser. A 'warm, happy pub' is how one couple described it. Food is high on the agenda, but the place still thrives as a local watering-hole, with a genuine 'pubby' bar and a splendid collection of up to ten real ales, which are generally chalked on a board. Typical tipples might include Bass, Hall & Woodhouse Tanglefoot, Black Sheep Bitter and Marston's Owd Rodger. Cider drinkers have a choice of Bulmers or Broadoak, while wine buffs can enjoy some excellent drinking from a well-spread list that breathes quality. The cooking shows plenty of imagination, as well as keeping faith with the pub classics. Typical dishes from the regularly changing menu might include macaroni cheese with leeks, mushrooms and 'proper' sauté potatoes, supreme of salmon with tomato fondue and mushroom cream sauce, roast topside of beef, and chicken Kiev; you can also get ploughman's and hot baguettes. If you fancy exploring the area, there are plenty of attractions nearby, including Corsham Court gardens, Bowood House and Castle Combe. SAMPLE DISHES: chicken liver parfait £4.75; spicy stir-fried beef fillet with egg noodles £5; vanilla crème brûlée with raspberries £3.

Open *11 to 3, 5 to 11, Sun 12 to 3, 7 to 11; bar food and restaurant 12 to 2, 7 to 10*
Details *Children welcome in dining-room Car park Wheelchair access Garden No music Dogs welcome Access, Amex, Delta, Diners, Switch, Visa Accommodation: 11 rooms, B&B £45 to £65*

FORDHAM **Cambridgeshire** **map 6**

White Pheasant

Market Street, Fordham TEL: (01638) 720414
on A142, 5m N of Newmarket

This white-painted seventeenth-century inn not far from Wicken Fen nature reserve is under the same ownership as the Red Lion, Icklingham, and the Pykkerell, Ixworth (see entries). Inside, tartan curtains, a motley mixture of old tables and chairs, prints and paintings on the walls, soft wall lights with candles on the tables, and muted classical music all create a relaxing and cosy ambience. Kick off with green-lipped mussels with cheese and herbs, or king prawn tails with garlic butter, and proceed with gammon glazed with honey and mustard, or peppered pork steak with sage and onion sauce. On the slightly more expensive printed menu wild mushroom and onion tart, and oak-smoked haddock feature alongside roast leg of lamb, and roast duck breast with cherry and cinnamon sauce. Daily specials could include fillet of bream with raspberry and peach sauce, or a pie of sausage-meat and herbs with onion gravy. On draught are Theakston Best, Courage Directors and a weekly-changing guest ale. The short, well-chosen wine list has some good-quality producers. SAMPLE DISHES: beef and pepper soup £3.25; lambs' liver and bacon with onion gravy £6.75; Bakewell tart £3.50.

Open *12 to 3, 6 to 11, Sun 12 to 3, 7 to 10.30; bar food 12 to 2.30, 6 (7 Sun) to 10; closed all day 25 and 26 Dec, and eve 1 Jan*
Details *Children welcome Car park Wheelchair access Garden Background music No dogs Access, Delta, Switch, Visa*

FORDWICH Kent map 3

Fordwich Arms

King Street, Fordwich TEL: (01227) 710444
off A28, 3m NE of Canterbury

The riverside garden by the banks of the Stour is an absolute joy for summer imbibing, but this mock-Tudor brick pub pulls in the crowds throughout the year. 'Plush' is probably the best description of the single long bar with its flowery wallpaper, fabrics and bygones on the walls. Best options if you are feeling peckish are the blackboard specials, which might include lamb and apricot curry, lemon and herb-crusted sea bass, and cider-braised beef. Otherwise there are eight varieties of ploughman's with home-made chutney, salads, filled jacket potatoes and sandwiches. Traditional hot puddings with custard round things off, along with gâteaux and 'elite ice-cream' sundaes. Sunday lunch is served in the restaurant, and theme nights are a regular feature of the place. Theobald's local cider is a fruity alternative to the hoppy line-up of Wadworth 6X, Flowers Original, Fremlins and Boddingtons; the 'own label' house wine is good value. Wildlife enthusiasts could set a course for Stodmarsh Nature Reserve or Brambles Wildlife Park at Herne Common. SAMPLE DISHES: melon with mango sorbet £3; Stilton chicken £6.50; spotted dick and custard £2.25.

Open *11am to 11pm, Sun 12 to 3, 7 to 10.30; bar food all week L 12 to 2.30, Mon to Sat D 6 to 10; restaurant Sun L 12 to 2, Fri and Sat D 6 to 10*
Details *Children welcome in dining-room Car park Wheelchair access (also WC) Garden and patio No smoking in restaurant Background music Dogs welcome Access, Delta, Switch, Visa*

FOSS CROSS Gloucestershire map 5

Hare and Hounds

Foss Cross TEL: (01285) 720288
on A429, between Circencester and Northleach

People tend to drive very fast along this stretch of the Fosse Way, and if you go with the flow you're likely to miss this isolated roadside pub set in rolling Cotswold hills. A sagging slate roof hangs low over the windows in the Cotswold-stone walls. Inside, it's low ceilings, basic furniture and a very friendly atmosphere; a more modern extension is at the back. 'Our food is prepared from fresh local produce to order,' announces one of the blackboards, and along with ploughman's and salads you will find 'quite gorgeous' taramasalata, grilled gammon, pan-fried trout, and devilled chicken, plus vegetarian offerings such as pancakes stuffed with spinach and feta in tomato sauce. Children have their own menu or can have a half-sized main course. Pies and tarts lead the pudding board. Shepherd Neame Spitfire, Hook Norton Bitter and Wadworth 6X may be among the real ales on draught, and interesting New World wines are sold by the glass. SAMPLE DISHES: Stilton pâté £2.25; steak and kidney casseroled in stout £6; bread-and-butter pudding £2.50.

Open *11 to 3, 6 to 11, Sun 12 to 3, 7 to 10.30; bar food 12.15 to 2.30, 7 to 10.15*
Details *Children welcome in bar eating area Car park Wheelchair access (also WC) Garden and patio No music Dogs welcome Access, Amex, Diners, Visa*

FOTHERINGHAY Northamptonshire map 6

Falcon Inn

Fotheringhay TEL: (01832) 226254
off A605, 4m NE of Oundle

Standing in the shadow of Fotheringhay's majestic church, with its lantern tower crowned by a falcon crest (the heraldic symbol of the House of York), this lively and popular pub manages to please all comers. The heart of the action is the lounge bar, with a dining-room and conservatory tacked on; there's also a separate public bar for serious drinking and chat. The handwritten menu changes daily and it's full of dishes from the heart of the country pub repertoire: soups, home-made pâtés and terrines, smoked fish, pies, roasts and so on. Typically you might find such things as gravlax with dill sauce, rabbit braised in cider with apples and walnuts, wild boar in orange and nutmeg sauce, and seafood gratin, as well as ploughman's and grills. Desserts are seasonal, fruity, home-made offerings, ranging from blackberry and apple crumble to fresh raspberries with raspberry sorbet. Monday lunch is limited to soup and sandwiches. Landlord Alan Stewart has assembled a first-rate, keenly priced wine list with the emphasis tilted away from France towards the New World, Chile, Argentina and so on; half-bottles are also well represented. The Falcon is also a great real ale pub, with brews from big East Anglian names such as Adnams, Greene King, and Elgood's of Cambridge, alongside Bass and Ruddles County. SAMPLE DISHES: sweet spiced herring salad £3.75; lamb steak in redcurrant sauce £8.50; summer pudding £2.50.

Open *10 to 3, 6 to 11, Sun 12 to 3, 7 to 10.30; bar food Tue to Sun 12.15 to 2, 6.45 to 9.45 (7 to 9 Sun)*
Details *Children welcome in bar eating area Car park Wheelchair access (also WC) Garden and patio No smoking while others eat No music Dogs welcome in 1 room Access, Visa*

FOWLMERE Cambridgeshire map 6

Chequers

High Street, Fowlmere TEL: (01763) 208369
off B1368, between A10 and A505, 5m NE of Royston

Since the sixteenth century this splendidly restored coaching-inn has had a colourful and chequered history. Once a chapel of rest for coffins *en route* from London to Cambridge, it was also a wartime rendezvous for pilots based at the nearby airfield. Mementoes are dotted around the neatly turned-out bar. The menu makes lively reading and dishes are pulled from all corners of the globe: grilled halloumi is served with aubergine dip, spring lamb is cooked the Arabic way with coriander and cumin, while roast duck is given the oriental treatment with ginger, star anise and chilli. Closer to home you will find chimney-smoked Bottisham ham with home-made banana chutney, and local pigeon breasts with braised red cabbage. The cheeseboard features some gems from Irish farmhouse producers. Tables need to be reserved for meals in the galleried restaurant. Adnams Bitter and Broadside are on draught, but most interest centres on the cracking wine list. Nine house wines are offered by the glass and the full slate offers the prospect of serious drinking from top-notch sources. Fans of malt whisky are also in for a treat: 30 corkers are available for those who love a dram. SAMPLE DISHES: chilled gazpacho £3; poached fillet of salmon on creamed watercress sauce £8; hot date sponge on sticky toffee sauce £3.75.

Open *12 to 2.30, 6 to 11, Sun 12 to 2.30, 7 to 10.30; bar food and*

restaurant 12 to 2 (2.30 Sun), 7 to 10 (9.30 Sun); closed 25 Dec
Details *Children welcome Car park Wheelchair access Garden No music No dogs Access, Amex, Delta, Diners, Switch, Visa*

FOWNHOPE Hereford & Worcester map 5

▲ *Green Man Inn*

Fownhope TEL: (01432) 860243
on B4224, 6m SE of Hereford

Since its birth in 1488, this classic half-timbered building has served as a staging-post for coaches travelling between Hertford and Gloucester as well as a courthouse-cum-prison. These days it plays the part of a welcoming hostelry, complete with oak beams and huge fireplaces. Customers in the bar can choose from a menu that runs from sandwiches and salads to fruit pies and crumbles. In between, the options could include roast local chicken, grilled trout with almonds, beef curry or gratin of courgettes and mushrooms. Fownhope is in apple orchard country, so it's no surprise that ciders are on tap; otherwise go for one of the real ales such as Marston's Pedigree, Hook Norton Best and Samuel Smith Old Brewery Bitter. House wines, by the glass or bottle, include Three Choirs from Gloucestershire. SAMPLE DISHES: chicken wings with garlic dip £2.25; steak sandwich with mushrooms and onions £6; profiteroles £2.25.

Open *11 to 3, 6 to 11, Sun 12 to 3, 7 to 10.30; bar food 12 to 2, 6 to 10; restaurant D only 7 to 9*
Details *Children welcome Car park Wheelchair access Garden No-smoking area No music Dogs welcome Access, Amex, Delta, Diners, Switch, Visa Accommodation: 19 rooms, B&B £32 to £53*

FRESHFORD Bath & N.E. Somerset map 2

Inn at Freshford

Freshford TEL: (01225) 722250
on A36, 4m S of Bath

It would be hard to pick a more beguiling setting than this. The Inn – a substantial house of Bath stone with a triple-gabled roof and a black Doric-pillared portico – can be found on a tiny lane, with glorious views overlooking water meadows and the River Avon. In summer the urns and hanging baskets overflow with blooms. The place can fill up quickly – especially at weekends – but luckily there's ample room in the comfortably modernised interior. Bar menus and blackboard specials provide plenty of choice, whether you are looking for a dish of New Zealand mussels or garlic mushrooms or fancy something a bit more substantial – chicken breast wrapped in bacon with Stilton sauce, or poached fillet of salmon with prawns and capers, for example. The pudding list runs to about 30 items (but only half are home-made, admits the landlord). Ushers Best, Bass, Marston's Pedigree, Theakston Best and Courage Best are on draught, and the wine list is workmanlike. SAMPLE DISHES: chicken liver parfait £3; mini-leg of lamb with redcurrant and mint sauce £8; treacle sponge £2.75.

Open *Mon to Sat 11 to 3, 5.30 to 11, Sun 12 to 3, 7 to 10.30 (summer Mon to Sat 11 to 11, Sun 12 to 10.30); bar food 11.30 to 2.30, 6 to 10*
Details *Children welcome Car park Wheelchair access (also WC) Garden No smoking in restaurant Background music Dogs welcome Access, Switch, Visa*

FRILSHAM Berkshire map 2

Pot Kiln

Frilsham TEL: (01635) 201366
off B4009; in Yattendon take road opposite church, left at next T-junction, go over M4 motorway bridge and straight on – don't turn right to Frilsham

The Pot Kiln is 'way off the beaten track' in the Berkshire countryside, but worth seeking out if you enjoy modest, unimproved hostelries. The pub takes its name from the old brick kilns that once stood on the site, and it continues to make a virtue of tradition; if you want a drink, you need to queue at 'what is virtually a hatch, rather than a proper bar'. The West Berkshire micro-brewery has its home here, and aficionados can sample Brick Kiln Bitter along with Morland Original, Old Speckled Hen and Arkell's 3B. Food is hearty, sustaining stuff precisely in tune with the mood of the place: grilled salmon fillet and sirloin steaks, chicken and mushroom or pheasant pies, for example, or perhaps pork steak in mustard sauce if you fancy something a little more ambitious. The kitchen doesn't cook chips, although roast potatoes are available most days. If you intend paying a trip to the Pot Kiln on Sunday, note that the menu is restricted to hot rolls. SAMPLE DISHES: leek and potato soup £2.25; lamb and rosemary casserole £6; treacle sponge pudding £2.25.

Open *12 to 2.30, 6.30 to 11, Sun 12 to 3, 7 to 10.30; bar food Mon and Wed to Sat 12 to 1.45, 7 to 9.30 (Sun L hot rolls only 12 to 2)*
Details *Children welcome in 2 areas Car park Wheelchair access Garden Live music Dogs welcome in public bar only No cards*

FRISTON Suffolk **map 6**

Old Chequers

Aldeburgh Road, Friston TEL: (01728) 688270
just off B1121, 3m SE of Saxmundham

Standing at a crossroads by the village green, the Old Chequers plays the role of genteel country pub right down to its farmhouse furniture. The end of 1996 marked landlord David Grimwood's 'second coming' (as one reporter described it) after a protracted sabbatical, but little has changed. The lunchtime carvery buffet is still going strong, offering the likes of juicy roast pork with vegetables and 'very welcome' broad beans, for example. Desserts range from chocolate roulade to summer pudding. In the evening there's a much more extensive 'restaurant-style' blackboard with dishes such as Aldeburgh cod with spinach and cheddar cheese, or pheasant stuffed with chestnut and bacon. Adnams Bitter is the resident brew, or choose from guests such as Marston's Pedigree or Wadworth 6X. The list of around 40 fairly priced wines is considered to be 'comprehensive for a pub'. SAMPLE DISHES: lunchtime buffet £7; ostrich en croûte £12.50; crème brûlée £3.25.

Open *11.30 to 2.30, 7 to 11, Sun 12 to 3, 7 to 10.30; bar food 12 to 2, 7 to 9*
Details *Children welcome Sun L only in bar eating area Car park Wheelchair access Patio Background music No dogs Access, Amex, Delta, Switch, Visa*

GARGRAVE North Yorkshire **map 8**

Old Swan Inn

20 High Street, Gargrave TEL: (01756) 749232
on A65, 4m NW of Skipton

Entering this unspoilt pub is like taking a trip back in time. Once through the door you are immediately in a world where rusticity rules and locals congregate for pints of Timothy Taylor Landlord, Greene King Abbot Ale and Morland Old Speckled Hen. If food is required, the best bets are to be found on the specials boards: one focuses on vegetarian dishes such as tagliatelle with herb and tomato sauce, or broccoli and cheese pie; the other pleases carnivores with venison and pheasant pie and the like. Alternatively, dip into the printed menu, which treads a familiar path with Yorkshire puddings, haddock and chips, and decent portions of steak pie with tender meat in a rich gravy. A modest range of wines is available by the glass. Nearby is the market town of Skipton and craft centres at Coniston and Ingleton. SAMPLE DISHES: minestrone soup £2; seafood platter £5.50; lemon tart £2.

Open *weekdays 11 to 3, 5.30 to 11, Sat 11am to 11pm, Sun 12 to 3, 7 to 10.30; bar food 12 to 2, 6 (7 Sun and winter) to 9*
Details *Children welcome Car park Wheelchair access (also WC) Garden Background music Guide dogs only No cards*

GEDNEY DYKE Lincolnshire map 6

Chequers

Main Street, Gedney Dyke TEL: (01406) 362666
just off B1359, from Gedney roundabout on A17, 3m E of Holbeach

Since taking over this agreeable Fenland free house, Rob and Judith Marshall have turned it into one of the top pubs in the region. It shines like a beacon in an area not overly endowed with high-class food pubs. The 'Just a Bite' menu is served in the bar, featuring such dishes as warmed goats'-cheese salad, ploughman's, or pasta; there is also a full menu on offer in the two dining-rooms. A basket of good-quality bread gives a foretaste of what follows: starters may include scampi in filo with curry sauce, and feuilleté of sole and salmon, to be followed by main courses such as beef casseroled in red wine, smoked chicken breast with pancetta on spinach, or rosettes of new season's lamb on a tagliatelle of vegetables. There's a special 'catch of the day' on the blackboard, and vegetarians are given a choice at each course: stuffed vine leaves, and spinach, mushrooms and asparagus in pastry, perhaps. Banoffi pie was described by one enthusiast as 'delectable – lovely caramel, excellent crisp pastry', and there may also be fruit pavlova, or baked Sauternes cream. 'This was pub food at its best,' concludes a report; 'exciting, worth travelling for, tasty and pleasurable.' Elgood's Pageant Ale, Morland Old Speckled Hen and Greene King Abbot Ale are among the real ales, and nine house wines and wines of the month are served by the glass from an interesting list of about 50 bins. SAMPLE DISHES: bang-bang chicken £4; smoked pork sausages with red cabbage and apple £5.50; cinnamon meringue with butterscotch sauce £2.75.

Open *12 to 2, 7 to 11, Sun 12 to 3, 7 to 10.30; bar food and restaurant 12 to 2, 7 to 9 (9.30 Thu to Sat); closed 25 and 26 Dec, no D 1 Jan*
Details *Children welcome Car park Garden and patio No smoking in 1 dining-room Background music No dogs Access, Amex, Delta, Diners, Switch, Visa*

GIBRALTAR Buckinghamshire map 3

Bottle and Glass

Gibraltar TEL: (01296) 748488
on A418, between Thame and Aylesbury

Drive along the A418 and you can't fail to notice the Bottle and Glass, with its thatched roof, hanging baskets and masses of flower-filled tubs. The interior creates a good impression, too: Windsor chairs are dotted around the bar, the floors are stone flags and red tiles, and a fire creates warmth. Fish is the mainstay of the daily-changing menu: you could start with moules marinière or sauté herring roes on toast, and then proceed to plaice Waleska, paella, or even something grand like lobster thermidor. Meat shows up in the shape of a warm salad of ham with lamb's lettuce and basil, beef Wellington, or calf's liver with spinach, rosemary and mint sauce. 'Skilfully cooked' lemon tart ends things on a high note; otherwise you might choose apricot pancakes or profiteroles. Morrells beers are on draught and three wines are served by the glass. SAMPLE DISHES: tomato and pesto soup £3; haddock Egyptienne £10; chocolate marquise with coffee-bean sauce £4.

Open *11 to 3, 6 to 11, Sun 12 to 3; bar food all week L 12 to 2.30, Mon to Sat D 6.30 to 10*
Details *Children welcome Car park Wheelchair access (also WC) Garden Background music Dogs welcome on a lead Access, Amex, Delta, Diners, Switch, Visa*

GLOOSTON Leicestershire map 5

▲ *Old Barn Inn*

Glooston TEL: (01858) 545215
off A6, 6m N of Market Harborough

'Local community spirit' is one of the keys to the success of this 400-year-old pub in a tiny hamlet well off the beaten track. Charles Edmondson-Jones, Stewart Burge and co. have been in residence since 1985, and their hands-on involvement is greatly appreciated; they are clearly 'well known and liked', observed one visitor. The interior of the building has been knocked through and an archway revealed to allow warmth from the log fire to permeate the place. A daily-changing blackboard offers such things as roast baby beetroot with horseradish and yoghurt sauce, poached skate with cucumber and fennel, and casseroled pheasant, while a separate menu changes from month to month. Creative ideas abound: in May, for example, you could be treated to medallions of pork in rhubarb and apple sauce, or poached turbot with anchovy sauce; in December expect dishes such as stuffed roast partridge with pink grapefruit sauce or fillet of beef in Guinness and port sauce. Chips are notable by their absence. As a finale, there are desserts such as coffee bavarois and passion-fruit soufflé. Real ales from Adnams, Hook Norton, Buckley, Hall & Woodhouse among others are regularly on draught; seven wines are sold by the glass and the short seasonal list promises plenty of sound, affordable drinking. Glooston is within reach of Rockingham Castle and Rutland Water, while the prospect of trekking the nearby Midshires Way attracts walkers. SAMPLE DISHES: chicken mousseline with red-pepper sauce £4.50; poached smoked haddock with spinach and a chive butter sauce £11; strawberry mille-feuilles £3.25.

Open *Mon to Fri 7 to 11, Sat and Sun 12 to 2.30 (3 Sun); bar food and restaurant Sat and Sun L 12 to 1.45, Mon to Sat D 7 to 9.30*
Details *Children welcome Car park Patio No smoking in restaurant No music Dogs welcome Access, Amex, Delta, Switch, Visa Accommodation: 3 rooms, B&B £37.50 to £49.50*

GODMANSTONE Dorset map 2

Smith's Arms

Godmanstone TEL: (01300) 341236
on A352, 4m N of Dorchester

Photographs of the Smith's Arms probably find their way into albums from Tokyo to Turin, for this converted fifteenth-century smithy is, by all accounts, the smallest pub in England. As a result, it's one sight that the tourists cannot miss. The inside is tiny, full of memorabilia and with just six tables lined up along its massively thick stone walls; a garden by a rushing stream takes care of the overflow. Landlord John Foster is an ex-jockey and an 'amazingly friendly host' who is often to be seen hopping nimbly between the tables 'cajoling people to eat up and then try the rhubarb crumble'. The menu is a no-nonsense canter through sandwiches, lasagne, home-cooked ham, steak and kidney pie, broccoli and leek gratin, and the like. 'My red wine came in a half-pint glass and stood up to the chilli con carne very well,' noted one reporter. Ringwood Best Bitter is drawn direct from the cask and this must be one of the few pubs with ouzo on optic. SAMPLE DISHES: cauliflower cheese £4; tuna and spicy tomato lasagne £4.50; walnut tart £2.

Open *11 to 3, 6 to 11, Sun 12 to 3, 7 to 10.30; bar food 12 to 2, 6.30 to 9.45; closed Jan*
Details *No children Car park Wheelchair access (also WC) Garden Background music No dogs No cards*

GOOSNARGH Lancashire map 8

Bushell's Arms

Church Lane, Goosnargh TEL: (01772) 865235
off B5269, 3m W of Longridge

The prospect of eating curried parsnip and banana soup, Moroccan-style roast lamb, or Lebanese kofta in a Lancashire pub opposite the village post office sounds almost outlandish, but that's the score at the Bushell's Arms. David and Glynis Best are forever cooking, reading and researching; forever dreaming up new recipes and ideas. Their standard printed menu sets the ball rolling, with samosas, falafel, Greek stifado and a South American version of chilli con carne, but the real invention is to be found on the list of daily specials. The north of England provides black pudding, mitton of pork (fillet in a mould layered with chestnuts and sage), farmhouse pasties and fresh fish from Fleetwood. The rest is a world tour, taking in Burma, Holland and Italy along the way. From the choice of side dishes, it's worth ordering a helping of O'Brien potatoes (cooked with peppers, cream, Parmesan, garlic and spices). Puddings stay, for the most part, with what is in the domestic tradition: gooseberry pie with elderflower cordial, damson cobbler, apple and sultana flapjacks, for example. David Best also takes time out to write about wine, and his list of about 50 bins has all the hallmarks of a knowledgeable enthusiast who has visited many of the producers in the flesh. For beer buffs, there's a choice of Boddingtons and Tetley Bitter. SAMPLE DISHES: tandoori chicken winglets £2.50; salmon and broccoli in puff pastry £6; apricot and date crumble £2.

Open *12 to 3, 6 to 11, Sun 12 to 3, 7 to 10.30; bar food 12 to 2.30, 7 to 9.30*
Details *Children welcome in bar eating area Car park Wheelchair access Garden and patio No-smoking area No music Guide dogs only No cards*

GOSFIELD Essex map 3

Green Man

The Street, Gosfield TEL: (01787) 472746
on A1017, 4m NE of Braintree

'This is our local and we eat here on average once a week throughout the year,' admit a couple of regulars. Long-serving landlord John Arnold and his neatly outfitted staff no doubt know their faces and names by now. The main attraction in the beamed bar (which also boasts fish tanks) is the menu of sound traditional English dishes along the lines of 'outstanding' Stilton and celery soup, 'perfectly cooked' lamb chops with port and cranberry sauce, and roast duck with orange sauce. At lunch-time there's also a popular cold buffet. Puddings confirm the patriotic theme with strawberry and apple tart, syllabub and so on. Greene King IPA and Abbot Ale are 'kept immaculately', according to one reporter. The separate restaurant also does a brisk trade. Paycocke's (National Trust) is worth a look if you fancy driving out to Coggeshall, about eight miles away. SAMPLE DISHES: crispy mushrooms £3; pheasant casseroled in red wine £7.25; lemon syllabub £3.

Open *12 to 3, 6.30 to 11, Sun 12 to 3, 7 to 10.30; bar food and restaurant all week L 12 to 2, Mon to Sat D 6.30 to 9*
Details *Children welcome in eating areas Car park Wheelchair access (also WC) Garden Jukebox No dogs in eating areas Access, Amex, Delta, Switch, Visa*

GRANGE MOOR West Yorkshire map 8

Kaye Arms 🍇

29 Wakefield Road, Grange Moor TEL: (01924) 848385
off A642 and B6118, 4m S of Dewsbury

The area around the Kaye Arms is pure countryside. There's a farm behind the pub, and the only other building on this stretch of road is a tea-room farmhouse. The inn's interior is divided into three areas, with wooden half-panelling, a mixture of plates and pictures on the walls, and a patterned carpet running throughout. An extensive menu taking in Cheddar cheese soufflé, wild boar and Black Sheep Ale sausages with butter-beans, poached smoked haddock on beetroot, for example, is backed up by a long list of daily specials. These might include queen scallops grilled with garlic butter and Gruyère, duck leg confit on apricot chutney, salmon with ginger and lime butter, or roast venison with a pear and rosemary sauce. A broad selection of sandwiches is also available. Dessert wines are listed alongside puddings like pear and almond tart, and strawberry crème brûlée. No draught beers are sold, but the wine list offers a decent choice, with several by the glass, including a white and red wine of the month. Towards Wakefield is the Yorkshire Mining Museum, which is well worth a visit. SAMPLE DISHES: warm smoked chicken with spiced pear salad £4; chicken breast in filo with a wild mushroom sauce £9; iced lemon curd parfait £3.25.

Open *Tue to Sat 11.30 to 3, 7 to 11, Sun 12 to 2, 7 to 10.30; bar food Tue to Sat L 12 to 2, Tue to Sun D 7.30 (7 Sat) to 10 (9.30 Tue and Sun)*
Details *No children Car park Wheelchair access (also WC) Background music No dogs Access, Delta, Switch, Visa*

GRASMERE Cumbria map 10

▲ *Travellers Rest*

Grasmere TEL: (01539) 435604
just off A591 Keswick road, ½m N of Grasmere

Sometimes it overflows, sometimes there isn't a queue in sight: such is life for a country pub in the tourist heartland of the Lake District. Walkers trudge the long-distance coast-to-coast path, others come to discover what inspired Wordsworth. It makes for a happy gathering. If food is required, the kitchen can deliver 'top-class' vegetable soup, baguettes and jacket potatoes with decent fillings, as well as poached trout, Mediterranean chicken with sun-dried tomatoes, garlic and basil, plus specials such as grilled salmon with hollandaise sauce. Sunday lunch is a 'roast of the day'. On handpump you will find beers from Jennings of Cockermouth, including Bitter, Dark Mild, Cumberland Ale and Sneck Lifter. Wines of the month are listed on a board. SAMPLE DISHES: vegetable dim-sum £3; Cumberland mixed grill £10; lemon crunch £2.75.

Open *Mon to Sat 11 to 11, Sun 11 to 10.30; bar food all week 12 to 3, 6 to 9.45 (12 to 9.45 Apr to end Oct)*
Details *Children welcome Car park Wheelchair access Garden No smoking in dining-room Background music No dogs in dining-room Access, Switch, Visa Accommodation: 8 rooms, B&B £16 to £58*

GREAT HAMPDEN Buckinghamshire map 3

Hampden Arms

Great Hampden TEL: (01494) 488255
off A4010 or A413, midway between Princes Risborough and Great Missenden

This is very much an 'eating' pub, and most of the wooden tables in the three interconnecting rooms are already set. It can get busy too, and reservations are taken for both lunch and dinner. Light dishes such as seafood pancake or cottage pie are available at lunch-time, but at both sessions you can expect the likes of baked king prawns or snails, boar pie, steaks, chicken or mixed vegetable curry, and baked Stilton avocado. Desserts take in, for example, hot cherries with brandy sauce, sticky toffee pudding, and apple crumble. Real ales include Wadworth 6X, Greene King Abbot Ale and Thomas Hardy Country Bitter, house wines are served by the glass, and more than a dozen liqueur coffees are on offer. The village is on a minor road in the Chilterns, in an area much used by walkers. Hughenden Manor,

Disraeli's home, is not far away. SAMPLE DISHES: mushrooms stuffed with pâté £5.50; Dover sole thermidor £16; sherry trifle £3.

Open *12 to 2.30, 7 to 11, Sun 12 to 3, 7 to 10.30; bar food 12 to 2, 7 to 9.30 (Sun 9); closed 25 Dec, Sun evening Jan and Feb*
Details *Car park Wheelchair access Garden No music Dogs welcome on a lead Access, Visa*

GREAT KIMBLE Buckinghamshire map 3

▲ *Bernard Arms*

Risborough Road, Great Kimble TEL: (01844) 346172
on A4010, 2m NE of Princes Risborough

In 1833, this Chiltern roadside pub changed its name from the Chequers to the Bernard Arms; at least it won't now be confused with the prime ministers' country residence nearby. As might be expected, photographs of famous – or infamous – statesmen who have nipped into the pub have pride of place on the walls: Harold Wilson in the '70s, and John Major and Boris Yeltsin with their wives from a more recent era. The kitchen takes its work seriously, offering all-comers a menu that keeps up with current trends: starters such as fried chorizo on a Stilton salad, or Chinese-style chicken with soy sauce, might be followed by more substantial dishes, including roast breast of duck with pomegranate sauce, grilled swordfish steak with a nutty dill and garlic sauce, or ten ounces of Scotch ribeye with prunes and shallots. Ice-creams are alternatives to home-made apple pie, syrup sponge pudding, or fruits of the forest cheesecake. A separate menu is served in the restaurant. Benskins Bitter is the house beer, otherwise choose between Fuller's London Pride and Wadworth 6X; several wines from the diminutive list are served by the glass. SAMPLE DISHES: chicken liver and port wine pâté £4; julienne of Scotch beef in a creamy cracked pepper and cognac sauce £8; chocolate torte £3.50.

Open *12 to 3, 6 to 11.30, Sun 12 to 3, 7 to 10; bar food and restaurant 12 to 2.30, 7 to 9.30*
Details *Children welcome Car park Wheelchair access (also WC) Garden Background music No dogs Access, Amex, Delta, Diners, Switch, Visa Accommodation: 5 rooms, B&B £35 to £45*

SAMPLE DISHES: listed in the main text of an entry indicate three typical dishes from the menu to give some idea of the style of cooking and prices.

GREAT KINGSHILL Buckinghamshire map 3

Red Lion

Great Kingshill TEL: (01494) 711262
on A4128, 3m N of High Wycombe

This modest building was jam-packed on the 'really dark, cold night, with torrential rain' when one reporter visited. A tiny vestibule leads directly into the L-shaped bar, where tables are crammed in, standing-room at the counter is minimal, and a mishmash of plates, prints and old pictures hang on the walls. 'Beer sales were virtually none. People come here to eat fish and drink white wine,' noted an inspector, although Tetley Bitter and Marston's Pedigree are on tap. A sign by the front door proclaims that all fish is fresh from Billingsgate, and one of the two large chilled cabinets in the bar is full of white wine bottles. The huge menu is painted on a blackboard; fish not available that day are marked with a cross, but if Billingsgate has it they'll have it here: lobster, brill, turbot, parrot fish and more besides. Starters are simple, and puddings like Danish apple tart and crème caramel are made in-house. The wine list reflects the Spanish owner's background, and house wines are sold by the glass. SAMPLE DISHES: grilled lemon sole £11; tiramisù £3.

Open *11 to 3, 6 to 9.30, bar food and restaurant 12 to 2, 6 to 9*
Details *Children welcome Car park Garden Background music No dogs No cards*

GREAT WHITTINGTON Northumberland map 10

Queens Head Inn

Great Whittington TEL: (01434) 672267
off A68, 4m N of Corbridge at Stagshaw roundabout, then 1½m to village

This stone-built pub is set in the unspoilt village of Great Whittington with rolling countryside all around. The two well-appointed rooms with their exposed-stone walls and open log fires have a relaxing atmosphere, and there's plenty of space for diners. Mushrooms in leek and Stilton sauce, or smoked mackerel with a salad of onion, tomato and basil, could kick off the bar menu, with leg of lamb with Pan Haggerty (whose origins are Northumbrian), or chicken breast in broccoli and cream sauce to follow. At dessert stage, old favourites such as banoffi pie and sticky toffee pudding could be joined by a fruit crumble. A good range of real ales includes Durham Magus, Hambleton Bitter and Courage Directors, plus Queens Head, the pub's own brew. Around 30 wines feature on the list, with four available by the glass. Corbridge, famous for its Roman site, is nearby. SAMPLE DISHES: avocado, bacon and tomato salad £3.50; local guinea-fowl in red wine sauce £9; fruit pie £3.50.

Open *Mon to Fri 12 to 2.30, 6 to 11, Sat 12 to 3.30, 6 to 11, Sun 12 to 3.30, 7 to 10.30; bar food and restaurant 12 to 2.30, 7 to 9*
Details *Children welcome in 1 bar and restaurant Car park Wheelchair access (also WC) Garden Background music No dogs Access, Amex, Switch, Visa*

GREAT WOLFORD Warwickshire map 5

▲ *Fox & Hounds Inn* 

Great Wolford TEL: (01608) 674220
off A44, 3m NE of Moreton in Marsh

'We have been a public house since 1590,' the licensees tell us, yet this gabled, flower-basket-hung building isn't immediately recognisable as a pub. It looks more like a group of newly restored Cotswold residences around a central courtyard car park, but the den-like, dim interior is basically untouched, with a rough stone inglenook, low beams hung with hop garlands, and a stuffed fox in a glass case. Real ales are clearly an enthusiasm – 'we've had over 150 different ones in a year and a half' – with about ten on draught at any one time, including Hook Norton and, from further afield, North Yorkshire Flying Herbert. The wine list has around two dozen bottles, with a handful by the glass, plus some country wines. Dishes on the printed menu are a predictable bunch: ploughman's and sandwiches, chicken Kiev, steaks, ice-creams and sorbets. More ambitious are blackboard specials such as deep-fried whitebait with tarragon mayonnaise, baked pork chop with apricot and sage stuffing, and grilled lemon sole with prawn sauce and profiteroles. SAMPLE DISHES: chicken liver pâté with Cumberland sauce £3.75; sauté chicken breast stuffed with saffron mousse £7; raspberry bombe £2.50.

Open *12 to 3, 7 to 11, Sun 12 to 3, 7 to 10.30; bar food and restaurant Sun to Fri 12 to 2.30, 7 to 9.30*
Details *Children welcome in dining-room Car park Wheelchair access (also WC) Garden and patio Background music Dogs welcome on a lead Accommodation: 4 rooms, room only £35*

indicates a pub serving food on a par with 'seriously good' restaurants, where the cooking achieves consistent quality.

indicates a pub serving better-than-average wine.

GREAT YELDHAM Essex **map 6**

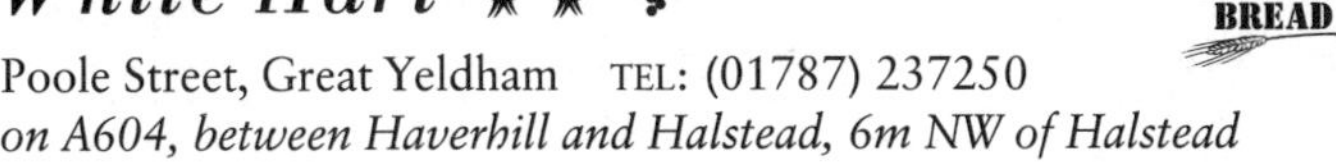

White Hart

BREAD

Poole Street, Great Yeldham TEL: (01787) 237250
on A604, between Haverhill and Halstead, 6m NW of Halstead

'It's the kind of place you really cannot miss,' noted one traveller on arrival at this rambling half-timbered Tudor edifice. This is the most recent acquisition of the Huntsbridge Group (see also the Three Horseshoes at Madingley and the Pheasant Inn at Keyston) and it seems set for great things. Inside, it is vastly spacious and slightly baronial in a domestic sort of way, with tables and chairs dotted around the massive, newly flagstoned bar. Puffs of smoke waft from the mighty open log fire in the bar, and the big counter has handpumps dispensing Adnams Bitter, Marston's Pedigree and Fuller's London Pride. 'Eat, drink and be merry is the message,' quipped one reporter.

Chef/proprietor Roger Jones transferred here from Keyston and you can expect plenty of Huntsbridge-style flexibility about the business of eating. Informality is the order of the day in the bar and the garden, while a slightly more measured approach marks out the restaurant (where you can book tables). One menu is served throughout. A list of snacks offers ploughman's, smoked salmon with toasted brioche, 'hot' chicken curry with lime pickle and 'green' Basmati rice, and so forth, and reporters are of one voice about the quality of the home-baked breads: the focaccia, in particular, is 'absolutely stunning', proclaimed one recipient, who went on to describe big chunks 'three inches high, warm, moist, rich, spongy, loaded with herbs and topped with barely brown onion threads'. The full menu is dazzlingly modern, with flamboyance and cohesion leaping out from every dish: hot mascarpone tart is accompanied by poached garlic and grilled radicchio, duck confit terrine comes with haricot bean purée and pickled beetroot. Ingredients are deployed with real confidence: oven-dried figs with grilled goats' cheese, sauté mooli as the embellishment for oriental-style poached turbot. There's also a feel for the classics in such dishes as breast of Deben duck with boulangère potatoes, leeks and plum sauce. Cheeses from Neal's Yard are kept in prime condition and the creativity carries through to desserts such as elderflower sorbet with a compote of plums.

As with all Huntsbridge addresses, the wine list is 'exceptionally interesting', offering a selection 'of fine wines from modern and old masters'; 13 house wines are served by the glass. SAMPLE DISHES: squid tempura with teriyaki sauce £4.50; roasted fillet of salmon with shredded courgettes, new potatoes and rosemary butter sauce £10; marinated exotic fruit with coconut ice-cream £4.75.

Open *11 to 3.30, 5.30 to 11, Sun 12 to 3, 5.30 to 10.30; bar food and restaurant 12 to 2, 6.30 to 10 (Sun D 7 to 9.30)*
Details *Children welcome in bar eating area Car park Wheelchair access (also WC) Garden and patio No smoking in dining-room No music No dogs Access, Amex, Delta, Diners, Switch, Visa*

GRETA BRIDGE **Co Durham** **map 10**

▲ *Morritt Arms* 🍇

Greta Bridge TEL: (01833) 627232
off A66, 6m W of Bowes

Dating from the seventeenth century, the Morritt Arms was used during Victorian times as the second overnight stopover by the London to Carlisle mail coach. Dickens stayed at Greta Bridge in 1839, and the Dickens Bar, with its Windsor chairs and stools, is well known for its striking murals depicting characters from *Pickwick Papers*. All the rooms are cosy and comfortably furnished. Bar food ranges from sandwiches – including the chef's speciality club sandwich, topped with a poached egg and dressed with red wine vinaigrette – and chicken liver pâté, to mixed grill, sausage and mash, vegetable Wellington, or fillet of cod in beer batter, all supported by a blackboard of daily specials. A fuller *carte* is offered in the Copperfield Restaurant, which also has an extensive wine list running to about 150 bins, including a strong New World contingent; a decent selection is also available by the glass. Real ales include Tetley Bitter, Theakston Best and Butterknowle Conciliation Ale. SAMPLE DISHES: avocado with prawns £3.25; lambs' liver with bacon £7; bread-and-butter pudding £3.25.

Open *11.30 to 11, Sun 12 to 3, 7 to 10.30; bar food 11.30 to 9.30; restaurant 11.30 to 2.30 (3 Sun), 6.30 to 9.30*
Details *Children welcome Car park Wheelchair access (also WC) Garden and patio No smoking in restaurant Background and live music; jukebox Dogs welcome Access, Amex, Delta, Diners, Switch, Visa Accommodation: 19 rooms, B&B £45 to £95*

GUNNISLAKE **Cornwall** **map 1**

Rising Sun 🍺

Calstock Road, Gunnislake TEL: (01822) 832201
just off A390, between Tavistock and Callington

'It is very English, very idiosyncratic and I wish it were my local,' remarks a reporter from Kent. No wonder – the pub, which dates from the seventeenth century, is a splendid, higgledy-piggledy place with terraced gardens overlooking the Tamar Valley. Inside, the clutter is magnificent – fresh flowers, *objets d'art*, chamber pots, jugs and teapots of every description, huge pottery pieces, cheese covers and more. There is real warmth here; 'everything...seems to glow.' Blackboards list the food on offer: one advertises the likes of local oak-smoked trout, 'trawlerman's stew' with garlic bread, baked brill with herb butter, and roast duck breast with a citrus glaze; another promotes sweets such as three-chocolate gâteau and special pavlovas served with home-made clotted cream; otherwise take advantage of the West Country cheeses. Excellent real ales are on offer: Jail Ale, St Austell Dartmoor Best, Hicks Cornish Bitter and others are available, as well as Inch's cider; five house wines are served by the glass. SAMPLE DISHES: chicken liver pâté £3; steak and ale pie £6; blueberry and raspberry cheesecake £2.75.

Open *Mon to Sat 11 to 3, 5 to 11, Sun 12 to 3, 7 to 10.30; bar food all week 12 to 2.30, 7 to 9.30*
Details *Children welcome in eating areas Car park Garden and patio Background music Dogs welcome in bar only No cards*

GUNWALLOE Cornwall **map 1**

▲ *Halzephron Inn*

Gunwalloe TEL: (01326) 240406
from A3083 1½m S of Helston take small lane towards Church Cove

'Halzephron was living up to its name when I visited,' begins a lively report. '[It is] derived from two Cornish words meaning "hell cliffs", [and] the wind was blasting straight off the boiling sea.' This part of Cornwall is known as the 'wrecking coast', a scene of plunder, destruction, contraband, smuggling; a shaft connecting this remote 500-year-old pub to an underground tunnel still exists. These days, however, most custom – even on a gale-ridden November day – is likely to come from tourists, and the pub puts on a reassuring, civilised face to welcome all comers.

One menu is served throughout, and it's a neat and convincing balancing act between tried-and-tested favourites and dishes that have bistro overtones. Delicately creamy crab pancakes were 'wonderful', thought one visitor, but the choice runs all the way from 'Mr Kearsley's crab salad platter' to 'Mr Retallack's chargrilled sirloin steaks'. Daily specials add variety in the shape of cheese and herb soufflé, scallops thermidor and braised lamb's liver with Dubonnet. Sticky toffee pudding with clotted cream makes an 'excellent' finish; otherwise there are Cornish ice-creams, sorbets and heartwarmers like treacle sponge pudding. Real ales are sound local names such as Dartmoor Best, Sharp's Own and Doom Bar; there's also a wide-ranging list of more than 40 wines supplemented by a further ten classy vintages ('The Guv'nors Selection') supplied by Corney & Barrow. Famished walkers should note that the pub is the only watering-hole on the coastal path between Mullion and Porthleven. SAMPLE DISHES: sauté mushrooms with herb and cream sauce £3.50; steak and kidney pudding £8; pecan pie £3.

Open *11 to 3, 6.30 to 11, Sun 12 to 3, 7 to 10.30; bar food 12 to 2 (1.45 Sun), 7 to 9.30 (9 Sun); closed 25 Dec*
Details *Children welcome in family room Car park Wheelchair access Garden and patio No smoking in dining-room Occasional live music Guide dogs only Access, Delta, Switch, Visa Accommodation: 2 rooms, B&B £35 to £56*

HAILEY Oxfordshire map 5

▲ *Bird in Hand*

Whiteoak Green, Hailey TEL: (01993) 868321
off B4022, Charlbury to Witney road, turn right ½m after Hailey village

Originally a coaching-house and farm, this Cotswold stone pub has evolved over the years into a high-class 'residential country inn' (as the licensees describe it). Heavy old beams and a huge inglenook set the tone in the main bar, and there are no fewer than six different dining areas, although one menu operates throughout the pub. The kitchen is firmly in tune with the times, delivering the likes of steamed asparagus and wild mushroom bruschetta, baked fennel and goats'-cheese tart with artichoke oil, and chargrilled lamb steak with roasted garlic bulbs, as well as pleasing the old guard with ham and eggs, and home-made burgers. Fresh fish specials vary from day to day. To finish choose either cold pâtisserie or one of the traditional hot puddings. Sunday lunch is a roast. The list of 20 drinkable wines includes half a dozen by the glass, and beer drinkers have a choice of Boddingtons, Marston's Pedigree or Wadworth 6X. While in the area, it's worth taking a trip out to admire the glories of Blenheim Palace. SAMPLE DISHES: Thai-style crab-cakes with sweet chilli sauce £5; guinea-fowl and mushroom pudding with a suet crust £7.50; chocolate elodie (three-colour layered chocolate mousse) £3.25.

Open *11 to 11, Sun 12 to 3, 7 to 10.30; bar food 12 to 1.45, 7 to 9.30*
Details *Children welcome in eating areas Car park Wheelchair access (also WC) Garden and patio Background music Dogs welcome Access, Delta, Switch, Visa Accommodation: 16 rooms, B&B £50 to £75*

HALFWAY BRIDGE West Sussex map 3

Halfway Bridge Inn

Halfway Bridge, Lodsworth TEL: (01798) 861281
on A272, midway between Midhurst and Petworth, just S of Lodsworth

This brick and tile-hung pub surrounded by fields is shielded from the main road by a pretty, brick-lined front garden with wooden tables and chairs. The interior has been well modernised, although diners may find the tables rather cramped. The menu offers much of interest: you could start with deep-fried Camembert with gooseberry and onion marmalade, or chicken liver and wild mushroom salad; go on to roast lamb with mint sauce, or smoked haddock with bubble and squeak and a poached egg; and finish with spotted dick, or treacle roly-poly. Alternatively, choose from the blackboard specials, which may include smoked salmon with scrambled egg, skate with black butter and capers, and orange and Grand Marnier ice-cream. Rabbit, pheasant, pigeon and venison all feature in season. Fuller's London Pride, Gale's HSB and Cheriton Pots Ale are on draught, together with guest ales. A regularly changing selection of wines is sold by the glass, as well as two house wines from the list of 20-plus bottles. Petworth House (National Trust) is just along the road. SAMPLE DISHES: spinach and prawn soup £3.25; calf's liver and bacon with mash £9; plum and honey crumble £3.50.

Open *11 to 3, 6 to 11, Sun 12 to 3, 7 to 10.30; bar food and restaurant 12 to 2 (2.30 Sat and Sun), 7 to 10; closed Sun evening winter*
Details *No children Car park Wheelchair access Garden and patio No-smoking area in dining-room No music Dogs welcome Access, Delta, Switch, Visa*

HALLATON Leicestershire map 5

Bewicke Arms

1 Eastgate, Hallaton TEL: (01858) 555217
off A47, 7m NE of Market Harborough

This sixteenth-century thatched inn is in a charming position, opposite the green, in a peaceful, unspoilt village surrounded by rolling countryside. The village itself boasts a conical butter cross, picture-postcard cottages and an interesting museum of local life; it's also famous for the legendary pagan customs of Hare Pie Scrambling and Bottle Kicking that bring sightseers to Hallaton on Easter Monday. The two beamed bars have a welcoming atmosphere, with old-fashioned cushioned settles and sturdy oak tables. Log fires burn in cold weather, and the décor consists of various farming implements and other artefacts. An additional room is opened at busy times and at weekends. Pub favourites are found on the printed menu: sandwiches and salads, pâté and prawn cocktail, deep-fried fillet of plaice, and grilled rump steak with Stilton butter, for example. The blackboard specials feature game in season – French-style rabbit casserole, or half a roast pheasant with mustard sauce – and also dishes like Somerset beef, and chicken Lady Jane (with bacon and mushrooms in port and rosemary sauce). Desserts are a pudding-lover's dream. On draught are Ruddles Best Bitter and County, and Marston's Pedigree, and house wines are sold by the glass. SAMPLE DISHES: goujons of plaice £4.25; grilled salmon fillet with honey, dill and mustard sauce £7.25; sherry trifle £3.

Open *12 to 2.30, 7 to 11, Sun 12 to 3.30, 7 to 11; bar food and restaurant 12 to 2, 7 to 9.45 (9.30 Sun)*
Details *Children welcome Car park Garden and patio Background music Guide dogs only Access, Delta, Switch, Visa*

HALSTEAD Leicestershire **map 5**

Salisbury Arms

Oakham Road, Halstead TEL: (0116) 259 7333
off B6047, 8m S of Melton Mowbray

A lot goes on at the Salisbury Arms, also known as the 'Tilton Hilton' (Tilton on the Hill is nearby): a number of special events, such as Italian evenings and savoury pie and sticky pudding nights, are held in the conservatory restaurant, and there may well be a private function taking place in the marquee. Bar food is served throughout the attractively furnished interconnecting rooms. The menu goes in for quirky descriptions: 'tatty hides' are deep-fried potato skins, while 'Salisbury snags' are sausages stuffed with apricots, wrapped in bacon and served with mash. Otherwise you can expect to find ham and leek soup, chicken piri-piri, lamb casserole, a range of fish, and sticky toffee sponge with clotted cream ice-cream. Adnams Broadside and Bass are on draught, and the wine list offers more than 30 bottles, with bin-ends listed on a board. SAMPLE DISHES: 'bobby' beans wrapped in bacon £4; cod fillet with parsley sauce £5; toffee chocolate pie £3.

Open *Tue to Sat and bank hols 11 to 3, 6 to 11, Sun 12 to 3; bar food and restaurant Tue to Sun 12 to 2, Tue to Sat D 6.30 to 10*
Details *Children welcome Car park Wheelchair access (also WC) Garden and patio No smoking in restaurant Background music Guide dogs only Access, Delta, Switch, Visa*

HAMSTEAD MARSHALL Berkshire map 2

▲ *White Hart*

Kintbury Road, Hamstead Marshall
TEL: (01488) 658201 *off A4, 4½m W of Newbury*

Little Italy in the middle of rural Berkshire – that's the White Hart. Owners Nicola and Dorothy Aromando, who have been here since 1982, are Italian and this is reflected in the food they serve and in the ambience of this smart-looking Georgian pub. A very comfortable atmosphere pervades, the welcome is warm and the service remains professional, polite and helpful. The standard printed menu offers a selection of pasta, omelettes, steaks, sole and chicken. But, according to reporters, the dishes to go for are those on the blackboard. They could include coniglio paesana (boned rabbit stuffed with herbs and pine-nuts, braised with wine, sweet peppers and black olives and served on spinach polenta), coda di rospo (monkfish sauté with tomatoes, brandy and cream with risotto), or cozze marinara (mussels cooked with wine and garlic accompanied by home-made bread). For one visitor, pernici (partridge with cherry sauce and sweet potato) was a 'star main course', and his Parma ham and melon starter and tiramisù dessert were 'best I've had'. Espresso coffee, in the words of one who enjoyed it, is the 'put hairs on chest' stuff. Not surprisingly, the wine list contains a reasonable selection of Italian bottles. Real ales include Wadworth 6X and, from Hall & Woodhouse, Badger Best, although bottles of Peroni beer are a good accompaniment to the food. SAMPLE DISHES: grilled goats' cheese with garlic and yoghurt £5.50; involtino di pollo (chicken breast stuffed with ham and asparagus and braised in wine sauce) £10.50; Italian almond tart with cherries £4.50.

Open *Mon to Sat 12 to 2.30, 6 to 11; bar food and restaurant 12.30 to 2, 6.30 to 9.45*
Details *Children welcome in eating areas Car park Wheelchair access Garden and patio No smoking in restaurant Background music No dogs Access, Visa Accommodation: 6 rooms, B&B £45 to £75*

HAROME North Yorkshire map 9

Star Inn

Harome TEL: (01439) 770397
off A170, 3m SE of Helmsley

The Star Inn began a near-miraculous transformation in June 1996, when keen new owners Andrew and Jacqueline Pern moved in with the determination to put the place back on the map after months of neglect. The building is much the same as it always was: 600 years old, thatched, with a low roof, 'wonky walls' and a stable-door entrance. Inside, it oozes atmosphere. Black settles and rustic tables have the carved rodent signature of Yorkshire craftsman 'Mouseman Thompson'; at one end of the bar is a black range, at the other a log fire.

What is remarkable is the change in the food. The Perns have resisted the temptation to crash headlong into the world of restaurant-style cuisine; instead, they balance the flexible requirements of pub eating with dishes that are emphatically classy. At lunch-time, in particular, you can call in for an unusual sandwich (perhaps rare sirloin steak with blue cheese shavings, or Brie with roasted peppers), have a plate of smoked salmon and scrambled eggs, or even a beautifully presented starter of creamy duck liver pâté with home-made nut bread and a salad of decently dressed, crisp leaves. Game features strongly in season: pheasant and armagnac terrine comes with apple and vanilla chutney; while half a bird might be roasted and served with baby carrots and turnips 'with tops on' plus a gutsy Burgundy-style sauce. Partridge comes with a risotto of black pudding, leeks and Lancashire cheese; peppered breast of mallard with Yorkshire sauce. Fish also shows up in the shape of, say, seafood hotpot with fennel and Pernod, or fillet of sea bass with mussels, leeks and saffron, while rump of lamb is given the North Country treatment with pickled red cabbage and bubble and squeak. Desserts might include things like a brûlée of rice pudding with mulled fruits. Four real ales, including Black Sheep Bitter and Theakston XB, are on draught, and the wine list generally includes around eight by the glass. Nunnington Hall (National Trust), Duncombe Park and Castle Howard are nearby attractions. SAMPLE DISHES: mushroom and Madeira soup £2.50; fillet of cod with boulangère potatoes and grain-mustard sauce £6.75; mille-feuille of raspberries £3.50.

Open *11.30 to 3, 6.30 to 11, Sun 12 to 10.30; bar food and restaurant Mon to Sat 12 to 2, 6.45 to 9.30, Sun 12 to 9.30*
Details *Children welcome Car park Wheelchair access (also WC) Garden No smoking in restaurant Background music Dogs welcome in bar only Access, Switch, Visa*

All details are as accurate as possible at the time of going to press, but pubs often change hands, and it is wise to check beforehand by telephone anything that is particularly important to you.

✿ indicates a pub serving outstanding bar food, backed up by all-round excellence in other departments, such as service, atmosphere and cleanliness.

HARRIETSHAM Kent map 3

Ringlestone Inn

Ringlestone Road, Harrietsham TEL: (01622) 859900
off A20, 3m NE of Harrietsham, take B2163 N signposted Sittingbourne, turn right towards Doddington at crossroads by water-tower after Hollingbourne

More than eight real ales are tapped from casks at this remote country inn on the North Downs, among them Fuller's London Pride, Shepherd Neame Bishops Finger and Spitfire, and Greene King Abbot Ale. The pub's speciality fruit wines – from sweet apricot to dry rose-petal – and liqueurs such as blackberry brandy can be bought by the bottle to take away, as can the directly imported house wines; fine wines are listed on a board. Food is taken as seriously as drinks. A help-yourself hot and cold buffet operates at lunch-time – cold pies and roast meats with salads, or perhaps macaroni with tuna and clams, or chicken casserole – with a full menu offered in the evening. This may embrace crab pâté, or mussels provençale to start, followed by a wide selection of Ringlestone pies, or spicy pork loin steaks, then local fruit crumble, or apple lattice flan. Meals can be eaten throughout the bars (reservations are taken for the restaurant). Oak beams, brick and flint walls, a huge inglenook, and centuries-old oak furniture testify to the age of the place. Four ponds linked by waterfalls feature in the splendidly peaceful garden. The licensees tell us that they plan to offer accommodation from summer 1997. SAMPLE DISHES: marinated herring fillets £5; breast of chicken stuffed with garlic, ham and Cheddar £9; treacle, orange and nut tart £3.25.

Open *Mon to Fri 12 to 3, 6 to 11, Sat 12 to 11, Sun 12 to 10.30; bar food and restaurant 12 to 2 (2.15 Sun), 7 to 9.30; closed 25 Dec*
Details *Children welcome Car park Wheelchair access Garden Background music Dogs in bar only Access, Amex, Delta, Diners, Switch, Visa*

HARRINGWORTH Northamptonshire map 6

▲ *White Swan*

Harringworth TEL: (01572) 747543
off B672, 6m N of Corby

In a pretty village dominated by the mighty 82-arch Harringworth Railway Viaduct, this fifteenth-century coaching-inn is handy for a trip to Rutland Water and Rockingham Forest. An enthusiastic team has given the whole place a lift, the atmosphere is described as 'peaceful and relaxed' and the food is well worth noting. The regularly changing blackboard offers a good choice ranging from various pastas and grilled halibut steak to chicken Harringworth (stuffed with mushrooms, onions and Stilton). Handpumps on the carved oak bar dispense Greene King IPA, Abbot Ale and Marston's Pedigree, and the walls are decorated with old photographs of the village and the nearby wartime airfield at Spanhoe. Outside is a Japanese-style patio for fine weather visits. SAMPLE DISHES: deep-fried mushrooms with garlic dip £4; grilled halibut steak £8; bread-and-butter pudding £2.

Open *11.30 to 2.30, 6.30 to 11, Sun 12 to 3, 7 to 10.30; bar food and restaurant 12 to 2, 7 to 10 (9 Sun)*
Details *Children welcome in 1 room Car park Wheelchair access No smoking in restaurant Background music No dogs Access, Amex, Delta, Switch, Visa Accommodation: 7 rooms, £38 to £50*

HASCOMBE Surrey **map 3**

White Horse

Hascombe TEL: (01483) 208258
on B2130, 3m SE of Godalming

Visit the National Trust Arboretum at nearby Winkworth and then repair to the White Horse to quench your thirst and have a bite to eat. With its hop-garlanded bar and motley collection of wooden pews and tables, the pub is very popular and apt to get crowded, but that adds to the atmosphere. Families are very welcome here. A printed menu listing the usual pub stalwarts is supplemented by blackboard specials that take in, for example, chicken curry, steak and kidney pie, and lamb and mint kebabs. Puddings might include hazelnut and raspberry meringue, and chocolate truffle cake. The separate restaurant offers a shorter but more expensive menu. Beers on draught include King & Barnes Sussex Bitter, Wadworth 6X and Badger Best. More than 40 bottles feature on the wine list, with a number available by the glass. SAMPLE DISHES: chicken liver pâté with French bread £4; charcoal-grilled lamb chump chops and salad £11; blackcurrant and apple crumble £3.

Open *11 to 3, 5.30 to 11, Sat 11am to 11pm, Sun 12 to 10.30; bar food 12 to 2.20, 7 to 10; restaurant all week L 12 to 2.30, Mon to Sat D 7 to 10*
Details *Children welcome Car park Garden and patio No music Dogs welcome Access, Amex, Switch, Visa*

If a pub has a special point of interest, this is indicated by a 'flashed' word or phrase at the top right of the entry.

HASSOP Derbyshire map 9

Eyre Arms

Hassop TEL: (01629) 640390
on B6001, 2m N of Bakewell

This rustic roadside pub, dating from the seventeenth century, takes its name from the one-time owners of Hassop Hall, which dominates the hamlet. Their coat of arms can be seen on the pub's sign, and above the impressive stone fireplace in the lounge. This room is welcoming and civilised, with cushioned wall settles, beamed ceilings, a longcase clock, and prints and photographs hanging on the stone walls. The printed menu is a list of pub favourites, among them filled jacket potatoes, garlic mushrooms, chicken Kiev and steak and kidney pie, though venison pie may be included in season. Daily specials, listed on a blackboard, extend the choice with roast breast of duck with cherry sauce, leg of lamb stuffed with apricots and honey, and perhaps beef in Guinness with pickled walnuts. A reporter describes the service as 'excellent; very friendly staff, very busy'. Black Sheep Special, John Smith's Bitter, Marston's Pedigree and a guest beer are on draught. Hassop is at the heart of the Peak District; nearby Bakewell is worth a visit, and those who've done Chatsworth could look to visit fourteenth-century Haddon Hall, one of the best-preserved manor-houses of its period in the country. SAMPLE DISHES: carrot and orange soup £2.50; halibut steak in orange and basil sauce £8.75; brandy-snap basket £2.50.

Open *11 (12 Sun) to 3, 6.30 to 11; bar food 12 to 2.30, 6.30 to 9.30*
Details *Children welcome in bar eating area Car park Wheelchair access (also WC) Garden Background music No dogs No cards*

HATHERLEIGH Devon map 1

▲ *Tally Ho*

Hatherleigh TEL: (01837) 810306
on A386, between Okehampton and Torrington

The Tally Ho Brewery operates in a converted bakery at the back of this 500-year-old pub overlooking the local church. Five 'additive-free' draught ales are always on sale in the heavily beamed bar – from weak to strong they are Master Jack's Mild, Potboiler's Brew, Tarka's Tipple, Nutters Ale and Thurgia, plus the even more potent Jollop at Christmas time; three are also available in bottles. A few Italian flag-wavers add colour to the menu in the shape of mozzarella in carrozza (a variation on cheese on toast), deep-fried calamari, pasta, and desserts such as cassata and tiramisù; pizzas are the main attraction on Wednesday. Otherwise the bar menu offers a Potboiler's lunch (Devon Cheddar with pickles, bread and a pint of beer), omelettes, steaks, and a chicken dish (home-smoked breast with wild mushrooms and warm raspberry dressing), fish (cod fillet with filo scallop parcels and a sauce of lemon, lime and Bacardi, for example), plus something for vegetarians. A full restaurant menu is served in the dining-room. Grappas, malt whiskies and a wine list with some Italian names complete the picture for drinkers. Exotic song birds warble away in the beer garden – where barbecues are occasionally staged in summer. The pub was undergoing refurbishment as we went to press, with a new extension planned for the restaurant. SAMPLE DISHES: mushrooms stuffed with Devon goats' cheese £4; mixed tagliatelle with capers, anchovies, olives and tomato sauce £6; chocolate banana pie £3.

Open *11 to 2, 6 to 11, Sun 12 to 2, 7 to 10.30; bar food 12 to 2, 7 to 9.30; restaurant Thur to Tue D only 7 to 9.30 (Fri to Tue summer)*
Details *Children welcome in bar eating area Car park Garden Background music Dogs welcome Access, Amex, Delta, Switch, Visa Accommodation: 3 rooms, B&B £30 to £60*

HAWKSHEAD Cumbria map 8

▲ *Queen's Head Hotel*

Main Street, Hawkshead TEL: (01539) 436271
on B5285, 4m S of Ambleside

This timbered, white-painted hotel is at the heart of the traffic-free, honey-pot tourist village of Hawkshead. Low oak-beamed ceilings, panelled walls, a log fire and stools at circular tables characterise the bar. The extensive menu, which exhorts people to share tables at busy periods, mixes traditional pub staples such as seafood cocktail, and beef in Guinness pie, with more unusual offerings: sweet and spicy chicken wings, baked haggis with black pudding, and roast rabbit with apple and gooseberry sauce, for example. On the weekly-changing fish menu you may find pan-fried monkfish with bacon and garlic, or dressed crab. There's a separate restaurant to the rear of the bar. Robinson's Bitter, Mild and Frederics are on draught, and house wines are sold by the glass, with plenty of choice on the full list. Wordsworth attended Hawkshead Grammar School, and you can see the desk in which he carved his name. The Beatrix Potter Gallery is another local attraction. SAMPLE DISHES: grilled goats' cheese £3.25; poached salmon with prawn and chive sauce £7.25; meringue nest with fruits of the forest and ice-cream £3.25.

Open *11am to 11pm, Sun 12 to 10.30; bar food and restaurant 12 to 2.30, 6.15 to 9.30, Sun 12 to 9.30*

Details *Children welcome in dining-room Wheelchair access (also WC) Garden No smoking in dining-room and children's room Background music No dogs Access, Amex, Delta, Diners, Switch, Visa Accommodation: 13 rooms, B&B £30 to £75*

HAWORTH West Yorkshire map 8

Quarry House Inn

Bingley Road, Lees Moor TEL: (01535) 642239
off A629, 1½m E of Haworth

Reputedly a quarry manager's house in its former life, this remote stone-built inn on the road between Keighley and Cullingworth is a handy pit-stop for tourists on the Brontë sisters' trail. Inside, all is thoroughly traditional. The bar menu offers good, wholesome North Country stuff and it's excellent value. Choose from such things as hot pork pie with mushy peas, home-made meat and potato pie, roast breast of chicken, rump steak sandwich with fried onion rings or order something from the grill. Seasonal fish and game appear on the blackboard and a more elaborate menu is served in the restaurant. Drink Timothy Taylor Landlord or Golden Best, or Tetley Bitter; otherwise there is a list of three dozen acceptable wines bolstered by a list of specials in the bar. SAMPLE DISHES: orange and grapefruit salad £2; deep-fried breaded haddock fillet £5; brandy-snap basket with ice-cream and fresh fruit £2.50.

Open *12 to 3, 7 to 12; bar food and restaurant 12 to 2, 7.30 to 10.30; closed 25 and 26 Dec, 1 Jan*
Details *Children welcome Car park Wheelchair access (also WC) Garden and patio Background music Dogs welcome Access, Visa*

HAWRIDGE COMMON Buckinghamshire map 3

Rose & Crown

Hawridge Common TEL: (01494) 758386
off A416 N of Chesham, take road towards Cholesbury

Up on the high reaches of the Chilterns in great walking country between Chesham and Cholesbury, this roadside pub caters equally for rambling types, locals and passers-by. A weathered wooden porchway leads to the low-beamed bar with its exposed brickwork and tables dotted here and there. A separate dining area is neatly laid-up away from the bar. New licensees took over in November 1996, and the cooking shows promise – judging from dishes such as salmon in chive sauce, confit of duck, fillet of beef with mushroom and Burgundy sauce, and chocolate truffle torte. Ruddles County, Wadworth 6X and Brakspear are on draught and wines are sold by the glass. SAMPLE DISHES: king prawns in garlic butter £5; best end of lamb £10.75; crème brûlée £3.25.

Open *Mon to Sat 11 to 3, 6 to 11, Sun 12 to 3, 7 to 10.30; bar food all week 12 to 2, 7 to 9; restaurant Tue to Sun L 12 to 2, Tue to Sat D 7 to 9*
Details *No children Car park Garden and patio Background music No dogs Access, Amex, Delta, Diners, Switch, Visa*

HAYDON BRIDGE Northumberland map 10

General Havelock Inn

Radcliffe Road, Haydon Bridge TEL: (01434) 684376
on A69, 8m W of Hexham, 100yds from junction with B6319

A good location in a village close to the River South Tyne is part of the attraction for visitors to this unprepossessing green-painted pub. Inside there's a bar with dark green walls, a lighter green carpet and the evidence of judicious and regular polishing. Ian and Angela Clyde are ever-present welcoming hosts whose friendliness and efficiency are much appreciated. The bar menu features the kinds of dishes that have proved their worth over the years – honest soups, a chunky terrine of chicken, gammon and duck liver wrapped in bacon, chicken with creamy tarragon sauce, roast turkey in season, and home-made sweets in the mould of poached pears with chocolate sauce. The lunch menu served in the 'well-cared-for' dining-room charts a similar course, and you can also eat this in the bar. In the evening a more formal four-course set menu takes over, although the repertoire is much the same. The house wine has been described as 'delightful' and the full list of around 30 bins stays well within the affordable bracket. Tetley Bitter is the sole beer on handpump. SAMPLE DISHES: cream of mushroom soup £2; baked fillet of plaice with lemon and parsley £6; Danish chocolate bar £3.

Open *Wed to Sun 11.30 to 2.30, 7 to 11; bar food Wed to Sun L only 12 to 1.30; restaurant Wed to Sun L 12 to 1.30, Wed to Sat D 7.30 to 8.30*
Details *Children welcome Wheelchair access (also WC) Garden and patio No music Dogs welcome No cards*

Prices quoted in an entry are based on information supplied by the pub, rounded up to the nearest 25 pence. These prices may have changed since publication and are meant only as a guide.

The Guide *is totally independent, accepts no free hospitality and carries no advertising.*

HAYFIELD **Derbyshire** **map 8**

▲ *Sportsman*

Kinder Road, Hayfield TEL: (01663) 741565
on A624 Glossop to Chapel-en-le-Frith road

Hayfield is at the foot of Kinder Scout, crisscrossed by the Pennine Way, and at the edge of the Peak District National Park, but also convenient for the Manchester conurbation – hence its popularity. Beams and open fires add character to the interior of the Sportsman, where menus are chalked on boards. Cauliflower soup with home-baked bread, or black pudding with mustard, might be followed by marinated spicy chicken pan-fried with honey and sherry, or pork fillet with apples braised in cider and juniper berries. Vegetarians might be offered parsnip sausage and a bulgar wheat pattie served with vegetables. Fish – poached salmon or grilled plaice, for example – plus steaks and grills are always a feature, as are ploughman's and filled baguettes. You could finish with bread-and-butter pudding or apple tart. The Sportsman is a Thwaites house, with the brewery's ales on draught. A selection of wines comes by the glass, and the pub is proud of its collection of at least 25 single-malt whiskies. SAMPLE DISHES: spicy parsnip soup £2.50; beef casseroled in peppercorn and white wine sauce £8; banana ice-cream with hot Jamaican rum £3.

Open *Tue to Sun and bank hol Mon 12 to 3, all week 7 to 11; bar food Tue to Sun L 12 to 2, Mon to Sat D 7 to 9*
Details *Children welcome in bar eating area Wheelchair access Garden and patio Background music Dogs welcome Access, Visa Accommodation: 6 rooms, B&B £24 to £45*

HAYTOR VALE **Devon** **map 1**

▲ *Rock Inn*

Haytor Vale TEL: (01364) 661305
off A382 or B3344, SW of Bovey Tracey

At 1,490 feet, Haytor Rocks dominate the high moorland on the edge of Dartmoor. Close by is the Rock Inn, a comfortable retreat with oak furniture and log fires. Local fish and game are strong points of the kitchen's repertoire: mussels in garlic butter, John Dory, and beef and venison pie, for example. Other dishes may include oak-smoked Cheddar and basil quiche, lemon sole with a mussel and prawn sauce, and strawberries with Devon cream in meringue, all backed up by steaks, and West Country cheeses. Thomas Hardy's Country Ale and Royal Oak, and St Austell

Dartmoor Best are on draught, and wines have been well chosen. SAMPLE DISHES: field mushrooms with garlic butter £4.75; mixed seafood platter £9; caramelised oranges with brandy-snaps £3.75.

Open *11 to 2.30, 6.30 to 11 (10.30 winter), Sun 12 to 3, 7 to 10.30; bar food and restaurant 11.30 to 2.15, 7.30 to 9.30*
Details *Children welcome in dining-room Car park Wheelchair access Garden Smoking in lounge bar only No music No dogs Access, Amex, Delta, Switch, Visa Accommodation: 10 rooms, B&B £30 to £46*

HEBDEN BRIDGE West Yorkshire **map 8**

Hare and Hounds

Wadsworth, Hebden Bridge TEL: (01422) 842671
off A6033 Hebden Bridge to Keighley road at Pecket Well, signposted Old Town, then 1m

No one hereabouts uses this pub's correct name; it's known as the 'Lane Ends', probably because it sits at the end of three fairly narrow roads. The Pennine Way runs north from here to Haworth and Keighley Moors, so you may well find walkers as well as locals in the L-shaped bar area, with its bench seating and upholstered chairs, diamond-patterned carpet and brick fireplace. No doubt they'll be here for the down-to-earth Yorkshire cooking: triple-decker sandwiches, home-made soup, or Yorkshire pudding with onion gravy to start, followed by poached salmon, griddled tuna, chicken and mushroom pie, or turkey curry, and then ginger sponge, or apple tart. Vegetarians get a look in with such things as five-bean chilli and spicy tomato pasta. Roast beef with all the trimmings is the obvious choice for Sunday lunch. Timothy Taylor ales are particularly well kept; wines are the basic kind. SAMPLE DISHES: pork, ginger and leek sausages £4; liver, bacon and onions £5; strawberry crumble £2.

Open *Wed to Sat (winter Fri and Sat) 12 to 3, Mon to Sat 7 to 11, Sun and bank hols 12 to 11; bar food Thur to Sun L 12 to 2, Tue to Sat D 7 to 9, Sun 12 to 8.30; no food Tue D winter*
Details *Children welcome Car park Wheelchair access Garden and patio No music Dogs welcome No cards*

HECKINGTON Lincolnshire map 6

▲ *Nags Head*

34 High Street, Heckington TEL: (01529) 460218
off A17, 5m E of Sleaford

Homity pie – a venerable recipe concocted from potatoes, cheese, herbs and onions – is so popular here that it will probably still be a best seller when the millennium arrives. Otherwise, long-serving licensees Bruce and Georgina Pickworth change and re-write their menu each day and tell us emphatically that 'all dishes are home-made'. Sit in the bar of this atmospheric village local and you could begin with pears and Stilton on toast, garlic mushrooms, or smoked halibut and scrambled egg, then proceed to avocado and prawn hotpot, or warm salmon in cream and parsley sauce. At lunch-time you can also order hot, meaty sandwiches, as well as the more usual kind, while puddings might embrace anything from chocolate biscuit brandy cake to seasonal fruit pies. Wards Best Bitter and Vaux Double Maxim are the standard draught beers, and the guest beer changes every two months. SAMPLE DISHES: home-made pâté £3; roast glazed gammon in cider £6; banoffi pie £2.50.

Open *11 to 3, 5 to 11, Sun 12 to 3, 7 to 10.30; bar food 12 to 2, 7 to 9*
Details *Children welcome Car park Wheelchair access (also WC) Garden Jukebox No dogs Access, Visa Accommodation: 4 rooms, B&B £22 to £32*

HENFIELD West Sussex map 3

Plough Inn

High Street, Henfield TEL: (01273) 492280
at junction of A2307 and A281

The Plough is an unprepossessing place on the main street of a pleasant little country town well supplied with decent food shops. The interior is essentially one large area with a bar at the back and a separate eating area to one side. The cooking is mostly English in style 'with minimal recourse to Italian stand-bys' so you can expect such dishes as liver and bacon casserole, steak and kidney pudding, locally made sausage and mash, followed by desserts like lemon sponge. Plough Special is the house bitter and the cheapest on offer, or choose from Fuller's London Pride, Flowers Original or a guest such as Hall & Woodhouse Badger Best; the wine list is a modest affair running to around 20 bins. Note that the pub doesn't have a car park, so you will need to leave your vehicle in the street or in one of the town car parks. SAMPLE DISHES: French onion soup £2.50; lamb steak with mustard sauce £5.75; spotted dick and custard £2.50.

Open *Mon to Sat 11 to 3, 6 to 11, Sun 12 to 3, 7 to 10.30; bar food and restaurant all week L 12 to 2, Tue to Sat D 6.30 to 9*
Details *Children welcome in dining-room Wheelchair access Garden and patio No music Dogs welcome Access, Amex, Delta, Switch, Visa*

HEPWORTH West Yorkshire map 9

Butchers Arms

Hepworth, nr Holmfirth TEL: (01484) 682857
off A616, 6m S of Huddersfield

A Yorkshire lady remembers the time when the local brass band used to play sessions outside this stone-built pub and it was the heartbeat of Hepworth. In its current incarnation the Butchers Arms still shows genuine respect and purpose. Improvements, such as they are, have been incorporated with some sensitivity. There isn't much in the way of horse brasses or tackle in the three interconnecting rooms that make up the interior: instead you will notice paintings by local artists (including the landlord's father), candles in sticks or bottles all around, maps of Brontë country, an ancient piano with a teddy bear sitting on top of it. The impression is of a genuinely traditional pub, with no barriers between eating and drinking. It is also the kind of place where customers feel 'really looked after'.

Menus are written on blackboards over the fireplace and the kitchen clearly knows what '90s pub cooking is all about. Spicy Thai crab-cakes, tinged with ginger and spring onions, are served with red pepper salsa (the same relish also perks up Cajun blackened halibut steak), while deep-fried goats' cheese comes with 'real' piccalilli. The menu also calls into play Cumberland sausage and black pudding, steak and kidney pie, and calf's liver (covered in crisp breadcrumbs and topped with a 'marmalade' of apples, onions and cheese). Plates are decoratively embellished with herbs, and vegetables are generous to a fault. Ginger sponge with double cream custard has been a pleasingly comforting dessert; otherwise the list could include tiramisù, lemon mousse and the like. Theakston Best and Marston's Pedigree are regularly on handpump, and the wine list is a serviceable selection at fair prices. SAMPLE DISHES: French leaf salad with sun-dried tomatoes, smoked chicken and bacon £4.25; tandoori monkfish with cucumber raita £10.50; coffee and Grand Marnier cheesecake £3.

Open *Mon to Thu 6 to 11, Fri 12 to 3, 6 to 11, Sat 12 to 11, Sun 12 to 10.30; bar food and restaurant Fri to Sun L 12 to 2, Mon to Sat D 6 to 9.30*
Details *Children welcome in dining-room Car park Wheelchair access (also WC) Patio Background and live music Dogs welcome Access, Delta, Switch, Visa*

HERTFORD HEATH Hertfordshire map 3

Silver Fox

16–18 London Road, Hertford Heath TEL: (01992) 589023
on B1197, 2m NW of Hoddesdon

Mr and Mrs Blackett have run this popular village pub since 1989, and it remains a reliable choice with locals and visitors to the area. It's a prettily decorated place, with flowers on the beams and many carefully thought-out touches all around: smart, but not at all posh, sums it up. The printed bar menu offers lots of scope in an unfussy way, with a choice ranging from sandwiches and French bread 'splits' to locally made sausages, salads and generous steaks with all the trimmings. Added to this are a handful of specials such as chicken curry and braised pork chop. Desserts – up to 15 of them – have a separate board all of their own: expect banoffi pie, huge bowls of sherry trifle, pavlova, and so on. The bar menu is available in the restaurant at lunch-times, but in the evening a more expensive *carte* comes into operation. Adnams Bitter, Theakston Old Peculier and Tetley Bitter are on handpump, and the wine list provides a decent choice. A Hertfordshire reporter reveals that there's a good walk nearby, taking in Roundings Wood (part of Hertford Heath Nature Reserve). SAMPLE DISHES: crispy mushrooms and garlic dip £2.50; grilled sirloin steak £7.25; crème brûlée £2.

Open *11.30 to 2.30, 5 to 11, Sun 12 to 3.30, 7 to 10.30; bar food 12 to 2, 6 to 9.30; restaurant 12 to 2, 6.30 to 11*
Details *No children Car park Wheelchair access Garden and patio No smoking in dining-room Background music No dogs Access, Visa*

HETTON North Yorkshire map 8

Angel Inn ✿✿ ❦

Hetton TEL: (01756) 730263
off B6265, 5m N of Skipton

The Angel is proud of its past. Five centuries ago it was probably a crofter's cottage; 300 years later it evolved into a farmhouse doubling as a pub, and the owners started to brew and sell beer to the drovers moving cattle from Grassington to Gargrove. In 1983 a new era began when Denis and Juliet Watkins took over and revolutionised the place. The tide of success and popularity can sometimes overwhelm ventures like this and, to be sure, the crowds pack in relentlessly. 'This is the first eating place that I have been to where the non-booked-in punters amass outside the doors half an hour before opening time,' commented one reporter who clearly did not mind waiting. Business can be frenetic in the bare-timbered bar/brasserie, but what another visitor called 'the feel-good factor' hits you even before you have managed to reach a table. Staff in black waistcoats and long white aprons somehow manage to keep pace with the action and are obviously eager to please.

The blackboard menu leaves you in no doubt that this is a pub whose loyalty is wholeheartedly in the gastro-world of the 1990s – even if the setting suggests something more antiquated. Mediterranean flavours and influences leap out from almost every dish: the terrine of Tuscan vegetables with tapénade crostini and balsamic dressing is a classic, but the repertoire also embraces carpaccio of beef, toasted ciabatta 'sandwich' filled with chargrilled lamb fillet, roasted peppers, rocket, Parmesan and pesto, and stuffed breast of chicken wrapped in pancetta with slow-roast tomatoes, crispy basil and fondant potatoes. There's also a fiery contemporary streak to dishes such as smoked salmon with red pepper, chilli and tomato ice-cream. Even staunchly traditional North Country ingredients are turned on their heads, as in the terrine which brings together ham shank and foie gras, or the salad of fresh salmon rolled in garden herbs with fromage blanc. Desserts, by comparison, are in the well-tried mould of sherry trifle, crême brûlée, and fresh raspberry and white chocolate mousse. A more sedate atmosphere prevails in the restaurant, which is open for evening meals and Sunday lunch.

The Angel wine list is a brilliant tome, with a strong contingent from Italy, plenty of classic stuff from France and a useful showing of half-bottles. The full slate runs to 300 bins, with 8 house wines and no fewer than 24 by the glass. If beer is what you fancy, the choice is between Tetley Bitter, Black Sheep Bitter and Special. SAMPLE DISHES: warm salad of crispy duck with chorizo and walnut-oil dressing £6; calf's liver on polenta with beetroot sauce and horse-radish shavings £11; summer pudding with crème fraiche £3.75.

Open *all week 12 to 2, 6 to 9.30 (10 summer); bar food 12 to 2, 6 to 9.30; restaurant Sun L 12 to 2, Mon to Sat D 7 to 9*
Details *Children welcome Car park Wheelchair access (also WC) Garden No smoking area in restaurant and snug No music No dogs Access, Amex, Delta, Switch, Visa*

✿ *indicates a pub serving outstanding bar food, backed up by all-round excellence in other departments, such as service, atmosphere and cleanliness.*

Many pubs have separate restaurants, with very different menus. These have not been inspected. A recommendation for the pub/bar food does not necessarily imply that the restaurant is also recommended.

HEXHAM Northumberland map 10

Dipton Mill

Dipton Mill Road, Hexham TEL: (01434) 606577
S of Hexham towards Blanchland and Hexham racecourse

'This is a cracking pub,' enthuses a reporter. 'We had lunch there twice during our week's holiday in Northumberland.' Those who wonder how a week's holiday may be spent should know that the Dipton Mill is in a delightful country setting with good walking opportunities. Hadrian's Wall runs near the town, Chesters Roman Fort and Housesteads Roman Fort are well worth a visit, and Hexham's ancient abbey contains a Roman tombstone. The stream running beside the pub confirms that this was once a mill; inside, the panelled bar with its open fires has a friendly atmosphere. Food is now served in the evening as well as at lunch-time, and everything is cooked on the premises. You can expect ploughman's with a variety of cheeses, chicken breast in sherry sauce (described by a reporter as 'delicious and succulent'), steak and kidney pie, lamb steak, and cheese and broccoli flan, followed by chocolate cake, or pavlova roulade. The local Hexhamshire Brewery supplies well-kept Shire Bitter, Devil's Water and Whapweasel Bitter; there's also Theakston Best, and a broad choice of malt whiskies. 'Worth a visit for a taste of the North!' concludes a report. SAMPLE DISHES: carrot and celery soup £1.50; turkey, bacon and mushroom crumble £4; syrup sponge with custard £1.50.

Open *12 to 2.30, 6 to 11, Sun 12 to 4.30, 7 to 10.30 (closed 25 Dec); bar food 12 to 2.30, 6.30 (7.15 Sun) to 8.30*
Details *Children welcome in games room Wheelchair access (also WC) Garden and patio No music No dogs No cards*

HIGHER BURWARDSLEY Cheshire map 7

▲ *Pheasant Inn*

Higher Burwardsley TEL: (01829) 770434
off A534, between Broxton, signposted Burwardsley

The log fire in the bar of this partly timbered seventeenth-century inn is reputed to be the largest in Cheshire: it's perfect to sit beside and recuperate after trekking the nearby Sandstone Trail (the walk from Frodsham to Whitchurch across the crest of the Peckforton Hills). Nautical bric-à-brac and brass line the walls, along with pictures and rosettes of Highland cattle: the owners have their own prizewinning herd, and you can see them grazing outside. The comprehensive bar menu ranges from cold platters, daily curries and pies (steak and Guinness has been exceedingly good) to more unexpected dishes such as grilled chicken breast stuffed with ginger and leek sausage. Fresh fish shows up well on the blackboard: expect anything from poached salmon with warm raspberries to casserole of monkfish, scallops and mussels with pink peppercorns and dill. Puddings are well-tried favourites such as lemon meringue pie. Bass and Felinfoel Double Dragon are on handpump, and the pub has a stock of 40 malt whiskies; house wines come by the glass. Next door to the pub is the Cheshire Workshops candle factory; further afield are Orton Park motor racing circuit and the castles of Beeston, Peckforton and Cholmondley. SAMPLE DISHES: half-melon filled with fresh crab £3.50; noisettes of lamb with orange and redcurrant sauce £9; Bakewell tart £2.25.

Open *12 to 3, 7 to 11, Sun 12 to 3, 7 to 10.30; bar food 12 to 2.30, 7 to 9.30*
Details *Children welcome Car park Wheelchair access Garden and patio No smoking in conservatory daytime when children are present Background music Dogs welcome exc in eating areas Access, Amex, Diners, Visa Accommodation: 10 rooms, B&B £35 to £45*

HILDERSHAM Cambridgeshire map 6

Pear Tree

VEGETARIAN

Hildersham TEL: (01223) 891680
off A604, 8m SE of Cambridge

The Pear Tree must be the major thing of interest in Hildersham, although the village itself, small and quite pretty, is pleasant to stroll around. The pub comprises just the one bar, with plenty of space for eating, and a wood-burner for when it gets cold. Ploughman's and basket meals – Lincolnshire sausages with chips, for example – are on the printed menu, while the blackboard may announce specials like chicken and sweetcorn soup, beef and mushrooms baked with Guinness and Stilton, steaks, or chicken tikka. The chef is a Vegetarian Society 'Professional Cordon Vert' certificate-holder, so at least two vegetarian dishes are offered every day: vegetable pasta Mornay, or blackeye-bean bourguignon are typical. Accompaniments, such as 'gorgeous' garlic bread, and 'first-class' vegetables, received the thumbs-up. Puddings are traditionally English crumbles and tarts, and the kitchen makes its own ice-creams. This is a Greene King house, with the brewery's ales, including Mad Judge, in excellent condition. 'The beer is so good, who needs wine?' ask a couple of aficionados, although there's a short list, with a handful by the glass. SAMPLE DISHES: deep-fried crispy vegetables with savoury dip £3.25;

poached salmon fillet with pink peppercorn sauce £8; bread-and-butter pudding £2.

Open *11.45 to 2.30, 6.30 to 11, Sun 12 to 3, 7 to 10.30; bar food 12 to 2, 6.30 to 9.30 (7 to 9 Sun)*
Details *No children Car park Garden No music Dogs welcome Access, Amex, Delta, Switch, Visa*

HILL TOP Leicestershire **map 5**

Nags Head Inn

Hill Top TEL: (01332) 850652
4m from M1, Jct. 24, on B6540, at S end of Castle Donington

'Easy to miss on a road out of Castle Donington,' warns a reporter who liked this low-ceilinged beamed pub and its range of 'excellent' food. The same menu is served in the bar and the two dining-rooms, and the kitchen often gives run-of-the-mill dishes a special twist: club sandwiches come in hot Italian bread, Cajun-style fillet of beef is served with tzatziki, stir-fried vegetables arrive with couscous. The repertoire also takes in warm salads, tricolore pasta with smoked haddock, blackened swordfish with crème fraîche, and pork steak in cheese and beer. Desserts are equally lively: apple crumble jazzed up with mangoes or blueberries, or fresh figs in butterscotch syrup, for example. Marston's Pedigree and Banks's Mild are on draught, and the list of around 40 wines offers pleasant drinking at fair prices; house wines are sold by the glass. The Nags Head is within reach of the East Midlands Airport and Castle Donington racing circuit and motor museum. SAMPLE DISHES: garlic mushrooms with Stilton sauce £4; baked cod with herb crust £9; treacle and oat tart £2.75.

Open *11.30 to 2.30, 5.30 to 11, Sun 12 to 3, 7 to 10.30; bar food all week L 12 to 2, Mon to Sat D 5.30 to 7; restaurant all week L 12 to 2, Mon to Sat D 6 to 9.15*
Details *No children Car park Wheelchair access (also WC) Garden and patio No smoking in dining-room No music Dogs on leads in bar only Access, Amex, Switch, Visa*

HILLTOP Shropshire map 5

▲ *Wenlock Edge Inn*

VIEWS

Hilltop, Wenlock Edge, nr Easthope
TEL: (01746) 785678 *on B4371, 4½m S of Much Wenlock*

'We offer sparkling water from our own borehole, 190 feet down through the Wenlock Edge,' states the menu: is this a first for British pubs? The Waring family takes as much trouble over its food, wine and beer as it does over its water. The same menu applies throughout the inn, although tables in the no-smoking dining-room are bookable. A reporter who stayed for a few days enthused over Orkney herrings, Shrewsbury lamb in spicy redcurrant sauce, Hereford chicken – 'a delicate dish cooked in apples and cider' – and Shropshire venison pie. Among the puddings may be Bakewell tart, chocolate chimney (a combination of chocolate ice-cream, flake and sauce), or tipsy banana with Tia Maria. Hobsons Best and Town Crier, and Ruddles Best are on draught, with usually around four wines by the glass, and a full list of over 30 bottles. The pub is near one of the highest points of Wenlock Edge and has superb views: west across Apedale towards the Cambrian mountains; and south towards Brown Clee, Shropshire's highest peak. SAMPLE DISHES: mushrooms with garlic and sherry £3.40; prawn and smoked haddock gratin £6.50; plum sponge £2.90.

Open *Tue to Sat 11.30 to 2.30, Mon to Sat 6 to 11, Sun 12 to 2.30, 7 to 10.30; bar food and restaurant Tue to Sun L 12 to 2, D 12 to 2, 7 to 9*
Details *Children welcome in eating areas Car park Wheelchair access Patio No smoking in restaurant No music Dogs welcome in bar only Access, Amex, Delta, Switch, Visa Accommodation: 4 rooms, B&B £45 to £70*

HINDON Wiltshire map 2

▲ *Lamb at Hindon*

Hindon TEL: (01747) 820573
on B3089, 16m W of Salisbury

Up to 300 horses were stabled in Hindon when it was an important staging-post for coaches travelling the London–West Country road – although William Pitt was discomfited to find no fresh horses for him on his journey of 1786. The Lamb sits comfortably with its stone-built neighbours in the little town, and the interior echoes with the past. Beams in the ox-blood ceiling, a great log-burning inglenook, panelling and ticking clocks give atmosphere to the bar, and a back room has another log-burning fire. Appropriately, the cooking has a homely, country feel, with dishes like broccoli and leek soup, game casserole, or pork chop with mustard sauce, for example. Fish dishes range from gratin of seafood with leeks and samphire, to cod with prawn mayonnaise, while puddings are English classics like plum fool. Wadworth 6X and Cottage Wheeltappers Ale are on draught, with ten wines announced on a blackboard and around 50 on the list. SAMPLE DISHES: mussels with garlic and cream £5; pigeon pie £6; summer pudding £3.

Open *11am to 11pm, Sun 12 to 3, 7 to 10.30; bar food and restaurant 12 to 2, 7 to 10 (9.30 restaurant)*
Details *Children welcome Car park Wheelchair access (also WC) Garden and patio No smoking in restaurant No music Dogs welcome Access, Amex, Delta, Switch, Visa Accommodation: 14 rooms, B&B £38 to £85*

HOLNE Devon **map 1**

▲ *Church House Inn*

Holne TEL: (01364) 631208
off A38 and A3357, just S of Ashburton

'Stunning countryside,' was one reporter's description of this fourteenth-century inn's setting, with Dartmoor National Park and the river Dart valley on its doorstep. Oliver Cromwell reportedly stayed here during the Civil War; nowadays customers tend to be holidaymakers and hikers, as well as locals popping in for a drink. A wide, pillared porch with benches leads into two bars, divided by a heavy, sixteenth-century oak partition. The printed menu offers good-value, homely food, and the kitchen makes good use of local produce: starters include soups, terrines and pâtés, mushrooms in garlic butter, and the like; while main courses are principally grilled fish and meat – trout, whole lemon sole, and ribeye steak, for example. More adventurous specials are listed on the blackboard, where you could find lambs' liver with cream and sherry sauce, 'very good' Dartmoor rabbit pie, or baked salmon with lemon herb butter. At lunch-time there are also pub staples like ploughman's, filled jacket potatoes and sandwiches. Local Salcombe ice-cream is available alongside fruit crumble and bread-and-butter pudding for dessert. The 'Maison de l'Eglise' restaurant offers Sunday lunch, and an à la carte menu in the evenings.

Beers on handpump include local Dartmoor Best and Butcombe Bitter as well as Old Speckled Hen and Wadworth 6X. Around 40 bins feature on the wine list, including a number of half-bottles; wines are also chalked on a board, and a selection is available by the glass. A few miles down the road is Buckfast Abbey. SAMPLE DISHES:

half a pint of prawns in the shell with bread and butter £4.25; casserole of pork with orange, sage and dumplings £6.25; treacle tart £3.

Open *11.30 to 3, 6.30 to 11 (10.30 Mon to Thur Nov to Feb), Sun 12 to 3, 7 to 10.30; bar food Mon to Sat 12 to 2.15, 6.30 to 9.15, Sun 12 to 2.30, 7 to 9; restaurant Sun L 12 to 1.30, Tue to Sat 7 to 9*
Details *Children welcome in bar eating area Car park Wheelchair access Patio No smoking in dining-room Live music Dogs welcome on a lead Access, Visa Accommodation: 6 rooms, B&B £20 to £28*

HOPTON WAFERS Shropshire map 5

▲ *Crown Inn*

Hopton Wafers, nr Cleobury Mortimer TEL: (01299) 270372
on A4117, between Kidderminster and Ludlow

A reporter sets the scene: 'It's a fantastic area, like a miniature Dartmoor, all small-scale extremely steep hills covered only in gorse.' The building is 'thoroughly creeper covered', the bar has beams heavy with hops and hunting prints on the walls. The bar menu features such things as sauté mushrooms with crispy bacon, Cumberland sausage and mash, and vegetable risotto, while the specials board moves into the realms of pan-fried local rabbit with wild mushroom and sloe gin sauce. To finish, there might be tiramisù, or bavarois with Greek yoghurt and toasted almonds. A great reason for calling in here is the classy wine list, which has 'unusually good' house wines by the glass bolstered by abundant half-bottles. Higsons Bitter, Boddingtons and Marston's Pedigree are on draught. For those with an appetite for history, Stokesay Castle (possibly the oldest fortified manor house in England), is within reach. SAMPLE DISHES: feta cheese, olives and mixed salad £4.25; mandarin chicken stir-fry £7.75; pan-fried strawberries with vanilla ice £3.75.

Open *12 to 3, 6 to 11, Sun 12 to 3, 7 to 10.30; bar food 12.15 to 2.30, 6.15 to 9.30; restaurant Sun L 12.15 to 2.30, all week D 7.30 to 9.30*
Details *Children welcome Car park Wheelchair access (also WC) Garden and patio No smoking in restaurant Background music No dogs Access, Delta, Switch, Visa Accommodation: 8 rooms, B&B £42 to £68*

Assessments of wine in pubs is based largely on what is available in the bar. Many pubs also have full restaurant wine lists.

Licensing hours and bar food times are based on information supplied by each establishment and are correct at the time of going to press.

HORNDON Devon **map 1**

Elephant's Nest

Horndon, nr Mary Tavy TEL: (01822) 810273
off A386 Tavistock to Okehampton road, 4m NE of Tavistock

This used to be the New Inn, but it was later re-named in honour of a rotund landlord with a huge, bushy beard who was always to be found seated behind the bar. That's the story, anyway. The building, which started life as a cluster of miners' cottages in a remote corner of Dartmoor, still bears witness to its age and history with a cosy stone-walled interior, polished slate floors, heavy old beams and boarded ceilings. It is a great summer destination for walkers and holidaymakers. Food is chalked on a big blackboard and in addition to standard offerings like ploughman's, steak and kidney pie, and chilli, you will find more exotic specials, including Greek salad with lemon dressing, Gujarati beef curry, and Mediterranean chickpeas with pitta bread. By contrast, desserts are familiar things like treacle and walnut tart, pineapple cheesecake, and steamed plum pudding; ice-creams are from Salcombe and Langage Farm. Boddington's, Palmers IPA and St Austell HSD are bolstered by two regularly changing guest ales, and you can also get Inch's cider on draught. The wine list runs to around 30 bins. SAMPLE DISHES: Stilton and walnut pâté £3.25; lamb and lentil hotpot £4.75; sticky butterscotch slice £2.25.

Open *11.30 to 2.30, 6.30 to 11, Sun 12 to 2.30, 7 to 10.30; bar food 11.30 (12 Sun) to 2, 6.30 to 10 (7 to 9.30 Sun)*
Details *Children welcome in dining-room Car park Garden Background music Dogs welcome on a lead No cards*

HORNDON ON THE HILL Essex **map 3**

▲ *Bell Inn*

High Road, Horndon on the Hill
TEL: (01375) 673154 *off M25 Jct. 30/31, signposted Thurrock, Lakeside; take A13, then B1007 to Horndon*

The construction of the Bell got under way during Tudor times and this historic coaching-inn has been a witness to many interesting incidents since then; a plaque records that a certain Thomas Higbed was burned at the stake here for heresy in 1555. The interior is awash with ancient timbers, but the pub's most bizarre feature is the collection of hot-cross buns nailed to one of the ceiling beams – a tradition that dates back almost a century (there's even a stone specimen donated during wartime, when supplies were scarce).

As for the food of today, 'there's a skilled hand in the kitchen', observed one reporter. Menus are peppered with up-to-the-minute brasserie ideas: the soup might be cream of ratatouille, or roast parsnip with honey; spicy crab-cakes come with creamed leeks; and the sauté chicken livers served with black pudding, poached egg and mayonnaise would make a quirky, up-market breakfast. In more substantial vein, you might find roast monkfish with shallot and garlic confit, knuckle of pork with apples and calvados, and breast of chicken with couscous, lemon and olive oil. The more conventional palate isn't ignored either: traditional dishes – albeit with a twist or two – include duck and venison terrine with home-made piccalilli, corned beef hash with oyster mushrooms, and steak and kidney pie. Desserts show the same blend of familiarity and fashion – plum tarte Tatin with crème anglaise, steamed chocolate pudding with chocolate sauce, for example. Thirteen wines, including fizz from the Czech Republic, are offered by the glass, and the full list of 100 bins is wide ranging and well constructed. The Bell dispensed 144 different guest beers in 1996, and Fuller's London Pride, Bass and Highgate IPA are always on draught. Hill House, a more recent building a couple of doors down the street, provides hotel accommodation in tandem with the inn. SAMPLE DISHES: hot tomato and basil pesto tart £4; fillet of salmon with mussels and chive butter £10; apple meringue pie with citrus sorbet £3.50.

Open *11 to 2.30, 6 to 11, Sun 12 to 3, 7 to 10.30; bar food and restaurant 12 to 2 (exc. restaurant Sat L), 6.30 to 10; no food 25 and 26 Dec*
Details *Children welcome in eating areas Car park Wheelchair access Patio No-smoking area No music No dogs Access, Amex, Delta, Switch, Visa Accommodation: 14 rooms, room only £45 to £60*

HORNINGSEA Cambridgeshire map 6

Plough and Fleece

Horningsea TEL: (01223) 860795
off A45, 4m NE of Cambridge

This three-hundred-year-old, Grade II-listed pub was built in the Dutch-style and stands in the high street of a quiet village. Inside, the charming main bar is beamed, with a quarry-tiled floor and rustic furniture, and the dining-room – a newer extension – is equally well appointed. Popular with locals, businessmen, students and shoppers escaping Cambridge city centre, the pub is well known for its friendly atmosphere and home-cooked food, which has a traditional flavour well in keeping with the ambience of the place – you won't find Muzak or electronic games here. On the menu, devilled crab rubs shoulders with home-made pâté and ploughman's, while main courses range from shepherd's pie, and honey-roast guinea-fowl, to beef Wellington. Desserts include traditional lemon cheesecake with sultanas, and 'figgy sly pie'. Greene King, IPA and Abbot Ale, are on draught and wines are available by the glass. Nearby is the War Museum at Duxford and Anglesea Abbey. SAMPLE DISHES: hot garlic cockles £3.25; Barbary duck breast £9.50; cherry cobbler £2.50.

Open *11.30 to 2.30, 7 to 11.30, Sun 12 to 2, 7 to 10.30; bar food and restaurant all week L 12 to 2 (1.30 Sun), Tue to Sat D 7 to 9.30*
Details *Children welcome in dining-room Car park Wheelchair access (also women's WC) Garden and patio No smoking in restaurant No music Dogs welcome in public bar only Access, Amex, Switch, Visa*

HORRINGER **Suffolk** **map 6**

Beehive

Horringer TEL: (01284) 735260
on A143, 3m SW of Bury St Edmunds

'Keep your eyes peeled' for this attractive flint pub, advises a regular, 'as it looks like a house.' Creepers climb the walls, and there's a little garden at the front as well as plenty of landscaped space at the back. Inside, it feels homely, with several 'deliberately dark' rooms where you can hide yourself away in a corner. Terracotta tiled floors add to the mood, and the whole place is run with friendly efficiency.

The printed menu changes four times a year and the kitchen is ever-ready to take on board new ideas, although some dishes are fixtures – by popular demand. The light side of things is represented by home-made taramasalata, scrambled eggs with wild mushrooms and horseradish, steak sandwiches and the like, but the kitchen proves its worth with more substantial stuff. 'Perfectly cooked' calf's liver comes with a splendid reduction of stock and double cream with plenty of chopped tarragon leaves ('This is what I expect in a sauce!' commented the recipient), while pan-fried escalope of beef is served with a genuine provençale sauce topped with cheese. Fish also shows up favourably in the shape of baked fillet of salmon with a peanut crust and ginger and chilli butter, or sauté of scallops, monkfish and crayfish tails. Puddings could be as simple as banoffi pie, or Greek yoghurt with honey. The Beehive is a Greene King pub with IPA and Abbot Ale kept in good condition, but it's worth taking time to explore the wine list: around 20 well-chosen bottles are backed up by a blackboard listing wines by the glass. Nearby is the Ickworth Rotunda (National Trust) as well as Rede Farm Park. SAMPLE DISHES: chicken liver and pistachio pâté £4; Cumberland sausages braised in red wine and bacon sauce £6; banana cheesecake with toffee sauce £3.

Open *11.30 to 2.30, 7 to 11, Sun 12 to 2.30, 7 to 10.30; bar food 12 to 2, 7 to 9.30 (9 Sun)*
Details *Children welcome Car park Wheelchair access Garden and patio No music No dogs Access, Switch, Visa*

HORSEBRIDGE Hampshire map 2

John of Gaunt

Horsebridge, nr Stockbridge TEL: (01794) 388394
1m off A3057, 8m W of Winchester

Its location on the Test Valley walk means that this agreeable village pub gets its share of ramblers – as well as anglers hoping for a catch in the river. Traditional pub fare features on the everyday menu: burgers, gammon with pineapple, steak and kidney pudding, deep-fried plaice, and so on. More enterprising dishes appear on the blackboard, and could include tuna fish-cakes, turkey à la king, leek and potato pie, and 'excellent' wild duck with red wine and black cherry sauce, with 'tender, just pink' meat. Orange bread-and-butter pudding and apple pie with custard may be among the desserts. Palmers IPA and Ringwood Best and Fortyniner are on draught, and house wines are served by the glass. Mottisfont Abbey Garden (National Trust), a few miles down the road towards Romsey, is a must for garden-lovers, particularly when its roses are in bloom. Plans are afoot to open a couple of bedrooms in 1997, the licensees tell us. SAMPLE DISHES: chicken and sweetcorn soup £1.50; fish pie £5.25; spotted dick £1.75.

Open *11.30 to 2.30 (3 Fri and Sat), 6 to 11, Sun 12 to 3, 7 to 10.30; bar food 12 to 2, 7 to 9.30*
Details *Children welcome Car park Wheelchair access (also WC) Patio Background music Dogs welcome No cards*

HOUGHTON CONQUEST Bedfordshire map 6

▲ *Knife & Cleaver*

The Grove, Houghton Conquest TEL: (01234) 740387
between A6 and B530, 5m S of Bedford

The Knife & Cleaver (so called because it was at one time an abattoir and butcher's shop) is in the centre of the village opposite the medieval parish church. The vast majority of people who come here eat in the spacious, plant-filled conservatory restaurant. A separate menu is served in the bar, with its panelling, open fires, exposed beams and tasteful old prints. The menu kicks off with a daily soup (perhaps tomato and sage), mixed hors d'oeuvre and interesting filled breads (a toasted muffin with crabmeat, for example) and moves on to salmon fish-cakes, pan-fried lamb's kidneys on tapénade toast, and lamb and leek pie. In addition there are daily specials like prawn and potato pasty, beef cobbler, or halibut rarebit. Caramelised orange slices, and pear tart are fruity alternatives to chocolate mousse or crème brûlée for those wanting a sweet. More than 20 wines, including champagne, are sold by the glass, while the full, sensibly chosen list runs to over 100 bins, with a handful of classic clarets. Beer-drinkers can go for either Adnams Extra or Bateman XB. SAMPLE DISHES: Loch Fyne oysters baked with Stilton £6; three-game casserole £5.25; sticky toffee pudding £2.50.

Open *11 to 3, 6 to 11, Sun 12 to 3; bar food and restaurant all week L 12 to 2.30 (exc restaurant Sat; last orders bar 2 Sat L), Mon to Sat D 7 to 9.30*
Details *Children welcome in dining-room Car park Wheelchair access (also WC) Garden and patio No smoking in restaurant while others eat Background and live music No dogs Access, Amex, Delta, Diners, Visa Accommodation: 9 rooms, B&B £38 to £69*

HUBBERHOLME North Yorkshire map 8

▲ *George Inn*

Hubberholme TEL: (01756) 760223
off B6160 at Buckden, 20m N of Skipton

J.B. Priestley loved Hubberholme so much that he chose to have his ashes scattered in its ancient churchyard. The attraction of the tiny hamlet is obvious: its setting at the head of Wharfedale is stunning, the waters of the Wharfe running past over limestone pavements. The pub itself is unspoilt, with rustic stone walls, flagged floors and beamed ceilings. It's highly popular in summer, especially with walkers and cyclists; and in winter, locals and hardened outdoor enthusiasts cluster around the open wood-burning stove. Theakston Black Bull Bitter, Morland Old Speckled Hen and Younger Scotch Bitter are among the well-kept real ales, and the wine list extends to around 40 bins. Snacks like sandwiches and ploughman's flesh out the menu at lunch-times, but those with heartier appetites could opt for vegetable soup, or garlic mussels followed by pan-fried duck breast in Madeira gravy, fillet of salmon with parsley sauce, or steak and kidney pie. A brandy-snap basket filled with ice-cream and berry sauce is a good way to end a meal. SAMPLE DISHES: trout pâté £3.25;

Dales lamb chops baked with garlic and rosemary £10; apple pie £2.50.

Open *11.30 to 3 (4 Sat), 6 to 11, Sun 12 to 4, 7 to 10.30; bar food 12 to 2, 6.30 to 9*
Details *Children welcome in bar eating area   Car park   Wheelchair access   Garden   No music   Dogs welcome   Access, Visa   Accommodation: 6 rooms, B&B £25 to £54*

IBSLEY   Hampshire **map 2**

Old Beams Inn

Salisbury Road, Ibsley   TEL: (01425) 473387
just off A388 between Fordingbridge and Ringwood

Originally a pair of medieval cottages, then a tearoom during the Second World War, this eye-catching timbered and thatched pub now does a roaring trade catering for visitors to the New Forest and the Avon Valley. The original part of the building is taken up with the restaurant, while those wanting drinks and more informal food head for the more modern open-plan bar with its dark wood furniture and central hooded fireplace. An excellent range of real ales is always on show: drinkers could opt for Ringwood Best or Old Thumper, Eldridge Pope Royal Oak, Gales HSB or other big names from breweries in the region. A cold buffet of meats, seafood and salads is a major draw on the food side of things; otherwise the extensive specials board lists steamed meat pudding, chargrilled steaks, beef bourguignon and various fresh fish such as Dover sole. More than 50 wines feature on the list and you can order 'wines of the world' by the glass. SAMPLE DISHES: chilled melon boat £2; pork fillet in mustard sauce £7.25; chocolate gâteau £2.50.

Open *10.30 to 2.30, 6 to 11, Sun 12 to 3, 6.30 to 10.30; bar food and restaurant 12 to 2.15, 7 to 9.45; closed 25 amd 26 Dec evenings; restaurant closed Sun D*
Details *Children welcome in family room   Car park   Wheelchair access (also WC)   Garden and patio   No-smoking area   No music   Dogs welcome away from food area   Access, Amex, Diners, Visa*

ICKLINGHAM Suffolk map 6

Red Lion

High Street, Icklingham TEL: (01638) 717802
on A1101, 7m NW of Bury St Edmunds

The Neolithic Icknield Way runs through the village of Icklingham, linking the Norfolk coast with southern England, although this spacious, thatched pub dates merely from the sixteenth century. Character is provided by beams, wooden tables and chairs, rugs and antiques, log fires and candlelight. Bar food is backed up by more ambitious daily specials, all of which are listed on blackboards. Typical dishes range from melon with prawns, smoked salmon and avocado, to Newmarket sausages, or grilled plaice and bonito. Readers have endorsed 'first-rate' Barnsley chop, huntsman's grill (wild boar bacon, venison steak, sausage and liver), and 'perfect' raspberry mousse. Greene King IPA, Rayments and Abbot Ale are well-kept, and the wine list is bolstered by a selection of up to 20 English country wines. SAMPLE DISHES: mixed hors d'oeuvre £6; pork chops glazed with honey and mustard £8.50; hot chocolate nut pudding £3.25.

Open *12 to 2.30, 6 to 10, Sun 12 to 2.30, 7 to 9; bar food and restaurant 12 to 2.30, 6 to 10 (7.15 to 9 Sun)*
Details *Children welcome Car park Wheelchair access (also WC) Garden and patio Background music Guide dogs only Access, Visa*

IGHTHAM Kent map 3

▲ *Harrow Inn* ✿

Common Road, Ightham Common TEL: (01732) 885912
just off A25 Sevenoaks to Borough Green road

'On an autumnal evening the scent of woodsmoke fills the air as you walk from the car park,' commented a traveller about this 300-year-old village pub covered in creepers. The log fire acts as a divider between the two bars: one has a pool table, with pop Muzak as an accompaniment; the slightly 'cramped' front bar comes complete with shelves of books along the window ledges, fresh flowers and candles. A racing-car enthusiast put up the pictures and an ancient dashboard is suspended over the counter. Tables are squeezed into both areas.

The kitchen works to a blackboard menu of manageable proportions, and dishes are diverse without resorting to voguish overkill. Prices are reasonable, and all produce is fresh. Voluminous tureens of soup are served with a whole brown cob on a bread board, complete with knife and a slab of butter. Alternatives are moules marinière, and platters of smoked fish, plus an eclectic mixed bag ranging from pork meatballs and dumplings, and Irish stew to flash-fried chicken satay with the accompanying spicy peanut sauce mixed into a commendably dressed salad ('a novel interpretation of what has become a pub staple,' concluded one reporter). As a finale, try 'excellent' sticky pear pudding on a base of single cream tinged with raspberry coulis, or raisin and apple brûlée. There's a 'popular' restaurant at the back of the pub dealing in more elaborate dishes, for those wanting dinner or Sunday lunch. Greene King IPA, Abbot Ale and Marston's Pedigree are on draught and six house wines are served by the glass in the bar. SAMPLE DISHES: spiced carrot and parsnip soup £2.75; Toulouse sausage and mash £5.50; chocolate marquise £3.

Open *12 to 3, 6.30 to 11, Sun 12 to 3, 7 to 10.30; bar food all week L 12 to 2, Tue to Sat D 7 to 9.30; restaurant Sun L 12 to 2.30, all week D 7 to 10*
Details *Children welcome in dining-room Car park Garden Background music Dogs welcome on a lead Access, Amex, Delta, Switch, Visa Accommodation: 2 rooms, B&B £28 to £45*

INGBIRCHWORTH South Yorkshire map 9

Fountain Inn

Wellthorne Road, Ingbirchworth TEL: (01226) 763125
just off A629 Huddersfield to Sheffield road, 6m W of Barnsley

In a peaceful setting off the A629, this white-painted stone pub is a popular and traditional haunt – much appreciated for its friendliness and good value. Displays of cups and crockery catch the eye in the spacious interior, although most interest centres on the blackboards and printed menus. The repertoire is noticeably lively for a country pub in South Yorkshire: crispy Peking ducks' legs with cucumber relish, deep-fried goats' cheese with home-made piccalilli, salmon and broccoli pancakes with lobster sauce, and marinated lamb steak with roasted shallots and rosemary gravy, for example. Otherwise expect haddock and chips with mushy peas, mushroom lasagne, grilled gammon, and bangers and mash, followed by seasonal fruit brûlées and crumbles as well as jam roly-poly and hot lemon pudding. Monday is 'steak and wine night', while on Tuesday there's a reduced-price menu that includes a fish dish with a free glass of bubbly; in addition, a two-course 'cheap menu' is served most lunchtimes and early evening. Fifteen wines provide sound everyday drinking, and beer drinkers can opt for Tetley Bitter or Marston's Pedigree. SAMPLE DISHES: Stilton croquettes with Waldorf salad and balsamic dressing £3; ham, leek and pasta bake £5.75; pear and almond tart with raspberry sauce £2.75.

Open *Mon to Sat 11.30 to 2.30, 5 to 11, Sun 12 to 10.30; bar food Mon to Sat 11.30 to 2, 5 to 9.30, Sun 12 to 9.30*
Details *Children welcome Car park Wheelchair access (also WC) Garden No smoking in 2 areas Background music No dogs Access, Switch, Visa*

ITCHEN ABBAS Hampshire map 2

▲ *Trout*

Itchen Abbas TEL: (01962) 779537
on B3047 between Winchester and New Alresford

Aptly named, as it stands a stone's throw from the River Itchen (a mecca for trout fishermen), this brick and tile-hung village hostelry is also a good base-camp if you fancy exploring the Itchen Way. The pub itself is a homely kind of place with plenty of village atmosphere. Trout from the river is poached and served as a speciality with new potatoes and vegetables; otherwise the short bar menu includes garlic mushrooms, lamb stew, steaks and roasts, backed up by sweets such as rhubarb crumble and treacle tart. Marston's Bitter, Pedigree and Owd Roger are regularly on draught, and a guest beer appears each week. Avington Park and The Watercress Line are within driving distance. SAMPLE DISHES: turkey and vegetable soup £2.25; half crispy duck £10; apple and blackberry pie £3.

Open *Mon to Sat 11 to 3, 6 to 11, Sun 12 to 3, 7 to 10.30; bar food all week 12 to 2, 7 to 9*
Details *Children welcome in eating areas Car park Wheelchair access (also WC) Garden smoking area in dining-room Background music; jukebox Dogs welcome in 1 bar only Access, Amex Accommodation: 6 rooms, B&B £30 to £57*

ITTERINGHAM Norfolk map 6

Walpole Arms

Itteringham Common, Itteringham TEL: (01263) 587258
off B1354, 4m NW of Aylsham

Landlord Paul Simmons has done a grand job in revitalising this attractive brick pub close to the River Bure. The opened-up cottagey interior has been 'recently tended to', although the rough brick walls, beamed ceilings and standing timbers are still in place; a new dining-room had just been completed as we went to press, and work is under way on the back garden. The owners grow their own organic vegetables and buy organic meat from a butcher and grazier in the neighbourhood. Norfolk produce shows up favourably in the shape of deep bowls of Morston mussels, casseroled local rabbit, pigeon pie and gammon stew with dumplings. Home-made soups are 'pleasing', pasta is the fresh kind. A separate blackboard lists desserts ranging from mixed fruit Bakewell tart to sticky toffee pudding. Beers on handpump are East Anglian favourites such as Adnams Bitter, Broadside and Woodforde's Great Eastern, as well as Bass. Six wines are offered by the glass. Itteringham is between Blickling Hall and the gardens, lakes and woods of Mannington Hall. SAMPLE DISHES: cream of broccoli soup £2; cod with cheese and prawn sauce £6.75; chocolate fudge cake £2.50.

Open *12 to 3, 6 to 11, Sun 12 to 3, 7 to 10.30; bar food and restaurant all week L 12 to 2, Tue to Sun D 7 to 9*
Details *Children welcome in eating areas Car park Wheelchair access (also WC) Garden and patio No smoking in restaurant Background and live music No dogs during food-serving times Access, Delta, Switch, Visa*

IXWORTH Suffolk **map 6**

Pykkerell

High Street, Ixworth TEL: (01359) 230398
off A143 Bury St Edmunds to Diss road

Day-trippers to Ixworth might be interested in the guided tours and demonstrations at Pakenham Watermill, and the fully operational Pakenham Windmill. Both are near this fifteenth-century coaching-inn. One menu is served in bar and restaurant alike, and there's much to whet the appetite: Cromer crab-cakes on red pepper coulis, linguine with prawn and bacon sauce, and smoked salmon with raspberry vinaigrette are among the starters; while main courses take in rack of lamb with blueberry and mint sauce, warm chicken and crispy pasta salad, and Gressingham duck with Victoria plum and stem ginger sauce. A seasonal fish dish is always chalked up, and sticky treacle tart may round things off. Beams and a log fire in the lounge are what you would expect of an inn of this age in rural Suffolk, but the Pykkerell also has an historic armoury, not to mention a timber-framed Elizabethan barn across the courtyard. Greene King Abbot Ale and IPA are on draught and the short but sensibly chosen wine list has something for everyone. SAMPLE DISHES: Arbroath smokies with tomato and ginger chutney £4; venison steak and liver with wild boar chop and sausage £12; crème brûlée £3.25.

Open *12 to 2.30, 6 to 11, Sun 12 to 2.30, 7 to 10.30; bar food and restaurant 12 to 2.30, 6 to 10*

Details *Children welcome Car park Wheelchair access (also WC) Patio Background music Dogs welcome Access, Delta, Switch, Visa*

KEYSTON Cambridgeshire map 6

Pheasant Inn

Keyston TEL: (01832) 710241
on B663, 1m S of junction with A604

'What a glorious old thatched pub,' commented one reporter as he approached the Pheasant. Inside, it is divided up into a series of open-plan rooms with beams and black-painted farm implements hanging from the ceiling. Informality reigns, menus are flexible: you can just eat, just drink, or do both; and you can choose to sit in the bar or reserve a table in the slightly more formal Red Room with its bigger tables and linen napkins.

The menu is a fiercely modern assemblage of up-to-the-minute ideas with noticeable Mediterranean overtones, plus a few sticks of lemon grass and other oriental flavours tossed in for good measure. Here you will find salad of chargrilled monkfish with roasted peppers, cherry tomatoes and a herb dressing sitting next to chicken, wild mushroom and basil sausage with braised lentils. There's also a hearty undercurrent to dishes such as roast pigeon breasts with braised cabbage and roast potatoes, and tenderloin of pork with a beetroot purée, caramelised apples and calvados sauce. Those wishing to by-pass meat are well served by grilled basil polenta with wild mushrooms, artichoke, tomatoes and herbs; or an onion tart with sweet peppers, courgettes and coriander. In the words of one reporter, chef Martin Lee 'has a very sure touch – delicious food, [with] intense flavours and attractively presented'. Desserts also get their share of praise: a caramel soufflé with prune and Armagnac ice-cream impressed one diner, while another was equally delighted by banana filo parcels. Alternatively, there are unpasteurised cheeses from Neal's Yard. The Pheasant is part of the independent Huntsbridge Group (see entries for the Three Horseshoes, Madingley, and the White Hart, Great Yeldham), so the wine list is top-class: 13 – including Pommery Champagne – are offered by the glass; the rest is a highly knowledgeable selection grouped according to style. Adnams Bitter pleases the beer drinkers, and guest ales provide a touch of variety. SAMPLE DISHES: terrine of poultry with marinated vegetables à la grecque £4; grilled fillet of salmon with Swiss chard, new potatoes, herb purée and olive oil £12; chestnut parfait with praline sauce and caramelised hazelnuts £4.50.

Open *11 to 3, 6 to 11, Sun 12 to 2, 7 to 10.30; bar food and restaurant 12 to 2, 6 (7 Sun) to 10*

Details *Children welcome Car park Wheelchair access No smoking in dining-room No music Dogs welcome in bar only Access, Amex, Delta, Diners, Switch, Visa*

KILVE Somerset map 2

▲ *Hood Arms*

Kilve TEL: (01278) 741210
on A39, 3m NW of Nether Stowey

That famous seafarer Admiral Hood was born and bred at nearby Kilve Court; hence the family name of this spick-and-span coaching-inn on the fringes of the Quantock Hills within a mile of the 'foaming brine'. Inside it is spacious and uncluttered, with plenty of tables dotted around and prints lining the walls. Best bets as regards bar food are the blackboard specials – a changing slate that might include such things as avocado and prawn 'medley', chicken with gammon and leeks in a puff pastry nest, or salmon and haddock bake, and spicy minced lamb in chilli sauce served on a bed of aubergines and topped with a cheese dumpling. 'Vanessa's Pudding Pantry' contains knickerbocker glory, treacle tart and old English trifle, to name but three. A short *carte* is also served in the Countryman restaurant. Cotleigh Tawny Bitter and Exmoor Ale are on handpump beside Flowers Original, and 15 everyday wines appear on the 'bar list'. Dodington Hall and Coleridge Cottage (National Trust) are two nearby attractions. SAMPLE DISHES: carrot and orange soup £2.50; steak, ale and mushroom pie £5.75; raspberry and apple pie £2.50.

Open *11 (11.45 winter) to 2.30, 6 to 11, Sun 12 to 2, 7 to 10.30; bar food and restaurant 12 to 2, 6.30 to 10*
Details *Children welcome in eating areas Car park Wheelchair access Garden and patio No-smoking area in restaurant Background music No dogs Access, Delta, Switch, Visa Accommodation: 5 rooms, B&B £20 to £62*

KIMBOLTON Hereford & Worcester map 5

Stockton Cross Inn

Kimbolton TEL: (01568) 612509
on A4112, 1m NE of Leominster

'The establishment so impressed us that we returned, driving from Cardiff, with the family,' wrote one couple after discovering this timbered cottage pub. Within, it is heavily beamed, with horse brasses, hops and firearms for decoration, and there's a wonderful fireplace. Three blackboards list the vast range of dishes coming out of the kitchen: there may be as many as 20 main courses on offer. You could start with black pudding with bacon and melted cheese, locally smoked duck breast, or curried prawns in crisp potato shells, then go on to salmon pasta, venison in red wine, leg of lamb with mint and onion sauce, or steak and kidney pie. Traditional desserts such as bread-and-butter pudding, or a brandy-snap fruit basket round things off. Flowers Original and Castle Eden Ale are on draught, along with two ciders and a small choice of wines by the glass. SAMPLE DISHES: smoked prawns £4.50; pork tenderloin stuffed with spinach £10.50; treacle tart £3.

Open *all week 12 to 3, Tue to Sun 7 to 11 (10.30 Sun); bar food all week 12 to 2.15, Tue to Sun 7 to 9.30*
Details *No children Car park Wheelchair access Garden No-smoking area Background music No dogs Access, Visa*

KINGSTEIGNTON Devon map 1

Old Rydon Inn 🍇

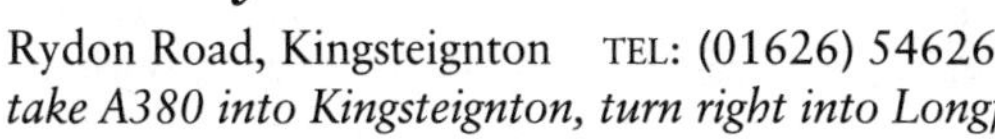

Rydon Road, Kingsteignton TEL: (01626) 54626
take A380 into Kingsteignton, turn right into Longford Lane, turn right again at base of hill into Rydon Road

The Devon name 'rydon' comes from the old English 'ryge dun', meaning hill of rye, and the sign outside this ancient converted farmhouse shows a former tenant harvesting his crop. The building, which dates from the times of Henry II, has been substantially renovated over the years: the pub part is in the former stables, with the old cider apple loft upstairs; there's also a flower-filled conservatory and dining-room, not to mention a sheltered walled garden for fine days. It's cheerfully atmospheric and highly popular, and generally produces food that is a notch above the local average. The blackboard menu is an exciting read, moving quickly from ploughman's and jacket potatoes into the eclectic world of mushroom risotto with fried black pudding, Indonesian nasi goreng, venison, pigeon and hare pie with red cabbage and spätzli, and warm salad of chicken breast with ginger, honey and mustard dressing. Puddings continue the same theme: apricot and raspberry trifle with mascarpone and amaretti topping, for example. More ambitious food is served in the restaurant. The wine list spans the globe for interesting, good-value drinking, and there's a useful showing of half-bottles. Beer drinkers have a choice of Bass, Wadworth 6X and a guest ale. SAMPLE DISHES: smoked salmon and egg mayonnaise £3.25; lamb chilli con carne £5; lemon meringue pie £2.50.

Open *11 to 2.30, 6 to 11, Sun 12 to 3, 7 to 10.30; bar food 12 to 2 (2.30 Sun), 7 to 9.30; restaurant Mon to Sat D only 7 to 9.30*
Details *Children in conservatory and upstairs only Car park Wheelchair access Garden and patio No smoking in dining-room Background music No dogs Access, Amex, Delta, Diners, Switch, Visa*

KINGSTON NEAR LEWES East Sussex map 3

Juggs

The Street, Kingston near Lewes TEL: (01273) 472523
off A27, 2m SW of Lewes

'They walked from Brighton/The Juggs ladies of old/With fish in their baskets/Their wares to be sold,' runs the rhyme which explains the unlikely name of this sympathetically modernised 500-year-old pub. The main bar is a long, low space with rooms at each end 'where the serious eating is done'. The kitchen used to house the occupants' livestock, but now it has a very different role. What it delivers is a short menu of mainly home-cooked dishes done with a splash of 'genuine skill': the sight of the food coming from the kitchen on baking trays 'cheered the spirit' of one eagle-eyed visitor. By-passing ploughman's, sandwiches and 'huge' starters such as vegetable soup and pots of prawns, he went straight for main-course specials – kedgeree of smoked salmon and spinach in a plait, and a Brie and leek quiche – both of which passed muster with flying colours. Desserts are equally appealing: the red berry brûlée 'looked wonderful' in its transparent dish, while the apricot and almond tart impressed with the quality of its shortcrust pastry. Only a limited menu is available Sunday lunch-time. Well-kept draught beers include reliable southern names such as Harveys Best and King & Barnes Festive; the modest wine list is notable for its low prices. SAMPLE DISHES: mackerel pâté with hot pitta bread £3.50; spaghetti bolognese £5.25; chocolate brownie with hot fudge sauce £3.

Open *11 to 2.30, 6 to 10.30, Sun 12 to 2.30, 7 to 10.30; bar food 12 to 2, 6 (7 Sun) to 9.30*
Details *Children welcome in family rooms Car park Wheelchair access Garden and patio No smoking in restaurant and 1 family room No music Dogs welcome on a lead Access, Switch, Visa*

If you visit any pubs that you think should appear in the Guide, *write to tell us* – The Which? Guide to Country Pubs, *FREEPOST,* 2 *Marylebone Road, London NW1 1YN.*

KINTBURY **Berkshire** **map 2**

▲ *Dundas Arms* ✿ 🍇

53 Station Road, Kintbury TEL: (01488) 658263
½m S of A4, between Newbury and Hungerford

There's nothing like a great waterside setting to bring in the crowds, and the Dundas Arms thrives on its position. It stands at a junction where the River Kennet meets the Kennet & Avon Canal, with trees all around and wildlife doing its thing before your very eyes. There's something engagingly atmospheric about it all – no wonder the tables on the jetty and towpath are snapped up with voracious eagerness. The crowds come for the scene, but also for the wine and the food.

'There has never been a day when we were unable to find something good to eat from the blackboard,' noted one couple after feasting happily on jugged hare, and hock of ham on the bone with parsley sauce and creamy mashed potato. The short bar menu has its fixtures – home-cured gravlax, warm smoked duck breast salad, steak and kidney pie, chocolate pavé with coffee bean sauce – but new dishes surface from time to time. These might be grilled flat mushrooms on Italian bread, hot white bean casserole, or iced orange soufflé with caramel sauce, to name but three tempting possibilities. The style sits comfortably between reassuring familiarity and zesty modernism. In similar vein there's also a restaurant menu offering additional dishes such as casseroled partridge with Chinese cabbage, and grilled fillets of red mullet with sweet saffron onions and carrots. Long-serving landlord David Dalzell-Piper's wine list is majestic: 200 bins span the globe, from clarets and burgundies of great distinction to more up-beat offerings from the New World, right down to some splendid house selections. 'And there can be nothing wrong with the beer,' added one contented visitor, judging by the number of people in the bar – locals, fishermen and river-boat sailors – ordering pints of Morland Original, Bass and Charles Wells Bombardier. SAMPLE DISHES: crab au gratin £4.25; avocado, smoked chicken and prawn salad £7; summer pudding £4.

Open *11 to 2.30, 6 to 11, Sun 12 to 2.30, 7 to 10.30; bar food and restaurant Mon to Sat L 12 to 2, Tue to Sat D 7 to 9*
Details *Children welcome in bar eating area Car park Garden and patio No music No dogs Access, Amex, Delta, Switch, Visa Accommodation: 5 rooms, B&B £55 to £65*

✿ *indicates a pub serving outstanding bar food, backed up by all-round excellence in other departments, such as service, atmosphere and cleanliness.*

KIRDFORD West Sussex map 3

▲ *Half Moon Inn*

Kirdford TEL: (01403) 820223
off A272, 2m W of Wisborough Green

Fish is the focus at this long, tiled pub opposite the village church, reflecting the family's enduring connections with Billingsgate market. Pan-fried baby squid and octopus with garlic butter, and crispy herring roes features among the starters, while main courses run from salmon and cod fish-cakes to baked sea bass stuffed with spring onions, ginger and soy, in addition to simply cooked plaice, skate and lemon sole. Carnivores may prefer pâté followed by spicy lamb kebab from the more restricted meat options. Either way, end the meal with an English pud – treacle sponge, or spotted dick with custard, for example. Fuller's London Pride, Boddingtons and Wadworth 6X are among the real ales, and four house wines are sold by the glass. Kirdford is approached by minor roads off the A272 between Petworth and Billingshurst. Petworth House is famous for its collection of Turners (the artist used to stay here) and its carvings by Grinling Gibbons; deer graze in the parkland laid out by Capability Brown. SAMPLE DISHES: gravlax with mustard and dill sauce £4.25; scallops and bacon salad with raspberry dressing £10.50; blackberry and apple pie £3.

Open *11 to 3, 7 to 11, Sun 11 to 11; bar food and restaurant 12 to 2, 7 to 9.15*
Details *Children welcome in eating areas Car park Wheelchair access Garden No smoking in restaurant Background music Dogs welcome Access, Switch, Visa Accommodation: 3 rooms, B&B £40 to £50*

KIRKBY LONSDALE Cumbria map 8

▲ *Snooty Fox* ✿ 🍇

Main Street, Kirkby Lonsdale TEL: (01524) 271308

'We would go again: it is only 18 miles away,' vowed one couple who are clearly happy to travel in search of good pubs. The Snooty Fox is the most recent incarnation of what was the Green Dragon, and its owners have transformed it from a high-street watering-hole into a stylish venue serving what they call 'gourmet' food. Don't be put off: you won't find any reverential lifting of cloches or hushed tones here. The open-plan interior consists of several distinct areas and 'room is made for kiddies in push chairs'. In the front are pews and tables where you can eat or just relax with a pint of 'creamy'

Theakston Best, Hartleys XB or Timothy Taylor Landlord; if you want to put money in the jukebox or play the games machine, go round the corner. Another area is for non-smokers, and in good weather you can sit out on the terrace.

In the kitchen serious work is in hand. A three-cheese soufflé comes straight from the oven, perfectly light and 'floating on a pool of garlic cream'; seven lightly cooked queen scallops are daintily arranged around a mound of spinach with a luxurious sauce laced with Napoleon brandy. Assured technique is also evident in roast pheasant breast stuffed with sweetbreads and apricots served on tagliatelle with a Madeira and truffle gravy and – to finish – another soufflé, this time iced white chocolate and liquorice with the juice of passion fruit served with sugar-snap biscuits and garnished with gold leaf. As the happy recipient of this lunch-time repast concluded, this is 'a huge cut above a standard bar/restaurant without a corresponding hike in price'. However, if complexity is not what you are looking for, there's also the prospect of deftly executed simple things like leek and potato soup ('tasting of both ingredients') and 'seriously chunky' steak and kidney pudding with first-rate chips and al dente vegetables.

The wine list is quite short but well selected, ranging from a fistful of house wines by the glass to a heady 1953 Chateau Haut Brion weighing in at £250. Kirkby Lonsdale is a charming little town well worth browsing in, and there are also good riverside walks by the banks of the Lune. SAMPLE DISHES: avocado mousse with prawns £3.75; chargrilled chicken breast with creamed leeks and oyster sauce £6; lemon tart £3.75.

Open *11am to 11pm, Sun 12 to 10.30; bar food and restaurant 12 to 2.30, 6.30 to 10, Sun 7 to 9.30 Sun*
Details *Children welcome in eating areas Car park Wheelchair access (also WC) Garden and patio Occasional background music; jukebox Dogs welcome Access, Amex, Delta, Diners, Switch, Visa Accommodation: 9 rooms, B&B £29 to £52*

KIRKBYMOORSIDE North Yorkshire map 9

▲ *George & Dragon*

17 Market Place, Kirkbymoorside TEL: (01751) 433334
off A170, between Helmsley and Pickering

The George & Dragon overlooks the market square of this old market town. Dating from the seventeenth century, it used to be a coaching-inn providing comfort and hospitality to travellers using the route between the old Great North Road and the east coast. Today it offers a warm welcome to visitors exploring the North York Moors National Park, Rievaulx Abbey and other nearby attractions.

Inside is a single, traditional bar with two civilised front rooms with stripped panelling, open fires, beamed ceilings and the landlord's collection of sporting prints and memorabilia. The candlelit restaurant is in the old brewhouse, though the same menu is served in the bar. Black pudding on apple purée, and venison sausages could be among the starters, with rack of lamb with mint gravy, chicken breast braised in Guinness, and salmon fish-cakes with dill sauce forming the centrepieces. Blackboard specials feature a lot of game, fish and vegetarian dishes: perhaps roast pheasant or partridge, fillet of brill with cucumber sauce, and spicy chickpea croquettes. Well-kept Theakston Best Bitter, Timothy Taylor Landlord and Black Sheep Bitter are on draught, and a blackboard lists around 15 wines by the glass. SAMPLE DISHES: pea and ham soup £2.25; jugged hare £9; chocolate and hazelnut roulade £3.

Open *11 to 3, 6 to 11, Sun 12 to 3, 7 to 10.30; bar food and restaurant 12 to 2.15, 6.30 to 9.15*
Details *Children welcome in eating areas Car park Wheelchair access (also WC) Garden and patio No smoking in restaurant Background music No dogs Access, Delta, Switch, Visa Accommodation: 19 rooms, B&B £45 to £85*

KIRTLING Cambridgeshire **map 6**

Queen's Head 🍇

Kirtling TEL: (01638) 731737
off B1063, 5m SE of Newmarket

Gary and Dianne Kingshott of the Beehive, Horringer (see entry) recently bought and revitalised this Elizabethan building dating from 1558. Gone is the run-down interior: in its place is a series of rooms on different levels, with stripped wood tables, comfortable Chesterfields and a plethora of antiques in keeping with the history of the place. Ceilings are mustard, walls 'greeny turquoise', and log fires burn. It has a rather affluent feeling.

The menu is written on blackboard 'strips' and it's a movable feast that changes daily as supplies come and go. Soups are splendid: the creamy fish version with croûtons was greatly enjoyed by one visitor. Elsewhere, there is a near perfect balance between sound traditional pub cooking and things current. So, you can expect steak sandwiches, and local butcher's sausages in red wine *jus* with potatoes to share the limelight with warm salad of chicken and bacon, breast of duck cooked pink with an 'excellent' raspberry and orange vinegar sauce, and braised lamb shank. Added to that you might see stir-fried chicken fillets with vegetables: so authentic 'I almost felt like asking for chopsticks,' commented one recipient. Desserts range from orange bread-and-butter pudding to blueberry cheesecake, not to mention the occasional experimental creation such as a warm crème brûlée-style base with halves of lightly cooked strawberries embedded into it. Greene King IPA and Abbot Ale are kept in good condition, and the short, well-considered wine list has six by the glass. The pub had been open only a few weeks when our inspector called, and Gary Kingshott was taking time off from the Beehive to get the kitchen up and running. The signs are encouraging: reports, please. SAMPLE DISHES: wild mushroom risotto £4; sauté chicken livers with bacon and cherry tomatoes £8; bitter chocolate tart £3.

Open *12 to 2, 6 to 11, Sun 12 to 3; bar food all week L 12 to 2 (2.30 Sun), Mon to Sat D 7 to 9.45, Sun 12 to 2.30*
Details *Children welcome Car park Wheelchair access Garden and patio No music No dogs Access, Delta, Switch, Visa*

Red Lion

Kirtling TEL: (01638) 730162

New owners have transformed this timber-framed building from a village watering-hole into a useful contender in the food stakes – equally popular with locals and punters *en route* to Newmarket Races. 'The bar is lovely,' commented one visitor: rugs are strewn over the quarry-tiled floors, and lighted candles illuminate stripped wood tables in the evening. Bar meals are a relatively recent addition, but the kitchen produces some creditable offerings, including 'silky smooth' chicken-liver pâté, grilled plaice with lemon butter, and Szechuan-style stir-fried beef with rice; there are also one or two more ambitious-sounding dishes such as venison 'olives' stuffed with sun-dried tomatoes and fresh herbs. To finish are desserts including home-made pavlova, and Cambridge burnt cream. The main menu (served in the restaurant in the evening) moves into the realms of roast guinea-fowl with hazelnuts and honeyed apricots, and pan-fried salmon fillet with pine kernels and Dijon mustard sauce. Greene King IPA is bolstered by guest brews such as Nethergate Old Growler and Fuller's ESB. Four house wines are served by the glass, and the list of around 30 is a useful slate from Adnams. SAMPLE DISHES: mussels in white wine, cream and garlic £4; ribeye steak with chips £7; lemon and ginger cheesecake £3.50.

Open *12 to 3, 5 to 11, Sun 12 to 3, 7 to 10.30; bar food Tue to Sun L 12 to 2.30 (3 Sun), Tue to Sat D 7 to 9.30; restaurant Tue to Sun L 12 to 2.30 (3 Sun), Tue to Sat D 7 to 10*
Details *Children welcome in dining-room Car park Patio Background music Dogs welcome in bar only Access, Visa*

KNAPP Somerset map 2

▲ *Rising Sun* 🍇

Knapp, North Curry TEL: (01823) 490436
off A358 Taunton to Langport road at Thornfalcon garage, signed North Curry

The Rising Sun really is off the beaten track: 'you should have seen my car after tackling those narrow muddy lanes,' commented one intrepid traveller. But don't be put off. The building is a lovely fifteenth-century longhouse in a tiny hamlet, with roses and shrubs crowding the front garden; enter by the back way into a room crammed with beams and standing timbers. Tables occupy virtually every inch of space, apart from an area around the enormous log-burning stove that has huge sofas to lounge in. Landlord Tony Atkinson is always on hand, chatting and supervising. Fish from Brixham and St Mawes is the thing to eat here and the blackboard lists all kinds of delights, from moules marinière, and bouillabaisse, to sea bass with mustard, or John Dory cooked the Mediterranean way with olive oil, sun-dried tomatoes, anchovies and capers. Carnivorous options tend to be steaks, chicken, or roast mallard, with various fruity sauces. Snacks such as Welsh rarebit, and ham and eggs are also available in the bar at lunch-time, while desserts could feature genuine 'chewy' treacle tart with Salcombe Dairy ice-cream. Bass, Boddingtons and Exmoor Ale are on handpump, along with local farmhouse cider, and the wine list includes some very decent and appropriate whites. A traditional willow and basket-making centre is one nearby attraction worth exploring. SAMPLE DISHES: stuffed mushrooms £3.75; brill topped with salmon mousse and cucumber with white wine sauce £11.50; Devil's Snow (meringue with ice-cream, fruit compote and cream) £4.

Open *11.30 to 2.30, 6.30 to 11, Sun 12 to 3, 7 to 10.30; bar food L only 12 to 2; restaurant 12 to 2, 7 to 9.30*
Details *Children welcome in dining-room Car park Wheelchair access (also WC) Patio Background music Dogs welcome in bars only Access, Delta, Switch, Visa Accommodation: 3 rooms, B&B £25 to £36*

KNEBWORTH Hertfordshire map 3

Lytton Arms 🍺

Park Lane, Old Knebworth TEL: (01438) 812312

Knebworth is known to thousands of devoted fans for its rock extravaganzas. Not to be outdone, the landlord of this Victorian-style pub backing on to the park stages his own festivals. In this case, however, the faithful come not for music, but for beer. Whatever the season, it's always possible to sample a splendid range of brews (including up to eight guest ales) – B&T Shefford Bitter, Nethergate Decadent, Cotleigh Tawny and Woodforde's Wherry, to name but a handful. In addition, there's a stock of 50 Belgian bottled beers, numerous malts to match, plus a workaday wine list. Photographs and cuttings relating to the Cobbold family (who own the big house) line the wood-panelled walls in the three bars, where food is also given proper attention. Speciality sausages are worth noting on the printed menu, but the best stuff is on the blackboard. Texas Toothpicks are head-blowing, deep-fried chillies with barbecue sauce; otherwise you might find anything from Brancaster mussels, and bobotie, to generous helpings of lamb and dill casserole, or pheasant in mushroom and wine sauce. Desserts range from rhubarb crumble and crêpes suzette to something called 'Kiss the Blarney'. Outside is a garden with a well-equipped play area. SAMPLE DISHES: watercress and parsley soup £2; chicken korma £5.50; sticky toffee pudding £2.

Open *Mon to Thu 11 to 3, 5 to 11, Fri and Sat 11am to 11pm, Sun 12 to 10.30; bar food 12 to 2, 6.30 to 9.30, Sun 12 to 2.30, 6.30 to 9*
Details *Children welcome in bar eating area Car park Wheelchair access (also WC) Garden and patio Background music No dogs Access, Amex, Delta, Diners, Switch, Visa*

KNIGHTWICK Hereford & Worcester map 5

▲ *Talbot Hotel*

Knightwick TEL: (01886) 821235 **LOCAL PRODUCE**
just off A44 after crossing River Teme, between Worcester and Bromyard

The bridge over the River Teme is the defining point for this white-painted 600-year-old coaching-inn. Across the road is the local church, and wooded slopes rise up beyond. It sounds pleasantly old-fashioned, yet this is a hostelry that moves healthily with the times – providing everything from a sauna to a visiting aromatherapist. A massive fireplace with a huge woodburning stove is the centrepiece of the busy main bar, with its comfortable wall benches, draped curtains at the windows and sporting prints on the walls.

The menu is chalked up on a long blackboard over the fireplace and it changes summer and winter: young nettle soup with oatmeal for warm days, and a red lentil broth laced with chilli, ginger and garlic to keep out the cold. The kitchen seeks out local produce avidly; game is from the pub's own 'farm', fish is fresh, and the countryside yields an abundance of 'food for free'. Fungi, in particular, receive special treatment: girolles are served on garlicky sourdough croûtes, slices of giant puffball are deep-fried and accompanied by tartare sauce and crispy bacon. The raw materials may be close to home, but culinary inspiration is global. Scallops are wrapped in Japanese nori (seaweed) and deep-fried in beer batter, fusilli pasta is turned in a home-made pesto sauce, while it's back home for rabbit cooked in local cider. There's also a dedication to free-range and traditionally reared meat and poultry, such as Herdwick and Jacob sheep, and Wild Blue pork (a cross between Gloucester Old Spot and a wild boar). Puddings range from lemon posset and home-made damson ripple ice-cream to tiramisù, while cheeses are from the English 'new wave'. Some 20 quality wines are sold by the glass, and the full list offers high-class drinking across the board ('We only serve Lieb if specifically requested,' notes the landlord). Those with a taste for real ale have a choice of Hobsons Bitter, Bass and Worthington Best. Knightwick is well placed for a visit to the moated manor house at Lower Brockhampton (National Trust). SAMPLE DISHES: smoked-chicken salad with tarragon and Morello mayonnaise £5; steamed fillet of brill with coconut, tomato and cream sauce £14; iced ginger and chocolate cake £4.

Open *11am to 11pm, Sun 12 to 3, 7 to 10.30; bar food 12 to 2, 6.45 to 9.30, Sun 12 to 2.30, 7 to 9*
Details *Children welcome if eating Car park Garden and patio Jukebox in 1 bar Dogs welcome Access, Visa Accommodation: 10 rooms, B&B £25 to £57*

KNOWL HILL Berkshire map 3

▲ *Bird in Hand* 🍇

Bath Road, Knowl Hill TEL: (01628) 826622
on A34, 3m NE of Twyford

Parts of the Bird in Hand date back to the fourteenth century, but it gained fame in the late 1700s when George III called in and granted the place a Royal Charter and the right to serve wine and beer day and night. This licence no longer exists, but the pub's current incumbents cater admirably for the needs of today's travellers. The panelled Oak Lounge bar is a popular rendezvous and the buffet is much sought after. Snacks, pasta and more up-market dishes such as breast of duck with shallot and port marmalade are augmented by daily specials along the lines of pan-fried turkey escalope 'draped with pineapple and whisky reduction'. A table d'hôte menu is also served in the restaurant. The wine list is a quality slate of around 60 bins spanning the globe, and 12 decent wines are available by the glass thanks to the installation of Le Verre de Vin preservation system. Beer drinkers have a choice of Brakspear PA, Fuller's London Pride and Timothy Taylor Landlord. SAMPLE DISHES: farfalle with chicken, leeks and tarragon £4; braised oxtail marinated with prunes and oranges £7; white chocolate and Amaretto truffle £3.25.

Open *11 to 3, 6 to 11, Sun 12 to 3, 7 to 10.30; bar food and restaurant 11.45 to 2.30, 6 to 10.30, Sun 11.45 to 2.30, 7 to 10*
Details *Children welcome in bar eating area Car park Wheelchair access Garden and patio No music Dogs welcome Access, Amex, Delta, Diners, Switch, Visa Accommodation: 15 rooms, B&B £55 to £95*

KNOWSTONE Devon map 1

▲ *Masons Arms Inn*

Knowstone TEL: (01398) 341231 and 341582
1½m M of A361, midway between South Molton and Tiverton

'Always our first-choice escape route from London,' commented a couple from NW5. The Masons Arms has many obvious attractions and history is on its side. For some, the thatched medieval building is imbued with an 'authentic ancient gloom' which shows in the blackened beams hung with 'old bottles, old keys and odd bits of piping', not to mention the bulging stone walls and tiny windows; others take a different view. The bar menu is short and to the point: ploughman's with West Country cheeses, a pie and a curry of the day, cold meats with salad, perhaps some pasta as well; added to this are specials that might range from cassoulet to salmon fish-cakes with tomato salsa. Desserts are things like summer pudding, damson crumble, and syllabub, and the menu also offers 'real dairy ice-creams'. Fixed-price dinners are served in the restaurant, and gastronomic theme nights feature regularly. Good real ales such as Cotleigh Tawny and Hall & Woodhouse Badger Best are tapped direct from the cask, and Inch's Stonehouse cider is also available. A decent range of up to eight wines are served by the glass and the full list includes around 30 reasonably priced bins from reliable sources. The pub is in a conservation area with easy access to National Trust properties such as Knightshayes and Arlington Court, and the Royal Horticultural Society Gardens at Rosemoor are close by. SAMPLE DISHES: moules marinière £3; Exmoor lamb chops £6; lemon posset with Chantilly cream £2.25.

Open *11 to 3, 7 to 11, Sun 12 to 3, 7 to 10.30; bar food 12 (12.30 Sun) to 2, 7 to 9.30 (9 winter); restaurant Sun L 12.30 to 2, Tue to Sat 7 to 9*
Details *Children welcome in eating areas Car park Wheelchair access Garden and patio No smoking in restaurant Background and live music Dogs welcome Accommodation: 5 rooms, B&B £21 to £38*

LACOCK **Wiltshire** **map 2**

▲ *Red Lion*

1 High Street, Lacock TEL: (01249) 730456
on A350, 3m S of Chippenham

The Red Lion, a large three-storey, red-brick building built in the early eighteenth century, dominates the end of the wide main street of this well-known, beautiful village of low grey-stone medieval cottages with stone-tiled roofs. The long bar has four seating areas, one dominated by a superb open fireplace; all are kitted out with a mixture of furniture and rural artefacts, and the warm red walls and wooden ceilings are covered with an eclectic display of ornaments. The printed menu is a round-up of traditional pub fare, from jacket potatoes to various pies, while daily specials include the likes of lamb with ginger and almonds, pork and mushroom in a cream and sherry sauce, and haddock, cod and prawn bake; 'massive helpings' of fruit pie or cheesecake could be a hearty way to finish. Wadworth 6X and IPA are on draught, along with seasonal guests such as Old Timer, and wines are sold by the glass. The village, with its famous abbey and Fox Talbot Museum, is owned by the National Trust and can get very busy in summer. SAMPLE DISHES: vegetable soup £2.25; chicken, pasta and Stilton bake £7; lemon meringue pie £2.50.

Open *11 to 3, 6 to 11, Sun 12 to 10.30 (summer 11am to 11pm); bar food all week 12 to 2.15, 6.30 to 9.30*
Details *Children welcome Car park Garden No-smoking area in dining-room Background music Dogs welcome Access, Delta, Switch, Visa Accommodation: 4 rooms, B&B £45 to £70*

LANERCOST **Cumbria** **map 10**

▲ *Abbey Bridge*

Lanercost TEL: (01697) 72224
off A69, 3m NE of Brampton; follow signs to Lanercost Priory

Wildlifers speak fondly of sitting on the 300-year-old bridge close to this sturdy old inn and watching the sun set behind Lanercost Priory. With birds flying overhead, kingfishers diving into the River Irthing and the occasional otter to see, it is a delightful prospect. To enter the pub you need to ring the door bell. The main bar is in a converted blacksmith's forge with horseshoes and collars on the rough stone walls, and a spiral staircase leading up to the balcony dining-room. Ploughman's might appear as a 'special' at lunch-time; or go for something like vegetable parcels with sweet-and-sour dip, mouth-tingling Cajun chicken, or a 'five rib' rack of lamb (although one reporter thought this was 'too terrible to contemplate' as a light repast). In the evening the menu is fleshed out with a few more dishes, including salmon and halibut Wellington, beef Stroganov and vegetable Kiev. To finish, you might try ginger sponge pudding with a zingy lemon and ginger sauce; you can also expect pies, ice-creams and home-made cheesecake. Yates Bitter is the house beer, although there's a constantly changing selection including, perhaps, Shepherd Neame Spitfire Ale and Hall & Woodhouse Badger Bitter; the wine list is short and serviceable. There are well-signed riverside walks in both directions from the pub, and Hadrian's Wall is not far away. SAMPLE DISHES: prawn and pineapple brochettes £3.50; beef and ale casserole £7.25; chocolate rum pot £2.25.

Open *12 to 2.30, 7 to 11, (10.30 Sun); bar food and restaurant 12 to 1.45, 7 to 8.45*
Details *Children welcome Car park Wheelchair access (also WC) Garden No smoking in restaurant Background music Dogs welcome Access, Amex, Visa Accommodation: 7 rooms, B&B £19 to £50*

LANGLEY Cheshire map 8

Leather's Smithy 🍺

Clarke Lane, Langley TEL: (01260) 252313
off A523, 2m SE of Macclesfield, 1¼m from village towards Macclesfield Forest

What's in a name? This old stone inn was actually a smithy, once manned by a certain William Leather, who in 1821 decided to obtain a licence so that he could sell beer and porter. The horses and anvil may have gone, but drinking is still serious business here. Banks's Mild and Bitter, Morrells Varsity and Graduate, and Camerons Strongarm are on handpump, while lager fans should be intrigued to see imported Zamek Ceska Republica on draught. The pub also has a prodigious stock of around 80 malt whiskies, plus plenty of drinkable wines, and there's glühwein to keep out the winter chills. Food is served in the beamed and stone-flagged bar, the value for money is excellent, and you can get everything from black pudding with mushy peas, roast beef and rhubarb pie, to red Thai chicken curry, and boned trout stuffed with prawns and asparagus. Facilities can be arranged for camping and short-stay caravans – which is good news for the walkers and anglers who frequent nearby Macclesfield Forest and Ridgegate Reservoir. SAMPLE DISHES: lasagne verde £4.75; mixed grill £6.75; sticky toffee pudding £2.50.

🍺 *indicates a pub serving exceptional draught beers.*

Open *12 to 3, 7 (5.30 Fri) to 11, Sun 12 to 10.30; bar food 12 to 2, 7 to 8.30 (9.30 Fri and Sat), Sun 12 to 8.30*
Details *Children welcome in family room Car park Wheelchair access Garden No smoking in family room Background and live music Dogs welcome in bar only Access, Delta, Switch, Visa*

LANGTON GREEN Kent map 3

Hare

Langton Green TEL: (01892) 862419
on A264, 2½m W of Tunbridge Wells

This buzzy roadside pub keeps faith with its Victorian origins, as you can see from the contemporary etchings, framed memorabilia, chamber pots and ornamental plates dotted around the interior. One eating area at the back has French windows opening on to the patio (with the village green beyond) although food can be eaten anywhere. Extensive, constantly changing, blackboard menus by-pass most pub clichés in favour of things like three-cheese tartlet with vegetable chutney, spinach and wild mushroom pancakes with roasted pine-kernels, Scotch salmon with a prawn and herb filling wrapped in pastry and served with lobster sauce, and much more besides. 'Good service, great atmosphere,' added one reporter. This is a Greene King pub dispensing IPA, Abbot Ale and Rayments Bitter, alongside Inch's cider. Wine is also taken seriously: two dozen bottles feature on the wine list, and no fewer than 12 are available by the glass, including a dessert wine. SAMPLE DISHES: chicken satay with peanut and grape dressing £4.25; roast half-shoulder of lamb with sherry and redcurrant sauce £11.25; bread-and-butter pudding with cream and apricot sauce £3.75.

Open *11.30 to 2.30, 6 to 11, Sun 12 to 10.30; bar food 12 to 2, 6 to 10 (Sun 12 to 9)*
Details *Children welcome in eating areas Car park Wheelchair access (also WC) Patio Background music Dogs welcome Amex, Delta, Diners, Visa*

LANGTON HERRING Dorset map 2

Elm Tree

Shop Lane, Langton Herring TEL: (01305) 871257
off B3157, 5m NW of Weymouth

Approach this large, whitewashed inn in the pretty village of Langton Herring through leafy lanes, and find within a comfortable, 'not too modernised' interior. Food is served throughout three beamed rooms, and might include daily specials of freshly made pastas, pork and apple casserole, or poached salmon in green peppercorn sauce. On the printed menu there are also plenty of pub stalwarts, from ploughman's and pies to steaks and chilli. In addition, snacks along the lines of BLTs, and hot garlic bread with roast beef, are available lunch-times only. Pineapple in coconut rum liqueur with coffee ice-cream is a good way to finish. Beer drinkers will find Boddingtons, Flowers and Greenalls Original on handpump; and wines, some by the glass, are chalked on a blackboard. The energetic will be happy to know that the Dorset coast path runs from the pub along the mainland side of the lagoon enclosed by Chesil Beach. SAMPLE DISHES: mussels in white wine and cream £6; baked Portland crab Mornay £8; butterscotch banana fritters £3.50.

Open *10.30 to 3, 6 to 11, Sun 12 to 3, 7 to 10.30 (Sun summer 12 to 10.30); bar food 12 to 2.15 (2.30 Sun), 7 (6.30 Sat) to 9.15*
Details *Children welcome in eating areas Car park Wheelchair access (also WC) Garden and patio Background music Guide dogs only No cards*

LANLIVERY Cornwall **map 1**

▲ *Crown*

Lanlivery TEL: (01208) 872707
off A390, 2m W of Lostwithiel

This rough-stone building with a slate roof, tucked away down a narrow country road, dates from the twelfth century and is reputedly Cornwall's oldest pub. It was clearly at one time a row of cottages, which accounts for the series of rooms leading off each other; it now has a conservatory at the end. Daily specials usually include a good showing of fish – locally smoked mackerel, local scallops and rainbow trout perhaps, or whatever else the boats have landed – and specialities such as Cornish Under Roast (thin strips of topside of beef, rolled and baked with onions, cheese and potatoes). Otherwise opt for liver and bacon with onion gravy, or – from the bar menu – a pasty or a curry. Fruit pavlova and nutty treacle tart are popular puddings. On draught are Bass and Cornish-brewed Sharp's Own and Cornish Coaster's, while farm cider is on tap and wines come by the glass. SAMPLE DISHES: leek and potato soup £2.50; battered haddock with chips and peas £4.25; syllabub £2.50.

Open *Mon to Sat 11 to 3, 6 to 11, Sun 12 to 3, 6.30 to 10.30; bar food and restaurant all week 12 to 2.15, 7 to 9.15*
Details *Children welcome in eating areas Car park Wheelchair access (also WC) Garden No-smoking room No music Dogs welcome Accommodation: 2 rooms, B&B £26 to £40*

LAVENHAM Suffolk map 6

▲ *Angel*

Market Place, Lavenham TEL: (01787) 247388
on A1141, 6m NE of Sudbury

The Angel is the kind of place that gives English country inns a good reputation. First licensed in 1420 and set at the very heart of this much-lauded market town, opposite the Guildhall, it breathes civility. The interior is spick and span, with scrubbed tables, shelves of books to browse through and often a fire blazing in the grate. Visitors can eat in the bar or the dining-room from a menu that changes daily and is firmly in the mould of generous country cooking. A couple who stayed in June enjoyed rough game terrine with Cumberland sauce and perfectly crisp toast, roast asparagus with bacon and hollandaise, and grilled emperor fish with lemon and samphire. Other choices might range from pork and leek sausages with onion gravy to hare braised in red wine with redcurrants, not to mention ploughman's, salads and pasta. According to reporters, kiwi pavlova, or crème brûlée, is an excellent way to finish. Adnams, Nethergate Bitter, Mauldons White Adder and Greene King IPA are guaranteed to 'sharpen the thirst of any real-ale lover', and there is some excellent drinking to be had from the admirable wine list; seven house wines come by the glass. SAMPLE DISHES: tomato, basil and Parmesan salad £4; chicken, bacon and mushroom pie £6; strawberry syllabub £3.25.

Open *11am to 11pm, Sun 12 to 10.30; bar food 12 to 2.15, 6.45 to 9.15; closed 25 and 26 Dec*
Details *Children welcome in bar eating area Car park Wheelchair access (also WC) Garden No smoking in 1 room No music Dogs welcome Access, Amex, Delta, Switch, Visa Accommodation: 8 rooms, B&B £38 to £100*

LAXFIELD Suffolk map 6

King's Head

Gorams Mill Lane, Laxfield TEL: (01986) 798395
on B1117, 6m N of Framlingham

'One of Suffolk's treasures' is one reporter's view of this gem of a Tudor thatched pub. Known to all and sundry as the 'Low House', it stands in a dip just below the village churchyard. Some scenes for the film *Akenfield* (based on the book about East Anglian village life) were shot here – and it's easy to see why. The interior consists of five little rooms virtually untouched by current fashion or convenience:

the seats are mostly high-backed settles and there's no bar. Pints and jugs of impeccably kept Adnams beers and Greene King IPA are drawn direct from casks in the taproom, and trays are brought to your table; regulars can recall when the banging of empty glasses was sufficient to summon the barman. In keeping with the spirit of the place, the cooking leans heavily towards English rustic: Norfolk dumplings filled with pork and thyme, game casserole with apricots, a salad of jellied bacon and parsley, and 'excellent' lemon syllabub. Occasionally the modern world intrudes – as in roast wild salmon with parsnip rösti, and tagliatelle with a sauce of pesto and roasted peppers – but tradition generally wins the day. Apart from beer, there is James White Suffolk cider and a short list of a dozen or so wines from Adnams. The Kings Head is owned by the incumbents of nearby Tannington Hall, who arrange regular horse and carriage rides to and fro between house and pub. SAMPLE DISHES: chicken liver parfait with cranberry relish £3.75; grilled plaice fillet £5.75; spotted dick £3.

Open *11 to 3, 6 to 11, Sun 12 to 3, 7 to 10.30; bar food 12 to 2, 7 to 9*
Details *Family room Car park Wheelchair access (also WC) Garden and patio Live music No dogs in eating areas No cards*

LEVINGTON Suffolk map 6

Ship

Levington TEL: (01473) 659573
off A45 to Felixstowe, 6m SE of Ipswich

Sit outside the front of this impressively thatched fourteenth-century pub and gaze across the Orwell estuary with its boats and waterscapes. The low-ceilinged bar is filled with nautical bric-à-brac of all kinds and there are now two non-smoking eating areas beyond the bar. Ploughman's, quiches and salads are supplemented by more heart-warming dishes such as lamb with honey and ginger, and venison in red wine. Desserts take in old-school hot puddings as well as cold items such as black cherry flan. A weekly guest ale is put on alongside Ind Coope Burton Ale, Flowers Original and Wadworth 6X, and the pub has a commendable list of 17 good-value wines drawn from Adnams' magisterial cellars. The Ship is a good starting point for walks to Rimley Marshes, where you might spy marsh harriers in summer and short-eared owls in winter. Note the pub's strict 'no children' policy. SAMPLE DISHES: chicken with spicy peanut sauce £6; Lancashire hotpot £6; jam sponge pudding £2.75.

Open *11 to 3, 6 to 11, Sun 12 to 3, 7 to 10.30; bar food and restaurant all week L 12 to 1.45, Wed to Sat D 7 to 8.45*
Details *No children Car park Wheelchair access (also WC) Garden and patio No smoking in 2 eating areas No music No dogs Access, Delta, Switch, Visa*

LIDGATE **Suffolk** **map 6**

Star Inn ✿

Lidgate TEL: (01638) 500275
on B1036, 6m E of Newmarket

Spanish cooking in the unlikely setting of a Suffolk country pub has put Lidgate firmly on the gastronomic map. Enthusiastic and chatty landlady and cook Maria Teresa Axon is Catalan by birth and she has brought a genuine taste of the region to this East Anglian backwater. Despite on-going renovation and reconstruction, the 500-year-old building is much as it was in earlier days, two massive log fires burn, the atmosphere is beguiling. Regulars congregate in the bar areas, others head for the little apricot-coloured dining-room. One menu is served throughout.

Highpoints from recent meals have been the splendid Mediterranean fish soup (reckoned to be worth every penny) and genuine paella (even though one reporter found the 'prawn whiskers in every mouthful' rather off-putting). The Spanish influence also shows in perfectly cooked Spanish omelettes, roast chicken subtly impregnated with herbs, strong garlicky prawns malaguena, and, of course, Catalan salad. One often reported success is carpaccio, a technique which is applied to everything from venison, and exemplary beef topped with Parmesan, to salmon with scampi and dill dressing. Elsewhere, correspondents have spoken highly of monkfish marinière, fillet of cod in honey, wonderfully tender roast pork with apricots and capers, and unusually moist quail on toast with red wine sauce. Desserts tend towards homespun offerings like hot raspberry pie, lemon cheesecake and chocolate roulade. Service is casual and friendly, exactly what you would expect from an easy-going pub. Greene King IPA and Abbot Ale are kept in good order, the house wines are eminently quaffable and the short list chalked on a board won't necessitate a bank loan. SAMPLE DISHES: squid in spiced sauce £4.50; roast leg of lamb in garlic and wine £8.50; treacle tart £3.50.

Open *all week 11 to 3, Mon to Sat 5 to 11; bar food all week L 12 to 2 (3 Sun), Mon to Sat D 7 to 9.30*
Details *Children welcome in bar eating area Car park Garden Background music Dogs welcome Access, Amex, Switch, Visa*

✿ *indicates a pub serving outstanding bar food, backed up by all-round excellence in other departments, such as service, atmosphere and cleanliness.*

Report forms are at the back of the book; write a letter if you prefer.

LIFTON Devon map 1

▲ *Arundell Arms*

TEL: (01566) 784666
just off A30, 3m E of Launceston

Now that the A30 no longer runs through it, Lifton has returned to rural tranquillity, with the sixteenth-century Arundell Arms at its heart. Anne Voss-Bark is still very much in evidence – just as she was when she took over the pub in 1960 – and the whole place breathes solidity and courtesy: it is 'tremendously well-run'. The sporting brigade turns up in numbers, attracted mainly by the 20 miles of fishing rights on the River Tamar and its tributaries, but the inn remains comfortably down-to-earth. If you are looking for high-quality pub food, make sure you go to the Arundell Bar through the main entrance (another pub, also owned by Anne Voss-Bark but leased to tenants, is in the same block of buildings).

The Arundell Bar is smart, well-heeled and gentrified: rugs and stylish fabrics set the tone, a log fire often crackles, and there are benches and Windsor chairs to sit on; look around and you will notice framed fishing flies and piscatorial photographs. The menu is straightforward: ploughman's comes with three local cheeses; otherwise there are soups and pâté with home-baked bread (help yourself from the communal basket on the side table), salads such as avocado with roasted artichoke, bacon in a tomato vinaigrette, plus a handful of more substantial dishes. Fritters of Cornish fish are coated in saffron batter and served with green mayonnaise, mignons of beef come with griddled vegetables and horseradish cream, while desserts might be chocolate mousse gâteau with vanilla sauce. More ambitious fixed-price meals are served in the restaurant. Six fine wines are served by the glass, thanks to a vacuum-preservation system, and the full list is 'sound' with a bias towards France, but with plenty of affordable stuff from the New World. SAMPLE DISHES: oxtail soup with parsley dumplings £3.50; Spanish omelette £6.50; caramelised rice-pudding with citrus fruits £3.50.

Open *Mon to Sat 11am to 11pm, Sun 12 to 2.30, 7 to 10.30; bar food all week 12 to 2.30, 6.30 to 9.30; restaurant all week 12 to 2, 7.30 to 9.30*
Details *Children welcome in bar eating area Car park Garden Background music Dogs welcome Access, Amex, Diners, Switch, Visa Accommodation: 29 rooms, B&B £61 to £97*

---

indicates a pub serving food on a par with 'seriously good' restaurants, where the cooking achieves consistent quality.

All details are as accurate as possible at the time of going to press, but pubs often change hands, and it is wise to check beforehand by telephone anything that is particularly important to you.

LINTON West Yorkshire **map 8**

Windmill Inn

Linton TEL: (01937) 582209
off A58, 1½m S of Wetherby

Visitors to Harewood House, Bramham Park and Wetherby Races often drop into this attractive stone pub in a village above the River Wharfe. The twin attractions in the two heavily beamed bars are good local hospitality and generous nourishment in both solid and liquid form. A varied blackboard menu offers homespun North Country sustenance, including Yorkshire pudding with onion gravy, lamb hotpot, 'poacher's partridge', and home-made rice pudding with strawberry jam; it also conjures up memories of Continental holidays, with spicy Italian meatballs, swordfish with tarragon sauce, and paella (for two or four people). Theakston Best Bitter, John Smiths and a weekly guest ale are suitable thirst quenchers; the pub also has what the landlord describes as an 'extensive' wine list. SAMPLE DISHES: chicken liver pâté with brandy and port £3; salmon fillet hollandaise £8.50; blackberry and apple pie £2.25.

Open *Mon to Thur 11.30 to 3, 5 to 11, Fri and Sat 11.30 to 11, Sun 12 to 10.30; bar food Sun L 12 to 5.30, Mon to Sat 12 to 2, 6.30 to 9*
Details *Children welcome in eating areas Car park Garden and patio Background music No dogs Access, Delta, Switch, Visa*

LITTLE ADDINGTON Northamptonshire **map 6**

Bell

High Street, Little Addington TEL: (01933) 651700
off A6 and A510, 6m SE of Kettering

'Gosh what a sight,' exclaimed a traveller coming upon this lavishly refurbished pub with its modern stone frontage. No expense has been spared outside, and the newness continues within: the smart, stylish bar area has been constructed with respect for quality materials – large tiles on the floor, lots of polished wood, bits of shiny brass, framed photographs of the village around the walls. 'An air of decorum prevails.'

The same attention to detail and eye for quality dictates activities in the kitchen. One menu is served throughout the pub, and customers are invited to eat just one course (even a starter) if so inclined. A basket of home-baked breads (including a really good onion focaccia) is brought to the table by 'cosmopolitan-looking' waitresses. Starters run to exemplary cream of celeriac soup, a refined chicken liver pâté with 'good depth and a silky texture' served with a neat dollop of shallot and orange relish, carpaccio of beef, and marinated seared chicken breast spiked with a drizzle of oily chilli dressing. Main courses are 'served as described' says the menu, which means that braised lamb shank is accompanied by boulangère potatoes and 'rustic ratatouille', and long-cooked casserole of pheasant comes with herb dumplings and winter vegetables. The highlight of one serious gastronomic work-out, however, was the sublime kidney pudding served as a complement to chargrilled fillet of Scotch beef. Desserts include a creditable version of glazed lemon tart, as well as passion-fruit délice, and white chocolate mousse encased in dark chocolate and topped with glazed raspberries; otherwise there are cheeses from Neals Yard Dairy. Six really good wines of the month are served by the glass and the offer of a 'taster' helps those who are unsure – a gesture which is to be applauded; a more extensive list can also be considered. Beer drinkers can choose between Theakston Best, XB and Hook Norton Best. SAMPLE DISHES: salad of Parma ham with artichoke hearts and cherry tomatoes £4.50; fillet of halibut with salmon and dill mousse £9; milk chocolate and orange torte £3.

Open *Mon to Sat 12 to 3, 6 to 11, Sun 12 to 3, 7 to 10.30; bar food and restaurant Tue to Sun 12 to 2.30, 7 to 10*
Details *Children welcome Car park Wheelchair access (also WC) Garden and patio No-smoking area Background music in bar and occasional live music No dogs in restaurant Access, Amex, Delta, Switch, Visa*

LITTLE BEDWYN Wiltshire map 2

▲ *Harrow Inn*

Little Bedwyn TEL: (01672) 870871
off A4, 4m SW of Hungerford

This welcoming brick Victorian inn is well off the main drag in a quiet village, just 200 yards from the Kennet & Avon Canal. It's popular among walkers, canal-users and a discerning clientele of diners, particularly in the evenings. Within is a series of three interconnecting rooms, homely and smartly decorated, with a comfortable mixture of furniture, attractive prints on the walls, and a wood-burning stove. The cosy front room, with linen cloths on the tables, houses the restaurant, although the menu – more expensive than the one in the bar – can be ordered throughout. In the bar you'll find baguettes and ploughman's, with perhaps beef Stroganov, or skate wing with peppercorns and capers; the restaurant menu offers dishes such as smoked quail with quail's eggs, lambs' sweetbreads, roast poussin on a ragoût of leeks and mushrooms, calf's liver with apples and calvados, traditional roasts, and game in season (partridge with a compote of pears and perry, say). Orange bread-and-butter pudding makes an unusual dessert. Hampshire King Alfred's, Ringwood Best and Fuller's London Pride might be among the weekly-changing real ales on draught, and a short but interesting wine list offers plenty by the glass. SAMPLE DISHES: cream of onion soup £3; best end of lamb with rosemary sauce £13; crème brûlée £3.

Open *11 to 3, 5.30 to 11, Sun 12 to 2.30, 7 to 10.30; bar food and restaurant Tue to Sun L 12 to 2.30, Mon to Sat D 7 to 9.30*
Details *Children welcome in eating areas Wheelchair access Garden No smoking in dining-room No music Dogs welcome Access, Delta, Switch, Visa Accommodation: 3 rooms, B&B £25 to £55*

LITTLE BOLLINGTON Cheshire map 8

Swan with Two Nicks

Park Lane, Little Bollington TEL: (0161) 928 2914
off A56, 3m E of Lymm

A footbridge runs from Park Lane over the River Bollin into the grounds and deer park of Dunham Massey (National Trust). This, and its proximity to the Manchester conurbation, accounts for the popularity of the Swan, which has been much enlarged over the years. The atmosphere is generated by sheer bustle, though a small bar has beams hung with brasses and old bottles. Order in the smartly decorated dining area and try to find a table. The menu lists standard items like cold platters, sandwiches and steaks, while the blackboard may feature such things as roast loin of pork with cinnamon-flavoured apple sauce, baked salmon with dill and cracked black pepper, and a vegetarian dish of goats' cheese with aubergine and tomato coulis. Trifles, crumbles and fruit pies figure among the puddings. Boddingtons, Marston's Pedigree and Flowers IPA are regularly stocked real ales, with a guest like Morland Old Speckled Hen joining them. There's also a separate restaurant with its own menu. SAMPLE DISHES: vegetable Stroganov £5.50; grilled fillet of plaice with lobster and cognac sauce £6.50; spotted dick £2.50.

Open *11.30 to 3, 5.30 to 11, Sun 12 to 10.30 (12 to 4, 7 to 10.30 Sun Jan and Feb); bar food 12 to 2.30, 6 to 9.30, Sun 12 to 4, 7 to 9.30; restaurant 12 to 2.30, 7 to 9.30*
Details *Children welcome in eating areas Car park Wheelchair access (also WC) Garden and patio Background music No dogs Access, Visa*

Prices quoted in an entry are based on information supplied by the pub, rounded up to the nearest 25 pence. These prices may have changed since publication and are meant only as a guide.

LITTLEBURY Essex map 6

▲ *Queens Head Inn*

High Street, Littlebury TEL: (01799) 522251
on B1383, 2m NW of Saffron Walden

Two beer festivals are staged each year in this refurbished sixteenth-century inn, and licensees Jeremy and Deborah O'Gorman keep an impressive cellar. Over 140 brews have been served during the course of a year, and eight handpumps are regularly at work: Friary Meux, Timothy Taylor Landlord and Bass are always on; others such as Butcombe Bitter come and go. The interior of the pub is 'Victorian country-style', with red quarry tiles, a polished wooden bar counter and lots of old-fashioned furniture dotted around. Jeremy buys fish and vegetables from the London markets, and herbs are grown under glass in the garden. The result is a blackboard menu advertising such things as pan-fried scallops with steamed rocket and a thin cream sauce, baked mackerel with damson chutney, sirloin steak, and chicken 'daube' casserole. The dessert list has some interesting possibilities, ranging from chargrilled banana and stuffed figs to 'well-made' chocolate fudge pudding. Coffee is a decent brew, and if you want an unlikely finish try a shot of cranberry vodka. House wines are reckoned to be 'remarkably good' and the short list has a fair selection from the Old and New Worlds. Audley End House is a notable attraction within striking distance. SAMPLE DISHES: baked avocado with Stilton butter £3; chicken with smoked salmon and basil cream £7; deep Bakewell tart £2.50.

Open *12 to 11, Sun 12 to 10.30; bar food and restaurant all week L 12 to 2, Mon to Sat D 7 to 9; reduced opening hours 25 and 26 Dec*
Details *Children welcome in eating areas Car park Wheelchair access (also WC) Garden and patio No-smoking area in dining-room Background music Dogs welcome in bar only Access, Amex, Delta, Diners, Switch, Visa Accommodation: 6 rooms, B&B £30 to £62*

LITTLE COMPTON Warwickshire map 5

▲ *Red Lion*

Little Compton TEL: (01608) 674397
off A44, 4m NW of Chipping Norton

Strikingly attractive gardens are a draw at this pub in a village near the northern edge of the Cotswolds. Inside there's as much exposed stone as out, with little by way of bric-à-brac. Meat is supplied by a local butcher, and the pub has a reputation for its steaks: rump, for example, is cut by weight and chargrilled to your liking, and lamb steak comes thick-cut and – if you prefer – marinated in olive oil, garlic, soy and chilli. Otherwise blackboard specials might take in nectarine stuffed with cottage cheese and chives, grilled cod with lemon butter, chicken with bacon and mushrooms in a white wine sauce, or venison casseroled with sherry, chestnuts and apricots, and the printed menu offers traditional pub grub like pies and pasta. A good way to finish could be whisky trifle or apple pie. Donnington BB and SBA are on draught, and the wines on the carefully selected list are grouped by style, with three served by the glass. SAMPLE DISHES: celery, apple and prawn salad £4; seafood pancake £6; treacle sponge £2.50.

Open *11 to 3, 6 to 11, Sun 12 to 3, 7 to 10.30; bar food 12 to 2, 7 to 8.45 (9.30 Sat)*
Details *Children welcome in dining-room Car park Wheelchair access Garden No smoking in dining-room Live music and jukebox No dogs Access, Delta, Switch, Visa Accommodation: 3 rooms, B&B £24 to £36*

LITTLE COWARNE Hereford & Worcester map 5

▲ *Three Horseshoes*

Little Cowarne TEL: (01885) 400276
off A465 Bromyard to Hereford road, 4m S of Bromyard

Set high on a windswept hillside between the Malvern Hills and the Golden Valley, the Three Horseshoes began life as a cottage before being turned into a country pub. One menu operates throughout the place, and customers can choose between the hop-garlanded bar, the restaurant or the patio. Janet Whittall's kitchen is a hive of activity, producing everything from pickles, chutneys and ice-creams to the spice powder used to make chicken balti. She also makes good use of local and seasonal produce: wild rabbit is served with blackberries, hare is cooked in red wine sauce, while damsons are spiced and added to ploughman's, served as a sauce with duck, and even made into a soufflé. Sandwiches are available at lunch-time, although the licensees tell us that devilled kidneys with sauté potatoes, or prawn and haddock smokies, are very popular alternatives. Rounding things off, there might be sticky toffee cakes, summer pudding, or strawberry pavlova. A guest beer is put on alongside Ruddles County, Webster's and John Smith's Bitter, and the wine list is sound, drinkable stuff. Caravanners can park their vehicles in the paddock. SAMPLE DISHES: melon with orange Muscat wine £3; salmon fillet in dill sauce £7.50; sherry trifle £2.50.

Open *11 to 3, 6.30 to 11, Sun 12 to 3, 7 to 10.30; bar food and restaurant 12 to 2.30, 6.30 to 10 (7 to 9.30 Sun); closed 25 Dec*
Details *Children welcome Car park Wheelchair access (also WC) Garden and patio Jukebox Dogs on leads in bar only Access, Switch, Visa Accommodation: 2 rooms, B&B £18 to £35*

LITTLE HAMPDEN **Buckinghamshire** **map 3**

Rising Sun ✿ ❦

Little Hampden TEL: (01494) 488393
from Great Missenden take road signposted Rignall and Butler's Cross; after 2m take turn marked 'Little Hampden only'

'When we left at 2pm, I counted 15 pairs of walking boots "parked" in the lobby and outside the front door,' reported one eagle-eyed correspondent. The Rising Sun continues to live up to its reputation as a well-heeled Chiltern rambler's bolt-hole: breeches and designer socks appear to be *de rigueur.* Outdoor types and others congregate in the deceptively large L-shaped bar or cluster round the huge log fire in an adjoining room; there's also a separate dining area for intimate meals away from the chatter.

The 'Woodman's lunch' is a good deal if you need sustenance without show (what you get is a bowl of soup with a hot crusty roll, plus pâté, cheeses, salad and pickles). The rest of the menu is laced with imaginative ideas: sweetcorn and caraway seed pancakes filled with creamy wild mushrooms, roast home-smoked Deben duck served with cinnamon and pear sauce, and 'escabetchi' – which is described as 'Philippine-style sweet-and-sour monkfish and cod'. Slightly less-daring dishes have been recommended of late – in particular hot dressed Norfolk crab served in the shell with a Gruyère cheese and mustard topping, and skilfully cooked salmon in a dill and cream sauce. Vegetables display the same sure touch: turnip purée and Brussels sprouts ('expertly "undercooked" by traditionally British standards', in the view of one reporter) have been singled out. To finish, French caramel, and plum tart with pastry that had 'an interesting suet-like texture and flavour' impressed one lunchtime visitor; or you might opt for blueberry, apple and almond crumble served with custard and ice-cream. Hot mulled wine and spiced cider are available during the winter; otherwise the wine list has ten well-described vintages by the glass. The list of real ales extends to Brakspears, Adnams, Marston's Pedigree and Morland Old Speckled Hen. SAMPLE DISHES: prawn and asparagus vol-au-vent with garlic bread and salad £4.50; chargrilled escalope of pork with apple and cider sauce £8; peach crême brûlée with blackcurrants in syrup £3.25.

Open *Tue to Sat 11.30 to 2.30, 6.30 to 11, Sun 12 to 3; bar food Tue to Sun 12.30 to 2, Tue to Sat 7 to 9*
Details *Children welcome in bar eating area Car park Wheelchair access (also WC) Garden and patio No-smoking area Background music No dogs Access, Switch, Visa*

❦ *indicates a pub serving better-than-average wine.*

LLANFAIR WATERDINE Shropshire map 5

▲ *Red Lion*

Llanfair Waterdine TEL: (01547) 528214
off B4355, 4m NW of Knighton, at Lloyney

'Remote is an understatement,' commented one traveller who thoroughly enjoyed the 'lovely drive' down B roads and narrow lanes to reach this atmospheric drovers' inn. The River Teme, which marks the border between England and Wales, runs along behind the building. Inside the inn, it feels instantly welcoming, and infectiously congenial: this is still very much 'the old-fashioned village local' and new licensees Chris and Judy Stevenson seem intent on keeping it that way. Logs are stacked neatly by the great fireplace, pretty bottles and china flasks dangle from the ceiling. The cooking doesn't aspire to great heights but you can get some interesting things such as spring rolls with chilli dip, Brie and broccoli pithiviers, and mushroom ravioli, alongside grills, curries and pasta. At weekends, the pâté may be home-made. In addition there are more ambitious blackboard specials along the lines of stuffed lamb en croûte, and steak chasseur. The landlord also knows his beer and keeps a good stock of ales, including Wye Valley Bitter and Dorothy Goodbody, as well as Tetley Bitter and Marston's Pedigree; house wines are 'acceptable'. Those fancying a hike should note that Offa's Dyke Path is a stone's throw away. SAMPLE DISHES: deep-fried mushrooms with blue cheese dip £2.50; glazed gammon steak with fresh nectarines £7.25; spicy fruit cake with Cheshire cheese £2.50.

Open *Wed to Mon 12 to 2 (longer in summer), all week 7 to 11 (10.30 Sun); bar food and restaurant Wed to Mon L 12 to 2, all week D 7 to 9.30*
Details *Children welcome in eating areas Car park Garden and patio No smoking in dining-room Background and live music No dogs No cards Accommodation: 3 rooms, B&B £35 to £50*

LLANYMYNECH Shropshire map 5

Bradford Arms

Llanymynech TEL: (01691) 830582
on A483, 6m S of Oswestry

'I have eaten at supposedly reputable restaurants charging twice this pub's prices and not had such good quality and range of selection,' enthuses a fan of this roadside mock-Tudor inn. The choice and standard of what's on offer in the bar will keep anyone happy. A starter of grilled eggs with Stilton and a main-course salad of Guinness-baked ham with apricot chutney and oranges are among the more unusual items. More familiar are grilled goats' cheese with toasted pine-nuts, and smoked chicken with avocado, to be followed perhaps by poached salmon with dill and white wine sauce, beef casserole, a variety of steaks, or suprême of guinea-fowl with blackberry sauce. 'Puddings are a must,' a reporter writes; choose from a list that includes crème caramel, blackberry and apple crumble, and rum and walnut gâteau. Those more savoury of tooth can pick three from about 20 quality cheeses, including Llanboidy and Shropshire Blue. One real ale on draught changes each month; it could be Greene King Abbot Ale. A Spanish cava is among the five wines available by the glass, and a section of fine wines on the full list includes two 1928 clarets at three-figure prices. SAMPLE DISHES: braised celery hearts with smoked ham and mushrooms £4; lamb in creamy mint sauce £6.50; chocolate mousse gâteau £2.50.

Open *Tue to Sat and bank hols 12 to 2.30, 7 to 11, Sun 12 to 2, 7 to 10.30; bar food Tue to Sun 12 to 2, 7 to 10 (9.30 Sun); restaurant all week D only 7 to 10 (9.30 Sun)*
Details *Children welcome Car park Wheelchair access (also WC) Patio Background music Guide dogs only No cards*

LODERS **Dorset** **map 2**

▲ *Loders Arms*

Loders TEL: (01308) 422431
off A3066, 2m NE of Bridport

'Farmers in boots, members of the local cricket team and invariably a large dog in front of the fireplace' are among the regulars in this 'genuine local' set amid delightful Dorset countryside. The walls are decorated with local prints (for sale); real ales from Palmers of Bridport are on handpump. Friendly licensees Roger and Helen Flint offer a straightforward, good-value bar menu that ranges from hearty soups and freshly baked baguettes with various fillings to pasta and chilli con carne, with desserts such as bread-and-butter pudding, or dark chocolate and brandy mousse, bringing up the rear. A more ambitious restaurant menu includes crab and coriander parcels, black pudding with chutney, and rack of lamb. The wine list is short, but well chosen, and house wines come by the glass. SAMPLE DISHES: carrot and lentil soup £2.50; spaghetti puttanesca £6; sticky toffee pudding £3.

Open *11.30 to 3, 6 to 11, Sat 11 to 3, Sun 12 to 10.30; bar food 12.30 to 2, 7.30 to 9; restaurant Mon to Sat 12.30 to 2, 7.30 to 9; closed Mon L winter, no D Sun winter*
Details *Children welcome Car park Wheelchair access (also WC) Garden and patio Background music Dogs welcome Access, Visa*
Accommodation: 2 rooms, B&B £25 to £40

LONG CRENDON **Buckinghamshire** **map 2**

▲ *Angel Inn*

FISH

Bicester Road, Long Crendon TEL: (01844) 208268
on B4011, 2m NW of Thame

The ancient core of this greatly extended 400-year-old country inn can be seen in the slab of exposed wattle and daub behind a glass screen in one of the dining-rooms. These days, the Angel is a pub of many parts. As you enter, there's a bar area with old couches, sofas and a fire; beyond is a 'very pubby', rustic eating area with high-backed settles, bare wooden tables and little white candles ('the kind you keep in reserve for power cuts') in flower pots. The place also boasts a conservatory bedecked with wickerwork and an old Bath chair suspended from the ceiling. It is all very endearing.

Everyone agrees that fish is the star turn here, and its freshness is seldom in doubt: 'the kitchen clearly knows how to cook and handle the stuff,' commented one reporter. Rich, plentiful provençale fish soup continues to win votes, and the repertoire stretches from the traditional and the classic ('really good' cod and chips, and well-timed salmon in shrimp sauce) to up-beat brasserie ideas (chargrilled squid with roasted peppers and chilli oil, or monkfish, mussel and scallop stew). Away from fish, crispy duck and bacon salad with plum dressing has been praised; otherwise order pasta, bangers and mash, steak with 'frites', or even ploughman's with English farmhouse cheeses. Chargrilled ciabatta or toasted bread topped with marinated anchovies are worth considering on the side. Desserts might include treacle tart, cheesecake and the like. The wine list continues to improve. Eight are available by the glass, wines of the month are chalked on a board by the bar and the full slate is arranged by style: choice is imaginative, pricing very reasonable. For beer drinkers, Brakspear Bitter and Flowers Original are on handpump. While in the village it's worth paying a visit to Long Crendon Courthouse (National Trust). SAMPLE DISHES: Caesar salad £5; brochette of lamb and beef with chargrilled vegetables £9.75; blackberry and cassis fool £4.25.

Open *12 to 2.30, 6 to 11; bar food all week L 12 to 2.30, Mon to Sat D 6.30 to 10*

Details *Children welcome Sat and Sun L only Car park Wheelchair access Patio No smoking in 1 dining-room Background music No dogs Access, Delta, Switch, Visa Accommodation: 3 rooms, B&B £40 to £50*

If a pub has a special point of interest, this is indicated by a 'flashed' word or phrase at the top right of the entry.

LONGROCK Cornwall map 1

Mexico Inn

Gladstone Terrace, Longrock TEL: (01736) 710625
off A30, just E of Penzance

The odd name of this old granite pub refers to the fact that way back in 1794 it was used as a counting house by a silver-mining engineer who had just returned from Mexico. He eventually obtained a beer licence and turned the front parlour of the house into a pub, which naturally became known as the Mexico Inn. Mining tools around the place are a reminder of the past, and the printed menu includes guacamole with tortillas, and potato skins with chilli alongside such things as pan-fried squid with chillies and ginger, lasagne and steaks with all kinds of sauces. Most intriguing of all are the daily specials, which feature unusual soups such as chickpea and coriander, plus seafood in abundance: baked sea bass with spring onions, white wine and ginger, and grilled haddock with smoked bacon and Stilton sauce are typical. Hot skillets, filled baguettes and jacket potatoes are also served at lunch-time. Bass, Boddingtons and Marston's Pedigree are bolstered by a guest ale, and the short wine list includes four house wines by the glass. St Michael's Mount is a nearby attraction. SAMPLE DISHES: poached green-lipped mussels in white wine and garlic cream sauce £3.50; pan-fried chicken breast with soy sauce, honey, pineapple and cashew nuts £7.50; cinnamon and apple crêpes £3.25.

Open *12 to 2.30, 6 to 11, Sun 12 to 3, 7 to 10.30; bar food 12 to 2, 6 to 9.30 (summer Fri and Sat 6 to 10, Sun 6 to 9)*
Details *Children welcome in eating areas Car park Wheelchair access (also WC) Garden No smoking in dining-room Background music Dogs welcome in bar area only Access, Delta, Switch, Visa*

LONGSTOCK Hampshire map 2

Peat Spade Inn

Longstock TEL: (01264) 810612
off A3057, 1m N of Stockbridge

It's all change at the Peat Spade. Julie Tuckett – who put the pub firmly on the gastronomic map – departed in 1996 to take over a restaurant in Devon. Her place has been taken by Sarah Hinman and Bernie Startup, formerly of the Plough, Sparsholt (see entry). Now read on.

The building is much as it was – solid and comfortable Victorian, in the centre of a well-heeled village. Inside, it is spick and span, with shelves of knick-knacks including entire collections of Toby jugs, an assortment of ancient pipes, and various prints and water-colours on the walls. The menu is imaginative, and one reporter was pleased to note that the new owners have maintained the fruitful contacts established by their predecessor with local suppliers. The principle of cooking to order remains. Go for a snack and you might order home-made faggots with onions, or moghlai chicken curry. The remainder of the menu is straight and true: pan-fried medallions of pork with gooseberry coulis, casserole of organic Aberdeen Angus beef with shallots and port, salmon fish-cakes with lemon crème fraîche. Vegetarians are treated to unusual creations such as Mediterranean-style roasted peppers with walnut and wild mush-room terrine and goat's cheese ('excellent...well-balanced flavours' was one reporter's verdict). Puddings might be chestnut ice in a brandy basket, or apple, sultana and ginger crumble. Everything is served 'with some thought and style'. The admirable list of two dozen reasonably priced wines includes seven served by the glass. Supporters of local breweries will also be pleased by the names on the handpump: Pope's Best, Richard Lionheart from the Hampshire Brewery and Fortyniner from Ringwood might feature in the varying line-up. Progress reports on the new regime would be very welcome. SAMPLE DISHES: minted pea soup £3; suprême of chicken on a bed of sweet red cabbage £8; chocolate truffle tart £3.

Open *Tue to Thur 11.30 to 2.30, 6.30 to 10.30, Fri and Sat 11.30 to 3, 6 to 11, Sun 12 to 3; bar food Tue to Sat 12 to 2, 7 to 9 (9.30 Fri and Sat)*
Details *Children welcome in bar eating area Car park Wheelchair access (also WC) Garden No-smoking area Background music Dogs welcome No cards*

LONGWORTH Oxfordshire map 2

Blue Boar Inn

Longworth TEL: (01865) 820494
off A420 at Kingston Bagpuize, 7m W of Abingdon

Pick a pleasant village setting not far from the River Thames where it is little more than a trickle, choose a thatched building with creeper-covered walls and you have the scenario for a hostlery with all the trade marks of a genuine Oxfordshire country pub. Walk into the Blue Boar and you will find a bar that oozes character and the kind of civilised charm that seldom fails to find favour. If drinking is on your mind, there are real ales from Morrells Brewery in Oxford, as well as a useful wine list with a good spread of decent names. The bar menu is also likely to entice, with such exotica as deep-fried squid, Chinese chicken salad, and Thai prawn curry, alongside smoked salmon and scrambled eggs, beef and Guinness pie, fish and chips, and grilled steaks. Home-made puddings range from apple crumble to lemon posset. SAMPLE DISHES: curried parsnip soup £3; smoked haddock and prawn pasta £7.25; chocolate mousse £3.

Open *11.30 to 2.30, 6 to 11, Sun 12 to 3, 7 to 10.30; bar food 11.30 to 2, 7 to 10, Sun 12 to 2, 7 to 9.30*
Details *Children welcome Car park Garden Background music Dogs welcome Amex, Visa*

LOSTWITHIEL Cornwall **map 1**

▲ *Globe Inn*

3 North Street, Lostwithiel TEL: (01208) 872501
off A390, 5m SE of Bodmin

A paved courtyard provides outdoor seating at this ancient tavern which is an amalgamation of three houses; inside, a wood-effect gas fire offers warmth and cosiness in gloomy weather. Local scallops pan-fried in garlic and parsley butter may be on the menu, which befits the pub's location at the head of the Fowey Estuary. Otherwise choose from daily specials such as steak and kidney pie, chicken casserole, or lamb korma. Available at lunch-time are things like prawn platter, ploughman's and all-day breakfast, while evening specials could take in rack of lamb, or boar in a Madeira sauce. For dessert, there's bread-and-butter pudding, perhaps, or treacle tart. Bass and Flowers IPA are on draught, along with two guest ales, and house wines are sold by the glass. Restormel Castle, dating from around AD 1100, is just north of Lostwithiel. SAMPLE DISHES: chef's pâté with salad and toast £2.25; rack of lamb with herb crust and mint gravy £8.75; peach gâteau £2.

Open *11.30 to 3, 6 to 11, Sun 12 to 3, 7 to 10.30; bar food and restaurant Tue to Sun L 12 to 2.30, all week D 6.45 to 9; no food Sun and Mon D winter*
Details *Children welcome in eating areas Wheelchair access Patio No music No dogs No cards Accommodation: 3 rooms, B&B £20 to £38*

▲ *Royal Oak*

Duke Street, Lostwithiel TEL: (01208) 872552

Real ale aficionados will find themselves in paradise at this solid stone pub: Marston's Pedigree, Fuller's London Pride, locally brewed Bass and Sharp's are joined by no fewer than three guest beers, normally from small, independent breweries, and there's a wide choice of bottled beers too. The pub – beams and timbers inside, with deep red banquettes, benches and dark wooden tables and chairs – looks Victorian but in fact dates from the thirteenth century (an underground passage reputedly once ran from the cellars to Restormel Castle). The place has a relaxed, local feel, though service is friendly to all comers. Regulars will know that 'Mrs Hine's cow pie' consists of steak and kidney marinated and cooked in real ale; other main courses could include curry of the day, locally reared pork chop, steaks, and a range of fish, from garlic king prawns to Dover sole. To start, there may be a tasty-sounding soup like tomato, lentil and orange; fruit pies and gâteaux are typical puddings. Blackboards announce the wines of the month, and the full list has plenty by the half-bottle. SAMPLE DISHES: cream of mushroom soup £1.75; grilled plaice £8.50; apple pie £1.75.

Open *11am to 11pm, Sun 12 to 3, 7 to 10.30; bar food and restaurant 12 to 2, 6.30 (7 Sun) to 9.30; closed 25 December*
Details *Children welcome in eating areas Car park Wheelchair access Garden and patio Jukebox No dogs in dining-room Access, Amex, Delta, Diners, Switch, Visa Accommodation: 6 rooms, B&B £29 to £55*

LOWER BEEDING West Sussex map 3

Crabtree

Brighton Road, Lower Beeding TEL: (01403) 891257
on A281, 4m S of Horsham

The pub logo, depicting a crab enfolded by the boughs of a tree, should prepare you for the highly idiosyncratic attractions of Jeremy Ashpool's roadside inn. The building is four-square Georgian, and inside are various rooms, bars and corridors complete with a 'beautiful old original' floor and fireplaces. To one side is the main dining-room with paintings for sale on the wall, pot plants and floral drapes. Customers are dressed up and down ('although the down is still classy,' noted one visitor), service is young and enthusiastic.

Bar food is served only at lunch-time, but there's no sense of its playing second fiddle to the restaurant. Ashpool is a bold, independent cook, always ready to take on board new influences: it's not difficult, for example, to spot echoes of the East in dishes such as spiced lamb rissoles with Basmati rice, yoghurt and cumin dressing, or tenderloin of pork with stir-fried vegetables, soy and ginger. Modern British and European trends also surface in pan-fried duck livers with spring vegetables and tarragon, seared tuna with cucumber and oregano, and grilled salmon with a polenta and marjoram topping. Herbs and flavours shine through. Ploughman's come with good butter, fabulous malty home-baked bread and unexpected cheeses such as Tornegus and Flower Marie; you can also have a sandwich if you wish. Desserts tend towards things like praline ice-cream, and stem ginger and lime cheesecake. In the evening the kitchen pulls out all the stops for uncompromising up-to-the-minute dishes such as roast corn-fed chicken breast with pesto on tagliatelle with a yellow pepper sauce and roasted sweet potato.

The Crabtree is a King & Barnes pub, serving Sussex Bitter and Festive Ale as well as the brewery's splendid and fascinating range of seasonal brews – one for each month of the year. The wine list is clued up and affordable ('prices are not over-greedy,' according to a reporter) and the Antipodes supplies some fine stuff. SAMPLE DISHES: Stilton and chicory tart with walnuts and cherry tomatoes £4.25; lamb's kidneys with Dijon mustard sauce £8.50; apple and cinnamon pie £3.

Open *11 to 3, 5.30 to 11, Sun 12 to 3, 5.30 to 10.30; bar food all week, L only 12.30 to 2; restaurant D only 7.30 to 9.30*
Details *Children welcome in bar eating area Car park Wheelchair access Garden and patio No smoking in dining-room Background music Dogs welcome in bar only Access, Amex, Delta, Switch, Visa*

LOWER ODDINGTON **Gloucestershire** **map 5**

Fox Inn

Lower Oddington TEL: (01451) 870555
off A436, E of Stow-in-the-Wold

The Fox has been given an air of civilised gentrification since it was taken over in 1992, and the interior bears evidence to what might be called 'the stripped wood, sisal matting generation'. The heart of the building is the flagstoned main bar area, which is uncluttered 'except by human beings' as one visitor on a busy day quipped. To be sure, the places buzzes with upper-crust affluence and is likely to be packed even at 8 o'clock on a Wednesday evening in November. The hum of conversation generally drowns out the background classical music. Beyond the bar are several interconnected rooms all centred around the kitchen, and outside is a half-acre walled garden.

The menu changes every two weeks, but some dishes are fixtures: salmon fish-cakes with parsley sauce, and warm chicken, bacon and avocado salad are too popular to be discarded. Raw materials are notably good: rack of lamb is served with onion sauce, kedgeree is the real thing made from smoked haddock, while chicken Santenay comes in a creamy basil and tomato sauce. Vegetables are nicely timed and 'decently restricted in number'. Puddings are a mixed bag, ranging from hot walnut tart to banana ice-cream with butterscotch sauce. You can also get several sorts of French bread sandwiches. The pub's owner was in the wine trade for many years and has put together a lively list, including six by the glass; the pub also has an allocation of Cloudy Bay, so expect some interesting stuff from 'down under'. Beer drinkers are equally well served: Hook Norton Best Bitter and Marston's Pedigree are bolstered by guests such as Bishop's Finger, Hall & Woodhouse Tanglefoot and Crown Buckley Reverend James. The area around Lower Oddington is prime country for those who like ancient village churches and gardens. SAMPLE DISHES: Caesar salad £3; pasta with wild mushrooms and crème fraîche £6; apple and cinnamon pie £3.

Open *12 to 3, 6.30 to 11, Sun 12 to 3, 7 to 10.30; bar food 12 to 2, 7 to 10 (9.30 Sun); closed 25 Dec and evening 1 Jan*
Details *Children welcome in bar eating area Car park Wheelchair access (also WC) Garden and patio Background music No dogs Access, Visa*

LOWER WIELD **Hampshire** **map 2**

Yew Tree Inn

Lower Wield TEL: (01256) 389224
off B3046 Alresford to Basingstoke road, at Preston Candover

Set in a very rural spot, this solitary country inn is reached via a narrow, single-track road running through woods and farmland, and yet Basingstoke is only a few miles away. Food is taken seriously here, with one of the two bars set aside for dining. Service is 'correct' but casual, and a civilised air prevails. The printed menu offers baked potatoes – including one with snails and garlic butter – ploughman's and warm crusty baguettes, alongside roasted suprême of Scottish salmon, steaks and light dishes such as avocado, tomato and crispy bacon salad. At dinner, the repertoire extends further to the likes of steamed suprême of sea bass with ratatouille, and roast partridge with wild mushrooms, lentils and port wine, while the short blackboard menu of imaginative daily specials may yield hock of Italian cured ham, rosette of Cornish crab, grilled venison sausages, or grilled fillet of Cornish plaice with spicy gazpacho and olive oil. Beers include Marston's Pedigree as well as Pots Ale and Diggers Gold from local Cheriton Brewhouse. About 30 wines feature on the list, with house wines available by the glass. Outside, mused one visitor, the large garden 'must be wonderful in summer'. SAMPLE DISHES: oak-smoked Scottish salmon with fresh lime £6.50; roast wing-rib of Angus beef salad £9; spotted dick and custard £3.25.

Open *all week 12 to 3, Tue to Sat 6 to 11; bar food and restaurant all week L 12 to 2, Tue to Sat D 7 to 9.30*
Details *Children welcome in bar eating area Car park Wheelchair access (also WC) Garden No music No dogs Access, Delta, Switch, Visa*

LOWICK Northamptonshire map 6

Snooty Fox

Main Street, Lowick TEL: (01832) 733434
just off A6116, 2m NW of Thrapston

The pub, a Colleyweston longhouse dating from the sixteenth century, is in the middle of the picturesque, one-lane village: you can't miss it, it's the only pub there. The entrance hall separates the restaurant from the main bar area, which is dominated by the heavy oak counter that dispenses an admirable choice of weekly-changing brews: perhaps Golden Newt, Theakston Best and Old Peculier, and Morland Old Speckled Hen. An impressive blackboard in the black-beamed bar displays the menu of the day. Daily-delivered fish is the main thrust: crab salad, Whitby cod fillet, lobster thermidor, shark steak and whole grilled plaice may all feature on the boards at any one time. Meat eaters are not neglected, either: there's rack of lamb, steaks, and chicken balti ('we make a bucket a day,' says the landlord). Banoffi pie might be among the puddings. The international wine list has plenty of choice, from the light and palatable to the more noble. While in the area, those with children may like to visit Lilford Park, a country park with many facilities appealing to youngsters, including a farm. SAMPLE DISHES: grilled prawns £6; sole in champagne sauce £8; raspberry cheesecake £2.50.

Open *11.30 to 4, 6 to 12, Sun 12 to 3, 7 to 11; bar food and restaurant 12 to 2 (2.30 Sun), 7 to 10*
Details *Children welcome Car park Wheelchair access (also WC) Garden and patio Background and live music Guide dogs only Access, Amex, Delta, Switch, Visa*

LOW NEWTON-BY-THE-SEA Northumberland map 10

Ship

Low Newton-by-the-Sea TEL: (01665) 576262
off B1340, 2m N of Embleton

The seaside setting brings the crowds to this honest-to-goodness local pub-cum-village shop in a row of whitewashed cottages owned by the National Trust. On warm summer days the place seems to be overrun by tourists and 'beach lovers'; in the winter it becomes the domain of locals and 'windswept walkers'. Whatever the season, the mood is infectiously conversational, and the setting is homely, with wall benches, prints and local photographs on the walls, and creels hanging above the bar. The food is in similar vein: the fresh crab sandwiches are – apparently – renowned for miles around. So is the genuine home-made vegetable soup: 'the landlady was making a new batch on a quiet winter night, ready for the next day,' observed one traveller. Otherwise expect ploughman's, burgers, beef curry and one or two other items on the menu. Ruddles Best is regularly on handpump and a guest ale appears from time to time; wine is served by the glass. SAMPLE DISHES: home-made vegetable broth £1.50; fresh crab sandwiches £1.75; ploughman's £2.75.

Open *11am to 11pm (winter 11 to 3, 7 to 11), Sun 12 to 3, 7 to 10.30; bar food all day*
Details *Children welcome to 9pm Wheelchair access Jukebox Dogs welcome No cards*

LUGWARDINE Hereford & Worcester map 5

Crown & Anchor

Cotts Lane, Lugwardine TEL: (01432) 851303
off A438, 3m E of Hereford

You can sit outside in a gravelled beer garden at this attractive, eighteenth-century inn. The cosy interior retains its old beams, fires burn in the grates, and each of the open-plan rooms has its own character. Buy a drink – a glass of house wine, a pint of Bass, Worthington or Hobsons, or a glass of draught cider – choose something to eat from the long menu, order at the bar and grab a seat. Start with roast root vegetables with a red pepper dressing, perhaps, or spicy chicken wings, and proceed to fillets of lemon sole with grapes, turkey and broccoli lasagne, or lentil and aubergine curry. Alternatively, opt for a monthly-changing special such as venison and pistachio terrine, pheasant in Madeira, or salmon fillet poached with cream and cucumber. Finish with, say, gingerbread pudding with ginger wine sauce, or pears baked in cider. SAMPLE DISHES: herrings in sweet dill sauce £2.75; chicken with apples and brandy £6.75; pancake with vanilla ice-cream and butterscotch sauce £2.50.

Open *11.30 to 11, Sun 12 to 10.30; bar food 12 to 2, 7 to 10 (9.30 Sun)*
Details *Children welcome Car park Wheelchair access Garden and patio Live music Guide dogs only No cards*

LUSTLEIGH Devon map 1

Cleave

Lustleigh, nr Newton Abbot TEL: (01647) 277223
off A382, 4m SE of Moretonhampstead

The local beauty spot of Lustleigh Cleave, after which this fifteenth-century thatched pub is named, is where the River Bovey runs under the rocks. In the heart of one of Devon's loveliest villages, the pub has a pleasant, sheltered front garden with a cobbled path, old-fashioned cottage flowers and shrubs. Children can play in a paddock away from the garden with swings, footballs and hoops. Within, all is immaculate in the two low-beamed bars, one of which houses an immense inglenook complete with bread oven, and in the spacious dining-room. Service is quick and efficient in this popular pub, where the focus is on careful and sound cooking, with more than a nod towards the use of local ingredients. While the printed menu offers the usual pub stuff, blackboard specials could take in cottage pie, banana curry, lasagne, or turkey à la king. A reporter enjoyed 'excellent' vegetable soup – 'the real thing' – and it came with two doorstops of granary bread of the sort 'you only ever get in pubs'. Evening specials might be steak, duckling or trout. Beers on draught are Flowers Original and IPA and Bass, and a few wines are served by the glass, litre or half-litre. SAMPLE DISHES: chicken liver pâté £4; locally made pork sausages £5.25; warm treacle tart £2.25.

Open *Summer Mon to Sat 11am to 11pm, winter 11 to 3, 6.30 to 11, Sun all year 12 to 10.30; bar food 12 to 2.30, 6.30 to 9; cold food available all day in summer*
Details *Children welcome in dining-room and family room Car park Wheelchair access Garden and patio No smoking in family room No music Dogs welcome Access, Visa*

LUXBOROUGH Somerset map 1

▲ *Royal Oak of Luxborough*

Luxborough TEL: (01984) 640319
off A396, 4m S of Dunster

Luxborough is a long, straggling Exmoor village, with houses hugging the road as it meanders through; you may think you've missed the Royal Oak when you come out into open countryside – persevere, for a turn in the road brings you to this pub, a few stone cottages, a bridge and a stream. A tiny flower-filled garden separates the pub from the road. Inside, it is marvellously unspoilt: thick walls, low beams, a rough flagged floor in the front bar, huge log-burning fireplace and a mishmash of pews, chairs and rustic tables. On the printed menu are staples like ploughman's, and beef and stout pie, though it is extended in the evening to include steaks, Barbary duck breast with cranberry and rosemary sauce, chicken breast poached in wine with a dill sauce, and grilled local trout. Blackboard specials major in the seasonal: generally a good range of fish and game – sea bass in lobster sauce, grilled Dover sole, venison fillets, or game pie, for instance – and among the desserts could be steamed treacle pudding and lemon cheesecake. The bar dispenses a wide choice of well-kept real ales, among them RCH Pitchfork, Moor Withycutter and Exmoor Gold, plus farm ciders, and there's a full wine list. SAMPLE DISHES: trout pâté £4.25; stalker's pie £6; Styles Farmhouse ice-cream £2.50.

Open *11 to 2.30, 6 to 11, Sun 12 to 3, 7 to 10.30; bar food and restaurant 11 to 2, 7 to 10*
Details *Children welcome in bar eating area Car park Wheelchair access (also WC) Garden and patio Live music Dogs welcome No cards Accommodation: 9 rooms, B&B £23 to £45*

LYDDINGTON **Leicestershire** **map 5**

Old White Hart

51 Main Street, Lyddington TEL: (01572) 821703
off A6003, 2m S of Uppingham

Follow the signs to Bede House (English Heritage) to find this honey-coloured stone pub in the Welland Valley. Tradition reigns here and the pub wears its patriotic colours on its sleeve. In a bucolic setting of dried flowers and old horse tackle the kitchen ploughs a furrow deep into the roots of British country cooking. The bar menu, which changes every two months, brings together such regional classics as meatless Glamorgan sausages with spiced plum chutney, Cornish potted salmon, Huntingdon fidget pie and Dorset jugged steak. Salmon is served with elderflower and gooseberry sauce, while hake comes with samphire and sorrel sauce. Mushrooms Lyddington – cooked with garlic and topped with Stilton – is a perennial favourite, while puddings continue the seasonal theme. A larger menu is served in the pub's three restaurants (Keepers, Poachers and Hunters). The White Hart dispenses Greene Abbot Ale and IPA as well as Marston's Pedigree; six house wines are served by the glass and there's also a creditable list with some interesting bottles, including Petite Sirah 1992 from Mexico. Given the Britishness of the whole place, it is surprising to find that the French game of pétanque is played with serious intent – ten pistes are in use. SAMPLE DISHES: smoked haddock with hot cream and onions £3.75;

fillet of pork with caramelised apples and a sage and cider gravy £7.25; brandied lemon syllabub £3.

Open *12 to 3, 6.30 to 11, Sun 12 to 3, 7 to 10.30; bar food and restaurants 12 to 1.45, 7 to 9.30*
Details *Children welcome in eating areas Car park Wheelchair access (also WC) Garden and patio No smoking in 2 dining-rooms Background music Dogs welcome Access, Switch, Visa*

LYDFORD **Devon** **map 1**

▲ *Castle Inn*

Lydford TEL: (01822) 820241/2
off A386, 7m N of Tavistock

The sixteenth-century inn with its vine-covered patio is next to Lydford Castle, an old stannary prison, and just a couple of hundred yards from stunning Lydford Gorge in the foothills on the fringe of Dartmoor. An old-world atmosphere pervades the bar, with its log fire, beams, antique settles, slate-flagged floor, and prints and plates on the walls. An Eastern influence can be seen in such dishes as Thai chicken and coconut soup, Burmese pork and banana curry, and Szechuan prawns, while from closer to home come wild boar pâté, steak and kidney pie, and salmon and cod plait with champagne and thyme sauce. Sticky toffee pudding 'melted in the mouth' of one reporter, and there could also be caramelised rice pudding. Badger Tanglefoot, Fuller's London Pride and a guest ale are on draught, and plenty of wines come by the glass. A separate restaurant serving a set-price menu is open for dinner. SAMPLE DISHES: mussel bisque £3.70; goujons of cod with tomato sauce £5.75; whiskied bread-and-butter pudding with apricot sauce £2.75.

Open *11.30 to 3.30, 6 to 11, Sun 12 to 3, 7 to 10.30; bar food 12 to 2.30, 7 to 9.30 (9 Sun); restaurant D only 7 to 9.30*
Details *Children welcome in dining-room and 1 bar Car park Wheelchair access (also WC) Garden and patio No-smoking area in restaurant No music Dogs welcome in bar only Access, Amex, Delta, Diners, Switch, Visa Accommodation: 10 rooms, B&B £29 to £70*

LYDGATE **Greater Manchester** **map 8**

White Hart ✿✿ ❦

51 Stockport Road, Lydgate TEL: (01457) 872566
on A670, 3m E of Oldham

There's been a pub on this site – high on the hillside overlooking Oldham and Manchester – since 1788, when the place had vast cellars for brewing its own beer using water from the well. A barn was added subsequently to hold the local foxhounds; in due course this became a police station and later a schoolhouse. Enter Charles Brierley and John Rudden, who took over the White Hart in 1994 and have dragged it emphatically into the present day. The ground floor is now a bar and 'brasserie' and it looks pristine, with its exposed stonework, bright wood, framed prints and immaculate paintwork. Drinkers can still call in for a pint of J.W. Lees, Phoenix Bonneville Bitter or Boddingtons, although one Lancastrian regular notes that locals may be 'shunted off to two side rooms' when tables are jam-packed.

Hefty doorstep sandwiches with roast ham, English mustard and home-made chutney, plus omelettes and bowls of soup are the nearest the place gets to old-school pub cooking; the rest is brasserie through and through. Platters of smoked fish and oysters; tian of wild mushrooms, spinach and pine-nuts; and crab risotto with Parmesan and basil represent the lighter side of things, while the treatment given to gravlax might raise an eyebrow or two: sometimes it is seared or pan-fried with sweet ginger, other times it turns up as a curious-sounding 'beetroot' version accompanied by capers and shallots. Otherwise, the kitchen heads straight for the cosmopolitan world of grilled fillet of hake with balsamic shallots, braised duck leg with peppered tongue and black pudding potato, and rump of lamb with garlic mash and tomato and olive *jus*. Desserts generally include a fruity crème brûlée, as well as apple crumble, hot banana muffins, and so on; there are also British farm cheeses to round things off. Dinners and Sunday lunch are served in the upstairs restaurant from a sensibly short menu that treads a similar path. The 'brasserie' wine list is keenly priced and lively, with ten by the glass; the full list ranges far and wide with confidence. The licensees tell us they will be offering accommodation from February 1997. SAMPLE DISHES: mushroom mousse topped with a seared king scallop £4.50; maize-fed chicken with truffle pasta £8.25; steamed blueberry sponge with cinnamon £3.50.

Open *weekdays 12 to 3, 5 to 11, Sat 12 to 11, Sun 12 to 10.30; bar food 12 to 2.30, 6 to 9; restaurant Sun L 12 to 2.30, Tue to Sat D 7 to 10*
Details *Children welcome in bar eating area Car park Wheelchair access (also WC) Garden No smoking in dining-room Background music No dogs in eating areas Access, Amex, Delta, Switch, Visa*

MADINGLEY **Cambridgeshire** **map 6**

Three Horseshoes

High Street, Madingley TEL: (01954) 210221
off A1303, 2m W of Cambridge, close to M11 Jct. 13

Madingley, it seems, holds many memories. A correspondent recalls when he was a lad attending Scout Camp at the nearby Hall: 'Several of us, all underage, went and drank cider and sang songs round the piano [in the Three Horseshoes].' That was 50 years ago. Today the pub is a much more affluent place and everything is definitely above board. Another reporter describes the place as 'immaculate as they come, demurely thatched and absolutely spotless'. Everywhere you'll see polished woodwork, gleaming glass and hoovered carpets – not to mention lovely old prints on the walls. All comers are happily accommodated – from leather-clad bikers to business types from Cambridge.

You can eat at bare tables in one of the bar areas, but the centre of the action is a 'stunning' conservatory dining-room, where tables can be booked and waiters serve with a degree of professionalism. The walls are festooned with weeping figs and passion-flowers creeping over trelliswork; billowing drapes hang at the windows. In this setting the kitchen delivers generous, enthusiastic cooking with a bold Mediterranean accent. Materials are of the highest quality – whether it be 'superb beef and marvellous fish' or cheeses from Neals Yard. The menu provides 'all kinds of everything' that is in fashion, a great deal often happens on the plate, but at its best the result is cohesive modern pub food of the highest order. The style shows up perfectly in dishes such as 'smokily grilled' chicken breast with pesto, lemon-tinged couscous, roasted pine kernels and salsa verde, or a 'mighty slab' of monkfish roasted with garlic, rosemary, 'outstanding' baby fennel and served with a tomato, onion and saffron compote. Elsewhere, you might encounter pressed skate terrine with anchovies and green beans, chargrilled beef flank with parsley purée, as well as salads and up-market pizzas. Desserts are of the kind that produces drools of ecstasy: sticky toffee pudding ('as good as they come'), caramelised lemon tart with lime ice-cream, pears baked with marsala, cinnamon and crème fraîche.

The Three Horseshoes is part of the Huntsbridge Group of independently run pub/restaurants (see also White Hart, Great Yeldham and the Pheasant, Keyston) and it benefits from the attitude of owner and Master of Wine John Hoskins. The wine list is a stunner; its Italian contingent is outstanding, as are the representatives for the New World. Thirteen fine wines – including champagne – are served by the glass. Three real ales are on show, including Adnams Bitter plus two guests such as Everards Tiger and Batemans XXXB. SAMPLE

DISHES: fricassee of foie gras, duck liver, sweetbreads, and garlic with rösti and parsley £6.75; pan-fried salmon with green curry shrimps, pak choi and Thai spices £11.50; grilled peaches with mascarpone, brandy syrup and vanilla sugar £3.50.

Open *11.30 to 2.30, 6 to 11, Sun 12 to 2.30, 7 to 10.30; bar food and restaurant 12 to 2, 6.30 to 10 (exc Sun D)*
Details *Children welcome Car park Wheelchair access Garden No music No dogs Access, Amex, Delta, Diners, Switch, Visa*

MAIDENSGROVE Oxfordshire map 2

Five Horseshoes

Maidensgrove TEL: (01491) 641282
off B480 and B481, 5m NW of Henley-on-Thames

Dating from the early seventeenth century and in an enviable setting on the high reaches of the Chilterns, this brick and flint hostelry is a great favourite – not least because it has some of the most impressive views of any pub in the vicinity. Customers come not only for the panoramas but for the food. The bar menu offers a wide choice, from Stilton soup and steaks to ploughman's, pasta, and filled pancakes, and dishes such as goats' cheese crostini, monkfish and tiger-prawn kebabs, and Creole-style chicken breast with pear chutney. Attached to the pub is Café Shoes, a bistro-style restaurant with an extended menu that might also take in dishes such as Louisiana-style catfish, and braised lamb shank with couscous. The Five Horseshoes is a Brakspear-tied house with PA and Special on handpump, alongside Theakstons XB. A blackboard advertises wines by the glass, and the full list is well-spread. Outside catering is a further string to the bow, and marquees can be erected on the land behind the pub. SAMPLE DISHES: chicken liver pâté with hot toast £5; chargrilled salmon steak with minted avocado sauce £10; double chocolate mousse cake with fresh fruit coulis £3.50.

Open *Mon to Sat 11.30 to 2.30, 6.30 to 11, Sun 12 to 3, 7 to 10.30; bar food and restaurant all week 12 to 1.45, 7 to 9.45*
Details *Children welcome in restaurant and 1 room of bar Car park Wheelchair access Garden and patio Background music Dogs welcome Access, Delta, Switch, Visa*

MARKET OVERTON Leicestershire **map 6**

▲ *Black Bull*

2 Teigh Road, Market Overton TEL: (01572) 767677
off B668 Oakham to Stretton road, 2½m N of Cottesmore

The core of this much-extended village pub is a neatly thatched building complete with a flower-decked porch. Licensees John and Valerie Owen look after the place well and have nurtured its local reputation as a sought-after eating venue. Fresh fish shows up promisingly in the guise of mussels, lemon sole with parsley butter, and grilled red sea bream with a creamy watercress sauce. The chef also makes a feature of sizzling Cantonese-style dishes as well as turning out the likes of breadcrumbed double breast of chicken filled with Rutland cheese and served with wild mushroom sauce. You could start with coarse home-made paté and finish with a fruit crumble. Ruddles Best and Theakston's Best and XB are on draught alongside relative newcomer Oakhams Grainstore 10.50; there's also a short list of carefully chosen wines. Rutland Water and Woolsthorpe Manor (National Trust) are within striking distance. SAMPLE DISHES: smoked salmon and mackerel roulade £3; garlic lamb steak with redcurrant and port sauce £8; apple crumble £2.50.

Open *11.30 to 2.30, 6 to 11, Sun 12 to 3, 7 to 10.30; bar food and restaurant 12 to 2, 6 to 10*
Details *Children welcome Wheelchair access (also WC) Patio Background music Dogs welcome in bar area only Access, Delta, Switch, Visa Accommodation: 2 rooms, B&B £25 to £42*

MARSDEN West Yorkshire **map 8**

Olive Branch

Manchester Road, Marsden TEL: (01484) 844487
on A62, 7m SW of Huddersfield

Owner John Lister treats us to a history lesson concerning the name of this miraculously revitalised Pennine pub: back in 1851, the inn was apparently taken over by entrepreneur and part-time preacher Jo Sykes. His avowed aim was to create a watering-hole for the respectable traveller looking for a peaceful retreat (no swearing and no alcohol on Sundays were two of his rules). Thus he named the pub the Olive Branch and he became known as Jo O'Tolive.

The place is now described as a 'bar/brasserie', although 'dining pub' might be nearer the mark. Tables are laid up in three areas, and Gerald Scarfe cartoons and Punch and Judy china figures form the decorative flourishes. The blackboard menu makes tasty reading:

game and pistachio nut terrine with Seville orange coulis, sea bream with samphire and coriander oil, confit of duck with onion and sultana marmalade, for example. There's also a hearty peasant-style undercurrent running through dishes such as braised hind leg of hare with celeriac purée, lamb shank with rosemary and garlic, and roast partridge with wild mushrooms and bacon. Pan-fried sirloin steaks come every which way, while pasta receives up-to-the-minute treatment. Puddings include home-made ices as well as the unusual-sounding treacle, oat and lime tart, which is a neat variation on an old theme. The 80-strong wine list roams the globe, picking up consignments from Israel, Romania and Oregon along the way; prices are extremely reasonable. Worthington Best Bitter is on hand-pump. A footpath leads from the pub to the remains of the Huddersfield Canal and Tunnel End with its tourist centre. SAMPLE DISHES: warm asparagus with balsamic dressing £4; tranche of Whitby cod with salsa verde £9; pear frangipane with strawberry coulis £4.

Open *12 to 2.15, 6.30 to 11; bar food Mon to Sat D only 6.30 to 9.30 (9.45 Sat), Sun L 12 to 1.45, D 4 to 9*
Details *No children Car park Wheelchair access Patio Background music No dogs Access, Delta, Switch, Visa*

MARSH BENHAM Berkshire map 2

Water Rat ✿

Marsh Benham TEL: (01635) 42879
off A4, 3m W of Newbury

The Kennet valley inspired Kenneth Grahame to write *The Wind in the Willows* and this attractive thatched pub pays homage to the author – not only in its name, but in the murals depicting characters and scenes from the book that adorn the opened-up interior. Two comfortable dining-areas with exposed brickwork, plus a bar with carved settles are the setting for light and inventive food. One menu is served throughout and the main inspiration is '90s Mediterranean, although the kitchen casts its net wide: antipasti (chargrilled and marinated peppers, tuna and olives), tagliatelle with mascarpone and spinach, and risotto nero (with squid ink) line up beside smoked haddock and herb omelette with carrot butter, *petit sale* (salt pork with lentils), and pot-roast shoulder of lamb with Moroccan spices accompanied by minted couscous.

The repertoire changes monthly to take account of seasonal supplies, and the attention to detail is impressive – right down to the quality of the oils used in salad dressings, and the fact that a complete vegan menu is offered in addition to numerous vegetarian dishes.

Reporters have singled out fish as a high point, whether it be char-grilled tuna with guacamole, roast cod basquaise or chilled poached salmon with fennel mayonnaise. Desserts call into play such things as apple and orange tart Tatin with cinnamon ice-cream, steamed lemon sponge with candied figs, and bread-and-butter pudding; otherwise go for cheeses like Cornish Yarg, Gubbeens and Cotherstone. Three real ales – Wadworth 6X, Brakspear Bitter and a guest brew – are on draught, and the pub stocks Belgian bottled beers, as well as plenty of malt whiskies. Five house wines are offered by the glass, and the full list runs to about 50 bins. SAMPLE DISHES: scrambled eggs with chorizo, Parma ham, asparagus and parsley £6.50; pan-fried rabbit loin with Greek salad and sauté potatoes £9.75; bitter chocolate and bourbon truffle cake with clotted cream £5.75.

Open *Mon to Sat 11.30 to 2.30, 6 to 11, Sun 12 to 3, 7 to 10.30; bar food and restaurant all week 12 to 2.30 (3 Sun), 7 to 9.30*
Details *Children welcome in eating areas Car park Garden and patio No smoking in restaurant Background music No dogs Access, Amex, Delta, Switch, Visa*

MARSH GIBBON **Buckinghamshire** **map 5**

Greyhound Inn

Marsh Gibbon TEL: (01869) 277365
off A41 Bicester to Aylesbury road, 4m E of Bicester

It may come as a surprise to find an exclusively Thai menu at this old, grey-stone pub set in a pretty village. Bare stone walls are also a feature of the two small, neat-looking rooms inside, where you may want to start your meal with wun-tun (commended for its 'nicely and subtly spiced minced chicken filling') with a spicy dipping-sauce, or a Thai salad. After that, carry on with, say, beef stir-fried with garlic, chillies, bamboo shoots and French beans, or roast duck curry. Even eight-ounce sirloin steak is cut into strips and cooked with coriander, garlic and peppers and served with a hot, spicy sauce. Many of the puddings involve exotic fruits, although ice-creams are a refreshing way to finish. Real ales are as English as they come, with Fuller's London Pride, Hook Norton Bitter and Greene King Abbot Ale on draught; wines are served by the glass. You can sit in the tiny garden at the front; at the back, beyond the car park, is a mini-football field with things to climb on for the children. SAMPLE DISHES: spring rolls £4; chicken with cashew nuts and mushrooms £6.25; chocolate torte £2.

Open *all week 12 to 3.30, 6 to 11.30 (10.30 Sun); bar food and restaurant all week 12.30 to 3, 6.30 to 10*
Details *Children welcome in eating areas Car park Wheelchair access (also WC) Garden No-smoking areas in bar and no smoking in restaurant Background music No dogs Access, Delta, Diners, Switch, Visa*

MARSHSIDE Kent **map 3**

Gate Inn

Marshside TEL: (01227) 860498
between A28 and A299, 3m SE of Herne Bay

The interior of this splendidly unimproved village local is as honestly rustic as they come, and the garden, by a stream, is lovely in summer, with picnic tables under shady trees and tame ducks waddling about. Inside, old photos of cricket teams line the walls, a log fire often blazes, and there are odd benches and settles to sit on; a venerable piano maintains its place. Food is of the 'filling and simple variety' that is exactly in keeping with the pub itself. Black pudding shows up in the mixed grill, ploughman's, doorstep sandwiches and as one of the toppings for the pub's famous spicy vegetable hotpots. 'Meat' pâté, pasta dishes, chunks of French bread with various fillings, not to mention bowls of home-made soup in the wintertime, complete the disarmingly unaffected picture. Landlord Christopher Smith is 'proud of his selection of beers', comments a local reporter. There are no handpumps on the bar: Shepherd Neame Masterbrew, Spitfire Ale and others are drawn direct from casks in the cellar. English fruit wines also show up well. SAMPLE DISHES: garlic mushrooms £2; pasta, pesto and bacon with garlic bread £4.75; vanilla ice-cream with sauce and chopped nuts £1.

Open *11 to 2.30 (3 Sat), 6 to 11, Sun 12 to 3, 6 to 10.30; bar food all week L 11.45 to 2 (2.30 weekends), Tue to Sun D 6 to 9 (9.30 Thur to Sat)*
Details *Children welcome in bar eating area and family room Car park Wheelchair access (also WC) Garden No-smoking area at lunch-time No music Dogs welcome No cards*

MELLOR Greater Manchester **map 8**

Devonshire Arms ✿

Longhurst Lane, Mellor TEL: (0161) 427 2563
off A626, 2m E of Marple

Brian Harrison's unprepossessing stone-built pub may occupy one of the 'duller stretches of Mellor', but nearby the open countryside rises towards the Derbyshire Hills and Kinder Scout for those wanting a breath of exhilarating fresh air. The Devonshire Arms is still decidedly a traditional pub, with live jazz on Thursdays, a mixed bag of customers and plenty of chat and conversation all around. On the walls are family photographs detailing links with the Royal Air Force and the Far East.

Oriental overtones are also easy to detect in the eclectic lunchtime menu, which looks to India for buttered chicken masala, shai korma and malaidar unday ('the finest egg curry yet,' according to the blurb). China has its say with kung po chicken and honey-layered duck, and you can also find Singapore noodles and spicy offerings from Malaysia. Not content with plundering the East, the kitchen also tries its hand with courgettes provençale, carbonnade of beef, and tortellini with home-made tomato sauce. Brian Harrison's mussel chowder is a best seller and it's easy to see why: it's a thick, hearty brew full of juicy molluscs in a saffron and tomato-flavoured broth loaded with potatoes and mushrooms. He also produces exemplary gravlax, which is beautifully firm and tender. If you want no more than a snack, the menu also advertises open sandwiches on French bread. Sweets are dominated by crêpes served in threes. 'It's a shame they don't serve food in the evenings except Monday,' concluded one Mancunian with a seasoned palate, 'because this would be an ideal, accessible location for city-dwellers like us who fancy a good, impromptu meal which isn't going to cost much.' Beer drinkers have a choice of Robinson's Best Bitter, Mild and Frederic's Premium, while those with a taste for New World wines will find plenty to please on the ever-changing list. SAMPLE DISHES: hummus with hot pitta bread £3.50; smoked sausage with sauté potatoes £5.25; summer pudding £2.50.

Open *11 to 3, 5.30 to 11, Sun 12 to 3.30, 7.30 to 10.30; bar food all week L 11.30 to 2.15, Mon D 6.45 to 9*
Details *Children welcome in eating areas Car park Wheelchair access Garden Live music No dogs No cards*

MELLOR Lancashire **map 8**

▲ *Millstone*

Church Lane, Mellor TEL: (01254) 813333
off A677, 3m NW of Blackburn

The Millstone, a substantial grey stone building, stands high up above the Ribble Valley within easy reach of the Forest of Bowland. Once an old coaching-inn, it still manages to feel like a pub although it clearly functions as a hotel. The centre of the 'pub' action is Millers Bar, a large, open-plan panelled room where you can quaff pints of Thwaites ales in an atmosphere that is lively and convivial. All ages mingle here. The menu, with additions on the blackboard, makes interesting reading and shows some brisk modern touches: terrine of Tuscan vegetables comes with a balsamic dressing, scallop and artichoke broth is a fixture, while confit of duck is served with cassoulet. Reports have also singled out creamy leek and spinach soup; chicken, ham and apricot pie 'chock a block' with meat; and Jamaican jerk chicken with peas, rice and home-made chutney. There are also some good sweets on offer, including mango and Grand Marnier sorbet and well-made treacle tart. A sandwich and baguette menu is also available, and full meals are served in the restaurant. Wines by the glass are 'very drinkable'. SAMPLE DISHES: salmon and smoked haddock fish-cakes £4; lamb balti £6.75; crème brûlée £3.50.

Open *11am to 11pm, Sun 12 to 10.30; bar food and restaurant 12 to 2, 7 to 9.30 (8.45 Sun and bank hols)*
Details *Children welcome Car park Wheelchair access (also WC) No smoking in restaurant Background music No dogs Access, Amex, Delta, Diners, Switch, Visa Accommodation: 24 rooms, B&B £49 to £100*

MELLS Somerset **map 2**

▲ *Talbot Inn*

High Street, Mells TEL: (01373) 812254
3m W of Frome

This rambling, fifteenth-century coaching-inn in the unspoilt village of Mells is close to the medieval church and next to an impressive manor-house, long associated with the Horner family. In fact, the nursery rhyme about Little Jack Horner is thought to have originated in the pub, though quite which corner he sat in is anyone's guess. The interior is comfortable and tastefully decorated, with pews, country prints and a good log fire in the beamed and half-panelled lounge. Other public areas include an adjacent room which also has a log fire, a lively bar and the 'Oxford Room'. Around half a dozen meat specials and the same number of fish dishes extend the printed menu; you could find monkfish and sea bass, and, in season, pheasant from the local shoot. Otherwise there's carrot and orange soup, mushrooms stuffed with walnuts and Stilton, lamb and potato stew, cheese and ratatouille flan, and game pie, for example, plus apple crumble to finish. Butcombe Bitter and Bass are on handpump, along with a beer of the week, and there's a full wine list. The planted, cobbled courtyard and garden are pleasant places for outdoor eating and drinking. SAMPLE DISHES: cauliflower and Stilton soup £2.25; grilled lemon sole with herb butter £8.75; tiramisù £3.25.

Open *12 to 3, 6 to 11, Sun 12 to 3, 7 to 10.30; bar food and restaurant 12 to 2, 7 to 10*
Details *Children welcome Car park Garden Background music No dogs in eating areas Access, Delta, Diners, Switch, Visa Accommodation: 7 rooms, B&B £24 to £53*

MELMERBY Cumbria map 10

Shepherds Inn

Melmerby TEL: (01768) 881217
on A686 Penrith to Alston road, 8m NE of Penrith

'The choice of cheeses should satisfy any fromage freak,' said one reporter. There's a choice of no fewer than 17 of them with 'our Ultimate Ploughman's, with biscuits or however you like'. North Country options include Cotherstone, Redesdale, Bewcastle, and Westmorland Smoked, to name a few, and then there's Cornish Yarg, Blue Vinney and two-year-old Cheddar. But non-cheese lovers will not be disappointed either, for the selection on the two printed menus – one is a 'menu of the day' – runs to steaks, pork tenderloin, pasta, curries, salads, Cumberland sausage hotpot, and fish such as local Ullswater trout. The drinks are of interest too. Jennings Cumberland Ale is permanently 'on' and others are changed regularly. You could find Joseph Holt Bitter, Black Sheep Riggwelter, Wadworth 6X, Mansfield Bitter, and Fuller's London Pride; among bottled beers are half a dozen or so from Belgium and the occasional German wheat beer. About 40 malt whiskies are on offer, and the wine list features around 30, a number available by the half-bottle – or opt perhaps for a glass of English fruit wine. The pub overlooks the village green at a crossroads in the foothills of the Pennines, and is in popular walking country; the start of the Roman Maiden Way is nearby. SAMPLE DISHES: lamb and vegetable soup £2; venison and Roquefort crumble £8; apricot lemon cheesecake £2.50.

Open *10.30 to 3, 6 to 11, Sun 12 to 3, 7 to 10.30; bar food 11 to 2.30, 6 to 9.45, Sun 12 to 2.30, 7 to 9.45; closed 25 Dec*
Details *Children welcome Car park Wheelchair access Patio Non-smoking area Live music; jukebox Dogs welcome in 1 bar only Access, Amex, Delta, Diners, Switch, Visa*

MEYSEY HAMPTON Gloucestershire map 2

▲ *Masons Arms*

Meysey Hampton TEL: (01285) 850164
off A417, 1½m W of Fairford

Conveniently situated between Lechlade and the historic sights of Cirencester, this seventeenth-century Cotswold inn is a popular haunt for travellers and locals, young and old. All comers are treated with kindness and courtesy. The building itself is Grade II listed and, inside, the authentic bucolic atmosphere seems to have been preserved with farming bric-à-brac on bare walls, oak settles, and dried hops dangling from the ceiling – although one reporter thought the place had 'tea-room' overtones. The menu is a mixed bag of pub stalwarts (baguettes, ham, egg and chips, lasagne), plus a few traditional dishes (game pie, grilled salmon) and a few more exotic sounding specials, including spicy lemon chicken fillet and breast of duck with sweet plum sauce. A separate board lists sweets such as blackcurrant and cassis crêpes, queen of puddings, and apple crumble. Wadworth 6X and John Smiths are on draught, along with a guest ale – maybe Marston's Pedigree or something from the local Wychwood brewery. The wine list (written on the labels of magnums of champagne) is a short, serviceable selection. SAMPLE DISHES: grilled mushrooms with Stilton and bacon £3.25; beef and Beamish casserole £5.50; apple and blackberry sponge £2.25.

Open *11.15 to 3, 6 to 11, Sun 12 to 3, 7 to 10.30; bar food and restaurant all week L 12 to 2, Mon to Sat D 7 to 9.30*
Details *Children welcome Car park Wheelchair access (also WC) Patio No smoking in restaurant Background music Dogs welcome Access, Delta, Switch, Visa Accommodation: 8 rooms, B&B £28 to £44*

MICKLEHAM Surrey map 3

King William IV

Byttom Hill, Mickleham TEL: (01372) 372590
off A24, between Leatherhead and Dorking, 2m S of Leatherhead

'A real walker's pub' on a hillside, with good views over Norbury Park and the Mole Valley, neatly sums up the major appeal of this popular Surrey pub. Those who have burned off a lot of energy can replenish their vigour with draughts of Adnams Bitter, Hogs Back TEA and a monthly guest such as Ringwood Fortyniner. If solid sustenance is required, there are fine-looking sandwiches plus big portions of lasagne, navarin of lamb, pasta with prawns, and so on, to quell the hunger pangs. Fruit crumble comes with ice-cream; otherwise look for the dessert of the day. Choice is limited on Sunday lunch-times and bank holidays, and a menu of 'starters' is served in the evening. Note that there are steep steps both inside the pub and outside. Not far away is Box Hill (owned by the National Trust). SAMPLE DISHES: jumbo sausage in French bread with salad £4.50; seafood pie £6.75; bread-and-butter pudding £3.

Open *11 to 3, 6 to 11, Sun 12 to 3, 7 to 10.30; bar food all week L 12 to 2, Tue to Sun D 7 to 9.45*
Details *Children under 14 in small eating area only (limited space) Garden and patio Background music No dogs Access, Delta, Switch, Visa*

MIDDLETON ONE ROW Co Durham map 10

▲ *Devonport Hotel*

16–18 The Front, Middleton One Row TEL: (01325) 332255
off A67, 4m E of Darlington

Although set in a peaceful, out-of-the-way spot high above the River Tees, with views over wooded farmland to the Cleveland Hills, the Devonport's proximity to the Teesside conurbation means it's a useful stopover for business people. Meals are served in two restaurants, one specialising in fish, and there is a separate menu in the bar – a plain, spacious room with red plush benches and chairs. On offer might be avocado and crab, or penne with Toulouse sausage to start, followed by salmon fillet glazed with tomato and pesto sauce, chicken and seafood paella, or pork fillet with wild mushroom sauce, and then cherry cheesecake, or jam roly-poly with custard. Beers on draught include Theakston Best, Boddingtons Bitter and John Smith's Magnet, and the list of 30 wines is supplemented by bin-ends. The locomotives in Darlington's Railway Museum should appeal to aficionados. SAMPLE DISHES: smoked chicken and bacon salad £4; grilled haddock with chive butter £6; lemon meringue roulade £3.25.

Open *11am to 11pm, Sun 12 to 10.30; bar food and restaurant 12 to 2.30, 6.30 to 9.30 (10 Fri and Sat)*
Details *Children welcome Car park Wheelchair access (also WC) Patio Background and live music Dogs welcome Access, Amex, Delta, Diners, Switch, Visa Accommodation: 16 rooms, B&B £50 to £80*

MIDFORD Bath & N.E. Somerset map 2

Hope & Anchor Inn

Midford TEL: (01225) 832296
on B3110, 3m S of Bath

Negotiating the steep hill and tricky bends on the B-road out of Bath, you might easily miss this unassuming stone pub altogether, which would be a pity. It's a comfortable and welcoming place with a sound reputation for interesting food. Warm colour schemes, attractive prints and an open fire in the stone hearth create the mood in the bar, where you can choose from a menu with strong Continental overtones: Spanish tortilla, a selection of tapas (including 'jamon', spicy mushrooms, olives and so on), and paella share the billing with tomato, feta cheese and avocado salad with basil dressing. Even more interesting is the list of fish specials – not only whole lemon sole, and skate with black butter, but also meaty fillets of monkfish 'draped' with chorizo and served with a herby tomato sauce garnished with mussels. A separate restaurant menu, which includes things like marinated lamb with prunes, ginger and coriander, is also available in the bar and the garden. Real ales in this free house are listed as Bass, Butcombe Bitter and Tisbury Best from Wiltshire. There are pleasant walks along the banks of the River Frome, and Westwood Manor (National Trust) is nearby. SAMPLE DISHES: provençale fish soup £3.75; sirloin steak with garlic, salad and fried potatoes £8; tarte Tatin £2.50.

Open *11.30 to 2.30, 6.30 to 11, Sun 12 to 3, 7 to 10.30; bar food and restaurant 12 to 2, 6.30 to 9.30*
Details *Children welcome Car park Wheelchair access Patio Background music No dogs Access, Switch, Visa*

MILTON ABBAS Dorset map 2

▲ *Hambro Arms*

Milton Abbas TEL: (01258) 880233
off A354, 6m SW of Blandford Forum

This low, thatched pub fits in well with the neat and orderly white-washed cottages that line the main street of the late-eighteenth-century village of Milton Abbas. Inside, the beamed front bar has a log fire and well-spaced dining tables. There's a separate dining-room called 'The Rib Room', and a terrace if the weather is warm. The menu includes pub staples such as ploughman's, sandwiches, salads, pies and grills. The all-day breakfast fry-up is still a feature. The blackboard offers more choice, along the lines of medallions of venison with pigeon breast, grilled pork steak with cider and Dijon mustard sauce, and chicken Rossini with mushroom sauce. A reporter was impressed by mushrooms in tomato and garlic ('lots of garlic'), and 'rich, gamey' roast partridge with rosemary and thyme sauce that came with 'decent, crisp, non-greasy' chips, but could only manage a third of the large portions. Boddingtons and Flowers Original are on handpump, and there's a decent selection of wines, including Australian and Spanish. Nearby are the rare breeds centre at Long Ash Farm and Park Farm Museum. SAMPLE DISHES: crispy coated Camembert with gooseberry sauce £4; steak and mushroom pie £7.25; peach and passion-fruit torte £3.

Open *11 to 2.30, 6.30 to 11, Sun 12 to 3, 7 to 10.30; bar food and restaurant 12 to 2, 7 to 9.30 (8.30 Sun)*
Details *Children welcome in dining-room Car park Wheelchair access (also WC) Patio Background music in bar only No dogs Access, Switch, Visa Accommodation: 2 rooms, B&B £25 to £50*

MILTON STREET East Sussex map 3

Sussex Ox

Milton Street, Alfriston TEL: (01323) 870840
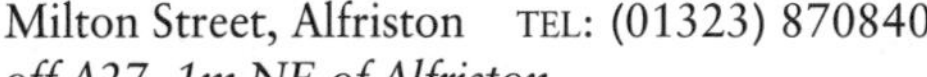
off A27, 1m NE of Alfriston

This large, rambling pub is 'suitable for almost anyone, from children and grannies to European visitors', notes a man of Sussex. Its attractions are obvious: as well as a huge outdoor adventure playground, there's a no-smoking family room called 'The Sty' and a bargain price for children's meals. Drusilla's Theme Park – which children will enjoy – is nearby. Added to that, the views across the Cuckmere Valley and South Downs are superb, attracting ramblers who may have just visited the ancient site of the Long Man of Wilmington. The menu will suit all palates, and the range includes everything from burgers, ploughman's and open sandwiches – called Sussex Ox Slabs – to oriental-style tiger prawns, garlic and herb chicken, and smoked fish platter. A specials board lists daily-changing dishes. There is a separate dining-room – The Harness Room – which serves the same menu. Real ales available include Harvey's Sussex Best, and Greene King Abbot Ale and IPA; guest beers also make an appearance, and the pub has a small wine list. SAMPLE DISHES: chive and mackerel pâté £3.25; steak, mushroom and ale pie £7; treacle sponge pudding £2.75.

Open *11 to 3, 6 to 11, Sun 12 to 3, 7 to 10.30; bar food and restaurant 11 to 2.15, 6 to 9.15*
Details *Children welcome Car park Garden No smoking in family room Background and live music No dogs in eating areas No cards*

MINCHINHAMPTON Gloucestershire map 2

Weighbridge Inn

Longfords, Minchinhampton TEL: (01453) 832520
on B4014, m E of Nailsworth towards Avening

This fascinating old inn, adjacent to the original packhorse trail to Bristol, takes its name from the weighbridge that served the mills and stone mines of the area. If you are interested in things past, you can visit the mines, once you have obtained permission from their custodians, the National Trust. '2 in 1' pies are the pub's renowned speciality: in one half is cauliflower cheese, and in the other a meaty mixture such as steak and mushroom, or turkey, sweetcorn and pepper topped with home-made pastry. Other options on the short but 'cooked to order' menu might include shepherd's pie, seafood bake, pizzas and salads, while sweets take in such things as banoffi pie and chocolate munchy cake. A decent choice of real ales includes Wadworth 6X, Smiles Best and Theakstons Best among others, and there are a handful of workaday wines too. SAMPLE DISHES: vegetable and lentil crumble £4.25; steak and mushroom pie £5.25; cherry meringue surprise £2.50.

Open *11 to 2.30, 7 (6.30 Sat) to 11, Sun 12 to 2.30, 7 to 10.30; bar food 12 to 2, 7 (6.30 Sat) to 9 (9.30 Fri and Sat)*
Details *Children welcome Car park Wheelchair access (also WC) Garden and patio No music Dogs welcome but not in garden No cards*

MITHIAN Cornwall **map 1**

Miners Arms

Mithian TEL: (01872) 552375
on B3285, 2m E of St Agnes

The decades roll by, but time seems to have little impact on the 400-year-old Miners Arms. Inscribed on one of the decorative ceilings is the date 1577; there's an alleged penance cupboard ('but we'd rather do our time in the bar!', says the brochure); and the presence of spirits has – apparently – been felt in various parts of the pub. The bar menu doesn't seek to court fashion: instead it offers a 'garlic bread collection' (including one version topped with tomato and basil), along with variations on the ploughman's theme, Cornish crab bake, curries and something called the 'Sou' Wester Supper', which consists of spinach, smoked haddock and white fish in a tarragon cream sauce with a cheese crumble topping. Bass and Marston's Pedigree are on handpump and the pub has a few familiar wines on display. SAMPLE DISHES: mushrooms in garlic butter £3.75; chilli tomato pasta £5.50; blueberry and apple pie £2.50.

Open *12 to 3 (2.30 winter), 6 to 11, Sun 12 to 3, 7 to 10.30 (11 winter); bar food and restaurant Mon to Sat 12 to 2.15, 7 to 9.30*
Details *Children welcome Car park Garden and patio No smoking in dining-room Background music Dogs welcome on a lead No cards*

MONKSILVER Somerset **map 2**

Notley Arms

Monksilver TEL: (01984) 656217
on B3188, 5m S of Watchet

This white-painted, sturdy-looking village pub is set in glorious countryside with a pretty stream running beside the garden. Inside, there's a relaxing country feel to the L-shaped bar area, with its motley collection of tables, settles and chairs. Log-burning stoves heat the room if it's cold, and fresh flowers and knick-knacks enhance the comfortable atmosphere. A light and cheerful family room has plenty of toys and games to amuse the children. Food is advertised on a blackboard and, besides the usual ploughman's and other pub staples, you will find perhaps Exmoor beef salad, filled pitta bread, fresh mussels, pasta with ham and cream, or chicken breast with apple and tarragon stuffing. Puddings could include treacle tart, meringue with ice-cream, or banana and chocolate sauce, and there's been praise for the malted bread-and-butter pudding served with local clotted cream. For beer drinkers Exmoor Ale, Ushers Best and Morland Old Speckled Hen are on handpump. A decent selection of wines is listed on the blackboard, with a number available by the glass – or opt for one of the country fruit wines. Within walking distance is Combe Sydenham Hall, which is open to the public. SAMPLE DISHES: smoked haddock fish-cakes with lemon sauce £5.50; 'old-fashioned' lamb with onion dumplings £6; brown-bread ice-cream £2.50.

Open *11.30 to 2.30, 6.30 to 11, Sun 12 to 2.30, 7 to 10.30; bar food 12 to 2, 7 to 9.30, Sun 12 to 1.45, 7 to 9; closed 2 weeks end Jan/early Feb*
Details *Children welcome in family room Car park Garden No smoking in family room Live music Dogs welcome on a lead No cards*

MONTACUTE Somerset **map 2**

▲ *Kings Arms Inn*

Montacute TEL: (01935) 822513
just off A3088, 4m NW of Yeovil

The Union Jack flutters outside this creeper-clad sixteenth-century inn, set in an unspoilt, quintessentially English village. Built of honey-coloured stone, the hotel can be found among the trees at the bottom of Ham Hill – panoramic views of the village and Montacute House await those who make the climb to the top. Relaxation and gentility are the hallmarks within, where the menu lists traditional favourites such as melon with Parma ham, smoked salmon, sirloin steak with mushrooms and tomatoes, and pies of turkey and apricot, or beef in ale with mushrooms; and more modern dishes which are given a lift by dressings and sauces – salad of tomato, mozzarella and basil with pink grapefruit dressing, grilled plaice fillet with shellfish sauce, and baked aubergines layered with duxelles of spinach and mushrooms with chilli and cashew-nut sauce, for example. The blackboard specials could feature pork and pigeon terrine among the first courses, chicken, ham and asparagus pie topped with mash as a main course, and perhaps lemon tart for pudding. Bass and Fuller's London Pride are on draught, and a blackboard lists some interesting and good-value wines by the glass. SAMPLE DISHES: smoked duck with pear chutney £4.25; rabbit and boar pie with juniper and gin £8; grape crème brûlée £3.50.

Open *11 to 2.30, 6 to 11, Sun 12 to 2, 7 to 10.30; bar food all week 12 to 2, Mon to Sat 7 to 9; restaurant Mon to Sat D only 7 to 9*
Details *Children welcome in bar eating area Car park Wheelchair access (also WC) Garden No smoking in eating areas No music Guide dogs only Access, Amex, Delta, Switch, Visa Accommodation: 30 rooms, B&B £53 to £85*

MORWENSTOW Cornwall map 1

Bush Inn

Crosstown, Morwenstow TEL: (01288) 331242
3m W of A39, between Bude and Clovelly, 6m N of Bude; from village follow signs to Morwenstow Church and then Bush Inn

Find the Bush Inn at the end of a single-track lane that stops just short of the cliffs with their dramatic sea views. The building itself looks like a farmhouse, though parts of it date back to AD 950, when it is thought the place was a chapel for Celtic hermits. Nowadays, within its two unassuming tiny bars with their heavy beams and rough stone floors, the pub offers homely, no-frills, good-value bar lunches – 'solid fuel for people who have just had a bracing clifftop walk' in the view of one reporter. In summer you're likely to find crab or mackerel ploughman's along with sandwiches, while in winter hearty stews – of lamb, perhaps, or turkey – and soups are on offer, with perhaps spotted dick to finish. Beer drinkers can opt for St Austell HSD or draught Guinness, and three wines are sold by the glass. Nearby is Morwenstow Church, known for its eccentric Victorian vicar, Robert Stephen Hawker; in the churchyard you will find the crew of one shipwreck that he buried with the ship's figure-head as a grave marker. SAMPLE DISHES: Cornish pasty £2.25; beef stew £3.50; sticky toffee pudding £2.

Open *12 to 3, 7 to 11, Sun 12 to 3, 7 to 10.30; bar food Mon to Sat L only 12 to 2*
Details *No children Car park Garden No music Dogs welcome No cards*

The Guide *is totally independent, accepts no free hospitality and carries no advertising.*

MOULSOE Buckinghamshire map 6

▲ *Carrington Arms*

Moulsoe TEL: (01908) 218050
1m E of M1 Jct. 14 towards Cranfield

Edwin and Trudy Cheeseman moved to this converted estate manager's residence in a straggling village seemingly on a road to nowhere in April 1995. They brought with them a very distinctive way of doing things, an idea that evolved during their time at the Black Horse, Woburn. Edwin's 'up-front style may not be to everyone's taste,' commented one reporter, 'but there's no doubt he's a natural-born achiever.' Holding centre stage in the open-plan interior is a 'bespoke Falcon Range' which goes hand in hand with what is virtually a mini-butcher's shop and fishmonger rolled into one. The procedure is as follows: find a table (there are no bookings), set up a tab at the bar, then order some drink. Four real ales, including local Charles Wells Bombardier plus Boddingtons and Adnams, are on draught, the wine list is typically idiosyncratic, and there are jugs of Pimms in summer. Next stop, the refrigerated counter, where all kinds of beefy joints, steaks, fish and game are laid out; take your pick, choose your weight and decide whether you want exemplary grilling, steaming or even the 'smoke pot'. While you wait, you can stand at the oyster bar, indulge in a bivalve or two with perhaps a glass of fizz or a shot of pepper vodka. Alternatively, order from a short menu of bar snacks that ranges from Brie and apple omelette, and beef and ale cobbler, to tom yum soup and other exotica inspired by holiday trips to the Far East. SAMPLE DISHES: hot Scotch kipper fillet roll £3.50; Cromer crab salad £6; pear and ginger sponge with butterscotch sauce £3.

Open *11 to 2.30, 6 to 11, Sun 12 to 3, 7 to 10.30; bar food 12 to 2, 6.30 to 10, Sun 12 to 2.15, 7 to 9.30*
Details *Children welcome Car park Wheelchair access (also WC) Garden and patio Background music No dogs Access, Amex, Delta, Diners, Switch, Visa Accommodation: 8 rooms, B&B £39 to £49*

MOULTON North Yorkshire map 9

Black Bull Inn ✿ 🍇

Moulton TEL: (01325) 377289
1m SE of Scotch Corner

For more than three decades the Black Bull has been the dominion of the Pagendam family, who have made it a long-established favourite with the citizens of North Yorkshire – not to mention travellers *en route* along the A1. Much of its fame resides with the Seafood Bar and its evening restaurant (quirkily housed in an original 1930s Pullman carriage), but find your way to the bar and you are immediately transported to a civilised country pub. Cushioned black settles and pews provide the seating, copper pots hang from the walls, and an open fire blazes when the weather closes in.

Bar food is limited to lunchtime light meals and snacks, but the quality never lapses. Freshness is the key. One reporter spotted 'deep tureens of soup, generously filled sandwiches and appetising salads', all geared to hearty Yorkshire appetites. Seafood is a strong suit, with everything from oysters and moules marinière to salmon fish-cakes with spicy tomato sauce, and feuilleté of smoked haddock, prawns, parsley and mash. Alternatives might appear in the shape of Welsh rarebit with bacon, steak baguettes, grilled black pudding with pork sausage and apple, or linguine with prawns, sun-dried tomatoes and cream. Rounding things off is a purposeful list of sweets, ranging from dark chocolate truffle terrine with orange sauce to pear and raspberry brûlée. France shows up strongly on the wine list, which is well-chosen and fairly priced across the range; house recommendations are particularly good value. Theakston Best and Tetley Bitter are on draught. SAMPLE DISHES: smoked salmon pâté £5; barbecued spare ribs £5.50; blackcurrant tart £2.50.

Open *12 to 2.30, 6 to 10.30, (11 Fri and Sat), Sun 12 to 2; bar food Mon to Sat L only 12 to 2; restaurant Mon to Fri 12 to 2, 6.45 to 10.15*
Details *No children under 7 Car park Wheelchair access Garden and patio No music No dogs Access, Amex, Delta, Diners, Switch, Visa*

MUCH WENLOCK Shropshire **map 5**

George & Dragon

2 High Street, Much Wenlock TEL: (01952) 727312
on A458, between Shrewsbury and Bridgnorth, 8m NW of Bridgnorth

Nothing much changes at the George & Dragon: the same snug, old-fashioned rooms with lots of nooks and crannies, and collections of bric-à-brac everywhere – old bottles, advertisements and pictures, and hundreds of water jugs hanging from the beamed ceiling. English country cooking is the style: expect the likes of pork and herb terrine, beef casseroled in stout, seafood Wellington, and rabbit in mustard and cider sauce. Home-baked ham with parsley sauce is the kitchen's signature dish, although it can also produce more exotic offerings such as Thai-style chicken. Sandwiches, ploughman's and jacket potatoes join the menu at lunch-times. On handpump you will generally find Hook Norton Best Bitter and Everards Best Bitter, with a range from the Wye Valley and Burton Bridge Breweries.

House wines are sold by the glass, as are three fruit wines from Lurgashall, Sussex, and the local speciality, Rogers Shropshire mead. Much Wenlock, with its medieval guildhall and ruins of an ancient priory, is worth exploring. SAMPLE DISHES: smoked halibut with lime mayonnaise £3.75; casserole of venison with orange and juniper £6; sticky toffee pudding £2.50.

Open *11 to 2.30, 6 to 11, Sun 12 to 2.30, 7 to 10.30; bar food and restaurant all week 12 to 2, 6.30 (7 Sun) to 9*
Details *Children welcome evenings only Wheelchair access Background music No dogs No cards*

▲ *Talbot Inn*

High Street, Much Wenlock TEL: (01952) 727077

'The Talbot Inn has ministered to the needs of the weary traveller for six centuries,' reads the brochure. Dating from 1360, the building was once part of Wenlock Priory (founded by St Milburga and re-built by Lady Godiva) and is thought to have been the Almoner's House. Through an alley is a brick courtyard, and a converted malthouse at the back is used for accommodation. Inside, it is 'unusually genteel', although there are signs of the past in the tiny windows and coat of arms over the ancient fireplace; the atmosphere reminded one visitor of a 'licensed ye olde tea-room'. The printed menu, which is supported by daily specials chalked on a board, offers the likes of Greek salad, black pudding with cider and apple sauce, and grilled sardines, followed by smoked loin of pork in gooseberry sauce, Shropshire pie (with pork, leek, apple and cheese in cider sauce), and haddock Mornay. Bread-and-butter pudding is the best-selling sweet, although you might also choose almond, cherry and pear tart, or fruit crumble. Everything appears to be 'freshly produced on the premises', concluded one visitor. Real ales are familiar names such as Courage Directors and Morland Old Speckled Hen, and wines by the glass are kept in good order. SAMPLE DISHES: Stilton and walnut pâté £3; grilled Barnsley chops with mint and garlic butter £8; treacle tart £3.25.

Open *10.30 to 2.30, 6 to 11, Sun 12 to 2.30, 7 to 10.30; bar food and restaurant 12 to 2, 7 to 9.30 (8.30 Sun)*
Details *No children Car park Wheelchair access Garden and patio No smoking in restaurant Background music Guide dogs only Access, Amex, Delta, Switch, Visa Accommodation: 6 rooms, B&B £40 to £90*

If you disagree with any assessment made in the Guide, *write to tell us why* – The Which? Guide to Country Pubs, *FREEPOST, 2 Marylebone Road, London NW1 1YN.*

MUNSLOW **Shropshire** **map 5**

Crown

Munslow TEL: (01584) 841205
on B4368, 8m N of Ludlow

The Georgian façade of this impressive-looking three-storey pub hides an interior that dates back to Tudor times. Flasgstone floors alternate with patterned carpets in the beamed bar riddled with nooks and crannies. Most of the space is devoted to eating, and the first-floor dining-room copes with any overspill. This is a family business: Adrian cooks with his mother's help, while dad runs the bar. Various chalkboards advertise the usual ploughman's, lasagne, cauliflower cheese and the like; but also note the disarmingly simple salad of white anchovies, as well as the handful of Thai dishes, including tom yum soup, and tiger prawns with noodles. In addition, a printed menu lists dishes that sound as if they have come straight out of a classic French cookbook: pork Dijon and trout grenobloise line up alongside 'poulet Calvi' – a colourful concoction of skinned chicken breast flamed in brandy with tomatoes, olives, bacon and garlic. From the bar you can view the landlord's own micro-brewery, which produces house beers such as Boy's Pale Ale and Munslow Ale, as well as a monthly special; otherwise drink Banks's Mild, Marston's Pedigree or Old Hazy cider. Nine house wines head the good-value list. Reporters have also singled out the coffee: 'the first time I've heard beans being ground in a pub,' commented one well-travelled observer of the scene. From Thursday to Sunday during the summer months, afternoon teas are served in what was once a courtroom. SAMPLE DISHES: smoked chicken and cream cheese soup £2.25; salmon Normandy £9; treacle tart £2.25.

Open *12 to 2.30, 7 to 11, Sun 12 to 3, 7 to 10.30; bar food 12 to 2, 7 to 9.30*
Details *Children welcome Car park Garden and patio Background music Dogs welcome on a lead Access, Amex, Delta, Switch, Visa*

MYLOR BRIDGE **Cornwall** **map 1**

Pandora Inn

Restronguet Creek, Mylor Bridge TEL: (01326) 372678
off A39 from Truro, take B3292 signposted Penryn, then Mylor Bridge road, and follow steep road down to Restronguet

The pub was named after the ship sent to pick up the mutineers of Captain Bligh's *Bounty*. The *Pandora* sank on her return voyage: the captain clearly didn't go down with his ship, for after his court martial he is said to have bought and renamed this inn. The nautical associations are appropriate, for the pub is in a beautiful waterside setting with its own moorings for yachts. Inside the ancient building is a series of flagstoned, low-ceilinged bars – tall people may have to duck to miss some of the beams. The bar menu is strong on fish – from a half-pint of prawns, and crab-cakes, to seafood pancake, and fish pie – and other dishes range from a wide selection of sandwiches and burgers to sausages and mash, and spinach and mushroom quiche; steak sandwich and mixed grill are also available in the evening, and a traditional roast on Sunday. The upstairs restaurant is open for dinner. St Austell Tinners and Trelawney's Pride are on draught, as is real Cornish scrumpy; more than 20 wines, including locally produced Polmassick, are sold by the glass. SAMPLE DISHES: deep-fried mushrooms £3.50; Restronguet fish pie £5.50; treacle tart £2.50.

Open *Mon to Fri winter 12 to 2.30, 7 to 11, summer 11am to 11pm, Sat all year 11am to 11pm, Sun all year 12 to 10.30; bar food 12 to 2, 6.30 to 9 (9.30 Fri and Sat); restaurant all week D only 7 to 9.30; closed 25 Dec*
Details *Children welcome in bar eating area Car park Wheelchair access (also WC) No-smoking areas in pub and restaurant No music Dogs welcome on a lead Access, Amex, Delta, Switch, Visa*

NANCENOY Cornwall map 1

▲ *Trengilly Wartha Inn*

Nancenoy TEL: (01326) 340332
off A394 Falmouth to Helston road, then follow signs to Constantine and Nancenoy

'Trengilly Wartha' is the old Cornish for 'settlement above the trees': it's a fitting description for this remote place nestling in the wooded valley of Polpenwith Creek surrounded by six acres of gardens and meadows in an 'Area of Outstanding Natural Beauty'. The building started life in the eighteenth century as a simple farm dwelling, and became a fully fledged inn only during the 1970s – making it quite a novice by country pub standards. Inside are two bar areas, with settles and stools around the counter and a wood-burning stove as the focal point of proceedings.

The owners of this pub believe in 'inventive food', noted one reporter. The printed bar menu is an interesting mix of pub staples and livelier modern ideas ranging from ploughman's with West Country cheeses and home-pickled vegetables, Cornish pasties, Trengilly sausages, and chilli, to grilled goats' cheese and olives on home-made ciabatta, 'fine' twice-baked leek and cheese soufflé, and steamed 'boudin noir' on a bed of creamed potatoes and spiced red cabbage. Daily specials bring fish to the forefront: Falmouth Bay scallops with ginger and spring onions, fillet of sea bass with tarragon butter, and 'outstanding' flash-fried crab-cakes with tiny baby turnips and a cream sauce, for example. Others have praised rare-roasted wild pigeon breast on a salad of bitter greens. Desserts might include 'appetising' steamed ginger pudding as well as meringues with 'wonderful' clotted cream. Fixed-price dinners and Sunday lunch are served in the separate restaurant. Wine is also taken very seriously here: the owners have recently set up their own retail business and hold regular tastings; their 200-strong list features a great selection of 15 by the glass available for bar customers. First-rate real ales are tapped direct from casks: Sharp's Cornish Coaster, Dartmoor Best and St Austell HSD are supplemented by regular guests; you can also drink Pothallon and Sheppy's ciders. SAMPLE DISHES: Stilton and spring-onion tartlet £3.50; Cornish lamb and flageolet bean casserole £6; passion-fruit cheesecake £2.75.

Open *11 to 3, 6 to 11, Sun 12 to 3, 7 (6.30 winter) to 10.30; bar food 12 to 2.15, 6.30 to 9.30, Sun 12.15 to 2, 7.15 to 9.30; restaurant all week D only 7.30 to 9.30*

Details *Children welcome in bar eating area, games room and conservatory Car park Wheelchair access Garden and patio No smoking in conservatory No music No dogs in restaurant Access, Amex, Delta, Diners, Switch, Visa Accommodation: 6 rooms, B&B £32 to £62*

NAUNTON Gloucestershire **map 5**

▲ *Black Horse*

Naunton TEL: (01451) 850565
off B4068, 5m W of Stow-on-the-Wold

'People come here to talk to each other and to the landlord,' noted one reporter describing the atmosphere in this 'villagey' Cotswold pub. The interior has a more distinctive character than most, with its 'rather blackened' old stone walls, a lovely old clock with a carved wooden surround above the fireplace, and one wall covered by drawings of nearby villages. Collections of china, flasks, pewter mugs and dried flowers are arranged in uncluttered fashion in a couple of niches. The printed menu doesn't stray far beyond pub standards such as potato skins and chicken Kiev, but a few more appealing home-made offerings show up on the blackboard: garlic mushrooms, roast duck with port and mushroom sauce, salmon and broccoli with pasta in a cream sauce are typical. Gâteaux and ice-creams dominate the desserts. 'Excellent' Donnington's BB and SBA are on draught and wines are served by the glass. Naunton is strung out along the River Windrush, a delightful spot for walking or contemplation.

SAMPLE DISHES: carrot and coriander soup £2; beef Stroganov £7; treacle sponge £2.25.

Open *11 to 3, 6 to 11, Sun 12 to 3, 7 to 10.30; bar food and restaurant 12 to 2, 7 to 9*
Details *Children welcome Car park Wheelchair access (also WC) Patio Background music Dogs welcome on a lead Access, Switch, Visa Accommodation: 2 rooms, B&B £20 to £35*

NAYLAND Suffolk map 6

White Hart

11 High Street, Nayland TEL: (01206) 263382

Take one fifteenth-century Suffolk village pub, bring in a chef with five years' experience heading the kitchen at Le Gavroche, support it all with the Roux Brothers' name and back-up, and you have the ingredients for a severe identity crisis. Is it a pub, is it a restaurant, is it perhaps a bit of both? The persuasive informality, the lack of tablecloths, the simply written plastic-coated menus and the 'thick' bistro-style wine glasses clearly signal 'new wave pub', even if dishes do appear in large, deep plates with elaborate Gavroche-style presentation.

The setting for all this is a heavily beamed, open-plan dining area with bare brick and painted walls hung mostly with nineteenth-century military portraits. Part of the floor is glassed over to reveal a cellar 'full of empty bottles, boxes, tins and cases, including one which once contained Château Pétrus'. The main man, chef/proprietor Mark Prescott, confines himself to the kitchen, while a mix of English and French staff keep the mood cheerfully animated out front. Prescott's cooking owes more to robust Englishness than Gallic haute cuisine and he has tailored his menus perfectly to the needs of pub customers as well as food buffs. He's not shy about using cheap or unfashionable cuts of meat, a lot of things are 'on the bone', dishes are often allowed to simmer slow and long. Leg of rabbit is served with a creamy mustard sauce and braised cabbage, shoulder of lamb is a mighty piece of meat roasted for a goodly length of time, while lamb shanks are braised and glazed with honey and rosemary sauce and served with savoyard potatoes. Occasionally a more eclectic modern idea surfaces, as in ravioli of goats' cheese with pesto and balsamic vinegar, or a salad of spiced tiger prawns around a mound of Japanese noodles.

Lunch is fixed-price for two or three courses, although you are welcome to order just a main dish. There are even sandwiches – although these are not your usual cheese-and-pickle variety: the version with chargrilled minute steak, red onions and fried egg in ciabatta smeared with mustard butter is a bumper bestseller. The evening *carte* offers similar dishes – apart from, say, plates of Irish oysters with a red wine vinegar dressing, or whole roast Dover sole. Prices of most main dishes are, remarkably, in single figures. To finish, the English tradition returns with Sussex pond pudding, and apple tart, alongside sablé of poached pears with kirsch sabayon and caramel sauce. The wine list is a cracking, imaginative collection of around 60 bins, with half a dozen by the glass, half-bottles a-plenty and big, juicy flavours abundant. Lest you forget this is still a pub, there are handpumps dispensing pints of Adnams Bitter, Greene King IPA and a guest ale. Accommodation is planned for late 1997. SAMPLE DISHES: game terrine with fig chutney £5; roast fillet of cod wrapped in prosciutto £9.75; crème caramel with sultanas and prunes in armagnac £4.

Open *12 to 3, 6.30 to 11, Sun 12 to 3, 7 to 10.30; bar food 12 to 2, 6.30 to 9.30*
Details *Children welcome Car park Wheelchair access (also WC) Garden and patio Background music No dogs Access, Amex, Delta, Diners, Switch, Visa*

NETTLECOMBE Dorset map 2

▲ *Marquis of Lorne*

Nettlecombe TEL: (01308) 485236
off A3066, 4½m NE of Bridport

A good, friendly atmosphere permeates throughout the traditionally furnished bars at this stone-built pub in the shadow of Eggardon Hill, an Iron Age rampart (worth the climb up). The bedrooms have recently been totally refurbished, and the beer garden with its herbaceous borders is now separated from the large and safe children's play area. The landlords tell us they've abandoned a printed menu (apart from one listing snacks like sandwiches and salads) and now rely on blackboards to inform customers of what's on offer – and a wide choice it is, too, with as many as 15 main courses. To start, there might be smoked mackerel with gooseberry and elderflower chutney, a tomato chutney to accompany deep-fried baby sweetcorn and courgettes, and minted yoghurt with onion bhajias. There's always a good choice of fish dishes among the main courses – smoked haddock and prawn pie, say, or crab salad – while meaty items may include lamb and apricot pie, meatballs in red wine and tomato sauce, and chicken breast topped with cheese and bacon. Favourite puddings run from fruit salad to tiramisù, as well as raspberry pavlova. Local brewery Palmers supplies Bridport Bitter and IPA, and at least seven wines are sold by the glass. SAMPLE DISHES:

melon with prawns £4; grilled pork chop with gravy and apple £6; white chocolate mousse £2.50.

Open *11 to 2.30, 6 (6.30 winter) to 11, Sun 12 to 3, 7 to 10.30; bar food 12 to 2, 7 to 9.30; no food 25 Dec*
Details *Children welcome in bar eating area Car park Garden No smoking in dining-room Background music No dogs Access, Delta, Switch, Visa Accommodation: 6 rooms, B&B £35 to £58*

NEWLAND Gloucestershire map 5

▲ *Ostrich Inn*

Newland TEL: (01594) 833260
on B4231, 4m SE of Monmouth

The name of the pub probably derives from the symbol of an ostrich used by a family well established in Newland during the eighteenth century, though the building itself dates from the sixteenth century. While the pub's location midway between the Forest of Dean and the Wye Valley is an undoubted attraction, so too are the wide-ranging menus, the real ales and the wines. Dishes are listed on blackboards hung around the bar, complemented at lunch-time by about 30 cheaper specials. Starters may range from whitebait to rabbit satay, main courses from Libyan chicken to stuffed roast grouse. Desserts, including an 'absolutely delicious' bread-and-butter pudding, are more European in scope. Eight frequently changing real ales, perhaps Shepherd Neame Spitfire, Bateman Victory Ale or RCH Old Slug Porter, are on offer, as are 60 wines, including six by the glass. There's also an interesting selection of about 30 malt whiskies, plus a choice of five cafetière coffees. 'The main charm' comes from the warm welcome, the old settles, the view of the fine church opposite, the inglenook, and lighting from the miners' lamps and candles in bottles. 'A very special place,' concludes a reporter. SAMPLE DISHES: Stilton and walnut pâté £4; venison medallions in wild mushroom sauce £13.50; hot toffee pudding £3.

Open *12 to 2.30 (3 Sat), 6.30 to 11, Sun 12 to 3, 6.30 to 11; bar food 12 to 2, 7 to 9.30; closed 25 Dec*
Details *No children Garden and patio Background music Dogs welcome Access, Amex, Delta, Switch, Visa Accommodation: 2 rooms, B&B £25 to £40*

Many pubs have separate restaurants, with very different menus. These have not been inspected. A recommendation for the pub/bar food does not necessarily imply that the restaurant is also recommended.

NEWNHAM Kent map 3

George Inn

44 The Street, Newnham TEL: (01795) 890237
off A2, 5m SW of Faversham

This brick and tile-hung village pub, dating from the sixteenth century, has 'a wonderful atmosphere'. It started life as a farmhouse, and all the striking rooms within have log fires and bare boards strewn with rugs. The walls are covered with prints, and there are displays of butterflies, stuffed birds and clay pipes, and cabinets filled with old glass bottles. Beams are garlanded with hops, flowers on the tables are fresh, and service is both courteous and efficient. Food has a traditional ring to it, with game in season, Whitstable fish and local fruit and vegetables featuring. On the specials blackboard you could find pheasant normande, local skate with black pepper and capers, or meaty lamb and apricot pudding, while the printed menu offers the likes of steaks, pies and ploughman's. To finish, try perhaps chocolate and brandy slice or coffee kahlua ice-cream. This is a Shepherd Neame pub, with the brewery's full range on handpump, including Bishop's Finger and Spitfire, and Original Porter in winter. There's a short wine list, and house wine is served by the glass. Nearby are Doddington Place Garden and the Fleur de Lys Heritage Centre at Faversham. SAMPLE DISHES: fried whitebait £3.75; rack of lamb with rosemary and garlic £10; chocolate, Grand Marnier and almond ice-cream £2.

Open *10.30 to 3, 6 to 11, Sun 12 to 3, 7 to 10.30; bar food Tue to Sun 12 to 2 (1.45 Sun), Tue to Sat 7 to 10*
Details *Children welcome in bar eating area Car park Wheelchair access (also WC) Garden Background music Dogs welcome No cards*

NEWTON-ON-THE-MOOR Northumberland map 10

▲ *Cook and Barker Inn* ✿

Newton-on-the-Moor TEL: (01665) 575234
¼m W of A1 in middle of village

There are views across rolling fields to the North Sea from this comfortable old stone inn (named after two local families who were joined by marriage). A lot has happened to the building in recent years, and current owners Phil and Lynn Farmer have done a great deal to turn it into what an informed source called 'one of Northumberland's top food pubs'. The place fairly packs them in – '150 for Sunday lunch' – but there's no suggestion that the kitchen is cooking by numbers or cutting corners.

The daily blackboard menu served in the bar is reckoned to be 'exceptional value for money' and it succeeds with its blend of simplicity and cutting-edge creativity. On the one hand, there are tureens of vegetable soup based on good stock, quenelles of creamy Stilton and walnut pâté, and liver and bacon with onions. On the other, you might find salad of wood pigeon with roasted peppers and balsamic vinegar, smoked salmon fish-cakes with chive and vermouth sauce, and breast of chicken with 'trompettes de mort' and ratatouille. Rounding things off are desserts like pavlova and sticky toffee pudding. House wines ('on draught or from a box') are served by the glass, and the full list is geared towards customers in the stone-walled restaurant, which is housed in a converted blacksmith's forge. Four real ales, including Stones Bitter and Theakston XB, are on draught. The pub is a useful stopover if you are *en route* to Scotland or fancy exploring nearby attractions such as Howick Hall and Dunstanburgh Castle (National Trust). SAMPLE DISHES: bouillabaisse £4; beef and Guinness pie £5; sticky toffee pudding £2.25.

Open *11 to 3, 6 to 11, Sun 12 to 3, 6 to 10.30; bar food 12 to 2, 6 to 8; restaurant 12 to 2, 7 to 9*
Details *Children welcome in eating areas Car park Wheelchair access Garden No smoking in 1 room No music No dogs Access, Amex, Delta, Switch, Visa Accommodation: 4 rooms, B&B £35 to £65*

NEWTON ST CYRES Devon map 1

Crown and Sceptre

Newton St Cyres TEL: (01392) 851278
on A377 Crediton to Exeter road

'We win awards for our flower displays each year,' announces landlord Graham Wilson with some pride; the blooms outside his white-painted pub and on the patio are a blaze of colour in summer. The interior was completely refurbished in 1996, incorporating locally made hardwood tables and chairs and antique light fittings. 'Local' also sums up the kitchen's approach to supplies. Fish from Brixham is a speciality (expect anything from whole plaice to John Dory and red mullet), while salmon is from the Teign Valley. Locally bought meat and poultry are used for dishes such as pork fillet in coarse-grain mustard sauce, lamb moussaka with home-made garlic bread, and steaks of various sizes and cuts. Vegetarians might be offered pasta in béchamel sauce with three types of mushrooms from nearby sources, while desserts such as apple and sultana crumble come with clotted cream. Cheese is from Quicke's farm in the village, ice-creams are from Salcombe Dairy. Bass, Boddingtons and Wadworth 6X are on draught, and eight wines are served by the glass. Outside is an enormous, safe garden with children's play equipment. SAMPLE DISHES: pork satay £3; chicken breast in five-peppercorn and whisky sauce £6; pear and butterscotch flan £3.

Open *11.30 to 2.30, 6 to 11, Sun 12 to 2.30, 7 to 10.30; bar food 12 to 2, 7 to 9 (9.30 summer)*

Details *Children welcome Car park Wheelchair access (also WC) Garden and patio No music Dogs welcome Access, Switch, Visa*

NEWTON UNDER ROSEBERRY **Redcar** **map 10**

King's Head

Newton under Roseberry TEL: (01642) 722318
on A173, 3m SW of Guisborough

Walkers passing by on the Cleveland Way could do worse than stop here for lunch: daily-changing set-price lunches throughout the week, with a handful of choices at each course, represent excellent value; while Sunday brings the full range of traditional roasts. Otherwise there's an extensive menu, plus a blackboard listing dishes of the day. Starters may include stir-fry of scallops and prawns, or a pot of Stilton and garlic mushrooms, followed by steak and stout pie, or paupiettes of lemon sole; finish with orange and Grand Marnier crème brûlée, or raspberry pavlova. Salads and sandwiches are available in many interesting varieties, and there's a wide range of steaks and grills. Vegetarians are not forgotten: they have a separate list of main courses, and plenty of choice among the starters on the main menu. Theakston Best and Black Bull, and John Smith's Magnet are on handpump, and the wine list of around 40-odd bottles includes five halves and a section for connoisseurs. SAMPLE DISHES: vegetable and Stilton soup £2.75; chicken breast stuffed with ham, mozzarella and tomato with cheese sauce £9.50; ginger sponge with ginger and lemon sauce £3.25.

Open *11.30 to 3, 7 to 11, Sun 12 to 3, 7 to 10.30; bar food 11.45 to 2.30 (3.30 Sun), 7 to 10*

Details *Children welcome in bar eating area Car park Wheelchair access (also WC) Garden and patio No-smoking area Background music Guide dogs only No cards*

NORTH NEWINGTON **Oxfordshire** **map 5**

Roebuck Inn

Banbury Road, North Newington TEL: (01295) 730444
just off B4035, 3m SW of Banbury

Graham Newton and Brian Watkins have been at the helm of this sizeable village pub since 1990 and have built up its reputation as 'a place for the *cognoscenti*'. This is a Mecca for the Banbury business community during the week and often bursts at the seams on sunny weekends. It's a clean, up-to-date hostelry that succeeds without trying to be fashionable, and service is reckoned to be 'faultless'. The constantly changing menu is chalked on three boards 'in obscure calligraphy'. The style is bistro, with chilli and lasagne being eclipsed by warm chicken livers and bacon tossed in balsamic vinegar, Thai chicken curry, and salmon steak served on pasta with beurre blanc. A starter of prosciutto with quartered fresh figs was praised at inspection, while a salad of crispy smoked duck with orange sauce earned full marks. As a fillip to the food there's a cracking little wine list embracing a petit chateau claret as well as Seaview Brut Australian fizz. The landlords are also proud of their beer cellar and keep a fine stock of real ales including Morland Original, Adnams Broadside and Theakston XB. Outside is 'a pretty little kiddies garden with slides'. SAMPLE DISHES: baked garlic and parsley mushrooms £3.25; steak and kidney pudding with onion gravy £7; chocolate roulade £2.50.

Open *Tue to Sun 12 to 3, 7 to 11 (10.30 Sun); bar food Tue to Sun L 12 to 2, 7 to 9 (9.45 Fri and Sat)*
Details *Children welcome in bar eating area Car park Wheelchair access (also WC) Garden and patio Background music No dogs Access, Delta, Switch, Visa*

NORTH NEWNTON **Wiltshire** **map 2**

▲ *Woodbridge Inn*

North Newnton TEL: (01980) 630266
on A345, 3m S of Pewsey

This unassuming-looking, cream-painted inn is set beside a roundabout and is surrounded by open farmland in an area of unspoilt thatched villages. A tiny dining-area is adjacent to the small, welcoming bar, with its rug-strewn boards, good mixture of furniture, and numerous prints, plates and china on the mellow pink and terracotta walls. Morning coffee and afternoon tea are served, and at other times you can expect an eclectic range of dishes: sandwiches, Mexican chilli, beef burritos, nachos, steak and ale pie, and fish and chips. Lamb sizzler with orange and ginger sauce, and liver with bacon and mash may be among the specials, and the restaurant menu can be served in the bar on request, with dishes like stincotto, smoked marlin, fish créole, and noisettes of lamb. Wadworth beers are on draught (the Woodbridge is tied to the brewery), and a blackboard lists around 15 wines by the glass. There are four pétanque pitches and a children's play area in the garden, and a camping and caravan site in a field behind. SAMPLE DISHES: broccoli and basil soup £2.50; Woodie's vegetable pie £5.75; treacle sponge £3.25.

Open *Mon to Sat 11am to 11pm, Sun 12 to 3, 7 to 10.30; bar food Mon to Sat 11 to 10.30, Sun 12 to 2.30, 7 to 10; restaurant all week 12 to 2.30, 6 to 10.30*
Details *Children welcome (no children under 5 after 8pm) Car park Wheelchair access (also WC) Garden No smoking in restaurant Background music No dogs Access, Amex, Delta, Diners, Switch, Visa Accommodation: 3 rooms, B&B £27 to £38*

NORTON Shropshire map 5

▲ *Hundred House Hotel*

GARDEN

Bridgnorth Road, Norton TEL: (01952) 730353
on A442, 6m S of Telford

'Perfectly splendid' was how one visitor summed up the atmosphere in this gloriously idiosyncratic inn. From the outside it looks immediately enticing, with its Georgian brickwork, tall chimneys and creepers enveloping the walls. Four members of the Phillips family are in control here and each brings a special passion to the place. Sylvia's enthusiasm shows up in the 'wonderfully charming gardens' full of unusual roses, shrubs and trees, not to mention more than 50 varieties of herbs. Her influence also defines the décor, and the effect is 'entrancing'. Everywhere are bunches of dried herbs tied in tassels, heady scents fill the air, jewel-like colours shine out from the patchwork fabrics.

Son Stuart heads the kitchen and brings to the cooking a fondness for things current, plus a devotion to what is seasonally appropriate. The brasserie menu also features 'extraordinary' soups such as chilled melon with summer fruits and sorbet, bruschetta and crusty home-made focaccia bread with garlic, onions and rosemary. Other dishes could be as simple as steak and kidney pie with stout, 'classical' lasagne with 'real chips', Bridgnorth sausages with mash, or ten ounces or prime chargrilled sirloin. The modern world also has its say with coriander-cured salmon with lime, peanuts and beansprouts; chilli-fried red mullet with salsa, or a flashy vegetarian charlotte filled with roast carrot mousse wrapped in courgettes. 'Good clean tastes' also show up in specials such as braised squid with fennel, white wine and tomatoes or 'petit sale' of duck with parsley mash and grain-mustard sauce. Intensely flavoured home-made ice-creams feature among the sweets.

Mr Phillips senior earned a reputation for real ale when the family ran the Greyhound, Marsh Gibbon (see entry), and beer buffs won't be disappointed by Heritage Bitter, Ailrics Old Ale, Brains SA or Everards Autumn Gold. Ten excellent wines are sold by the glass and you will be hard-pressed to find a dud on the list; look for the bottles from Bodenham vineyard. SAMPLE DISHES: Caesar salad £4.50; slow-braised shin of beef with horseradish cream £9; home-made chocolate ice-cream in a brandy-snap basket £3.50.

Open *11 to 3, 6 to 11, Sun 12 to 3, 7 to 10.30; bar food and restaurant 12 to 2.30, 6 to 9.30; Sun 12 to 2.30, 7 to 9*
Details *Children welcome Car park Wheelchair access (also WC) Garden Background music Guide dogs only Access, Amex, Delta, Switch, Visa Accommodation: 23 rooms, B&B £65 to £90*

NORTON HEATH Essex **map 3**

White Horse

Norton Heath TEL: (01277) 821258
just off A414 Ongar to Chelmsford road, 3m E of Chipping Ongar

In an outpost of rural Essex, to the west of Chelmsford, this 400-year-old coaching-inn draws a good trade from its neighbourhood as well as the conurbations. The place is kept in good order and service is reckoned to be 'the best'. Bar food is served only at lunch-times, but the menu is on a blackboard and the kitchen rings the changes with the likes of fillet of salmon in white wine, cream and mushroom sauce, and roasted tomatoes with garlic and thyme dressing, plus desserts such as home-made chocolate terrine with whipped cream. The White Horse also has its own restaurant, which is open for more elaborate meals. Tolly Cobbold Original is the only beer on hand-pump, but the pub has a realistically priced wine list, including house wines by the glass. SAMPLE DISHES: cream of leek soup £2; calf's liver with grain mustard sauce £5.50; baked apple sponge and custard £2.50.

Open *11 to 3, 6 to 11, Sun 12 to 3, 7 to 10.30; bar food Tue to Sat L 12 to 2; restaurant Tue to Sun L 12 to 2, all week D 7 to 9*
Details *Children welcome Car park Wheelchair access (also WC) Garden and patio No music No dogs Access, Delta, Switch, Visa*

NORTON ST PHILIP Somerset map 2

George

High Street, Norton St Philip TEL: (01373) 834224
on A366 at junction with B3110, 6m S of Bath

The George is a magnificent ancient building with a wealth of architectural features: Gothic doorway, cobbled courtyard, timbered galleries and an external Norman staircase. The main bar is full of historical charm. Mullioned windows, stone walls, half-timbered, bare wooden floor, beams and simple furnishings set the tone. Supporters of the Duke of Monmouth were imprisoned in the Dungeon Bar off the courtyard after his defeat at Sedgemoor in 1685. The George is tied to Wadworth, and has 6X, IPA and Old Timer on draught, and there's a good collection of malt whiskies and a full wine list. Here, there's an emphasis on the use of local produce, and food has been reckoned by reporters to be of good value. You might expect Stilton and broccoli terrine, turkey breast stuffed with mozzarella and ham, smoked pork loin cutlets in cider sauce ('lean meat – good cut and decent sauce and served with a huge dish of crisp vegetables'), and desserts like light and dark chocolate terrine. SAMPLE DISHES: wild boar pâté £4; pan-fried duck breast with plum sauce £11; fruits of the forest pancake £3.50.

Open *11 to 3, 5.30 (5 Sat) to 11, Sun 12 to 3, 7 to 10.30; bar food Mon to Sat 12 to 2.30, 6.30 to 10, Sun 12 to 2.30, 7 (6.30 summer) to 9.30; restaurant Sun L 12 to 2.30, Fri and Sat D 7 to 10*
Details *Children welcome in eating areas Car park Wheelchair access Garden and patio No smoking in 1 room Live music Dogs welcome on a lead Access, Delta, Switch, Visa*

NUNNINGTON North Yorkshire map 9

Royal Oak

Church Street, Nunnington TEL: (01439) 748271
B1257, 2m N of Hovingham

The Royal Oak is a stone building on the hill leading down from the parish church in this peaceful backwater of a village, where a three-arch bridge spans the Rye. The larger of the two bars is the main one for diners, with its exposed-stone walls, beams in the ceiling, log fires, dried flowers and lots of rustic tools and bygones. Bread is made on the premises, and a sample meal could consist of coronation chicken, followed by roast duck with orange sauce, and then vanilla ice-cream in a brandy-snap basket with toffee sauce. Theakston Old Peculier, Tetley Bitter and Ind Coope Burton Ale are on draught. Nunnington Hall (National Trust), Gilling Castle, the castle at Helmsley, Rievaulx Abbey and Castle Howard are all nearby and worth a visit. SAMPLE DISHES: spicy mushrooms £3.75; fish stew £8; sticky toffee pudding £3.

Open *Tue to Sat 11.45 to 1.45, 6.30 to 11, Sun 11.45 to 1.45, 7 to 10.30; bar food Tue to Sun 12 to 1.45, 6.30 to 8.45*
Details *Children welcome in dining-room Car park Wheelchair access (also WC) Patio Background music No dogs Access, Switch, Visa*

OAKWOOD HILL Surrey **map 3**

Punch Bowl Inn

Oakwood Hill TEL: (01306) 627249
off A29 Dorking to Horsham road, 5m NW of Horsham

With its slate roof, attractive half-tiles, and vivid flowers crowding the doors in hanging baskets and vast tubs, the Punch Bowl is a very pretty sight, especially in summer. The pub, which dates from the fifteenth century, shows its age in the nicest possible way: floors are uneven and in winter the huge inglenook is ablaze. Beers on hand-pump include Hall & Woodhouse Badger Best and Tanglefoot, as well as Wadworth 6X; house wines are available by the glass. Food is served all day and ranges from 'light bites' such as chicken 'wings of fire', calamari, chicken goujons, and cheeseburgers to main courses in the steak, gammon, and trout genre; otherwise choose an 'old favourite' such as ploughman's or the all-day breakfast. Daily specials could include field mushrooms filled with ham, garlic and herbs and topped with melted Stilton, or beef and beer stew with dumplings. SAMPLE DISHES: prawn cocktail £4; chicken Kiev £6; Punchbowl hot raspberries £3.25.

Open *11am to 11pm, Sun 12 to 10.30; bar food and restaurant 12 to 10*
Details *Children welcome Car park Wheelchair access (also WC) Garden and patio Background music; jukebox Dogs welcome Access, Amex, Delta, Switch, Visa*

OARE Kent **map 3**

Shipwrights Arms

Ham Road, Oare TEL: (01795) 590088
on the northern outskirts of Faversham

'Most people arrive by boat!' observed one traveller after deciding to walk across the lonely marshes to this extraordinary creekside pub.

The 300-year-old brick and clapboard building stands three feet below sea level and you need to clamber up the bank to see the water. 'This is one of the most genuine pubs I've visited,' added the same reporter: standing timbers divide up the interior, there are well-worn settees and armchairs to sit on, and nautical paintings to look at. Warmth comes from open fires or bulging pot-bellied stoves; the hum of the generator reminds you that the place is without mains electricity. The mood is one of great relaxation, the atmosphere is 'timeless'. Pints of Shepherd Neame Masterbrew, Spitfire and Goacher's Mild are tapped from casks behind the bar; also don't miss the excellent unpasteurised cider from nearby Pauley Farm. Food is honest, filling and good value, with the emphasis on refuelling sustenance for famished walkers or boating types. The all-day breakfast is a well-cooked, grease-free plateful, sandwiches come in doorsteps of white bread, steak and kidney pie has a sound reputation. To finish are puddings of the school-dinner variety, such as spotted dick. SAMPLE DISHES: mushroom soup £1.50; steak and kidney pie with mash and peas £4.75; treacle sponge £2.

Open *11am to 11pm; bar food 12 to 3, 7 to 9.30*
Details *Children welcome Car park Garden No smoking in 1 room Occasional live music Dogs welcome No cards*

ODELL Bedfordshire map 6

Bell

Horsefair Lane, Odell TEL: (01234) 720254
off A6, 8m NW of Bedford

Plenty of seats on the large patio and a garden overlooking the River Ouse are attractions in summer at this extended stone-and-thatch village pub. An aviary and Lucy, the pet goose who loves lettuce and carrots, are added appeals for children. Inside, log fires in winter add comfort to the five interconnecting low-beamed rooms, while a décor of warm, mellow colours and a comfortable mixture of old and new furniture add to the atmosphere. A printed menu runs from sandwiches and salads to omelettes, home-made flans – with, for example, anchovies, onions, tomatoes and olives – pies and favourites such as cod and chips, and liver and bacon with onion rings. This is enhanced by a short list of daily specials: fish, broccoli and mushroom pie, perhaps, or chicken casseroled with lemon and tarragon, with a variety of good-quality sausages supplied by a local butcher. A separate board lists puddings along the lines of syrup and jam sponge, lemon mousse, and apple pie. Greene King Abbot Ale, IPA and Rayments Special Bitter are on draught along with a seasonal ale like Black Baron. A footpath links the pub to nearby

Harrold-Odell Country Park. SAMPLE DISHES: pork and apple sausages £5; beef, bacon and red wine casserole £6.25; banana split £2.25.

Open *11 to 2.30, 6 to 11, Sun 12 to 2.30, 7 to 10.30; bar food 12 to 2, 7 to 9.30 (9 Sun May to Sept)*
Details *Children welcome in bar eating area   Car park   Wheelchair access   Garden and patio   Background music   No dogs   No cards*

OFFHAM East Sussex — map 3

Blacksmith's Arms

London Road, Offham TEL: (01273) 472971
off A275, 2m N of Lewes

Food follows the seasons in this village pub opposite the church. The printed menus offer the likes of mussels in a pastry case, steamed fillet of brill wrapped in Parma ham and cabbage leaves, and poached figs. A vegetarian dish is always available, and daily-changing blackboard specials may include grilled sea bream in ginger butter, and duck breast bigarade; snacks are sold too (except on Friday and Saturday evenings). Food is served throughout the bar, with its photographs and prints on the walls and plenty of tables. Harveys Best Bitter and Armada Ale are well kept, and Old Ale is sold in season. There's a range of wines to choose from on the list, with four house wines by the glass, quarter-litre and bottle. SAMPLE DISHES: garlic woodland mushrooms in cream, wine and herbs £4.25; lamb fillet roasted with honey, lime and thyme £8.25; terrine of oranges with dark chocolate sauce £3.25.

Open *11 to 3, 6 to 11, Sun 12 to 3, 7 to 10.30; bar food 12 to 2.15, 7 to 9.15*
Details *No children   Car park   Wheelchair access (also WC)   Patio   No music   Dogs welcome   Access, Delta, Visa*

OLD DALBY Leicestershire — map 5

Crown Inn

Debdale Hill, Old Dalby TEL: (01664) 823134
off A46 Nottingham to Leicester road; turn at Upper Broughton and follow Old Dalby signs

Having negotiated the signs and turnings until you reach the end of Debdale Hill, you might think you have come to the wrong place. The Crown looks like an 'ordinary red-brick farmhouse', which is exactly what it was in days gone by. Go in by the back way and you are immediately in the tiny old bar. Real ale is taken so seriously here that current brews are chalked on blackboards hung above the casks. The line-up is vast, taking in everything from Adnams and Bateman's XXXB to Timothy Taylor Landlord and Woodforde's Wherry. For those seeking wine, there's a decent list of 30 bins supplied by Lay & Wheeler. Away from the bar is a warren of little rooms with open fires, dark wooden beams and fresh flowers. The bar menu is ambitious in its intentions and effusively explained. Sandwiches, open baguettes and ploughman's with Melton Mowbray pork pie and Colston Bassett Stilton are safe choices for a snack; otherwise delve into dishes such as prawn and smoked salmon frittatas, spiced vegetable pithiviers, open scallop ravioli served in a bamboo basket, or roast loin of pork filled with a sweet mango farce, accompanied by a piquant Armagnac and pear sauce. Elaboration continues through to the puddings. A similar menu – with higher prices – is available in the dining-room. SAMPLE DISHES: apple, cashew and celery salad with grilled olive crostinis £5.50; marinated spatchcock of pigeon served on a pearl barley rösti £11; brazil and hazelnut lattice pie £3.50.

Open *12 to 3, 6 to 11, Sun 12 to 3, 7 to 10.30; bar food all week L 12 to 2, Mon to Sat D 6 to 10; restaurant Mon to Sat D only 7 to 9.30*
Details *Children welcome in games room Car park Wheelchair access Garden and patio No smoking in 1 room No music No dogs No cards*

OLD HEATHFIELD **East Sussex** **map 3**

Star

Old Heathfield, nr Heathfield TEL: (01435) 863570
off B2203 or B2096, just S of Heathfield

'It really is the quintessential English country pub,' writes an inspector of this ancient pub with its roughly hewn golden stone, marvellous garden and lovely views. The interior is equally atmospheric, with log fires, low beams, some panelling, and tables with pews and benches everywhere. Blackboards all over the place announce what's on the menu: home-made soups, turkey and ham pie, pan-fried marinated salmon, lobster tails in white wine, bubble and squeak, and venison sausages with juniper berries, for instance, with banana nut sundae, and hot chocolate fudge cake among the puddings. Fuller's London Pride, Harveys Best Bitter and a weekly-changing guest ale are on draught. House wines come by the glass, and the full list features a locally produced rosé. Bateman's, Kipling's home from 1902 until his death in 1936, is a short drive away; get there before lunch to avoid the hordes at busy times. SAMPLE DISHES: mussels in saffron sauce £5.50; shoulder of lamb £8; crème caramel £3.

Open *11.30 to 3, 5.30 to 11, Sun 12 to 3, 7 to 10.30; bar food and restaurant Sun to Fri 12 to 2.30, 7 to 9.30*
Details *Children welcome Car park Wheelchair access Garden Background music Dogs welcome Access, Delta, Switch, Visa*

OMBERSLEY Hereford & Worcester map 5

Kings Arms

Ombersley TEL: (01905) 620315 and 620142
off A449 Worcester to Kidderminster road, 4m W of Droitwich

The interior of this sprawling, half-timbered fifteenth-century inn consists of a warren of little rooms warmed by open fires and decorated with horse brasses and copper pans. Carvings of a coat of arms, a Yorkist rose and a mermaid adorn the ceilings. Among the enterprising dishes on the long menu may be cream cheese and cashew-nut pâté, wok-fried chicken livers with bacon, and chicken breast poached in orange and lemon sauce. The pub's steak and kidney pie is 'famous throughout the world', according to the menu, and vegetarians normally have plenty of choice. Sweets range from fruit tarts to ice-creams. Bass, Worthington and Brew XI are on handpump, and the short wine list includes four half-bottles. The pub can get busy, but the garden and patios – 'where every available brick-wall-inch and pergola-wood-inch is crammed with climbers' – take some of the strain. SAMPLE DISHES: grilled lemon-marinated sardines £4.25; chicken and leek crumble £7.25; Bakewell tart £3.50.

Open *11 to 2.45, 5.30 to 11, Sun 12 to 10.30; bar food 12.15 to 2.15, 6 to 10, Sun 12 to 10*
Details *No children Car park Garden and patio No music No dogs Access, Amex, Delta, Switch, Visa*

OSMOTHERLEY North Yorkshire map 9

▲ *Three Tuns Inn*

Osmotherley TEL: (01609) 883301
1m off A19, 6m NE of Northallerton

Serious walking is a passion for many who trek up to the wilds of North Yorkshire, and this minuscule stone-built inn makes a perfect base camp if you are aiming to tackle the Lyke Wake, Hambleton Hobble or the Cleveland Way. Hugh and Juliet Dyson know all about providing nourishment, and much of their cooking is centred on local produce, whether it be Filey lobster or new season's grouse from the moors. The specials board has clear restaurant overtones:

starters such as black pudding with tomato and coriander sauce are served with the 'bread board', while main courses could include anything from grilled salmon with creamed leeks, to pan-fried ostrich steak with mushrooms and sun-dried tomatoes. Soups, sandwiches and other pub old-stagers form the backup, while desserts are mostly of the crumble and trifle kinds. Theakston Best, XB and Old Peculier are on handpump, and the short wine list is sound. SAMPLE DISHES: cream of lemon sole and lobster soup £3; roast mini-rack of local pork with apricot and sage sauce £9.50; orange and brandy pudding £3.25.

Open *12 to 3.30, 6.45 to 11.45, Sun 12 to 3, 7 to 10.30; bar food and restaurant all week L 12 to 2.30 (2 for hot food), Mon to Sat D 7 to 9.30*
Details *Children welcome Garden No music Dogs welcome in snug bar only Access, Switch, Visa Accommodation: 3 rooms, B&B £48 to £60*

OVER PEOVER Cheshire map 8

▲ *Dog Inn*

Well-Bank Lane, Over Peover TEL: (01625) 861421
off A50 between Knutsford and Holmes Chapel; turn at Whipping Stocks pub and continue for 1½m

A friendly, relaxed atmosphere pervades this eighteenth-century, attractive pub in a rural setting, and pretty hanging baskets attest to the fact that it's as well maintained outside as in. The kitchen has earned a reputation for quality cooking, producing such starters as Manx kippers, spare ribs, and salade niçoise, and main courses like poached salmon with cucumber sauce, chicken breast in mushroom and brandy sauce, and steak and ale pie. There is a range of traditional roasts and a good choice of sandwiches, as well as ploughman's and salads. Puddings are picked from a trolley: apple pie, or raspberry pavlova, perhaps. 'Dinner was a huge affair,' writes a satisfied reporter. Greenall Original, Boddingtons and Flowers IPA are on draught, and the wine list, with its helpful descriptions, offers more than 30 wines at competitive prices. SAMPLE DISHES: tomato, carrot and coriander soup £2.50; roast Cheshire turkey with stuffing £7.50; bread-and-butter pudding £2.50.

Open *11.30 to 3, 5.30 to 11, Sun 12 to 3, 7 to 10.30; bar food 12 to 2, 7 to 9*
Details *Children welcome in bar eating area Car park Wheelchair access Garden and patio No-smoking area Background and live music; jukebox Dogs by arrangement Access, Delta, Switch, Visa Accommodation: 3 rooms, B&B £48 to £65*

OVER STRATTON Somerset map 2

Royal Oak

Over Stratton TEL: (01460) 240906
off A303, take Illminster town centre turning away from South Petherton, turn left after 300yds

Even in winter the garden at the Royal Oak looks inviting, and in summer children can be left to play in safety among the various amusements set up for them. Inside is as equally appealing: two bars are decorated with hop-bines and dried flowers, and comforting fires burn in winter. 'We loved the whole atmosphere,' was the verdict of one couple. The bar menu offers ploughman's with Dorset Blue Vinney, local Cheddar and Somerset Brie; you could also choose calf's liver with sage and lemon sauce, chicken and broccoli lasagne, or Chinese lamb. Specials are listed on boards – expect casseroled rabbit with mustard and tarragon sauce, say, or pasta with mussels – and the restaurant menu is also served in the bars. Game features in season: roast pheasant with thyme and brandy sauce, or venison steak, for instance. Puddings include a seasonal fruit brûlée – the raspberry version has been described as 'deliciously creamy and smooth'. The pub is tied to Badger Inns, with Dorset Best, Tanglefoot and Stratton Ale on draught; house wines are served by the glass, the full list running to more than 60 bins. SAMPLE DISHES: langoustines with fruit salad £4.50; Swedish-style meatballs £5.25; tarte Tatin £2.25.

Open *11 to 3, 6 to 11, Sun 12 to 3, 7 to 10.30; bar food and restaurant 12 to 2.15, 7 to 10*
Details *Children welcome in dining-room Car park Wheelchair access Garden and patio No smoking in dining-room Background music Guide dogs only Access, Delta, Switch, Visa*

OVINGTON Hampshire map 2

Bush Inn

Ovington TEL: (01962) 732764
off A31, 2m W of Alresford

In summer you can sit on the benches in the front garden and enjoy the rose-covered façade of this unspoilt seventeenth-century village pub tucked down a quiet country lane. The more energetic would enjoy a stroll along the footpath, overhung by trees, beside the gently flowing River Itchen. The interior of the pub is dark and cosy, with green-painted walls, rustic scrubbed pine tables, high-backed settles and an interesting collection of artefacts, from stuffed fish to pictures and old bellows; a blazing log fire adds another welcoming dimension in winter. A blackboard of specials offering, say, smoked chicken and mango salad, and Chinese noodles in plum sauce, broadens the range of the bar menu, which features Thai beef salad, grilled trout almondine, and tiger prawns in filo with coriander and chilli mayonnaise, for example. Wadworth 6X, Strong Country Bitter, Gale's ESB and a guest are on draught, and around half a dozen wines are available by the glass, with an extensive choice of English country wines. SAMPLE DISHES: greenlipped mussels with garlic butter £4.50; bream en papillote £8; raspberry and Drambuie mousse £3.25.

Open *11 to 2.30, 6 to 11, Sun 12 to 3, 7 to 10.30; bar food 12 to 2, 6.30 to 9.15; restaurant Sun L 12 to 3, Mon to Sat D 7.15 to 9.15*
Details *Children welcome in eating areas Car park Wheelchair access Garden and patio No music Dogs welcome on a lead Access, Switch, Visa*

PATTISWICK Essex map 3

Compasses Inn

Compasses Road, Pattiswick TEL: (01376) 561322
off A120, 3m NW of Coggeshall

Signs on the stretch of the A120 that was once Stane Street direct you to Pattiswick and the Compasses, set in rolling fields with just a couple of cottages and a long-converted church for company. Considering its countryside setting, the place can get very busy; a large garden with a play area accounts for its appeal among families. Plenty of vegetarian choices are on offer – cream cheese, courgette and broccoli bake, and Thai-style vegetable and cashew-nut risotto, for example. Meat eaters could opt for lambs' kidneys in sherry gravy, and fish lovers might try traditional battered cod, or sea bass in Chablis, tomato and basil sauce. A meal may end with raspberry pavlova, or hangover gâteau (layers of rum, brandy and orange liqueur mousse sandwiched between sponge). Coffee comes in cafetières unless you specify otherwise: alternatives are listed on a board. Greene King Rayments Special Bitter, IPA and Abbot Ale are on draught, with house wines served by the glass. SAMPLE DISHES: mussels marinière £4.50; liver and bacon suet pudding £8; treacle sponge pudding £3.

Open *11 to 3, 6.30 (6 Sat) to 11, Sun 12 to 3, 7 to 10.30; bar food and restaurant 12 to 3, 7 to 10 (12 to 10 Sun Easter to Sept)*
Details *Children welcome in eating areas Car park Wheelchair access (also WC) Garden Background music Guide dogs only Access, Delta, Switch, Visa*

Recommendations for good country pubs will be very welcome.

PEMBRIDGE **Hereford & Worcester** **map 5**

▲ *New Inn*

HISTORY

Market Square, Pembridge TEL: (01544) 388427
on A44, between Kington and Leominster, 6m E of Kington

Dating from the early 1300s, this black and white timbered inn stands opposite the old covered market and the parish church. Three atmospheric rooms give a sense of age with their huge timbers and flagged floors; a large open fire burns in the public bar. The fare is homespun and hearty: fish pie, minted lamb, or vegetable hotpot, for example. A summer special might be a salad of smoked turkey and avocado, a winter one game pie. Snackier items could include a croissant filled with smoked salmon and scrambled eggs, and goujons of chicken with garlic dip. Treacle and orange tart is an interesting variation on a traditional theme, and other desserts could be French chocolate flan, or orange and brandy pudding. Locally made Weston's Stowford Press cider is on tap, Ruddles Best and County are on draught, and there's a decent choice of malt whiskies as well as English country wines. SAMPLE DISHES: half-pint of garlic prawns £6; steak and mushroom pie £5.25; banana and apple crumble £2.50.

Open *11 to 3, 6 to 11, Sun 12 to 3, 7 to 10.30 (6.30 winter); bar food 12 to 2, 7 to 9.30; restaurant Wed to Sun 12 to 2, 7 to 9.30 (booking essential for restaurant)*
Details *Children welcome in bar eating area Car park Wheelchair access (also WC) Patio Live music in winter Dogs welcome in bar only Accommodation: 8 rooms, B&B £19 to £37*

PETER TAVY **Devon** **map 1**

Peter Tavy Inn

Peter Tavy TEL: (01822) 810348
off A386, 2m NE of Tavistock

A degree of modernisation and restoration has done nothing to smother the atmospheric quality of this two-storey stone inn along a lane that seems to be going nowhere. The building once housed the masons working on the local church, but later served as a cottage for a farmer, then a blacksmith and also a cobbler (who repaired the shoes worn by local mine workers). The heavy front door still has its original sixteenth-century lock and there's a 'lookout window', set into the back wall, from where people kept watch for beacons during the time of the Spanish Armada. Overall, massive walls, heavy beams and slate floors set the tone. New licensees John and Gill Diprose, formerly of the Durant Arms in Ashprington, arrived in late 1996, and although the chefs remain the same, Gill supervises in the kitchen and, we are told, has added a few new dishes. Lunch still brings everything from steak sandwiches and baguettes to sizzling crab-cakes and steak and kidney pudding; in the evening you will also find prawn and Pernod crêpes, carpaccio, and fricassee of chicken with asparagus. Daily specials might now take in paella, green Thai curry, and pot-roast pheasant; fish features strongly – grilled lemon sole or monkfish provençale, for example. Puddings range from Scottish Atholl brose to old-English trifle. Tip-top ales such as St Austell HSD and Princetown Jail Ale are always on draught, and there are regular West Country guests like Sharps and Exmoor. Around 40 wines offer great-value drinking. From the pub's raised garden you can look across to Brentor Beacon. SAMPLE DISHES: smoked salmon and scrambled eggs £5; haddock and broccoli gratin £4.95; chocolate mousse £2.50.

Open *11.30 to 2.30 (3 Fri to Sun), 6.30 (7 winter) to 11 (7 to 10.30 Sun), all day Aug bank hol Mon; bar food 12 to 2 (3 Fri to Sun), 6.30 (7 Sun and winter) to 9.30*
Details *Children welcome Car park Wheelchair access Garden and patio No smoking in 1 room at weekends Occasional background music Dogs welcome on a lead Access, Delta, Switch, Visa*

PHILLEIGH Cornwall **map 1**

Roseland Inn

Philleigh TEL: (01872) 580254
off B3289, 4m NE of St Mawes

The best way to get to this lovely, little seventeenth-century inn is to take the King Harry Ferry across the River Fal, then drive for a couple of miles. Inside, the décor is very simple – flagstone floors, standing timbers, oak settles and antique chairs around large tables. A coal fire warms the bar in the winter, while outside is a pleasant, well-planted paved terrace. The straightforward, homely food matches the style of the pub. Philleigh Angels (scallops) feature on the menu alongside traditional beef stew, 'proper' Cornish pasty, chicken, sweetcorn and broccoli pie, crab salad, and chilli devils. Rice-pudding, fruit crumble, and treacle tart might be among the desserts. This is a Greenalls pub, with the brewery's Bitter on handpump, as well as Bass, Marston's Pedigree and Morland Old Speckled Hen, and there are a handful of wines. The Roseland Peninsula, where the pub is set, is lush and green with sub-tropical plants and plenty of colour. SAMPLE DISHES: Stilton and celery soup £2.50; seafood Mornay £5.50; bread-and-butter pudding £3.

Open *11.30 to 3, 6 (6.30 winter) to 11, Sun 12 to 3, 7 to 10.30; bar food 12 to 2.15, 7 to 9; no food 25 Dec*
Details *Children welcome Car park Wheelchair access (also WC) Garden and patio No music Dogs welcome No cards*

PICKERING North Yorkshire map 9

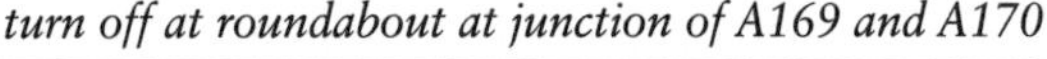

▲ *White Swan* 🍇

Market Place TEL: (01751) 472288
turn off at roundabout at junction of A169 and A170

For more than 12 years various members of the Buchanan family have been the incumbents of this congenial town-centre inn, and have made it a popular venue for locals and for visitors taking in the sights of the Dales. The focus of the place is the traditional front bar, where lively banter takes place in a setting of wood panelling and tasteful prints. Bar lunches move beyond sandwiches and croque-monsieur to more imaginative offerings such as smoked-chicken salad with baby vegetables, venison sausage cassoulet, and Whitby crab-cakes with pesto mayonnaise and sauté apples. In the evening a more elaborate menu is served in both bar and restaurant: expect such things as seared fillet of sea bass with sage risotto, or braised lamb shank with olive-oil mash. The pub also has a forward-looking vegetarian menu that includes, say, French fried aubergines with curried lentils and herb rice, beetroot fritters with hot mustard cream and caramelised onions, and stir-fried Chinese leaves, artichokes and peppers with soy butter. Puddings range from dark chocolate terrine to tarte Tatin. The Buchanans have a special interest in the wines of St Emilion, and around 70 feature on the substantial list of around 300 bins. Otherwise you will find Black Sheep Best Bitter and Special Bitter on handpump, along with Cropton Two Pints from Pickering. SAMPLE DISHES: chargrilled sardines £3.50; baked breast of chicken with buttered noodles, red pimento sauce and crisped leeks £5.50; bramble and apple pie £2.75.

Open *11 to 3, 6 to 11, Sun 12 to 3, 7 to 10.30; bar food and restaurant 12 to 2.30, 7 (7.30 restaurant) to 9.30*
Details *Children welcome in eating areas Car park Wheelchair access Patio No music Dogs welcome Access, Amex, Delta, Switch, Visa Accommodation: 12 rooms, B&B £55 to £98*

PICKHILL North Yorkshire map 8

▲ *Nags Head* 🍇

Pickhill TEL: (01845) 567391 and 567570
off A1, 5m SE of Leeming

This former coaching-inn in the heart of 'Herriot country' provides a comfortable retreat for hungry travellers using the A1. The tap bar is popular with locals and features a collection of jugs and hanging neckties above the bar, while the more plush lounge bar has numerous prints and water-colours on the walls, many of which are for sale. Inventive bar food is listed on two daily-changing menus and is served throughout the pub. The repertoire will suit most tastes: you might find casserole of grouse with red wine and autumn berries, pan-fried venison fillet with port and juniper-berry sauce, smoked haddock and prawn kedgeree, and fillet of beef Wellington, alongside mainstays of Barnsley chop, chicken and chips, cottage pie, and home-made burgers. Tea, coffee and sandwiches are served in the afternoon. Real ales include Black Sheep Bitter, Hambleton Best, Black Bull, and Theakston Old Peculier. The wine list is global and good value, running to 87 bins, with six served by the glass. Nearby are the abbeys of Fountains, Jervaulx and Rievaulx; Brimham Rocks, Mother Shiptons cave and Aysgarth waterfalls are also within easy reach. SAMPLE DISHES: fresh crab bisque £3; grilled duck breast with plum sauce £10; almond crème brûlée £3.

Open *11am to 11pm, Sun 12 to 10.30; bar food and restaurant 12 to 2, 6 to 10 (exc restaurant Sun D)*
Details *Children welcome in bar eating area Car park Wheelchair access (also WC) Garden No smoking in restaurant Background music No dogs Access, Delta, Switch, Visa Accommodation: 17 rooms, B&B £34 to £48*

PILLEY Hampshire map 2

Fleur de Lys

Pilley Street, Pilley TEL: (01590) 672158
off A337, 1½m NW of Lymington

'The oldest pub in the New Forest' was fashioned from a pair of workers' thatched cottages in 1096; as you go through the door into the stone-flagged hallway you will see a list of landlords dating back to the end of the fourteenth century, and the site of the original fireplace. Evocative historical touches are everywhere: there's a medieval wishing well and a dovecote in the garden, not to mention a couple of 'lively' ghosts (including a mischievous grey-haired lady). Hams were once smoked in the chimney (you can still see the pulley), but today the main attraction is the cooking of nutritious soups and stews in cauldrons over the fire. Otherwise the kitchen delivers a varied assortment of dishes, ranging from the 'finest dish of potato skins' one reporter had ever encountered, to venison and wild boar sausages, turkey curry and some promising vegetarian ideas including a 'hotch-potch' of New Forest mushrooms with sun-dried tomatoes and a creamy basil sauce. As a finale, try the home-made 'fruit cake' ice-cream or 'Molly's' chocolate pudding. Ringwood Bitter, Morland Old Speckled Hen and others are drawn direct from casks, and Thatcher's cider is also on tap. House wines are sold by the glass from a short list of around 20 bins. There is a children's play area in the garden, and an outdoor marquee doubles as a family room in summer. While in the area, it's worth making a detour to see nearby Boldre church with its Fleur de Lys window. SAMPLE DISHES: game and port pâté £4; ginger prawns with steamed rice £7; lemon brûlée £3.25.

Open *12 to 3 (4 summer), 6 to 10.30 (11 summer), Sun 7 to 10.30; bar food 12 to 2.30, 6 to 9.30*
Details *Children welcome in eating areas Car park Wheelchair access (also WC) Garden Background and occasional live music Access, Delta, Switch, Visa*

PITTON Wiltshire map 2

Silver Plough 🍇

Pitton TEL: (01722) 712266
off A30, 5m E of Salisbury

Originally a private residence and farmhouse, this striking 250-year-old building gained its licence in 1947 – much to the relief of the local residents who had been without a local pub since the turn of the century. Antique china and glass rolling pins hang from the beams, alongside jugs and bottles of every description. A wood-burning stove provides heat and there are comfortable oak settles to recline on. Bar food is ordered from 'the cheesebar'. A printed menu offers the likes of pan-fried lamb's kidney with mustard sauce, various pastas and salads, and grilled rump steak topped with Stilton; in addition, there's a specials board listing daily dishes such as breast of chicken with pink peppercorn sauce, and pork chop with sweet pepper and tomato coulis. Desserts don't stray far beyond banoffi pie and spotted dick. A separate, full menu is available in the restaurant. The Silver Plough was acquired by Badger Inns in autumn 1996, so the resident real ales are now Hall & Woodhouse brews such as Tanglefoot and Dorset Best Bitter. Ten wines are served by the glass, and the full list is a global selection with a good showing from the

New World and plenty of quality drinking for under £15 a bottle. SAMPLE DISHES: beef, tomato and potato soup £2.75; steak and oyster pie £6; apricot and orange cheesecake £3.25.

Open *11 to 3, 6 to 11, Sun 12 to 3, 7 to 10.30; bar food and restaurant 12 to 2.30, 6.30 to 9.30*
Details *Children welcome in eating areas Car park Wheelchair access (also WC) Garden Background music Dogs welcome in bar only Access, Amex, Delta, Switch, Visa*

PLAYLEY GREEN Gloucestershire map 5

Rose & Crown

Playley Green, Redmarley TEL: (01531) 650234
on A417, 1m S of M50 Jct. 2

'The garden is my particular passion,' writes landlady Kathy Bunnett, who tells us that all her tubs and hanging baskets are 'home-grown and home-made'. Everything about this endearingly unpretentious pub is as neat and lovingly tended as can be. The Bunnetts also take care when it comes to buying ingredients for their kitchen: meat is from the local butcher, fish is delivered up to three times a week and vegetables are from the market. There is a run-of-the-mill printed menu, but the hub of the cooking is the list of specials: venison broth or Stilton mushrooms could start things off, while main dishes might include grilled haddock with parsley sauce, sauté chicken with sherry and tarragon sauce, or cold roast loin of pork – not to mention ever-popular fish and chips. Also, don't miss out on the special Rose & Crown salads with the pub's own-recipe dressings. Lemon and ginger tart is a typical sweet. Sunday lunch is built around a trio of roasts, and a full menu is offered in the restaurant. Flowers Original and Fremlins Bitter are on draught, and the pub has a short wine list. SAMPLE DISHES: Camembert pancake £3.25; lamb and apricot curry £5.50; banoffi pie £2.25.

Open *11 to 2.30, 6 to 11, Sun 12 to 3, 7 to 10.30; bar food all week L 11.30 (12 Sun) to 2, Mon to Sat D 6.30 to 9.30; restaurant Sun L 12 to 3, Tue to Sat D 6 to 9.30; closed 25 Dec*
Details *Children welcome in eating areas Car park Garden and patio No smoking in restaurant Background music Dogs welcome Access, Visa*

PLUCKLEY Kent map 3

▲ *Dering Arms* 🍺

Station Road, Pluckley TEL: (01233) 840371
off B2077, close to Pluckley railway station

It's difficult to believe that this lovely old stone building houses a pub until you find out that it was built as a hunting-lodge: then the unusual shape, the mullioned and leaded windows, and the Dutch gables begin to make more sense. The interior is comfortable, welcoming and well furnished, though one reporter described it as 'somewhat austere', with an exposed-brick fireplace, a stag's head, fishing-rods and a hunting theme. Bar food ranges from sandwiches and ploughman's, through sausages or ham with chips, to all-day breakfast, and a pie of the day: perhaps pork with apples and cider, or chicken with banana. Daily blackboard specials are common to both bar and restaurant. These may run from cheese and red wine pâté, or crab Newburg, to salmon fish-cakes with sorrel sauce, braised oxtail, or rabbit in mustard and ale; and desserts might include tarte Tatin or sherry trifle. Dering Ale, the house bitter, and Goacher's Maidstone Ale and Dark Mild are dispensed from the bar, as is Biddenden cider. Six house wines are served by the glass, while the full list runs to over 80 bottles. SAMPLE DISHES: garlic bread with cheese £2; grilled plaice £7; caramel rice pudding £2.50.

Open *11 to 3, 6 to 11, Sun 12 to 3, 7 to 10.30; bar food and restaurant Tue to Sun L 12 to 2, Tue to Sat D 7 to 9.30 (10 Fri and Sat)*
Details *Children welcome in dining-room and games room Car park Wheelchair access Garden Live music Dogs welcome Access, Amex, Visa Accommodation: 3 rooms, B&B £28 to £40*

PLUSH Dorset map 2

Brace of Pheasants

Plush, nr Dorchester TEL: (01300) 348357
off B3143, 2m N of Piddletrenthide

Down narrow lanes and surrounded by clumps of woodland, open fields and high hedges, the Brace of Pheasants is reputedly 'one of Dorset's prettiest sixteenth-century thatched inns'. The long, low pub is white and adorned with wrought-iron pheasants and flowers. At the back is a mature garden with a large aviary, so there's plenty of space for children in summer. The low-beamed main bar has real character and charm, with a massive inglenook where on cold days you are likely to find Bodger, the pub's black labrador, having a snooze. The printed menu is imaginative, listing restaurant-type dishes such as steamed breast of chicken filled with Parmesan, garlic and parsley in a wine and cream sauce, and 'sirloin steak Capetown' with prawns and garlic butter. Supplementing that is the daily specials board, where you might find seasonal game – pheasant with apple and calvados, or venison sausages, for example. Fish is also well represented with, perhaps, grilled salmon with lime and ginger butter, or red bream with a black pepper crust and cream sauce. Set-price three-course meals are served in the dining-room, and two-course theme nights focus on pasta, curry, and 'Surf or Turf'. On handpump are Fuller's London Pride, beers from Smiles Brewery, and a guest beer, and for cider fans there's Inch's Stonehouse. House wines are sold by the glass, and nine half-bottles feature on the short list. SAMPLE DISHES: warm salad of queen scallops and lardons of bacon tossed in garlic butter £5; roast loin of venison with an elderberry and redcurrant sauce £13.50; bread-and-butter pudding £3.

Open *11.30 (12 winter) to 2.30, 7 to 11, Sun 12 to 3, 7 to 10.30; bar food 12 to 1.45, 7 to 9.45; restaurant 12 to 1.30, 7 to 9.30*
Details *Children welcome in restaurant and family room Car park Garden and patio No smoking in restaurant and family room No music Dogs welcome on a lead Access, Delta, Switch, Visa*

PORTHLEVEN Cornwall **map 1**

Ship Inn

Porthleven TEL: (01326) 572841
off B3304, 2m SW of Helston, on W side of harbour

From the road that winds through the town down past the harbour, a few steps lead up to the Ship, a simple stone building built into the side of a cliff; the view overlooking the harbour mouth is terrific. Within the small bar with its two log fires, bare boards are strewn with rugs and rough stone walls are hung with a few local watercolours and photographs – plus a map of the wrecking coast of Cornwall, 'which I completely understood after seeing the 100-foot waves crashing against the cliffs opposite the pub,' writes a reporter. Nets and other nautical memorabilia create a crowded look. A handful of real ales on draught includes Sharp's Doom Bar Bitter and Cornish Coaster and Greene King Abbot Ale. Crab is a speciality – there's everything from claws to crab and prawn Mornay, and crab thermidor. Alternatively, you can opt for things like jacket potatoes, steaks, curries, steak and kidney pudding, seafood platter, or chicken, sweetcorn and broccoli lasagne – plus, say, apple tart for dessert. SAMPLE DISHES: prawn cocktail £3.50; fish pie £5.75; bananas in rum £2.75.

Open *11.30 to 3, 6.30 to 11 (11.30 to 11 summer), Sun 12 to 3.30, 7 to 10.30; bar food all week 12 to 2, 7 to 9*
Details *Children welcome in family room Garden Background music Dogs welcome No cards*

POWERSTOCK Dorset map 2

▲ *Three Horseshoes*

Powerstock TEL: (01308) 485328
off A3066 at Gore Cross, 4m NE of Bridport

The setting is breathtakingly beautiful: although the Three Horseshoes stands on a high point in the village and has views of the surrounding hills, the serpentine lanes in and out of the village burrow deep into the ancient Dorset countryside. This is Thomas Hardy's Wessex at its most atmospheric, and not far away is Eggardon, site of an Iron Age fort. Landlord Pat Ferguson focuses his attention elsewhere, however, and plunders the catch of the day from boats working out of Weymouth. This is a fish pub without compromise. The kitchen's philosophy is spelt out on the menu: 'We bought some cracking fish today,' it reads. 'This is what we bought and how we propose to cook it.' The result could be seared scallops with fresh peach chutney, Tabasco sauce and a dash of white wine, or shark steak with herb hollandaise, or grey mullet with mustard butter. Whole sea bass roasted with fresh fennel and served with garlic sauce is billed as 'a feast for two'.

Alternatives come in the shape of, say, marinated lamb steak with grilled Mediterranean vegetables, chicken breast stuffed with air-dried ham and cheese, or pasta with button mushrooms, cream and herbs from the garden. A bowl of mussels, a grilled goats'-cheese salad, or even a baguette would suit well for a light lunch. Desserts could be anything from almond flan to steamed fruit pudding. You can eat in the little dining area at the front of the pub or the larger room at the back, and there's a garden for sunny days. The Fergusons' wine list continues to evolve; 20 wines are now served by the glass and the full slate is a lively tour of the world's vineyards, with special attention given to the southern hemisphere. Real ale fans can quaff pints of locally brewed Palmer's IPA and Bridport Bitter. SAMPLE DISHES: roasted tomato and basil soup £3.50; pan-fried tuna steak provençale £10.50; lemon tart £3.50.

Open *11 to 3, 6 to 11, Sun 12 to 3, 7 to 10.30; bar food and restaurant 12 to 2.30 (3 Sun), 7 to 9.30*
Details *Children welcome in eating areas Car park Garden and patio No smoking in restaurant No music Dogs welcome Access, Amex, Delta, Switch, Visa Accommodation: 3 rooms, B&B £40 to £60*

---

indicates a pub serving outstanding bar food, backed up by all-round excellence in other departments, such as service, atmosphere and cleanliness.

PRESTWOOD **Buckinghamshire** **map 3**

Polecat Inn

170 Wycombe Road, Prestwood TEL: (01494) 862253
on A4128 Great Missenden to High Wycombe road, 2m W of Great Missenden

'It's large, but it's a gem,' enthused a Bucks reporter. One plus is the great expanse of attractively laid-out garden, while four separate dining-rooms score because of their 'personalised décor' – in this case stuffed birds and animals in glass cases are a feature. The standard menu changes twice each year and it's backed up by a list of daily specials, which could be anything from magret of duck with a light, skilfully executed honey and cinnamon sauce to kingfish in Thai pastry. Smoked haddock bake is prepared in 'the classic style', home-made pies are topped with shortcrust pastry (you need to wait 30 minutes for it to be cooked), and wild boar sausages are served on an 'apple ratatouille' with sauté potatoes; otherwise take comfort in cottage pie or lasagne. As a finale, there might be 'really light' sticky toffee pudding, passion-fruit syllabub or almond sables with apricot sauce. Beers on handpump include familiar names such as Ruddles Best and County, Marston's Pedigree and Morland Old Speckled Hen; several wines are offered by the glass, specials are on a blackboard and the modestly priced list takes few risks. SAMPLE DISHES: double-baked Stilton soufflé with red onion marmalade £4; brochettes of marinated fish on jasmine-scented rice £7; lemon and lime sponge pudding £3.

Open *11.30 to 2.30, 6 to 11, Sun 12 to 3; bar food all week L 12 to 2, Mon to Sat D 6.30 to 9*
Details *Children welcome in dining area Car park Wheelchair access (also WC) Garden No-smoking area Background music Dogs welcome No cards*

PRIORS DEAN **Hampshire** **map 2**

White Horse Inn

Priors Dean TEL: (01420) 588387
from Petersfield, take road signposted Steep and Froxfield for 5m, turn right at crossroads signposted East Tisted, then second right; from A32, 5m S of Alton, turn on to Steep and Froxfield road, left at crossroad, then second right

This remote inn, in a lofty Downs position, is known as 'The Pub With No Name' because there's no sign outside. On top of this, the White Horse is difficult to find, but it's well worth making the effort.

Long-serving landlord Jack Eddlestone has retired after more than 20 years, but nothing much has changed, and the classic old farmhouse retains its seventeenth-century charm. Each of the two rustic parlours has an open log fire fronted by rocking-chairs and sofas a grandfather clock and an array of antique furniture. Old pictures and farming implements hang on the walls. The range of real ales is as broad as ever, including two ales specially brewed for the pub – No Name Best and No Name Strong Bitter – as well as Wadworth 6X, Ringwood Fortyniner and Gales HSB. Blackboard specials might include kidneys sauté in port sauce, Stilton-stuffed pear, spicy Italian meatballs with tagliatelle, pork steak with apple and blackberry sauce, or rump steak with wild mushrooms. Ginger sponge and chocolate flake pavlova are two good ways to finish. Around 20 English country wines are on offer, plus a reasonably priced conventional wine list. SAMPLE DISHES: moules marinière £4.25; lamb cutlets with cherry and almond sauce £7.50; brandy-snap basket with fruits of the forest £3.75.

Open *11 to 2.30 (3 Sat), 6 to 11, Sun 12 to 3, 7 to 10.30; bar food all week L 12 to 2, Mon to Sat D 7 to 9*
Details *Children welcome Car park Garden No music Dogs welcome on a lead Access, Delta, Switch, Visa*

RAMSBURY Wiltshire map 2

Bell 🍇

The Square, Ramsbury TEL: (01672) 520230
off A4192, 6m E of Marlborough

'It's well worth the short detour off the A4,' said one visitor. Set in a charming village, the Bell is a popular choice for reliable pub food, and handy too, if you are visiting nearby Littlecote House, the Kennet & Avon Canal or Marlborough. Inside there's a comfortably furnished rambling series of rooms, with several eating areas tacked on to the bar, plus a separate dining-room. A relaxed and civilised atmosphere prevails, helped along by wood-burning fires, tasteful prints on the walls and popular window seats with views down the village street through Victorian stained-glass panels. As well as pub grub, the bar menu takes in a host of interesting dishes such as fillets of red mullet with a tomato and basil sauce, venison pie, and shish kebab. Fish pie appears as 'a large bowl of stew crammed with prawns, white fish and chunks of salmon with breadcrumbs for topping'. There's a short list of daily specials, too, which could include liver and bacon, trout fillets, or seared tuna steak with basil on a sweet potato cake. Puddings have their own board and you could find maple and walnut sponge, lemon tart, or rich chocolate mousse. Beers on draught are Wadworth Henry's Original IPA and 6X, and Hook Norton Best Bitter, plus regular guest brews; or choose from 20 malt whiskies. The wine list is a truly international affair and includes house wines by the glass. SAMPLE DISHES: Brie and Camembert fritters on a plum sauce £4; pesto chicken £8.50; treacle tart £3.

Open *12 to 3, 6 to 11, Sun 12 to 3, 7 to 10.30; bar food and restaurant 12 to 2 (2.15 Sat and Sun), 7 to 9 (9.30 Fri and Sat); no food Sun eve Oct to March*
Details *Children welcome in dining-room and in 1 area of bar Car park Wheelchair access Garden and patio No-smoking area Background music Dogs welcome in bar only Access, Amex, Delta, Switch, Visa*

RAMSHOLT Suffolk map 6

▲ *Ramsholt Arms*

Dock Road, Ramsholt TEL: (01394) 411229
off B1083, 5m SE of Woodbridge

'In the summer over 200 boats are moored here,' writes landlord Michael Bartholomew – and no wonder. This eighteenth-century ferryman's cottage and one-time smugglers' inn stands in one of the most enchantingly beautiful locations in Suffolk, on the banks of the River Deben, with wondrous waterscapes in both directions. Of course, 'on a cold, dark, wet, windy night in late October it's a very different story!' The days of beer in enamel jugs and light from paraffin lamps may have gone, but the place still looks the part: log fires burn, the curtain in the bar is a ship's sail. The kitchen makes proper use of local fish and seasonal game from the nearby estate for a menu that ranges from big bowls of steamed mussels, and fillet of halibut in lemon butter, to warm salad of breast of woodcock with mushrooms, and pot-roast partridge with red wine and onion sauce. Desserts are things like treacle tart and Belgian chocolate mousse. Fans of ethnic food should make a note that Thursday night is a special event featuring Indian and Thai cuisine. This a free house with well-kept Adnams Bitter, Flowers Original and Theakston on draught. Sutton Common and Rendlesham Forest are nearby, and wildlife enthusiasts could follow the footpaths upstream through the Deben Ramsar Site and 'environmentally sensitive' river valleys. SAMPLE DISHES: spinach and cummin filo parcels £3.75; steak and kidney pudding £6; banana cheesecake with toffee sauce £3.50.

Open *11 to 3, 6.30 to 11, Sun 12 to 10.30; bar food and restaurant 12 to 2.30, 7 to 9.30*
Details *Children welcome Car park Wheelchair access (also WC) Garden No smoking in dining-room No music Dogs welcome Access, Visa Accommodation: 4 rooms, B&B £30 to £60*

RATTERY Devon map 1

Church House Inn

Rattery TEL (01364) 642220
off A385, from A38 S of Ashburton, 4m W of Totnes

One of the oldest inns in Britain, the Church House dates from 1028, when it was built as accommodation for the workers on the Norman church next door. It later became a hostel for travelling monks, and has now been scheduled for preservation as a monument of special architectural and historic interest. Enter through the arched doorway into the one long bar with its massive beams, impressive standing timbers, oak screen and fireplaces; walls are thick, windows are small, and horse brasses and copper implements adorn the walls. The printed bar menu is fairly standard fare – ploughman's, pies, salads, grills and the 'Church House fry-up'. But the blackboard is more adventurous and may list spicy red pepper chicken, roast guinea-fowl with a blackcurrant, cranberry and port sauce, or venison casserole, for example. To finish off, there's a very good selection of locally made ice-creams. Beers on handpump include Dartmoor Best Bitter and Legend, Tetley Imperial plus a guest beer. There are also over 30 malt whiskies to choose from. House wine is available by the glass, and the lengthy list comprises a worldwide selection. SAMPLE DISHES: hot and spicy prawns £3.50; chicken Wensleydale £6.25; treacle tart £2.50.

Open *11 to 2.30, 6 to 11, Sun 12 to 2.30, 7 to 10.30; bar food 12 to 2, 7 to 9 (10 Fri and Sat)*
Details *Children welcome in eating areas Car park Wheelchair access (also WC) Patio Background music Dogs welcome on a lead No cards*

RATTLESDEN Suffolk map 6

Brewers Arms

Lower Road, Rattlesden TEL: (01449) 736377
off A14, 5m W of Stowmarket

'If you can find Rattlesden then you can find the pub,' advised one reporter. The Brewers Arms stands in a little village near Stowmarket; from the outside, the building looks Victorian, with its cream stucco walls and green sash windows – in contrast to most of its neighbours, which are rustic thatched cottages. Inside there are signs of antiquity, although restoration has yielded clean brickwork, black painted beams and shelves lined with 'what looked like sets of encyclopedias'. The whole place is run with a degree of friendly efficiency, and if you arrive on Thursday evening you are likely to hear live jazz. The kitchen takes its cue from good raw materials – witness thick carrot and coriander soup, and a medley of game in red wine sauce served with 'two oblongs' of fresh herby mashed potatoes. Otherwise, the menu takes in starters such as spicy chicken pancakes with garlic bread, and main dishes ranging from stuffed chicken breast with tarragon sauce to monkfish thermidor. To finish, there are half a dozen puddings along the lines of treacle and nut pie, and hazelnut meringues with butterscotch sauce. Greene King IPA and Abbot Ale are impeccably maintained, and the short wine list offers a dozen or so affordable bins. SAMPLE DISHES: duck and orange pâté £3; medallions of beef with wild mushroom sauce £8; brandy-snap basket with strawberries £3.

Open *12 to 3, 6.30 to 11, Sun 12 to 3, 7 to 10.30; bar food and restaurant Tue to Sun L 12 to 2, Tue to Sat D 7 to 9.30*
Details *Children welcome if eating Car park Wheelchair access (also WC) Garden Background and live music Dogs welcome in bar only Access, Switch, Visa*

REACH Cambridgeshire map 6

The Kings

8 Fair Green, Reach TEL: (01638) 741745
off B1102, 5m W of Newmarket

The curiously named hamlet of Reach is on the southern edge of the Cambridgeshire Fens: the 'Devil's Dyke' stretches from the village south-east to Ditton Green. Inherited wealth from the river trade means that the architecture hereabouts seems rather affluent. The pub itself – overlooking the green – has a nicely proportioned Georgian façade with a 'rampantly shrub-bordered' lawn out front. Landlord Mr Lester went to school near the Hook Norton brewery in Oxfordshire and he dutifully ensures that the Old Hooky is kept in tip-top condition when it's on; other reliable draught beers in his cellar might be Elgood's Cambridge Bitter, Greene King IPA and Mauldons Humble Pie. Matching the beer is a blackboard menu of dishes ranging from spicily aromatic chicken and sweetcorn soup, and potato skins with sweet chilli sauce, to prawns with garlic and coriander, lasagne, Thai pork, and beef Stroganov. Desserts tend to be nursery offerings such as jam roly-poly – 'a well-made suet crust Swiss roll filled with blackberry jam,' noted one recipient. SAMPLE DISHES: smoked salmon £4; herby chicken £6; treacle tart £2.

Open *Tue to Sun 12 to 3, all week 7 to 11 (10.30 Sun); bar food Tue to Sat and bank hol Mon L 12 to 2, Tue to Fri and bank hol Mon D 7 to 9*
Details *Children welcome Car park Wheelchair access Garden No music No dogs No cards*

REDE Suffolk map 6

Plough

Rede TEL: (01284) 789208
off A143 Bury St Edmunds to Haverhill road

The setting is a beautiful Suffolk village complete with a traditional working farm and shire horses: the thatched and pinkwashed Plough fits in perfectly. 'An air of tranquillity' fills the bar, which has all the atmosphere of an 'olde tea-shoppe' – with furniture to match. The kitchen 'keeps a weather eye on new trends', according to one reporter, and it's equally at home with traditional country dishes and stylishly eclectic specialities. On the one hand you might find rabbit casserole cooked with wholegrain mustard, cider and prunes, or a gamey mixed grill consisting of venison steak and liver, plus wild boar sausages and bacon from nearby Denham estate; on the other, you could try 'aptly named' spicy Italian meatballs with spaghetti, sauté lamb with basil, or chicken di funghi. Fish shows up favourably in the shape of cod and salmon Mornay, or medallions of monkfish with cucumber, cream and sherry sauce. Puddings span everything from pecan and treacle tart to Paris Brest. Service is 'exactly what one would expect for a country restaurant/pub – friendly, smiling, attentive', noted one satisfied couple. Greene King IPA and Abbot Ale are kept in good condition, and wines are sold by the glass. SAMPLE DISHES: carrot and orange soup £2.25; guinea-fowl in red wine and port sauce £7.50; blueberry cheesecake £3.

Open *11 to 3, 7 to 11, Sun 12 to 3, 7 to 10.30; bar food and restaurant 12 to 2, 7 to 9.30*
Details *Children welcome in bar eating area Car park Wheelchair access Garden Background music No dogs Access, Amex, Diners, Switch, Visa*

REDMILE Leicestershire map 5

▲ *Peacock Inn* ✿ 🍇

Main Street, Redmile TEL: (01949) 842554
off A52, 7m W of Grantham

'An excellent venue' for visitors to nearby Belvoir Castle (family seat of the Duke of Rutland) 'and for anybody else', enthuses a reporter. At first sight you might think the Peacock is a dyed-in-the-wool English pub: it has beams, log fires and low ceilings in most of the interior, and even a canal running past the garden. However, the 'wonderful' newish extension at the back – with 'sun-kissed' colour schemes, settles and bookcases, an assortment of glass-topped wicker tables and chairs, and glass doors opening on to a terrace – and the allegiance of the chef, Franc Garbez, will prove you wrong. Garbez's classical French training dictates the style of the food, so the bar menu includes chicken liver with garlic cream cheese and toasted brioche, salade niçoise, sauté confit of duck with leeks, and mustard and herb-crusted lamb shank with cassoulet. A few Mediterranean influences also creep in, in the form of pastas and dishes such as a risotto of oven-dried tomatoes, white truffles and morels, and poached monkfish stuffed with red capsicum wrapped in Parma ham. At lunch-time you can also order sandwiches in the bar.

Traditional Sunday lunch has been lauded as 'the best...for miles around'; roast beef and Yorkshire pudding has 'just that little hint of "Frenchness" while remaining a true English experience'. More ambitious dishes with a forthright Gallic accent are served in the restaurant. A useful selection of real ales comprises representatives from Bass, Tetley, Theakston and Timothy Taylor, among others. Not surprisingly, France shows up strongly on the list of around 40 wines, several of which are available by the glass. SAMPLE DISHES: smoked salmon and leek pancake with chive sauce £4.50; pork tenderloin with orange, walnuts and cranberry *jus* £8.50; apple tart with calvados sorbet £3.50.

Open *11am to 11pm, Sun 12 to 10.30; bar food 12 to 2, 6 to 10, Sun 12 to 3, 7 to 10.30*
Details *Children welcome in eating areas Car park Wheelchair access (also WC) Garden Background music No dogs Access, Delta, Diners, Switch, Visa Accommodation: 8 rooms, B&B £65 to £75*

RICKLING GREEN Essex map 6

▲ *Cricketers Arms*

Rickling Green TEL: (01799) 543210
off B1383 at Quendon, 6m N of Bishop's Stortford

Allow yourself at least 15 minutes to read the menu in this Essex village pub: it is both extensive and inventive, and visitors are encouraged to take it away and pass it on to their friends. Produce is from the London markets, and dishes of the day on blackboards reflect what landlord Tim Proctor has bought on his trips. For a starter, you might pick gambas, Rickling pâté, or Bayonne ham. And then there are the mussels – served five different ways. Mains take in grills, beef Wellington, vegetable Stroganov, duck, and lamb, as well as plenty of fish. Real ales include Flowers IPA and local brews like Mauldons, Crouch Vale, Ridleys and Nethergate. No fewer than 12 house wines are available by the glass, and the short list of others is augmented by a couple of monthly specials. As its name suggests, the Cricketers overlooks a cricket green – one of the oldest in north-west

Essex; Audley End house is nearby, as is Mole Hall wildlife centre at Widdington. SAMPLE DISHES: a smokery of fish (salmon, halibut, eel and tuna) £5.50; chicken in apricot and cream sauce £5.75; pineapple fritters £2.

Open *11 to 3, 6 to 11, Sun 12 to 3, 7 to 10.30; bar food 12 to 2 (2.30 Sat and Sun), 7 to 9.30*
Details *Children welcome in eating areas Car park Wheelchair access Patio No-smoking area Jukebox Dogs welcome in public bar only Access, Amex, Diners, Visa Accommodation: 10 rooms, B&B £50 to £60*

RIDGEWELL Essex **map 6**

White Horse

Mill Road, Ridgewell TEL: (01440) 785532
on A604, 10m N of Halstead

A pretty village on the Essex/Suffolk borders, Ridgewell is awash with thatch, low white cottages – and it also boasts a village green. Outside, the White Horse has tubs of flowers and a secluded garden where children can play, while within, the main bar gives plenty of scope for a quiet chat. Although there is a separate restaurant, during the week diners generally opt for one of the four tables set aside by the bar, while at weekends the dining-room fills up. The straightforward bar menu concentrates on sandwiches, ploughman's and pies; or choose from the restaurant menu with its good choice of fish – there's praise for monkfish provençale and 'gorgeous crispy chips'. A small list of blackboard specials might include chicken curry, steak and ale pie, and burgers. Among beers on draught are local Nethergate IPA plus guest beers such as Adnams Broadside and Bitter. Fifteen wines fill out the list, and there's a good range on sale by the glass. Gin and ginger beer, the licensees tell us, is a favourite summertime tipple at the inn: 'tall glass, lots of ice, very refreshing'. SAMPLE DISHES: steak sandwich £4; chicken Dijon with rice and salad £5.50; fruit pavlova £2.50.

Open *11 to 3, 6 to 11, Sun 12 to 3, 7 to 10.30; bar food and restaurant 12 to 2.15, 7 to 10; morning coffee from 10.30; closed 25 Dec*
Details *Children welcome Car park Wheelchair access (also WC) Garden and patio Background music No dogs Access, Delta, Switch, Visa*

RIPPONDEN West Yorkshire map 8

Old Bridge Inn

Priest Lane, Ripponden, nr Sowerby Bridge
TEL: (01422) 822595
off A58, 6m S of Halifax

The setting by a cobbled bridge is lovely, despite its proximity to a major A-road. Go inside the ancient, white-painted inn and you may find a log fire burning in each of the three unspoilt bar areas, which still have their original wooden beams; metal lamps hang from high ceilings, and copper kettles are dotted about. At lunch-time during the week a popular help-yourself set-price cold buffet operates; otherwise a blackboard menu offers the likes of home-made soup, mushrooms parisienne, salmon, leek and pasta bake, seafood pancake, or meatballs with garlic bread. A choice of five puddings might include cranberry cheesecake or lemon meringue pie. A good showing of real ales includes Timothy Taylor Best Bitter, locally brewed Ryburn Bitter, and Black Sheep Special, plus a guest beer. Several wines are offered by the glass, and a blackboard lists additional bottles. On the other side of the bridge is the Over the Bridge restaurant, under the same ownership; you can order wine from its list of 100-plus bins. SAMPLE DISHES: smoked trout pâté £3.50; meat and potato pie with pickled red cabbage and mushy peas £4.50; banana and toffee pancakes £2.25.

Open *weekdays 12 to 3, 5.30 to 11, Sat 12 to 11, Sun 12 to 3, 7 to 10.30; bar food all week L 12 to 2, Mon to Fri D 6 to 10; restaurant Mon to Sat D only 7 to 9.30 (booking essential)*
Details *Children welcome in bar eating area Car park Wheelchair access Patio No music Guide dogs only Access, Visa*

ROCKBEARE Devon map 1

Jack in the Green

London Road, Rockbeare TEL: (01404) 822240
on A30, 3m NE of Exeter

You could easily drive straight past this roadside pub – unless you're stuck in a traffic jam. Either way, it's worth stopping off here, for the place has a well-deserved reputation in the area as a serious dining pub. The blackboard menu offers classy food with all the right modern touches: seafood soup with 'excellent, garlicky' rouille could start a meal, followed perhaps by salmon and dill fish-cake, braised faggots with bubble and squeak and onion gravy, or lamb and vegetable hotpot; or you could try ploughman's with a choice from ten West Country cheeses. Puddings are a strong suit: raspberry and white chocolate trifle, figs baked in honey served with ginger ice-cream, or 'superb' classic crème brûlée. The set-price restaurant menu is also served in the bar, offering perhaps chickpea soup drizzled with basil olive oil, followed by loin of English lamb. The bar is neat and well maintained, decorated with fresh flowers and hunting prints. Three local real ales are always on draught, including perhaps Cotleigh Tawny and Exe Valley Dob's Best Bitter. About a dozen wines are sold by the glass, and the full list offers a choice from around the world, including Mexico. SAMPLE DISHES: tomato and basil soup £2.25; smoked turkey and ham carbonara £5; rice pudding with spiced plums £3.

Open *11 to 2.30, 6 to 11, Sun 12 to 3, 7 to 10.30; bar food 12 to 2, 6.30 to 10; restaurant 12 to 1.45, 7 to 10*
Details *Children welcome in bar eating area Car park Wheelchair access (also WC) Patio No smoking in some areas Background music No dogs Access, Delta, Switch, Visa*

ROCKBOURNE Hampshire **map 2**

Rose & Thistle

Rockbourne TEL: (01725) 518236
off B3078, 3m NW of Fordingbridge

Rockbourne is one of those impeccably tasteful, immaculately maintained up-market villages in rolling downland on the Hampshire/ Wiltshire border. It's worth taking a walk around to admire the lovely thatched cottages, the little stream and the famous Roman Villa. The Rose & Thistle is thatched, too, and looks picture-postcard pretty. It should come as no surprise that the interior is a typically charming mix of heavy oak beams and timbers, carved benches and a flagstone floor. The kitchen makes good use of local produce for a bar menu that is forever changing. Light lunch dishes such as grilled avocado with Stilton cheese, sausages and mash with onion gravy, and tagliatelle carbonara are backed up by specials along the lines of game pie, French-style rabbit casserole with a 'cheese croûte top', and chicken curry. Evening brings more ambitious stuff in the shape of venison in black cherry and tarragon sauce, for example. Also note the fresh fish, such as poached salmon in chive sauce, crab salad, and fillet of sea bass fried in lemon butter. Seasonal ales supplement the line-up of Courage Best, Ushers, Wadworth 6X and so on. The wine list has been put together with an eye for quality as well as value; six house wines come by the glass. SAMPLE DISHES: soft herring roes on toast £4.50; grilled lamb steak with warm mint and orange sauce £9; raspberry cheesecake £3.50.

Open *11 to 3, 6 to 11, Sun 12 to 3, 7 to 10.30; bar food and restaurant 12 to 2.30, 7 to 9.30*
Details *Children welcome Car park Wheelchair access Garden and patio No-smoking area No music No dogs Access, Delta, Switch, Visa*

ROKE Oxfordshire **map 2**

Home Sweet Home

Roke, nr Wallingford TEL: (01491) 838249
turn at the signpost 'Home Sweet Home' on B4009, between Benson and Watlington

Tucked away in a peaceful village, this partly thatched, white-painted pub stands in a pretty row of sixteenth-century cottages. Prints hanging on the rough, painted walls give a homely feel to the place, with its central fireplace, beams, standing timbers and assorted armchairs and sofas. Ploughman's, salads and filled jacket potatoes kick off the bar menu, which also offers things like Stilton and mushroom pancakes, plaice fillet, beef curry, baked prawns, and burgers. The comfortable dining-room has its own vast menu, but this is also available in the bar: smoked halibut with prawns, and Caesar salad might be among the starters, with main courses along the lines of half a roast duck with honey and orange sauce, trout with almonds, and traditional roasts and steaks. Daily specials, listed on a board, may include rabbit and celeriac pie, and salmon in filo with chive sauce. Brakspear Bitter and Hardy Royal Oak are on draught, and the wine list of 20 bins features own-label French wines. SAMPLE DISHES: vegetable soup £2.50; chicken stuffed with Gorgonzola, spring onions and sun-dried tomatoes £9; bread-and-butter pudding £2.50.

Open *11 to 3, 5.30 to 11, Sun 12 to 3, 7 to 10.30; bar food 12 to 2, 6 to 9.30 (10 Fri and Sat); restaurant 7 to 9.30*
Details *Children welcome Car park Wheelchair access (also WC) Garden Background music No dogs in eating areas Access, Visa*

ROMALDKIRK Co Durham **map 10**

▲ Rose and Crown

Romaldkirk TEL: (01833) 650213
on B6277, 5m NW of Barnard Castle

The setting is pure English village – two greens, ancient church, stocks, old water pumps (which, within living memory, supplied Romaldkirk with its water). The Rose and Crown, dating back to 1733, is nothing if not handsome – a coaching-inn of the old school that has survived the years and continues to improve, thanks largely to the efforts of present incumbents Christopher and Alison Davy. A fire often blazes and the panelling gleams in the snug bar, where farming implements decorate the walls.

Locals drive through the back lanes for a taste of oxtail, calf's liver, mallard breasts with green peppercorn sauce, and smoked haddock fish-cakes (which are 'brilliant served with a chive cream sauce'). Others come from much farther afield. Christopher Davy's cooking is in tune with the seasons and he knows what the region can produce. His lunch-time ploughman's contain what he calls 'real' cheeses (including Cotherstone), as well as home-made plum chutney and pickled onions; Theakston Old Peculier is used to lace steak, kidney and mushroom pie, asparagus may be from nearby Richmond, Whitby woof comes with grain mustard and fresh tarragon. Home-made soups embrace everything from smoked chicken and celeriac to creamed turnip; puddings take in hot midwinter Bakewell tart, lime meringue pie, and stem ginger ice-cream with rhubarb compote. Fixed-price menus are available in the restaurant. Beer drinkers have a choice of Theakston Best, Marston's Pedigree and Morland Old Speckled Hen; wine buffs can stay with the six house wines (by the glass or bottle) or dip into the full list, which begins in the New World and ends in Spain. SAMPLE DISHES: ballottine of corn-fed chicken £4; roast cod with braised new potatoes £7.25; hot apple and calvados tart £3.25.

Open *11.30 to 3, 5.30 to 11, Sun 12 to 3, 7 to 10.30; bar food 12 to 1.30, 6.30 to 9.30; restaurant all week L 12 to 1.30, Mon to Sat D 7.30 to 9; closed 25 and 26 Dec*
Details *Children welcome Car park Wheelchair access (also WC) Patio No smoking in dining-room No music No dogs Access, Switch, Visa Accommodation: 12 rooms, B&B £58 to £88*

ROSEDALE ABBEY North Yorkshire map 9

▲ *White Horse Farm Hotel*

Rosedale Abbey TEL: (01751) 417239
turn off A170 to the right, 3m NW of Pickering, then 7m to village

High on the western flank of Rosedale overlooking moors, dales and the village below, this popular stone-built pub boasts some of the finest views in all Yorkshire. No wonder it attracts sightseers and walkers exploring the National Park. First licensed in 1702, it still has an air of genuine history. A huge horned animal's skull and hunting trophies decorate the walls around the fireplace in the bar, where drinkers congregate for pints of Theakston's XB, Old Peculier and Tetley Bitter, or enjoy a dram of malt whisky to keep out the moorland chills. Soups such as lobster bisque come with hunks of home-baked bread, and the bar menu also extends to chicken Caesar salad, Yorkshire rarebit, pork and apple sausages with mash, and grilled salmon. Formal dinners are served amid ecclesiastical furnishings in the aptly named Misericord Restaurant. The well-spread list of about 40 wines includes five by the glass. SAMPLE DISHES: tomato and mozzarella salad £4; pigeon in redcurrant sauce £7.50; sticky toffee pudding £2.50.

Open *weekdays 12 to 2.30, 6.30 to 11, Sat 12 to 11, Sun 12 to 3, 7 to 10.30; bar food Sun to Fri 12 to 2, 6.30 (7 Sun) to 9.30, Sat 12 to 9.30; restaurant Sun L 12 to 1.30, all week D 7 to 8.45*
Details *Children welcome in bar eating area Car park Garden and patio No smoking in restaurant Background music Dogs welcome Access, Amex, Switch, Visa Accommodation: 15 rooms, B&B £40 to £70*

ROTHERWICK Hampshire map 2

Coach and Horses

The Street, Rotherwick TEL: (01256) 762542
off B3349, 2m NW of Hook

Tubs of flowers in summer brighten up this solid-looking, white-painted brick pub standing squarely on the main village street. Within is a series of heavily beamed rooms (log fires in every one) with old prints on the walls. As many as seven real ales are hand-pulled at the bar, including Gribble Ale and Reg's Tipple, Badger Dorset Best and Tanglefoot, and Wadworth 6X. There's also a decent showing of wines by the glass and bottle. Bar food, served all day, ranges from home-made soup to steak and kidney pudding, Cumberland sausage, or potato and Stilton bake; the dinner menu in the dining area to the rear of the pub may include stockpot soup, or moules marinière to start, followed by Badger pie (beef marinated in Badger beer), halibut provençale, or duck à l'orange. Puddings are along the lines of Black Forest gâteau, trifle, or fruit in liqueur. Stratfield Saye House, built for the Duke of Wellington after Waterloo, is nearby. SAMPLE DISHES: mushroom and broccoli soup £2.50; lambs' liver in red wine £6; oranges in Cointreau £2.

Open *11am to 11pm, Sun 12 to 10.30; bar food 11.30 (12 Sun) to 9.45; restaurant Sun L 12 to 4, all week D 6 to 9.45*
Details *Children welcome Car park Wheelchair access Patio Background music Dogs welcome Access, Amex, Delta, Diners, Switch, Visa*

ROTHWELL **Lincolnshire** **map 9**

Nickerson Arms

Rothwell TEL: (01472) 371300
off B1225, 2m SE of Caistor

Inside this long, low, white pub set in a small village in a peaceful valley, the bars with their copper-topped tables have an old-fashioned feel, log fires burn and a friendly atmosphere prevails. Herbs are grown in the lovely garden, which also has children's play equipment. On the bar menu you will find dishes such as chicken and brandy pâté with warm redcurrant jelly, Grimsby haddock, and scampi, while specials may run to monkfish with lemon and caper butter, venison steak forestière, or ribeye steak with asparagus. Sunday lunch is a traditional affair. Bateman XB and XXXB, Boddingtons and a guest beer are among the real ales on draught, house wines are served by the glass, and two wines come in 'two-glass' bottles. SAMPLE DISHES: asparagus and avocado salad £4; beef, Guinness and smoked mussel pie £6.50; chocolate truffle ice-cream £3.

Open *12 to 3, 7 to 11, Sun 12 to 4, 7 to 10.30; bar food and restaurant 12 to 2.30, 7 to 9.30*
Details *Children welcome Car park Wheelchair access (also WC) Garden and patio Background music Dogs welcome Access, Amex, Delta, Switch, Visa*

ROWDE **Wiltshire** **map 2**

George & Dragon ✿✿ ❦

High Street, Rowde TEL: (01380) 723053

No one should be in any doubt that the George & Dragon is a pub through and through. It may put on an inauspicious face, but what happens inside is remarkable. Tim and Helen Withers have kept the place as it should be: drinkers are happily accommodated in the bar, and those wanting to eat can seek out a table – perhaps in the restaurant, with its functional wooden furniture and panelled walls hung with paintings, prints and plates. One menu is served throughout and the mood is affectionately chatty. Everyone seems to single out the service for special mention: it hits precisely the right note, balancing friendliness and good humour with capable efficiency.

Fish is the star turn here, and deliveries come up daily from Cornwall to this corner of landlocked Wiltshire. What impresses is not only the range and the freshness of the raw materials, but also the razor-sharp timing and the balance between the fish itself and its accompaniments: a pleasantly sweet cider sauce with baked red gurnard, or a 'tasty' assemblage of mixed peppers, onions and capers for grilled fillets of red mullet. Elsewhere, the list of piscine specials shows off the full range of cooking techniques in such things as roast hake with aïoli, pan-fried snapper with basil and Muscat, and Thai curry of scallops, cod and John Dory. Away from fish, the menu also deals in premier-league stuff, whether it be aubergine caponata, wild mushroom tart with quails' eggs and chervil mayonnaise, or lambs' kidneys cooked with sherry vinegar. Even something as traditionally 'pubby' as lamb pie is a dish of real class, with 'unusual and piquant flavours under its duvet of pastry'.

Meals conclude on a suitably refined note with classic crême brûlée, lemon curd tart 'with real bite', and delicately prepared poached peaches in a raspberry champagne sauce. The George & Dragon is a Wadworth-tied house, with IPA and 6X augmented by seasonal brews such as SummerSault, Malt & Hops and Old Timer. Sixteen good wines are sold by the glass and the full list fizzes with possibilities for those seeking adventurous drinking at prices that are temptingly affordable. SAMPLE DISHES: cheese soufflé baked with Parmesan and cream £4.50; monkfish with mustard, cucumber and bacon £12.50; chocolate St Emilion £4.

Open *Tue to Sat 12 to 3, Mon to Sat 7 to 11, Sun 12 to 3, 7 to 10.30; bar food and restaurant Tue to Sat 12 to 2, 7 to 10*
Details *Children welcome in restaurant Car park Garden No smoking in restaurant No music Dogs welcome in bar only Access, Delta, Switch, Visa*

ROYDHOUSE West Yorkshire map 8

▲ *Three Acres Inn*

Roydhouse TEL: (01484) 602606
off B6116 (from A629), 1m E of Kirkburton

During the day the views of the green Pennine countryside make the trip here worthwhile, and at night the pub looks 'really pretty and inviting'. Food is the main thrust of the enterprise; a seafood bar is a recent addition to the place. In the evening, candles on some of the tables in the warm and cosy bar give it a brasserie/bistro feel. Otherwise it's traditionally furnished, with dark wooden tables and spindleback chairs, some walls of bare stone, others painted, decorated with a mixture of plates and pictures. Daily specials are listed on a blackboard – grilled halibut with cucumber and lime butter, or confit of duck – while the menu runs from a splendid selection of interesting sandwiches (Whitby crab with lemon and ginger dressing, for example) to dishes like daube of beef, parsnip and leek crumble, or salmon with a herb crust; there's always a daily roast. Morland Old Speckled Hen and Timothy Taylor Bitter are among the real ales, and house wines are sold by the glass, with wines of the month written on a board. SAMPLE DISHES: Yorkshire pudding with caramelised onion gravy £3; pork, apple and mustard sausages, black pudding and colcannon £7; marmalade sponge with lemon curd ice-cream £3.75.

Open *12 to 3, 7 to 11, Sun 12 to 10.30; bar food and restaurant Sun to Mon L 12 to 2, all week D 7 to 9.45*
Details *Children welcome Car park Garden and patio Background music No dogs Access, Amex, Delta, Switch, Visa Accommodation: 19 rooms, B&B £48 to £58*

RUNSELL GREEN Essex map 3

Anchor

Runsell Green TEL: (01245) 222457
just off A414 (from A12), 4m W of Maldon; take Woodham Walter turn in Runsell Green, pub is 200yds N of main road

A recently opened no-smoking conservatory (complete with high chair) adds to the all-round family appeal of this 500-year-old pub in a row of houses overlooking fields and hedges. Beams and brasses set the tone in the bar, where an 'elegantly chalked' blackboard advertises the day's dishes. The kitchen shows a few inventive touches in, say, 'excellent' stir-fried monkfish and scallops with noodles or French wild boar steak with a splendid 'gamey' gravy and plentiful fresh vegetables. Otherwise familiarity wins the day with ploughman's, lasagne, steak and kidney pie plus desserts such as 'death by chocolate', summer pudding, and blackcurrant cheesecake. This is a Ridleys pub with IPA and ESX Best on draught; workaday house wines are served by the glass. SAMPLE DISHES: garlic mussels £3.25; chicken, ham and mushroom pie £5.50; spotted dick £2.25.

Open *Mon to Fri 11 to 3, 6 to 11, Sat 11am to 11pm, Sun 12 to 10.30; bar food and restaurant 12 to 2.30 (3 Sun), 6.30 to 9.30 (10 Sat)*
Details *Children welcome in eating areas Car park Wheelchair access Garden and patio No smoking in 1 room Background and live music Dogs welcome in public bar only Access, Switch, Visa*

RYE East Sussex **map 3**

Ypres Inn

Gun Gardens, Rye TEL: (01797) 223248

This seventeenth-century pub occupies a fine position, tucked away behind the historical Ypres Tower (from which it takes its name), and its sheltered garden enjoys views along the River Rother to Rye Harbour. Bar snacks, which are served all afternoon in summer, include soup of the day (perhaps cream of courgette), baguettes, ploughman's, and prawn platter. For lunch or dinner you could start with the likes of oak-smoked chicken breast, smoked salmon and soft cheese roulade, or garlic mushrooms. Much is made of lamb and fish – appropriately, given the proximity of Romney Marsh and the sea. Redcurrant jelly, mint and wine are used to glaze rack of lamb, and noisettes come with a grain mustard crust, while Dover sole, or monkfish and potato gratin, might be among the fish options. A handful of vegetarian alternatives, such as penne with Stilton and walnut sauce, is also on offer. Desserts range from clementines in brandy to treacle and walnut tart. Six cask-conditioned ales on handpump include Hook Norton Best and Old Hooky, and guest beers such as Fuller's London Pride and Pett Progress from the local Old Forge brewery; there's also a short wine list. SAMPLE DISHES: broccoli and watercress soup £2; roast fillet of cod with parsley sauce £7.50; apple and blackberry pie £2.25.

Open *12 to 11; bar food 12 to 2.30, 7 to 10.30 (summer 12 to 10.30)*
Details *Children welcome in dining-room Garden and patio Background and live music Dogs welcome Dogs welcome on a lead Access, Amex, Delta, Switch, Visa*

ST MARGARET'S AT CLIFFE Kent **map 3**

▲ *Cliffe Tavern*

High Street, St Margaret's at Cliffe TEL: (01304) 852400
off B2058, 4m NE of Dover

Around seven real ales are dispensed at the bar of this three-storey, clapboarded hotel, among them Fuller's London Pride, Greene King IPA and Abbot Ale, and Morland Old Speckled Hen. A Grade II listed building, it became a hostelry towards the end of the nineteenth century. The front bar is reached from an attractively decorated hallway, while french windows in the lounge and dining-room lead out into a walled rose garden. The lunch-time blackboard may announce such starters as spinach and nutmeg soup, and duck liver pâté, and main courses of pasta, curry, and steak and ale pie, while more ambitious dishes are chalked up in the evening: perhaps spinach-stuffed mushrooms with goats' cheese and tomato sauce, followed by Barbary duck breast with rosemary butter and onion jam, or chicken breast with a herb crust. Evenings also see a good choice of fish, from pan-fried cod with mustard and basil sauce to local sea bass with dill and butter sauce. You could round things off with lemon tart or, in season, summer fruit pavlova. The wine list, extending to nearly 40 bottles, includes a clutch of halves. The hotel is ideally placed for people catching ferries from Dover or Ramsgate and for the Eurotunnel Centre. SAMPLE DISHES: wild mushroom tart £4; grilled lemon sole with smoked salmon butter £8.50; treacle and walnut tart £4.

Open *11 to 3, 6 to 11, Sun 12 to 3, 7 to 10.30; bar food and restaurant 12 to 2, 7 to 9.30*
Details *Children welcome in eating areas Car park Wheelchair access (also WC) Garden No smoking in dining-room Live music Dogs welcome Access, Amex, Delta, Switch, Visa Accommodation: 12 rooms, B&B £28 to £45*

ST MARY BOURNE Hampshire map 2

▲ *George Inn*

St Mary Bourne TEL: (01264) 738340
on B3048, 3m NW of Whitchurch

A 'proper sense of place' is a vital key to the success of any renovated country pub. When Simon and Fiona Bradley took over the run-down George Inn, they wheeled in a serious architect to turn things around. The 'village bar' is still the focus for local goings-on, with re-laid flag floors, oak woodwork and appropriate photographs of life in the village. Beyond is a saloon bar – dubbed the Long Room because of its cricketing memorabilia – and beyond that an oyster and seafood bar where Helford natives (oysters), plates of gorgeous thick-cut smoked salmon and other smoked fish are the order of the day. If you choose to eat in one of the bars, there's the prospect of a decently varied menu ranging from provençale fish soup, and salads (grilled goats' cheese and watercress, for instance) to sausages and mash, kedgeree, lamb casserole with spicy beans, and chargrilled steaks. You can also get ploughman's, BLTs and the like, while desserts are mostly traditional favourites such as caramelised rice pudding, and apple crumble tart. Mark Robertson, who came here from the country-house elegance of Fifehead Manor, Middle Wallop, heads the kitchen; full menus served in the three 'themed' dining-rooms have also been favourably endorsed. The George dispenses a notable selection of real ales including Hop Back Summer Lightning and Ringwood Fortyniner, alongside Courage

Best Bitter, Charles Wells Bombardier Premium Bitter and Theakston Old Peculier. The wine list has been put together under the expert eye of Freddy Price and it displays fair prices across the range. SAMPLE DISHES: Welsh rarebit £2.75; salmon fish-cakes £6; sticky toffee pudding £2.

Open *11 to 3, 6 to 11, Sun 12 to 3, 7 to 10.30; bar food 11.30 to 2.30, 7 to 10; restaurant 12 to 2, 7 to 10*
Details *Children welcome in eating areas Car park Wheelchair access (also WC) Garden No smoking in restaurant Background and live music No dogs in eating areas Access, Delta, Switch, Visa Accommodation: 2 rooms, B&B £45 to £55*

SAWLEY North Yorkshire **map 9**

Sawley Arms

Sawley, nr Ripon TEL: (01765) 620642
off B6265 Pateley Bridge to Ripon road, 5m SW of Ripon

Fountains Abbey – the remains of one of the largest Cistercian monasteries in Europe – is in a magnificent setting just down the lane from this unassuming stone pub. The outside of the Sawley Arms is decked with banks of colourful flowers in summer, while the comfortably furnished main bar has a fire to keep you warm in winter. The majority of people come here to eat, although Theakston Best Bitter is on draught, and there's a short wine list, with house wines by the glass. Sandwiches and salads feature on the menu, and among the starters you will find 'interesting' soups such as celery, apple and tomato, plus things like salmon and herb pancakes glazed with cheese, or duck liver pâté with Cumberland sauce. A sensibly short list of main courses may include chicken curry, halibut with prawns and white wine sauce, or braised lamb with fennel. To finish amaretti Schokoladentorte flies the flag for the European Union. SAMPLE DISHES: smoked Nidderdale trout £5.75; plaice Mornay on a bed of leeks £7; meringue swans £3.50.

Open *all week 11 to 3, Tue to Sat and bank hol Mons 6.30 to 10.30; bar food and restaurant all week L 11.45 to 2, Tue to Sat D 6.45 to 9*
Details *No children under 9 Car park Wheelchair access (also WC) Garden No smoking in dining-room Background music No dogs Access, Visa*

If you visit any pubs that you think should appear in the Guide, *write to tell us* – The Which? Guide to Country Pubs, *FREEPOST, 2 Marylebone Road, London NW1 1YN.*

SAXTON **North Yorkshire** **map 9**

Plough Inn

Headwell Lane, Saxton TEL: (01937) 557242
off A162, between Tadcaster and Sherburn in Elmet

'Excellent "restaurant"-quality food which can be eaten in a small "pub" bar' just about sums up the attraction of this converted nineteenth-century farmhouse in a tiny village a few miles from the A1. There is no standing on ceremony whether you are at the bar or in the cosy dining-room, but service is ever pleasant and the cooking is reckoned to be 'brilliant'. Menus are chalked on large blackboards that advertise anything from Cumberland sausage and mash to red mullet with couscous and sorrel sauce. Here is a kitchen that can look smart for the likes of fillet of lemon sole with fennel and onion compote and lobster sauce, or change into peasant gear for home-made pork rillettes, or breast of pigeon with braised cabbage. Lunch specials broaden the repertoire by offering such simple things as hot chicken and salad baguettes, first-rate ploughman's, and club sandwiches (the version with St Agur cheese went down a treat for one traveller). Otherwise there are hot dishes along the lines of Thai fishcakes with chilli dressing, lamb patties with apple and apricot compote, and perfectly executed cod fillet baked with a herb crust redolent of dill. Puddings are beautifully presented creations such as strawberry and almond strudel, or chocolate mousse that comes fruitily embellished with a sharp raspberry sauce, a spray of redcurrants, sliced strawberries and Chinese gooseberries.

The wine list is a real corker with some great drinking at really affordable prices. The range is catholic with plenty of serious stuff from the New World; the half-bottle selection is well worth considering. The Plough is also raising its real ale profile and the handpumps now include such names as Woodhams Old Chopper. Saxton is within reach of the Wars of the Roses battlefields as well as the Biggin Nature Trail. SAMPLE DISHES: confit of duck with balsamic dressing £4.75; fillet of lamb with haricots vert and a garlic and basil *jus* £12; crème brûlée £3.50.

Open *Tue to Sun 12 to 3, Tue to Sat 6 to 11; bar food Tue to Sat L only 12 to 2; restaurant Tue to Sun 12 to 2, Tue to Sat 6.30 to 12*
Details *Children welcome lunch-time and early evening Car park Wheelchair access (also WC) Garden No smoking in restaurant Background music No dogs Access, Delta, Switch, Visa*

indicates a pub serving food on a par with 'seriously good' restaurants, where the cooking achieves consistent quality.

SCALES Cumbria map 10

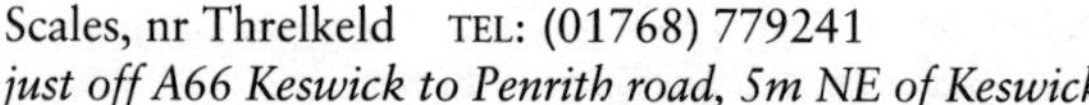

White Horse Inn

Scales, nr Threlkeld TEL: (01768) 779241
just off A66 Keswick to Penrith road, 5m NE of Keswick

Locally brewed real ales are a strong point at this isolated cluster of buildings off the A66: Best and Cumberland from Jennings, Yates Bitter, Blencathra and occasionally Skiddaw from the Hesket Newmarket Brewery are names to look out for. An excellent selection of farmhouse cheeses is a feature too, from Allerdale goats' to Pencarreg Blue. As you'd expect of this ex-farmhouse in a stunning location, the interior is beamed, cosy and comfortable, with open fires in winter. Lunch may consist of dishes like peach filled with herb cheese, Borrowdale trout, and blackcurrant sundae. The dinner menu offers a broader choice, including perhaps potted Flookburgh shrimps, or air-dried Waberthwaite ham, honey-glazed stuffed duckling, and Eve's pudding. Three house wines from the good-value list are sold by the glass. Paths behind the pub lead up to Blencathra Fell, and both Bassenthwaite Lake and Derwent Water are nearby. SAMPLE DISHES: broccoli and Cashel Blue soup with soda bread £2.75; salmon fillet with spring onions, garlic, ginger, lemon grass and prawns £8.50; damson sponge pudding with ice-cream £2.50.

Open *12 to 2.30, 6.30 to 11, Sun 12 to 3, 7 to 10.30; bar food 12 to 1.45, 6.45 to 9; closed Mon (exc bank hols) Nov to Easter*
Details *Children welcome Car park Patio No-smoking area Background music No dogs Access, Visa*

SEAHOUSES Northumberland map 10

▲ *Olde Ship Hotel*

9 Main Street, Seahouses TEL: (01665) 720200
on B1430, 3m SE of Bamburgh

Built as a farmhouse around 1745, the Olde Ship is now a highly popular waterside pub with emphatic nautical associations. The saloon and cabin bars are festooned with all manner of ships' figureheads and wheels, lifeboat oars, highly polished brass lamps and much more besides; if you fancy even more of the same, there is also a boat gallery upstairs with a collection of model ships, a seaman's chest, maritime paintings and so forth. Food from the sea shows up well on the bar menu, which includes such things as crab soup, and smoked fish chowder, alongside braised steak, and chicken and asparagus casserole. Landlady Mrs Glen's 'special pudding' sounds temptingly enigmatic;

otherwise you might order cloutie dumpling – a dessert from across the Scottish border. Fixed-price dinners are served in the dining-room. Beers from Theakston, Morland and Ruddles are generally on show, and some everyday wines are stocked, along with Lindisfarne Mead. From Seahouses you can arrange a boat trip to the Farne Islands, famous for their bird sanctuary and colonies of seals. SAMPLE DISHES: vegetable soup £1.50; bosun's fish stew £4.75; apple Geordie £2.

Open *11 to 3, 6 to 11, Sun 12 to 3, 7 to 10.30; bar food and restaurant 12 to 2, 7 to 8.30 (no food 25 Dec, sandwiches only 1 Jan); closed Dec and Jan*
Details *No children Car park Wheelchair access (also WC) Garden and patio No smoking in dining-room Background music Guide dogs only Access, Delta, Switch, Visa Accommodation: 16 rooms, B&B £30 to £37*

SEAVIEW Isle of Wight — map 2

▲ *Seaview Hotel*

High Street, Seaview TEL: (01983) 612711
on B3340, 2m E of Ryde

With flags and ensigns flying, this long-standing Victorian hotel feels distinctly nautical – especially if you are sitting out on the terrace, inhaling the sea breezes and watching the lines of clinker-built dinghies bobbing about on the water. Inside, the Seaview might be described as 'Tardis-like', although the 'pub' side of things centres on the main bar and the bare-boarded public bar – both stuffed with all kinds of maritime memorabilia, including prints and models of ships, oars, lifebelts and much more besides. The short bar menu always features a home-made soup, such as celeriac, as well as the house special – hot crab ramekin. Fresh local fish is invariably top of the bill, closely followed by some modern-sounding dishes such as rocket and Roquefort salad with pine kernels. In more familiar territory – but with a twist in the tail – you might find prawn cocktail with Pernod and fennel dressing, or chargrilled ham steak accompanied by 'crunchy new potatoes with garlic and fresh herbs'. Similarly, sweets might range from apple cake and cinnamon crème fraîche to pear William water-ice. A greatly extended menu is served in the restaurant. Goddards Special Bitter (brewed on the island) lines up alongside Flowers IPA, while the wine list has Corney & Barrow house wines by the glass and a Brading '92 from the local Adgestone vineyard. SAMPLE DISHES: chicken liver and wild mushroom pâté £4; crispy plaice fillet with chips £5.25; frozen peach yoghurt £2.75.

Open *10.30 to 3, 6 to 11, Sun 12 to 3, 7 to 10.30; bar food 12 to 2, 7 to 9.30; restaurant all week L 12 to 2, Mon to Sat and bank hol Sun D 7 to 9.30*
Details *Children welcome in bar eating area Car park Garden and patio No smoking in 1 dining-room Background music No dogs Access, Amex, Diners, Switch, Visa Accommodation: 18 rooms, B&B £45 to £95*

SEEND CLEEVE Wiltshire map 2

Barge Inn

Seend Cleeve TEL: (01380) 828230
between A361 and A365, 5m W of Devizes

The old wharf house and stables by the towpath on the Kennet & Avon Canal has been doing its stuff as a hostelry since 1805, and it lives and breathes the world of the 'bargee'. Inside it is covered from wall to ceiling with 'rose and castle' designs and artwork (the colourful ornamentation of barges and narrowboats), and brightly painted milk churns are used as bar stools. The menu makes much of the pub's special setting and associations: 'from the bilge' is soup, 'lock-jaw specials' are mammoth open sandwiches, 'wharfman's bake' is tagliatelle with asparagus, garlic and crème fraîche sauce. The evening menu is fleshed out with lamb kebabs, Thai chicken curry, pork Stroganov and the like. Wadworth 6X and IPA are on handpump along with Hall & Woodhouse Tanglefoot and a regular guest ale. Several wines are offered by the glass. SAMPLE DISHES: niçoise salad £3.50; oriental steamboat £6; hot pancakes with morello cherries, dairy ice-cream and hot chocolate sauce £3.

Open *11 to 2.30, 6 to 11, Sun 12 to 3, 7 to 10.30; bar food and restaurant 12 to 2, 7 to 9.30 (10 Fri and Sat)*
Details *Children welcome Car park Wheelchair access (also WC) Garden No smoking in restaurant No music Dogs on leads welcome, in bar only Access, Amex, Delta, Diners, Switch, Visa*

SELLACK Hereford & Worcester map 5

Lough Pool Inn

Sellack TEL: (01989) 730236
off A49, 3m NW of Ross-on-Wye

Tucked away down narrow lanes in peaceful rolling countryside close to the River Wye, this sixteenth-century, black and white timbered cottage is a favoured re-fuelling point for walkers and people exploring the Wye Valley. The interior has been opened up to make a main room with a flagstoned floor, open fires and a comfortable mixture of tables and chairs, and cushioned window seats; two dining-areas are adjacent to this. The bar menu offers a decent choice, from traditional steak and kidney pie, or gammon with pineapple, to more enterprising dishes such as prawns with mushrooms in tomato, cream and sherry sauce, poached salmon steak with a sauce of Dijon mustard, horseradish and chives, and barley and ale strudel. A board highlights daily specials, which may even run to ostrich and goat. Those with a sweet tooth will be spoilt for choice when it comes to puddings, although oranges in Grand Marnier are there for those inclined to the more fruity. Wye Valley Supreme, Bass and John Smith's are on draught, Stowford Press cider from local Weston's is on tap, and house wines are sold by the glass. SAMPLE DISHES: pea and ham soup £2.25; spiced lamb casserole £8; Dutch apple pie £2.75.

Open *12 to 3, 6.30 to 11, Sun 12 to 3, 7 to 11; bar food and restaurant 12 to 2, 7 to 9.30 (9 Sun); closed 25 Dec all day and 26 Dec evening*
Details *Children welcome in dining-room and some bar areas Car park Wheelchair access Garden No smoking in restaurant Background music No dogs Access, Delta, Switch, Visa*

SELLING Kent map 3

White Lion

The Street, Selling TEL: (01227) 752211
3m from M2, Jct. 7, or off A451 S of Faversham

In a landscape of apple orchards and hop fields, the White Lion feels every inch the rural pub, Kentish style. Flowers adorn the frontage in summer, while the interior is all bare floorboards and hop-festooned beams. Two log fires dominate the bars. Jazz nights and curries are features of the place; otherwise the blackboards advertise such things as pork fillet in cream, mustard and brandy sauce, Mexican specialities, steaks, and vegetarian dishes including mushroom Stroganov. 'We only use fresh local vegetables,' says landlord Anthony Richards. Puddings are mostly home-made crumbles, pies and trifles, prepared with seasonal fruit from the neighbourhood. The White Lion is a Shepherd Neame pub with Spitfire and Masterbrew on draught and Original Porter in bottles; around 40 malt whiskies and a comprehensive wine list complete the picture. SAMPLE DISHES: chicken liver, brandy and garlic pâté £3; beef suet pudding £5.75; lemon meringue pie £2.50.

Open *11 to 3, 6.30 to 11, Sun 12 to 3, 7 to 10.30; bar food and restaurant 12 to 2.15, 7 to 9.30; no food 25 Dec*
Details *Children welcome Car park Wheelchair access (also WC) Garden and patio Background and live music Dogs welcome Access, Visa*

SHAMLEY GREEN Surrey map 3

▲ *Red Lion Inn*

Shamley Green TEL: (01483) 892202
on B2128, 4m SE of Guildford

A main road separates this 200-year-old coaching-inn from the village green and the cricket pitch, which means that parking may a problem – particularly as the Red Lion seems to be riding high on popularity. If you want to eat in the light, airy bar with its pretty floral curtains and neat wooden tables, you need to book. Staff are charming, capable and helpful, and the kitchen delivers good-quality food. Reporters reckon that prices are somewhat on the high side, but everyone agrees that the results on the plate are well worth any extra outlay. Sandwiches, jacket potatoes and ham, egg and chips represent the traditional side of things; otherwise the menu goes in for seafood crêpes, sea-bass parcels, and lemon sole and scallop florentine topped with Gruyère cheese. Away from fish, you can expect fillet of beef Wellington and tender pan-fried chicken with a creamy leek sauce that is attributed to 'gastronaut' Keith Floyd. To finish, there is sticky toffee pudding, tiramisù, treacle tart and Grand Marnier gâteau. Flowers, Ansells Bitter and Greene King Abbot Ale are normally on draught and drinkable house wine is served by the glass. SAMPLE DISHES: ploughman's £4.25; half a roast duck with black cherry sauce £11.75; raspberry trifle £3.25.

Open *11am to 11pm, Sun 11 to 10.30; bar food all week L 12 to 2.30, Sun to Fri D 7 to 9.30*
Details *Children welcome Car park Wheelchair access (also WC) Garden Background music Guide dogs only Access, Switch, Visa Accommodation: 3 rooms, B&B £40 to £55*

SHEEPWASH Devon map 1

▲ *Half Moon Inn* 🍇

Sheepwash TEL: (01409) 231376
off A3072, 4m W of Hatherleigh

Sheepwash is an attractive village, and its centrally located pub is a delight: 'solid, comfortable and just right,' observes a reporter. A log fire may be blazing in the large inglenook, and a magnificent wooden wall clock ticks away in the beamed and flagged bar. A ten-mile stretch of the River Torridge reserved exclusively for guests means that a fishing theme prevails, with photographs of proud anglers and their catches; a small shop off the simple back bar sells everything a fisherman could need, and instruction can be arranged. Simple food of a high standard is available in the bar at lunch-times, from plain and toasted sandwiches, through ploughman's to home-made pasties and home-cooked ham salads; and a reporter writes in praise of the full set-price dinners served in the restaurant. Marston's Pedigree, Courage Best and Mainbrace – brewed specially for the pub – are on handpump, but wine's the thing to go for here. Apart from a decent selection of good-quality house wines, the list offers over 200 bins from around the world. The cellars are open for inspection too, and the pub also has a wide collection of malt whiskies. SAMPLE DISHES: ham and cheese toasted sandwich £2; pâté with salad and hot rolls £3.25; ice-cream £1.50.

Open *10.30 to 2.30, 6 to 11, Sun 12 to 2, 7 to 10.30; bar food all week L only 12 to 1.45; restaurant all week D only 8 (1 sitting, booking essential); closed evening 25 Dec*
Details *Children welcome Car park Wheelchair access Patio No music Dogs welcome Access, Switch, Visa Accommodation: 14 rooms, B&B £36*

SHENINGTON Oxfordshire — map 5

▲ *Bell Inn*

Shenington TEL: (01295) 670274
off A422, 6m W of Banbury

The Bell, dating from the early eighteenth century, can get surprisingly busy for such an apparently off-the-beaten-track sort of place. People come for the food, and a regularly changing blackboard proclaims what's on offer. Starters may take in king prawns with garlic, a terrine of four cheeses, or kipper pâté, while main courses could include plaice in Stilton sauce, steak and kidney pie, and lamb and lime casserole. Game crops up in season – venison casserole, for instance – and among the vegetarian choices could be spinach and ricotta lasagne. Warm morello cherries with kirsch, and crème brûlée are possible dessert choices. Hook Norton and Boddingtons are on draught, and a short wine list has three by the glass. SAMPLE DISHES: prawn mousse £3.25; duck with port and prunes £9; sticky toffee pudding £2.50.

Open *12 to 3, 7 to 11, Sun 12 to 3, 7 to 10.30; bar food 12 to 2 (later Sun L), 6 to 10*
Details *Children welcome Garden No music Dogs welcome Access, Delta, Visa Accommodation: 4 rooms, B&B £15 to £40*

Prices quoted in an entry are based on information supplied by the pub, rounded up to the nearest 25 pence. These prices may have changed since publication and are meant only as a guide.

SHERE Surrey **map 3**

White Horse

Middle Street, Shere TEL: (01483) 202518
just off A25, midway between Guildford and Dorking

In the eighteenth century this black and white, half-timbered pub was used by smugglers, and in 1955, while the cellar was being repaired, a second bricked-up cellar full of casks of contraband brandy was discovered. Parchment documents from 1605 were also found behind a wall, and are now on display. Inside is a series of heavily beamed bars, with log fires, leaded windows and stone floors, and it can get very busy – one Friday lunch-time, a reporter found it 'packed to the gunnels' with people eating and drinking. The reasonably priced menu is divided into 'Little Meals' and 'Big Meals'. Traditional-sounding dishes such as steak sandwich, beef, Guinness and mushroom pie, coronation chicken salad, and barbecue platter (with ribs, chicken, sausage, fries and salad) are listed alongside a few spicier alternatives – jambalaya, Moroccan-style lamb with cumin and apricots, and filo parcels filled with curried vegetables, for example. Beers on draught include Wadworth 6X, Theakston Best and Ruddles Best, while the short wine list is competitively priced. The White Horse doesn't have a car park, so arrive early to make sure you can find a space in the village. SAMPLE DISHES: salad niçoise £4.25; chicken suprême wrapped in bacon with sage and onion sauce £7; walnut and honey flan £2.25.

Open *11am to 11pm, Sun 12 to 10.30; bar food 12 to 2.30, 7 to 9.30 (9 Sun)*
Details *Children welcome in dining-room Garden and patio No-smoking area No music Dogs welcome Access, Amex, Visa*

SHIPSTON ON STOUR Warwickshire **map 5**

▲ *White Bear*

4 High Street, Shipston on Stour TEL: (01608) 661558
just off A429 Ettington to Moreton-in-Marsh road

'It's a townee pub, albeit small rural townee,' observed one reporter after a visit to this historic hostelry on the market square. The Bear is very much a local rendezvous, whether it be for a pint of Marston's Pedigree, Bass or Brew XI or something from the seasonal bistro-style menu. As a starter or side order you might try a basket of 'rustic' bread with herbed olive oil and a baked head of garlic. Warm salads (scallops with spring onions and ginger, for example) and a few pasta dishes are fixtures, otherwise go for confit of duck with stir-fried vegetables, Thai chicken curry, or pan-fried chicken breast with creamy mushroom and white wine sauce. Daily specials add a touch of seasonality – roast partridge in port wine sauce, a cold pie of organic Malvern guinea-fowl, or – to finish – plum crumble. As an alternative to dessert, it's refreshing to see savouries such as Welsh rarebit, or Gentlemen's Relish on hot buttered toast. A decent list of around 50 wines includes several by the half-bottle. SAMPLE DISHES: terrine de Provence £4; chargrilled tuna steak au poivre £8; bread-and-butter pudding £2.50.

Open *Mon to Thur 11 to 4, 6 to 11, Fri and Sat 11am to 11pm, Sun 11 to 10.30; bar food and restaurant all week L 12 to 2.30, Mon to Sat D 6.30 to 9.30*
Details *Children welcome in eating areas Car park Wheelchair access Garden and patio Background and live music Dogs welcome Access, Amex, Delta, Switch, Visa Accommodation: 10 rooms, B&B £23 to £45*

SHIPTON-UNDER-WYCHWOOD Oxfordshire map 5

▲ *Lamb Inn*

High Street, Shipton-under-Wychwood TEL: (01993) 830465
on A361, 4m NE of Burford

The Lamb is one of those venerable Cotswold inns that one imagines will go on forever without change. One expects it to be unaffected by style, fashion or improvement. But, lo and behold, new owners in the shape of The Old English Pub Company acquired the place in the summer of 1996. At the time of our visit, the same redoubtable barman was still pulling pints of Wadworth 6X and Hook Norton Bitter in the stone-walled bar; there were still newspapers on sticks to read and the blackboard menu continued to stay with the tradition of baked ham in cider sauce, Cotswold pie, roast duck with orange sauce, and sherry trifle, with an occasional dash of Mediterranean sunshine thrown in. There's also a hot and cold buffet every lunch-time except Sunday, when the roast takes centre stage. 'Very decent' house wine is served by the glass. SAMPLE DISHES: tomato and mozzarella salad £3.50; seafood tart £9; chocolate mousse £3.

Open *11 to 3, 6 to 10.30 (11 Fri and Sat), Sun 12 to 2.30, 7 to 10.30; bar food and restaurant 12 to 2, 7.30 to 9.30*
Details *Children welcome in dining-room Car park Wheelchair access (also WC) Garden and patio No smoking in restaurant No music No dogs Access, Amex, Delta, Switch, Visa Accommodation: 5 rooms, B&B £58 to £73*

SHOBDON **Hereford & Worcester** **map 5**

Bateman Arms

Shobdon TEL: (01568) 708374
on B4362, 6m W of Leominster

Shobdon is in a sparsely populated and very attractive area of steep little hills and meandering rivers. The pub's interior is personal, domestic and old-fashioned. Daily-delivered fresh fish is a strong point of the blackboard menu, which may offer cod fillet in beer batter with chips, Scottish salmon with dill sauce, and poached sea bass. Other dishes steer a course between the traditional and the trendy: smoked chicken and potato relish, or Dorset crab pot to start; and pork fillet in mustard sauce, chargrilled venison steak, or leek and potato crumble among the main courses. You could finish with pear frangipane, or steamed lemon and ginger sponge. Orange juice is freshly squeezed at the bar; Bass and locally brewed Wood Parish Bitter are on draught; and four house wines from a short list are served by the glass. SAMPLE DISHES: mushroom tartlet £3.25; beef and Guinness sausages £4.50; Bailey's cheesecake £3.

Open *12 to 2.30, 7 to 11, Sun 12 to 3, 7 to 10.30; bar food and restaurant 12 to 2, 7 to 10 (9.30 Sun)*
Details *Children welcome in eating areas Car park Garden and patio No smoking in dining-room Background music Guide dogs only Access, Visa*

SHORTBRIDGE **East Sussex** **map 3**

Peacock

Shortbridge, Piltdown TEL: (01825) 762463
just off A272 SW of Uckfield

A good range of real ales is served at this half-timbered pub in a tiny hamlet, among them Boddingtons, Morland Old Speckled Hen, Marston's Pedigree and Wadworth 6X. 'Comforting' and 'unaffected' are the words that spring to mind to describe the bar, with its mixture of furniture and bench seats, and a large hooded fireplace with a log fire, while other eating-areas are more formal. Food in the bar ranges from sandwiches and ploughman's, through soup – vegetable with cheese, for instance – to pancakes with various fillings (such as seafood, or chicken and asparagus), and perhaps Dover sole, with profiteroles with Cointreau sauce among the puddings. A traditional roast is served on Sundays, and there may be themed evenings on special occasions like St Valentine's Night. House wines are sold by the glass. Sheffield Park, with its famous garden, is nearby.

SAMPLE DISHES: smoked chicken and bacon salad £3.50; vegetable-filled pancake £5.25; tiramisù £2.50.

Open *11 to 4, 6 to 12, Sun 12 to 2, 7 to 11; bar food 12 to 3, 6 to 10; restaurant all week, D only 7 to 10*
Details *Children welcome throughout pub L, in dining-room only D Car park Garden Background music Dogs welcome Access, Delta, Visa*

SIXPENNY HANDLEY Dorset map 2

Roebuck

High Street, Sixpenny Handley TEL: (01725) 552002
on B3081, 1m off A354 between Salisbury and Blandford Forum

'Sixpenny Handley is the plainest of the half-dozen former estate villages in Cranborne Chase, which makes the discovery of the Roebuck's brilliant individuality all the more fun,' writes a visitor to this turn-of-the-century pub. The comfortable L-shaped bar has open fires, an eclectic collection of furniture, some easy chairs, and knick-knacks on shelves. A short blackboard menu of simple but satisfying food is displayed at lunch-times: sandwiches, ploughman's, a freshly made soup, and salads backed up by fish pâté, poached salmon, and spinach tart. In the evening the reverse of the same board lists a more ambitious dinner menu: perhaps a starter of smoked duck breast, followed by pot-roast quail stuffed with smoked pork, or stincotto (roast shank of salted pork in red wine sauce). A meal might end with something like treacle and apple crumble. Ringwood Fortyniner and Best Bitter are on draught, backed up by frequently changing guest ales, including those from the local Hop Back Brewery. Several wines are offered by the glass from a short but interesting selection. SAMPLE DISHES: vegetable soup £2.75; pot-roast guinea-fowl £9.25; caramel parfait £3.

Open *Tue to Sat 11 to 3, 6.30 to 11 (7 to 11 Mon in summer), Sun 12 to 3, 7 to 10.30; bar food Tue to Sun L 12 to 1.45, Tue to Sat D 7 to 9 (Sun D by arrangement)*
Details *Children welcome until 8pm Car park Wheelchair access (also WC) Garden No music No dogs No cards*

SKIRMETT **Buckinghamshire** **map 3**

Old Crown

Skirmett TEL: (01491) 638435
off A4155 Henley-on-Thames to Marlow road, 5m N of Henley-on-Thames

Step over the threshold of this rather unassuming roadside pub and you are immediately in an 'old curiosity shop': the little rooms are crammed full with bits and pieces of every description – jugs and mugs hang from the low ceilings, while ginger-beer bottles, old photos, dried flowers, plates and so forth take up every imaginable surface. The place operates rather like a restaurant, especially when it's booked up for Sunday lunch. As one reporter noted, 'If you turned up for a casual drink, you would not be able to sit down because all the tables are taken up by diners and [you would] feel rather out of place as everyone else is eating.' The kitchen delivers honest, high-class pub food: the new world of salsas and wilted greens is far away. Instead there are liberally garnished jacket potatoes, home-made pâtés and smoked fish terrine, plus generous portions of main dishes ranging from poached Scotch salmon in prawn and dill sauce to guinea-fowl with shallots, calvados and caramelised apples ('good, hearty winter fare...well prepared and efficiently served', commented one customer). Desserts could include home-made treacle tart. Landlord Peter Mumby dispenses Brakspear Bitter and Special straight from the cask, and has no truck with the 'gimmickry' of lager or designer bottled beers; the house wine is good quaffable stuff, though. He is also strict about children: none under ten is allowed anywhere – and that includes the garden. SAMPLE DISHES: deep-fried Camembert with gooseberry conserve £4.50; lamb cutlets with rosemary and redcurrant jelly £10.25; apple, sultana and cinnamon pie £3.25.

Open *11 to 2.30, 6 to 11, Sun 12 to 2.30, 7 to 10.30; bar food and restaurant Tue to Sun L 12 to 2, Tue to Sat D 7 to 9.30; open bank hol Mons*
Details *No children under 10 Wheelchair access Garden and patio No smoking No music No dogs Access, Delta, Switch, Visa*

The Guide *is totally independent, accepts no free hospitality and carries no advertising.*

Many pubs have separate restaurants, with very different menus. These have not been inspected. A recommendation for the pub/bar food does not necessarily imply that the restaurant is also recommended.

SLAIDBURN **Lancashire** **map 8**

▲ *Hark to Bounty* 🍇

Slaidburn TEL: (01200) 446246
on B6478, 7m N of Clitheroe

'The story behind the name', the licensees tell us, is as follows: until 1875, this medieval inn was known as the Dog. Then the local squire (who was also the village parson) stopped off with his pack of hounds. The hunters' drinking was disturbed by a loud and prolonged baying from outside, especially from the squire's own dog, which prompted him to proclaim 'Hark to Bounty'. These days, most of the action still takes place in the oak-beamed lounge bar, although it's worth taking a look at the court room that was visited by justices from the fourteenth century until 1937 and is now used for functions. Bread is baked daily and the kitchen works to a hearty menu of home-made soups, 'gradely' (that's Middle English for 'excellent') pork chop grilled with mustard and brown sugar, steak and kidney pie with genuine butter-rich shortcrust pastry, plus a blackboard of daily specials. Theakston's Mild, Best and Old Peculier are on draught and the pub boasts a better-than-average wine list from award-winning merchants D. Byrne & Co of Clitheroe. Slaidburn is in rugged moorland country deep in the Forest of Bowland. SAMPLE DISHES: mixed salad with hot crispy bacon £3.50; Cumberland sausage with apple sauce £5; jam roly-poly and custard £2.

Open *10.30am to 11pm, Sun 12 to 3, 7 to 10.30; bar food and restaurant 12 to 2, 6.30 to 9 (Fri and Sat 9.30), Sun 12 to 8, additional restaurant Sun L 12 to 2*
Details *Children welcome Car park Wheelchair access Garden Background music No dogs when food is being served Access, Delta, Switch, Visa Accommodation: 8 rooms, B&B £22.50 to £45*

SLAPTON **Buckinghamshire** **map 3**

Carpenters Arms

Slapton TEL: (01525) 220563
off A4146, 3m S of Leighton Buzzard

This must be one of the few country pubs with its own bookshop. Customers are welcome to browse through the shelves of second-hand tomes at any time during licensing hours. The building stands on a road through the village – houses here, open spaces there – and it fills up quickly (booking is essential on Saturday evenings, say the licensees). Luckily, the interior has been opened up to allow for plenty of eating room; blackboards are dotted around the place.

Snacks and ploughman's with home-made pickles are served most of the time (except Saturday evening and Sunday lunch); otherwise the menus try to move with the seasons: poached salmon steak with a helping of fresh asparagus and new potatoes made an apt summertime supper for one reporter. In addition, there are mighty pies, good salads, and dishes such Parma ham with ricotta cheese and pesto, Dutch fish stew, and whole roast spring chicken coated in curry spices. To finish, look for white ladies pudding (a coconut-flavoured version of bread-and-butter), as well as apple, honey and rum syllabub. Portions are hefty, although prices 'seem slightly steep for the area', noted a correspondent from the Home Counties. Real ale from the local Vale Brewery and weekly guests are on handpump; the promising wine list was due to change as we went to press. Slapton is convenient for walks on the Ridgeway Path, and the Grand Union Canal is not far away. SAMPLE DISHES: courgette and Brie soup £3; oak-smoked haddock with spinach and a cheese and mustard sauce £9.25; chocolate and brandy mousse £3.50.

Open *12 to 3, 7 to 11; bar food 12 to 2, 7.30 to 10*
Details *No children Car park Wheelchair access Patio No music Dogs welcome Access, Switch*

SLAPTON Devon **map 1**

▲ *Tower Inn* 

Slapton TEL: (01548) 580216
off A379, 5m SW of Dartmouth

Founded in the fourteenth century to accommodate workmen building the adjacent monastic college, of which only a ruined tower now remains (hence the pub's name), this ancient inn fits snugly into the base of a hill. Within is a series of interconnecting, atmospheric rooms with tiny windows and thick walls, all decorated with stylish simplicity. The village is only half a mile from Slapton Sands, where you could work up an appetite for one of the chef's specials: seafood marinara, say, or ham alla genovese. Otherwise, the menu encompasses starters such as devilled whitebait, or deep-fried Camembert, and main courses like trout stuffed with prawns, chicken provençale, and steak and ale pie, with the Italian influence resurfacing in pizza and lasagne, and in vegetarian dishes like penne piccante. Lunchtime sees the addition of ploughman's and sandwiches. An impressive range of real ales is dispensed, among them Gibbs Mew Bishop's Tipple, Dartmoor Best and Exmoor Ale, and there's a full wine list. SAMPLE DISHES: prawn cocktail £3.50; tagliatelle milanese £6; sticky toffee pudding £3.

Open *12 to 3.30, 6 to 11, Sun 12 to 3.30, 7 to 10.30; bar food and restaurant 12 to 2.30, 7 to 9.30; closed Mon L Nov to Feb*
Details *Children welcome Car park Garden No-smoking area in dining-room Background music Dogs welcome Access, Delta, Switch, Visa Accommodation: 3 rooms, B&B £20 to £40*

SMARDEN Kent map 3

▲ *Bell*

Bell Lane, Smarden TEL: (01233) 770283
off A274, 7m SW of Charing

This 'smashing little pub, all on its own' about a mile out of the village, was once a blacksmith's forge. Dating from the early 1500s, it is a white, tile-hung building with a rambling interior where flagged floors, beams, and candles in bottles add to the 'great atmosphere'. Energetic young staff help to keep things cheerful even when the bar is heaving. Alongside the draught milk – yes, that's milk – you'll find a great line-up of real ales, including Morland Old Speckled Hen, Goacher's Maidstone, Fuller's London Pride, Flowers, Shepherd Neame, Harveys and Fremlins, to name a few. Food majors in chips with just about everything – including steaks, gammon, chicken, scampi and sausages. Daily specials could be chicken satay with wild rice, or vegetable curry, and desserts take in the likes of apple crumble and bread pudding. It's all honest, no-frills stuff and portions are large. The wine list runs to 30 bins, with a choice of six by the glass. SAMPLE DISHES: clam fries £2.25; steak, kidney and mushroom pie £5; chocolate crunch cake £1.75.

Open *11.30 to 2.30 (3 Sat), 6 to 11, Sun 12 to 3, 7 to 10.30; bar food 12 to 2, 6.30 to 10 (10.30 Fri and Sat)*
Details *Children welcome in 1 bar Car park Garden No smoking in 1 bar Jukebox Access, Amex, Delta, Switch, Visa Accommodation: 4 rooms, B&B £20 to £32*

SMART'S HILL Kent map 3

Bottle House Inn

Smart's Hill TEL: (01892) 870306
off B2188, 1m S of Penshurst

Dating from 1492, but dressed up with a smart, modern frontage, this pub is in good company with the nearby tourist hot spots Penshurst Place and Chiddingstone Castle. Food is served throughout and you can choose to eat in either the low-beamed bar with its inglenook and ancient timbers or in the separate restaurant. The menu is long and eclectic, dividing almost equally between meat and fish, with a scattering added for vegetarians. Starters range from chicken satay to chargrilled black pudding with mild pepper sauce. Carnivores could continue with beef bourguignon with tagliatelle, or pork fillet with red plum and peppercorn sauce, while piscophiles might fancy sizzling scallops and scampi with black-bean sauce, or monkfish poached in coconut milk with coriander and Thai spices. Puddings such as spotted dick and pecan pie are listed on a separate board. The wine list includes some impressive names from good sources (note the Müller-Thurgau from nearby Penshurst vineyard) and half-bottles are not neglected. Larkins, Harveys and Ind Coope Burton Ale are on draught. SAMPLE DISHES: tomato, basil and onion salad topped with mozzarella cheese £4; breaded lemon sole with chips £7; apricot frangipane £3.25.

Open *11 to 2.30, 6 to 11, Sun 12 to 3, 7 to 10.30; bar food and restaurant 12 to 2, 6.30 to 10 (7 to 9.30 Sun)*
Details *Children welcome Car park Garden and patio Background music Dogs welcome Access, Amex, Switch, Visa*

Spotted Dog

VIEWS

Smart's Hill TEL: (01892) 870253

Chiddingstone Castle, with its village of Tudor half-timbered houses, and Penshurst Place are both very near Smart's Hill, and both very popular, so you can expect crowds at this weatherboarded and white-painted brick pub, which also dates from Tudor times. Plenty of swift and efficient staff are at hand within the characterful interconnecting rooms with their timbers, low ceilings and rustic wooden furnishings. In summer people may want to eat outside to enjoy the far-reaching views from the rear terrace over Penshurst village and the Medway Valley. Grills and salads could be strong points at that time of year: halibut steak, langoustines, or penne with a cold sauce of basil, sun-dried tomatoes and mozzarella, with fresh sardines, or gazpacho to start. Blazing log fires are the attraction in winter, when a meal could start with a soup like leek and potato and go on to game (guinea-fowl braised in red wine, say), or pork in cider and apple sauce. Five real ales include King & Barnes Sussex, Adnams Best and Hardy Royal Oak, and there's a comprehensive wine list. SAMPLE DISHES: minted pea and ham soup £2.75; shoulder of lamb braised in red wine with garlic and rosemary £10; jam roly-poly £3.55.

Open *11.45 (11 summer) to 3, 6 to 11, Sun 12 to 4, 7 to 10.30 (12 to 10.30 Sun in summer); bar food 12 to 2.15 (3 Sun), 7 to 9.30*
Details *Children welcome Car park Garden Background music No dogs Amex, Switch, Visa*

SNAPE Suffolk map 6

▲ *Crown Inn*

Main Street, Snape TEL: (01728) 688324
off A1094, on way to Snape Maltings

Snape is now synonymous with The Maltings and the world-renowned Aldeburgh Festival, and this 500-year-old pub serves the needs of culture-hungry incomers as well as the local drinking fraternity. The interior is archetypal East Anglian: a double Suffolk settle frames a little alcove, the floors are old brick and there are beams in the ceiling.

As befits the setting, local fish is a strong suit on the chalked-up bar menu, which ranges far and wide for inspiration. 'Plump, luscious' herring roes on bruschetta sprinkled with herbs and capers was reckoned to be 'a dish to die for'; otherwise the kitchen offers grilled squid with soy dressing, and fillet of sea bass with aïoli and roasted red peppers. The cosmopolitan tone extends to meat and game: honey-glazed confit of duck with creamed polenta and spinach is pure '90s brasserie, while cassoulet is a forthright assemblage including Toulouse sausage and spicy beans. Desserts are mostly classics such as crème brûlée and strawberry pavlova; alternatively, there are home-made ice-creams (prune and marsala, for example). The Crown is an Adnams tied house, with Bitter, Broadside and seasonal Tally-Ho on handpump; Adnams also supplies the list of three dozen classy wines, including around ten by the glass. If you fancy a break from the artistic junketings, drive out to Tunstall Forest or Minsmere RSPB Reserve and soak up the countryside. SAMPLE DISHES: leek and coriander soup £2.50; chicken breast with mozzarella and basil filling and sun-dried tomato cream £7.50; summer pudding £3.

Open *11 to 3, 6 to 11, Sun 12 to 3, 7 to 10.30; bar food and restaurant 12 to 2, 6.30 to 9.30 (also pre- and post-theatre bookings)*
Details *No children Car park Wheelchair access (also WC) Garden and patio No cigars or pipes in restaurant No music Guide dogs only No cards Accommodation: 3 rooms, B&B £35 to £50*

SNETTISHAM Norfolk map 6

▲ *Rose & Crown*

Old Church Road, Snettisham TEL: (01485) 541382
just off A149, 4m S of Hunstanton

Find the cross monument in Snettisham and you've found the Rose and Crown, which is just behind it. The fourteenth-century freehouse is rather quaint, with flowers and hanging baskets outside, and it's very popular. Families are attracted by the well-equipped play area in the secure garden (which comprises two forts, a swinging walkway, a playhouse and slide) – so there's plenty to keep youngsters amused while you enjoy a pint of Bass, Adnams, Greene King Abbot Ale, or Shepherd Neame Spitfire. New landlord Anthony Goodrich has upgraded the wine list: two dozen are now featured, courtesy of Adnams, and most are served by the glass, thanks to the Verre de Vin preservation system: 'A victory for the pub wine connoisseur,' proclaimed one reporter. Meals can be eaten in the bar, restaurant or garden room where steaks, burgers and fish are barbecued to order. Bar food is staple fare – salads, filled baguettes, curry, casseroles and the like. Specials on the blackboard could include rack of lamb, crab salad, toad-in-the-hole, or fillet steak with wild mushrooms and port sauce. There are log fires in winter, and the walled garden for the summer. The pub is well placed to visit west Norfolk beaches, Sandringham House and gardens, and the Heacham lavender fields. SAMPLE DISHES: local mussels in garlic and white wine sauce £3.75; Armenian lamb £7.50; home-made pecan pie £3.

Open *all week 11 to 11; bar food and restaurant 12 to 2.30, 6 to 9.30*
Details *Children welcome in eating areas Car park Wheelchair access Garden and patio No-smoking in 1 room Live music No dogs Access, Switch, Visa Accommodation: 3 rooms, B&B £35 to £55*

SOUTH GODSTONE Surrey map 3

Fox and Hounds

South Godstone TEL: (01342) 893474
off A22 at South Godstone, follow signs for Godstone farm; pub is 3/4m from farm, 1/2m from railway bridge

A wood-burning stove stands in the main bar here, an area dominated by blackened, seemingly ancient high-backed settles forming little dining booths around kitchen tables. Up some steps is a tiny bar area, with oak screens and standing timbers, leading through to a pleasant dining-room. The kitchen's policy is to use 'only home-grown produce where possible' – this means free-range meat from Kent, local vegetables, fish from British ports and eggs from across the road; and the menu changes almost daily. Bar food is served only at lunch-time, when the choice includes sandwiches, snacks such as croque-monsieur, and main courses of free-range gammon and eggs, for example. There's also a selection of imaginative 'Gourmet Luncheon' dishes – perhaps loin of venison on rösti with sloe berry *jus*, or deep-fried lobster-cake with hollandaise. In the evening, food is served only in the restaurant from a more formal (and more expensive) menu. Toffee-apple crumble, served with a jug of cream, has been a 'fresh tasting and light' dessert; other options might include treacle tart, or home-made ice-creams. Greene King IPA and Abbot Ale are on draught, and four house wines are served by the glass. SAMPLE DISHES: canapé anglais (mushroom, bacon, sausage and fried egg on toast) £4; Romney Marsh lambs' liver with crispy bacon and sauté onions £5.75; Grand Marnier rice brûlée £4.

Open *11 to 3, 6 to 11, Sun 12 to 3, 7 to 10.30; bar food all week L only 12 to 2; restaurant all week L 12 to 2, Tue to Sat D 7 to 9; no food 25 and 26 Dec*
Details *Children welcome in eating areas at L only Car park Wheelchair access Garden Background music Dogs welcome in bar only on a lead Access, Delta, Switch, Visa*

SOUTH LEIGH Oxfordshire map 2

▲ *Mason Arms*

South Leigh TEL: (01993) 702485
off A40, 3m SE of Witney

'Gerry Stonhill's individual Mason Arms', as the menu proclaims, is a splendid fifteenth-century thatched inn tucked away in a peaceful village. The owner has indeed stamped his personality all over the place – signs request no dogs, children or mobile phones – and the ambience has been described as that of a gentleman's club, with an exclusively French wine list based in Bordeaux and Burgundy, a cover charge in the dining-room, and Cuban cigars offered after dinner. A comfortable and civilised atmosphere pervades the three rooms, with rugs on flagstones, inglenook fireplaces, antique furniture and hessian-covered walls hung with tasteful paintings. The restaurant menu, served throughout, is bolstered by daily specials, plus sandwiches at lunch-times. 'Farm-fresh' duck is a speciality – with apple sauce, stuffing and gravy, say – and fish is delivered daily. Otherwise there could be lamb and plum casserole, game in season – venison and pheasant, perhaps – spit-roast over the fire, and steaks, with French apple tart and cheese and biscuits to conclude a meal. 'Ducks crossing' says the sign outside – and look out, too, for the peacocks strutting about the garden. SAMPLE DISHES: potted shrimps £6; lemon sole £10; crème caramel £3.50.

Open *Tue to Sat 12 to 3, 6 to 11, Sun 12 to 2; bar food and restaurant Tue to Sun L 12 to 2, Tue to Sat D 7.30 to 10*
Details *No children Car park Wheelchair access Garden and patio No music No dogs Access, Amex, Visa Accommodation: 2 rooms, B&B £35 to £65*

Use the maps and index at the back of the Guide *to plan your trip.*

SOUTH POOL **Devon** **map 1**

Millbrook Inn

South Pool TEL: (01548) 531581
1½m S of A379 at Frogmore, SE of Kingsbridge

Fish is a strong point at this small white-painted inn dating from the sixteenth century, as you might expect from its setting at the head of a creek running into the Salcombe Estuary. Poached salmon might come as a sandwich or with salad; crab may be plainly dressed, served with avocado, or made into a bisque; smoked trout could also be an option. Home-made soup, a platter of seafood, steaks, and pasta (with pesto and Parmesan, say, or tomato and vodka) may be on the menu too, with treacle tart among the puddings. Both bars are welcoming and full of character: the front one is more of a public bar, with a dartboard, while the back bar has tapestry-covered stools and wheelback chairs, beams, horse brasses, and old and new photographs and prints on the walls; french windows lead from here to a delightful terrace by a mill stream. Bass, Wadworth 6X, Ruddles Best Bitter and a guest beer are on draught, and Churchward's cider is on tap. SAMPLE DISHES: lamb broth £2.25; halibut au poivre £7.25; sticky toffee pudding £3.

Open *11.30 (11 summer) to 2.30, 6.30 (5.30 summer) to 11, Sun 12 to 3, 7 (6.30 summer) to 10.30; bar food all week L 12 to 2, Tue to Sat D 7 to 9 (6.30 to 9.30 summer; also open Mon and Sun D summer)*
Details *Children welcome in 1 bar Patio No music No dogs No cards*

SOUTHROP **Gloucestershire** **map 2**

Swan Inn

Southrop TEL: (01367) 850205
2m off A361 Lechlade to Burford road

Seriously creeper-clad and sedately Cotswold in style, this Swan continues to glide under the supervision of landlord Patrick Keen. Drinkers tend to head for the public bar, others choose the lounge or the little dining-room. One menu is served throughout. Bar lunches consist of hearty, straightforward stuff, including Stilton and onion soup, fish pie served with a helping of cauliflower cheese and potatoes, shepherd's pie made with lamb, and a plate of Gloucester sausages with peas, crispy courgettes, red cabbage and garlic potatoes. In the evening the kitchen delivers more elaborate restaurant-style dishes along the lines of warm goats'-cheese salad and roast duck breast with kumquat sauce; added to that is a fish menu, which ranges from mussels with white wine to whole sea bass or fillet of turbot for two. Bringing up the rear are home-made ice-creams, tiramisù and so on. Morland Original, Archers Best and a guest beer are on draught, beside Czech Budvar lager, Weston's cider and bottles of elderflower presse. Fifteen keenly priced 'house selections' top the wine list. SAMPLE DISHES: chicken liver and smoked garlic pâté £3; grilled lamb chops with cranberry and mint sauce £10; sticky toffee pudding £2.25.

Open *12 to 2.30, 7 to 11, Sun 12 to 3, 7 to 10.30; bar food and restaurant all week L 12 to 2, Mon to Sat D 7 to 9.30*
Details *Children welcome Wheelchair access No smoking in 1 room Background music Dogs welcome Access, Amex, Delta, Switch, Visa*

SOUTH STOKE Oxfordshire map 2

Perch & Pike Inn 🍇

South Stoke TEL: (01491) 872415
off B4009, 1 m N of Goring

Not far from the River Thames and in the heart of the Chilterns, this diminutive 300-year-old pub attracts visitors not only because of its setting and its pleasingly cluttered interior, but also because of its cooking. The food is undoubtedly imaginative, although one reporter thought the place seemed more like a restaurant: 'silver napkin rings are whisked away once you've liberated your napkin'; dishes are beautifully presented and service is suitably discreet. From the chargrill come squid (with a salad and marinated chicory), venison and juniper sausages (served with parslied mash), and lamb cutlets (with a mustard and herb crust and minted pea purée), not to mention lunchtime snacks such as beef in garlic bread. Dishes like smoked haddock on Welsh rarebit, roasted fillets of red mullet with tapénade, and lasagne with wild mushrooms, ceps and truffle oil give the food a more fashionable edge. 'Luxury' bread-and-butter pudding features among the desserts, along with warm lemon tart and banana cheesecake. Brakspear Pale Ale and Special are on draught, and 12 wines are offered by the glass from a short, but thoughtfully assembled, list. SAMPLE DISHES: spinach and Parmesan cheese tart £5; rösti crab-cakes with mango and coriander salsa £9.50; brown-bread ice-cream with raspberry coulis £4.

Open *12 to 2.30, 6 to 11, Sun 12 to 3, 7 to 10.30; bar food all week L 12 to 2, Mon to Sat D 7 to 9; closed 25 Dec and evening 26 Dec*
Details *Children welcome in bar eating area Car park Wheelchair access Patio No music Dogs welcome Access, Visa*

🍇 *indicates a pub serving better-than-average wine.*

SOUTH ZEAL **Devon** **map 1**

▲ *Oxenham Arms*

South Zeal TEL: (01837) 840244
off A30, 4m E of Okehampton

One of the oldest and most atmospheric inns in the country, this creeper-clad, solid stone pub was built by monks at the end of the twelfth century. It is designated as an Ancient Monument and was first licensed as a coaching-inn in 1477. A stone-flagged corridor, with rooms off, runs through the centre of the pub. There are beams everywhere, doorways are arched, the woodwork is oak, windows are tiny and multi-paned, and the walls are thick, rough and uneven. Log fires blaze in the bars, and there's a garden for warm days. In the lounge bar is a stone monolith, thousands of years old, which is reckoned to extend 20 feet below ground. Express an interest in the pub's history and there's a good chance one of the friendly staff will give you a quick tour. Food is simple, and the blackboard menu could list unpretentious fare such as turkey and ham pie, Devon squab pie (made with lamb, apple and sultanas), and salmon and broccoli Mornay. Sandwiches and ploughman's are available too, and puddings – cherry pie, or chocolate and brandy fruit slice, for example – come with clotted cream. A set-price menu is served in the restaurant. Beers, tapped from casks behind the bar, include award-winning local brew Dartmoor Gold from the Princetown Brewery, and Dartmoor IPA. Local Inch's Stonehouse cider is also on draught, and a good selection of half-bottles feature on the nearly-50-strong wine list; house wines are sold by the glass. SAMPLE DISHES: Oxenham pork and liver pâté £3.25; steak, kidney, Guinness and mushroom pie £5; ice-cream sundae with walnuts £2.50.

Open *11 to 2.30, 6 to 11, Sun 12 to 2.30, 7 to 10.30; bar food and restaurant 12 to 2, 7 to 9*
Details *Children welcome in eating areas Car park Wheelchair access Garden and patio No smoking in dining-room and family room Background music No dogs in dining-room Access, Amex, Diners, Visa*
Accommodation: 8 rooms, B&B £40 to £60

SPARSHOLT **Hampshire** **map 2**

Plough

Sparsholt TEL: (01962) 776353
off B3049 1½m W of Winchester

A feeling of space and comfort fills the Plough, its characterful bar decorated with plates, prints, a collection of old bottles, and hops strewn along the beams. A log fire and bare brick walls add to the atmosphere. Two blackboards proclaim the dishes of the day – generally a good mixture of pub staples, plus some more imaginative fare. Fillet of salmon comes with lemon and dill sauce, with pork fillet there is whisky and apple cream, and 'excellent' wild mushroom tagliatelle contains an excellent selection of fungi, including chanterelles and ceps. Or you might find lasagne, herby sausages with mash, or a pie of beef in ale with mushrooms. Eve's pudding, traditional fruit crumbles, and hot chocolate fudge cake may feature on the separate desserts board. Wadworth ales are on draught, along with a guest beer, and wines are sold by the glass. Service comes from an 'on-the-ball landlord and very pleasant staff'. A lovely large garden and a peaceful setting all add to the appeal of the place. SAMPLE DISHES: celery and Stilton soup £2.75; chicken breast stuffed with mushrooms, garlic and basil £8.50; bread-and-butter pudding with apricots and whisky £3.25.

Open *11 to 3, 6.30 to 11, Sun 12 to 3, 7 to 10.30; bar food*
Details *Car park Wheelchair access (also WC) Garden and patio No-smoking area Background music Dogs welcome on a lead Access, Switch, Visa*

SPEEN Buckinghamshire **map 3**

King William IV

Hampden Road, Speen TEL: (01494) 488329
off A4010, 3m SE of Princes Risborough

In the heart of a peaceful village nestling among Chiltern beechwoods, the King William is set back from a narrow lane and makes for an attractive watering-hole. The interior is homely with its open brick fireplace, sofas and chairs, while outside are a terrace and garden for warmer days. Food is taken seriously here. One menu is available throughout, with lighter lunches and suppers listed on the specials board; these could include garlicky mushrooms on toast, smoked chicken and tarragon crêpes, or smoked haddock kedgeree. More substantial dishes from the printed menu come in the form of Tuscan chicken, roast half-duckling with hedgerow berry sauce, and baked halibut steak topped with prawn thermidor sauce, to name a few. Puddings are home-made by a certain 'Mrs Owen': expect anything from spotted dick to St Clements sponge with orange sauce. Service is of the 'no-trouble-at-all type', with one late visitor arriving just as the pub was closing and being served excellent coffee with a smile. Real ales include Adnams Bitter, Brakspear Bitter, and Marston's Pedigree, while the wine list features a good selection of English wines, and runs to 35 bins in all. Nearby is Hughenden

Manor and the National Trust's West Wycombe Park. SAMPLE DISHES: Pacific greenshell mussels £4.25; grilled sea bream with a parsley butter sauce £9; sticky toffee pudding with hot caramel sauce £3.50.

Open *Tue to Sun 12 to 3, Tue to Sat 6.30 to 11; bar food and restaurant 12 to 2, 7 to 10*
Details *Children over 8 welcome in bar eating area Car park Wheelchair access (also WC) Garden and patio No smoking in dining areas Background music No dogs Access, Switch, Visa*

STALISFIELD GREEN Kent map 3

Plough

Stalisfield Green TEL: (01795) 890256
off M20/A20, 8m NW of Ashford

To bring 'uncompromisingly French' bistro cooking to a great little country pub in Kent takes some nerve, but it also requires a respect for the hostelry itself. Landlady Mrs Gross and her French chef/husband have succeeded admirably and deserve full marks for sticking to their guns: it would have been very easy for them to turn the whole place into a restaurant in all but name. The Plough, which is some way off the beaten track, has as its focus a large, airy bar with hop-garlanded beams, wooden tables and a log fire; beyond is a smaller area with a sofa and armchairs by the fire, a big wooden table surrounded by high-backed pews, and patio doors leading to the child-friendly garden.

The menu is a daily-changing blackboard written entirely in French. It's a classic read – escargots, crème de légumes, charcuterie omelettes, salade aux lardons (with poached egg), crêpes fruits de mer, carré d'agneau, filet de boeuf and so on; lobster has also made an appearance, served 'hot with calvados'. The cooking here is 'wonderful', enthused a reporter after sampling a dozen delicate mussels with a rich buttery stuffing tinged with garlic, and confit of duck that 'really fell off the bone'. Others have sampled a 'magnificent' platter of mixed shellfish and partridge with a strong gamey farce – a dish that was 'eaten in happy, contented silence'. Vegetables might include new potatoes 'cooked in duck fat' (a real jolt for the taste buds), sublime celeriac prepared rather like dauphinois, and sauté courgettes. Desserts are in the same staunchly Gallic vein: home-made ice-creams, tarte aux prunes, and îles flottantes of incomparable class. The grapes for the house wine are grown by a cousin in France, and the regularly changing list of 36 bins is patriotically French to a fault. Then it's back to England for Shepherd Neame Master Brew, Harveys Best and local Pateley Farm unpasteurised cider. SAMPLE DISHES: French onion soup £3; breast of duck with ginger and honey sauce £11; tarte Tatin £3.50.

Open *Tue to Sat 12 to 3, 7 to 11, Sun 12 to 3; bar food and restaurant Tue to Sun L only 12 to 1.45*
Details *No children Car park Garden Background music Dogs welcome on a lead Access, Delta, Switch, Visa*

STANDLAKE Oxfordshire **map 2**

Bell

Standlake TEL: (01865) 300784
off A415, 5m SE of Witney

This 300-year-old pub, set back from the road in the heart of the village, has been refurbished by the licensees who took over in 1995. The small main bar is attractively decorated and simply furnished with pine tables, cushioned chairs and wall benches. Bar food is available only at lunch-times; dinner is served in the separate restaurant. 'All our menus are written on blackboards, as they change constantly, and as we use only fresh ingredients they have a strong seasonal bias,' the licensees tell us. Game in season may include a pie of wild rabbit, leek and smoked bacon, doorstep sandwiches could be filled with free-range turkey, avocado and tomato salsa, and fish runs to mussels steamed with Thai spices. Other options in the bar may include brisket of organic beef with mustard mash and onion gravy, salmon fish-cakes with parsley and lemon sauce, and 'farm-made' pork and leek sausages, with desserts ranging from lemon tart to bread-and-butter pudding. Morland Original and perhaps Old Speckled Hen plus a guest ale are on draught, and there's a good choice of wines by the glass. SAMPLE DISHES: cream of forest-mushroom soup £3; black pudding with spiced red cabbage, apple and fried potatoes £5; spiced ginger pudding with stewed rhubarb £3.50.

Open *Mon to Sat 12 to 3, 6 to 11, Sun 12 to 3, 7 to 10.30; bar food Tue to Sat L only 12 to 2.30; restaurant Sun L 12 to 2.30, Tue to Sat D 6.30 to 9.30; food also served L and D bank hol Mons and D Easter Sun*
Details *Children welcome in eating areas Car park Garden No smoking area in restaurant Background music in restaurant No dogs in eating areas Access, Delta, Switch, Visa*

STANFORD DINGLEY **Berkshire** **map 2**

Old Boot Inn

Stanford Dingley TEL: (0118) 974 4292
off A4, 5m SW of Pangbourne

A delightful garden, complete with wishing-well and dovecote, is a draw in good weather at this 200-year-old pub in an up-market village on the River Pang. The range of real ales on draught is an attraction, too, with guest beers joining Brakspear Special, Fuller's London Pride, and Morland Old Speckled Hen. Within is a large bar with a beamed ceiling, comfortable furnishings, country prints on the walls, and a large inglenook with a log fire; the side bar is popular with locals, and there's a dining-room to the rear. Various blackboards announce what the kitchen has prepared: there are old favourites such as beef and ale pie, and gammon steak with pineapple or egg, as well as more innovative options along the lines of lambs' kidneys with black pudding, salmon and crab wrapped in vine leaves with lime and ginger, or partridge roasted with chestnuts and cabbage. Puddings might be banoffi pie, home-made ice-creams, or pecan maple tart. SAMPLE DISHES: buttered haggis bites with Cumberland dip £3.75; crab salad £9; crème brûlée £3.

Open *Winter Mon to Sat 12 to 3, 7 to 11, summer Mon to Fri 11 to 3, 6 to 11, Sat 11am to 11pm, all year Sun 12 to 3, 7 to 10.30; bar food and restaurant all week 11 to 2, 6 to 10*
Details *Children welcome in eating areas Car park Garden and patio No music Dogs welcome Access, Delta, Switch, Visa*

STANTON HARCOURT **Oxfordshire** **map 2**

Harcourt Arms

Stanton Harcourt TEL: (01865) 881931
off A40, 3m SW of Eynsham

The Harcourt Arms is a striking and elegant former coaching-inn, dating from the eighteenth century. The open-plan interior was refurbished following the takeover by the Old English Pub Company, and the three comfortable and relaxing areas are distinguished by open log fires, beams, and numerous Spy cartoons and other prints on the walls. This is an inn very much geared to dining, with one main restaurant area, though the menu on offer there can be served throughout. A board proclaims an extensive list of baguettes and doorstop sandwiches, with another announcing the daily specials: smoked mackerel with horseradish, or pumpkin soup to start, followed by perhaps Oriental lamb, pork and leek sausages in onion gravy, and a good choice of seafood, from fish and chips to skate wing with capers. Finish with traditional English puddings. Wadworth 6X, Theakston XB and Ruddles Best, plus two guest ales, are on draught, and the wine list has around half a dozen by the half-bottle. SAMPLE DISHES: cream of vegetable soup £2.75; salmon steak with Parmesan and basil sauce £9; banana and toffee crumble £3.50.

Open *12 to 3, 6 to 11, Sun 12 to 2.30, 7 to 10.30; bar food and restaurant 12 to 2.30, 7 to 10*
Details *Children welcome in eating areas Car park Wheelchair access (also WC) Garden No-smoking area in restaurant Background music Dogs welcome in bar only Access, Amex, Delta, Diners, Switch, Visa*

STANTON WICK Bath & N. E. Somerset map 2

▲ *Carpenters Arms* 🍇

Stanton Wick, nr Pensford TEL: (01761) 490202
off A368, ½m W of junction with A37 Bristol to Shepton Mallet road

Converted from a row of stone-roofed miners' cottages, the Carpenters Arms is now a model of affluent comfort. Outside, visitors can sit on the patio amid the hanging baskets and flower-beds which make the pub a mass of colour. Inside, the stone walls are adorned with old prints, and blue and white vases fill the window sills. Bar food is served in Coopers Parlour, where you can choose imaginative dishes such as sardines baked in onion, garlic, tomato and chive sauce, or deep-fried Brie on a caramelised onion confit, or simpler food like local trout, fish pie or a baguette. Daily specials might include home-made chicken liver pâté, or pork stir-fry. More expensive à la carte meals are available in the restaurant. The wine list is well spread and catholic, with plenty of better-than-average drinking by the glass. Local Butcombe Bitter, Wadworth 6X and Bass are on draught. Birdwatchers should note that Stanton Wick is within reach of Chew Valley Lake. SAMPLE DISHES: chicken and salmon terrine wrapped in bacon with apple and sultana chutney £4; grilled chargrilled lamb steak coated with garlic, herb and cream sauce £8.25; chocolate fudge cake £3

Open *11 to 11 (10.30 Sun); bar food 12 to 2, 7 to 10; restaurant all week L 12 to 2, Tue to Sat D 7 to 10*
Details *Children welcome Car park Wheelchair access (also WC) Patio Background and live music Dogs welcome in bar only Access, Amex, Delta, Diners, Switch, Visa Accommodation: 12 rooms, B&B £49 to £73*

The details under the text are taken from questionnaires sent to all pubs that feature in the book.

STAPLE FITZPAINE **Somerset** **map 2**

▲ *Greyhound Inn*

Staple Fitzpaine TEL: (01823) 480227
between A358 and B3170, 5m SE of Taunton

In an earlier incarnation this sturdy, creeper-clad seventeenth-century building was a hunting lodge, although it has been vastly extended over the years to include several bars, a restaurant and a skittle alley. 'The overall effect is of large, airy rooms, solidly furnished in quiet good taste,' remarked one visitor. The Greyhound is also children-friendly, and there's a climbing frame and play area in the large garden. A printed bar menu promises home-made burgers, fish and chips, tacos, and 'crowlers' (sausages, to you and me), with a special section devoted to what are modestly called 'large portions' (which might include 24oz mixed grill, or 16oz T-bone steak), but the real action is to be found on the blackboard *carte* of daily specials. Here, the kitchen aims high. Smoked salmon is marinated in lime and coriander, chicken breast is stuffed with 'Somerset Stilton' and served on a pear coulis, 'male' breast of duckling is filled with walnuts and a pomegranate paste. Among the desserts, you could expect, say, summer pudding, Bakewell tart or apple strudel. The pub is also a sterling purveyor of West Country beers, offering Exmoor Ale, Cotleigh Tawny Bitter and Otter Ale as well as Bass and regular guest brews; Lane's traditional cider is served during the summer months. Five house wines are sold by the glass and the list runs to 30 serviceable bins. SAMPLE DISHES: asparagus tart £3.75; seared spiced salmon steak with cranberry and red wine sauce £8; lemon syllabub £3.

Open *12 to 3, 5 (6 Sat) to 11, Sun 12 to 3, 7 to 10.30; bar food 12 to 2, 7 to 10 (Sat 2.15, Sun 2.30);*
Details *Children welcome Car park Wheelchair access (also WC) Garden/patio Background and live music Dogs welcome Access, Switch, Visa Accommodation: 3 rooms, B&B £30 to £45*

STARBOTTON **North Yorkshire** **map 8**

▲ *Fox & Hounds*

Starbotton, Upper Wharfedale TEL: (01756) 760269
on B6160, 16m N of Skipton

The setting of this 400-year-old limestone pub, amid the beautiful Dales countryside, makes it a perfect base for walkers. The River Wharfe and the Dales Way are nearby, while Aysgarth Falls, Malham Cave and Hardraw Force are within easy reach. The cosy interior is unspoilt, with flagged floors throughout; in winter there's a roaring fire, while outside seating is provided in the summer months. The comprehensive and varied blackboard menu lists a range of tried-and-tested dishes plus a few daily specials, and additional, more expensive choices in the evening. You might find curried cauliflower soup, and twice-baked cheese soufflé, among the starters; main courses of Thai-style chicken curry, lamb and mint burgers, and chicken and leek crumble; and good vegetarian options such as mixed bean and peanut chilli. Desserts include whisky marmalade bread-and-butter pudding, and Ecclefechan butter tart with maple ice-cream. Real ales, include Theakston Best, Old Peculier and Black Sheep Best, and the pub stocks a vast range of whiskies. SAMPLE DISHES: deep-fried king prawns with lemon mayonnaise £4.25; Moroccan-style lamb £7.25; brown bread ice-cream in a brandy-snap basket with blackberry sauce £2.25.

Open *Mon to Sat 11.30 to 3, Tue to Sat 6.30 to 11, Sun 12 to 3, 7 to 10.30; bar food all week L 12 to 2, Tue to Sat D 7 to 9; closed Mon Nov to Mar*
Details *Car park Wheelchair access Patio No smoking in dining-room Background music No dogs Access, Delta, Switch, Visa Accommodation: 2 rooms, B&B £30 to £50*

STAVERTON Devon map 1

▲ *Sea Trout*

Staverton TEL: (01803) 672258
off A385, 2m N of Totnes

This fifteenth-century pub in the lush Dart Valley was called the Church House Inn until a previous landlord caught a large sea trout in the nearby river. So runs the story. The solid, white-painted building has over the years spread into adjoining cottages and a smart hotel-style extension. An air of solid, respectable comfort permeates the open-plan bar, with its beams, thick walls, red banquettes, Windsor chairs, and fish in glass cases. The printed bar menu offers standard pub fare along the lines of sandwiches, burgers, and steak and kidney pie, although the pub's own sausages – pork with herb, pork with sun-dried tomato and garlic, for instance – are a highlight. Game pie may feature on the blackboard of specials, along with pork casserole, grilled guinea-fowl with port and orange sauce, and grilled Torbay scallops with cheese and tomato sauce. To finish there are West Country cheeses and Salcombe Dairy ice-creams. Dartmoor Best Bitter, Wadworth 6X and Bass, plus a guest ale, are on draught, and wines are sold by the glass. A different menu operates in the restaurant. SAMPLE DISHES: Cajun squid rings £3; half a duckling roasted with hoisin £10; bread-and-butter pudding £2.50.

Open *11 to 3, 6 to 11, Sun 12 to 3, 7 to 10.30; bar food and restaurant 12 to 2, 7 to 9.45*
Details *Children welcome in bar eating area Car park Wheelchair access (also WC) Garden and patio No music Dogs welcome Access, Amex, Delta, Switch, Visa Accommodation: 10 rooms, £39.50 to £62*

STEDHAM West Sussex map 3

Hamilton Arms

School Lane, Stedham TEL: (01730) 812555
off A272, 2m W of Midhurst

Pull off the A272 at the Hamilton Arms for a pint and you'll be in for a surprise: in addition to typical pub fare, it serves authentic Thai meals. The hard-working owners have succeeded in making their cuisine popular in rural Sussex; the food, in the words of one reporter, 'should not disappoint even the unsuspecting customers'. The main bar is simply furnished but has various Thai artefacts dotted around. A selection of authentic ingredients and spices are on sale in the bar area. There is a separate dining-room, called Nava Thai, with a comprehensive menu, but bar meals are a good introduction to the cuisine for uninitiated palates. The illustrated menu lists such delicacies as fried noodles with shrimps, wun-tun with honey-roasted pork, red or green curries, and roast duck with light sesame sauce and pickled ginger with rice. However, if you really do fancy an English meal you can have steak, cottage pie, or a sandwich. The atmosphere is welcoming, and the owner is often around to give you advice. Beers naturally include bottled Singha Thai, but real-ale buffs can enjoy local Ballard's Best, Fuller's London Pride or Courage Directors; wine is available by the glass. The landlords import Beer Ching, a malt liquor, and Meakong, a Thai rum. SAMPLE DISHES: fried noodles with soya sauce, bean sprouts and spring onion £4.75; sweet and sour chicken with rice £5.25; exotic fruit cocktail with five flavour ice-cream £3.50.

Open *Tue to Sun 11am to 11pm; bar food and restaurant 12 to 2.30, 6 to 10.30 (10 Sun)*
Details *Children welcome in eating areas Car park Wheelchair access (also WC) Patio Background music Dogs welcome on a lead Access, Delta, Switch, Visa*

If a pub has a special point of interest, this is indicated by a 'flashed' word or phrase at the top right of the entry.

Report forms are at the back of the book; write a letter if you prefer.

STEEPLE ASTON Oxfordshire map 5

Red Lion

South Street, Steeple Aston TEL: (01869) 340225
just off A4260, or B4030, 4m S of Deddington

Steeple Aston, a small village in rolling countryside, isn't far from the Banbury–Oxford Canal and the Cherwell. Tables on the terrace at the front of the red-brick pub become a sun-trap in summer while, inside, nothing much seems to change, with sewing-machine tables and a large fireplace in the bar. This is essentially a two-person operation developed over 25 years, with Colin Mead organising the bar and wife Margaret the kitchen. Sandwiches and ploughman's, home-made pâté, hotpots in winter, and salads – salmon, or crab, say – in summer are what to expect on the bar-food front, all well executed and made with fresh and top-quality ingredients. There is also a separate restaurant, open most evenings, with a more ambitious set-price menu. Beer connoisseurs come here for Hook Norton Best Bitter, Wadworth 6X and Badger Tanglefoot, while those who prefer wine can delve into the wide-ranging list that concentrates on France; house wines are sold by the glass. Nearby Rousham Garden, landscaped by William Kent in the early eighteenth century, is full of interest. SAMPLE DISHES: smoked salmon platter £6; moules marinière £5; Macallan's Craigellachie cream £3.

Open *11 to 3, 6 to 11, Sun 12 to 3, 7 to 10.30; bar food Mon to Sat L 12 to 2, Tue to Sat D 7.30 to 9.15; restaurant Tue to Sat D only 7.30 to 9.15*
Details *No children Car park Patio No smoking in restaurant No music Dogs welcome Access, Amex, Visa*

STIFFKEY Norfolk map 6

Red Lion

44 Wells Road, Stiffkey TEL: (01328) 830552
on A149, 4m E of Wells-next-the-Sea

Stiffkey is 'the genuine article', a picturesque north Norfolk village much favoured by walkers and birdwatchers. Its local pub is also the real thing: the brick and flint cottage has a thoroughly rural feel, whether you choose to sit in the bar, conservatory or what looks like a converted barn turned into a vaulted dining-room. Local fish (some from King's Lynn market) appears in the shape of Blakeney white-bait, soft herring roes on toast, crab salad and 'superbly fresh' grilled lemon sole. Blackboard menus also include things like a salad of 'perfectly ripe' grilled goats' cheese, Thai spring rolls, chunky Norfolk game pie, and broccoli and Stilton quiche. The pub specialises in beers from some of East Anglia's top independent breweries, including Greene King Abbot Ale, Wolf Bitter, Woodforde's Wherry and 'pale, hoppy' Great Eastern (brewed to celebrate 150 years of the Great Eastern Railway). The short, cosmopolitan wine list (from Adnams) includes ten by the glass. SAMPLE DISHES: Stiffkey moules marinière £5; home-baked ham with onion and caper sauce £6; autumn fruit pudding £2.50.

Open *11 to 3, 6 to 11 (summer 5 to 11), Sun 12 to 3, 7 to 10.30; bar food 12 to 2, 7 to 9 (school hols and bank hols 6.30 to 9, summer 6 to 9)*
Details *Children welcome Car park Garden and patio No music Dogs welcome Access, Delta, Switch, Visa*

STILTON Cambridgeshire map 6

▲ *Bell Inn*

Great North Road, Stilton TEL: (01733) 241066
off A1, 6m SW of Peterborough

The Bell has grown a great deal since the sixteenth century, when it was a coaching-inn serving the needs of travellers on the Great North Road. Both Dick Turpin and Clark Gable stayed here, and today the inn doubles as a fully fledged hotel and conference centre. Its greatest claim to fame, however, is its connection with Stilton cheese, which was first served and sold during the 1720s. One glance at the menu in the Village Bar tells its own story: the cheese appears with celery in soup, is made into a pâté, appears in a dip for breaded mushrooms and even turns up as a glaze for vegetarian pasta bake. The best way to sample it is also the simplest – either with plum bread or as the centrepiece of a ploughman's. Cheese aside, you might also be tempted by spicy coriander lamb, cod fillet with a crisp coating of breadcrumbs, paprika and almonds, or something called chicken pomanda (with a mushroom, garlic and peppercorn sauce on a bed of stir-fried vegetables). A separate restaurant operates every session except Saturday lunch. Tetley Bitter and Marston's Pedigree are on handpump and the inn has a varied, well-spread wine list. SAMPLE DISHES: avocado salad £4; steak, ale and mushroom pie £8; sticky toffee pudding with toffee sauce £2.50.

Open *weekdays 12 to 2.30, 6 to 11, Sat 11 to 3, 6 to 11, Sun 12 to 3, 7 to 10.30; bar food 12 to 2, 6.30 to 9.30 (7 to 9 Sun); restaurant Sun to Fri L 12 to 2, all week D 7 to 9.30 (9 Sun)*
Details *Children welcome in bar eating area Car park Garden and patio Background music No dogs Access, Delta, Switch, Visa Accommodation: 19 rooms, B&B £59 to £94*

STOCKLAND Devon map 2

▲ *Kings Arms Inn* 🍇

Stockland TEL: (01404) 881361
signposted from A30 Chard to Honiton road, or from A35 take Shute garage exit W of Axminster

'We have now installed a Verre de Vin system for more wines by the glass,' the proprietors tell us, so you should be able to sample even more delights from the big names on the well-chosen list. You won't be disappointed if you restrict yourself to the house wines and bin-ends either. The nucleus of this thatched pub in an off-the-beaten-track, attractive village is the Cotley restaurant/bar, with its inglenook. A long blackboard menu ranges far and wide for chicken broth, and fish soup, a platter of seafood, trout meunière, chicken tikka masala, and tournedos Rossini. A 'rollover hotdog' is now served in the evening for those who don't want too much, and at lunch-time the full menu is fleshed out with sandwiches, salads, and 'snacks' like steak and kidney pie, and pork braised in ale. Puddings may take in an unusual apple and cheese strudel, and Swiss chocolate gâteau, as well as old English trifle. Ruddles County and Exmoor Ale are among the real ales on draught. SAMPLE DISHES: devilled whitebait £3; rack of lamb £9.50; passion-fruit ice-cream gâteau £3.

Open *12 to 3, 6.30 to 11, Sun 12 to 3, 7 to 10.30; bar food and restaurant all week L 12 to 1.45, Thur to Sun D 6.30 to 9; snack menu all week L only 12 to 1.45*
Details *Children welcome in bar eating area Car park Wheelchair access Garden and patio Background and live music Dogs welcome Access, Delta, Switch, Visa Accommodation: 3 rooms, B&B £25 to £40*

STOGUMBER Somerset map 2

▲ *White Horse* 🍺

Stogumber TEL: (01984) 656277
off A358, 4m SE of Watchet

Since 1981, Peter Williamson has held the reins at this likeable pub in the heart of the village, and it is a place much appreciated for its atmosphere as well as its sustaining food and drink. Mr Williamson tells us that all his food is home-made, apart from the sausages and burgers. The menu has its share of salads, omelettes and grills, but you will also find some more unusual offerings in the shape of chicken breast with peaches and an extraordinary-sounding oriental pasty stuffed with ten different vegetables including miniature sweet-corn, water chestnuts, mange-tout, bamboo shoots and celery.

Puddings range from home-made pineapple ice-cream to steamed sultana sponge, and there's plenty of local clotted cream to add that touch of richness. Real ale fans do well with a line up that includes Cotleigh Tawny Bitter, Exmoor Ale, Wheeltappers and Otter Ale. There is also Sheppy's cider on tap. A handful of workaday wines satisfies the grape-loving fraternity. SAMPLE DISHES: salmon mousse £2.50; steak and kidney pudding £6; walnut tart and cream £1.50.

Open *11 to 2.30, 6 to 11, Sun 12 to 3, 7 to 10.30; bar food and restaurant Mon to Sat 11 to 2, 6 to 10, Sun 12 to 2, 7 to 10; closed 25 Dec evening*
Details *Children welcome in dining-room and garden Car park Wheelchair access (also WC) Garden and patio Background music Dogs welcome in bar only Access, Delta, Visa Accommodation: 2 rooms, B&B £17.50 to £25*

STOKE-BY-NAYLAND Suffolk map 6

▲ *Angel Inn*

Polstead Street, Stoke-by-Nayland TEL: (01206) 263245
on B1068, 5m SW of Hadleigh

'There should be pubs like this one all across Britain,' commented one correspondent; another reckons that the Angel delivers 'some of the most sophisticated pub food in East Anglia'. This 'outstandingly attractive' building with its centuries-old beams and fireplace still welcomes drinkers, but its main business is with the kitchen. Be warned, the bar can become what one reporter called 'a scrimmage': 'we arrived at 12.30pm and people were halfway through their meals!' Thankfully, staff seem to cope with the pressure in a pleasant, businesslike way.

You can take pot luck in the bar or reserve a table in the slightly more sedate restaurant. One menu operates throughout and dishes on the wall boards change twice daily depending on what is available. Fish from the east coast ports makes a noteworthy appearance and there's not much fancy dressing or trendy frippery to the style or treatment: steamed mussels in white wine, 'beautifully cooked' large lemon sole, and griddled wing of skate are typical. 'Excellent' home-made fish-cakes might come with a ramekin of mayonnaise with apple, lime and mango or with a highly distinguished rémoulade sauce. Away from fish there might be clear German pea soup with ham, ballottine of duckling with Cassis sauce, or steak and kidney pudding with onion gravy. Vegetables regularly receive a round of applause – especially new potatoes in their skins: 'it is difficult to imagine a simpler dish which can give such pleasure when it is done well,' mused one contented soul. Great-looking french fries have also been noted. The kitchen makes a big show of presentation, which runs through to desserts (raspberry mousse in a chocolate cup, steamed apple pudding with vanilla sauce, for example), while one six-year-old thought the ice-cream and strawberry shortcake 'the best she had ever tasted'. Greene King IPA and Abbot Ale plus Adnams Bitter and a guest brew are on draught, and the wine list holds plenty of interest – the range is global, quality is high and prices are very fair. Needless to say, Dedham Vale and Constable country make this area a tourist hot spot. SAMPLE DISHES: mushroom and pistachio pâté £4; chicken and king prawn brochette with yoghurt and mint dip £8.50; dark chocolate ganache gâteau £3.50.

Open *11 to 2.30, 6 to 11, Sun 12 to 3, 7 to 10.30; bar food and restaurant 12 to 2, 6.30 (7 Sun) to 9; closed 25 and 26 Dec*
Details *No children Car park Patio No smoking in 1 room No music No dogs Access, Amex, Delta, Diners, Switch, Visa Accommodation: 6 rooms, B&B £45 to £59*

STOKE HOLY CROSS Norfolk map 6

Wildebeest Arms

Norwich Road, Stoke Holy Cross TEL: (01508) 492497
from Norwich take A140 Ipswich road; directly after roundabout take the left turn signposted Stoke Holy Cross

A Norfolk pub with a name that comes 'out of Africa' sounds slightly bizarre and there aren't many clues to be found – apart from the tribal spears over the fireplace. Otherwise, the interior of this roadside hostelry strikes a laid-back and modern rustic note, with bare tables to the right and left of the bar, high-backed wicker dining chairs, and a real log fire in the far wall. Piped music keeps pace with the eclectic mood of the times.

Chef Eden Derrick came here after working at David Adlard's highly rated restaurant in Norwich. His technique and imagination are not difficult to detect. Needless to say, current trends dictate much of the shortish menu and the kitchen is noticeably keen on vivid accompaniments: lime pickle and yoghurt dressing for salmon tartare, home-made zucchini pickles with chicken liver parfait, banana salsa with blackened Cajun salmon. The Mediterranean brings such things as red pepper pizza with mozzarella, or grilled polenta with braised mixed mushrooms in a sauce of white wine, olive oil, basil and sun-dried tomatoes. Big-city brasserie influences also surface in warm salad of wild duck, black pudding and chicken livers with toasted pine kernels, or home-made venison and beef sausages with carrot and parsnip purée. Side orders include hand-cut chips with their skins on. Desserts are true to fashion: glazed lemon tart, chocolate marquise with mint custard, for example. In addition to the main menu, there's also a good-value three-course fixed-price lunch. The wine list is eminently attractive, with some tantalising up-to-the-minute names from around the world, all at very realistic prices. Courage Directors, Adnams Best and John Smith's are on handpump. SAMPLE DISHES: brochette of tiger prawns wrapped in Parma ham with basil sauce and aïoli £5.25; rump of lamb with creamy mash, pesto and confit of garlic £12.50; passion-fruit and blackberry parfait with orange crème anglaise £4.

Open *11 to 3, 6.30 to 11, Sun 12 to 3, 6.30 to 11; bar food Mon to Sat 12 to 2, 7 to 10, Sun 12.30 to 2.30, 7 to 9.30*
Details *Children welcome Car park Wheelchair access (also WC) Garden No-smoking area in dining-room Background music No dogs Access, Amex, Delta, Diners, Switch, Visa*

STOKE ROW Oxfordshire map 2

Crooked Billet ✿

LOCAL PRODUCE

Newlands Lane, Stoke Row TEL: (01491) 681048
off B481 Reading to Nettlebed road, 5m W of Henley-on-Thames

The Crooked Billet looks every inch like the real thing, as far as country pubs go: no wonder it has featured in countless commercials and TV programmes. What you notice from the outside are the green shuttered windows, the two dormers, the crooked tiled roof and the wonky-looking chimneys. Inside, it is a vision of organised chaos: much of the front room seems to be used as an overspill larder, piled with sacks of pasta and heaps of vegetables; empty champagne bottles are everywhere. At the back of the pub is a rambling garden, complete with a little cherry orchard – a reminder of the time when the sale of fruit and other village produce used to pay for the upkeep of the famous Maharajah's Well (donated by the Maharajah of Benares during Victorian times), still an attraction for visitors to Stoke Row.

Paul Clerehugh's dedication to local produce is remarkable. He bakes bread with flour from ancient Mapledurham Mill, organic meat and dairy produce are from a farm in Whitchurch, while a herb grower in Sonning supplies whatever is needed; added to this are the green-fingered efforts of helpful gardeners and friends. Hives in the pub garden provide honey, and meat is smoked on the premises. To celebrate this rich diversity, Paul stages occasional 'gourmet evenings' based on ingredients procured from a ten-mile radius of the pub. By contrast, the inspiration for his regular, weekly-changing menus is the encyclopedia of world cookery. You might find, for example, Thai mussels with red curry; a version of salad niçoise with smoked salmon; yellow-fin tuna with soy butter sauce and 'a little green chilli pickle on the side'; and pork fillet with spicy gumbo sauce, gratinated nachos, jalapeños and salsa – not to mention patriotically British pigeon breast with braised red cabbage and a baby haggis. Successes mentioned in recent reports have included grilled fillet of brill with Puy lentils, mash and spring onions, and shoulder of lamb with pearl barley and Savoy cabbage. 'Sound cooking, hefty portions, strong flavours' was how one reporter summed up the experience. The Crooked Billet is a pub with no bar: pints and pitchers of locally brewed Brakspear ales are drawn direct from casks in the cellar. The 100-strong wine list is a global as the food; the choice is sharp, accompanying notes are wacky, but where are the vintages? SAMPLE DISHES: pan-fried baby squid with pak-choi greens and lemon pepper £5; oxtail casserole with mash £10; coffee cheesecake with fudge sauce £5.

Open *12 to 2.30, 7 to 11, Sun 12 to 10; bar food 12 to 2.30, 7 to 10 (10.30 Fri), Sat 12 to 10.30, Sun 12 to 10*
Details *Children welcome in bar eating area Car park Wheelchair access Garden No music No dogs Access, Visa*

STOPHAM West Sussex map 3

White Hart

Stopham Bridge TEL: (01798) 873321
on A283 Pulborough to Petworth road, just W of Pulborough

Standing next to the medieval bridge over the River Arun, this plain stone-built pub seems fixed in a landscape virtually untouched by time. There's been a building on the site since 'Domesday', and the whole place emanates a kind of half-forgotten charm with its panelling and low beams. In this cheerful atmosphere, you can quaff real ales such as King & Barnes Sussex Bitter, Flowers and – perhaps – Morland Old Speckled Hen, and choose from a no-frills repertoire of home-made soups, chicken liver, bacon and hazelnut terrine, roasts and casseroles, plus a fair showing of fish (smoked haddock Mornay, or cod in beer batter, for example). Puddings, such as lemon and sultana sponge, continue the same theme. Tables can be booked in the restaurant. Monthly theme nights are a regular attraction, and in summer there may be live music in the riverside garden. SAMPLE DISHES: mushroom and tarragon soup £2; roast pork with vegetables £4.75; bread-and-butter pudding £2.25.

Open *11 to 3, 6.30 to 11, Sun 12 to 3, 7 to 10.30; bar food and restaurant Mon to Sat L 12 to 2.30, all week D 7 to 9.30 (no food Sun D winter)*
Details *Children welcome Car park No smoking in some areas Garden Background music; live music in garden summer Dogs welcome in bar only Access, Amex, Visa*

STOUGHTON **West Sussex** **map 3**

Hare & Hounds

Stoughton TEL: (01705) 631433
off B2147 at Walderton, 5m NW of Chichester

Stoughton is set in an extremely quiet and very beautiful spot on the lower slopes of the South Downs; the village church dates from Saxon times and has fine Romanesque features. The Hare & Hounds, a creeper-covered brick and flint building, is itself more than 300 years old. To the front of the pub is a terrace where chickens peck about the plant tubs and trees; tables here and in the rear garden allow for outdoor eating and drinking, and for enjoying the views. The atmosphere inside is comfortable, log fires ensuring a warm welcome in winter. A line of bars and hatches is surrounded by various blackboards listing daily-changing specials: there could be venison (used in sausages or a pie), Dover sole, or skate wing, for example. A printed menu offers a range of standard bar meals such as locally dressed crab salad, cheese and onion flan, shepherd's pie, and ploughman's. Spotted dick and treacle sponge with custard were both described as 'absolutely correct' by one reporter. There is also a good-value set-price dinner in the evening. A choice of six real ales on draught includes Timothy Taylor Landlord, Gale's HSB, Ballard's Wassail and Harveys Sussex Best Bitter, while the wine list runs to around 35 bins. SAMPLE DISHES: Mediterranean fish soup £3.50; steak and mushroom pie £6; lemon meringue pie £2.75.

Open *11 to 3, 6 to 11, Sun 12 to 4, 7 to 10.30; bar food Mon to Sat 11 to 2.30, 6 to 10.30, Sun 12 to 3.30, 7 to 10; no food 25 Dec*
Details *Children welcome Car park Wheelchair access (also WC) Garden and patio No music Dogs welcome Access, Amex, Delta, Switch, Visa*

STOW BARDOLPH **Norfolk** **map 6**

Hare Arms

Stow Bardolph TEL: (01366) 382229
off A10, 2m N of Downham Market

This attractive, creeper-clad country pub, built during the Napoleonic wars, is set in a picturesque village which is part of the local Stow Hall estate. It is named after the Hare family, who have lived at the hall since the 1550s. Inside, the main bar has a pleasant array of traditional, comfortable furnishings and a wealth of memorabilia, from old advertising signs to brass blow torches, which all add up to the homely and welcoming atmosphere. As for bar food, the printed menu offers the usual range of pub staples, but old hands head straight for the more unusual dishes available on the blackboard. You might find chicken breast wrapped in bacon with a whisky sauce; braised beef in red wine; skate wing with a mustard sauce; or sea bream with a red pepper sauce. The Hare is a Greene King-tied house serving IPA, Abbot Ale and Rayments, as well as seasonal brews. Wines are sold by the glass in the bar, and about 30 bins are available on the list, plus a good choice of half-bottles. Outside there's a splendid summer garden in which peacocks roam, while in the winter fires blaze in the bar. 'It warrants making a scheduled stop,' said one visitor. Nearby is the National Trust property of Oxburgh Hall. SAMPLE DISHES: prawn mousse with toast £6; chicken breast wrapped in oak-smoked bacon with a Stilton and mustard sauce £6.25; bread-and-butter pudding £2.50.

Open *11 to 2.30, 6 to 11, Sun 12 to 2.30, 7 to 10.30; bar food 12 to 2, 7 to 10; restaurant Mon to Sat D only 7.30 to 9.30; closed 25 and 26 Dec*
Details *Children welcome in 1 room Car park Garden No-smoking area No music No dogs Access, Delta, Switch, Visa*

STOW-ON-THE-WOLD **Gloucestershire** **map 5**

Queens Head

Market Square, Stow-on-the-Wold TEL: (01451) 830563
at junction of A429, A436 and A424, 8m W of Chipping Norton

Opposite 'ye olde' stocks on a small green and diagonally across from the Town Hall, the Queens Head is a terraced pub surrounded by antique and gift shops. 'One certainly gets one's fill of Cotswold-style personalities here,' noted one reporter. Inside is a classic mix of very large black ceiling beams, flagstoned floors and exposed stone walls, lots of bare wood and a fire. The two small bars are intimate and dark, and at the back is an attractive walled courtyard filled with plants in pots. Food is particularly good value for such a well-known market town. There's a short list of daily blackboard specials but nothing is too fancy – tomato and basil soup, lamb and apricot pie, salmon steak and dill sauce and lamb kleftiko, for example. On the printed menu are ploughman's, jacket potatoes, smoked fish pasta, and pork and chive sausages served with crusty bread and mustard. The pub is tied to the local Donnington Brewery and, naturally enough, serves their brews. French and South African wines are served by the glass. Note that the pub doesn't have a car park, so you have to leave your vehicle at the roadside. SAMPLE DISHES: lamb broth £2; chicken and mushroom pie £5.25; fruit crumble £2.

Open *11 to 2.30, 6 to 11, Sun 12 to 3, 7 to 10.30; bar food Mon to Sat L 12 to 2, Tue to Sat D 6 to 9*
Details *Children welcome in bar eating area and games room Wheelchair access (also WC) Garden and patio Background music Dogs welcome Access, Delta, Diners, Switch, Visa*

STRINESDALE **Greater Manchester** **map 8**

Roebuck Inn

Brighton Road, Strinesdale TEL: (0161) 624 7819
from Oldham take A62 Huddersfield road, then left on to A672 Ripponden road, then right after 1m on to Turf Pit Lane; follow for 1m

A dramatic setting, high on the bleak hills above Oldham, is part of the allure of this friendly no-nonsense country pub. The menu roams far and wide, but its heart is in the North Country: black pudding comes with a hot roll, beef is braised in a pint of 'Boddies' ale, meat and potato pie is served with beetroot or red cabbage. Added to that are steak and cowheel pie topped with shortcrust pastry, stuffed marrow, mighty roasts and chops, and deep-fried cod with mushy peas. Typically for the area, curries come with rice or chips, and sandwiches are made of thick white bread or muffins. If you want to splash out, there are also seasonal specials such as breast of chicken stuffed with pistachio nuts and mango, or salmon fillet wrapped in bacon and served on a bed of spinach with prawn sauce. Desserts range from jam roly-poly, and strawberry and gooseberry pie, to ice-cream sundaes. Boddingtons and Oldham Bitter are on draught and the affordable wine list runs to more than 30 bins. SAMPLE DISHES: rollmop and sweet herrings £2.50; braised lamb with cream, wine and green peppercorns £6.50; pear and frangipane tart £2.25.

Open *12 to 3, 6 to 11, Sun 12 to 10.30; bar food and restaurant 12 to 2.30, 6 to 9.45, Sun 12 to 9.45*
Details *Children welcome Car park Wheelchair access (also WC) Garden Background music Dogs welcome in bar only Access, Amex, Delta, Switch, Visa*

SUMMERHOUSE Co Durham map 10

Raby Hunt Inn

Summerhouse TEL: (01325) 374604
on B6279, 6m NW of Darlington

Handily placed between Teesside and the Dales, this pleasant-looking stone pub is just the job if you are looking for brilliant-value lunch-time sustenance. The atmosphere in the snug and the lounge is comforting and chatty, the food is genuinely home-cooked. There's always a daily roast, plus a few salads and quiches, bulked out by ham and pheasant pie, chicken breast in leek and bacon sauce, and cold poached salmon with new potatoes. Desserts couldn't be simpler: apple pie, warm lemon meringue pie, peach Melba. Theakston Black Bull Bitter is on draught, and a handful of wines are also available by the glass. Summerhouse is only five miles from the Medieval splendour of Raby Castle, and the Darlington Railway Centre and Museum is also within reach. SAMPLE DISHES: pâté and toast £2.50; shepherd's pie £4; almond sponge £1.25.

Open *11.30 to 3, 6.30 to 11, Sun 12 to 3, 7 to 10.30; bar food Mon to Sat L only 12 to 2*
Details *Children welcome in bar eating area Car park Wheelchair access Garden and patio No music No dogs L No cards*

SUTTON Cheshire map 8

▲ *Sutton Hall*

Bullocks Lane, Sutton TEL: (01260) 253211
off A523, ½m S of Macclesfield

Early-sixteenth-century oak beams and pillars feature in the bar of this country hotel, although parts of the building are even older than that; flagstones, three open log fires and a suit of armour all add to its character. Marston's, Stones and a weekly-changing guest ale are on draught, and bar food may include feta, olive and tomato salad, spinach pancakes with ratatouille, steak and kidney pie topped with oysters, and a selection of desserts from a trolley; there is also a choice of daily-changing specials. The inn has its own-label French house wines by the glass, and the full list includes over 40 bins. The hall, whose walls are up to four feet thick in places, is surrounded by extensive gardens. SAMPLE DISHES: onion soup £1.75; pâté-stuffed chicken suprême in puff pastry £5.25; banana fritters with ice-cream and apricot glaze £2.

Open *11am to 11pm, Sun 12 to 4, 7 to 10.30; bar food and restaurant 12 to 2.30 (2 Sun), 7 to 9.45*
Details *Children welcome only on Sat, Sun and bank hols in dining-room Car park Wheelchair access Garden Background music Dogs welcome Access, Amex, Delta, Switch, Visa Accommodation: 10 rooms, B&B £69 to £85*

SUTTON BASSETT Northamptonshire map 5

Queens Head

Main Street, Sutton Bassett TEL: (01858) 463530
on B644, 3m NE of Market Harborough

The tally of real ales dispensed in this unpretentious village pub continues to soar: licensees Vince and Nicky Powell tell us that they have put on more than 850 of them since 1994. Adnams Bitter, Ruddles Best and County are fixtures, but the list is an ever-changing extravaganza for beer buffs. As well as pulling pints, the Powells are also dab hands in the kitchen, and their blackboard specials are particularly eye-catching. Partridge pudding and oven-baked duck breast with plum and brandy sauce are likely to please devotees of things gamey, while fish lovers might be tempted by grey mullet with Gruyère and mustard, or scallops with beurre blanc and chervil. Snacks include jacket potatoes (two of them, weighing up to sixteen ounces) and club sandwiches, and the menu also promises smoked fish pot, kromeskies, beef Stroganov and steaks. As a finale, look for the ambitious-sounding brandy basket filled with chocolate mousse served with crème caramel on a vanilla cream. On Friday and Saturday evenings, and Sunday lunch-time, the upstairs restaurant is open for more formal meals. Six interesting wines are offered by the glass – in addition to the house selections – and the short, affordable list is well worth exploring; English country wines are also available. SAMPLE DISHES: avocado and tuna mayonnaise £3.75; salmon and spinach in filo pastry £9.50; strawberry tartlet filled with mascarpone cheese £3.00.

Open *11.45 to 3, 6.30 to 11, Sun 12 to 3, 7 to 10.30; bar food all week L 11.45 (12 Sun) to 2, Tue to Sun D 7 to 9.30 (10 Fri and Sat); restaurant Sun L 12 to 3, Fri and Sat D 7 to 9.30*
Details *Children welcome in eating areas Car park Wheelchair access (also WC) Patio Background and live music Guide dogs only Access, Visa*

Assessments of wine in pubs is based largely on what is available in the bar. Many pubs also have full restaurant wine lists.

SUTTON GAULT Cambridgeshire map 6

▲ *Anchor Inn*

Sutton Gault TEL: (01353) 778537
off B1381 Sutton to Earith road, 6m W of Ely

Built around 1650 in the shelter of the banks of the New Bedford River (or the Hundred Foot Drain, as it is more evocatively known), the Anchor was for years a ferry inn providing lodgings for the men working on the new waterways. Visit the pub today and it's easy to conjure up a few spirits of the past as you sit at scrubbed pine tables in the glow of old-fashioned gas lights. The flagstone floors slope this way and that.

Licensees Robin and Heather Moore make a real effort to procure what is local and seasonal: hand-dressed Cromer crab and young lamb in spring; strawberries, asparagus, Brancaster oysters and mussels through the summer; and wild duck from the marshes in winter. Also on the menu you might notice a fondness for rare breeds: roast loin of Castlemilk Morrit lamb with port and cranberry sauce, loin of Gloucester Old Spot pork with cream and mustard sauce, Tamworth hams served with gooseberry chutney, for example. 'Rare' fish such as pike and, occasionally, zander (a relative of the perch) are also hauled from the river and used in invigorating ways. Good soups (cream of leek and tarragon, for example), pâtés and terrines are reckoned to be high points, as are daily blackboard specials such as sausages with braised red cabbage, and wild mushroom omelette with hot olive bread. Excellent British farmhouse cheeses will be brought out and allowed to come to room temperature if you order them at the beginning of your meal. Otherwise there are organic ice-creams from Rocombe Farm in Devon, as well as pecan and maple tart, and chocolate terrine with orange sauce. The 100-strong wine list from Lay & Wheeler always has at least six by the glass; the choice is global, and prices are very fair. Nethergate IPA, Adnams Bitter and Wadworth 6X are on handpump. From the terrace you can gaze across the Fenland waterscapes and do a spot of bird-watching, and the Ouse Washes, Welney Wildlife Centre and Wicken Fen Reserve (National Trust) are also worth exploring. SAMPLE DISHES: warm salad of king scallops, crisp bacon and cumin £5; wild rabbit, cider and mustard pie £10; mango mousse with shortbread £4.25.

Open *12 to 3, 7 (6.30 Sat) to 11, Sun 12 to 3, 7 to 10.30; bar food 12 to 2, 7 to 9 (6.30 to 9.30 Sat)*
Details *Children welcome in bar eating area Car park Wheelchair access (also WC) Patio No-smoking in some areas No music No dogs Access, Amex, Delta, Switch, Visa Accommodation: 2 rooms, B&B £45 to £78*

SUTTON-ON-THE-FOREST North Yorkshire map 9

Rose & Crown Inn

Main Street, Sutton-on-the-Forest TEL: (01347) 810351
on B1363, 8m N of York

'I could not recommend the Rose & Crown more highly for food, attentive service and atmosphere at an affordable price,' writes a reporter of this large, ivy-covered, portico-entranced inn. The interior is smart, stylish and comfortable, with a mixture of furniture, and prints on the walls. The blackboard menus are varied and the kitchen takes care with the cooking. Salmon fish-cakes are a popular starter; others might be warm smoked chicken salad, or goujons of haddock. Main courses run from a good choice of fish dishes, to items like black pudding on rösti, braised pigeon breasts with bacon, or celery hearts with ham. Vegetables received good notices from one reporter: 'definitely no soggy overcooked veg here!' Desserts are generally traditional: bread-and-butter pudding, or rum and raisin ice-cream, for instance. Lunch-times see the addition of lighter meals and sandwiches. Theakston Bitter is on draught, and there's a wide selection of wines by the glass. SAMPLE DISHES: tomato soup £2.25; king prawns wrapped in bacon £10.75; sticky date and walnut pudding £3.20.

Open *Tue to Sat 11 to 2.30, 6 to 11, Sun 11 to 3; bar food and restaurant Tue to Sun L 11 to 2.30, Tue to Sat D 6 to 9.30*
Details *Children welcome Car park Wheelchair access Garden No smoking in restaurant Background music No dogs Access, Delta, Diners, Switch, Visa*

SWAN BOTTOM Buckinghamshire map 3

Old Swan

Swan Bottom, The Lee TEL: (01494) 837239
off A413, between Great Missenden and Wendover, just N of The Lee

'A cracking country pub of the log-fire, low-beam and settle variety,' notes a regular. The building dates from the sixteenth century, but it's 'visibly clean', with new curtains and a fresh lick of paint adding to the appeal of the place. Two open fires often blaze in the bar. Chatty, long-serving chef/landlord Sean Michaelson-Yeates changes his blackboard menu each day and seafood shows up particularly well. Cod, chive and parsley fish-cakes taste really home-made and come with fresh tomato salsa, squid is fired up with chilli, and there are big bowls of mussels to be had. On the meat front, a portion of steak and kidney pie 'cut from a larger beast' is a sound version with 'first-rate shortcrust pastry cooked "on"', while boiled bacon with parsley sauce is 'a great slab of gammon'. Soups are wholesome, and puddings such as deep-filled apple tart or fruit crumble are in the homespun tradition. In all, it's pub grub done with a bit of flair. Real ales including Butcombe Bitter, Brakspear and Adnams Bitter are kept in good order and the chalked-up wine list is 'modest, cheap and tolerable'. The Lee is a great haunt for serious Chiltern walkers, especially on Sundays. SAMPLE DISHES: chicken liver and brandy pâté £3.75; pasta in tomato and herb sauce with Parmesan £4.75; chocolate fudge cake £2.75.

Open *Mon to Fri 12 to 3, 6.30 to 11, Sat 12 to 11, Sun 12 to 5; bar food all week 12 to 2 (2.30 Sun), Tue to Sat D 6.30 to 9*
Details *Children welcome Car park Wheelchair access (also WC) Garden Background music Dogs welcome on a lead Access, Delta, Visa*

TANGLEY Hampshire map 2

▲ *Fox Inn* 🍇

Tangley TEL: (01264) 730276
off A343, 5m NW of Andover

'This is a lovely, warm, welcoming, genuine rural pub, and I would go again,' concluded one reporter. Situated at a crossroads without a house in sight, this cosy and comfortable old inn is a popular place with all age groups, who have the choice of a couple of low-ceilinged bars and a dining-room to eat in. A huge lunch menu offers the likes of ploughman's, pastas, pies and casseroles like lamb, leek and rosemary. A salt beef sandwich got the thumbs-up from one reporter, as did the mushroom and sun-dried tomato lasagne with its 'lovely gooey cheesy top'. A good choice of puddings includes 'Bleeding Heart' (an 'alcoholic porridge' with brandy, cream, raspberry coulis, oats and almonds), 'Millionaire's Mousse' (a rich chocolate mousse log covered in amaretti biscuits), summer pudding and strawberry cheesecake, to name a few. Main courses on the more expensive dinner menu include fish dishes such as Brixham skate with black butter, and various steaks. Service, in the words of one correspondent, is both 'well informed' and 'charming'. Wines rate more emphasis than real ales here, with the list running to around 30 bins from around the world and eight house wines available by the glass; beers on draught include Courage Best, Bass and Hardy Royal Oak. SAMPLE DISHES: crab and prawn bake £5.25; steak, kidney and Guinness pie £5.50; banana toffee pancake £2.

Recommendations for good country pubs will be very welcome.

Open *11 to 3, 6 to 11, Sun 12 to 3, 7 to 10.30; bar food and restaurant 12 to 2, 6 to 10*
Details *Children welcome in eating areas Car park Wheelchair access Patio Background music Dogs welcome No cards Accommodation: 1 room, B&B £32 to £40*

TARRANT MONKTON Dorset map 2

▲ *Langton Arms*

Tarrant Monkton TEL: (01258) 830225
on Tarrant Valley thoroughfare, 1m off A354, 4m NE of Blandford Forum

Viewed from the front, the seventeenth-century thatched building looks like a sleepy little village pub. The front bars confirm this image, with its low beams, tiled floors, window seats and cushioned benches, and an inglenook in the main bar. But the pub has been much extended, and the old skittle alley is now a massive family room with its own bar, children's play area and a buffet-style children's menu: 'It's busy, busy, busy,' noted one visitor. Grown ups may find crab soup, battered prawns, steak pie, chicken breast in lemon and bacon sauce, and seasonal fruit crumbles. Goff's White Knight, Morland Old Speckled Hen and Shepherd Neame Spitfire Premium Ale are among the real ales on handpump, and some wines are sold by the glass. SAMPLE DISHES: carrot and orange soup £2.25; venison sausages with onion and redcurrant gravy £5.50; chocolate and Cointreau mousse £2.50.

Open *weekdays 11.30 to 2, 6 to 11, Sat and bank hols 11.30 to 11, Sun 12 to 10.30; bar food all week L 12 to 2 (3 Sat and Sun), Wed to Sat D 6 to 10; restaurant Tue to Sat D only 6 to 10*
Details *Children welcome in family room Car park Wheelchair access Garden No smoking in dining-room and family room Occasional background music; jukebox Dogs welcome in 1 bar Access, Visa Accommodation: 6 rooms, B&B £35 to £54*

TEMPLE GRAFTON Warwickshire map 5

▲ *Blue Boar*

Temple Grafton TEL: (01789) 750010
off A422, 5m W of Stratford-upon-Avon

To find this early seventeenth-century stone and brick pub you need to head eastwards out of the village; it stands at a crossroads, away from it all, in undeveloped Warwickshire countryside. Inside, the place conveys the impression of 'Olde Worlde' in a suitably understated way. The bar menu has a few familiar offerings such as ploughman's, gammon, and leg of chicken curry alongside things that strike a more enterprising note – devilled herring roes, Thai crab-cakes with lobster sauce, and marinated stir-fried lamb with noodles, followed by tiramisù and chocolate whisky pudding, for example. Separate lunch and dinner menus are also available in the restaurant. Landlord Seán Brew keeps a good stock of real ales, including Donningtons SBA, Hook Norton Bitter and Theakston Old Peculier. The wine list is also worth considering: a dozen house wines provide sound, affordable drinking and the full slate includes a very promising 'connoisseur's selection'. Devotees of comedies and tragedies might like to know that Shakespeare was married in Temple Grafton church in 1582. SAMPLE DISHES: chicken liver mousse with Cumberland sauce £3; seafood tagliatelle with fresh herbs £6.75; charlotte Malikoff £3.

Open *11.30 to 2.30, 6 to 12, Sun 12 to 3, 7 to 11; bar food and restaurant 12 to 2.15 (3 Sun), 6.30 to 10*
Details *Children welcome Car park Wheelchair access Patio No smoking in 1 room No music No dogs Access, Amex, Delta, Diners, Switch, Visa Accommodation: 4 rooms, B&B £30 to £60*

TESTCOMBE Hampshire map 2

Mayfly

Testcombe TEL: (01264) 860283
on A3057, between Stockbridge and Andover

This former farmhouse, built in the nineteenth century, has an idyllic setting on the banks of the River Test, one of the most famous trout-fishing rivers in the country. Picnic benches outside make the most of the views, while inside there may be a scramble for the window seats and tables in the airy conservatory. A relaxing atmosphere permeates throughout, and staff are always chatty and helpful, even when the place is packed to the gunnels on sunny summer weekends. Service is from a buffet where waitresses carve rare roast beef, ham, and smoked chicken. There are also quiches, a 'famous' selection of about 30 cheeses, pasta, and tandoori chicken; and the kitchen offers a hot dish of the day, plus help-yourself salads. Treacle tart, and sticky toffee pudding may be among the desserts. Whitbread Castle Eden Ale, Boddingtons and Flowers are on draught, and around 14 wines are sold by the glass. SAMPLE DISHES: smoked chicken (buffet) £4.25; roast leg of lamb £7.50; maple and walnut tart £2.50.

Open *all week 10am to 11pm; bar food all week 11.30 to 10*
Details *Children welcome Car park Wheelchair access (also WC) Garden and patio Background music Dogs welcome on a lead Access, Switch, Visa*

THELBRIDGE **Devon** **map 1**

▲ *Thelbridge Cross Inn*

Thelbridge TEL: (01884) 860316
off B3137; from Tiverton, before Witheridge, take left fork on to B3042 for 2m

'A welcoming sight on such a rainy, misty day,' commented a reporter of the large log fire blazing in the main bar of this isolated roadside inn which has views over both Exmoor and Dartmoor. Sofas and armchairs around the fire contribute to the comfort, and the bar and restaurant areas provide plenty of space for eating. A printed menu offers snacks of the standard sort but most visitors go for the daily-changing blackboard specials where the focus is no-nonsense cooking of fresh ingredients in ample portions. There's leek and potato soup, for example, steak and kidney pie, roast beef with Yorkshire pudding, or battered cod. 'Help, my figure!' writes a reporter who happily succumbed to the clotted cream that accompanied a well-made banoffi pie. Other desserts could include strawberry pavlova, or spice apple and sultana crumble. Bass, Butcombe Bitter and a guest ale are on draught, country wines are among those served by the glass, and more than 60 whiskies are stocked. SAMPLE DISHES: vegetable and chicken soup £2; roast pork with apple sauce £4.50; chocolate and orange torte £2.50.

Open *11am to 11pm, Sun 12 to 10.30; bar food 12 to 2, 7 to 9; closed 26 Dec*
Details *Children welcome in eating areas Car park Wheelchair access (also WC) Garden No smoking in 2 dining-rooms Background music Guide dogs only Access, Amex, Delta, Diners, Switch, Visa Accommodation: 8 rooms, B&B £35 to £70*

THORNTON **West Yorkshire** **map 8**

Ring O'Bells

Thornton TEL: (01274) 832296
just off B6145, 3m W of Bradford

The stone exterior of this nineteenth-century former chapel is unassuming, but within the modern and comfortably furnished interior there's a delightfully inviting atmosphere. The pub can become very busy, especially in the evening, when it is advisable for diners to book; the same menus operate in the bar and in the restaurant. Among the dishes produced by the 'enthusiastic kitchen', where the emphasis is on use of local ingredients, is the 'Ring O'Bells Reviver' – the pub's 'award-winning' steak and kidney pie – which, according to one who tried it, is truly a 'worthy winner'. The regularly changing blackboards offer an imaginative range: half a roast duckling with a rhubarb and ginger sauce, scallops sauté with shallots served on saffron rice, or mixed game and vegetable pie topped with puff pastry, for example. To finish you can have steamed roly-poly with vanilla custard, or perhaps warm pear and apple tart with vanilla ice-cream and butterscotch sauce. A range of decent ales includes Webster's Yorkshire Bitter, Black Sheep Bitter, and Theakston XB. The comprehensive wine list has over 100 bins and a good handful of half-bottles; wines available by the glass are listed on a blackboard. SAMPLE DISHES: pan-fried button mushrooms in garlic butter £2.75; chicken florentine £7; Belgian chocolate cups filled with orange and white chocolate mousse and served with a duo of fruit sauces £3.25.

Open *11.30 to 3.30 (3 Sat), 5.30 to 11, Sun 12 to 3, 6.30 to 10.30; bar food and restaurant 12 to 2, 5.30 (6.30 Sat and Sun) to 9.30; closed 25 Dec*
Details *Children welcome Car park Wheelchair access (also WC) Patio No smoking in restaurant Background music No dogs Access, Delta, Switch, Visa*

THORNTON WATLASS **North Yorkshire** **map 9**

▲ *Buck Inn*

Thornton Watlass TEL: (01677) 422461
off B6268, 3m SW of Bedale

Only minutes from the A1, Thornton Watlass is a picturesque village with houses built of local stone grouped around the green. The inn overlooks the green too, and cricket fans can watch matches in summer through its windows. The lounge, with upholstered wall settles, a shelf lined with old bottles, and numerous foxes' brushes and masks on the walls, is comfortably old-fashioned; adjacent to it is a homely dining area. The lunch-time menu consists of dishes such as chickpea and potato curry, steak and kidney pie, Masham rarebit (toast topped with Wensleydale, ale and bacon), and ploughman's and baguettes. The menu moves up a gear in the evening: cauliflower soup, game pâté, duck breast roasted in honey and soy, and pork chop casseroled with mushrooms, apple and sage. Plum crumble with custard, or crème caramel could be options at pudding stage. A guest ale, usually from a small local brewery, joins Theakston Best, Black Sheep Bitter, Tetley and John Smith's, dispensed by hand-pump, and the wine list runs to 20-plus bins. SAMPLE DISHES: mussels with cream and pesto sauce £4; crumbed breast of mustard chicken £7.75; orange cheesecake £2.50.

Licensing hours and bar food times are based on information supplied by each establishment and are correct at the time of going to press.

Open *Mon to Fri 11 to 3, 6 to 11, Sat 11am to midnight, Sun 12 to 3, 6.30 to 10.30 (all day Sun summer); bar food and restaurant 11.45 to 2, 6.30 to 9.30*
Details *Children welcome in eating areas and games room Car park Wheelchair access Garden No smoking in restaurant Background and live music No dogs Access, Amex, Delta, Diners, Switch, Visa Accommodation: 7 rooms, B&B £30 to £52*

THREE LEGGED CROSS East Sussex map 3

Bull

Dunster Mill Lane, Three Legged Cross TEL: (01580) 200586
take Three Legged Cross road signposted in centre of Ticehurst, off B2099

'On a drizzly Sunday morning in early November, with the pub lights winking through the tiny paned glass windows', this great old hostelry seemed like a Sussex nirvana for one traveller. The core of the building is a centuries-old Wealden Hall house, and inside it still seems 'impressively dark and heavy' with sturdy black beams, timbers and exposed stone walls. Natural colours abound, garlands of dried hops dangle all around, and every inch of floor space is 'stuffed with tables, benches, chairs – some pieces of real character'. The kitchen produces safe-and-sound food, ranging from cream of cauliflower soup, and baguettes filled with thick slices of bacon and hunks of sausage, to individual steak and kidney pies, whole plaice, and pepperpot pork. On Sunday there's also a choice of roasts. Among home-made desserts are 'hokey-pokey ice-cream' and bread-and-butter pudding. Rother Valley Level Best is worth noting among the line-up of real ales, which also includes Morland Old Speckled Hen and Harveys Best and Old. Outside is a children's play area and there's a fish pond in the garden. SAMPLE DISHES: baked Brie £2.75; garlic chicken in pastry £5.25; summer pudding £2.50.

Open *11 to 3, 6 to 11, Sun 12 to 3, 7 to 10.30; bar food and restaurant all week L 12 to 2.30, Tue to Sat D 7 to 9.30*
Details *Children welcome Car park Wheelchair access Garden No pipes in restaurant Live music Dogs welcome Access, Delta, Switch, Visa*

THRESHFIELD North Yorkshire map 8

Old Hall Inn

Threshfield TEL: (01756) 752441
on B6265, 1m W of Grassington

Once the manor in a tiny Dales village, Old Hall dates from the fifteenth century and consists of a series of rooms: two bars, a family room in the conservatory, and a separate dining-room which serves the same menu as the bar. The place is popular – visitors and locals are joined by walkers who may have just traversed Wharfedale, and at busy times you may have to wait for a table. While you are doing so, you could examine the chamber pots hanging from the ceiling, or count the numerous cups and brass plates alongside them. Food is advertised on a blackboard over the fireplace and varies daily. Starters could include barbecue spare ribs, a warm salad of chicken livers and smoked bacon with a raspberry and hazelnut vinaigrette, chilled melon with a raspberry sorbet, or deep-fried mushrooms. Mains are equally interesting: wild boar and pheasant pie, pan-fried chicken breast filled with mozzarella served with a tomato and basil sauce, and Goan hot-and-sour chicken rub shoulders with ploughman's, seafood bake, and liver and onions. Puddings have their own blackboard and can run to lemon sponge with lemon sabayon, pear Belle-Hélène, or Bakewell tart. Real ales on draught are Timothy Taylor, Theakston and guest beers such as Black Sheep and Tetley. House wines are on 'draught', too, but there is also a wine list. Holiday accommodation is available adjacent to the inn. SAMPLE DISHES: filo parcels with bacon, leeks and Camembert £4; pan-fried venison on a bed of garlic mash with caramelised onions £9.50; brandy-snap basket filled with peach cream £2.50.

Open *Tue to Sat 11.30 to 3, Mon to Sat 6 to 11, Sun 12 to 3, 7 to 10.30; bar food and restaurant Tue to Sun L 12 to 2, Tue to Sat D 6 to 9.30, and Sun D Easter to Oct*
Details *Children welcome in bar eating area and family room Car park Wheelchair access (also WC) Patio Background music Dogs welcome in some areas No cards*

TILLINGHAM Essex map 3

▲ *Cap & Feathers*

South Street, Tillingham TEL: (01621) 779212
off B1021, 5m NE of Burnham-on-Crouch

A local reporter sums up the appeal of this out-of-the-way inn within sight of the Essex salt marshes: 'a cheery enough local pub by a small, neat village green with weatherboarded cottages and a good sense of local pride.' New landlord and chef Tony Bardfield took over just before we went to press and he seems intent on keeping the place much as it was. Inside it is stoically rural – but friendly with it – and there are games of bar billiards and skittles. Top of the bill, as regards food, are the products from the smokehouse – anything from fillet of beef (slightly reminiscent of Parma ham, thought one recipient) to trout, haddock and whiting. Otherwise expect Tillingham pie made with game from the marshes, chilli, and lemon sole Breton (fried in butter with crabmeat), as well as ploughman's, pasta and a few home-made puddings. The pub is tied to the diminutive Crouch Vale Brewery based at South Woodham Ferrers and the full range of draught beers are on handpump (including seasonal brews like Willy Warmer); added to that are guests such as RCH Steam Beer and Hook Norton Old Hooky. Wines come by the glass. There might also be hot elderberry punch in winter. SAMPLE DISHES: celery and Stilton soup £2; 8 oz. grilled rib-eye steak £8; bread pudding £2.25.

Open *Easter to Sept 11am to 11pm, Sun 12 to 10.30, Oct to Easter 11 to 3, 6 to 11, Sun 12 to 3, 7 to 10.30; bar food Easter to Sept 12 to 10, Oct to Easter 12 to 2, 7 to 10; restaurant 12 to 2, 7 to 9.30*
Details *Children welcome in eating areas Car park Garden and patio No-smoking in family room No music Dogs welcome Access, Visa Accommodation: 4 rooms, B&B £20 to £35*

TILLINGTON West Sussex map 3

▲ *Horse Guards Inn* 🍇

Upperton Road, Tillington TEL: (01798) 342332
just off A272, 1m W of Petworth

Both printed and blackboard menus change twice daily at this white-painted, seventeenth-century village inn. Interesting light snacks such as courgette and Cheddar mousse are sold at lunch-time alongside moules marinière, smoked duck breast, grilled plaice, or roast loin of pork. Dinner tends to be more ambitious: grilled langoustines, roast partridge, whole lobster thermidor, or escalope of veal stuffed with Camembert and onions. Puddings are recited by the staff: perhaps white chocolate mousse, or raspberry and mascarpone tart. Meals are served throughout the pub, and there are plenty of tables in the softly lit beamed and panelled rooms. Wines are treated as seriously as the food, with plenty of choice by the glass, two pages of the list devoted to fine wines, and a blackboard of bin-ends. Hall & Woodhouse Badger Best, and King & Barnes Sussex Bitter are on handpump. SAMPLE DISHES: cauliflower and blue cheese soup £3.25; venison steak with port and cranberry sauce £11; apple and fig strudel £3.50.

Open *11 to 3, 6 to 11, Sun 12 to 3, 7 to 10.30; bar food and restaurant 12 to 2 (12.30 to 2.30 Sun), 7 to 10*
Details *Children welcome in bar eating area Car park Garden and patio Background music Dogs welcome in 1 area Access, Delta, Switch, Visa Accommodation: 3 rooms, B&B £55 to £60*

TIRRIL Cumbria **map 10**

▲ *Queens Head*

Tirril TEL: (01768) 863219
on B5320, 2m S of Penrith

Dating from 1719, the Queen's Head is a long, rambling, white-washed building which over the years has absorbed adjacent cottages. Within is what you'd expect for a village pub of this age: beams in the low ceilings, thick walls, plenty of old English oak, brasses, and four open fireplaces, one of which still has the hooks that were once used for smoking meat. Snacks and light meals are listed on a blackboard in the bar, where you can also order from the full restaurant menu. Starters might include king prawns sauté in garlic and white wine; among the main courses may be venison ragoût, crab strudel, and chicken breast stuffed with mangoes and lemon sauce. Ostrich (perhaps chargrilled and flambé in cherry brandy) and kangaroo also appear regularly on the menu. Desserts are from the school of crumbles, cheesecakes, and sticky toffee pudding. Theakston Best and Younger's Best are joined by two guest ales, over 20 malt whiskies are available, and about six wines plus some bin-ends are served by the glass. Before you leave, take a look at the debenture signed by Wordsworth, on display in the bar: it's proof that the poet owned this property in the 1830s. SAMPLE DISHES: garlic mushrooms in cream and Stilton £3; Barbary duck breast with damson and redcurrant sauce £9.25; steamed syrup pudding £2.50.

Open *12 to 3, 6 to 11, Sun 12 to 3, 7 to 10.30; bar food and restaurant 12 to 2.30, 6 to 9.30 (12 to 9.30 Fri and Sat summer)*
Details *Children welcome Car park Patio No-smoking area in dining-room Background music; jukebox Dogs welcome in bar only Access, Delta, Switch, Visa Accommodation: 7 rooms, B&B £27 to £42*

TORCROSS Devon **map 1**

Start Bay Inn

Torcross TEL: (01548) 580553
on A379 Dartmouth to Kingsbridge coast road

Right on the beach, this solid-looking thatched pub, with a large patio for outdoor eating and drinking, and a big family room, attracts crowds in summer – so much so that queues can start to form before the place is open. People are drawn not just by its location, but also by enormous portions of fish and chips. 'The cod was spanking fresh, the batter light,' comments a reporter, while other offerings – perhaps delivered to the back door by a local crabber or the skipper of a trawler – include plaice, haddock, monkfish and local scallops. Predictably, seafood and shellfish feature strongly in starters and salads, while meat dishes run along the lines of chicken-burger and gammon with pineapple. Sandwiches and ploughman's are also available. Salcombe dairy ice-creams figure among the puddings and gâteaux for dessert. Flowers Original and IPA and Bass are on draught; wines are sold by the glass. SAMPLE DISHES: prawn cocktail £3.25; battered skate wing £5.25; spotted dick £2.50.

Open *11.30 to 2.30, 6 to 11 (summer 11.30 to 11), Sun 12 to 2.30, 6 to 10.30 (summer 12 to 10.30); bar food 11.30 to 2.15, 6 to 10 (9.30 winter); bar snacks all day July 23 to Sept 6*
Details *Children welcome in dining-room Car park Patio Jukebox Dogs welcome on a lead No cards*

TREBURLEY Cornwall **map 1**

Springer Spaniel ✿

Treburley TEL: (01579) 370424
on A388 halfway between Launceston and Callington

The solid, squat exterior may be unprepossessing, but as soon as you walk inside you'll find a warm, pleasant hostelry that no doubt gets quite buzzy when the crowds descend. A log-burning stove holds centre stage in the main bar, with a huge settle and a couple of Windsor chairs nestling up to it. Prints of dogs and country scenes line the walls, and the floor is wood-block. Everything about this extremely well-run place suggests that it is serious about what goes on in the kitchen.

The bar menu offers 'the sort of comfort food which fits in with the relaxed, laid-back style of the pub', commented one reporter. By and large it consists of rolls, sandwiches and dishes such as cod with parsley sauce, pasta provençale, cassoulet and plates of cold roast beef or ham with chips. Added to this are soups, starters, salads and pies from the full *carte*. Seafood chowder continues to elicit rave reviews: a recently sampled version was 'the real thing – huge chunks of all sorts of fish in a rich creamy soup and served with a hunk of good bread and a slab of butter'. Otherwise you might go for pan-fried scallops with smoked bacon, a plate of smoked salmon, or Parma ham with melon. The pub's own garden provides much in the way of fruit and vegetables, and the hedgerows yield their own harvest. It shows in appropriate accompaniments: gooseberry and elderflower chutney for duck liver terrine, crabapple and sloe jelly with grilled lamb chops, and blackberry sauce for pan-fried duck breast, for instance. As a finale, look for unusual ice-creams such as lemon meringue with a sauce of fresh oranges, or coconut as a refreshing foil to caramelised exotic fruits. There is also plenty of substance in steamed vanilla sponge with marmalade sauce, and cherry and almond tart. St Austell HSD and Dartmoor Best Bitter fly the flag for West Country breweries, while the list of 18 wines takes a quick dip into the world's cellar. SAMPLE DISHES: fillet of smoked trout with apricot chutney £3.25; venison pie £7; chocolate mousse tartlet with light and dark chocolate sauce £4.

Open *11 to 3, 5.30 to 11, Sun 12 to 3, 6.30 to 10.30; bar food and restaurant 12 to 2, 6.30 (7 Sun) to 9*
Details *Children welcome in eating areas and games room Car park Patio No music No dogs in dining-room No cards*

TREGADILLET Cornwall **map 1**

▲ *Eliot Arms*

Tregadillet TEL: (01566) 772051
off A30, 2m W of Launceston

This seventeenth-century creeper-clad pub was 'modernised' in 1840, making the maze of little rooms 'a Steptoe's Yard of bric-à-brac'. Look around and you will see 'a blaze' of gleaming horse-brasses, clocks, advertising artefacts, candles stuffed into candlesticks of all kinds, as well as perhaps the largest collection of snuff boxes in the country. 'Who cleans it all?' mused one visitor, with an eye for good housekeeping. Then there are the antique settles, *chaises longues* and tables of all shapes and sizes. The printed bar menu is long and all-embracing, but the form here – according to reporters and locals in the know – is to go straight to the specials board: here you will find home-made dishes such as honeyed beef casserole, spicy chicken and apricot crunch, lasagne and so forth. The chargrill is switched on for steaks, kebabs and burgers, and the pub has its own smoker for ham and fish. Desserts are mostly in the 'gâteau and cheesecake' mould. Familiar names such as Morland Old Speckled Hen, Marston's Pedigree and Flowers Original are on handpump. Four wines are sold by the glass, and the list of 30 bins is global (a couple from England are worth noting). SAMPLE DISHES: chicken and leek soup £2; baked local trout with horseradish sauce £8; coffee and hazelnut pavlova £2.50.

Open *11 to 2.30 (3 Sat), 6 to 11, Sun 12 to 2.30, 7 to 10.30; bar food 12 to 2 (1.45 Sun), 7 to 9.30*
Details *Children welcome in dining-room and games room Car park Wheelchair access Garden Background music Dogs welcome in front bar area Accommodation: 2 rooms, B&B £22 to £40*

TROTTISCLIFFE Kent **map 3**

Plough

Taylors Lane, Trottiscliffe TEL: (01732) 822233
off M20 Jct. 2, between A20 and A227, 2m S of Culverstone Green

Families making a trip to Trosley Country Park ought to keep in mind this 500-year-old, white weatherboarded pub at the foot of the North Downs. Licensees Peter and Denise Humphrey happily welcome children and offer a menu that has plenty for young and old alike. As well as jumbo hot crusty rolls, and jacket potatoes with all kinds of fillings, there are various curries, home-made steak and kidney pie, grills and 'international dishes'. Fresh fish is always available. To round things off you will find nursery favourites such as spotted dick and bread-and-butter pudding. Well-known southern brews including Wadworth 6X, Fuller's London Pride and Young's Special often appear on the handpumps, and a dozen cheap and cheerful wines are also on display. SAMPLE DISHES: deep-fried potato skins with mozzarella cheese dip £3; prawns à la maison £5; jam sponge pudding £2.50.

Open *11.30 to 3, 6 to 11, Sun 12 to 4, 7 to 10.30; bar food all week L 12 to 2, Mon to Sat D 6.30 to 9.30*
Details *Children welcome Car park Wheelchair access Garden and patio Background and live music Dogs welcome Access, Delta, Switch, Visa*

TROUTBECK **Cumbria** **map 8**

▲ *Queens Head Hotel*

Troutbeck, nr Windermere TEL: (01539) 432174
at start of Kirkstone Pass, 2½m from junction of A591 and A592

The views over the Troutbeck Valley across the Garburn Pass to Applethwaite Moors must rank as some of finest in the Lake District, and this 400-year-old inn makes the most of them. The interior of the Queen's Head is strikingly atmospheric, with its oak beams, stone-flagged floors, and even an extraordinary bar counter fashioned from a genuine Elizabethan four-poster bed. The cooking, however, zooms straight into the modern world of warm salads, sun-dried tomatoes and confits. Florid descriptions abound: home-cured gravlax is 'lavished' with honey and mustard vinaigrette, cod steak pan-fried in curry spices is served with 'a collage' of wild mushrooms and wild rice. At lunch-time you can also get sandwiches and one-dish specials such as lemon chicken fillets on a bed of leaves with a hazelnut and citrus dressing. Although the emphasis is on fashionable elaboration, you can still find simpler things such as spaghetti bolognese, and steak, ale and mushroom cobbler. To finish, there might be raspberry and mascarpone mousse, or sticky toffee pudding; otherwise, a trio of cheeses is served with home-made sesame biscuits and bread. In the evenings you can book a table in the Mayor's Parlour restaurant and choose from the same menu. Three guest brews supplement a fine selection of real ales, including Mitchell's Lancaster Bomber, Tetley Bitter and Boddingtons. The wine list consists of two dozen well-chosen bins arranged by style. SAMPLE DISHES: Cajun spiced sausage and black pudding with tomato marmalade and home-made cheese and chive bread £4.50; paupiette of lemon sole baked with crab mousse served on saffron mash with watercress cream £8.25; crème brûlée with home-made shortbread £2.75.

Open *11am to 11pm, Sun 11 to 10.30; bar food 12 to 2, 6.30 to 9; restaurant all week D only 6.30 to 9; sandwiches 12 to 2.30*
Details *Children welcome Car park Wheelchair access Patio No-smoking area Background music Dogs welcome Access, Delta, Switch, Visa Accommodation: 8 rooms, B&B £40 to £60*

All details are as accurate as possible at the time of going to press, but pubs often change hands, and it is wise to check beforehand by telephone anything that is particularly important to you.

If you disagree with any assessment made in the Guide, *write to tell us why* – The Which? Guide to Country Pubs, *FREEPOST, 2 Marylebone Road, London NW1 1YN.*

TRUSHAM Devon map 1

▲ *Cridford Inn*

LOCAL PRODUCE

Trusham TEL: (01626) 853694
off B3193 Chudleigh to Exeter road, 3m NW of Chudleigh

'There is so much going for this pub,' noted one couple who stayed overnight. To begin, the building lays claim to be 'Devon's oldest domestic dwelling', dating from AD 825. It was 'improved' in 1081 – a feat commemorated by a mosaic date-stone in the dining-room. Antiquity also shows in the mighty, centuries-old beams etched with the marks of the masons who worked on the house; in the bar you can also view the 'earliest-surviving example' of a stained-glass domestic window in Britain.

Landlord David Hesmondhalgh makes admirable use of West Country produce for a 'bistro menu' that brings together fish from Brixham, Riverford Farm pork and herb sausages, free-range veal, ice-creams from Langage Farm and regional cheeses procured from the Ticklemore cheese shop in Totnes. Home-smoked salmon is served with dill and mustard sauce, while reports have also mentioned 'first-class, abundant smoked eel' as a starter. There are no great flashes of elaboration here, but the results are 'exemplary': correspondents have praised warm vichyssoise, and chicken liver pâté with Cumberland sauce, as well as grilled plaice with herb butter, and lamb chops that were both, quite simply, 'faultless'. A touch of eclecticism also surfaces here and there, as in Thai-style lamb kebabs, and spinach, courgette and tomato pancakes. Desserts have included apple strudel and a gem of a summer pudding 'full of firm fruit and with a crust that was well soaked in juice'. Dinners are served by candlelight in the restaurant. The short list of 30 wines, from top-notch Devon merchants Christopher Piper Wines of Ottery St Mary, has a really impressive selection of 20 by the glass, all kept in prime condition with the Verre de Vin system. Equally drinkable are the real ales: Bass, Adnams Broadside and Trusham Ale (brewed especially for the pub). SAMPLE DISHES: marinated herrings in juniper and spice *jus* £3.25; steak and kidney pie topped with a suet crust £6.25; brown sugar meringue with apricot coulis and ginger ice-cream £3.50.

Open *12 to 2.30, 6 to 11, Sun 12 to 2.30, 6 to 10.30; bar food and restaurant 12.15 to 1.45, 6.45 to 8.45*
Details *Children welcome in eating area Car park Patio No-smoking area Background music Dogs on leads welcome in bar Access, Visa Accommodation: 4 rooms, B&B £40 to £60*

indicates a pub serving exceptional draught beers.

TURVEY **Bedfordshire** **map 5**

▲ *Three Cranes*

High Street, Turvey TEL: (01234) 881305
on A428, 7m W of Bedford

Acquired and re-furbished by the Old English Pub Company in late 1996, this 300-year-old village inn (complete with a Victorian front portico and jettied gable) emanates a friendly, welcoming atmosphere – although the interior shows 'designer' influences, with its neat shelves of books, decent prints and methodically arranged furniture. Six real ales are normally on display, including Smiles Golden Brew, Theakston XB, Fuller's London Pride and others which are rotated weekly. Complementing these is a varied menu highlighted by specials such as curried parsnip soup, smoked seafood platter, Italian lamb casserole served on a pile of tricolour fusilli, plus fruit pies and crumbles to round things off. Theme nights and special events are staged regularly. Turvey is a picturesque village within striking distance of Chicheley Hall and the Great Ouse valley. SAMPLE DISHES: deep-fried Camembert with cranberry sauce £3; steak, mushroom and ale pie £6; treacle tart £2.50.

Open *11 to 2.30, 6 to 11, Sun 12 to 3, 7 to 10.30; bar food and restaurant 12 to 2, 6.30 (7.15 Sun) to 9.30 (10 Fri and Sat)*
Details *Children welcome in restaurant and 1 bar Car park Wheelchair access Garden Background music No dogs Access, Amex, Switch, Visa Accommodation: 4 rooms, B&B £30 to £45*

TURVILLE **Buckinghamshire** **map 3**

Bull and Butcher

Turville TEL: (01491) 638283
between B480 and B482, 5m N of Henley-on-Thames

Turville is a long, narrow Chilterns hamlet, with a pretty little village green, a church – and often crowds, as it's popular with walkers, horse-riders and day-trippers. The pub's two small, beamed bars, with a little dining area beyond, can get busy too, and you may have to share a table if you don't arrive early or make a reservation. Customers are here for the food as well as for the range of Brakspear ales dispensed at the bar. Balti curries with nan bread are a trade mark of the menu, as are steaks and grills and a good showing of vegetarian dishes. Starters may range from garlic mushrooms to smoked duck breast; main courses from Cumberland sausage to venison pie, or calf's liver and bacon. Fish is well represented – pan-fried halibut steak with lemon and capers, say – and among the specials may be lemon chicken, and rack of lamb with mint and rosemary. Cheesecakes and ice-creams figure prominently among desserts. About ten good wines are sold by the glass, and the full list is extensive. SAMPLE DISHES: home-smoked pastrami £4.50; steak and kidney pie £6.75; treacle tart £3.

Open *11 to 3, 6 to 11, Sun 12 to 3, 7 to 10.30; bar food 12 to 2 (2.30 Sat, 3 Sun), 7 to 9.45*
Details *Children welcome Car park Wheelchair access Garden Background music Dogs welcome on a lead Access, Delta, Switch, Visa*

TUTBURY Staffordshire **map 5**

▲ *Olde Dog & Partridge*

High Street, Tutbury TEL: (01283) 813030
off A50 and A38, 4m NW of Burton upon Trent

A civilised inn 'in fine fettle', is how one visitor described this half-timbered, fifteenth-century hostelry. The fact that it is privately owned may account for the 'lovingly renovated' interior, which comprises two comfortable 'pubby' bars decorated with sporting pictures, plus extensions towards the back housing the immensely popular dining-areas and carvery. The operation ticks over like clockwork thanks to good organisation and smart, courteous staff, and the food is reckoned to be 'exceptional' for this kind of set-up. Beautifully presented pâtés, salads, Scottish smoked salmon from Blar Mhor Estate, and dishes such as woodland mushrooms on a bed of polenta start the ball rolling. Main courses centre on freshly carved roasts: local turkey, 'perfectly cooked' rib of beef and so on with all the necessary trimmings. Alternatives appear in the shape of a steak and kidney pie, lamb shank, and salmon and prawn tagliatelle with chive sauce. Completing the picture are fruit pies, cheesecake and assorted cheeses. Locally brewed Marston's Pedigree is on handpump, alongside a guest brew such as Marlow Rebellion. Six wines are sold by the glass and it's worth looking for the 'wine of the month'. While in Tutbury, take a trip to its historic castle; otherwise venture out to Sudbury Hall (National Trust) or the Bass Brewery Museum in Burton-on-Trent. SAMPLE DISHES: warm 'country' salad of black pudding with sauté potatoes £3.25; poached salmon with Pernod sauce £7.50; hot treacle sponge with custard £3.

Open *11 to 3, 6 to 11, Sun 12 to 10.30; bar food all week L only 12 to 2; restaurant Mon to sat 12 to 2, 6 to 9.45 (10 Sat), Sun 12 to 9.30*
Details *Children welcome Car park Wheelchair access (also WC) Garden and patio No-smoking area in restaurant; no smoking in restaurant Sat and Sun Background and live music Access, Amex, Delta, Switch, Visa Accommodation: 17 rooms, B&B £36 to £78*

ULVERSTON Cumbria map 8

▲ *Bay Horse Inn*

Canal Foot TEL: (01229) 583972
off A590, 8m NE of Barrow-in-Furness, take Canal Foot turn in Ulverston, then next signed left turn following lane to pub

The approach past the Glaxo factory may be uninspiring, but the views are not. 'Canal Foot' is the spot where the canal empties into Morecambe Bay, and you can gaze out towards Cartmel, the sea and the sands of Morecambe. Some people fish, others train their binoculars on the bird life. On a beautiful summer's day, with full sun, blue skies and the tide coming in, it's blissful.

The pub divides into two: the civilised bar is all beams and brasses, and there's a full-length conservatory dining-room where the serious gastronomic action takes place. The whole set-up has an air of unfailing professionalism. Bar meals are limited to lunch-times and the style owes much to chef/proprietor Robert Lyons's mentor, John Tovey of Miller Howe. Tureens of soups, various pâtés and terrines, cornucopias of salads and vegetables, and a fondness for local supplies are what you notice most of all. Kick off with Galia melon with royal air-dried ham and Cumberland sauce, or chicken liver pâté served with cranberry and ginger purée, then proceed to something more substantial such as Waberthwaite smoked Cumberland sausage with onion marmalade and sage and onion sauce, cottage pie, or prawn, leek and water-chestnut pancake. You can also get sandwiches. Home-made desserts are in the Tovey tradition of fresh comice pear filled with butterscotch sauce, served with hot chocolate sauce, and strawberry chocolate shortbread tartlet, while plates of cheese come with home-made biscuits and soda bread. There are a few Old World wines on offer, but the really exciting drinking is on the list of 50 cracking bottles from the southern hemisphere. Real ale also receives a thorough airing, with a line-up that could include fine North Country names such as Mitchell's and Moorhouse's, as well as Everards, Hook Norton and Shepherd Neame. SAMPLE DISHES: smoked haddock and sweetcorn chowder £4.50; braised lamb, apricot and ginger with an almond and suet crust topping £7.75; brown sugar meringue with mango and paw-paw £3.25.

Open *11am to 11pm, Sun 12 to 10.30; bar food Tue to Sun L only 12 to 2; restaurant Tue to Sat L 12 to 1.30, all week D 7.30 for 8 (1 sitting)*
Details *Children welcome in bar eating area Car park Wheelchair access (also WC) No smoking in dining-room Background music Dogs in 1 bar only Access, Visa Accommodation: 7 rooms, B&B £55 to £80*

The Guide *is totally independent, accepts no free hospitality and carries no advertising.*

UPTON Nottinghamshire map 5

Cross Keys

Main Street, Upton TEL: (01636) 813269
on A612, 2m E of Southwell

Real ale is taken very seriously in this converted eighteenth-century farmhouse towards the outskirts of the village. Landlord Mr Kirrage stages regular beer festivals, where the accent is firmly on the output of enterprising micro-breweries: expect such esoteric names as High Force Forest XB from Durham, Little Avenham Clog Dancer from Preston, and Iceni Deire of the Sorrows, produced in Thetford. Regular tipples in the beamed bar of the Cross Keys include Springhead Bitter and Bateman's XXXB not to mention draught Hoegaarden, a Belgian wheat beer flavoured with coriander and curaçao. Food also gets a good airing, with a printed bar menu offering smoked salmon cigars filled with asparagus and cream cheese; cassoulet; halibut cooked with orange and tarragon; and braised liver and bacon. Fish specials, casseroles and the like add variety on the blackboard, and there's a good line-up of home-made sweets such as summer pudding. The upstairs restaurant is open for Sunday lunch and evening meals on Friday and Saturday. Mr Kirrage tells us that business is booming as regards wine sales: several house wines come by the glass and the list is well considered. SAMPLE DISHES: blue cheese parcels in filo pastry £3.75; steak and mushroom pie £5.25; chocolate torte £2.75.

Open *11 to 3, 5.30 to 11 (summer Sat 11am to 11pm), Sun 12 to 3, 7 to 10.30 (summer 12 to 10.30); bar food 11.30 to 2, 6 to 9.30 (all day Sat and Sun in summer); restaurant Sun L 12 to 2, Fri and Sat D 7.15 to 9.30*
Details *Children welcome in 1 area of bar Car park Wheelchair access (also WC) Garden No smoking in restaurant Background and live music Dogs welcome (guide dogs only in restaurant) No cards*

UPTON BISHOP Hereford & Worcester map 5

Moody Cow

Crow Hill, Upton Bishop TEL: (01989) 780470
just off B4215, 4m NE of Ross-on-Wye

The Moody Cow is a smart beast, tended by a 'dapper, highly professional landlord', and befriended by an equally smart clientele. It doubles as pub and 'bistro' (in fact, there are two dining-rooms – one cosy and countrified, the other in bare-wooded provençale style). One menu covers the whole set-up. The kitchen is keen on artistic presentation, although portions across the board are in the trencherman mould. Reporters have enjoyed appetising melon balls and prawns with yoghurt and dill dressing, warm shellfish salad 'with Thai overtones', home-made fish-cakes with rich parsley sauce, and breast of 'sweet roasted' duck with ginger and orange sauce. Fish and chips is served the old-fashioned way in newspaper. Desserts have included a version of bread-and-butter pudding that one couple thought was the best they had eaten outside their own home; banoffi pie has also hit the button. Sunday lunch brings a much appreciated roast. A decent line-up of draught beers includes Bass, Wye Valley Bitter, Flowers West Country Pale Ale and others; 40 wines span the globe. SAMPLE DISHES: feta filo parcels with lemon mayonnaise £4; sauté lambs' liver with onion and red wine gravy £7.25; steamed syrup sponge £3.

Open *12 to 2.30, 6.30 to 11, Sun 12 to 2.30, 7 to 10.30; bar food and restaurant Tue to Sun L 12 to 2, Tue to Sat D 6.30 to 9.30 (10 Fri and Sat)*
Details *Children welcome Car park Wheelchair access Garden No smoking in dining-room Background and live music No dogs Access, Amex, Delta, Diners, Switch, Visa*

WADDESDON Buckinghamshire **map 3**

▲ *Five Arrows Hotel*

Waddesdon TEL: (01296) 651727
on A41 between Bicester and Aylesbury

In 1894 the periodical *The Woman at Home* described the Five Arrows as 'a hostelry apart' and singled out 'its quaint gables and wall decorations; its masses of twining plants; its quiet and freshness, and its cool garden with enormous birds clipped in living green'. This is not a run-of-the-mill watering-hole. Even today the grandiose Gothic exterior, with its chimneys, turrets and balconies, looks more like a country mansion than a hotel. In fact, it was built in 1887 as a residence for the artisans working on nearby Waddesdon Manor – part of the Rothschild dynasty. Step through the rather imposing entrance, however, and you are immediately back on terra firma. The first thing you notice is the handpumps dispensing Fuller's London Pride and ESB as well as local offerings such as Beechwood Bitter from the Chiltern Brewery. Your eye might also be caught by the intriguing collection of historical photographs that are dotted around the walls.

The menu is chalked on boards framing the entrance to the dining-room, although you can eat anywhere throughout the pub. Wherever you sit, the table-mats are – appropriately – labelled slabs from wooden wine boxes. The kitchen is prepared to try out plenty of ideas with both peasant and cosmopolitan overtones: a really gutsy minestrone with pancetta could start things off alongside marinated smoked venison with quince confit; equally classy main courses take in succulent roast partridge from Waddesdon Estate, seared marlin steak with spiced tomato salsa or something as simple as fillet steak with shallot butter, or chargrilled chicken breast with tsatsiki. Home-made ice-creams appear as an accompaniment to desserts such as treacle tart and poached pears; otherwise opt for mocha pots or brioche bread-and-butter pudding. A 'sandwich and burger' menu is also available Monday to Saturday lunch-times: the former might feature chicken-liver pâté with wild plum jelly. As you might expect, the wine list digs deep into the output of Rothschild vineyards, not only in France but Portugal and Chile as well; there's also plenty of decent drinking from other sources. Visitors to the manor are welcome to tour the cellars or purchase something from the wine shop. SAMPLE DISHES: tomato and basil soup £4; pan-fried escalope of veal with orange and rosemary £10; crême brûlée £4.

Open *Mon to Sat 11 to 3, 6 to 11, Sun 12 to 3, 7 to 10.30; bar food and restaurant 12 to 2.30, 7 to 9.30, Sunday 12.30 to 2, 7.30 to 9*
Details *Children welcome in eating areas Car park Wheelchair access (also WC) Garden and patio No smoking in restaurant Background music No dogs Access, Switch, Visa Accommodation: 6 rooms, B&B £55 to £70*

WADENHOE Northamptonshire map 6

▲ *King's Head*

Church Street, Wadenhoe TEL: (01832) 720024
off A605, 4m SW of Oundle

Built in 1662, the mellow stone and partly thatched inn nestles down a pretty dead-end lane. Inside are two warmly decorated bars, one with a coal fire and a rustic boarded floor, the other with a quarry-tiled floor and a wood-burner in a large inglenook. Traditional skittles is played in the bottom room, and there's a comfortable dining-room. At lunch-times a blackboard lists such dishes as sandwiches and ploughman's, Welsh rarebit, and perhaps cassoulet or Irish stew. The kitchen changes gear in the evenings, producing perhaps tomato and basil soup, chicken-liver parfait with a confit of shallots, and leek tart with spicy tomato sauce to start, and main courses of ragoût of salmon and mange-tout in dill sauce, Dover sole with olive butter, and honey-roast leg of pheasant with creamed leeks and rösti. Bread-and-butter pudding is a firm favourite. Marston's Pedigree and three ales from Adnams are on draught, and the wine list is global, with house wines by the glass and around ten by the half-bottle. The paddock with benches beside the River Nene is a peaceful and scenic spot to relax in; otherwise take a walk along the nearby Nene Way. SAMPLE DISHES: vegetable soup £1.75; roast breast of pheasant with rich pheasant sauce £8.75; lemon tart £2.75.

Open *Tue to Sun 12 to 3, all week 7 (6 Fri and Sat and all week in summer) to 11; bar food and restaurant Tue to Sun and bank hols L 12 to 2, all week D 7 to 9*
Details *Children welcome in some areas of bar Car park Limited wheelchair access (also WC) Patio No smoking in restaurant Occasional live music Dogs welcome Access, Visa Accommodation: 2 rooms, £25 to £60*

WALBERSWICK Suffolk **map 6**

▲ *Bell Hotel*

Ferry Road, Walberswick TEL: (01502) 723109
on B1387, off A12, S of Southwold

Dubbed by wags as 'Hampstead by the Sea' because of its artistic and intellectual connections, Walberswick stands across the water from its auspicious Regency neighbour, Southwold. Two-way traffic is part and parcel of the scene. The fourteenth-century Bell occupies a prime site near the village green and a few doors from Valley Farm (the adopted home of water-colourist Phillip Wilson Steer); a quick stroll will take you to the beach or the jetty by the River Blyth – scene of the National Crabbing Contest held each August. Sue Ireland-Cutting took over as landlady in 1996 and has raised the food profile of the pub noticeably. Locally caught fish shows up in the shape of pan-fried herrings with granary bread, and smoked sprats, as well as cod or plaice and chips. The kitchen also casts its net wider for toasted bagels with smoked salmon and cream cheese, chicken-liver and pistachio-nut pâté, and green chicken curry, while desserts might include banana fritters with butterscotch sauce. A separate restaurant is open for weekday lunches and evening meals on Friday and Saturday. This is an Adnams tied house, with the full range of draught beers kept in excellent order for sampling in the old-fashioned bar or the vast sun-trap of a garden; Adnams also supplies the short but serviceable list of around 20 wines. SAMPLE DISHES: carrot and coriander soup £2.25; chilli with rice £5; sticky toffee pudding £2.50.

Open *summer 11am to 11pm, winter 11 to 3, 6 to 11, all year Sun 12 to 3, 7 to 10.30; bar food all week L only 12 to 2; restaurant D only 7.30 to 9; closed Sun D Nov to Mar*
Details *Children welcome in eating areas Car park Wheelchair access Garden No smoking in restaurant No music Dogs welcome on a lead Access, Delta, Switch, Visa Accommodation: 7 rooms, B&B £25 to £30*

WALCOTE **Leicestershire** **map 5**

Black Horse

Lutterworth Road, Walcote TEL: (01455) 552684
on A427, 1m E of M1 Jct. 20

From the outside you might think this was just another black-and-white English roadside pub. Once you are in the bar, you will find that a fire often burns in the grate, the mood is thoroughly local, and the line-up of real ales is an aficiondo's choice – there's HOB Bitter from the Hoskins & Oldfield Brewery in Leicester, as well as Timothy Taylor Landlord, Hook Norton Old Hookey and Timothy Taylor Landlord, among others. The menu, however, tells a very different story. The lady of the house, Saovanee Tinker, hails from Thailand and she cooks a short selection of straightforward dishes from her native land; the repertoire doesn't venture far beyond a handful of curries, stir-fries, mixed fried rice tinged with 'nam pla' fish sauce and khao mu deang (marinated leg of pork served in its own juices with a side dish of chilli and ginger sauce), although blackboard specials broaden the range. You can also book for five-course banquets in the restaurant and eat from a menu planned by the chef. SAMPLE DISHES: stir-fried mixed vegetables £4.85; kaeng pla (Thai fish curry) £6; banana and coconut cream £2.

Open *Wed to Sun 12 to 2 (3 Sun), all week 6.30 to 11; bar food Wed to Sun L 12 to 2, all week D 7 to 9.30*
Details *Children welcome in eating areas Car park Wheelchair access (also WC) No smoking in one room No music Guide dogs only No cards*

WAMBROOK **Somerset** **map 2**

▲ Cotley Inn

Wambrook TEL: (01460) 62348
off A30, just W of Chard

David and Sue Livingstone have been in residence at this welcoming, out-of-the-way pub since 1988 and have turned it into a local haven for decent food and drink. Their menu offers plenty of choice for appetites large and small, which means that you can plump for, say, mushroom fritters or a plate of devilled kidneys on toast as a snack or take the plunge and boost your protein intake with a mighty mixed grill. You might also find anything from baked plaice with dill and tarragon, or sweet and sour chicken, to vegetable and Stilton crumble. Puddings are home-made daily and there may be as many as 14 on offer, perhaps including Black Forest roulade or luxury bread-and-butter pudding, in 'large or extra large' portions.

Sandwiches, ploughman's and jacket potatoes complete the picture. Flowers Original, Boddingtons and Oakhill Best Bitter are on draught, and there are 18 good-value wines to choose from. SAMPLE DISHES: creamed mushrooms with tarragon £4; sauté chicken in ginger and pumpkin sauce £7; hazelnut and raspberry meringue £2 (small), £2.75 (large).

Open *11 to 3, 7 to 11, Sun 12 to 3, 7 to 11; bar food and restaurant 12 to 2, 7 to 10*
Details *Children welcome Car park Garden No smoking in restaurant Background music Dogs welcome in bar only Access, Visa*
Accommodation: 3 rooms, B&B £20 to £30

WARDLOW MIRES Derbyshire map 8

Three Stags Heads

Wardlow Mires TEL: (01298) 872268
at junction of B6465 and A623, 2m E of Tideswell

A relaxed atmosphere, thanks to friendly owners, pervades this modest, unsophisticated pub at the heart of the splendid walking country of the Peak District. The two-room interior has a rustic, homely charm; in one of the rooms a range provides warmth in winter. Game – perhaps in the form of rabbit and pigeon pie – features on the blackboard menu in season; otherwise you may find a sustaining home-made soup, steak and kidney pie, lamb and spinach curry, and a vegetarian dish such as pasta with aubergine and tomato sauce. Matins and Absolution from the new Abbeydale brewery in Sheffield, along with Springhead Best Bitter, are dispensed from the barrel, and house wines come by the glass. You're as likely to encounter pot-holers as walkers in the area, as the peaks to the north are riddled with caves. Both Buxton and Bakewell are worth visiting, and Chatsworth and Haddon Hall are in the vicinity. SAMPLE DISHES: leek and Stilton hotpot £5.50; gardener's chicken £7.50; plum crumble £1.75.

Open *Tue to Fri 7 to 11, Sat and Sun 12 to 11; bar food Tue to Fri 7.30 to 9.30, Sat and Sun 12.30 to 9.30*
Details *Children welcome Car park Patio No smoking in dining-room Live music Dogs welcome No cards*

---

indicates a pub serving exceptional draught beers.

SAMPLE DISHES: *listed in the main text of an entry indicate three typical dishes from the menu to give some idea of the style of cooking and prices.*

WARHAM ALL SAINTS Norfolk **map 6**

▲ *Three Horseshoes*

Bridge Street, Warham All Saints TEL: (01328) 710547
off A149 or B1105, 2m SE of Wells-next-the-Sea

'One of my favourite Norfolk pubs,' writes a reporter. 'Traditional, unspoilt, good country cooking, real ale drawn from cask, friendly welcome and atmosphere.' The eighteenth-century flint and brick building has changed little over the years, and features a very old-fashioned series of rooms with stone floors, scrubbed tables, open fires, leatherette benches and a pianola – even the lighting is still by gas. The food is in keeping with the style, its starting-point fresh local produce and, in season, game from nearby estates. Norfolk crab soup, salmon pâté, rabbit pie (with a spoon 'to ladle the delicious contents – chunks of rabbit and vegetables in tasty, herby gravy – on to the plate'), and gamekeeper's pie might be on offer, along with skate in seafood sauce, and Warham fish pie. Other main courses on the menu are liver and onions, and roast duck, with sticky toffee and syrup sponge puddings among the desserts. Wherry Best Bitter, Nelson's Revenge and Great Eastern Ale from Woodforde's are pulled by handpump. Home-made lemonade is a non-alcoholic alternative. The north Norfolk coastal path runs along Warham Marsh, an area of outstanding natural beauty. SAMPLE DISHES: crab and samphire mousse £3.25; pork and apple suet pudding £6; maids-of-honour tart £2.25.

Open *11.30 to 2.30, 6 to 11, Sun 12 to 3, 6 to 10.30; bar food and restaurant 12 to 2, 7 to 9*
Details *Children welcome in eating areas Car park Wheelchair access (also WC) Garden No smoking in restaurant No music Dogs welcome No cards Accommodation: 4 rooms, B&B £18 to £48*

WARSLOW Staffordshire **map 5**

▲ *Greyhound Inn*

Warslow TEL: (01298) 84249
off B5053, 7m E of Leek

On the main road through this pretty moorland village, the Greyhound is a much-liked pub. The kitchen doesn't go in for grand gestures, but ingredients are handled well and the deep-frying – so often difficult to get right – is particularly good. Jackets, ploughman's, burgers and sandwiches make up the printed menu. For something more substantial, the blackboard lists good-value dishes such as steak, mushroom and ale pie, smoked haddock and prawn

Mornay, or pork and peaches in a peppercorn sauce. There's a log fire for cold days and a beer garden if it's warm. Note that the pub puts on its glad rags for boisterous live entertainment on Saturday nights. Beers, including Marston's Pedigree and Worthington Best Bitter, are well kept, 'decent' house wine is served by the glass, and a selection of eight other wines is available. Nearby is the Manifold Valley and the Peak District, popular destinations for hikers, who make up some of the pub's customers. SAMPLE DISHES: Hartington Stilton ploughman's with salad £4.50; minted lamb casserole £5.50; raspberry and apple crumble £2.25.

Open *Tue to Sun 12 to 2.30 (Wed to Sun 12 to 2 Oct to Apr), all week 7 to 11 (10.30 Sun); bar food Wed to Sun L 12 to 2, Tue to Sun D 7 to 9*
Details *Children welcome Car park Wheelchair access (also WC) Garden Background and live music Dogs welcome Access, Delta, Visa*
Accommodation: 4 rooms, B&B £17 to £33

WASS North Yorkshire **map 9**

▲ *Wombwell Arms*

Wass TEL: (01347) 868280
off A19 to Coxwold, then follow signs for 2m to Ampleforth and Wass

Once part of a granary tucked away in a hamlet at the base of the Hambleton Hills, this whitewashed eighteenth-century inn has undergone a remarkable transformation of late. Gone is the hard-drinker's boozer: instead the place now has a reputation as one of the élite dining pubs in this affluent part of North Yorkshire. Full marks to welcoming hosts Alan and Lynda Evans, who moved in during 1990 and have never looked back.

The interior of the pub now consists of four interconnecting rooms dotted with pine furniture; one area has flagstones, another an old black range. Books, magazines and papers are left out to be perused. A few snacks such as ploughman's, open sandwiches and soups (courgette and mint, for example) are always available, but the real strength is the list chalked up on the two blackboards – one for lunch, another for dinner. Lynda Evans cooks with a sure hand and she takes her cue from what is in season and what the region can produce. Venison might be casseroled or served in its smoked form with a little pot of onion marmalade. Some dishes have brasserie overtones (as in goats' cheese and walnut salad, or tuna steak with lime and fennel butter); elsewhere it is back to the roots, with Whitby haddock fillet, freshly made salmon fish-cakes with a herby tomato sauce, and 'drunken rabbit' (cooked with red wine, mush-rooms, bacon and shallots). Excellent vegetables come in a separate dish. Desserts are mostly traditional stalwarts such as treacle tart, lemon posset and caramelised rice pudding. Alan Evans is a wine enthusiast and his list generally includes at least seven by the glass, plus a good showing of half-bottles. Guest ales from local breweries regularly feature – Dalesman's Delight is one example – alongside well-kept Yorkshire classics like Black Sheep Bitter and Timothy Taylor Landlord. Byland Abbey is worth a visit while you are in the area. SAMPLE DISHES: pan-fried chicken livers £3.25; cod with a garlic crust £7.25; blackcurrant and cassis fool £3.

Open *Tue to Sat 12 to 2.30, 7 to 11, Sun 12 to 2, 7 to 10.30; bar food 12 to 2, 7 to 9 (9.30 weekends); closed Sun eve in winter*
Details *Children welcome in dining-room Car park Wheelchair access Occasional live music Sun eve No dogs Access, Delta, Switch, Visa Accommodation: 2 rooms, B&B £24.50 to £49*

WATH-IN-NIDDERDALE North Yorkshire map 8

▲ *Sportsman's Arms*

Wath-in-Nidderdale TEL: (01423) 711306
off B6265, 2m NW of Pateley Bridge

The ornithological attractions of Gouthwaite Reservoir are not far from this old stone inn close to the meandering River Nidd. Long-serving proprietors Ray and Jane Carter have been in residence since 1978 and still have the knack of making visitors feel right at home in calming, pleasurable surroundings.

Fish is the star turn on the bar menu and freshness is the keynote. Whitby haddock is steamed and set on a bed of spinach with tomato and basil sauce, while Scottish salmon is roasted with a sesame crust and served with hollandaise sauce. The blackboards also advertise glazed king scallops, lobster thermidor, and lemon sole grenobloise. Local Nidderdale trout appears in its fresh form with bacon and capers, or smoked with horseradish as its accompaniment. Apart from fish you might also encounter interesting-sounding soups (cream of parsnip and apricot, for example), while meat and game feature in the shape of roast best end of lamb with tomato concassé and spring onions, or breast of duckling in blackcurrant and orange sauce. Speciality sandwiches and rolls are also available and ploughman's comes with fine farmhouse cheeses. Summer pudding is the signature dessert (one reporter nominated this against all comers as 'the best in the UK – possibly the world!'), but the choice also extends to tarte au citron, and ginger sponge with custard. Full meals are served in the 'restful' dining-room. The wine list is a classy selection with France as the main contender; the value for money across the range is outstanding. Beer drinkers have Theakston Best Bitter for a taste of real ale. SAMPLE DISHES: sauté Halloumi cheese on a bed of tomato with caper dressing £4.75; stuffed breast of chicken with garlic sauce £8; chocolate roulade £3.

Open *12 to 2.30, 7 to 11 (10.30 Sun); bar food and restaurant 12 to 2.30, 7 to 9.30*
Details *Children welcome Car park Wheelchair access (also WC) Garden No smoking in dining-room No music Dogs welcome Access, Switch, Visa Accommodation: 7 rooms, B&B £39 to £70*

WATTON-AT-STONE Hertfordshire map 3

George & Dragon 🍇

High Street, Watton-at-Stone TEL: (01920) 830285
on A602, 5m SE of Stevenage

Travellers on the A1 often make a detour to this 'very pleasant, yet very busy' village pub. The building itself is large and imposing, but it feels cheerfully relaxed and comfortable inside, especially when the log fire is blazing. One menu covers the bar and the dining-room, and reporters have been happy with the kitchen's output. Gamey pheasant soup warms the cockles on a cold winter's day, and there is generally plenty of fresh fish on offer: 'generous' sea bass with good, crisp vegetables has been praised. Otherwise, you will always find George & Dragon smokies and Millionaire's and Billionaire's buns (fillet steak in a bread roll), plus smoked salmon and mackerel roulade, savoury pancakes, lamb's kidneys with cream and Madeira; if you want to splash out, try the navarin of mixed seafood with garlic and herb dumplings, or roast duck breast with cognac and plum sauce. Home-made desserts are mostly nursery favourites such as sherry trifle, treacle tart, and lemon meringue pie. Thirty well-chosen wines offer plenty of options from reliable sources, and five house wines are served by the glass and half-litre or litre carafe. This is a Greene King pub with well-kept IPA, Abbot Ale and seasonal brews on handpump. SAMPLE DISHES: prawn and crab bisque £5; pan-fried medallions of pork with calvados, sage and apple £8.75; chocolate brandy biscuit cake £2.75.

Open *11 to 2.30, 6 to 11, Sun 12 to 3, 7 to 10.30; bar food and restaurant all week L 12 to 2, Mon to Sat D 7 to 10*
Details *Children welcome in eating areas Car park Wheelchair access (also WC) Garden and patio No smoking in 1 room No music No dogs Access, Amex, Delta, Diners, Switch, Visa*

🍇 *indicates a pub serving better-than-average wine.*

WELL **Hampshire** **map 2**

Chequers Inn

Well TEL: (01256) 862605
off A31, 5m W of Farnham

This sixteenth-century pub is on the edge of the out-of-the-way village. Inside, the welcoming main bar boasts an excellent log fire in winter; bare floorboards, panelled walls, a beamed and part-boarded ceiling, old scrubbed tables and pews define the décor. The blackboard menu in the bar changes daily and offers a varied and reliable choice with some imaginative touches. Among the starters may be Thai fish-cakes with pickled cucumber, kidneys sauté with bacon and mushrooms, and a salad of bacon, Stilton and poached egg, while main courses might feature braised lamb shank with creamed mash, salade niçoise made with fresh tuna, wild-boar sausages with onion sauce, and sea bream meunière. Sticky toffee pudding or pear cobbler could conclude a meal. Sauté scallops with samphire and saffron butter, followed by red mullet on olive-oil mash with roast peppers and fig tapénade are just two of the ideas on the separate restaurant menu. Hall & Woodhouse beers are on draught (the pub is now owned by Badger Inns). A weatherproof vine-covered pergola at the front makes an appealing place to sit in, and there's a large garden to the rear. SAMPLE DISHES: minestrone soup £2.75; wild rabbit in tomato, red wine and olive sauce £6.25; chilled rice pudding with fruit compote £3.

Open *Mon to Fri 11 to 3, 6 to 11, Sat 11am to 11pm, Sun 12 to 10.30; bar food all week 12 to 2.30, 7 to 10 (9.30 Sun); restaurant Fri and Sat D only 7 to 9.30*
Details *Children welcome Car park Garden and patio No music Dogs welcome Access, Switch, Visa*

WENTNOR **Shropshire** **map 5**

▲ *Crown*

Wentnor TEL: (01588) 650613
off A489, 6m NE of Bishop's Castle

Eight miles from Stokesay Castle and surrounded by bare, round Shropshire hills, Wentnor lies just to the west of the Long Mynd and is in the heart of popular walking country. The seventeenth-century pub is traditional white, and adorned with a mass of flowers, both at the front and on the small stone patio and garden at the back. Log fires blaze in winter, and the atmosphere is welcoming. The printed menu changes regularly but always includes steaks, chops and what licensees Jane and David Carr describe as their 'very popular' ocean crumble. The emphasis here is on country-style cooking, which is borne out in daily blackboard specials along the lines of smoked lamb steak with a spicy apricot sauce, monkfish with a red pepper sauce, or Normandy pheasant with calvados. Vegetarians are well looked after too, with specials that may take in Brie, apricot and onion bake. For dessert, keep an eye out for the whimberry lattice tart – it's a speciality during the short season for these dark berries, which grow high on the surrounding moorland. Food can be eaten either in the bar or dining-room. Beers include Wadworth 6X, Wood Shropshire Lad and Morland Old Speckled Hen. There's also a wine list of around 20 bins, mainly French, but with a smattering from the New World and some fruit wines from Kent. SAMPLE DISHES: garlic mushrooms with cream £3; Shrewsbury-style lamb chops with redcurrant sauce £9.75; brandy alexander pie £2.50.

Open *12 to 2.30, 7 to 11, Sun 12 to 3, 7 to 10.30; bar food and restaurant 12 to 2, 7 to 9; closed 25 Dec*
Details *Children welcome Car park Wheelchair access Garden and patio No smoking in restaurant Background music Dogs by arrangement Access, Delta, Switch, Visa Accommodation: 4 rooms, B&B £22 to £40*

WEOBLEY Hereford & Worcester map 5

▲ *Ye Olde Salutation Inn* 🍇

Weobley TEL: (01544) 318443
just off A4112 Leominster to Brecon road, in village centre, 12m NW of Hereford

Weobley is one of the most picturesque medieval villages in Herefordshire with a wealth of black and white timber-framed buildings. Dating from the fifteenth century, the comfortable and civilised Salutation comprises a former ale and cider house and an adjoining cottage. Bar food is well above average and excellent value for money. The printed menu features chicken and mushroom pancake, and warm seafood salad among the starters, followed by pan-fried lambs' kidneys with barbecue sauce, baked fillet of cod florentine, and roast loin of pork with apple, cider and sultana sauce. Specials are listed on a board: grilled trout with herb sauce, and lamb cutlets with minted redcurrant sauce may be among them. An admirable selection of farmhouse cheeses could round off a meal, or there may be home-made ice-creams or lemon tart ('melt-in-the-mouth pastry' effuses a reporter). Hook Norton Best, Flowers Original and locally brewed Hole-in-One are on draught; around six wines are served by the glass from an impressive list of around 100 bins. SAMPLE DISHES: prawn and red pepper salad £4.50; lamb's liver with red wine, onions and bacon £6.25; bread-and-butter pudding with apricot coulis £4.

Open *11 to 3, 7 to 11, Sun 12 to 3, 7 to 10.30; bar food 12 to 2, 7 to 9.30 (9 Sun and Mon); restaurant Tue to Sun L 12 to 2, Tue to Sat D 7 to 9; closed 25 Dec*
Details *Children welcome in bar eating area Car park Wheelchair access Garden and patio Jukebox in public bar Dogs welcome but guide dogs only in lounge bar and restaurant Access, Amex, Delta, Diners, Switch, Visa Accommodation: 4 rooms, B&B £35 to £65*

WEST BEXINGTON Dorset map 2

▲ *Manor Hotel*

Beach Road, West Bexington TEL: (01308) 897616
on B3157, 3m NW of Abbotsbury

From the garden of this handsome stone manor house you can see the weather sweeping in off the sea by Chesil Beach. Inside, a Jacobean, oak-panelled hall leads down to the pubby cellar bar via a twisting, stone staircase. Through the bar is a comfortable, no-smoking conservatory. Fresh fish is a speciality and a long list on the blackboard includes crab thermidor, whole local plaice, poached fillet of Dover sole with salmon and chardonnay sauce, and a skilfully executed timbale of assorted shellfish in a chive and Noilly Prat sauce. If fish isn't your fancy, choose perhaps liver and bacon, chicken curry, pastas or ploughman's. There is also a separate, formal dining-room. On handpump are Manor Bitter, St Austell Dartmoor Best and Wadworth 6X, while the very healthy wine list includes a decent selection of half-bottles. House wine is served by the glass. Abbotsbury Gardens and the Thomas Hardy monument are nearby. SAMPLE DISHES: gravlax £5.25; pork Stroganov £9; strawberry meringue roulade £3.50.

Open *11am to 11pm, Sun 12 to 3, 7 to 10.30; bar food and restaurant 12 to 2, 6.30 to 10*
Details *Children welcome Car park Wheelchair access (also WC) No smoking in conservatory Background and live music Dogs welcome Access, Amex, Diners, Switch, Visa Accommodation: 13 rooms, B&B £40 to £86*

WESTBURY-SUB-MENDIP Somerset map 2

Westbury Inn

Westbury-sub-Mendip TEL: (01749) 870223
on A371, 3m NW of Wells

Thickly planted window-boxes and hanging-baskets brighten up the stone exterior of this pub in summer, while inside is a series of three interconnecting, old-fashioned rooms, one set for dining. Curries, pastas and Mediterranean king prawns find a place on the menu among dishes from nearer home: Cheddar ploughman's (naturally), deep-fried Stilton and walnuts, smoked salmon with dill sauce, steak and kidney pie, chicken breast with leek sauce, and beef casseroled in ale, for example. Daily specials are listed on blackboards. Round things off with something like chocolate mousse, or apricot and almond tart. Around five frequently changing real ales are dispensed in summer, three in winter; among them might be Jennings Sneck Lifter, Fuller's London Pride and Wells Bombardier. A short but serviceable wine list has something to suit most tastes. While in the area, take a trip to Cheddar Gorge or the historic city of Wells with its magnificent cathedral. SAMPLE DISHES: deep-fried tiger prawns in filo £4; pan-fried duckling breast with honey, soya and ginger sauce £9.50; bread-and-butter pudding £2.50.

Open *11.30 (12 Sun) to 3, 6.30 to 11; bar food and restaurant 12 to 2 6.45 to 9.30 (7 to 9 winter)*
Details *Children welcome in dining-room and games room Car park Wheelchair access (also WC) Garden and patio No smoking in dining-room Background music Dogs welcome Access, Amex, Visa*

WEST CAMEL Somerset map 2

▲ *Walnut Tree*

West Camel TEL: (01935) 851292
off A303, between Sparkford and Ilchester

The restaurant may be the main focus of the kitchen's efforts here, but you can also get interesting, well-cooked food in the bars. Scallops on a bed of pasta with mushroom and white wine sauce for lovers of shellfish; chicken breast wrapped in bacon with asparagus cream sauce for meat eaters. Sticky toffee pudding with caramel sauce, or brandy-snap baskets with seasonal fruit and ice-cream, will nicely round off a meal. The Walnut Tree has been considerably modernised and extended, and its comfortably furnished series of rooms with beams and bare stone walls have a relaxing and friendly atmosphere. Butcombe Bitter and Bass are on draught; the wine list runs to around thirty bins, and five house wines are served by the glass. The area is rich in places to visit, with nearby attractions including Fleet Air Arm Museum, the gardens of Tintinhull House, Brympton d'Evercy, Montacute House and Lytes Cary Manor. SAMPLE DISHES: chicken livers in Madeira with grapes $4.25; salmon fillet with prawn and crab sauce £9; chocolate cups with white and dark chocolate mousse £4.

Open *11 to 2.30, 5.30 to 11, Sun 12 to 3, 7 to 10.30; bar food and restaurant 12 to 2, 7 to 9.30*
Details *Children welcome in eating areas Car park Wheelchair access Garden and patio Background music Guide dogs only Access, Amex, Delta, Diners, Switch, Visa Accommodation: 7 rooms, B&B £40 to £80*

WEST CHILTINGTON West Sussex map 3

Five Bells

Smock Alley, West Chiltington TEL: (01798) 812143
off A283 2½m W of Pulborough

It may be in a seemingly isolated spot, but this pleasant looking brick-and-tile pub succeeds in drawing in a fascinating and mixed crowd of young and old alike. The reasons for its popularity are not hard to spot. Real ale is the main business here and the pub's philosophy is a good one: always on tap are one 'session bitter', two best bitters, a premium brew and a mild, plus an ever-changing line-up of guests that could include Rayments Special, Palmers Best, King & Barnes Sussex Bitter and Gale's HSB; for those who prefer cider, there's a choice of Weston's Old Rosie or Biddenden. Food is also given due attention: 'We do not have a freezer!' insists landlord William Edwards, who adds that his menus tend to follow the seasons. The fixed items tend to be things like ploughman's, fish and chips, rack of lamb, and steaks with various sauces; you might also find fish soup, 'old English' sausages cooked in cider, and vegetable lasagne, backed up by some home-made puddings. SAMPLE DISHES: gravlax with horseradish and mustard dressing £5; steak and kidney pudding £7; toffee meringue roulade £4.

Open *11 to 3, 6 to 11, Sun 12 to 3, 7 to 10.30; bar food and restaurant all week L 12 to 2, Mon to Sat D 7 to 10*
Details *Children welcome in eating areas Car park Wheelchair access Live music Dogs welcome Access, Amex, Delta, Switch, Visa*

Many pubs have separate restaurants, with very different menus. These have not been inspected. A recommendation for the pub/bar food does not necessarily imply that the restaurant is also recommended.

WEST HUNTSPILL Somerset map 2

▲ *Crossways Inn*

Withy Road, West Huntspill TEL: (01278) 783756
on A38, 3m S of Burnham-on-Sea

The owners have been here for almost a quarter of a century, and reporters have nothing but praise for the way they run their pub. 'A Mecca for lovers of good beer,' writes one: with three guest beers changing each week, and Butcombe Bitter, Brains SA Best Bitter, Exmoor Stag and Flowers IPA among the regulars, drinkers have decisions to make. Diners do too. An extensive menu is supported by a blackboard of daily specials. Sandwiches and ploughman's are on offer, and for a full meal you could kick off with deep-fried white-bait, or perhaps fresh and smoked salmon pâté; then go on to Brixham plaice, lamb and apricot pie, local faggots with marrowfat peas, or steak and kidney pie. Bring things to a conclusion with lemon cheesecake, apple pie, or treacle tart. House wines, from a short list with helpful tasting notes, come by the glass, and there's also a clutch of high-quality 'classic wines'. SAMPLE DISHES: tomato and basil soup £2.25; venison and mushrooms casseroled in stout £5.25; sherry trifle £2.25.

Open *11 to 3, 5.30 to 11, Sun 12 to 3, 7 to 10.30; bar food 12 to 2, 6.30 to 9.30 (10 Fri and Sat); bistro Fri and Sat 6.30 to 10; closed 25 Dec*
Details *Children welcome Car park Wheelchair access Garden and patio No-smoking area Live music Dogs welcome on a lead Access, Visa Accommodation: 3 rooms, B&B £24 to £34*

WESTLETON Suffolk map 6

Crown

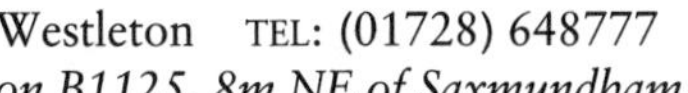

Westleton TEL: (01728) 648777
on B1125, 8m NE of Saxmundham

In 1997 ornithologists will be toasting the 50th anniversary of avocets at Minsmere RSPB Reserve. The up-market Crown will no doubt be involved in the celebrations: the reserve itself is only a walk or a bike-ride away, and landlady Rosemary Price is its 'head-teacher naturalist' – so she knows her stuff. From the front it looks like a 'typical country pub' on the village green, although it opens out at the back to include accommodation and a restaurant. The interior is bedecked with fishing and nautical memorabilia; a log fire burns and you can play games of shove ha'penny. Lunchtime bar food always includes local fish, from seafood thermidor to 'long-lined' cod in beer batter. Soups come with home-baked bread; also note more unusual items such as baked 'Kasseler' (cured pork loin) with wild mushrooms, wild boar and venison casserole, and 'braden rost' (hot-smoked salmon served with prawns and a creamy white wine sauce). Rounding things off are plenty of hot sponge puddings as well as ices and sorbets. The same menu is also available in the bar most evenings, although the restaurant side of the operation takes priority. Half a dozen real ales are on handpump, including Adnams Bitter, Woodforde's Wherry and Black Sheep Bitter alongside three guests. The extensive wine list is well worth considering: the New World contingent is particularly appetising, and one of the house wines is from the local Bruisyard vineyard. The impressive gardens behind the pub were landscaped by Chelsea Flower Show gold medallists Blooms of Bressingham. SAMPLE DISHES: smoked venison with whiskied cranberry compote £3.50; suprême of chicken stuffed with cream cheese and leeks in grain mustard sauce £6; rum and raisin sponge pudding £2.75.

Open *11 to 2.30, 6 to 11, Sun 12 to 3, 7 to 10.30; bar food all week L 12 to 2.15, 7 to 9.30*
Details *Children welcome in dining-room Car park Wheelchair access (also WC) Garden No smoking in restaurant Background music Dogs welcome in bar only Access, Amex, Delta, Diners, Switch, Visa Accommodation: 19 rooms, B&B £54 to £98*

WEST MARDEN **West Sussex** **map 3**

Victoria Inn

West Marden TEL: (01705) 631330
on B2146 Emsworth to Petersfield road, 9m NW of Chichester

The Victoria can be found at the heart of this small village of attractive brick-and-flint cottages in rolling South Downs countryside. Inside, homely prints and knick-knacks adorn the walls; and there's a good open log fire which proves popular on cold days. A printed menu features such things as chicken liver pâté, salads, chilli, and steak, with the addition of ploughman's and sandwiches at lunch-times, while a blackboard announces the daily specials: perhaps mussels, mushroom soup (described by a reporter as 'splendid and delicious'), moussaka, garlic chicken, and chocolate and amaretti torte. Gibbs Mew Bishop's Tipple, Overlord and Deacon are on draught, and house wines come by the litre, half-litre and glass. The Weald and Downland Open-Air Museum, at Singleton on the A286, where typical Downs buildings have been re-erected on-site, is a fascinating place for a visit. SAMPLE DISHES: baked avocado baked with Stilton £4.25; seafood lasagne £7; treacle tart with custard £3.

Open *11.30 to 3, 6 to 11, Sun 12 to 3, 7 to 10.30; bar food and restaurant 12 to 2, 7 to 9.30 (9 Sun)*
Details *Children welcome in dining-room Car park Wheelchair access (also WC) Garden and patio No music Guide dogs only Access, Amex, Delta, Switch, Visa*

WESTON Devon map 2

Otter Inn

Weston TEL: (01404) 42594
just off A30 Exeter to Honiton road, N of Honiton bypass

'The children love it,' write a family who are effusive in their praise for this 'superb' pub. Part of its appeal is the enchanting setting, with landscaped gardens running down the banks of the River Otter and – at the last count – '150 ducks' wandering about. Inside, the atmosphere is reckoned to be 'terrific', service is 'second to none' and the whole place has a beguiling charm. The kitchen delivers ample helpings of dishes such as Peking duck with pancakes, steamed mussels with orange, ginger, saffron and cream, home-made pork sausages and mash, and turkey curry, backed up by sweets like chocolate nut sundae and fresh fruit pavlova. More elaborate dishes, such as pheasant cooked with bacon, cranberries and red wine or rump of beef topped with Stilton, appear in the evening. Spit-roasting takes place in the fireplace every Thursday night, and a full restaurant menu is also available each day. Draught beers include Bass, Boddington and Hardy Country Bitter, and wines are given the thumbs-up. SAMPLE DISHES: carrot and ginger soup £2.50; chicken in red wine with apricots £6.25; bread pudding £3.

Open *11 to 3, 6 to 11, Sun 12 to 3, 7 to 10.30; bar food 12 to 2, 7 to 10, Sun 12 to 2, 7 to 9.30*
Details *Children welcome Car park Wheelchair access Garden Background and live music Dogs welcome on a lead Access, Switch, Visa*

WESTON TURVILLE Buckinghamshire map 3

Chequers Inn

Weston Turville TEL: (01296) 613298
from A41 midway between Aylesbury and Tring, take B4544 then Bates Lane and Church Lane

The Chequers is an attractive, cream-painted building in a quiet backwater of a village; an attractive canal-side walk to Wendover can be picked up at the nearby village of Halton. Inside, the stone-flagged floor and bare brick and flint walls set off the mixture of benches and chairs, while a log fire, ceiling-beams, old prints and other wall-hung bits and pieces complete the décor. The separate restaurant has its own menu, but the daily-changing blackboard menu in the bar delivers the goods too and offers plenty of choice. Celery and Stilton soup could start things off, followed by cod in beer batter with mushy peas and chips, dressed crab, or grilled lemon sole, while meat eaters could go for beef in ale, chicken, ham and leek pie, or gammon steak. Caramel soufflé with caramel sauce has been described as a 'light and tasty' way to end a meal, and there may also be passion-fruit délice. Brakspear PA, Wadworth 6X and Ridleys IPA on draught are joined by a guest ale, and wines are sold by the glass with a full list in the restaurant. SAMPLE DISHES: broccoli and ginger soup £2.25; pork, bacon and mushrooms in mustard sauce £6.25; chocolate and fudge gâteau £2.50.

Open *Tue to Sat 12 to 3, Mon to Sat 6 to 11, Sun 12 to 3, 7 to 10.30; bar food Tue to Sat L 12 to 2.30; restaurant Tue to Fri L 12 to 2.30, Tue to Sat D 7 to 9.30*

Details *Children welcome in bar eating area Car park Patio Background music No dogs Access, Amex, Delta, Switch, Visa*

WEST WYCOMBE Buckinghamshire map 3

▲ *George & Dragon*

High Street, West Wycombe TEL: (01494) 464414
on A40, 3m W of High Wycombe

A log fire warms the large, rectangular main room at this Grade II listed building in a National Trust village. Old prints, a collection of china plates, upholstered benches and plain tables with wheelback chairs set the tone. Specials of the day are written on blackboards and might include home-made soup, pork steak with apple and calvados sauce, or ham, leek and cider pie, as well as game in season. The printed menu concentrates on such dishes as grilled goats'-cheese salad, chicken Madras, grilled lamb cutlets with mint sauce, and wild mushroom and bean goulash. There are also pies: maybe venison, beef and mushroom, for example. You could finish with a selection of English cheeses, or traditional puddings like spotted dick or fruit crumble; alternatives from further afield might include baklava. A good showing of real ales includes Marston's Pedigree, Wadworth 6X and Ushers Founders Ale. Wine comes by the glass, and the list is international. SAMPLE DISHES: devilled goujons of chicken £4.25; Cumberland lamb pie £6; lemon meringue pie £2.25.

Open *weekdays 11 to 2.30, 5.30 to 11, Sat 11 to 11, Sun 12 to 3, 7 to 10.30 (12 to 10.30 Sun summer); bar food 12 to 2 (2.30 Sun), 6 to 9.30*

Details *Children welcome in dining-room Car park Wheelchair access Garden No smoking in 1 room No music Dogs welcome Access, Amex, Delta, Diners, Switch, Visa Accommodation: 8 rooms, B&B £48 to £58*

WHEPSTEAD Suffolk map 6

White Horse

Rede Road, Whepstead TEL: (01284) 735542
just off B1066, 4m SW of Bury St Edmunds

Set in the centre of the village with a delightful orchard garden at the back, this 300-year-old white painted pub makes a popular pit-stop for travellers *en route* to Ickworth Park and Rotunda. The menu is chalked on a board and it ranges far and wide. Starters are 'conspicuous by their absence', but you can kick off with a hefty portion of garlic bread. The repertoire takes in everything from well-timed sirloin steak with 'beautifully dry' chips to oriental exotica such as balti turkey curry, chicken tikka masala, and spicy Thai pork. Desserts are mostly cold creations like home-made coconut vacherin, or chocolate and brandy cheesecake. The White Horse is a Greene King tied house with IPA and Abbot Ale bolstered by seasonal brews such as Black Baron and Winter Hell; and the wine list is fleshed out with a blackboard of specials. SAMPLE DISHES: garlic bread with cheese £1.50; salmon steak with orange sauce and coriander £5.25; white chocolate and Cointreau gâteau £2.25.

Open *11.30 to 3, 6.30 to 11.30, Sun 12 to 3, 7 to 10.30; bar food 11.30 to 2, 6.30 to 9.30*
Details *No children Car park Wheelchair access Garden No music No dogs No cards*

WHITCHURCH Hampshire map 2

Red House

Whitchurch TEL: (01256) 895558

Shannon and Caroline Wells took over this 'rather ordinary village pub' in May 1996 and have worked minor miracles since their arrival. The flag-floored public bar and the lounge bar/dining-room, with its smart beech floor and large mirrors, both have their own entrance – as well as their own style. Service is chatty at the bar, and swift and efficient to the table. Chef Shannon made his name at Harveys restaurant in Winchester and has brought with him a talent for presentation but, more important, an uncompromising modern approach to cooking. This is a kitchen that goes headlong into the world of chargrilled tuna with pesto and black-olive marinade, and chump of lamb served on saffron creamed potato with wilted spinach. The attention to all-round detail shows up in, say, salmon and crab fish-cakes fashioned into neat balls and accompanied by fresh salad leaves dressed with chilli salsa, plus home-made bread rolls and a dish of herb butter on the side. Seasonal dishes and daily specials run hand in hand: Asian chicken salad with fried noodles and ginger soy dressing, and pan-fried halibut with smoked salmon butter sauce sit alongside warm salad of avocado and pancetta, and brochette of monkfish, scallops and salmon with black pasta. Desserts range from home-made ice-creams, and a duo of chocolate terrines with sour cherries to bread-and-butter pudding. The pub has a separate restaurant.

Four real ales are on handpump: Cheriton Brewhouse Pots Ale tops the list followed by Fuller's London Pride, Courage Best Bitter and Theakston XB. Two dozen well-chosen wines from around the world include six house wines by the glass; prices are admirable. Accommodation is promised for 1997. Whitchurch Silk Mill is worth a visit while you are in the village, and the River Test is close by. SAMPLE DISHES: semolina gnocchi with Gorgonzola and wild mushrooms £3.75; roast pheasant breast with pearl barley and a rich Madeira sauce £7.25; French lemon and honey tart £2.25.

Open *11 to 3, 6 to 11, Sun 12 to 3, 7 to 10.30; bar food Tue to Sun L 12 to 2, all week D 6.30 to 9.30; restaurant 12 to 2, 6.30 to 9.30*
Details *No children Car park Wheelchair access (also WC) Garden and patio No pipes in restaurant Background and live music; jukebox No dogs in restaurant Switch, Visa*

WHITEWELL Lancashire **map 8**

Inn at Whitewell 🍇

Whitewell, Forest of Bowland TEL: (01200) 448222
off B6243 Clitheroe to Longridge road, 6m NW of Clitheroe

The Inn *at* Whitewell? The inn *is* Whitewell: there's nothing else for miles. Enter through a large hallway and the bar is to the left, but those in the know head for a dining-room at the back; as this fills, other eating-areas are opened up. The inn has the appearance inside of a genteel country hotel, its walls covered with horsy prints, and there's a grand piano in the hall. A blackboard lists the daily specials; among them might be cauliflower soup, or confit of duck terrine, followed by chicken breast baked with bananas, or plainly grilled salmon, then Irish whiskey chocolate cake, or lemon cheesecake. From the printed menu you could order the likes of chicken liver pâté, seafood pancake, fish pie (the inn's signature dish), roasted lamb steak, or leek, potato and mushroom gratin. Marston's Pedigree and Boddingtons Bitter are on draught, and blackboards list wines by the glass and bottle, with a comprehensive list of good-quality wines in the separate restaurant. Service is described as 'remarkably good and speedy' even when the place is hectic. SAMPLE DISHES: gravlax £5.50; halibut topped with Welsh rarebit £5; white chocolate mousse with raspberry coulis £3.

Open *11 to 3, 6 to 11, Sun 12 to 3, 7 to 10.30; bar food 12 to 2, 7.30 to 9.30*
Details *Children welcome in eating areas Car park Wheelchair access (also WC) Garden and patio Dogs welcome Access, Amex, Delta, Diners, Switch, Visa Accommodation: 11 rooms, B&B £50 to £79*

WHITNEY **Hereford & Worcester** **map 5**

▲ *Rhydspence Inn* 🍇

Whitney-on-Wye TEL: (01497) 831262
off A438 Hereford to Brecon road, 4m E of Hay-on-Wye

Built in the fourteenth century as a manor house, the Rhydspence was famous as an assembly point for generations of Welsh drovers and Irish cowboys on the 'Black Ox Trail'. More recently, diarist Francis Kilvert described it as 'bright with lights and gaiety'. Today's visitors would, no doubt, agree. Two heavily beamed bars are in the oldest part of the building, the elegant restaurant is more modern, and for fine days there's a pleasant garden with a stream. The bar menu lists robust offerings in the shape of sausages from Heal's Farm in Devon, seafood pie, lasagne and home-made burgers. It is backed up by a few more ambitious specials, such as pan-fried scallops on a toasted crouton dressed with roasted pepper oil, or grilled tuna salad with guacamole and chilli. Children have their own menu. The wine list is a well-spread, interesting slate of around 50 bins including a couple from nearby Bodenham vineyard. Bass, Brains SA and Robinson's Best Bitter are on draught and you can also get Dunkerton's organic cider. SAMPLE DISHES: mushroom provençale with fresh tagliatelle £5.50; sizzling Cajun chicken with stir-fry rice £6.50; whimberry pie £4.

Open *11 to 2.30, 7 to 11, Sun 12 to 2.30, 7 to 11; bar food 11 (12 Sun) to 2, 7 to 9.30*
Details *Children welcome in eating areas Car park Wheelchair access Garden and patio No smoking in restaurant No music No dogs Access, Amex, Switch, Visa Accommodation: 7 rooms, B&B £33 to £75*

If a pub has a special point of interest, this is indicated by a 'flashed' word or phrase at the top right of the entry.

WHITTLESFORD **Cambridgeshire** **map 6**

Tickell Arms

Whittlesford TEL: (01223) 833128
off A505, or M11 Jct. 6, 7m S of Cambridge

Some of the house rules for which this good-looking blue-painted pub gained much of its former reputation now seem to have been relaxed: children are allowed across the threshold and can sit inside (provided they are away from the bar), cigarette smokers won't be castigated provided they seek refuge in the conservatory, and dogs are tolerated on leads. Even so, a few quirks remain: 'The barman could only give us one drink at a time (not a full order) and we had to pay for every course separately as we ate it,' noted one reporter. Apart from that, this bastion of deep-rooted eccentricity still rings with 'grand opera', service is from 'beautiful young people in aprons' and the garden remains as enchantingly delightful as ever. The home-made bread and coffee continue to elicit praise, while the menus – plus blackboard specials – still promise such things as kidneys in horseradish cream sauce with rice, pheasant casserole with vegetables, pavlova, and meringues with cream and chestnuts. Adnams Bitter and Old Ale are on draught; several wines are served by the glass and the list runs to about 80 bins. SAMPLE DISHES: game soup £2.75; ragoût of lamb £6; crème brûlée £3.

Open *Tue to Sat 11 to 2.30, 7 to 11, Sun 12 to 4, 7 to 10.30; bar food Tue to Sat 11 to 2.30, 7 to 11, Sun 12 to 4, 7 to 10.30; closed Sun evening Nov to March*
Details *Children welcome in bar eating area Car park Garden and patio No smoking in bar Background music Dogs welcome on a lead No cards*

WHITWELL **Leicestershire** **map 6**

▲ *Noel Arms*

Main Street, Whitwell TEL: (01780) 460334
on A406, 4m E of Oakham

This stone and part-thatched building has been much extended and modernised, though the bar retains a traditional atmosphere, with a stone fireplace, pew benches and rugs on flagstones. The plush open-plan lounge leads through to the candlelit dining-room. Lunchtime snacks include croque-monsieur, omelettes, ploughman's and steak baguette, with an extensive choice of starters and main courses ranging from chicken liver pâté to rabbit casserole or deep-fried fillet of cod. Also on offer in the evenings might be pan-fried pigeon breast with duxelles to start, fillet of brill with saffron and chives, rack of lamb with redcurrant and rosemary, and seafood pancake. A traditional English pud like treacle tart or apple pie could round things off. Marston's Best and Pedigree and Wadworth 6X are typical of the regularly changing real ales on draught, house wines come by the glass, and there's a smattering of half-bottles on the full list of 50 bins. The inn is very handy for Rutland Water and is within easy reach of Stamford and Burghley House, one of the best examples of Elizabethan domestic architecture in the country. SAMPLE DISHES: tomato and basil soup £2.50; steak and kidney pie £6.50; tiramisù £3.

Open *10 to 11, Sun 12 to 10.30; bar food and restaurant 12 to 2, 7 to 10 (9 Sun)*
Details *Children welcome Car park Wheelchair access (also WC) Garden and patio Background music Dogs welcome in 1 bar Access, Delta, Switch, Visa Accommodation: 8 rooms, B&B £45 to £65*

WIDECOMBE IN THE MOOR Devon map 1

Old Inn

Widecombe in the Moor TEL: (01364) 621207
from Bovey Tracey take Haytor road and continue to Widecombe in the Moor, 5m NW of Ashburton

Tourists from far and wide clearly know the score about 'Uncle Tom Cobley and all', because hordes descend on the village each year to seek out the famous fair. The Old Inn – which originally dates from the fourteenth century – is a focal point and popular rendezvous, especially during the festive season, high days and holidays. Visitors are well fed from a lengthy menu that covers just about everything in the standard pub repertoire (plus one or two unexpected dishes such as haggis with neeps and tatties, or lamb in redcurrant and gin sauce). Specialities are more adventurous: rabbit pie with cider and coarse-grain mustard, grilled sea-bass steak served on julienne of carrot with a 'coulis of smoked salmon sauce', for example; desserts such as spiced apple bread-and-butter pudding come with clotted cream. Sunday lunch is a choice of three roasts (standard or bumper versions). Widecombe Wallop is the house bitter; otherwise you can sample Ushers Best or Grey's farmhouse cider; around three dozen wines are realistically priced. SAMPLE DISHES: deep-fried potato skins with blue cheese and garlic dip £3.50; venison casserole £7.25; summer fruit fool £2.50.

Open *Mon to Fri 11 to 2.30, 7 (6 summer) to 11, Sat 11 to 2.30, 6.30 (6 summer) to 11, Sun 12 to 3, 7 to 10.30; bar food Mon to Sat 11 to 2, 6.30 to 8.30 (10 summer), Sun 12 to 2.30, 7 to 9 (10 in summer)*
Details *Children welcome in eating areas Car park Wheelchair access Garden and patio Background music Dogs welcome on a lead Access, Delta, Switch, Visa*

WINCLE **Cheshire** **map 8**

Ship Inn

Wincle TEL: (01260) 227217
1m S of A54, between Congleton and Buxton, 5m SE of Macclesfield

It may seem miles from anywhere, but this diminutive sandstone pub is well worth seeking out, especially if you're fond of unaffected North Country hostelries. Everything about the place is 'great', noted one correspondent after a dark autumnal visit. The mood is chatty as walkers and hikers mingle with regulars in the bar. Seasonal and local produce is used for comforting old-style dishes ranging from home-made meat and potato pie to greengage crumble. Fresh fish is delivered on Wednesdays and the menu also runs to a few more exotic things like feta cheese with herby marinated olives and vegetable 'fritto misto'. A roast is served on Sunday lunch-times during the winter. Boddingtons and a guest beer are on draught and the pub has a useful wine list from around the world. SAMPLE DISHES: chicken and vegetable soup £2; gammon and eggs £6; ginger and lemon sponge £2.50.

Open *12 to 3, 7 to 11, Sun 12 to 3, 7 to 10.30; bar food 12 to 2 (2.30 Sat and Sun), 7 to 9.30; closed Mon Nov to March*
Details *Children welcome in family room Car park Wheelchair access (also WC) Garden No music Dogs welcome in family room only No cards*

WINDLESHAM **Surrey** **map 3**

Brickmakers Arms 🍇

Chertsey Road, Windlesham TEL: (01276) 472267
on B386, off A30 Bagshot to Sunningdale road

Deep in Surrey's affluent golfing country, not far from Sunningdale and Wentworth, the Brickmakers Arms puts on a civilised face. The building is, quite naturally, brick with a modern extension tacked on and a pleasant patio and garden for fine days. The only music is likely to be occasional live jazz. The emphasis is mostly on restaurant meals although bar food is 'generally available but may be slow', warns landlord Gerry Price. Fresh fish is the kitchen's trump card, with up to ten kinds generally available. You can also get 'Brickies Big Bites' (hunks of ciabatta bread with various fillings), as well as things like black pudding with grain mustard sauce, warm chicken liver salad, meatballs in tomato sauce with tagliatelle, and smoked haddock kedgeree with poached egg. Desserts could be anything from crème brûlée to apple and blackberry pudding. An admirable selection of wines is available in the bar and the complete list is an enthusiast's choice, full of good stuff from around the world, much of it bought at auction. If beer is your tipple, choose between Courage Best, Fuller's London Pride and Theakston XB. SAMPLE DISHES: smoked mackerel pâté £4; pork sausages with onion gravy and mash £7.25; chocolate sponge and chocolate sauce £3.75.

Open *11.30 to 3, 5 to 11, Sun 12 to 3, 7 to 10; bar food and restaurant 12 to 2.30, 6 to 10*
Details *No children Car park Garden and patio No smoking in dining-room Live music Dogs in bar only Access, Amex, Delta, Diners, Switch, Visa*

WINFORTON Hereford & Worcester map 5

▲ *Sun Inn*

Winforton TEL: (01544) 327677
on A438 Hereford to Brecon road, 6m S of Kington

Brian and Wendy Hibbard's gem of a pub stands in the middle of 'superb English-cum-Welsh country scenery', and their bright white-washed cottage looks the part, with its 'rather overgrown' grassy garden and an attractive entrance full of plants. To one side of the long central bar is a lounge with horse brasses and other equestrian paraphernalia tacked to the wooden beams; to the other is a farm-house-style dining-area complete with a high settle and a jumble of plates, ornaments, wine racks and mirrors. There's even a piano. The mood is welcoming: one immediately feels at ease.

Wendy Hibbard's cooking is true to the Welsh tradition, but she is also a magpie-like plunderer of the world larder. The result is an enticing and eclectic mix with touches of real imagination: warm chicken tikka salad, Singapore prawns, 'outstanding' marrow stuffed with couscous, lamb in blackberry sauce, and grilled fillet of sea trout; beans and herbs sit alongside wild rabbit cooked in Herefordshire cider. Her trade mark is the way she uses accompaniments to lift a dish: tip-top smoked duck breast is balanced by 'gently sweet' melon salsa and 'strongly sharp' banana chutney; game pâté is served with 'lovely' onion marmalade; and Camembert filo parcels come with gooseberry and elderflower sauce ('an uplifting combination', according to one recipient). Best of all, perhaps, are her ploughman's, eight varieties in all, with brilliant local cheeses and an array of home-made pickles and chutneys: 'You couldn't do better,' enthused a reporter. Desserts are in a similar vein, everything from tipsy bread-and-butter pudding to greengage tart with custard. The strength and commitment of this set-up also shows in the choice and range of real ales – Wood Shropshire Lad from Winstanstow, Jennings from Cumbria, Hook Norton from Oxfordshire; the wine list may be short, but every bottle is a carefully chosen winner. SAMPLE DISHES: Carew mussels with leek, bacon and ginger sauce £4.25; breast of maize-fed guinea-fowl with wild mushroom sauce £10; Turkish delight charlotte £3.50.

Open *11.30 to 3, 6.30 to 11, Sun 12 to 3, 7 to 10.30; bar food Wed to Mon 12 to 2, 7 to 9.30*
Details *Children welcome in bar eating area Car park Wheelchair access (also WC) Garden and patio No smoking in some areas Background music No dogs No cards Accommodation: 3 rooms, B&B £30 to £55*

WING Leicestershire **map 6**

▲ *King's Arms*

Top Street, Wing TEL: (01572) 737634
off A47, 4m SE of Oakham

Set in a peaceful, out-of-the-way village close to Rutland Water, and convenient for Oakham and Stamford, this Grade II listed building, dating from 1649, was renovated and refurbished in 1996. The bar has retained its character, with old beams, open fires, sturdy oak tables, nooks and crannies, and a Georgian-style bar counter; an attractive stone-walled dining-room has been created from an old barn. The bar menu lists snacks like prawns and mushrooms pan-fried in garlic and herb butter, and various burgers, pasta dishes, and a mixed-grill, while a specials board offers, for example, toad-in-the-hole with bubble and squeak, or pheasant breast in port and cranberries. The dining-room menu is served throughout the pub too: you could start with venison pâté, or fish stew, and go on to pot-roast guinea-fowl, or duck breast with grapefruit and ginger wine sauce. Bateman XB, Bass and a guest ale are on draught, and about half a dozen wines come by the glass. SAMPLE DISHES: pan-fried lambs' kidneys, black pudding and smoked bacon £4.50; chicken breast stuffed with wild mushrooms and bacon in tarragon sauce £8; raspberry and Drambuie syllabub £2.75.

Open *summer Mon to Thur 11.30 to 3, 6.30 to 11, Fri to Sun 11am to 11pm, winter Sat to Thur 12 to 3, 6.30 to 11, Fri 11am to 11pm; bar food and restaurant 12 to 2.30, 6.30 to 9.30*
Details *Children welcome in bar eating area Car park Wheelchair access Garden and patio No smoking in restaurant Background and occasional live music Guide dogs only Access, Amex, Delta, Switch, Visa Accommodation: 4 rooms, B&B £30 to £55*

If you disagree with any assessment made in the Guide, *write to tell us why* – The Which? Guide to Country Pubs, *FREEPOST, 2 Marylebone Road, London NW1 1YN.*

WINSFORD Somerset map 1

▲ *Royal Oak Inn*

Winsford, Exmoor National Park TEL: (01643) 851455
off A396, 5m N of Dulverton

This ancient thatched inn nestles in a picture-postcard village within the wonderful scenery of Exmoor National Park, and there are plenty of walks nearby – including one up Winsford Hill. The back bar is pleasantly furnished with cushioned window seats and back-to-back settles, while the front bar has an inglenook with a log fire in winter and – aptly for this area – prints of hunting and shooting scenes. The atmosphere is civilised, up-market and chatty. Bar food is reliable stuff, embracing sandwiches and ploughman's, a daily soup such as watercress, and main courses like seafood pancake, steak sandwich, and chicken and leek pie, plus a selection of puddings served with clotted cream. On draught are Flowers Original and IPA, and among guest beers may be Shepherd Neame Spitfire. The wine list is geared to the set-price meals in the separate restaurant. SAMPLE DISHES: deep-fried Somerset Brie £3.75; grilled local trout £8.50; chocolate and whisky mousse £2.50.

Open *10.30 to 2.30, 6 to 11, Sun 12 to 3, 7 to 10.30; bar food 12 to 2, 6.30 to 9; restaurant Sun L 12 to 1.15, all week D 7.30 to 9.30*
Details *Children welcome in eating areas Car park Wheelchair access (also WC) Garden and patio No music Dogs welcome Access, Amex, Diners, Switch, Visa Accommodation: 14 rooms, B&B £68 to £95*

WINTERTON-ON-SEA Norfolk map 6

▲ *Fishermans Return*

The Lane, Winterton-on-Sea TEL: (01493) 393305
on B1159, 8m N of Great Yarmouth

The Fishermans Return, dating from the seventeenth century and built of brick and flint, was once a row of fishermen's cottages. At the heart of a popular holiday village and only a short stroll from the beach, it is an ideal spot to relax in after a walk across the dunes or a day exploring the Broads. The low-ceilinged lounge has an open wood-burner, red leatherette seating, and local prints and old photographs on the walls, while the spacious bar has another wood-burner and pew seating; a rear extension acts as a games room. An excellent range of real ales includes locally brewed Wolf Best Bitter, John Smith's, Adnams Bitter and, in season, Adnams Old Ale. James White Suffolk cider is on tap too. A printed menu offers straightforward pub fare: toasted sandwiches, fish pie, burgers, steaks and so on. This is enhanced by a blackboard of daily specials, which may run to moules marinière, goulash, and smoked haddock Mornay. Vegetarian dishes are interesting – aubergine and sweet potato in coconut on rice, say – while puddings could include black cherry cheesecake. Own-label French wines come by the glass and bottle, and a blackboard lists alternatives. SAMPLE DISHES: game and vegetable soup £3.50; spiced beef with wild rice £5.50; lemon and lime mascarpone torte £2.25.

Open *11 to 2.30 (3 summer), 6.30 (6 summer) to 11, Sun 12 to 10.30; bar food 12 to 2, 6.30 to 9.30*
Details *Children welcome in dining-room and games room Car park Garden and patio No-smoking areas Background music and jukebox Dogs welcome Accommodation: 3 rooms, B&B £30 to £45*

WISWELL Lancashire map 8

Freemasons Arms

8 Vicarage Fold, Wiswell TEL: (01254) 822218
1m off A680 near Whalley

Nestling in a little hamlet at the foot of Pendle Hill, this unpretentious village pub makes much of its cosy intimacy. New licensees Jeff and Pauline Livesey took up residence in March 1996, and their specials menu follows a similar path to that of their predecessors. Fresh fish shows up in the shape of, say, fillet of salmon with lemon butter sauce, and lemon sole filled with smoked salmon and salmon mousse served with saffron sauce. Otherwise the repertoire ranges from spinach pancakes, and smoked duck with avocado to medallions of beef au poivre, and rack of lamb with sherry gravy. To finish, try caramel meringue with toffee sauce, or chocolate truffle torte with Cointreau cream. Jennings Bitter and Cumberland Ale, plus Belhaven Mild are on handpump, and the pub has a stock of over 100 malt whiskies; four house wines head the list. Although the pub has no car park, parking is available in the village. SAMPLE DISHES: local black pudding with mustard sauce £3; salmon fish-cakes with parsley sauce £6.75; strawberry shortcake £2.75.

Open *Wed to Sun 11.30 to 2.30, 6.30 to 11; bar food and restaurant Wed to Sun 12 to 2, 6.30 to 9.30*
Details *Children welcome in dining-room Wheelchair access Patio Background music No dogs Access, Switch, Visa*

All details are as accurate as possible at the time of going to press, but pubs often change hands, and it is wise to check beforehand by telephone anything that is particularly important to you.

WITHYHAM East Sussex map 3

Dorset Arms

Withyham TEL: (01892) 770278
on B2110, 2m E of Hartfield

The exterior of this tile-hung pub on the village green is festooned with hop-bines in season, and window boxes add colourful displays of flowers. Enter through a traditional public bar to the pink-carpeted lounge, with its small round tables, wooden chairs and low, button-backed settees. The restaurant, which has a separate menu, is beyond. Sunday lunch is generally a choice from the traditional range of roasts; the rest of the time the menu offers sandwiches, jacket potatoes, ploughman's and dishes such as crispy mushrooms with a garlic dip, battered cod, omelettes, and sirloin steak. The daily-changing blackboard specials may run to lambs' liver with bacon and onions, ratatouille, chicken curry, and 'amazingly good' chocolate truffle torte. Harveys ales are on draught, and house wines are sold by the glass with a full list in the restaurant. Withyham is on the edge of Ashdown Forest, the setting for *Winnie-the-Pooh*. SAMPLE DISHES: whitebait £3.50; lamb and apricot pie £4.75; lemon soufflé £3.

Open *11.30 to 3, 5.30 to 11, Sun 12 to 3, 7 to 10.30 (Sat 11 to 3, 6 to 11); bar food and restaurant all week L 12 to 2.15, Tue to Sun D 7.30 to 9 (Oct to Mar closed Sun D)*
Details *Children welcome in dining-room Car park Garden and patio Background music Dogs welcome Access, Amex, Delta, Visa*

WITHYPOOL Somerset map 1

▲ *Royal Oak Inn*

Withypool TEL: (01643) 831506
off B3223, 2m S of Exford

The Royal Oak is a squat-looking, white-painted village pub that specialises in huntin' and fishin'. The owners can arrange both if you're a resident, but drinking customers can't fail to notice the sporting theme in the beamed Rod Room bar, which has sets of antlers, trophies and hunting pictures on the walls. The pub is a popular one, and the staff are pleasant, but on a busy day service can come under pressure. The bar menu lists the usual jackets and ploughman's alongside more unusual items such as Danish open sandwiches with prawns or smoked salmon, and venison steak with chips. Blackboard specials – which continue the theme of honest, plain cooking – might include chicken suprême with peas and french fries, or salmon steak with potatoes and salad. Set-price dinners and

Sunday lunch are served in the restaurant. On handpump are Flowers IPA and Marston's Pedigree Bitter; there are also bottles of Tiger Beer and Elephant Beer as well as over 30 different brandies and two dozen malt whiskies. Eight different wines are sold by the glass, and the list runs to 60 bins from around the world. The pub is situated in the middle of Exmoor, within easy reach of the ancient footbridge at Tarr Steps and historic Dunster Castle. Author R.D. Blackmore stayed at the Royal Oak while writing *Lorna Doone* in 1866. SAMPLE DISHES: half-pint of North Atlantic prawns £3.50; sirloin steak and chips £10; kiwi and ginger pavlova £2.75.

Open *11 (12 Sun) to 3, 6 to 11; bar food 12 to 2, 6.30 to 9.30; restaurant Sun L 12 to 2, all week D 7 to 9*
Details *Children welcome in dining-room Car park Wheelchair access Patio No music No dogs in dining-room Access, Amex, Delta, Diners, Switch, Visa Accommodation: 8 rooms, B&B £32 to £80*

WOLTERTON Norfolk map 6

▲ *Saracen's Head* 🍇

Wolterton TEL: (01263) 768909
off A140 Aylsham to Cromer road, through Erpingham and Calthorpe

Landlord Robert Dawson-Smith bills the Saracen's Head as 'North Norfolk's Lost Inn', and it's easy to see why. The pub itself, designed in the style of a Tuscan farmhouse, seems to be in the middle of nowhere 'twixt Erpingham and Itteringham; in fact, it stands adjacent to Wolterton Hall, not far from Mannington Hall and its gardens. This is a quirkily idiosyncratic place with a fun-loving atmosphere plus an attractive courtyard at the back. The kitchen has no truck with 'chips, peas or fried scampi'; instead, visitors might be offered Morston mussels with cider, grilled goats' cheese on toast, lamb's kidneys with bacon, or a layered ratatouille and brown bread pudding. Seasonal game shows up strongly in the shape of braised pigeon with prunes and marsala, salmis of rabbit and ham with mustard sauce, and a brace of roast woodcock on a croûte. Locally produced Prospero ice-creams and sorbets are alternatives to chocolate pots, and treacle tart. Monthly feasts are a special attraction. Adnams Bitter and a guest brew are always on draught, and Adnams also supplies the lively list of 16 affordable wines. SAMPLE DISHES: filo-wrapped prawns with olive mayonnaise £4.50; wok-sizzled lamb's liver with mushrooms and sherry £7.50; baked pineapple and dark rum £3.

Open *11 to 3, 6 to 11, Sun 12 to 3, 7 to 10.30; bar food and restaurant 12.30 to 2.15, 7.30 to 9.30*
Details *Children welcome Car park Wheelchair access Garden and patio No music No dogs Access, Amex, Visa Accommodation: 4 rooms, B&B £35 to £50*

WOOBURN COMMON Buckinghamshire map 3

▲ *Chequers Inn*

Kiln Lane, Wooburn Common TEL: (01628) 529575
just S of M50 Jct. 2

Deep in some of the most rural expanses of the Chilterns close to Burnham Beeches, this sympathetically extended seventeenth-century inn is perfect if you feel like getting away from it all. The bar still echoes with history: note the massive oak post and beam framework, plus open fireplace blackened with age. This is an extremely popular venue for bar food, and the kitchen aims high. Up-market pub snacks such as open turkey and avocado sandwich glazed with cheese share the billing with more brasserie-style dishes that may include sauté chicken livers on a bed of leaves, or collops of monkfish and king scallops in ginger and garlic butter. Desserts tend towards bread-and-butter pudding and the like. A more sophisticated menu is offered in the restaurant. Timothy Taylor Landlord, Fuller's London Pride and Marston's Pedigree are typical of the names on the handpumps, and the pub has an abundant choice of wines by the glass. During the summer there may be barbecues in the sunken garden. SAMPLE DISHES: cream of cucumber and mint soup £2.50; deep-fried pork escalope on tagliatelle with tomato sauce £8; summer pudding with clotted cream £2.75.

Open *all week 11am to 11pm; bar food and restaurant 12 to 2.30, 6.30 to 9.30*
Details *Children welcome Car park Garden Background music No dogs Access, Amex, Switch, Visa Accommodation: 17 rooms, B&B £78 to £83*

WOODHILL Somerset map 2

▲ *Rose and Crown*

Woodhill, Stoke St Gregory TEL: (01823) 490296
between A361 and A378, 8m E of Taunton, via North Curry

'One gets a strong impression of what country inns were like before electricity,' commented one visitor to this 'tremendous' eighteenth-century pub. Inside is a cluster of dimly lit, atmospheric rooms with beams, low ceilings, dark wood everywhere and 'nicotine yellow' colour schemes. Every inch of space seems to be covered with a higgledy-piggledy jumble of old bills, posters, photographs and prints. In one corner is a glass-covered well. The lunchtime menu offers unpretentious, homely stuff ranging from ham, egg and chips to scrumpy chicken, and there are also blackboard specials including, say, ribeye steak, codling in parsley sauce, and rich game pie with 'velvet brown gravy' and crumbly shortcrust pastry. Puddings, such as cherry cheesecake, and apple pie, come with home-made ice-cream or Somerset clotted cream. Evening heralds a shorter repertoire with slightly higher prices. Fixed-price dinners are served in the stone-floored restaurant. Thomas Hardy (formerly Eldridge Pope) Royal Oak and Country Bitter are on handpump alongside Moor Withycutter and Exmoor Ale; the short wine list is from the same suppliers. Outside is a lovely sheltered garden; the pub is convenient for a trip to the Somerset Levels and the nearby Willow Craft Centre. SAMPLE DISHES: ravioli and garlic bread £3.50; grilled skate wings £6.50; chocolate mousse cake £2.50.

Open *11 to 3, 6.30 to 11, Sun 12 to 3, 7 to 10.30; bar food and restaurant 12.30 to 2, 7 to 10*
Details *Children welcome in eating areas Car park Garden and patio No smoking in 1 dining-room Background music Dogs welcome exc in eating areas Access, Delta, Switch, Visa Accommodation: 3 rooms, B&B £23 to £38*

WOOLHOPE Hereford & Worcester map 5

▲ *Butchers Arms*

Woolhope TEL: (01432) 860281
off B4224, 7m SE of Hereford

This ancient half-timbered building is in an idyllic country setting, on a quiet lane just outside the village, surrounded by meadows and wooded hills. The patio garden, by a stream, makes a perfect spot for eating and drinking in summer, while, inside, log fires add warmth and cosiness to the beamed bars in winter. Leek and hazelnut terrine in vine leaves sounds like an interesting starter. Tried-and-tested main courses could include chicken curry, grilled gammon, lasagne, and battered cod, while desserts are of the school of bread-and-butter pudding and apple pie. There's also a range of salads and ploughman's, with a page of vegetarian options on the menu. Hook Norton Best Bitter and Old Hooky are on draught, as is local Weston's cider, and there's a comprehensive wine list. SAMPLE DISHES: chicken liver pâté £3.75; steak and kidney pie £6.75; peach mousse £3.

Open *11.30 to 2.30, 7 to 11, Sun 12 to 2.30, 7 to 10.30; bar food all week L 12 to 2, Mon to Sat D 7 to 10; restaurant Sat D only 7 to 10*
Details *Children welcome Car park Wheelchair access Garden and patio Occasional live music Guide dogs only No cards Accommodation: 3 rooms, B&B £30 to £39*

Food mentioned in the main entries is available in the bar, although it may be possible to eat in a dining-room.

Crown Inn

Woolhope TEL: (01432) 860468

Woolhope is a village on high land from which beautiful views are obtained of woodlands and rolling fields. The old stone pub is on top of the hill next to the church. The bar is furnished with red velvet banquettes and stools, with timber half-cladding on the walls and lots of old photographs of the village. Service has been described as 'very efficient' – as it needs to be, for this is a popular place, with most people eating. The long menu encompasses such starters as mussels in tempura, and potted Stilton with mushrooms, and main courses like local steaks, lamb stew with dumplings, and cauliflower and potato bake. Asterisks denote healthier options – grilled plaice, for instance, and Flora is available instead of butter if requested. Most of the puddings will appeal to those with a sweet tooth: toffee apple pie is typical. Hook Norton Best, Tetley and Smiles Best Bitter are on draught, and there's a choice of reasonably priced wines. SAMPLE DISHES: grilled sardines £2.75; faggots in onion gravy £5.25; pear and almond tart £2.50.

Open *12 to 2.30, 6.30 (7 winter) to 11, Sun 12 to 2.30, 7 to 10.30; bar food all year L 12 to 2, summer D 6.30 (6 Sat) to 10, winter D 7 (6.30 Sat) to 10; closed 25 Dec*
Details *No children after 8pm Car park Wheelchair access Garden and patio No smoking in restaurant Background music No dogs Access, Delta, Switch, Visa*

WOOLLEY MOOR Derbyshire map 5

White Horse Inn

Badger Lane, Woolley Moor TEL: (01246) 590319
on W side of Ogston Reservoir, off B6014, between Matlock and Stretton

Fans of real ale set a course for this low, stone building on a hill in the middle of nowhere. Since 1983 landlord Bill Taylor has championed the cause: four brews, including Bass and Jennings Mild, are regularly on show, and a quartet of guests are judiciously chosen for their different strengths and styles. Consult the blackboard to see what is available. The wine list now includes some decent New World bins plus a 'wine of the week'. Best bets on the food side of things are the daily specials, which might take in salmon and leek fricassee, chicken in smoked bacon and Stilton sauce, and ratatouille strudel. Alternatively, there is a printed menu offering everything from ploughman's to pies. Puddings range from home-made fruit crumble to ice-cream sundaes. Children are given colouring books, pencils and puzzles while they are waiting for their fish fingers and Mars Bar ice-cream. The pub has great views of the Amber Valley and is close to Ogston Reservoir as well as Calke Abbey (National Trust). SAMPLE DISHES: cauliflower with chopped nut and cheese sauce £2; pork and wild mushroom Stroganov £5.50; jam roly-poly with custard £2.25.

Open *Mon to Fri 11.30 to 2.30 (3 Sat), 6 to 11, Sun 12 to 3.30, 5 to 10.30; bar food and restaurant 11.30 to 2, 6.30 to 9, Sun 12 to 2.15, 5.30 to 8.30*
Details *Children welcome in dining-room Car park Wheelchair access Garden and patio No smoking in dining-room Background music Dogs welcome in bar only No cards*

WOOTTON Oxfordshire map 2

▲ *Kings Head*

Chapel Hill, Wootton TEL: (01993) 811340
off A44 Chipping Norton to Woodstock road

The great treasure houses of Blenheim and Woodstock are within easy reach of this neatly turned-out beige stone inn. Inside, bar and dining-room are divided by a genteel little area where you can sip preprandial drinks on sofas. The two worlds – boozing and dining – seem to co-exist happily. Fish cookery takes centre-stage, and in the bar you can sample blackboard specials such as grilled mullet on a bed of cabbage and baked tomato, salmon fillet with julienne of vegetables, and stuffed trout with prawns grilled in garlic butter, not to mention scampi and fries with home-made tartare sauce. Starters might include warm goats'-cheese salad with bacon and garlic croûton, sausages lyonnaise should please meat eaters, while desserts range from Boodle cream to cinnamon pear tart, and lemon icebox pudding. The full restaurant menu adopts a serious French accent, and there's a substantial wine list which seems to be tailored to the needs of dining-room customers. Real ales are Morland Original Bitter and Old Speckled Hen. SAMPLE DISHES: macaroni carbonara £4.50; chicken breast in tarragon and cream sauce £6.25; meringue with red fruits £3.

Open *11.30 to 3, 6 to 11, Sun 12 to 3, 7 to 10.30; bar food and restaurant Sun to Fri L 12 to 2.30, all week D 7 to 10*
Details *Children welcome in eating areas Car park Wheelchair access Garden No pipes Background music No dogs Access, Delta, Switch, Visa Accommodation: 3 rooms, B&B £50 to £90*

After the main section of the Guide *is the 'Out and about' section listing additional pubs that are well worth a visit. Reports on these entries are most welcome.*

WOOTTON RIVERS Wiltshire map 2

▲ *Royal Oak*

Wootton Rivers TEL: (01672) 810322
off A346, 3m NE of Pewsey

The setting, in a village close to the Kennet & Avon Canal and Savernake Forest, is 'quite unreasonably idyllic', noted one visitor to this quintessential sixteenth-century thatched inn. Inside, it has all the expected trappings – 'head-crackingly' low beams, neatly arranged settles and armchairs, wood-burning stoves. The printed menu includes ploughman's, snacks and salads, as well as a noticeable contingent of basket meals and things with chips. More promising is the daily specials menu, which offers such international dishes as Thai crab-cakes with chilli sauce, Turkish lamb with coriander and cumin, and home-made ratatouille topped with toasted Brie. Sorbets provide a refreshing alternative to richly calorific puddings such as hot chocolate fudge cake and sherry trifle. Wadworth 6X, IPA and a guest ale are tapped from casks behind the bar, and an interesting range of malt whiskies is on display. Eight wines are served by the glass, and the short list has a fair showing of Burgundies. Those considering tying the knot might like to know that the pub is licensed for wedding ceremonies. SAMPLE DISHES: Greek salad with feta cheese and black olives £4.25; venison sausages with redcurrant jelly £7.50; green figs laced with Pernod £3.

Open *11 to 3, 6 to 11, Sun 12 to 4, 7 to 10.30 (12 to 11 in summer); bar food and restaurant 12 to 2, 6.45 to 9.30 (10 weekends)*
Details *Children welcome in eating areas Car park Patio Jukebox Small dogs welcome on a lead Access, Amex, Switch, Visa Accommodation: 5 rooms, B&B £20 to £40*

WORTH Somerset map 2

Pheasant

Worth, Wookey TEL: (01749) 672355
on B3139, 3m W of Wells

Ebullient landlord Mr Dovidio keeps the atmosphere bubbling at this re-vamped roadside pub – and he's ably supported by smart bow-tied waiters. What one reporter called 'a truly exciting menu' attracts the crowds and the kitchen seems equally at home with everything from toasted cheese sandwiches ('made with real bread') to alligator kebabs. In between you will find an array of dishes including 'Filipino' pork and orange spring rolls, pan-fried liver, and medallions of pork in cider and cream sauce. As befits the pub name, pheasant appears in season along with a plethora of other game such as roast woodcock served on a bed of couscous. Draught real ales are supplied by the local Bath and Butcombe breweries. Chilean, Australian, French and even English wines feature on the list, and house wines are also available by the glass. Worth is handy is you are intending to make a trip to Wookey Hole or Cheddar Gorge. SAMPLE DISHES: potato skins filled with cheese, mushrooms and bacon £3; steak and kidney pie £5.50; profiteroles £2.75.

Open *11 to 3.30, 5.30 to 11, Sun 12 to 3, 7 to 10.30; bar food and restaurant 12 to 2.30, 6 to 10*
Details *No children in bar after 8 Car park Garden and patio Background and live music Dogs in bar only No cards*

WYRE PIDDLE Hereford & Worcester map 5

Anchor Inn

Main Street, Wyre Piddle TEL: (01386) 552799
on B4084, 2m NE of Pershore

Roses, shrubs, fragrant lavender and herbs abound in the idyllic garden sloping down to the River Avon behind this seventeenth-century pub; plenty of tables allow for outdoor eating and drinking, and give wonderful views over the countryside to Bredon Hill and Pershore Abbey. People are drawn here for the food as much as for the garden and views. A long printed menu encompasses snails bourguignon, garlic prawns, chicken fricassee, Herefordshire steaks, and Dover sole grilled with garden herbs and lemon butter. You may be spoilt for choice when you also spot the blackboard of specials: perhaps grilled goats' cheese on spinach, rabbit braised in mustard and cream, skate wings in caper butter, shoulder of lamb glazed with mint and redcurrant jelly, or even haggis with Drambuie. Puddings include fruit pies and crumbles served with custard. House wines are sold by the glass from a list numbering more than 30 bottles; and a reasonable choice of real ales includes Marston's Pedigree, Flowers IPA and Original, and Boddingtons. SAMPLE DISHES: venison pâté with Cumberland sauce £3.25; fillet of sole stuffed with scallops and crab £8.25; hot peaches with almond butter, brandy and cream £2.75.

Open *Mon to Fri 11 to 2.30, 6 to 11, Sat 12 to 3, 6 to 11, Sun 12 to 3, 7 to 10.30; bar food and restaurant 12 to 2.15, 7 to 9.30 (restaurant closed Sun D)*
Details *Children welcome in bar eating area Car park Garden and patio Background and live music Dogs on leads welcome Access, Amex, Switch, Visa*

Use the maps and index at the back of the Guide *to plan your trip.*

YATTENDON Berkshire map 2

▲ *Royal Oak* ✿ 🍇

The Square, Yattendon TEL: (01635) 201325
off B4009, 5m W of Pangbourne

Yattendon has been an estate village since Norman times, although this resolutely English inn is of slightly less venerable pedigree. Oliver Cromwell and his Roundheads planned their strategy for the Battle of Newbury in the bar; ironically, the pub was re-named in memory of King Charles who sought refuge here after the bloody confrontation. Today, the Royal Oak puts on a civilised face, although it wears its history well. A log fire often crackles in the bar, where the décor is all oak-beams and quarry tiles.

Menus were about to change as we went to press, but Robbie Macrae's style can be gauged from current dishes. On the one hand there's a fondness for pub/bistro classics – Caesar salad, croque-monsieur, home-made gala pie with piccalilli, deep-fried plaice with chips, steak and kidney pudding. But his training with Marco Pierre White means that his sympathy is also with the contemporary repertoire of carpaccio, chargrilled tuna niçoise, and salad of Chinese dumplings filled with spicy duck. Additional fish specials broaden the choice. The result – according to one report – is 'Big, really big portions, realistic prices and earthy flavours' in, for example, mussel, saffron and fennel stew, navarin of lamb, and honey-glazed hock of ham with casseroled lentils. Rounding things off are desserts ranging from treacle tart with clotted cream to rhubarb and ginger brûlée and tiramisù. More elaborately crafted modern dishes are served in the restaurant, with its flowers and summery yellow colour schemes. The well-spread list of around 90 bins offers quality across the range, with plenty of above-average drinking by the glass; regularly changing real ales on draught might include Ruddles Best and Wadworth 6X. Yattendon attracts its share of punters *en route* to Newbury Races, as well as sightseers heading for Basildon Park (National Trust). SAMPLE DISHES: smoked chicken, avocado and prawn salad £5.25; chargrilled Barnsley chop £9.25; summer pudding £4.25.

Open *all week 11am to 11pm; bar food 12 to 2 (2.30 Fri to Sun), 7 to 9.30 (10 Fri and Sat); restaurant Tue to Fri and Sun L 12 to 2, Mon to Sat D 7 to 10; closed 26 Dec and 1 Jan*

Details *Children welcome Car park Wheelchair access Background music Dogs welcome Access, Amex, Diners, Visa Accommodation: 5 rooms, B&B £75 to £90*

✿✿ indicates a pub serving food on a par with 'seriously good' restaurants, where the cooking achieves consistent quality.

YEALAND CONYERS Lancashire map 8

New Inn 🍇

40 Yealand Road, Yealand Conyers
TEL: (01524) 732938
off A6, 2m N of Carnforth

The old ivy-covered building reminded one couple of a double-fronted house rather than a pub, but its business is definitely the provision of food and drink. There's a cheerful intimacy about the place, tables are packed close together, and service is casual. Ian and Annette Dutton's earlier connections with John Tovey and Miller Howe are well known, but now they go their own way. On the bar menu you will find the classic Miller Howe-style cheese and herb pâté, hot nourishing soups, and, of course, famously gargantuan salads ('we managed one between us,' confessed one couple, 'and tipped the other into a greaseproof bag and enjoyed it immensely next day with cold chicken'). Local Waberthwaite ham comes in thick juicy slices, the meat of the day might be spicy Caribbean pork, while South African bobotie is a fixture. Desserts are extravagantly good: redcurrant and blackberry claret jelly 'that let you know there was claret in it', rice pudding with home-made jam or marmalade, even apple and Stilton farmhouse pie with clotted cream. More ambitious meals are served in the stylish beamed dining-room. Ian Dutton has put together an impressive list of around 60 wines that repays consideration. Otherwise, Hartley's Hatters Mild, Frederics and Robinson's ales are kept in good order. A two-mile trip will take you to Leighton Hall, home of the Gillow family of furniture-making fame. SAMPLE DISHES: vegetable soup with garlic croutons £2.25; beef in beer £5.50; cream toffee and walnut pie £3.

Open *11am to 11pm (11 to 3, 5.30 to 11 Mon to Fri end Aug to Easter); bar food 11 to 10; restaurant D only 6 to 10*
Details *Children welcome Car park Wheelchair access Garden No smoking in restaurant Background music Guide dogs only Access, Delta, Switch, Visa*

SCOTLAND

APPLECROSS Highland map 11

▲ *Applecross Inn*

Applecross TEL: (01520) 744262
off A896, 18m W of Loch Carron

The road to Applecross is Bealach na Ba – the highest mountain pass in Britain, rising to 2,054 feet in the space of six miles. It takes some degree of resolution to embark on such a journey, but birdwatchers, mountain bikers, fishing types and lovers of grand scenic vistas all make the trip. Their destination is, more often than not, Bernard and Judith Fish's congenial little inn. Atmosphere counts for a great deal here: visitors and locals all crowd together happily in the bar, and in summer the overspill is to the tables outside, where the views across the Sound of Raasay towards the Isle of Skye are spectacular. Turn to the west and you can see the Cairngorms; to the south there are views of Ben Nevis. The sea's harvest determines what the kitchen produces, and the bar menu is loaded with dishes conjured up from the local catch: squat lobsters appear as a 'cocktail', turn up in a curry and are served cooked in garlic butter. Added to that are oysters, queen scallops in a creamy wine and mushroom sauce, and grilled salmon served with salad and new potatoes. The carnivorous tendency is satisfied by burgers, steaks and chicken, while vegetarians might go for soup, macaroni cheese or meatless samosas with chilli dip. Desserts range from raspberry cranachan to home-baked apple crumble. Tables need to be booked for fixed-price dinners in the restaurant. Beer drinkers can sup Theakston or McEwan 80/-, whisky lovers have 50 brands to choose from, and there are 20 wines on the list. SAMPLE DISHES: garlic mushrooms £2.50; dressed local crab salad £7.50; hot chocolate fudge cake £2.

Open *summer all week 11am (12 Sun) to 11pm, winter Mon to Thur 11.30 to 2.30, Fri 11am to midnight, Sat 11am to 11.30pm, Sun 12 to 11; bar food Apr to Oct all week 12 to 9, Nov to Mar Sun to Fri 12 to 2.30, 5 to 9 (7 Sun), Sat 12 to 9; restaurant all week D only 6.30 to 8.45 (not Sun Nov to Mar); closed 1 Jan*
Details *Children welcome to 8.30pm Car park Wheelchair access (also WC) Garden and patio No smoking in restaurant Jukebox Dogs welcome Access, Visa Accommodation: 5 rooms, B&B £23 to £50*

If you visit any pubs that you think should appear in the Guide, *write to tell us* – The Which? Guide to Country Pubs, *FREEPOST, 2 Marylebone Road, London NW1 1YN.*

Use the maps and index at the back of the Guide *to plan your trip.*

ARDFERN **Argyll & Bute** **map 11**

▲ *Galley of Lorne*

Ardfern TEL: (01852) 500284
on B8002, reached from A816 N of Lochgilphead

Named after the galley that once cruised on the Firth of Lorn, this converted eighteenth-century drovers' inn is now a favourite with yachtsmen and lovers of the great outdoors. The views across Loch Craignish are a delight to behold. At the heart of the place is the Galley Bar, where visitors can enjoy a pint of Theakston Best Bitter or choose from the line-up of around 20 malt whiskies. Staples such as garlic mushrooms, steak pie, and bread-and-butter pudding are bolstered by more ambitious specials, with local seafood as the strong suit. At lunch-time you can also get ploughman's, baked potatoes and open sandwiches. A children's menu is available until 7.30 in the evening, while more formal restaurant menus take in anything from roast beef to monkfish provençale. A short list of youthful wines provides the back-up. SAMPLE DISHES: haggis, neeps and tatties £5; poached salmon with tomato and basil sauce £9.50; coconut cheesecake £3.

Open *11am to 1am, Sun noon to 1am; bar food and restaurant summer 12 to 2, 6.30 to 9.15 (8 Nov to Apr); restaurant closed Nov to Easter; pub closed 25 Dec*

Details *Children welcome in eating areas Car park Wheelchair access (also WC) Garden and patio Background and live music No dogs in eating areas Accommodation: 7 rooms, B&B £29 to £38*

ARDUAINE **Argyll & Bute** **map 11**

▲ *Loch Melfort Hotel*

Arduaine TEL: (01852) 200233
on A816, 4m SW of Kilmelford

Broad views over the Sound of Jura are one of the bonuses at this solid-looking hotel. Wood dominates the Chartroom Bar: wooden furniture, ceiling rafters, and panelled bar. A nautical theme runs throughout. The menu ranges from snacks and ploughman's through Aberdeen Angus steaks, and chicken breast with garlic and coriander, to puddings such as hot chocolate fudge cake. Seafood is, predictably, a strong point: oysters, North Atlantic prawns by the half-pint and pint, Islay scallops and lobster all feature. Daily specials are listed on a blackboard, and may include the likes of Loch Etive moules marinière. House wines are sold by the glass, and five half-bottles are among the 20-odd on the list. A set-price dinner menu, with supplements, operates in the restaurant. Arduaine Gardens (National Trust for Scotland), open all year, are next door. SAMPLE DISHES: grilled langoustines £9.50; venison sausages with caramelised onions £6; chocolate and ginger cream pie £2.50.

Open *all week 10am to 11pm; bar food 12 to 2.30, 6 to 9; restaurant all week D only 7.30 to 9; closed 4 Jan to end Feb*
Details *Children welcome in bar eating area Car park Wheelchair access Garden No smoking in restaurant Background music No dogs Access, Amex, Switch, Visa Accommodation: 26 rooms, B&B £35 to £99*

AUCHENCROW Borders map 11

▲ *Craw Inn*

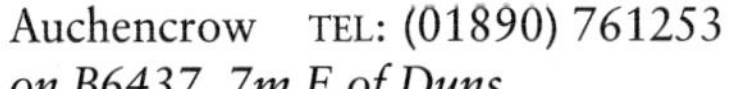

Auchencrow TEL: (01890) 761253
on B6437, 7m E of Duns

Landlady Kirsty Low seems to have made a dramatic impact on this diminutive village pub tucked away in a hamlet not far from the coast and the A1. Trade is brisk, she reports. Much of the interest, no doubt, centres on the food, which is now dominated by fish – some of it from local waters. Eyemouth contributes crabs and lobsters, and the menu also includes shrimps, jumbo prawns and langoustines. There's a distinct touch of ambition about dishes such as a trio of red mullet in fresh ginger, leeks and spring onions, or whole sea bass with garlic, herbs and olive oil; although herrings in oatmeal, fillets of lemon sole with beurre blanc, and coquilles St Jacques strike a more familiar note. Meat eaters have a fair choice, ranging from pork cutlets in apples, cream and cider, or roast duck with black cherry sauce, to Borders beef with Stilton sauce. Desserts also show some flair – chocolate calvados pots, or St Clements mousse, for example – and there are some smoked specimens on the cheeseboard. The list of real ales is better than average for a Scottish country pub, with names such as Broughton Greenmantle, Border Brewery Special and Old Kiln alongside Morland Old Speckled Hen on the handpumps. The short list of around 20 wines reads enticingly: choice is well considered, prices are very fair. SAMPLE DISHES: smoked salmon mousse £4; chicken breast in white wine, cream and mushroom sauce £8; dark chocolate terrine £3.

Open *11 to 2.30, 6 to 11, Sat 11am to 11.30pm, Sun 12.30 to 10; bar food and restaurant 12 to 2.15, 6 (7 winter) to 9*
Details *Children welcome in bar eating area Car park Wheelchair access (also WC) Garden and patio No-smoking area Live music Dogs welcome Access, Visa Accommodation: 7 rooms, B&B £25 to £30*

AUCHTERLESS **Aberdeenshire** **map 11**

Towie Tavern

Auchterless TEL: (01888) 511201
on A947, 4m S of Turriff

Castle spotters and tourists admiring the local sights should make the detour to this white pebble-dash cottagey pub if sustaining food and drink is required. The daily blackboard menus revolve around fresh supplies, and you can expect a strong showing of fish as well as seasonal game. Typical supper-time offerings in the winter months, for example, might include poached haddock in Dugléré sauce, whole lemon sole grilled with parsley butter, and pheasant casserole. Puddings could range from chocolate rum torte to honey and walnut tart, while the cheeseboard is 100 per cent Scottish. A slightly more expensive menu is served in the restaurant. Beer drinkers have a choice of Theakston Best Bitter or a guest ale, and whisky fans are admirably accommodated; there's also a list of 60 wines, with several from the New World. SAMPLE DISHES: deep-fried mushrooms stuffed with haggis £2.50; suprême of chicken with Arran mustard £8; toffee and banana crumble £3.

Open *Mon to Fri 11 to 2.30, 6 to 12, Sat 11am to midnight, Sun 12.30 to 11; bar food and restaurant 12 to 2, 6 to 9.30*
Details *Children welcome Car park Wheelchair access (also WC) Patio No smoking in restaurant Background music Dogs welcome Bar only Access, Visa*

BOWMORE **Argyll & Bute** **map 11**

▲ *Harbour Inn*

The Square, Bowmore, Isle of Islay TEL: (01496) 810330

Scott and Wendy Chance are making quite a name for themselves in this refurbished inn by the quayside. Drinkers crowd into the friendly bar, where bistro-style meals are served at lunch-time. Typical offerings from the menu might include local seafood in the form of stir-fried scallops with lemon sauce, and baked haddock fillet in parsley sauce; seasonal game such as potted Dunlossit pheasant with garlic and sage, or Jura venison in rich wine gravy topped with puff pastry also shows up well. These are backed up by dishes 'from the griddle', including Islay lamb cutlets, and langoustines in garlic and herb butter, and vegetarian options such as mushroom, celery and walnut strudel. Desserts take in the likes of flamed bananas in rum sauce with ice-cream, and steamed apple and toffee sponge with custard.

In the evening there's a full restaurant menu with an equally strong emphasis on local produce. MacEwan 60/- and 80/- are on draught, together with Younger Tartan Special and – as you might expect – the full range of Islay whiskies is on show. Note the long licensing hours; the pub also serves breakfast and morning coffee from 10 until noon. SAMPLE DISHES: twice-baked Islay cheese soufflé £3.75; honey roast pork loin with braised red cabbage £5.50; rich Drambuie cream with praline £2.

Open *all week 11am to 1am; bar food and restaurant Mon to Sat 12 to 2, 7 to 9*
Details *Children welcome lunch-time only Wheelchair access No music Dogs welcome Access, Switch, Visa Accommodation: 4 rooms, B&B £27 to £55*

BRIG O'TURK Stirling map 11

Byre Inn

Brig o'Turk TEL: (01877) 376292
on A821, between Callander and Aberfoyle

As its name suggests, this whitewashed stone building in attractive woodland was once a byre. For a pub/restaurant, it's on a minute scale, although the interior is relaxed and welcoming, with painted beams, gargoyle heads and pew-style seating. A wisp of smoke from the chimney is evidence of a welcoming fire in winter, while tables and chairs outside make a pleasant spot for eating and drinking in summer. The bar menu varies slightly between lunch and dinner, with salads, baked potatoes and sandwiches on the former, alongside starters of haggis, neeps and tatties, farmhouse pâté, and a home-made soup served with 'excellent' freshly baked soda bread. Haggis crops up again among main courses, this time with chicken and bacon in whisky and mustard sauce; otherwise there may be 'very good' steak pie, haddock deep-fried in beer batter, smoked fish pie, and pasta with mild blue cheese sauce. A short list of puddings might include spotted dick with custard. It may not seem possible in such a confined space, but there's also a separate restaurant open for dinner: expect more elaborate food and higher prices. Broughton Black Douglas and Special Bitter are on draught, and wines come by the glass. SAMPLE DISHES: onion soup £2.25; game casserole £6; bread-and-butter pudding £3.

Open *summer noon to midnight, winter 12 to 3, 6 to 11, Sun noon to midnight; bar food 12 (12.30 Sun) to 2.30, 6.30 to 9; restaurant D only 6.30 to 9*
Details *Children welcome Car park Wheelchair access (also WC) Garden No smoking in dining-room Background music No dogs Access, Delta, Switch, Visa*

CANONBIE Dumfries & Galloway map 11

▲ *Riverside Inn*

Canonbie TEL: (01387) 371295 and 371512
just off A47, 6m S of Langholm

Robert and Susan Phillips run this 'splendid' Borders hostelry with the kind of grace and good humour that is the accumulated experience of more than 20 years' innkeeping. She is restrained and efficient, he is jovial. From the outside, the building – by a river, of course – looks substantial, with its white walls, slate roof and the Union Jack fluttering from a flagpole. Inside it is bright and warm; converted sewing machines make up the tables and there are black irons and prints as decoration.

The kitchen's philosophy is disarmingly simple: search out seasonal and local produce, treat it with respect and cook it in ways that are suited to its natural character; also be prepared to change the menu twice daily. 'Keep faith with freshness' might be the motto. Soups set the tone: game broth, parsnip and apple, leek and potato. Grouse is potted, pheasant is made into a terrine, chops and steaks from Aberdeen Angus beef and Highland lamb are chargrilled. Fish of the day – anything from brill and skate to glorious queenies – are cooked in beer batter and served with 'damn fine' fat chips. Or you might encounter roast chunky cod with red onion and Cheddar crust, grilled ham and eggs, and assorted cold cuts with salads; a traditional cassoulet is one dish that doesn't speak immediately of Scotland. Puddings are in the same vein: damson crumble, toffee apple bake, blackberry and apple pie; otherwise, the home-made ice-creams are worth considering. Fixed-price three and five-course dinners are offered in the restaurant.

Real ales are also selected with care and an eye for what is true to the region: Yates and Deuchars IPA are regulars, but guests are many and varied; also note the range of bottled beers, which include everything from Caledonian Golden Promise to Fraoch Heather Ale. By contrast, the Phillipses look south – to Adnams – for their wine list: the result is a meticulously chosen slate with a strong French presence but a global outlook and hardly a dud in sight. SAMPLE DISHES: smoked trout pâté £4.75; beef hash with baked red cabbage £6; spiced bread pudding £3.

Open *11 to 2.30, 6.30 to 11; bar food and restaurant all week L 12 to 2, Mon to Sat D 7 to 9*

Details *Children welcome Car park Wheelchair access Garden No smoking in dining-room and 1 area of bar No music Dogs welcome by arrangement Access, Delta, Switch, Visa Accommodation: 7 rooms, B&B £55 to £85*

CLACHAN Argyll & Bute **map 11**

▲ *Tigh an Truish Hotel*

Clachan Bridge, Isle of Seil TEL: (01852) 300242
on B844, 12m S of Oban

This eighteenth-century whitewashed stone pub stands beside the dramatically arched Atlantic Bridge and – curiously – has its own petrol station. A reporter explains the procedure: 'When somebody wants petrol, a bell rings in the bar and the barmaid goes out to serve, and comes back to pull pints.' The atmosphere is chatty, the pace is leisurely. There are two boards in the genuine old wooden bar: one for darts, the other advertising the day's menu. The kitchen makes a brave attempt to produce down-to-earth home-cooking, and fish is a major theme – it might be anything from locally smoked salmon or locally caught prawns to seafood pie or even squat lobster curry. Elsewhere, expect things like game pie, spicy bean casserole, and pork chop with grain mustard sauce. Soup comes in half-pint mugs, while desserts could include the bizarre-sounding chocolate puddle pudding with Mars Bar sauce, or ice-cream laced with malt whisky. McEwan's 80/- and a guest ale are on draught, and there's also a short wine list. SAMPLE DISHES: sweet pickled herring and salad £2.75; steak and ale pie £6.50; rhubarb crumble £2.

Open *summer 11am to 11.30pm, winter 11 to 2.30, 5 to 11.30; bar food 12 (12.30 Sun) to 2.15, 6 to 8.30; no D Nov to Mar, limited L Nov to Apr*
Details *Children welcome in dining-room Car park Wheelchair access Garden Background music Dogs welcome No cards Accommodation: 2 rooms, B&B £40*

COLONSAY Argyll & Bute **map 11**

▲ *Isle of Colonsay Hotel* 🍇

Colonsay TEL: (01951) 200316
2 hrs 15 mins by ferry from Oban

Kevin and Christa Byrne's 250-year-old hotel is a lifeline for the tiny local community and a godsend for visitors to this most remote outpost of the Hebrides. The weather forecast is faxed through every morning, the local phone box is in the car park, and the hotel also has its own bookshop specialising in local tomes, as well as an off-licence. You can even hire a bike or arrange a cruise or fishing trip during your stay. Bar lunches could not be simpler: bowls of home-made soup, filled baguettes, steamed Colonsay mussels, perhaps jumbo prawns with home-made brown bread, or tuna and pasta salad, with a dessert such as chocolate roulade to finish. In low season the menu is pared down to the bare essentials.

Suppers are a touch more ambitious: venison in red wine, duckling à l'orange, not to mention fish and chips. Tables must be booked for fixed-price evening meals in the restaurant. The location means that real ale is not a realistic option, but bottles and keg beers are on offer, and the shelves of island malt whiskies are a great tempter. Otherwise dip into the lengthy list of around 100 wines. Adjoining the hotel is Virago's – a restaurant and craftshop providing light meals all day. The island is a wildlife enthusiast's paradise: almost 200 species from the British bird list, over 400 species of flora, not to mention feral goats, otters and colonies of grey seals. As the brochure points out, 'In a day's walk you can see cliffs and moorland, sandy beaches and lily-filled lochs, rhododendron woods, cultivated land and hill.' Natural diversity rules. SAMPLE DISHES: pâté £2.75; salmon and asparagus sauce £8; Alabama chocolate fudge cake £2.50.

Open *11 to 2.30, 6 to 11, Sun 12 to 2.30, 6.30 to 11; bar food 12.30 to 1.30, 7 to 8.30 (no D Nov to Feb); restaurant all week, D only 7.30 (1 sitting)* **Details** *Children welcome in bar eating area Car park Wheelchair access Garden No smoking in hotel restaurant No music No dogs Access, Amex, Delta, Diners, Switch, Visa Accommodation: 11 rooms, B&B £40 to £100*

COMRIE Perthshire & Kinross **map 11**

Deil's Cauldron 

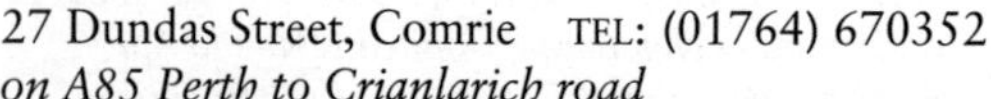

27 Dundas Street, Comrie TEL: (01764) 670352
on A85 Perth to Crianlarich road

Named after a nearby waterfall that you can reach by walking through beautiful beech and pine forests, the Deil's Cauldron stands at the edge of Comrie at the entrance to Glen Lednock. This is not a pub for 'the hearty boozer or adventurous foodie' (at least at lunchtime), but the atmosphere is delightful and the cooking is sound. In the low-ceilinged, stone-walled bar you can enjoy food from a sensibly short lunch menu with a noticeable Scottish flavour. 'Their haggis would convert the most timid Sassenach,' noted one reporter – especially as it comes with 'sweet and smooth' bashed neeps and 'chappit tatties'. Soups, such as hearty golden pea, are 'of a consistently high standard', and apple pie is likely to evoke fond childhood memories. In between is a straightforward selection of 'Lunches': the Gamekeeper's is a casserole with fresh vegetables, while the Trawlerman's brings in West Coast langoustines with herb and cream sauce. In the evening a few more elaborate offerings appear in the shape of chargrilled scallops with sesame dressing, Aberdeen Angus steaks, and fillet of venison with honey and gin sauce. Belhaven Best and Export are on draught, and the catholic list of 28 wines includes Californian house wines by the glass. Not far away are Drummond Castle Gardens, Lord Melville's Monument and the

Tartan Museum. SAMPLE DISHES: pâté with Cumberland sauce and oatcakes £3.75; fillet of herring in oatmeal with cider and apple sauce £5.50; steamed ginger pudding £2.50.

Open *Mon and Wed to Sat 11 to 2.30, 6 to 11, Sun 12.30 to 2.30, 7 to 11; bar food Wed to Mon 12 to 2, 6.30 to 8.30*
Details *Children welcome in bar eating area Garden No smoking in 1 dining-room No music No dogs Access, Delta, Switch, Visa*

CROMARTY Highland map 11

▲ *Royal Hotel*

SEASIDE

Marine Terrace TEL: (01381) 600217
from Inverness cross Kessock Bridge, follow signs for Cromarty for approx 17m

The chance to see an inhabitant of Scotland's only dolphin colony is reason enough to stop at the Royal, which is in a splendid location by the jetty on the edge of Cromarty Firth. The town is steeped in history, and the hotel pays homage with very early photographs of locals-made-good and ancient sites. Although ownership of the Royal changed in 1995, Scottish fare is still predominant on the printed bar menu, which features dishes such as mussels Albert (named after a local who supervises the gathering of these molluscs), venison in a whisky and cream sauce, and wild salmon. A daily specials board lists up to four extra dishes in each course: these might include ceps with garlic and cream, or grilled haddock and mushrooms, and a choice from this board is the best option, according to one reporter. A full menu is available in the dining-room. Beers include Belhaven Best and Theakston XB. House wine is sold by the glass. The beach is across the road, and there's plenty of scope for walking and bird-watching. SAMPLE DISHES: deep-fried haggis with Drambuie sauce £4; lamb cutlets Cromarty with honey, lemon and herbs £8.25; apple pie and cream £2.75.

Open *11 to 11, Sun 12.30 to 11; bar food 12 to 2 (2.30 Sat and Sun), 5.30 to 9 (9.30 Fri and Sat); restaurant 12 to 2, 5.30 to 8.30*
Details *Children welcome in eating areas Car park Wheelchair access (also WC) Patio No-smoking area Background music and jukebox Dogs welcome Amex, Visa Accommodation: 10 rooms, B&B £32 to £60*

Food mentioned in the main entries is available in the bar, although it may be possible to eat in a dining-room.

If a pub has a special point of interest, this is indicated by a 'flashed' word or phrase at the top right of the entry.

DRYMEN **Stirling** **map 11**

Clachan Inn

2 Main Street, Drymen TEL: (01360) 660824
off A811, 20m W of Stirling

Derek George and Elizabeth Plank have been running this historic village pub for more than 15 years and still maintain it as a genuine traditional hostelry. The building was first licensed in 1734, making it one of the oldest watering-holes north of the border. The bar menu is an assortment of unshowy dishes along the lines of lamb hotpot, seafood pasta, and trifle, with the occasional Scottish flourish for good measure. A decent line-up of real ales is thoroughly in keeping with the style of the place: expect such names as Belhaven Best, St Andrew's 80/- and Deuchars Pale Ale on the handpumps. Those wanting to explore the area could set their sights on Buchanan Forest. SAMPLE DISHES: haggis with oatcakes £3; half roast chicken £4.50; hot fudge sundae £2.50.

Open *all week 11am to midnight; bar food 12 to 4, 6 to 10*
Details *Children welcome in bar eating area Wheelchair access (also WC) Background music Dogs on leads welcome in bar only Access, Switch, Visa*

DYSART **Fife** **map 11**

Old Rectory

West Quality Street, Dysart TEL: (01592) 651211
off A955 Methil road, N of Kirkaldy

This cosy, low-beamed old pub near the tiny harbour has a collection of cigar-boxes, a stove giving real heat, sturdy, comfortable chairs and well-polished tables. 'The whole atmosphere was of friendliness and real efficiency,' commented one reporter, who tucked into a lunch of smooth chicken liver pâté, followed by a 'superb piece' of smoked ham shank with sauerkraut and sauté potatoes. The lunchtime menu is strong on starters, including potted beef, soused herrings, and deep-fried Camembert with gooseberry sauce; there's also a cold buffet, and hot dishes such as venison and mushroom casserole. Evenings see a change of emphasis: soups (including vegetable mulligatawny and prawn bisque), pasta, steaks, and chicken, ham and mushroom vol-au-vent, for example. Sticky toffee pudding is a perennially popular dessert, as are fruit pavlovas. A full à la carte menu is available in the separate restaurant. McEwan 80/- is on draught, and about five wines are sold by the glass, with around forty on the full list. The National Trust for Scotland has restored a row of fishermen's cottages in the village. SAMPLE DISHES: smoked mackerel mousse £1.75; poached salmon with mushrooms, grapes and prawn sauce £8.75; treacle sponge pudding with ginger sauce £2.50.

Open *Tue to Sat 11 to 12, Sun 12 to 2.30; bar food and restaurant Tue to Sat L 12 to 2, D 7 to 9.30, Sun L only 12.30 to 2.30*
Details *Children welcome in eating areas Car park Wheelchair access (also WC) Garden No music Guide dogs only Access, Amex, Visa*

EAGLESFIELD Dumfries & Galloway map 11

▲ *Courtyard*

Eaglesfield TEL: (01461) 500215
off A74, 3m E of Ecclefechan

Eaglesfield is essentially no more than a row of houses, but nearby tourist attractions include Gretna Green and Ecclefechan, birthplace of essayist and historian Thomas Carlyle. The Courtyard is relaxed and welcoming, with a front bar where you can have just a drink, and a room beyond for bar meals; another door leads to the separate restaurant, which has its own set-price menu. The bar menu offers plenty of choice: start with a soup – carrot and orange, perhaps – or pear with walnuts and tarragon dressing, and go on to grilled fillets of salmon in oatmeal with chive and lemon butter, pork fillet with grain mustard sauce, or sirloin steak, and finish with an ice-cream or one of the home-made puddings. McEwan 60/- and 70/- and Theakston Best are on draught; house wines are sold by the glass, and prices on the full list of predominantly New World wines are very reasonable. SAMPLE DISHES: twice-baked cheese soufflé with piquant sauce £2.75; baked cod with cheese and mustard topping £7; chocolate and Tia Maria pot £2.

Open *Tue to Sun 12 to 11; bar food and restaurant Tue to Sun 12 (12.30 Sun) to 2, 7 to 9*
Details *Children welcome Car park Wheelchair access (also WC) Patio No smoking in restaurant Background music Dogs welcome Access, Delta, Switch, Visa Accommodation: 3 rooms, B&B £20 to £34*

EDDLESTON Borders **map 11**

Horseshoe Inn

Eddleston TEL: (01721) 730225
on A703, 4m N of Peebles

The Horseshoe Inn, a low, whitewashed building, is described by the proprietors as a bar and bistro, although the anvils and horseshoes round the fireplace give the impression of an old blacksmith's forge. The bar area is small, but there are two spacious, well-furnished rooms for eaters and drinkers. 'The whole place felt right,' commented one reporter; 'clean, airy and stimulating the gastric juices.' A précis of the longish menu appears on blackboards, which also list the daily specials. On offer may be chicken wings with a rich, spicy sauce, spaghetti napolitaine, chicken bonne femme, baked plaice with asparagus sauce, and puddings like Bakewell tart and lemon cheesecake. Bar meals are served throughout the day on Sunday. Broughton Best and Greenmantle Ale are on draught, and blackboards display wines by the glass (the full list in the separate restaurant groups wines by grape variety rather than country of origin). Eddleston is a tiny, 'completely rural' village, perfectly placed for visits to the houses and castles of the Borders. SAMPLE DISHES: tomato soup £2; lamb osso buco £5.25; strawberry sponge £2.75.

Open *12 to 3, 6 to 12, Sun 12.30 to 12; bar food and restaurant Mon to Sat 12.30 to 2.30, 6 to 9.30, Sun 12.30 to 9.30*
Details *Children welcome Car park Wheelchair access Patio No-smoking area Background music Dogs welcome Access, Amex, Diners, Switch, Visa*

ELIE Fife **map 11**

Ship Inn

The Toft, Elie TEL: (01333) 330246
on A917, 5m W of Anstruther

Cricket and rugby matches on the sandy beach, summertime barbecues, and even an international jazz and beer festival are some of the attractions dreamed up by get-up-and-go licensees Richard and Jill Phillip. Their popular free house overlooking Elie Bay is a great place for families, and children are well catered for. The building has been a hostelry since 1838 and now has three dining-areas as well as an outdoor bar and beer garden. The printed menu – which is served throughout the pub – takes in things like grilled boneless kippers, tuna and peach salad, seafood crêpes, and steak with various sauces, followed by desserts ranging from banoffi pie to lemon pavlova meringue. Back-up is provided by daily specials. Belhaven Best and 80/- are on handpump, along with Theakston Best Bitter, and the wine list is dependable. Elie is close to one of the finest water sports centres in Scotland, as well as other attractions, such as Lady Anstruther's Bathing Tower and Deep Sea World. SAMPLE DISHES: sweet herring salad £4; spicy fried chicken with tomato sauce £6.25; fresh fruit salad £3.

Open *11am to midnight (11 winter), Sun 12.30 to 11; bar food and restaurant 12 to 2.30 (3 Sun), 6 to 9 (summer 9.30); closed 25 Dec*
Details *Children welcome in eating areas Wheelchair access (also WC) Garden and patio No music Dogs welcome Access, Delta, Switch, Visa*

GLENDEVON Perthshire & Kinross map 11

▲ *Tormaukin Hotel*

Glendevon TEL: (01259) 781252
on A823, 6m SE of Auchterarder

The Tormaukin is within an hour's drive of over 100 golf courses, with Gleneagles just ten minutes away. Not everyone who comes here is a golfer; the clientele ranges from locals to hunters, hill-walkers and tourists. The low, white-painted hotel framed by trees is a former drovers' inn, and in those days sheep markets were held in the surrounding fields. The bars are comfortable and cosy, with low-beamed ceilings, red patterned carpet, bare stone walls housing open log-burning fires, and cushion-seated wooden chairs around wooden tables. The bar menu reflects some foreign influences – feta cheese marinated with basil and garlic, hot-and-sour prawns, chicken, ham and asparagus crêpe, and sweet-and-sour pork – but its emphasis remains firmly in Scotland: Arbroath smokie pâté, east coast haddock, fillet steak with haggis and whisky sauce, and collops of venison are typical. Vegetarian dishes are listed separately, and children have their own section on the menu. Desserts range from banoffi cheesecake, and sticky gingerbread pudding, to strawberry and peach mousse, and fruit salad. Local Harviestoun 80/- and Ptarmigan, and Ind Coope Burton Ale are on draught, and house wines are sold by the glass. SAMPLE DISHES: mini smoked haddock fish-cakes £4; cassoulet of Highland game £8.25; squidgy cinnamon meringue with raspberries £3.25.

Open *11 to 11, Sun 12 to 11; bar food 12 to 2, 5.30 to 9.30, Sun 12 to 9.30; restaurant 6.30 to 9.30; closed 25 Dec and 10 days Jan*
Details *Children welcome in dining-room Car park Wheelchair access (also WC) Patio Background and live music No dogs Access, Amex, Delta, Switch, Visa Accommodation: 10 rooms, B&B £30 to £49*

GLENELG Highland map 11

▲ *Glenelg Inn*

Glenelg, by Kyle of Lochalsh TEL: (01599) 522273
on mainland at head of Sound of Sleat, off A87 at Loch Duich

Follow the single track road through the hills of Wester Ross to reach this remote inn overlooking the Isle of Skye. Once you are there, the first impression is of a welcoming bar with a huge blazing log fire. Folk musicians and singers often perform in the Glenelg Bar where the spirit of the ceilidh lives on. Sustenance comes in the shape of leek and tattie soup, locally smoked salmon, herrings in oatmeal, fresh salmon stuffed with pepper mousse, chicken, leek and mushroom pie, and assorted 'hoagies'. To finish, there are desserts such as chocolate bavarois and cheesecake; alternatively, you can have scones and shortbread with a pot of tea. In the evening, bar food is restricted to main courses (all at the same price); otherwise a fixed-price menu is available in the restaurant. No real ales are served, but there are plenty of whiskies (some cask strength) and a short, reasonably priced wine list to consider. Boat trips can be arranged for guests wanting to explore the local scenery. Sandaig, the setting for of Gavin Maxwell's *Ring of Bright Water*, is nearby. SAMPLE DISHES: lentil and bacon soup £1.50; seafood cassolette £5; bitter chocolate terrine with coffee bean sauce £2.

Open *Mon to Sat 12 to 2.30, 5 to 11 (Sun residents only); bar food Mon to Sat 12.30 to 2, 8 to 9; restaurant Sun 12.30 to 2, all week 7.30 to 9*
Details *Children welcome in bar eating area Car park Wheelchair access (also WC) Garden and patio No smoking in restaurant Background and live music Dogs welcome on a lead Accommodation: 6 rooms, B&B £28 to £80*

GLENFARG Perthshire & Kinross map 11

▲ *Bein Inn*

Glenfarg TEL: (01577) 830216
on A90 Perth to Kinross road, 8m S of Perth

This one-time drovers' inn by the roadside stands on its own in a delightful glen. The setting attracts, as does the comfortably furnished bar. A few traditional pub dishes, such as breaded haddock, gammon steak, and roast chicken, show up on the bar menu, but Italy steals the show. All kinds of pizzas and pastas are backed up by tuna salad, fungi ripieni (mushrooms stuffed with pâté, served in garlic and red wine sauce), sirloin steak pizzaiola, chicken cacciatora, and so on. Sweets are mostly based around ice-creams and liqueurs. A full evening *carte* dominated by seafood and steaks is served in the restaurant. Belhaven Sandy Hunter's is on handpump, house wine is served by the glass, and the full list runs to 40 bins. Glenfarg is well placed for a trip to Perth, St Andrews or Edinburgh. SAMPLE DISHES: devilled whitebait £3.25; beef Stroganov £9; vanilla ice-cream with warm white chocolate in Tia Maria cream £3.

Open *summer 11am to 11pm, winter 11 (12 Sun) to 2.30, 5 (6 Sun) to 9.30; bar food 12 to 2, 5 to 9; restaurant D only 7 to 9*
Details *Children welcome in bar eating area Car park Garden and patio Background music No dogs Access, Switch, Visa Accommodation: 13 rooms, B&B £32 to £76*

HADDINGTON East Lothian map 11

Waterside

1–5 Nungate, Waterside, Haddington TEL: (01620) 825674
off A1, 16m E of Edinburgh

'A fantastic location as the evening sun sets over the ancient churchyard opposite, and the swans swim close to the river bank,' is how one reporter lyrically describes the scene outside this convivial, child-friendly establishment. The place has bistro overtones, but there's no mistaking its pub roots. A good selection of regularly changing real ales is served in the long, low-ceilinged bar: Belhaven and Deuchars IPA might be supplemented by, say, Adnams Broadside and Mitchells Lancaster Bomber. 'The menu is a model of late-'70s and -'80s style,' noted one visitor, no doubt referring to dishes such as deep-fried Brie with redcurrant jelly, devilled whitebait, salmon in puff pastry, and pork fillet with smoked cheese and whisky sauce. Old favourites such as beef and Guinness pie, and haddock in beer batter, have been well received. Upstairs is a silver-service restaurant. The long wine list embraces everything from 'quite pleasant' house wines to champagne. SAMPLE DISHES: cream of Stilton soup £2.25; chicken with pepper sauce £7; lemon soufflé £2.75.

Open *11.30 to 2.30, 5 to 11, Sun 12.30 to 11; bar food 11.30 to 2, 5.30 to 10; restaurant 12 to 2, 6.30 to 10*
Details *Children welcome Car park Wheelchair access (also WC) Garden and patio No smoking in 1 room Background music No dogs Access, Amex, Delta, Diners, Switch, Visa*

After the main section of the Guide *is the 'Out and about' section listing additional pubs that are well worth a visit. Reports on these entries are most welcome.*

indicates a pub serving exceptional draught beers.

INNERLEITHEN **Borders** **map 11**

▲ *Traquair Arms*

HOME BREW

Traquair Road, Innerleithen TEL: (01896) 830229
off A72, 6m SE of Peebles

Traquair Bear Ale is brewed less than 100 yards from this splendid-looking stone-built inn at the gateway to the Borders. Visitors can sample the stuff in the stylishly comfortable bar, along with Broughton Greenmantle and bottles of Traquair House and Jacobite Ale. Beer aside, there's also plenty to tease the palate on the bar menu: hot-smoked Teviot salmon is served with tarragon mayonnaise, chicken is baked Basque-style with spiced risotto, olives and orange, while venison sausages are casseroled in red wine with mushrooms, garlic and redcurrant jelly. Local lamb cutlets and Aberdeen Angus steaks are grilled, and vegetarians are offered a fair choice, from oat and bulgar loaf to stir-fried noodles flavoured with soy, honey and spices. Desserts range from bread-and-butter pudding to cold confections. A slightly more ambitious repertoire is offered in the dining-room. Around 20 wines are bolstered by a good showing of halves; also look for the Scottish silver birch and fruit wines. Nearby Traquair House with its historic Bear Gates is worth a look, and the pub makes a good staging point for a trek along the Southern Upland Way. SAMPLE DISHES: spinach and filo parcel £3; braised lamb with tomatoes £5.25; steamed ginger and apple pudding £2.25.

Open *11 to 12; bar food all week 12 to 9; restaurant all week D only 7 to 9*
Details *Children welcome Car park Wheelchair access Garden and patio Live music Dogs welcome No cards Accommodation: 10 rooms, B&B £38 to £64*

KILBERRY **Argyll & Bute** **map 11**

▲ *Kilberry Inn*

Kilberry, by Tarbert TEL: (01880) 770223
on B8024, between Lochgilphead and Tarbert

The Kilberry Inn isn't the sort of pub you come upon by chance: to reach it you need plenty of time and a good map. The white-painted crofter's cottage with the red roof is halfway round the single-track coast road – a winding 16-mile drive that provides some of the most breathtaking scenery in Scotland. Yorkshire-born Kath and John Leadbeater run the place almost as a restaurant-with-rooms, which is just as well given the remote location. John serves and keep things moving out front, while Kath holds sway in the kitchen. Her cooking is in the domestic country tradition, but it's done with a highly personal touch. She is also very enterprising: breads (including an unusual garlic version), cakes and shortbread are always on the go, jars of home-made chutney and marmalade line the shelves. As for the meals, soups, mousses and pâtés kick things off, followed by a constantly changing list of dishes, including venison in red wine, beef cooked in Theakston Old Peculier Ale, and Kath's renowned country sausage pie, which consists of layers of sausage, stuffing and apple. As a finale, there's a remarkable range of cheesecakes, plus apple pie, and banana and toffee shortcake. No real ale is stocked (the place is too far out of the way), but you can dip into bottled beers such as Old Jock and Greenmantle Ale (both from the Broughton brewery) and Oatmeal Stout (King & Barnes); malt whiskies and a decent assortment of wines provide suitable alternatives. SAMPLE DISHES: port and Stilton pâté £4.25; salmon fish pie £9; hot chocolate fudge pudding £3.75.

Open *11 to 2, 5 to 11; bar food Mon to Sat 12.15 to 2, 6.30 to 8.30; closed mid-March to Easter*
Details *Children welcome in dining-room and family room Car park No smoking in family room No music Guide dogs only Access, Switch, Visa Accommodation: 2 rooms, B&B £37 to £63*

KILMAHOG **Stirling** **map 11**

Lade Inn

Trossachs Road, Kilmahog TEL: (01877) 330152
on A281 at junction with A84, 1m N of Callander

'Kilmahog is not really a place,' noted one traveller, 'just a couple of houses, a woollen mill and the pub.' The building looks 'wonderful' from the outside when it is clad in snow, while the interior is clean and bright, with pine panelling, an open fire and photographs of the pub (with and without winter whiteness) dotted around. A few Scottish gestures show up on the bar menu: haggis is served with neeps and tatties or deep-fried with whisky and grain-mustard sauce; herrings are marinated in tomatoes and Madeira; whole trout is accompanied by lime butter. Otherwise the kitchen looks further afield for tortellini with garlic and thyme sauce, chicken curry, or Lancashire hotpot. Sandwiches and jacket potatoes are also available at lunch-time, while desserts include a few old stalwarts like bread-and-butter pudding. Full evening meals are also available in the restaurant. Real ale from up-and-coming Scottish breweries is patriotically supported here: Broughton Greenmantle and Black Douglas and Orkney Red MacGregor are bolstered by a couple of guest brews such as Magic Mushroom Mild and Old Isaak. The wine list is a reasonable slate, with own-label house wines by the glass. SAMPLE DISHES: chicken liver pâté with cranberry sauce and oatcakes £3; smoked fish pie £6; treacle sponge and custard £3.

Open *11am to 11pm, Sun 12.30 to 11; bar food 12 to 2.20, 5.30 to 9.15; Sun 12.30 to 3.30, 5.30 to 9.15; restaurant D only 7 to 9.15; closed 1 Jan*
Details *Children welcome in bar eating area Car park Wheelchair access (also WC) Garden No-smoking area Background and live music Dogs welcome Access, Switch, Visa*

KILMELFORD **Argyll & Bute** **map 11**

▲ *Cuilfail Hotel*

Kilmelford TEL: (01852) 200274
on A816 at head of Loch Melfort, 12m S of Oban

Handily placed *en route* to Oban and the ferries to the Scottish isles, this substantial stone-built inn is very much the focal point of Kilmelford. Landlord David Birrell prides himself on using the best and freshest local produce and changes his menu each day to take account of supplies. Up to six kinds of seafood are generally advertised and the menu boasts, 'It's always Kilmelford Salmon Festival.' Starters include some intriguing ideas such as potted rib of Scotch beef, and warm black pudding salad with peach vinaigrette, while main courses centre on home-made pies, breast of chicken cooked every which way, steaks and grills, plus options for vegetarians. Sticky toffee pudding is a fixture: 'There would be a riot if we did not have this on the menu,' admits Mr Birrell. McEwan's 80/- and Younger No. 3 Ale are on handpump, and a few wines complete the picture. SAMPLE DISHES: 'Cuilfail' Cullen skink £2.50; salmon pie £6.50; upside-down fruit pudding with Carolina fudge sauce £3.

Open *12 to 3, 6 to 11 (summer 11.30 to 11.30); bar food 12 to 2.30, 6.30 to 9.30*
Details *Children welcome Car park Wheelchair access Garden Background music Dogs welcome Access, Amex, Delta, Switch, Visa Accommodation: 14 rooms, B&B £25 to £70*

KINNESSWOOD Perthshire & Kinross map 11

▲ *Lomond Country Inn*

Kinnesswood TEL: (01592) 840253
on A911, 4m SE of Milnathort

On the slopes of the Lomond Hills with panoramic vistas of Loch Leven beyond, this two-hundred-year-old country inn is a favourite with wildlife buffs and ornithologists. Vane Farm Nature Reserve attracts wildfowl and other birds by the thousand (the site is equipped with observation rooms holding powerful telescopes), while anglers have over a dozen stillwater fisheries to choose from. Needless to say, this is also great walking country. In summer you can also take a boat across the water to Leven Castle – prison home of Mary Queen of Scots. After a dose of fresh air, the log fires that often burn in the bar are more than welcome. The menu offers plenty of variety in the shape of Cullen skink, East Neuk seafood pancake, steak pie, and spicy minced lamb with tomatoes and peppers, followed by, say, raspberry cranachan, or crème brûlée laced with Grand Marnier. A full *carte*, plus a Scottish menu, are served in the restaurant. The bar is open throughout the day for the provision of draught beers, including Jennings Bitter, Bass, and a guest ale such as Harviestoun 70/-; there's also a well-spread list of around four dozen wines at realistic prices. SAMPLE DISHES: chicken liver pâté with Cumberland sauce £3.50; tagliatelle with smoked salmon and prawns £4.75; summer pudding with raspberry coulis £2.50.

Open *all week 11am to 11pm; bar food and restaurant weekdays 12 to 2.30, 6 to 9, Sat and Sun 12 to 9*
Details *Children welcome Car park Wheelchair access (also WC) No-smoking area in bar; no smoking in dining-room No music Dogs welcome in bar only Access, Amex, Delta, Diners, Switch, Visa Accommodation: 12 rooms, B&B £37 to £60*

KIPPEN Stirling map 11

▲ *Cross Keys*

Main Street, Kippen TEL: (01786) 870293
on B822, 10m W of Stirling

Established in 1703 and still going strong, the Cross Keys is every inch the family-run village inn. Angus and Sandra Watt manage to keep things ticking over nicely and have a welcoming approach to families. The kitchen stays with what it knows and does best, and the bar menu is neatly tailored for all tastes and appetites (a note says that small portions are available for senior citizens and children). 'Humble haddie pancakes', and sweetcorn fritters with chilli dip are typical starters, while main courses could include lasagne, beefburgers, chicken breast with lemon and tarragon sauce, or poached salmon with ginger and lime sauce. Omelettes, pasta and quiche are offered for vegetarians. Desserts always feature a few things that are home-made, such as cloutie dumpling and apple pie with cinnamon. Formal evening meals are served in the Vine Restaurant (named after the world famous Kippen Vine – 'the largest vine in the world under glass' until its demise in 1964). Broughton Greenmantle and Younger 70/- are on draught, and the varied wine list has four house wines by the glass. SAMPLE DISHES: bramble and port liver pâté £2.50; Kashmiri-style chicken korma with rice £5.75; fresh fruit sorbet £2.50.

Open *all week 12 (12.30 Sun) to 2.30, 5.30 to 11.30; bar food Sun to Fri L 12 (12.30 Sun) to 2, all week D 5.30 to 9.30; restaurant all week D only 7 to 8.45; closed 1 Jan*

Details *Children welcome in dining-room and family room Car park Wheelchair access Garden No smoking in family room Jukebox Dogs welcome Access, Switch, Visa Accommodation: 3 rooms, B&B £20 to £39*

KYLESKU Highland map 11

▲ *Kylesku Hotel*

Kylesku TEL: (01971) 502231

on A894, at S side of old ferry crossing, by new bridge linking Ullapool and Kylkestrome

Locally caught fish and shellfish are the strong suit on the menu of the busy, popular bar at this unassuming, informal hotel: mussels in garlic and lobster sauce, Lochinver haddock with chips, home-smoked salmon with salad, and grilled langoustines all feature. Meat options may include venison terrine, roast chicken, and steak, while puddings run to the likes of apple pie and apricot tart. No real ales are served, but the bar stocks a wide selection of malt whiskies, and the wine list is long, with some top-quality clarets. The restaurant, open for dinner, 'has one of the great views in Scotland': the hotel is in a superb location, looking up a loch to mountains, with waves lapping the jetty outside. For birdwatchers and walkers, this must be paradise; for the less energetic, boat-trips can be arranged to Eas Coul Aulin, Britain's highest waterfall. SAMPLE DISHES: chicken liver parfait £3.25; grilled monkfish with lobster sauce £6.75; banoffi pie £2.50.

Open *10am to 11pm; bar food 12 to 2.30, 6 to 9.30; snacks 2.30 to 5.30; restaurant all week D 7 to 8.30, L bookings only*

Details *Children welcome Car park Garden and patio No smoking in restaurant Background music Dogs welcome Access, Visa Accommodation: 8 rooms, B&B £25 to £55*

LIMEKILNS **Fife** **map 11**

Ship Inn

Halketts Hall, Limekilns TEL: (01383) 872247
on N bank of Firth of Forth, 3m W of Inverkeithing

Seats outside this white-harled, four-square building on the Firth of Forth look over the waters to the fine parklands of Hopetoun House and the House of the Binns on the opposite bank, with a grand view of the Forth bridges downstream. The interior has a strong nautical theme, with ships' wheels, scuttles and lifebelts; there are also pictures of ships and rugby players. Good value is the hallmark of the unpretentious menu, and the repertoire is pretty much standard pub fare. A tiny blackboard proclaims the soup of the day, and the kitchen produces dishes along the lines of fisherman's pie, vegetable curry, and old favourites like steak and ale pie, chilli, and traditional roast beef. Rolls and ploughman's are also served, and a short list of puddings includes an apple and cinnamon pastry. The pub's own Ship Inn Heavy, plus Orkney Dark Island, Belhaven 80/- and St Andrew's are among the real ales on draught, and wines are on sale by the glass. Service is described as 'quick, smiling and obliging'. SAMPLE DISHES: lobster bisque £2; chicken balti £4.50; sticky toffee pudding £1.50.

Open *Mon to Wed 11am to 11pm, Thur to Sun 11am to midnight; bar food L only 12 to 2 (2.30 Sat and Sun)*
Details *Children welcome Wheelchair access (also WC) Garden No-smoking area Background and live music Dogs welcome No cards*

LOCH CLUANIE **Highland** **map 11**

▲ *Cluanie Inn*

Loch Cluanie, Glen Moriston TEL: (01320) 340238
on A87, between Loch Ness and Skye ferry, at W end of Loch Cluanie

The 'nearest neighbour is two miles away', according to the staff of this seriously out-of-the-way inn. 'Remote' is an understatement, but that is precisely the appeal of the place – particularly for those who relish walking and climbing. If refuelling is required, the kitchen can deliver heartwarming Highland stuff, including such things as haggis with neeps and tatties, Angus mince with tatties, venison casserole, and the like, along with fruit crumbles and fudge cake to finish. A separate menu is served in the restaurant. The pub's location means that deliveries of real ale are out of the question, but drinkers can settle for kegs, bottled beers, or a dram or two of whisky. SAMPLE

DISHES: vegetable soup £2; steak and ale pie £6.50; apple and raisin crumble £3.

Open *11am to 11pm, Sun 12 to 11; bar food and restaurant 12 to 2.30, 6 to 8.30*
Details *Children welcome Car park Wheelchair access (also WC) Garden and patio Background music Dogs welcome Access, Visa Accommodation: 13 rooms, B&B £30 to £77*

MELROSE Borders map 11

▲ *Burts Hotel* 🍇

The Square, Melrose TEL: (01896) 822285
on A6091, midway between Galashiels and St Boswells

Deep in the heart of the Borders, almost within the shadow of the Eidon hills, this 250-year-old inn is a long-standing asset to the community. It puts on an affluent face. Bar lunches have an international flavour: Scotch beef is cooked rare and served cold with salad, home-smoked chicken is flavoured with curry mayonnaise, while sauté chicken receives Chinese treatment with pineapple, ginger and egg fried rice. A few more elaborate dishes appear at supper-time: parfait of local game is served with pink grapefruit marmalade or minted apple chutney, roast fillet of salmon is 'presented on a pillow of buttered spinach drizzled with a tomato and saffron dressing', while desserts might include baked apple curd tart with gingerbread and lime sorbet. A separate lunch and dinner menu is served in the restaurant. Regular guest beers augment Belhaven 80/- and Courage Directors; ten house wines top the well-spread list of around 70 bins. The area around Melrose is peppered with abbeys, stately homes and gardens worth visiting. SAMPLE DISHES: smoked salmon pâté with cucumber vinaigrette £3.50; casseroled pheasant in port sauce on herb mashed potato £6; summer pudding £3.25.

Open *11 to 2.30, 5 to 11, Sun 12 to 2.30, 6 to 11; bar food and restaurant 12 to 2, 6 to 9.30 (10 Fri and Sat)*
Details *Children welcome Car park Wheelchair access Garden and patio No smoking in dining-room Background music Dogs welcome Access, Amex, Delta, Diners, Switch, Visa Accommodation: 20 rooms, B&B £46 to £84*

🍇 *indicates a pub serving better-than-average wine.*

Many pubs have separate restaurants, with very different menus. These have not been inspected. A recommendation for the pub/bar food does not necessarily imply that the restaurant is also recommended.

MINNIGAFF **Dumfries & Galloway** **map 11**

▲ *Creebridge House Hotel* 🍇

Minnigaff TEL: (01671) 402121
off A75, just N of Newton Stewart

Named after the nearby River Cree and once owned by the Earls of Galloway, this traditional country house stands peacefully in three acres of landscaped gardens and woodland hard by the Penninghame and Kirroughtree Forests. At first glance it may not seem much like a pub, although the Bridges Bar is emphatically the real thing. Casual informality reigns. Real ales such as Orkney Dark Island and Calder's 70/- are on tap, and the food is tailor-made for snacks or full meals. Galloway steaks in various guises are the star attraction, but the menu offers everything from Cullen skink, and steak pie with mushy peas and chips, to Chinese dim-sum, and grilled red pepper risotto. There are also a few flashy specialities such as Solway scallops on a crab-cake with parsley and watercress sauce. Savoury croissants, salads and sandwiches are available most lunch-times, and Friday is fish day. Dinners and a Sunday lunch carvery are served in the Garden Restaurant. The wine list is an impressive slate drawn from Whighams wine cellars, which are virtually on the hotel's doorstep; half-bottles are particularly appetising. SAMPLE DISHES: filo parcels of wild mushrooms £3.25; Indonesian-style pork fillet £8; Ecclefechan butter tart £2.50.

Open *12 to 2.30, 6 to 11, Sun 12.30 to 2.30, 7 to 11; bar food 12 to 2, 6 (7 Sun) to 9; restaurant Sun L 12 to 2, all week D 6 (7 Sun) to 9*
Details *Children welcome Car park Wheelchair access Garden and patio No smoking in restaurant Background music Dogs welcome Access, Delta, Switch, Visa Accommodation: 20 rooms, B&B £40 to £75*

NETHERLEY **Aberdeenshire** **map 11**

Lairhillock Inn 🍇

Netherley TEL: (01569) 730001
on B979, 4m S of Peterculter

A log fire with a hooded chimney in the middle of the lounge is an unusual feature of this pub, which also has a traditional bar, a conservatory with superb views over the countryside, and a separate restaurant. The bars may be traditional and comfortable, but the menus travel the globe for dishes such as crêpes fruits de mer 'St Michel', Chinese-style meatballs, and chicken hongroise. These are supported by more traditional fare: oak-smoked salmon, escalope of pork, baked haddock, and sticky toffee pudding – the last described by the proprietors as 'home-made, yummy' and by a reporter as 'perfect'. Freddie the wild boar is a local star: he has sired all the 130-strong herd at the nearby farm which supplies Lairhillock. The predominantly French wine list runs to over 70 bottles, with clarets from some of the best vintages; a shorter version is offered in the bar, with three house wines by the glass. Real ales include Boddingtons, Flowers and a revolving guest brew. Nearby, and well worth a visit, is Muchalls Castle, a seventeenth-century mansion with a secret staircase and an underground passage leading to a cove. SAMPLE DISHES: gambas créole £5; suprême of chicken écossais (stuffed with haggis and topped with malt whisky) £9; cranachan £3.

Open *11 to 2.30, 5 to 11, Sun 12 to 2.30, 6 to 11; bar food 12 to 1.50, 6 to 9.30 (10 Fri and Sat); restaurant Sun L 12 to 2, all week D 7 to 9; closed 25 and 26 Dec, 1 and 2 Jan*
Details *Children welcome in 1 room Car park Wheelchair access (also WC) Garden and patio Background music Dogs welcome in 1 bar only Access, Amex, Delta, Diners, Switch, Visa*

PORTPATRICK Dumfries & Galloway map 11

▲ *Crown*

North Crescent, Portpatrick TEL: (01776) 810261
off A77, 6m SW of Stranraer

The Crown takes advantage of its location on the harbour of this picturesque village facing westwards towards the Irish Channel. Locally landed fish and shellfish figure prominently on the menu, as does Scotch beef. Mussels, prawns with pickled herring, and scallops in bacon are up among the starters, along with avocado with crab, and salade niçoise. Main courses range from Portavogie cod and haddock, and baked monkfish tails and lobster, to Barbary duck breast and vegetarian pasta bake. The traditional bar, where a fire burns in winter, has photographs of the hotel almost being washed away by waves. Theakston Best Bitter and McEwan 70/- and 80/- are on draught; more than 70 malt whiskies are available, and there's an extensive wine list. The smartly decorated dining-room leads into a non-smoking conservatory. SAMPLE DISHES: Scottish smoked salmon £5.75; seafood pancake £10; ice-cream £1.75.

Open *11am to 11.30pm, Sun 12 to 11; bar food and restaurant Mon to Sat 12 to 2, 6 to 10, Sun 12 to 2.30, 6.30 to 10;*
Details *Children welcome Garden No-smoking area in dining-room Background music Dogs welcome Access, Delta, Diners, Switch, Visa*
Accommodation: 12 rooms, B&B £38 to £72

RATHO **Edinburgh** **map 11**

Bridge Inn

27 Baird Road, Ratho TEL: (0131) 333 1320
off M8 and A8, 8m W of Edinburgh; follow signs for Edinburgh Canal Centre from Newbridge roundabout; pub is alongside canal

Built as a farmhouse before becoming a staging-post for passenger boats, the Bridge has been run as a pub and restaurant in its present form for more than 25 years. It stands right by the Edinburgh Canal Centre and offers all kinds of cruises and special trips (some with dinner and dancing included). This is very much a family pub, with first-rate children's facilities, ranging from high chairs and a baby-changing area to a special 'junior' menu. Bar food is served in a modern extension known as the Pop Inn and the menu is a mix of 'auld' Scottish favourites and eclectic specialities. Expect such things as bargee's broth, Newhaven haddock in batter, and cranachan, alongside pasta with smoked cheese and chive sauce, pork korma, and deep-fried jalapeño peppers stuffed with cream cheese. A full *carte* is served in the main dining-room. Belhaven 80/- and a guest ale are on handpump and the pub has a short list of well-chosen wines. SAMPLE DISHES: deep-fried Brie with autumn plum coulis £4.25; steak, ale and mushroom pie £5.75; apple and sultana pie £3.

Open *12 to 11, Sun 12.30 to 11 (Fri noon to midnight, Sat 11 to midnight); bar food 12 to 9 (Sun 12.30 to 8); restaurant 12 (12.30 Sun) to 2, 6.30 to 9; closed 26 Dec, 1 and 2 Jan*
Details *Children welcome in eating areas Car park Wheelchair access (also WC) Garden and patio No-smoking areas in bar and restaurant Background music Guide dogs only Access, Amex, Diners, Switch, Visa*

STRACHUR **Argyll & Bute** **map 11**

▲ *Creggans Inn*

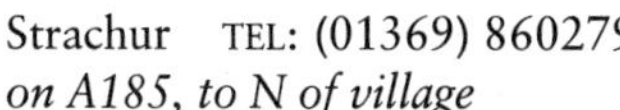

Strachur TEL: (01369) 860279
on A185, to N of village

Sir Charles – son of the late Sir Fitzroy – is now the custodian of this converted farmhouse that looks out across Loch Fyne to the hills and the sea. Its situation, in the swathes of open countryside that form the family estate, means that local produce is the kitchen's driving force. Lady Maclean, author of recipe books on the subject, heads the cooking team. The bar menu tells its own Scottish tale: the loch yields mussels, oysters and salmon (which might be smoked, turned into fish-cakes or made into a cassoulet with leeks); prawns are from Oban, and the waters also provide everything from sea bass to langoustines. Game from the estate also shows up in the shape of venison casserole and the like. Home-baked 'hoggie rolls' are filled with everything from mature Mull of Kintyre cheese with leek, onion and chive mayonnaise to roast sirloin of beef with tomato chutney. Desserts include home-made ice-creams and sorbets. More formal evening meals are also served in the restaurant. Sir Fitzroy's cellar stores some fine wines and the range of malt whiskies includes the house dram – Old MacPhunn ('a fine ten-year-old vatted malt'). 'Archeological and garden tours, and visits to stately homes and private collections can be arranged by Lady Maclean,' says the brochure. SAMPLE DISHES: Creggans pâté £4; roast chicken breast wrapped in smoked bacon £7; pear and apple tart £3.25.

Open *11 to 12; bar food 12 to 2.30, 5.30 to 9; restaurant all week D only 7 to 9*
Details *Children welcome in bar eating area Car park Wheelchair access (also WC) Garden and patio No smoking in restaurant; no-smoking area in bar Background and live music; jukebox No dogs in eating areas Access, Amex, Diners, Switch, Visa Accommodation: 19 rooms, B&B £40 to £100*

SWINTON Borders map 11

▲ *Wheatsheaf Hotel*

Main Street, Swinton TEL: (01890) 860257
on A6112, Coldstream to Duns road

Hotel by name, but not by nature, Alan and Julie Reid's inn by the village green seems to be on an upward curve. Much attention is focused on the food in the Four Seasons Restaurant, but there is also plenty to delight in the bar. One family who turned up with progeny aged five and one-and-a-half received really swift, friendly service and food that was spot-on. The bar menu embraces sandwiches, 'excellent' sausages, and tournedos Rossini, but the real thrust of the cooking shows in dishes such as fresh quail salad with Thai dressing, breast of chicken with mushrooms, bacon and Puy lentils, pork and apricot Stroganov, and broccoli and oyster mushroom fricassee. Fish also appears in the shape of 'The Wheatsheaf Smokie', grilled fillet of salmon with prawns, and roasted monkfish tails wrapped in bacon provençale.

Desserts are reckoned to be star turns: summer pudding, raspberry and Drambuie cream, and 'the best vanilla ice-cream' one youngster had ever tasted, for example. Alan Reid's wine list is an admirable selection to please those with a taste for the grape: six house wines can be drunk by the glass, and the full slate of around 70 bins includes some vigorous New World tipples plus a page devoted to halves. Broughton Greenmantle and Caledonian 80/- are available for beer drinkers in the bar. SAMPLE DISHES: smoked salmon and crayfish bisque £2.50; braised oxtail with root vegetables £6.50; iced honey and ginger parfait with raspberry coulis £3.75.

Open *Tue to Sun 11 to 2.30, 6 to 11; bar food and restaurant 11.45 to 2 (2.30 Sun), 6 to 9.30 (8.30 Sun)*
Details *Children welcome in bar eating area Wheelchair access (also WC) Garden and patio No smoking in restaurant and sun lounge No music Dogs in bedrooms only Access, Visa Accommodation: 4 rooms, B&B £25 to £44*

TAYVALLICH Argyll & Bute map 11

Tayvallich Inn

Tayvallich TEL: (01546) 870282
on B8025, off B841, reached from A816 N of Lochgilphead

A couple who lunched in the bar of John and Pat Grafton's beguiling inn by the shores of Loch Sween feasted memorably on plates of prawn sandwiches and locally smoked salmon, all washed down with a bottle of Chablis. 'Excellent – just what we wanted,' they concluded. The setting has its own special attraction, with boats bobbing on the water and the hills providing a backdrop, and the kitchen draws heavily on the fruits of the sea. Oysters and mussels are high points on the bar menu, scallops and jumbo prawns come from the Sound of Jura, and you are also likely to find such things as warm salad of smoked haddock and prawns, or Cajun salmon with black butter. Alternatives come in the shape of hot tomato salad, steak-burgers and grilled ciabatta rolls topped with ham, capers and mozzarella. A more ambitious repertoire shows up in the restaurant: stir-fried prawns and scallops with ginger and peppers was commended by one reporter. Beers are keg, but there are also plenty of local Islay malts to sample, as well as some creditable wines. SAMPLE DISHES: chicken liver pâté £3; fillet of haddock and chips £4.50; banoffi pie £3.

Open *summer all week 11am to midnight (1am Fri and Sat), Nov to Easter Tue to Sun 11 to 2.30, 6 to 11 (1am Fri and Sat); bar food and restaurant 12 to 2, 6 to 8.30*
Details *Children welcome Car park Wheelchair access Garden and patio No smoking in conservatory during meal-times No music Dogs welcome No cards*

✿ indicates a pub serving outstanding bar food, backed up by all-round excellence in other departments, such as service, atmosphere and cleanliness.

WEEM **Perthshire & Kinross** **map 11**

▲ *Ailean Chraggan*

Weem TEL: (01887) 820346
on B486, ½m N of Aberfeldy

A private house until 1963, Ailean Chraggan doesn't look much like a pub. Within, the atmosphere is 'unstuffy' and there's a 'friendly word for all customers, from lairds to hikers'. In the comfortable bar with its photographs of local scenes taken by landlord Alastair Gillespie, service is prompt and considerate. One menu is available throughout the pub and it features local fish such as Loch Etive prawns, salmon fillet with parsley butter, and pan-fried monkfish with Cointreau and orange dressing alongside venison casserole, pork fillet with a Stilton sauce, and steak and mushroom pie. One visitor thought the Cullen skink 'well worth making the detour for'. The pub's declared policy of providing 'quality food imaginatively prepared and well served' succeeds. The pub does not stock real ale, but the landlord hopes to rectify that situation in the near future; for the time being drinkers can seek solace in the list of around three dozen wines. At the other end of the village are Castle Menzies (the clan centre of the Menzies) and Blair Castle, not to mention lochs and glens aplenty. SAMPLE DISHES: moules marinière and garlic bread £4; chicken breast with white wine and tarragon sauce £7.50; crème brûlée £3.25.

Open *11am to 11pm; bar food and restaurant 12 to 2, 6.30 to 9.30 (8.30 winter)*
Details *Children welcome Car park Wheelchair access Garden and patio No music No dogs in dining-room Access, Delta, Switch, Visa Accommodation: 5 rooms, B&B £28 to £70*

WESTRUTHER **Borders** **map 11**

▲ *Old Thistle Inn*

Westruther, nr Gordon TEL: (01578) 740275
from A697, between Lauder and Greenlaw, take B6456

Curious opening hours dictate proceedings at this whitewashed village pub by the local church. Most business takes place in the evening, when the menu is dominated by 'certified' Aberdeen Angus steaks from a butcher in Galashiels. Sirloins, fillets and T-bone are available in a range of different weights and you can have a side order of mushrooms and onion rings if there's room on the plate. Otherwise the kitchen can provide gammon, scampi and a couple of sorbets. Weekend lunches are straightforward offerings like cheeseburgers, lasagne and sandwiches, although a note says that 'the evening menu is available on request'. Only bottled beers are available, and the wine list is limited to nine everyday tipples. SAMPLE DISHES: prawn cocktail £3.25; 16oz T-bone steak with chips £12; sticky toffee pudding £2.50

Open *Mon to Fri 5.30pm to midnight, Sat and Sun 12.30 to 11; bar food Mon to Fri 5.30 to 9, Sat and Sun 12.30 to 9*
Details *Children welcome in dining-room Wheelchair access (also WC) Patio No music Dogs welcome No cards Accommodation: 2 rooms, B&B £23 to £45*

W·A·L·E·S

ABERDOVEY Gwynedd map 7

▲ *Penhelig Arms Hotel* 🏵 🍇

Aberdovey TEL: (01654) 767215
on A493 Tywyn to Machynlleth road, opposite Penhelig station

'The wine list is what attracts us here,' noted one correspondent who made the trip to this pleasurable eighteenth-century inn by the harbour. The cellar is proprietor Robert Hughes's 'baby' and he has lovingly nurtured it over the years. Ten wines – including champagne – are offered by the glass, and the full slate runs to 250 bins. Enthusiasm, style and an eye for good value show up across the range. Those who prefer something 'hoppy' could opt for a pint of Marston's Pedigree, Greenall's Original or Theakston Bitter.

Drinking may be the main business, but the kitchen also takes its work seriously. Bar lunches are tailored to the needs of all comers, with just enough unexpected touches to keep adventurous palates intrigued. Pâtés and roulades (smoked chicken, or tuna and caper, for example) are regularly on show; otherwise you might begin with salmon en croûte with mayonnaise, or Italian mushroom, pepper and tomato gratinée. Main dishes plough a similar furrow: omelettes, lasagne and lamb curry on the one hand, chargrilled lamb steak with sun-dried tomato butter on the other. You can also get a range of sandwiches and warm baguettes filled with such combinations as Cumberland sausage, home-made mustard and onion. Rounding things off is a quartet of puddings that could span everything from lemon and lime soufflé to treacle tart. A similar menu is generally available in the evenings, although one reporter warned that it might only be served on quiet nights, when the kitchen isn't being stretched by restaurant orders. Three-course Sunday lunches are reckoned to be a fair bargain. SAMPLE DISHES: cream of broccoli, pea and mint soup £2; coq au vin £6.50; apple frangipane tart £2.50.

Open *11 to 3, 6 to 11, Sun 12 to 3, 6 to 10.30; bar food 12 to 2, 7 to 9*
Details *Children welcome in bar eating area Car park Patio No smoking in dining-room No music Dogs welcome in bar only Access, Delta, Switch, Visa Accommodation: 10 rooms, B&B £39 to £78*

ABERGORLECH Carmarthenshire map 4

Black Lion

Abergorlech TEL: (01558) 685271
on B4310, S of Llansawel

Standing by the Roman stone bridge on the banks of the Cothi river, this black and white village pub is – not surprisingly – a popular rendezvous when the sun shines. Barbecues are held in the waterside garden and the licensees also have fishing rights on a stretch of the water. Food served in the traditional bar includes the usual omelettes, jacket potatoes and things with chips, alongside more interesting dishes such as chicken breast filled with leeks and Stilton, minted lamb chops, and pork escalope cooked with lemon and peppers. A plate of pancakes stuffed with spinach, mushrooms and walnuts is among the starters and a fruit-filled version brings up the rear – along with ice-creams, orange sorbet and apple pie. Worthington Best Bitter and Buckleys are on draught, and a handful of wines are stocked. Walkers should keep in mind that the pub makes a welcome oasis if you are *en route* along the Cothi Tour. SAMPLE DISHES: deep-fried garlic and ginger prawns £3.25; beef bourguignon £7.25; white chocolate chip cheesecake £2.50.

Open *12 to 3, 7 to 11, Sun 12 to 3, 7 to 10.30; bar food and restaurant Tue to Sun 12 to 2, 7 to 9.30, bank hols 12 to 3*
Details *Children welcome in eating areas Car park Wheelchair access Garden Background music Dogs welcome Access, Amex, Visa*

AFON-WEN Flintshire **map 7**

Pwll Gwyn Hotel

Denbigh Road, Afon-Wen TEL: (01352) 720227
off A541, 10m NW of Mold

A Chinese banquet, an Italian night, a Cajun dinner, even 'a gastronomical trip around the world' – these are just some of the themed evenings organised here. The building and the setting may not be the best features of this eighteenth-century coaching-inn, but its food certainly draws the crowds to the beamed bar, with its horse brasses and other brass and copper artefacts. There is a printed menu plus a daily-changing blackboard of about five or six dishes: mussels baked with smoked cheese and cream is now a signature dish among the starters, or you could opt for avocado with chicken, celery and garlic in curried mayonnaise. Roasted lamb shank with port and cranberry sauce, or fillet of cod grilled in lemon pepper may be on the blackboard; otherwise try something like tagliatelle with salmon and broccoli, or oriental spiced pork with rice. Fruit melba, rice pudding, or syrup sponge with custard bring meals to a traditional close. The pub is tied to Greenalls, with that brewery's range of ales on draught; house wines are sold by the glass, half-litre and litre. SAMPLE DISHES: smoked salmon goujons £3.50; duck breast with orange and lemon sauce £6.50; chocolate brandy truffle £2.25.

Open *12 to 3, 7 to 11 (10.30 Sun); bar food 12 to 2.15 (2 winter), 7 to 9.30 (9.45 Sat)*

Details *Children welcome Car park Wheelchair access (also WC) Garden and patio No smoking in 1 dining-room Background music No dogs Access, Delta, Visa*

ALLTWEN Neath Port Talbot map 4

Butchers Arms

Alltwen Hill, Alltwen TEL: (01792) 863100
on A474, 1m SE of Pontardawe

There are splendid views across the Tawe Valley towards the Gower Peninsula from the garden of this exceedingly well-run pub. Locals support the place vigorously and the mood inside is friendly. The cooking has its roots in the homespun tradition of cockles with laverbread and bacon, lamb and mint pie, and chicken in leek sauce, but it also makes forays into what the landlord calls 'various ethnic regions'. The result might be Singapore chicken, Kenya beef, or something described as chicken rushda. Most dishes are served with chips or garlic potatoes. You can also order steaks in the bar and a full menu is available in the restaurant. The Butchers Arms has a long-standing reputation for the quality and range of its real ales: at any time you might find Everards Old Original, Courage Directors, Fuller's ESB and more besides. A few everyday wines are also stocked. SAMPLE DISHES: Hungarian beef £5.50; half-chicken in barbecue sauce £6; bread-and-butter pudding £1.75.

Open *all week 12 to 3, 6.30 to 11; bar food and restaurant all week L 12 to 2, Mon to Sat D 6.30 to 9 (10 Fri and Sat)*
Details *Children welcome Car park Wheelchair access Garden and patio Background music No dogs Access, Visa*

BEAUMARIS Isle of Anglesey map 7

▲ *Ye Olde Bulls Head Inn*

Castle Street, Beaumaris TEL: (01248) 810329

The Bulls Head – a redoubtable old inn 100 yards from Beaumaris Castle – has every reason to be proud of its past. Built in 1472 and improved in 1617, it still clings to its uneven floors, twisting staircases and little archways. It also boasts the largest single-hinged gate in the British Isles ('I saw it and it is, well, big,' was the view of one visitor). With a guest list that has included Samuel Johnson and Charles Dickens over the centuries, you can expect the place to hum with historical echoes. Downstairs is still resolutely a pub, upstairs is the restaurant, open for dinner and Sunday lunch. Bar food is limited to lunch-times, but the kitchen succeeds in balancing a sliver of fashion with a solid slice of old-school familiarity. Traditionalists can take their pick from ploughman's with Welsh cheeses, game terrine with pickled walnuts, casseroled rabbit with baby onions and root vegetables, or seafood pie made with shortcrust pastry. Those looking for up-to-the minute distractions might home in on home-cured bresaola, smoked breast and confit of duck with green tomato relish, or saffron tagliatelle with local seafood and red pesto. Sweets span everything from bread-and-butter pudding to hazelnut praline parfait. The wine list is a mighty impressive slate peppered with reputable names from around the world; half-bottles show up favourably, and five house wines are sold by the glass. SAMPLE DISHES: cream of leek and potato soup £2; local mussels in white wine, garlic and bacon £5; vanilla crème caramel £2.

Open *11am to 11pm, Sun 12 to 10.30; bar food Mon to Sat L only 12 to 2.30; restaurant Sun L 12 to 1.30, all week D 7.30 to 9.30*
Details *Children welcome Car park No smoking in dining-room Live music Guide dogs only Access, Amex, Delta, Switch, Visa Accommodation: 15 rooms, B&B £47 to £89*

BETWS-Y-COED Conwy map 7

▲ *Ty Gwyn Hotel*

Betwys-y-Coed TEL: (01690) 710383
on outskirts of village, at junction of A5 and A470 by Waterloo Bridge

A great setting, overlooking the River Conwy in the heavily wooded Conwy valley, is a major plus for visitors to this centuries-old coaching-inn. Jim and Shelagh Ratcliffe run the place as a family affair with help from their two sons, and have filled the comfortable lounge bar with all manner of antiques and other curios. Local Welsh lamb shows up on the bar menu (perhaps roasted with mint and honey) alongside a healthy selection of fish dishes ranging from fillet of trout with cucumber and prawn sauce to sea bass thermidor. Alternatives come in the shape of, say, deep-fried jalapeño peppers with garlic mayonnaise, pheasant braised in Beaujolais with red wine sauce, and whole roast mallard, while mushroom and nut fettucine has been 'fine' as a vegetarian option. Desserts feature things like pavlova and profiteroles. Evening meals and Sunday lunch are served in the restaurant. There's plenty of variety on the well-spread wine list, and Theakston Best Bitter is on draught. The pub stands at 'the gateway to Snowdonia National Park' with all its outdoor inducements and challenges. SAMPLE DISHES: moules marinière £3.50;

suprême of chicken with lemon and garlic butter £7; raspberry cheesecake £2.50.

Open *all week 12 to 3, 7 to 11.30; bar food 12 to 2, 7 to 9 (8.30 Nov to March); restaurant Sun L 12 to 2, all week D 7 to 9*
Details *Children welcome Car park Wheelchair access (also WC) Background music No dogs Access, Delta, Switch, Visa Accommodation: 13 rooms, B&B £19 to £80*

BONTDDU Gwynedd map 7

Halfway House

Bontddu TEL: (01341) 430635
on A496, between Barmouth and Dolgellau

Magnificent walks above the Mawddach estuary in Snowdonia National Park afford splendid views over both the water and the Cambrian Mountains. There are no spectacular vistas from the Halfway House itself, but hikers and everyone else are assured of a friendly, cheerful welcome. Bontddu ('Black Bridge' in English) is a picturesque village, and the black-and-white, timbered pub, is open-plan and airy. Plenty of fish and seasonal game feature on the menu: there could be pot-roast woodpigeon with smoked bacon and red wine, poached cod in curry and coconut milk sauce, or baked turbot with whole-grain mustard and Welsh cheese. Basket meals include salmon fish-cakes, lasagne is made with Welsh lamb and mint, and sandwiches are served at lunch-times. Marston's Bitter and Pedigree are on draught, and four house wines are served by the glass. Barmouth is a popular seaside resort, and the remains of Cymer Abbey (dating from the twelfth century) are worth a visit. SAMPLE DISHES: garlic mushrooms £4; deep-fried plaice with tartare sauce £5.75; chocolate ice-cream sundae £2.75.

Open *12 to 2.30 (3 summer), 7 (6 summer) to 11; bar food and restaurant 12 to 1.45, 6 to 8.45*
Details *Children welcome in eating areas Car park Garden and patio Background and occasional live music No dogs Access, Visa*

BRECON Powys map 4

▲ *George Hotel*

George Street, Brecon TEL: (01874) 623421 and 623422

The renowned Brecon Jazz Festival brings hordes of enthusiasts to this 'busy rural city' during August, and the place seems perpetually alive with farmers, holidaymakers, golfers and, of course, climbers and back-packers intent on overcoming the Beacons. The George is justifiably popular, and is 'probably the top place of its kind' locally, notes a traveller. The pink-painted, Georgian-fronted building is festooned with hanging baskets, often still blooming in October. Inside, it's a cheery sort of place, with open fires, light wood fittings and chatty staff who are generally on-the-ball. A 'just a snack' menu is served all day in the bar (and up to 6pm in the separate restaurant): wholesome soups such as parsnip and apple, deep-fried Teifi cheese, 'good-looking pasta, curries and pies' are backed up by stuffed local trout wrapped in leeks and the like. Evening specials include a few more showy offerings, such as a trio of fish mousses, and medallions of beef with whisky, cream and mustard sauce, while puddings range from home-made lavender sorbet on mango coulis to a fruity 'samosa' filled with cinnamon-dusted pear. Well-kept real ales like Marston's Pedigree and Bass are bolstered by seasonal guests (Snowman's Revenge in wintry November, for example); a fair selection of wines is also available. SAMPLE DISHES: sesame chicken wings £3.25; loin of pork in cider sauce £5.75; chocolate profiteroles £3.75.

Open *11am to 11pm, Sun 12 to 10.30; bar food and restaurant 12 to 10*
Details *Children welcome Car park Wheelchair access (also WC) Patio No smoking in restaurant Background and live music Guide dogs only Access, Switch, Visa Accommodation: 8 rooms, room only £35 to £55*

BWLCH-Y-CIBAU Powys **map 7**

Stumble Inn

Bwlch-y-cibau TEL: (01691) 648860
on A490, 3m SE of Llanfyllin

'This pub was a very nice surprise indeed, with a chef who really enjoys his job,' said one visitor, who also noted with interest the emphasis on 'Cajun and other exotic' dishes. That is not to say you'll only find spicy food: steaks, grills, burgers and filled baguettes all feature on the printed menu, but if you want something more adventurous, look out for the daily specials. You might find Parisian chicken (in a brandy and cream sauce), Thai prawns with a Creole sauce, grilled swordfish steak with Cajun spices and fresh lime, or spicy vegetarian burritos. Staff know exactly what the daily specials entail, and in quiet moments there's a chance you'll catch the chef, who is also the landlord, reading a cookbook behind the bar. Real ales include Worthington Best Bitter plus weekly-changing guest beers. Wines are chalked up on their own board, with Jacobs Creek as the house tipple. Hanging from the walls and heavily beamed ceiling are old farm implements, while models of ancient motorcycles are an unusual addition. Nearby is Lake Vyrnwy. SAMPLE DISHES: spicy parsnip soup £2.25; grilled hake fillets with saffron and prawn sauce £8; hazelnut meringue £2.50.

Open *11 to 3, 6 to 11, Sun 12 to 3, 7 to 10.30; bar food 12 to 2, 6 to 9; closed Mon Oct to March*
Details *Children welcome until 9pm Car park Garden No-smoking areas Background music Dogs welcome daytime only No cards*

CAPEL CURIG Conwy map 7

▲ *Bryn Tyrch Hotel*

Capel Curig TEL: (01690) 720223
on A5, 5m W of Betws-y-Coed

Don't be taken aback if you if find yourself rubbing shoulders with a management team, a gathering of art enthusiasts or even some geology students: this popular pub in the heart of Snowdonia caters for all comers. The interior has a well-worn, lived-in look, which isn't surprising since many of its customers are also energetic outdoor types, complete with boots and rucksacks. What singles the place out is its menu, which is almost entirely vegetarian and vegan. Japanese tempura with garlic and tahini sauce has been enjoyed; otherwise you might find apple and Stilton soup, Greek spinach pie, and cider nut roast with Italian tomato sauce. Meat and fish eaters get a look-in with, say, smoked chicken with Malayan sauce, or grilled trout. Puddings are made on the premises, ice-creams come from a producer on Anglesey. If you are looking for a snack, there are also sandwiches (before 6pm), plus jacket potatoes, quiche and so on. Flowers IPA, Castle Eden Ale and Marston's Pedigree are on draught, and a handful of wines are geared to good-value 'quaffing'. SAMPLE DISHES: vegetable samosas with mango chutney £3.50; smoked haddock and mushroom pie £8; crunchy treacle tart £3.

Open *12 to 11, Sun 12 to 10.30; bar food and restaurant 12.30 to 9.30 (9 Sun)*
Details *Children welcome Car park Garden No music Dogs welcome Access, Visa Accommodation: 15 rooms, B&B £17 to £20*

The Guide *is totally independent, accepts no free hospitality and carries no advertising.*

If you disagree with any assessment made in the Guide, *write to tell us why* – The Which? Guide to Country Pubs, *FREEPOST, 2 Marylebone Road, London NW1 1YN.*

CAREW Pembrokeshire **map 4**

▲ *Carew Inn*

Carew TEL: (01646) 651267
off A477, 4m E of Pembroke

To find the Carew Inn, look for the ninth-century Celtic cross and the ruined Norman castle that are the focal points of the village. The pub itself is large and square with no fewer than three eating-areas – a lounge bar and two dining-rooms (non-smokers upstairs). One menu is served throughout and the kitchen puts on some decent-sounding fish specials, including salmon steak with tarragon sauce, and baked king scallops with cheese and breadcrumb topping. Elsewhere, look for Thai chicken curry and regular offerings ranging from steaks and pasta to potato, leek and mushroom pie. Sandwiches and ploughman's are available at lunch-time. Hot and cold sweets range from blackberry and cinnamon pudding to hazelnut meringue nest. Worthington Best Bitter and Crown Buckley Reverend James are on tap throughout the year, and you will find a guest beer from Easter to September (it might be anything from Main Street Bitter, from the local Pembroke micro-brewery, to Young's Ram Rod); the short wine list also provides plenty of variety. The music is live on Thursday nights. SAMPLE DISHES: mussels provençale £4; chicken in white wine sauce £6; Bakewell tart £2.

Open *summer all week 11am to 11pm, winter Mon to Fri 12 to 2.30, 4.30 to 11, Sat 11am to 11pm, Sun 12 to 3, 7 to 10.30; bar food and restaurant 12 to 2 (2.30 summer), 7 to 9 (9.30 summer)*
Details *Children welcome in eating areas Car park Garden and patio No smoking in 1 dining-room Background and live music Dogs in bar only No cards Accommodation: 1 room, B&B £15 to £25*

CLARBESTON ROAD Pembrokeshire **map 4**

Picton Inn

Clarbeston Road TEL: (01437) 731615
off B4329, 5m N of Haverfordwest; take right turn signposted Llys-y-fran and Clarbeston Road

This white-painted, slate-roofed inn has an unspoilt country-pub atmosphere in its open-plan bar with exposed stone walls, beams, pine furniture and a wood-burning stove in the fireplace. A printed menu runs from salads, sandwiches, omelettes and Stilton quiche, to hot smoked mackerel with horseradish mayonnaise, grilled Welsh lamb chops, and liver with bacon and onions; puddings include banana baked in Malibu, and coffee and brandy cake. The list of daily specials moves into more adventurous territory with, perhaps, pan-fried boar with mushrooms, mustard and cream, or local trout stuffed with prawns, followed by Captain Morgan's rice-pudding. Crown Buckley Reverend James Original Ale, Boddingtons and Worthington Best Bitter are on draught, and three wines are sold by the glass. Picton Castle, with the adjacent Graham Sutherland Gallery, is well worth visiting while you're in the area. SAMPLE DISHES: ham and vegetable soup £2; venison steak with cranberry Cumberland sauce £9; rum and raisin bread-and-butter pudding £3.25.

Open *11am to 11pm (winter 11 to 2.30, 4.30 to 11), Sun 12 to 3, 7 to 10.30; bar food 12 to 2.30, 6 (7 Sun summer) to 9.30; no food Sun D, and L and D Mon in winter*
Details *Children welcome Car park Wheelchair access Patio Background music Dogs welcome No cards*

CLYTHA Monmouthshire map 2

▲ *Clytha Arms*

Clytha TEL: (01873) 840206
on old Abergavenny to Raglan road, S of A40, 6m SE of Abergavenny

Set in its own grounds, on the fringes of Clytha Park (National Trust), this former dower house has what one reporter described as 'an Edwardian flavour'. Inside, everything seems a little 'rickety', but civilised with it. Two large rooms are for drinkers and bar meals, where you can sit at pitch pine church-pew furniture and consider the menu. The kitchen delivers dishes with a highly distinctive character and a patriotic Welsh flavour: leek and laverbread rissoles are something of a speciality, although they don't appear all the time. The cooking is confident, honest and sharp. Andrew and Beverley Canning are capable of turning out home-made pasties and sausages, as well as producing plates of faggots and peas with beer and onion gravy, smoked sewin with scrambled eggs, and huge helpings of black pudding with fried apples and mustard sauce. There are also some unexpected eclectic touches in the shape of mini-spring rolls, chicken and lentil curry, and Parma ham with salami and Tuscan garlic bread. Sandwiches are also available and it's back to Wales for the ploughman's, which features a trio of cheeses with names such as Pencarreg, Llanboidy and Teifi Caerphilly. If you fancy a pudding, you might be offered raspberry and Chianti sorbet, Sauternes cream with spiced prunes, or treacle pud; otherwise finish in savoury mood with Y-Fenni rarebit. Things move up yet another gear for meals in the restaurant.

The Cannings take real ale seriously: Brains Bitter, Hook Norton and Bass are supplemented by three guest ales drawn from independent breweries – often including a mild. The wine list is also worth considering: the selections are concise, French regions are covered with discernment and there's also a brief foray into the New World. SAMPLE DISHES: ham with parsley sauce £4; wild mushroom ragoût with pasta £5.50; ginger syllabub £3.50.

Open *Tue to Fri 11.30 to 3.30, Mon to Fri 6 to 11, Sat 11.30 to 11, Sun 12 to 3.30, 7 to 10.30; bar food Tue to Sat L 12.30 to 2.15, Mon to Thu D 7.30 to 9.30; restaurant Tue to Sun L 12.30 to 2.15, Mon to Sat D 7.30 to 9.30*
Details *Children welcome Car park Wheelchair access Garden and patio No smoking in dining-room Background music No dogs Access, Delta, Switch, Visa Accommodation: 3 rooms, B&B £40 to £65*

CREIGIAU Cardiff — map 4

Caesar's Arms

Cardiff Road, Creigiau TEL: (01222) 890486
2m N of M4 Jct. 33

'Wonderful atmosphere. Pub ambience but with space and comfort,' enthused one correspondent from England. Complete redecoration was under way as we went to press, but you can be assured of informality and a very distinctive approach to food. The formula is straight and true: fish, meat and game are displayed in refrigerated cabinets; make your choice and then wait while it is cooked in the open kitchen. Grilling, poaching and frying are the main techniques brought into play.

Whole sea bass cooked in rock salt is the signature dish, but you can also get lobster, salmon, monkfish, and hake, or opt for something meaty such as braised lamb's liver and onions, marinated beef kebabs, or fillet of venison with port and redcurrant sauce. Chips or new potatoes come with everything, and you can choose salad or vegetables as extras. Start with game terrine, cockles and laverbread, Bajan fishcakes with Barbados sauce, or even monster crawfish tails, and round off with chocolate gâteau, mille-feuilles, or apple and strawberry crumble. Sunday lunch is an all-day affair, with three roasts added to the normal menu. Hancock's HB is on handpump, and the wine list is a well-chosen and wide-ranging slate. SAMPLE DISHES: hot garlic shrimps £4; honeyed crispy duck £10; raspberry pavlova £3.50.

Open *all week 12 to 3, Mon to Sat 6 to 12; bar food and restaurant all week L 12 to 2.30, Mon to Sat D 7 to 10.30*
Details *Children welcome Sun L in restaurant and other times by arrangement Car park Wheelchair access Garden and patio No music No dogs Access, Amex, Diners, Visa*

CRICKHOWELL Powys map 4

▲ *Bear Hotel* ✿ 🍇

Crickhowell TEL: (01873) 810408
on A40, 6m NW of Abergavenny

With more than six centuries of history under its belt, the Bear still feels very much like a traditional coaching-inn: there are all the expected accoutrements in the shape of flagstone floors, prints and antiques. It fairly buzzes with life, especially on a Saturday evening. You can eat in the downstairs bar from a menu that takes account of local produce and gives an occasional nod to eclectic fashion. Gratin of cockles and mussels with laverbread, and stuffed shoulder of lamb fly the flag for Wales, while fingers of olive pesto ciabatta with garlic, chervil and tomato dip, or poached chicken with apricots, capers and flaked almonds are from the cook's world tour. Boiled ham is served with mustard seed sauce and braised lentils, shepherd's pie comes with spicy potato wedges. Sandwiches are also available. Desserts tend to be old faithfuls like treacle sponge or sticky toffee pudding.

Menus in the panelled, baronial-style dining-room upstairs show a touch more flamboyance, as in breast of guinea-fowl filled with black pudding mousse on a bed of buttered spinach with marsala. Eleven wines are available by the glass from a list of around 50 keenly chosen bins at eminently reasonable prices. Beer drinkers are likely to be offered Bass, Ruddles Best and County, and John Smith's Bitter. Crickhowell is a useful staging-post if you are planning to explore the myriad attractions of the Brecon Beacons. SAMPLE DISHES: ragoût of mushrooms, leeks and garlic £3.50; baked Cornish mackerel with sage and lemon sauce and onion compote £6.25; Belgian chocolate and raspberry pavé with chocolate sauce £3.25.

Open *11 to 3, 6 to 11, Sun 12 to 3, 7 to 10.30; bar food all week L 12 to 2, Mon to Sat D 6 to 10; restaurant Mon to Sat D only 7 to 9.30*
Details *Children welcome in bar eating area Car park Wheelchair access (also WC) Garden No-smoking area in bar Background music Dogs welcome Access, Amex, Delta, Switch, Visa Accommodation: 38 rooms, B&B £42 to £90*

Nantyffin Cider Mill Inn ✿✿ 🍺 🍇

LOCAL PRODUCE

Brecon Road, Crickhowell TEL: (01873) 810775
1½m W of Crickhowell at junction of A40 and A479

On the edge of the Black mountains, in the heart of the Brecon Beacons sits this converted sixteenth-century house; it is now one of the premier-league pub/restaurants in Wales. Inside, it still looks and feels like a proper hostelry, even though there's a slightly more formal dining-room attached to the bar. Messrs Gerrard and Bridgeman are crusading supporters of local produce and it remains at the heart of their enterprise. A relative's farm outside Crickhowell provides an ever-growing supply of organic vegetables and salad leaves, plus unexpected harvests of wild fungi; Glanusk Estate is a magnificent source of game, and the kitchen now makes use of home-reared lamb and pork. The commitment is remarkable, the results on the plate brim over with neat modern touches.

Printed bar menus are supplemented by a blackboard of specials; there's also a separate list of so-called 'dining-room main courses'. Two dishes enjoyed by a reporter in early spring sum up the style perfectly: a slab of creamy local goats' cheese served on bruschetta with salad leaves and strips of chargrilled leeks, followed by succulent rack of lamb with crisp artichokes and caramelised onion confit. The rest is a bonzana of ideas: sauté flat mushrooms in a curry sauce wittily served in a poppadom basket; red mullet with home-made pumpkin ravioli and sage butter; saddle of rabbit wrapped in pancetta and basil breadcrumbs and served with sauté spinach and pine kernels – to name but three examples. And if you want steak, kidney and stout pie, they do that too.

As for drinks, the inn has a splendid stock of real ales: from the 'rotational pool' you might choose Felinfoel Double Dragon, Ushers Spring Fever or Crown Buckley Reverend James; traditional ciders such as Scrumpy Supreme and Weston's Old Rosie are also on tap. The wine list is an ever-improving modern slate now that several new suppliers have been taken on board; eight wines are available by the glass from 14 house selections. Even the home-made lemonade 'put other soft drinks to shame', raved one visitor who thought everything about the place was 'quite amazing'. The demand for accommodation in the National Park means that planning permission is in the pipeline for a five-bedroom barn conversion. SAMPLE DISHES: autumn salad of figs, Parma ham, roast tomatoes and spinach £4.50; chargrilled calf's liver with cabbage savoyade and smoked bacon £10.50; raspberry torte with Cointreau and raspberry cassis sauce £3.25.

Open *all week 12 to 3, 6.30 to 11; bar food and restaurant 12 to 2.30, 6.30 to 9.45; closed Mon Jan to Mar and Sept to Nov, restaurant closed D winter*
Details *Children welcome   Car park   Wheelchair access (also WC)   Garden   No music   Guide dogs only   Access, Amex, Delta, Switch, Visa*

✿✿ *indicates a pub serving food on a par with 'seriously good' restaurants, where the cooking achieves consistent quality.*

EAST ABERTHAW **Vale of Glamorgan** **map 4**

Blue Anchor Inn

East Aberthaw TEL: (01446) 750329
off B4265, between St Athan and Barry

The Blue Anchor's interior lives up to the promise of its ancient thatch and heavyweight stone walls; go through the door and you'll come upon wooden beams, blazing fires and a warren of little rooms with small windows and low lighting. The fact that the pub is 'within spitting distance' of a cement works and power-station is neither here nor there. Beer-drinkers have around six to choose from, including Boddingtons Bitter, Flowers IPA and Theakston Old Peculier, while those who prefer wine can drink it by the glass or choose a bottle from a list of nearly 40 bins. 'We grow many of our own vegetables and herbs,' writes the publican; these are put to good use in, say, provençale lasagne, or the creamy leek and tarragon sauce that accompanies steamed salmon. A harvest festival of good things is also served with main courses such as steak and kidney pudding, baked cod, or braised lambs' liver. There may be mussels to start, and steamed syrup sponge to finish. A longer menu is available in the separate restaurant. Porthkerry Country Park, with an impressive railway viaduct spanning the valley, is just along the coast, and you can view military and civil planes at Wales Aircraft Museum. SAMPLE DISHES: ploughman's with Welsh cheeses £4.25; stuffed roast pork with apple sauce £4.75; apple and raspberry crumble £2.25.

Open *11am to 11pm, Sun 12 to 10.30; bar food Mon to Sat L 12 to 2, Mon to Fri D 6 to 8; restaurant Sun L 12.15 to 2.30, Mon to Sat D 7 to 9.30*
Details *Children welcome in eating areas Car park Wheelchair access (also WC) Patio No music No dogs in eating areas Access, Delta, Visa*

ERBISTOCK **Wrexham** **map 7**

Boat Inn

Erbistock TEL: (01978) 780143
just S of A539, 2m W of Wrexham

The setting is a dream: this 400-year-old inn stands right by the banks of the River Dee, with tables overlooking the water and pleasant woodland walks nearby. No wonder it is open all day in the balmy summer months. Bar food is confined to lunch-times, but the kitchen is prepared to step boldly into the world of black pudding thermidor and the like. Fish shows up well in the shape of, say, deep-fried sea bream or fillet of red snapper, while puddings are along the lines of Eton mess. A separate restaurant operates throughout the week. New owner Terry Whalley is keen on real ale, and his regularly changing line-up could include beers from Mitchell's of Lancaster, as well as Young's Ram Rod and Cambrian Best Bitter. The wine list features 40 bins from around the world, with a selection of house wines by the glass. SAMPLE DISHES: cream of broccoli, smoked bacon and lentil soup £3; game pie £6.50; Eton mess £3.50.

Open *11 to 3, 6 to 11, Sun 12 to 3, 7 to 10.30 (summer Mon to Sat 11am to 11pm); bar food all week L only 12 to 2; restaurant 12 to 2, 7 to 9.30*
Details *Children welcome in eating areas Car park Garden and patio Background music Guide dogs only Access, Delta, Switch, Visa*

GLANWYDDEN Conwy **map 7**

Queen's Head

Glanwydden TEL: (01492) 546570
just off B5115 Colwyn Bay to Llandudno road

Robert and Sally Cureton's neatly converted wheelwright's cottage runs like clockwork. Crowds descend from all parts and you are well advised to arrive early – particularly at weekends. Despite the pressure, service is well-trained, efficient and speedy. There's not much in the way of traditional 'adornments' in the plush carpeted bar: eating is the main business and food is ordered at a desk by the kitchen door.

Lunch and slightly more showy dinner menus suggest that the kitchen likes things local and Welsh: deep-fried Pencarreg cheese comes with cranberry preserve, while smoked Caerphilly is used as a topping for field mushrooms with hollandaise. Dressed Conwy crab gets the thumbs-up as a salad, ultra-fresh plaice is served with Pernod sauce, and succulent pink cutlets 'with the sweetness of Welsh mountain lamb' arrive with a well-balanced port and plum sauce. You can also get open rolls and sandwiches; otherwise splash out on the speciality seafood platter. Most enthusiasm, however, is reserved for the prodigious assortment of hot and cold desserts. Chocolate brandy trifle has been endorsed, while a 'marvellously gooey-centred' pavlova with an expertly made coulis was thought to be worthy of a serious restaurant; as an alternative there are also Swiss ice-creams and sorbets. The wine list, 'selected in association with Rodney Densem Wines of Nantwich, Cheshire', is a better-than-average collection of about three dozen keenly priced bins; the house wine is also eminently drinkable. Draught beers are Tetley Bitter, Benskins Bitter, Ind Coope Burton Ale and one guest brew. SAMPLE DISHES: smoked trout pâté £3.75; braised beef carbonnade £7.25; coffee and walnut fudge pie £2.50.

Open *11 to 3, 6 to 11, Sun 12 to 2, 6 to 10.30; bar food 12 to 2, 6 to 9*
Details *No children under 7 Car park Wheelchair access Patio Background music No dogs Access, Switch, Visa*

GRESFORD Wrexham map 7

Pant yr Ochain

Old Wrexham Road, Gresford TEL: (01978) 853525

'A cross between a conservatory and a library with book-lined walls' is how one reporter described the interior of this fascinating old building in rural surroundings a few miles from Wrexham. A relaxed, airy feel pervades the place, and staff go about their business with friendliness and confidence. The menu is imaginative and wide-ranging, with dishes that suggest plenty of skill in the kitchen. Mushrooms with port and Stilton sauce are presented with Parmesan choux pastry, while salmon is tinged with coriander, wrapped in a puff pastry lattice and served with lime and vermouth sauce. On a simpler level, there might also be venison pâté, Cumberland sausage with mash and onion gravy, tagliatelle with sun-dried tomatoes, black olives and basil, and vanilla crème brûlée. A good stock of real ales includes Plassey Bitter, as well as Timothy Taylor Landlord and Boddingtons. Gresford is in what was once the coal mining heart of north Wales. SAMPLE DISHES: feta cheese, spinach and pine kernel strudel £4.75; braised half-shoulder of lamb with rosemary gravy £9.75; chocolate truffle torte £3.50.

Open *11.30 to 3, 5.30 to 11, Sun 12 to 10.30; bar food 12 to 2, 6 to 9.30, Sun 12 to 9.30*
Details *Children welcome L only Car park Wheelchair access (also WC) Garden and patio No smoking in 1 room Background and occasional live music Guide dogs only Access, Amex, Delta, Diners, Switch, Visa*

HAY-ON-WYE Powys map 4

▲ *Old Black Lion*

26 Lion Street, Hay-on-Wye TEL: (01497) 820841

Situated in this renowned mecca for bibliophiles, the Old Black Lion provides a good base for those wishing to browse through the many second-hand book shops, or to attend the literature festival held every May. Built in the thirteenth century near one of the main entrances to the old walled town, this former coaching-inn has played host to several famous personages, including Oliver

Cromwell, it is claimed. Customers heading for food in the King Richard bar, with its blackened beams, plates and cartoons on the walls, will find it well geared for dining. As well as the usual range of pub grub you will find an eclectic selection of dishes on the printed menu, from seafood vol-au-vent, and spicy peppered venison casserole, to tempura-battered cod, and turkey and herb lasagne. Vegetarians are well catered for, with Thai coconut stir-fry, for example. The blackboard menu is equally interesting, and you could find ragoût of wild boar with masala and oranges; venison, port and cranberry pie; or pheasant and calvados terrine with an apple and truffle confit. Desserts are of the traditional variety – treacle tart, sticky toffee pudding, to name two. Beers on handpump include Flowers Original, plus the pub's own Old Black Lion Ale, as well as Supreme from the Wye Valley Brewery. The wine list travels the world – there's even an offering from Mexico and one from China – and French house wines come by carafe. A separate list for the restaurant features bottles selected by Tanners. SAMPLE DISHES: smoked applewood duck salad with a plum sauce £5; spiced chicken with rice £7.75; steamed lemon and rhubarb pudding with a citrus custard £3.50.

Open *11 to 3, 6 to 11, Sun 12 to 3, 7 to 10.30; bar food and restaurant 12 to 2.30, 7 to 9 (9.30 Sun and all week spring and summer)*
Details *Children over 5 welcome in eating area of bar, over 8 in restaurant Car park Wheelchair access Patio No smoking in restaurant No music Dogs welcome Access, Amex, Visa Accommodation: 10 rooms, B&B £21 to £50*

LAMPHEY Pembrokeshire map 4

Dial Inn

The Ridgeway, Lamphey TEL: (01646) 672426
off A4139 Tenby to Pembroke road

Apart from the Dial, the focal point of Lamphey is the impressive ruins of Lamphey Palace, formerly a residence of the Bishops of St David's. The entrance to the inn leads straight into the large bar, which occupies the whole of the front of the building. Welcoming and warm, it also has an extraordinarily eclectic display of pottery and china. A printed 'Trencher Menu' lists snacks like pâté, mussels with garlic and herb butter, and prawn salad, while the blackboard announces more substantial fare: gammon with damson compote, crispy duck breast with caramelised orange sauce, chicken curry, or crab and pesto lasagne, for example, with chocolate and almond tart among the puddings. Worthington and Hancock's HB are on draught, and there's a good showing of half-bottles on the wine list of 30-plus bins. Manorbier Castle, set on a promontory in a cleft running down to the sea, is just a few miles away. SAMPLE DISHES: Glamorgan sausages £5; local sewin with laverbread and cream £9; lemon soufflé £3.

Open *11 to 3, 6 to 11, Sun 12 to 3, 7 to 10.30; bar food and restaurant 12 to 2, 7 (6.30 summer) to 9*
Details *Children welcome in eating areas Car park Wheelchair access Garden and patio No smoking in dining-room Background and live music No dogs Access, Amex, Delta, Switch, Visa*

LITTLE HAVEN **Pembrokeshire** **map 4**

Swan Inn

Point Road, Little Haven TEL: (01437) 781256
off B4341, 6m W of Haverfordwest

The Swan is beside the sea in the centre of Little Haven. A low wall on the other side of the Pembrokeshire coastal path, which runs past the front door, separates the pub from the cove. 'Good value' bar food is served only at lunch-time, with a separate restaurant open for dinner most evenings. The menu offers pâtés, ploughman's with 'a huge portion' of Cheddar, and sandwiches, alongside garlic mushrooms, cawl, and local crab or smoked salmon with salad. Worthington Best, Wadworth 6X and Watkin OSB are served in the bar, with its low beams, decorative jugs, dried flowers and an open fire in winter. A new wine list was in preparation as the *Guide* went to press. The village has striking views across St Brides Bay towards St David's. SAMPLE DISHES: crab bake £4.50; chicken and broccoli gratin £4.50; Irish coffee meringue gâteau £2.75.

Open *11 to 3, 6 (7 winter) to 11, Sun 12 to 3, 7 to 10.30; bar food all week L only 12 to 2; restaurant Wed to Sat D only 7 to 9 (booking advised); closed 25 Dec evening*
Details *No children Patio Background music Dogs welcome on a lead No cards*

LLANARMON DYFFRYN CEIRIOG **Wrexham** **map 7**

▲ *West Arms Hotel*

Llanarmon Dyffryn Ceiriog TEL: (01691) 600665
off A5 Llangollen to Oswestry road at Chirk, then follow B4500 for 11m

You can't get much more remote than this hotel, and from the extensive gardens you can soak up wonderful views of the Berwyn mountains, 'populated solely by the pine trees of Ceiriog Forest', observed one reporter. The bar area is made up of two rooms, one bare, the other with much-carved dark wood, including a love seat. Food is listed on both a printed menu and a blackboard of chef's specials. 'Raw materials and freshness were top-class,' noted an inspector. You may find sauté wild mushrooms, local game terrine, wok-fried vegetables and black-bean sauce, venison escalopes in red wine, steak and kidney pie, or grilled cod fillets. Finish with blackberry pie, steamed jam pudding with custard, or home-made ice-cream. Some classy names appear on the long, reasonably priced wine list, with house wines by the glass. Flowers IPA is on draught. Walkers will be in seventh heaven here; those who want to travel further afield should allow plenty of time: winding, narrow lanes can make for slow driving. SAMPLE DISHES: home-smoked duck breast £4; grilled Welsh lamb cutlets with redcurrant sauce £6.75; Bakewell tart £2.75.

Open *winter 12 to 3, 6 to 11, Sun 12 to 3, 7 to 10.30, summer all week 12 to 11 (10.30 Sun); bar food and restaurant 12 to 2, 7 to 9.30*
Details *Children welcome in bar eating area Car park Wheelchair access (also WC) Garden and patio No smoking in dining-room No music No dogs in eating areas Access, Delta, Switch, Visa Accommodation: 12 rooms, B&B £35 to £45*

LLANDWROG Gwynedd map 7

▲ *Harp Inn*

Llandwrog TEL: (01286) 831071
off A499, 5m SW of Caernarfon

Weekend walking breaks and guide-led treks through Snowdonia are just two of the attractions offered by landlord Colin Downie in this stone-built inn opposite Llandwrog village church. Sustenance is geared to the needs of those with appetites sharpened by exercise and the open air. Big bowls of home-made soup share the billing with filled wholemeal 'hoagies' and a contingent of spicy dishes such as lamb rogan josh, beef dopiaza, vegetable curry, and chilli. Breakfast platefuls, chicken and leek pie, and pork Normandy are less exotic alternatives, and the sweet menu displays full-colour photos of the inn's banana split, knickerbocker glory and the like. A slightly more ambitious menu is served in the restaurant. Fans of Welsh beers will be delighted at the sight of New Cambrian Ale, Dr Johnson's Draught and Archdruid from Dyffryn Clwyd in Denbigh, plus more familiar names such as Felinfoel Double Dragon. A Welsh wine also shows up on the short, workmanlike list. The pub is one mile from the beach at Dinas Dinlle. SAMPLE DISHES: pan-fried garlic mushrooms and toast £2.75; a trio of lamb chops £8; sticky toffee pudding £2.50.

Open *high season Mon to Sat 11am to 11pm, Sun 12 to 10.30, low season Tue to Fri 12 to 3, Mon to Fri 6 to 11, Sat 12 to 11 Sun 12 to 3, 7 to 10.30; bar food Tue to Sun 12 to 2, 6.30 to 9; restaurant high season Sun L 12 to 2, Tue to Sat D 6.30 to 9, low season Sun L and Sat D only*

Details *Children welcome in dining-room and games room Car park Wheelchair access (also WC) Garden and patio No smoking in restaurant and 1 area of bar Background and occasional live music; jukebox No dogs in restaurant Access, Delta, Switch, Visa Accommodation: 4 rooms, B&B £17 to £22*

LLANFIHANGEL NANT MELAN Powys map 4

▲ *Red Lion Inn*

LOCAL PRODUCE

Llanfihangel nant Melan TEL: (01544) 350220
on A44 Rhayader to Kington road, 3m W of New Radnor

In the hands of the Johns family, this old drovers' inn by the New Radnor hills has proved itself to be the Welsh pub *par excellence*. The interior is no-frills, but the welcome is as warm and friendly as you could wish for. Gareth Johns's cooking is based resolutely on Welsh produce, whether it be excellent smoked salmon from Rhydlewis, cockles with bacon, or steaks from Welsh Black cattle. The value for money – both at lunch and dinner – is outstanding.

The menu is written up on a blackboard; it changes daily, and you can eat the same food in the bar or conservatory dining area. Red Lion pâté – a rich smooth gamey parfait – is one of the specialities of the house, gravlax is cured on the premises, and the repertoire also encompasses grilled Pencarreg goats' cheese, wild boar and apple sausages, and local lake trout. Elsewhere, the kitchen rings the changes with fresh fish – offering anything from halibut and sea bream to tilapia and shark. What impresses is the quality and the refreshing lack of pretension; there's no sense of the kitchen over-reaching itself simply for effect. Desserts are similarly forthright – raspberry tartlets, gooseberry crumble, tiramisù, plus locally made dairy ice-creams and sorbets; otherwise there's a generous spread of farmhouse cheeses from nearby dairies and further afield. Hook Norton Bitter is on draught; also look for Welsh mead, and even a Welsh whisky. The short wine list is notable for its low prices and quaffability. SAMPLE DISHES: cream of vegetable soup £2.50; cod with tarragon sauce £6; bread-and-butter pudding £2.50.

Open *Mon and Wed to Sat 11.30 to 3, 6.30 to 11, Sun 12 to 3, 7 to 10.30; bar food Mon and Wed to Sat 12 to 2, 6.30 to 9 (9.30 Sat)*

Report forms are at the back of the book; write a letter if you prefer.

Details *Children welcome Car park Garden No smoking in 1 dining-room No music Dogs in bar only Access, Delta, Visa Accommodation: 3 rooms, B&B £18 to £32*

LLANGATTOCK Powys map 4

Vine Tree Inn

The Legar, Llangattock TEL: (01873) 810514
off A40, SW of Crickhowell

Just outside Crickhowell, on a junction facing the River Usk, the Vine Tree pulls in the crowds with its extensive menu of freshly cooked food. Stuart and Cynthia Lennox and family plunder the world's recipe books for a repertoire that roams far and wide: baked egg provençale, chicken and prawn curry served in half a pineapple, rabbit in wine, celery and almond sauce, and monkfish flavoured with Pernod and leeks are typical. You can also get steaks and pies as well as a handful of vegetarian dishes. Ploughman's and the like are also served Monday to Saturday lunch-time, while Sunday heralds a traditional roast. Desserts include a vast range of ice-creams and everything from fruit trifle to hot Jamaican pancakes filled with rum, and custard cream. Fremlins Bitter, Boddingtons and Wadworth 6X are on draught, and the wine list is a useful selection of familiar names. Hikers can set off for the challenging slopes of the Black Mountains; others might prefer a more leisurely stroll from the village along the Monmouth & Brecon Canal. SAMPLE DISHES: smoked venison with cranberry sauce £4.50; trout in chive sauce £8.50; rhubarb crumble £2.75.

Open *12 to 3, 6 to 11, Sun 12 to 3, 7 to 10.30; bar food 12 to 2.30, 6 to 10*
Details *Children welcome Car park Wheelchair access Patio No music No dogs Access, Delta, Switch, Visa*

LLANGYBI Monmouthshire map 4

▲ *White Hart*

Llangybi TEL: (01633) 450258
just off A449, between Newport and Usk

Built in the twelfth century for Cistercian Monks and later commandeered by Henry VIII as part of Jane Seymour's wedding dowry, this secluded whitewashed pub still displays remnants of its past. Two original fireplaces remain in working order, the beams are dark, and there's exposed stonework to be seen; it is friendly, informal and has 'plenty of authentic, unspoilt character', concluded one reporter. The bar menu ranges far and wide, with black pudding with mustard sauce, breaded loin of pork in pineapple, coconut and Malibu sauce, and chicken and leek pie, and challenges trenchermen with marinated ribeye steaks. At lunch-time you can also get quick snacks in the shape of hot dogs, steak rolls, omelettes and so on. Puddings are mostly sticky things, sorbets and sundaes. Bass, Wadworth 6X and Hancocks HB are on draught, and the wine list is modestly priced. The pub is set in lovely countryside in the Usk vale. SAMPLE DISHES: fan of melon with apricot coulis £2.25; rack of lamb with redcurrant sauce £8; toffee and apple pie £2.25.

Open *Mon to Fri 11.30 to 3.30, 6 to 11, Sat 11am to 11pm, Sun 12 to 4, 7 to 10.30; bar food and restaurant 12 to 2.30, 7 to 10*
Details *Children welcome in bar eating area Car park Wheelchair access Patio Background music No dogs Access, Visa Accommodation: 2 rooms, B&B £25 to £35*

LLANGYNWYD Bridgend **map 4**

Old House

Llangynwyd TEL: (01656) 733310
off A4063, 2m S of Maesteg

The Old House is, according to the pub's literature, 'probably one of the oldest premises in Wales, dating back to 1147'. History is part and parcel of the inn: the building, which nestles behind the church and a Celtic cross, boasts literary associations with the 'legendary' Wil Hopkin and is the setting for the re-enactment of that ancient Welsh ritual, the Mari Lwyd. The roof is thatched, the stone walls are dauntingly thick. 'The bar is a gem,' wrote one enthusiastic visitor, who went on to talk about the blackened inglenook fireplace and the beamed ceilings festooned with ceramic drinking pots. This is the kind of place where you come to sit and relax and enjoy yourself: 'When we were there on a wet and windy lunch-time at the end of October, we estimated that over 100 people were doing just that,' noted the same correspondent. The food is 'respectable and generous', and there's always a good showing of fish from the market in the shape of, say, lightly grilled sardines, pan-fried hake tails, and poached salmon. Half a dozen specials, such as roast lamb fillets with orange and mint sauce, are also available; otherwise the printed menu trawls its way through cold meats, beef curry, boiled ham with parsley sauce, and grills. Draught beers include Flowers Original and IPA as well as Brains Bitter; 180 whiskies are kept in stock and the wine list is bolstered by monthly specials. Outside is a large garden with plenty of diversions for the children. SAMPLE DISHES: prawns in garlic sauce £4; chicken fillet with mushroom and white wine sauce £6.50; banana split £2.25.

Open *11.30 to 2, 6 to 10, Sun 12 to 3, 6 to 9; bar food and restaurant 11.30 to 2, 6 to 10*
Details *Children welcome Car park Wheelchair access (also WC) Garden and patio No-smoking area Background music No dogs Access, Delta, Switch, Visa*

LLANVAPLEY Monmouthshire **map 2**

Red Hart

Llanvapley TEL: (01600) 780227
on B4233, 4m E of Abergavenny

Four generations – including grandmother and grand-daughter – plus two cats make this unassuming roadside pub a genuine home-from-home, a 'truly family-run affair'. Most of the business of the day takes place in the stone-walled bar with its collection of plates and horse brasses; there's also a newish dining-room in what was once a cider press. The menu roams the world for influences, taking in Cajun chicken with sliced garlic potatoes, several versions of chilli ('Great Lakes', 'Cincinnati' and 'California'), roast haddock, various pastas and vegetable Stroganov, while pumpkin pie, chocolate bread-and-butter pudding, and jazzed-up ice-creams round things off. Landlord Mr Sharpe is always seeking out unlikely sounding real ales such as Warden Brewery CHB, Steam Packet Blow Job and Mendip Gold, which appear alongside Bass, Smiles Best and Hancocks HB; his wine list is due to be expanded in response to demand. SAMPLE DISHES: prawn Madras cocktail £3.50; pheasant in cider and brandy £7.50; treacle sponge and custard £2.75.

Open *Mon and Wed to Fri 12 to 3, Mon to Fri 5.30 to 11, Sat 12 to 11, Sun 12 to 3, 7 to 10.30; bar food Mon and Wed to Fri L 12 to 3, Mon to Fri D 5.30 to 9.30, Sat 12 to 9.30, Sun 12 to 3, 7 to 9.30; restaurant all week D only 5.30 to 9.30*
Details *Children welcome in bar eating area Car park Wheelchair access Garden No smoking in restaurant Background music Dogs welcome No cards*

LLANVIHANGEL CRUCORNEY Monmouthshire map 4

▲ *Skirrid Mountain Inn*

Llanvihangel Crucorney TEL: (01873) 890258
off A465, 4½m N of Abergavenny

You enter this ancient pub – dating from 1110 and said to be the oldest in Wales – via a wonderful creaking door and immediately face a small bar servery. The main room, with its old pews and dark furniture, a large open fire, smoking candles and high ceiling, leads to the dining area. A feeling of age permeates the place: panelling is said to be Elizabethan, and the carved wooden staircase is where criminals were hanged for sheep-stealing – the last in the seventeenth century, when the inn acted as a court-house. The same menu is served throughout, with much use made of fresh local produce in the form of trout, gammon with free-range eggs, wild rabbits served with herb and cream sauce, and venison sausages casseroled with porter. The inn is also known for its savoury accompaniments: raspberry preserve with deep-fried Camembert, and damson jelly with lamb chops, for example. Puddings might include apple pie or mandarin pavlova. The full complement of Ushers ales is on draught and in bottles (look for IPA and 1824 Particulars Ale), and house wines are sold by the glass. SAMPLE DISHES: smooth pâté £4; vegetarian Skirrid loaf £6.50; Merlyn's cream liqueur ice-cream £2.50.

Open *11 to 3, 6 to 11, Sun 12 to 3, 7 to 10.30 (12 to 10.30 summer); bar food all week L 12 to 2, Mon to Sat D 7 to 9*
Details *Children welcome Car park Garden and patio No music Dogs welcome No cards Accommodation: 2 rooms, B&B £50 to £70*

LLANYRE Powys map 4

▲ *Bell Inn*

Llanyre TEL: (01597) 823959
just off A3081, 1m W of Llandrindod Wells

A century brings many changes: the Bell was once a pit-stop and watering-hole for drovers *en route* to the markets of Gloucester and Hereford; now it's an 11-bedroom inn complete with two restaurants. Vegetarian food is taken seriously here, although the short bar menu pleases both camps with the likes of river trout cooked in butter, steak and stout pie, Stilton, apple and celery en croûte, or ratatouille suet pudding. Curries and meatless kebabs come with brown rice. Full vegetarian dinners are also available for those frequenting the dining-rooms rather than the bar. Hancocks HB,

Tomos Watkin Bitter, Wood's Woodcutter and Brain's SA suggest that this is an address worth noting in the drinker's diary, and the pub has what it calls a 'world-wide wine list' loaded with classics and champagnes. Llanyre is well placed for a jaunt to the Elan Valley. SAMPLE DISHES: corn on the cob with butter £2; turkey in tarragon sauce £5.50; spotted dick £2.50.

Open *11am to 11pm, Sun 12 to 3, 7 to 10.30; bar food and restaurants 11.30 to 2, 6.30 (7 Sun) to 9.30*
Details *Children welcome in bar eating area Car park Wheelchair access (also WC) Garden and patio No smoking in 1 restaurant Background music Dogs welcome in some rooms Access, Amex, Switch, Visa Accommodation: 9 rooms, B&B £35 to £70*

LLYSWEN Powys map 4

▲ *Griffin Inn*

Llyswen TEL: (01874) 754241
on A470 Builth Wells to Brecon road

One reporter's description of the Griffin as a 'large hairy pub' no doubt refers to the hirsute growth of Virginia creeper that clings and climbs over the exterior of the building. This 500-year-old inn stands in the beautiful expanses of the Wye Valley, although its position 'on a busy corner where the A470...joins the A479' may detract from the feeling of peace and solitude. Over the years Richard Stockton and family have turned the place into a renowned rendezvous for country sportsmen in search of fish and game. The immaculately maintained beamed bar on two levels is, in the words of one visitor, 'definitely a fisherman's bar, bristling with stuffed fish and framed displays of salmon and trout flies', although its main feature is a huge inglenook fireplace. It feels civilised and atmospherically convivial in an old-fashioned way.

The Griffin must be one of the few pubs that is 'twinned' – in this case it is paired with the auberge 'La Diege' in the Vallée de Lot; the kitchen even produces a warm salad in honour of its French counterpart. A chargrill is one recent addition to the inn's culinary armoury, and it might be used for everything from squid and salmon to Mediterranean vegetables. There are also modern overtones to dishes such grilled fillet of sea bass with pimento sauce and deep-fried leeks, or breast of woodpigeon with bubble and squeak. Welsh cockles with laverbread and home-made salsa is an impressively constructed dish of many colours and varied textures, but the main thrust of the cooking is still in the home country: bowls of 'smoothly liquidised' broccoli and basil soup, wild venison in a stew with mushrooms and chestnuts, ragoût of wild rabbit, roast pheasant with a compote of caramelised shallots, for example. Puddings make much of the fruit larder – wimberry pie with 'delicious' locally made ice-cream, autumn raspberries in a white chocolate mousse for example. The ever-evolving wine list includes 15 house selections by the glass as well as some French classics and a healthy assortment from the Antipodes. Beer drinkers have a choice of Flowers IPA and Boddingtons. SAMPLE DISHES: Cornish mussels in white wine with garlic and leeks £5.50; braised lamb shanks on boulangère potatoes £10; passion-fruit and lime cheesecake £3.25.

Open *12 to 3, 7 to 11, Sun 12 to 3, 7 to 10.30; bar food Mon to Sat 12 to 2, 7 to 9; restaurant Sun L 12.30 for 1, Mon to Sat D 7 to 9 (booking essential)*
Details *Children welcome Car park Wheelchair access (also WC) Patio No smoking in dining-room No music Dogs welcome Access, Amex, Delta, Diners, Switch, Visa Accommodation: 10 rooms, B&B £35 to £70*

MAENTWROG Gwynedd **map 7**

▲ *Grapes Hotel*

Main Street, Maentwrog TEL: (01766) 590365
off A496, 5m S of Blaenau Ffestiniog

Listen for the other-worldly tinklings of the piano-playing ghost. This highly popular coaching-inn makes much of its history and has seen some famous visitors over the years: George Borrow wrote about the parlour in his classic book *Wild Wales*, statesman Lloyd George stayed, Lilley Langtry took tea. Bar food is served in a setting of pitch pine pews and heavily carved oak, and the menu roams far and wide for Chinese hors d'oeuvre, vegetarian fajitas, pork balls stuffed with mozzarella cheese, and chicken korma. There are also fish specials such as Anglesey oysters, and fresh crab with malt whisky and mayonnaise. Sandwiches are available Monday to Saturday, and Sunday lunch is a roast. Five real ales, including Pedwar Bawd and Cambrian Original, are usually on tap, and the pub has a short list of affordable wines. There are especially fine views of the mountains of Snowdonia and the River Dwyryd from the covered verandah, and the Ffestiniog narrow gauge railway is within easy reach. SAMPLE DISHES: prawn and apple salad £4; rack of local Welsh lamb £7.75; white and dark chocolate gâteau £3.25.

Open *11am to 11pm, Sun 12 to 10.30; bar food Mon to Fri 12 to 2.15, 6 to 9.30, Sat and Sun 12 to 9.30*
Details *Children welcome in dining-room Car park Wheelchair access (also WC) No smoking in dining-room Jukebox in bar Dogs welcome Access, Amex, Diners, Switch, Visa Accommodation: 8 rooms, B&B £25 to £50*

indicates a pub serving exceptional draught beers.

MARFORD Wrexham map 7

▲ *Trevor Arms Hotel*

Marford TEL: (01244) 570436

Once a coaching-inn, but now updated to suit the needs of today's travellers, the Trevor Arms continues to provide welcome sustenance in agreeable surroundings. The printed bar menu embraces everything from garlic mushrooms, and barbecued spare ribs, to salads and chargrilled steaks; also look for the 'curry of the day' and blackboard specials such as sweet-and-sour pork. At lunch-time (except Sundays) sandwiches, ploughman's and jacket potatoes are also available. Some more ambitious offerings along the lines of 'rustic' chicken, ham and asparagus terrine, and rack of lamb with creamed leeks and pink peppercorn sauce, feature on the restaurant menu. A carvery operates from 6 to 8 evenings. Greenalls and Tetley Bitter are augmented by two guest ales each week, and the pub has a short, serviceable wine list. SAMPLE DISHES: sauté king prawns with garlic and herb butter £5; beef bourguignon £5.50; apple crumble £2.50.

Open *all week 11.30 to 11; bar food and restaurant 12 to 2.30, 6 (7 Sun) to 9.45*

Details *Children welcome in eating areas Car park Wheelchair access (also WC) Garden and patio No-smoking area in dining-room Background music Guide dogs only Access, Amex, Visa Accommodation: 20 rooms, B&B £29 to £42*

PEMBROKE FERRY Pembrokeshire map 4

Ferry Inn

Pembroke Ferry TEL: (01646) 682947

off A477, N of Pembroke at southern end of Cleddau Bridge

As its name suggests, the Ferry Inn stands right by Pembroke dock, with excellent waterside views of the nautical action on the busy estuary. On the food front, the main attraction is the list of fresh seafood specials: you can expect anything from whole plaice, and fish, prawn and mushroom crumble, to more exotic offerings such as salmon en croûte, or fillets of sea bass with hollandaise sauce. For those with a taste for meat, there are steaks, 'old-fashioned' spiced beef, lamb kebabs marinated with honey and mint, curries and casseroles. Breaded mushrooms, and potato skins filled with blue cheese mayonnaise, are typical starters, while sweets might include coffee meringue or chocolate roulade. A hot carvery is served Sunday lunch-time in the restaurant, which is also open for more formal evening meals. Bass and Hancocks HB are on draught, Staropramen

Czech lager comes in bottles, and five house wines are sold by the glass. Pembroke Castle is a short drive away. SAMPLE DISHES: garlic tiger prawns £4; bacon steak with parsley sauce £5; raspberry and hazelnut roulade £2.25.

Open *11.30 to 2.45, 6.30 (7 Mon) to 11, Sun 12 to 2.45, 7 to 10.30; bar food 12 to 2, 7 to 10 (9.30 Sun); restaurant Sun L 12 to 2.45, Tue to Sat D 7 to 10; closed 25 and 26 Dec*

Details *Children welcome in dining-room Car park Wheelchair access Patio Background music in dining-room No dogs Access, Amex, Diners, Visa*

PENALLT Monmouthshire map 2

Boat Inn

Long Lane, Penallt TEL: (01600) 712615

just across footbridge from Redbrook (car park off A466 Monmouth to Chepstow road in Redbrook)

Eight to ten daily-changing real ales are a hallmark at this stone-built pub: Theakston Old Peculier, Freeminer Speculation Ale, Hook Norton Old Hooky, and Greene King Abbot Ale might be among those available. Country wines get a good look-in too – parsnip, for example. Inside, it is unspoilt, with plain stone walls, a red-tiled floor, a wood-burner and an old piano; the atmosphere is very friendly – as it needs to be, for space is limited. The menu ranges from ploughman's and baked jacket potatoes to curries (beef and spinach, say) and dishes such as rabbit and orange pie, or turkey and mushroom crumble, with a fair showing of vegetarian options along the lines of pan haggerty, or leek and parsnip Lancashire bake. Bread-and-butter pudding may be among the desserts listed on a blackboard. The pub is only just over the border in Wales, with its car park in England on the opposite bank of the River Wye; it can be reached by crossing a narrow footbridge. Tables in the terraced gardens make the most of the waterside location. Tintern Abbey is downstream, and Offa's Dyke long-distance footpath is on the English side of the water. SAMPLE DISHES: Welsh rarebit £1.75; prawn curry with noodles £4.75; apple crumble £2.

Open *11 to 3, 6 to 11 (Sat Easter to Sept 11am to 11pm), Sun 12 to 3, 7 to 10.30; bar food 12 to 2.30, 6 to 9.30*

Details *Children welcome Car park Wheelchair access Garden and patio Live music Dogs welcome No cards*

If a pub has a special point of interest, this is indicated by a 'flashed' word or phrase at the top right of the entry.

PENMAENPOOL Gwynedd map 7

▲ *George III Hotel*

Penmaenpool TEL: (01341) 422525
on A493, 2m W of Dolgellau

The setting is a stunner. This seventeenth-century hotel – once a ship chandler's and local pub rolled into one – overlooks the glorious Mawwdach Estuary and the Diffwys mountains beyond; great walks, fishing and birdwatching on the adjacent RSPB Centre are prime inducements for visitors. Two bars, including one for children, have fine views of the water. The menu is a straightforward slate that kicks off with Welsh rarebit, smoked trout, and ploughman's (try the version with Pen-y-Bryn cheese); to follow, there might be grilled lamb cutlets with fresh tomato and mint sauce, tuna steak with Spanish salad, and Cumberland sausage with onion gravy, as well as omelettes. Also look for specials such as moules marinière, and Cardigan Bay crab. Desserts range from baked Alaska for two to rhubarb and apple crumble. A full menu is also available in the restaurant. Locally brewed Cambrian Ale is on draught, along with John Smith's and Ruddles Best Bitter; five house wines are served by the glass, and the full list suits the needs of customers in the dining-room. SAMPLE DISHES: hot shrimps with toast £5; roast spare-ribs with barbecue sauce £6.75; raspberry Romanoff £4.

Open *11am to 11pm, Sun 12 to 3, 7 to 10.30; bar food 12 to 2.30, 6.30 (7 Sun) to 9.30; afternoon tea 2.30 to 6.30; restaurant D only 7 to 9*
Details *Children welcome in 1 bar Car park Wheelchair access (also WC) Garden and patio No smoking in restaurant and 1 bar Background music No dogs in restaurant Access, Delta, Switch, Visa Accommodation: 11 rooms, B&B £38 to £88*

PWLLGLOYW Powys map 4

Seland Newydd

Pwllgloyw TEL: (01874) 690282
on B4520, 4m N of Brecon

The name is Welsh for 'New Zealand', which is where the landlord's wife is from. Since moving here in 1996, Maynard and Freya Harvey have transformed this roadside hostelry (formerly the Camden Arms) into a stylish dining pub. The public bar, with its flagstone floor and plain wooden furniture, still has the feel of a 'farmers' bar', observed one reporter. Here you can sample heart-warming dishes such as stew and dumplings, or Welsh faggots with mash, peas and onion gravy, as well as home-made hummus with nan bread, salmon fish-cakes with provençale sauce, and breast of chicken with a shallot, rosemary and garlic sauce. The well-laid-out restaurant offers more ambitious stuff, along the lines of wild mushroom soup with pistachio nuts, king scallops with crab, ginger and spring onion sauce, and banana and toffee crême brûlée. Some of these dishes also appear as specials in the bar. Brains SA, Courage Directors and Ruddles should satisfy the real-ale brigade, while the list of around 30 wines is reckoned to be 'excellent value'. SAMPLE DISHES: chicken liver parfait with sweet-and-sour sauce £3; venison and brown ale pie £6; chocolate and Grand Mariner torte £4.

Open *11 to 3, 6 to 11, Sun 11 to 3, 6 to 10.30; bar food and restaurant 12 to 2.30, 7 to 9.15*
Details *Children welcome Car park Garden Background music Dogs welcome Access, Delta, Diners, Switch, Visa*

RED WHARF BAY **Isle of Anglesey** **map 7**

Ship Inn

Red Wharf Bay TEL: (01248) 852568
off A5025, 6m N of Menai Bridge

With its spectacular views over Red Wharf Bay on the south-eastern promontory of Anglesey, this unpretentious sixteenth-century whitewashed inn, run for the past 25 years by landlord Andrew Kenneally, draws the crowds in summer. Chairs and tables on the front terrace look out over the wide, sandy bay and the numerous boats moored there. Open fires blaze in winter, the dining-room at the back becomes a no-smoking family room by day, and a 'friendly informality pervades'. Among the imaginative bar food might be baked half-shoulder of Welsh lamb, parsnip and mushroom Stroganov, grey mullet on a bed of local mussels, or venison sausages; otherwise choose from pub staples such as ploughman's, pies, and baguettes. Real ales include Friary Meux, Tetley Bitter and Ind Coope Burton Ale. House wines are sold by the glass, and the list is better than average for a pub; there's also a good selection of about 20 malt whiskies. SAMPLE DISHES: leek and potato soup £2.50; chicken breast with Stilton and bacon £6.50; summer pudding £2.75.

Open *summer 11am to 11pm, winter 11 to 4, 6 to 11; bar food 12 to 2.30, 7 (6 summer) to 9.30; restaurant Thurs to Sun D, and special occasions, 7 (6 summer) to 9.30*
Details *Children welcome in dining-room Car park Wheelchair access Garden and patio No smoking in 1 room Background music No dogs Access, Delta, Switch, Visa*

RHYD-DDU Gwynedd map 7

Cwellyn Arms

Rhyd-ddu TEL: (01766) 890321
on A4085, between Caernarfon and Beddgelert

The Cwellyn Arms has splendid views towards Snowdon, and the pub is at the start of the Nantlle Ridge, a popular route for hikers. The proprietors are dedicated to providing food, drink and hospitality to all comers of all ages – locals, tourists, walkers and climbers. Inside, the pub is comfortable rather than stylish, with a huge log fire the focus of the two bars; there's a separate food-ordering area and restaurant tables beyond. The extensive menu of sustaining dishes runs from soup to the likes of pork spare ribs, a range of pies, pizzas and curries, and 'hot and spicy' Mexican beef. A reporter singled out ribeye steak, chicken tikka masala and chicken korma as 'all good', and desserts might include trifle, and summer pudding. Children have a separate menu, and barbecues are held outside in summer. The pub is renowned for its wide choice of draught beers: up to nine may be on offer, including Saddlers Best Bitter, Adnams Broadside, Gales HSB and Vaux Waggle Dance. House wines from a short list are sold by the glass. SAMPLE DISHES: vegetarian pâté £4; chicken and prawn pie £6.50; bread-and-butter pudding £2.50.

Open *all week 11am to 11pm; bar food and restaurant 11 to 10.30*
Details *Children welcome Car park Wheelchair access Garden No smoking in restaurant Background music Dogs welcome in snug bar only No cards*

ROSEBUSH Pembrokeshire map 4

Tafarn Newydd

Rosebush TEL: (01437) 532542
on B4313, 8m SE of Fishguard

Tafarn Newydd, Welsh for 'New Inn', is way out in the sticks, by a crossroads at the foot of the pass that cuts through the highest part of the Preseli hills. Remote it may be, but judging by the crowds, aficionados know exactly where to come. Go through the door and you are immediately in a traditional country pub with flagstone floors, a real log fire burning in the ancient stone hearth (even in May) and beams over the ceiling. Favourable first impressions are reinforced by the line-up of handpumps on the bar, with Buckley's Best and Reverend James alongside guest ales such as Merlin's Oak, Greene King Abbot Ale and Charles Wells Bombardier, not to mention Weston's Old Rosie cider. And if you turn up on Monday evening, there's likely to be live music – probably folk.

Chef/landlady Diana Richards is an enthusiastically eclectic cook who leapfrogs around the globe for culinary inspiration. The blackboard in the bar tells its own story: cawl with cheese, gratin of cockles with bacon and laverbread, and rarebit of Rosebush goats' cheese fly the flag for the Welsh dragon, but patriotism is tempered with an international curiosity. The result is a menu that also includes Thai fish-cakes with cucumber salad, oxtail with olives, Irish stew, and Vietnamese chicken with lemon grass – although a half-pint of 'succulent' fresh prawns is also a contender for anyone who wants a snack. Puddings are in similar style: gooseberry fool fragrant with rosewater, tangy lemon posset, coconut crème caramel, spumoni amaretti, for example. Beyond the bar is a modern, bistro-style dining-room with a bare tiled floor and walls ragged in shades of blue-green; this is the setting for more ambitious evening meals. France and Australia are the main contributors to the lively modern wine list, which has bags of high-quality drinking at reasonable prices. SAMPLE DISHES: crostini of garlic mushrooms £4; seafood lasagne £6; banana sticky toffee pudding £3.

Open *11am to 11pm, Sun 12 to 10.30; bar food 12 (12.30 Sun) to 2.30, 6.30 to 9.30; restaurant Tue to Sat D only 7 to 9.30*
Details *Children welcome in eating areas Car park Wheelchair access (also WC) Garden and patio No smoking in restaurant Live music Dogs welcome in public bar only Access, Visa*

RUTHIN Denbighshire **map 7**

▲ *Ye Olde Anchor*

Rhos Street, Ruthin TEL: (01824) 702813
at junction of A525 and A494

Once a stopover for drovers *en route* between Shropshire and Holyhead, this eighteenth-century inn is at the heart of Ruthin – which is rated as one of most attractive market towns in Wales. Don't miss the craft centre, the half-timbered courthouse or Nantclwyd House (a gem of a medieval building). Ye Olde Anchor is smart, neat and white with colourful window boxes; judging by the inglenook fireplace, beams and abundant copper and brass, the interior is clearly the genuine article. Most of pub's business is built around its restaurant and accommodation, but the food served in the lounge bar is highly commendable. Various ploughman's and excellent savoury pancakes are the mainstays, backed up by spannakopita ('a good lunch-time filler'), toasted steak sandwiches, omelettes and so forth; desserts are recited at the table. Bass and Hancocks HB are on draught, and the inn has a sound list of around two dozen wines courtesy of Tanners of Shrewsbury. Snowdonia National Park is virtually on the doorstep. SAMPLE DISHES: garlic mushrooms in Boursin cheese sauce £3; beef lasagne £4.25; chocolate fudge cake £2.

Open *12 to 2, 5.30 to 11, Sun 12 to 2, 7 to 10.30; bar food Mon to Sat L 12 to 2, all week D 7 to 9; restaurant D only 7 to 9*
Details *Children welcome Car park Wheelchair access (also WC) No smoking in restaurant Background music Dogs welcome Access, Amex, Delta, Diners, Switch, Visa Accommodation: 14 rooms, room only £23 to £65*

ST HILARY Vale of Glamorgan **map 4**

▲ *Bush Inn* 🍇

St Hilary TEL: (01446) 772745
off A48 Cardiff to Bridgend road

Half a mile from this striking sixteenth-century pub deep in the Vale of Glamorgan is Stalling Down, where Roman legions camped, Owain Glyndwr won a famous victory and, according to the licensees, a local highwayman called Ianto Ffranc was hanged. His ghost is said to haunt the inn – a sturdy edifice of bare stone walls and original oak beams. Food is a major attraction and the value for money is hard to beat. Starters such as Welsh rarebit, ratatouille, or spinach and cheese crêpes could be followed by steak and ale pie, tagliatelle provençale, liver and onions, or grilled plaice. Home-made puddings such as raspberry and sherry trifle, or coffee and almond charlotte, round things off. Three-course bar lunches and suppers are also highly affordable; in the evening you can also order from the restaurant menu, which features dishes like rack of Welsh lamb, and pan-fried trout in sherry. The wine list is a carefully chosen slate taking in reliable names from around the globe; note the Welsh Croffta. Beer drinkers have a choice of Hancock's HB, Bass and Morland Old Speckled Hen. SAMPLE DISHES: laverbread with bacon £2.50; baked ham and parsley sauce £4.25; lemon tart £2.50.

Open *all week 11.30 to 11; bar food and restaurant 12 to 2.30, 7 to 10, Sun 12 to 10.30*
Details *Children welcome in dining-room Car park Wheelchair access (also WC) Garden and patio Background music No dogs Access, Switch, Visa Accommodation: 3 rooms, B&B £17 to £35*

🍇 *indicates a pub serving better-than-average wine.*

SHIRENEWTON Monmouthshire **map 2**

Carpenters Arms

Shirenewton TEL: (01291) 641231
off B4235, 4m W of Chepstow

Originally a carpenter's shop, blacksmith's and public house all rolled into one, this sixteenth-century pub might now be mistaken for an antique shop, with its clutter of curios of every description. The interior is a maze of rooms on various levels, with the promise of a blazing fire if winter closes in. To warm the inner man, there's a menu of home-cooked dishes with an international flavour, ranging from liver and bacon, and suprême of chicken in leek and Stilton sauce, to paella; desserts are the comforting kind – bread-and-butter pudding, blackberry and apple crumble and so on. Landlord James Bennett keeps a good cellar, with half a dozen real ales usually on tap: expect Fuller's London Pride, Timothy Taylor Landlord, Marston's Owd Rodger and Greene King Abbot Ale, among others. Forty malt whiskies and a few wines complete the picture. Shirenewton is set in spectacular scenery between Chepstow and Usk. SAMPLE DISHES: garlic mushrooms £2; steak and mushroom pie £5.50; ice-cream and ginger-snaps £2.50.

Open *11 to 2.30, 6 to 11, Sun 12 to 3, 7 to 10.30; bar food 11.45 to 2, 6.45 to 9.30 (10 Fri and Sat), Sun D summer only*
Details *No children Car park Patio Background music Dogs welcome on a lead No cards*

SOLVA Pembrokeshire **map 4**

Cambrian Inn

Solva TEL: (01437) 721210
off A487, 3m W of St David's

Solva takes its tourism seriously and the Cambrian Inn is very much part of the scene. It is ideally placed at the bottom of a steep valley, with a river snaking its way out towards the sea. Eating is the prime business of the day in the three main rooms, and the printed menu and specials board advertise plenty that is 'home-made'. You might start with a bowl of cawl, or fish chowder with garlic bread, and finish with orange bread-and-butter pudding laced with Amaretto; in between you could find beef cobbler, fish pie, fusilli and tuna bake, and vegetable lasagne. Sandwiches, ploughman's, and jacket potatoes are served at lunch-time, and a few more ambitious dishes such as halibut with Dijon mustard sauce, and Welsh Black steak with red wine and mushroom sauce appear in the evening. Worthington Best Bitter and Tetley Bitter are usually on handpump, and the pub has a short, serviceable wine list. SAMPLE DISHES: French onion soup £3.75; salmon fish-cakes £5.25; pears with ice-cream and hot chocolate sauce £3.25.

Open *12 to 3, 7 to 11, Sun 12 to 2, 7 to 10; bar food and restaurant 12 to 2, 7 to 9.30 (9 winter)*
Details *No children under 10 Car park Wheelchair access (also WC) Patio Background music Guide dogs only No cards*

STACKPOLE Pembrokeshire map 4

Armstrong Arms

LOCAL PRODUCE

Jasons Corner, Stackpole TEL: (01646) 672324
off B4319, 3m S of Pembroke; follow signs for Stackpole Village

Lovers of brisk exercise and bracing breezes should beat a path to Peter and Senga Waddilove's sixteenth-century pub in the Pembrokeshire National Park. The walking in these parts is great: set your sights on Barafundle Bay, Stackpole Quay and the coastal footpath. The Waddiloves are keen on local produce and make use of everything from fish and game to Pembrokeshire sausages and Welsh cheeses. High aspirations and a global outlook are the hallmarks of their lunch and slightly more elaborate dinner menus: lamb meatballs come with tomato sauce and spaghetti, baked hock of ham is served with spiced lentils, while fillet of sea bass is steamed with lemon grass, coriander and vermouth. Puddings 'by Maria and Laura' range from chocolate and rum torte to blackcurrant bavarois. Half a dozen handpumps now dispense the likes of Worthington Best Bitter, Charles Wells Bombardier and Bateman's XB, and the pub has a short but promising wine list. Do not confuse Stackpole with Cheriton (otherwise known as Stackpole Elidor), which is just up the road. SAMPLE DISHES: Piedmont roasted peppers with crusty bread £3.50; breast of Barbary duck with spiced red cabbage £9; pear and almond tart £3.

Open *11.30 to 3, 6 to 11, Sun 12 to 3, 7 to 10.30; bar food and restaurant 12 to 2, 7 to 9 (July to Aug 6.30 to 9.30)*
Details *Children welcome Car park Wheelchair access by arrangement (also WC) Garden Jukebox Dogs welcome in bar only No cards*

Licensing hours and bar food times are based on information supplied by each establishment and are correct at the time of going to press.

TRELLECH Monmouthshire map 2

▲ *Village Green*

Trellech TEL: (01600) 860119
on B4293, 5m S of Monmouth

At first glance, the Village Green may seem more like a brasserie/restaurant than a pub: as you go into the solid three-storey building, there's a small but cosy bar to the left, and to the right an equally small lounge, with a large two-level dining-room further on. Beamed ceilings adorned with dried flowers, scythes and sickles, exposed stone-walls with old tin advertising signs, stone fireplaces and a profusion of knick-knacks set the style. Lunchtime bar snacks are the usual sandwiches, jacket potatoes, and deep-fried potato skins with perhaps sun-dried tomatoes, mozzarella and pesto, but you can always order from the printed list of starters and the blackboard menu of main courses. Flair and imagination are apparent in choux buns with wild mushrooms and Madeira, or venison sausage with sage-and-onion sauce to start; otherwise you could try plainly baked sewin, pork with apple and calvados, or chicken with prawns and mushrooms. To finish, there may be citrus pudding with lemon-curd ice-cream, apple brûlée, or a fruit crumble. Bass is on draught and house wines are served by the glass from a short list. SAMPLE DISHES: pigeon and basil terrine with apple sauce £3.75; seafood chowder £10; pear and honey mousse £3.50.

Open *Tue to Sat 10 to 3, 6.30 to 11, Sun 12 to 3; bar food and restaurant Tue to Sun L 12 to 1.45, Tue to Sat D 6.45 to 9.45*
Details *Children welcome Car park Wheelchair access (also WC) Patio Background music Guide dogs only Access, Delta, Switch, Visa Accommodation: 2 rooms, B&B £35 to £45*

ISLE OF MAN

PEEL **Isle of Man** **map 8**

Creek Inn

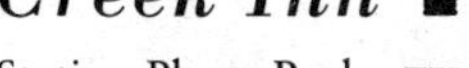

Station Place, Peel TEL: (01624) 842216

The quayside setting is a dream and the Creek Inn makes the most of it. You can look out over the water to Peel's venerable harbour and ruined castle or sit inside and feast on local seafood. Manx queenies, crab and lobsters (in summer) appear in various guises, but don't miss the kippers from local curer John Curtis. Other items on the short blackboard menu might include a tropical salad bowl topped with creamy yoghurt dressing, club sandwiches, steak and kidney pie, and lasagne. Desserts are things like Alabama fudge cake, or apple pie. Okells Bitter and Mild from the Isle of Man Brewery are bolstered by Post Horn Premium and various guest brews; a dozen wines are sold by the glass, bottle or carafe. The licensees tell us that they will be offering accommodation from Easter 1997. SAMPLE DISHES: pâté with redcurrant jelly £4; fisherman's pie £5.25; sticky toffee meringue £2.

Open *10am to 11pm (midnight Fri and Sat), Sun 12 to 3, 7 to 10.30; bar food 10am to 11pm (midnight Fri and Sat), Sun 12 to 3, 7 to 10.30*
Details *Children welcome in bar eating area Car park Wheelchair access (also WC) Patio Background and live music; jukebox No dogs Access, Visa*

OUT AND ABOUT

OUT AND ABOUT

Country pubs have all kinds of attractions, and people use them for all kinds of reasons. Pubs in 'Out and About' are a mixed bag, but each has some special quality that makes it well worth visiting; those marked with a ◆ have that little bit extra that makes them a cut above the rest.

Some of the pubs listed here are superlative outlets for real ale; others have fascinating history and architecture. There are hostelries close to public gardens, castles, rivers and canals; walkers, bird-watchers, climbers and fishermen will also find plenty of establishments that are handy for their own interests. Many places are also excellent family venues, and some may offer decent accommodation.

Most of these pubs serve food, although that is not the main reason for their inclusion in 'Out and About'. Food is often incidental to the proceedings, and some places provide only limited snacks; a few serve no food at all.

Pubs are listed on the basis of readers' recommendations, backed up in many cases by inspectors' reports. Further feedback on these places is most welcome.

ENGLAND

ABBOTS BROMLEY

Staffordshire map 5

Bagot Arms

Bagot Street
TEL: (01283) 840371
on B5104, 6m W of Uttoxeter
The famous Horn Dance brings enthusiasts to this eighteenth-century pub around the first week in September. Anglers also use the place as a meeting point between trips to the nearby reservoir. Brewing memorabilia fills the bar, where ales from Marston's and Bateman are on draught alongside some interesting bottled beers. Children are welcome if eating.
Open *12 to 3, 5.30 to 11 (7 to 10.30 Sun)*

ABBOTSBURY

Dorset map 2

Ilchester Arms

Market Street
TEL: (01305) 871243
on B3157, 9m W of Weymouth
An excellent, atmospheric pit-stop if you are exploring the 'stunning' village of Abbotsbury, with its ruined abbey, famous Swannery and 'the largest tithe barn in England'. Inside, the look is old-fashioned and Flowers Original and Wadworth 6X are on handpump. Children are welcome, and the pub offers accommodation.
Open *11am to 11pm, Sun 12 to 3, 7 to 10.30*

AINSTABLE

Cumbria map 10

New Crown

TEL: (01768) 896273
take A6 from M6 Jct. 41, follow signs to Armathwaite, then 2m to Ainstable
Usefully placed for a trip to some of the lesser-known corners of the Eden Valley and Talkin Tarn. New licensees have improved the list of real ales, which now includes North Country brews such as Mitchell's Lancaster Bomber and Doris's 90th Birthday Ale from the Hesket Newmarket Brewery. Children can eat in the dining-room, and the pub provides accommodation.
Open *12 to 3, 6 to 11, Sun 12 to 3, 7 to 10.30*

ALDEBURGH

Suffolk map 6

Ye Olde Cross Keys Inn

Crabbe Street
TEL: (01728) 452637
on A1094, 8m E of A12
Great in summer, when you can sunbathe on the shingle beach by the lifeboat station or put your feet up in the gravelled garden and sup Adnams beer. In winter the beamed bar provides cosy solace from the North Sea gales. Children are welcome in eating areas.
Open *11 to 3, 5.30 to 11, Sun 12 to 3, 7 to 10.30, summer 11am to 11pm, Sun 12 to 10.30*

ALMONDSBURY

South Gloucestershire map 2

Bowl Inn

16 Church Road
TEL: (01454) 612757
off A38, 7m N of Bristol
Old stone-built inn – parts of it date from the twelfth century, we are told – named after its location on the edge of the Severn estuary. The setting – within reach of Slimbridge Wildfowl Reserve – is one attraction, the pub's function facilities are another. Six real ales might include Smiles Best and Otter Bright (the list changes regularly) and there is Somerset cider brandy on show. Children are welcome, and the inn has ten *en suite* bedrooms.
Open *11 to 3, 5 (6 Sat) to 11, Sun 12 to 3, 7 to 10.30*

ALSTON

Cumbria map 10

Turk's Head Inn

Market Place
TEL: (01434) 381148
at junction of A686/A689/B6277, 16m NE of Penrith
A favoured destination if you have scaled Hartop Fell and have found

your way to the 'highest market town in England' with its magnificent moorland scenery all around. In the bar the mood is chatty and the draught beers (from Bentley, Boddingtons, Theakston and others) are fine. Children are welcome if eating.
Open *11 to 4, 6.30 to 11, Sun 12 to 3.30, 7 to 10.30*

ALVESTON

Warwickshire map 5

Ferry Inn

Ferry Lane
TEL: (01789) 269883
off B4056, between Stratford-upon-Avon and Wellsbourne
Popular as the target for trips out from Stratford (only two miles away) and close to the River Avon and Charlecote Park (National Trust). The interior is neat and tidy, the atmosphere is unpretentious and familiar real ales are on tap. A change of licensee was imminent as we went to press.
Open *11 to 2.30, 6 to 11, Sun 12 to 2.30, 7 to 10.30 (9 to 10.30 winter)*

AMBLESIDE

Cumbria map 8

Kirkstone Pass Inn

TEL: (01539) 433624
on A592, 4m NW of Ambleside
Remoteness and beautiful views down towards Windermere are what inspire travellers to trek out to this 'quaint' but welcoming 500-year-old inn. Depending on the weather, there might be Tetley Bitter, Fuggles Imperial and Calders on draught. Children are welcome away from the bar, and each bedroom boasts a four-poster.
Open *11am to 11pm, Sun 12 to 3, 7 to 10.30*

ANICK

Northumberland map 10

Rat Inn

TEL: (01434) 602814
just N of A69, 1½m NE of Hexham
A weird name for a pub, but one worth earmarking if you are fond of esoteric real ales. The line-up here includes Rat Bitter and King Rat, as well as Vaux Waggle Dance and Samson, Ward's Best and Thorne Best. Children can use the conservatory, dining-room and garden. The pub has splendid views across the Tyne Valley.
Open *11 to 3, 6 to 11, Sun 12 to 3, 7 to 10.30*

APPLETON ROEBUCK

North Yorkshire map 9

Shoulder of Mutton

Chapel Green
TEL: (01904) 744227
3m SE of A64 Leeds to York road, turn off at Colton Lane End
'We went three times in one week and enjoyed every moment,' admitted one couple who fell in love with this bustling village local overlooking the green and the square. Samuel Smith real ales are hand-pulled from wooden casks. Children are welcome in the dining area, and there's a garden at the back of the pub.
Open *11 to 3, 6.30 to 11, Sun 12 to 3, 7 to 10.30*

ARNCLIFFE

North Yorkshire map 8

Falcon

TEL: (01756) 770205
off B6160, 7m NW of Grassington
Landlord Robin Miller has carried on the tradition of family ownership in this Dales pub for more than 20 years. Younger's beer is gravity-fed, cider comes in bottles. Food is limited to snacks at lunch-time – when families are welcome to sit in the conservatory. The pub offers B&B in summer.
Open *12 to 3, 6.30 (7 Sun) to 11 (10.30 Sun, 9 all week in winter)*

ASHBURNHAM

East Sussex map 3

Ashtree Inn

TEL: (01424) 892104

just off B2204 (off A271), 4m W of Battle

Delightfully unspoilt pub in the midst of 'beautiful East Sussex countryside' close to the historic town of Battle and Ashburnham Park. Seafood gets the thumbs-up on the menu and the there's a decent choice of drinks. Children are welcome in the restaurant.

Open *Tue to Sun and bank hols 12 to 3, 7 to 11 (10.30 Sun)*

ASHENDON

Buckinghamshire map 2

Gatehangers Inn

TEL: (01296) 651296

off A41, midway between Bicester and Aylesbury

The name has changed (it used to be the Red Lion), but the panoramic views of the Vale of Aylesbury from this 400-year-old pub are unaltered. A new regime was settling in as we went to press, so progress reports are welcome. Hollands Bitter, Wadworth Henry's Original IPA and Hook Norton Bitter are typical real ales. Children are welcome, and the pub offers *en suite* accommodation.

Open *all week 12 to 2.30, 7 to 11*

ASHLEWORTH

Gloucestershire map 5

Boat Inn ◆

Ashleworth Quay

TEL: (01452) 700272

off A417, 5m N of Gloucester

Five-centuries-old riverside gem by the quay and the site of the ancient chain ferry across the Severn – once also the haunt of salmon netters. Inside is all cottage-style simplicity, outside is the old brewhouse and benches where visitors can enjoy the waterscapes. Excellent real ales might include Arkell's 3B, Smiles Best, Oakhill Yeoman 1767, Brandy Snapper and others; the full range of Weston's ciders is also on show. Food is confined to filled rolls and lunchtime snacks.

Open *11 to 2.30, 7 to 11 (11 to 3, 6 to 11 in summer), Sun 12 to 3, 7 to 10.30*

ASTON CREWS

Hereford & Worcester map 5

Penny Farthing

TEL: (01989) 750366

Just off B4222, 4m SW of Newent

An 'excellent' garden with views across the valley to the Forest of Dean is a plus point at this smartly refurbished seventeenth-century inn (originally a blacksmith's shop). Inside, a comfortable atmosphere pervades the pine-furnished bar, where Marston's ales are on draught. Children are welcome.

Open *12 to 3, 6 to 11, Sun 12 to 3, 7 to 10.30*

AYOT ST LAWRENCE

Hertfordshire map 3

Brocket Arms

TEL: (01438) 820250

off B656/B651, 2m W of Welwyn

Enjoy a pint of Greene King IPA, Wadworth 6X or Morland Old Speckled Hen in the atmospheric bars of this fourteenth-century inn (once the monastic quarters for the Norman church). But beware: a ghostly priest is said to haunt the place. The walled garden is a sun-trap and the pub provides accommodation.

Open *11am to 11pm, Sun 12 to 10.30*

BARBON

Cumbria map 8

Barbon Inn

TEL: (01524) 276233

just off A683, 3m N of Kirkby Lonsdale

Seventeenth-century coaching-inn nestling in prime walking country between the Dales and the Lake District. Theakston Best and Old Peculier are on draught and the wine list has a noticeable antipodean accent. Children are welcome, and the pub has useful family accommodation.

Open *12 to 3, 6.30 (7 Sun) to 11*

BARTON

Warwickshire map 5

Cottage of Content

15 Welford Road
TEL: (01789) 772279
off A439, just S of Bidford-on-Avon
Right on the River Avon and handily placed seven miles from Stratford-upon-Avon. Theakston Best, Courage Directors and Flowers IPA are on handpump. This is 'the home of espetada' (grilled meats on skewers), claims the menu. Children are welcome throughout the pub.
Open *11 to 2.30, 6 to 11, Sun 12 to 3, 7 to 10.30*

BECK HOLE

North Yorkshire map 9

Birch Hall ◆

TEL: (01947) 896245
off A169, 2m S of Grosmont
First licensed in 1860 as pub-cum-village store, this glorious little pub rings with echoes of the past. In the cellar there are casks from breweries near and far, plus Theakston Bitter, XB and Mild Ale, as well as Black Sheep Bitter. Simple food is served in the tiny bar, and there's a family area for children. Quoits pitches are laid out on the village green and local teams contest trophies fiercely. Excellent walking and sightseeing nearby.
Open *May to Oct 11am to 11pm, Sun 12 to 10.30, Oct to Apr 11 to 3, 7.30 to 11, Sun 12 to 3, 7.30 to 10.30*

BERKSWELL

West Midlands map 5

Bear Inn

Spencers Lane
TEL: (01676) 533202
off A452, 6m W of Coventry
Recently refurbished sixteenth-century inn named after the emblem of the Earl of Warwick. Inside, the walls are of local brick, the beams are low and a grandfather clock is on display. Also note the Russian cannon brought back after the Crimean War. The menu is extensive, real ales are on draught and the entire wine list is available by the glass. Reports, please.
Open *11am to 11pm, Sun 12 to 10.30*

BERRYNARBOR

Devon map 1

Ye Olde Globe

TEL: (01271) 882465
off A399, 4m E of Ilfracombe
Four-hundred-year-old lime-ash floors are one of the features of this splendidly atmospheric pub converted from three medieval cottages. This is an excellent address for holidaymaking families, with good children's facilities and an attractive garden. Courage Directors and Ushers Best are on handpump; otherwise try one of Rock's country wines.
Open *11.30 to 2.30, 7 to 11 (6 to 11 summer), Sun 12 to 2.30, 7 to 10.30*

BETCHWORTH

Surrey map 3

Dolphin

The Street
TEL: (01737) 842288
off A25, 2m W of Reigate, in centre of Betchworth
Homely village pub overlooking Betchworth Forge and the local church. Young's draught beers are kept in good order, and the bar also has a useful stock of wines kept using the Verre de Vin preservation system. Children aren't allowed inside, but there's space on the terrace at the back of the building.
Open *11 to 3, 5.30 to 11, Sun 11 to 3, 7 to 10.30*

BEWDLEY

Hereford & Worcester map 5

Little Packhorse

High Street
TEL: (01299) 403762
3m W of Kidderminster
Reputedly the oldest pub in Bewdley, with a quirkily idiosyncratic atmosphere and a sound reputation for good beer. Lumphammer Bitter is the house tipple; otherwise expect guests such as Tetley Wild Rover, as well as Ind Coope Burton Ale. Home-made pies are the stars of the menu. There are two rooms at the back for kids.
Open *11 to 3, 6 to 11, Sat 11am to 11pm, Sun 12 to 10.30*

BILDESTON

Suffolk map 6

Crown

104 High Street
TEL: (01449) 740510
just off B1115/B1708, 4m NW of Hadleigh

Once deemed 'the most haunted public house in Britain', this fifteenth-century beamed inn still boasts a ghostly resident. To take your mind off things, there are draught ales from Adnams and Nethergate, guest brews and Timmerman's imported fruit beer from Belgium. Children are welcome and accommodation is praised. Handily situated for Constable country.

Open *11 to 3, 6 to 11, Sun 12 to 3, 7 to 10.30*

BINSEY

Oxfordshire map 2

Perch ◆

Binsey Lane
TEL: (01865) 240386
off A420, 2m NW of Oxford

A wonderfully serene retreat away from the city of dreaming spires. This 600-year-old thatched pub stands by a river in Port Meadow – the spot where Gerard Manley Hopkins penned his verses about the Binsey poplars. Apart from the setting and nearby walks, there's a good outdoor play area for youngsters and a '95-table' beer garden. The landlord keeps a decent stock of real ales such as Tetley Bitter and Marston's Pedigree, plus a regularly changing guest brew. New licensees in July 1996; reports, please.

Open *summer 11.30 to 11, Sun 12 to 10.30, winter 11.30 to 2.30 (3 Sat), 7 to 11, Sun 12 to 3, 7 to 10.30*

BISHOP BURTON

East Riding of Yorkshire map 9

Altisidora

Main Street
TEL: (01964) 550284
just off A1079, 3m W of Beverley

Punters might be interested to know that Altisidora – the first horse to win (in 1813) the St Leger – was owned by the local squire: hence the odd name of this much-photographed pub. The place also has a resident ghost, currently called Coco. To steady the nerves, customers can order a pint of Mansfield Bitter or a seasonal brew from Deakin. Children are welcome.

Open *11am to 11pm, Sun 12 to 10.30*

BISHOP'S CASTLE

Shropshire map 5

Three Tuns ◆

Salop Street
TEL: (01588) 638797
on B4385 just off A488, 8m NW of Craven Arms

One of the oldest home-brew pubs in the land, first licensed in 1642, and boasting a classic 'four-storey tower' brewhouse. The building is timber-framed and in the heavily beamed bar you can sample Mild, XXX Bitter, and seasonal beers like Robert's Summer Special and Old Scrooge. The pub changed licensee in summer 1996: food looks to be on the up, and accommodation is in the pipeline. Children welcome.

Open *12 to 11, Sun 12 to 10.30*

BLACKAWTON

Devon map 1

Normandy Arms

Chapel Street
TEL: (01803) 712316
off A381 and B3207, 5m W of Dartmouth

Handy if you wish to sample the output of the local Blackawton Brewery and also wines from the nearby vineyard on their home ground. The pub's name is a reference to the Normandy D-Day landings: practice sessions took place on Slapton Sands, a few miles away. Children are allowed in the restaurant, and there are five bedrooms for overnight visitors.

Open *12 to 3, 7 to 11, Sun 7 to 10.30*

BLAKENEY

Norfolk map 6

King's Arms

Westgate Street
TEL: (01263) 740341
on A149, 5m W of Holt
'The smallest cartoon gallery in England' – housed in an old telephone kiosk – is one novel feature of this cheery brick-and-flint pub just round the corner from Blakeney quay. Woodforde's Wherry, Marston's Pedigree and Ruddles County are on handpump; the bedrooms have views out towards Blakeney Point and its seal colonies. Children are happily accommodated.
Open *11am to 11pm, Sun 12 to 10.30*

BLETCHINGLEY

Surrey map 3

William IV

Little Common Lane
TEL: (01883) 743278
on A25, 2m W of Godstone
Five real ales attract dedicated drinkers to this brick and tile pub in a quiet Surrey lane: expect to find Shepherd Neame Masterbrew, Fuller's London Pride, Harveys Best, Morland Old Speckled Hen and Pilgrim's Progress, a local brew from Reigate. Children are welcome in the various eating areas away from the bar, and there's a garden outside.
Open *11 to 3, 6 to 11, Sun 12 to 3, 7 to 10.30*

BLICKLING

Norfolk map 6

Buckinghamshire Arms

TEL: (01263) 732133
off B1354, from A140, 2m NW of Aylsham
Leased from the National Trust and a favoured detour for visitors who have come to view the splendours of Blickling Hall (its gates are virtually opposite the pub). Real ales from the local Reepham Brewery are on draught alongside Adnams, which also supplies the wines. Children are welcome in the restaurant and there'a big garden outside. Accommodation includes three four-poster rooms.
Open *11 to 3, 6 to 11, Sun 11 to 3, 7 to 10.30*

BLYTHBURGH

Suffolk map 6

White Hart Inn

London Road
TEL: (01502) 478217
on A12, 4m W of Southwold
Recently restored by new licensees, this former medieval courthouse is once again a true country pub catering equally for locals, families and travellers. Vast gardens, stupendous views and walks along the Blyth estuary are added attractions, and Blythburgh Church stands the other side of the A12. Adnams beers are on handpump, fish is a good choice from the menu.
Open *11 to 2.30, 6 to 11, Sun 12 to 3, 7 to 10.30*

BODICOTE

Oxfordshire map 5

Plough

TEL: (01295) 262327
just off A4260, 2m S of Banbury
In 1997 the Blencowe family will be celebrating four decades as custodians of this village pub close to the River Cherwell and Broughton Castle. This is also the home of the Bodicote brewery, and four beers are produced on the premises: Bitter, No. 9 and two winter brews, Old English Porter and Triple X.
Open *11 to 3, 5.45 to 11, Sun 12 to 3, 7 to 10.30*

BOLDRE

Hampshire map 2

Red Lion Inn

TEL: (01590) 673177
off A337, 2m N of Lymington
A useful staging-post for visitors to the lower reaches of the New Forest. Outside is a farm cart brimming over with flowers in summer, inside is a mass of chamber pots, antiques and farm implements. Thomas Hardy Country Bitter and Royal Oak are on

draught and several wines are offered by the glass. No children or dogs in the pub, please.
Open *Mon to Fri 11 to 3, 6 to 11, Sat 11am to 11pm, Sun 12 to 10.30*

BOTTOM-OF-THE-OVEN

Cheshire map 8

Stanley Arms

TEL: (01260) 252414
just S of A537, between Buxton and Macclesfield
'A welcome refuge after an invigorating walk' around the nearby reservoirs or up the slopes of Shuttingsloe. The views are good, and there's a garden at the back for hikers who do not want to remove their boots. Marston's Pedigree and Bitter are on draught and children are accommodated if eating.
Open *Mon to Fri 12 to 3, 5.30 to 11, Sat and Sun 12 to 11*

BOURTON

Dorset map 2

White Lion Inn

High Street
TEL: (01747) 840866
just off A303, 4m E of Wincanton
Known locally as 'The Bush', this 200-year-old coaching-inn has a good reputation for its range of drinks. Ushers Best, Morland Old Speckled Hen, and Theakston XB are backed up by Thatcher's cider and Harvest Gold, plus a full range of wines by the glass. Children are 'very welcome' (kids' food is at reduced prices); one of the bedrooms has a four-poster.
Open *12 to 3, 6 to 11 (12 to 11 Sat summer), Sun 12 to 10.30*

BOUTH

Cumbria map 8

White Hart Inn

TEL: (01229) 861229
off A590, 4m NE of Ulverston
'No keg beers,' insists the landlord of this old stone pub on the edge of Grizedale Forest, between Lake Windermere and Coniston. Instead, drinkers can choose Theakston, Boddingtons, Highgate and Tetley Bitter, plus a guest ale. Children are welcome in the eating areas and games room.
Open *all week 12 to 2 (3 Sun), 6 to 11*

BOWLAND BRIDGE

Cumbria map 8

Hare & Hounds Inn

TEL: (01539) 568333
off A5074, 8m S of Windermere
A secluded Lakeland setting in the Winster Valley brings crowds to this whitewashed 300-year-old inn surrounded by Cartmel Fells. This is a useful family destination with plenty of accommodation. Tetley Bitter is on handpump.
Open *11am to 11pm, Sun 11 to 10.30*

BRADFIELD

South Yorkshire map 8

Strines Inn ◆

Mortimer Road
TEL: (0114) 285 1247
2m off A57 (not in village), 6m NW of Sheffield
'Strines' means 'meeting of the waters' and this ancient pub (with modern additions) stands high atop Bradfield Moors on the edge of the Peak District; below is Strines Reservoir. The inn was built as a manor house in 1275 and still boasts massive beams, as well as a veritable taxidermist's museum of stuffed specimens. Live animals populate the pub's own sanctuary, and children have a playground in the garden. Lancaster Old Dambusters, Boddingtons and Castle Eden Ale are typical beers on draught. Three of the bedrooms boast four-posters.
Open *Mon to Fri 10.30 to 11 (10.30 to 3, 6 to 11 in winter), Sat 10.30am to 11pm, Sun 10.30am to 10.30pm*

BRADFORD-ON-TONE

Somerset map 2

White Horse Inn

TEL: (01823) 461239
off A38, 3m NE of Wellington
Five minutes' drive from the M5, and handy if you fancy a trip to Sheppy's 'gold medal' cider farm and museum.

Their brews are on tap in the bar, alongside real ales from local sources. The atmosphere is congenial, there's a garden for sunny days and the pub has a skittle alley.

Open *details unavailable as we went to press*

BRANCASTER STAITHE

Norfolk map 6

Jolly Sailors

TEL: (01485) 210314

on A149, between Hunstanton and Wells-next-the-Sea

A boon for Norfolk holidaymakers, families with children, boating people and bird-watchers: the dunes and salt-flats, plus Scolt Head Reserve, are a walk away. Bass and Greene King IPA are on draught and the 50-strong wine list includes some very decent stuff. Order a mug of soup or a dish of mussels if you're hungry.

Open *11 to 3, 6 (7 winter) to 11, Sun 12 to 3, 7 to 10.30; closed 25 Dec*

BRETFORTON

Hereford & Worcester map 5

Fleece Inn ◆

The Cross

TEL: (01386) 831173

on B4035, 4m E of Evesham

One of the most remarkable country pubs in Britain, an extraordinary museum of living history overseen by the National Trust. The timber-framed building began life as a farmhouse in medieval times, and was first licensed in 1848. Today, crowds come to marvel at the details of the place, and its evocation of rural life and labour: the Brewhouse, the Dugout (originally the pantry) and the Pewter Room are endlessly fascinating. The Fleece acknowledges its pub roots with guest beers from all over Britain, and it holds a festival in celebration. Morris dancers perform in the orchard gardens and medieval battles are sometimes re-enacted. Children are welcome throughout the inn.

Open *11 to 2.30, 6 to 11, Sun 12 to 2.30, 7 to 10.30*

BRINDLE

Lancashire map 8

Cavendish Arms

Sandy Lane

TEL: (01254) 852912

on B5256 between Leyland and Blackburn

Seventeenth-century hostelry in an ancient Lancashire village a few miles from the Leeds & Liverpool Canal and the urban sprawl of Blackburn. Inside there is modern stained glass, outside is a little garden with a waterfall. Beers from the Burtonwood Brewery are on draught. Children are welcome where food is eaten.

Open *11 to 3, 5.30 to 11, Sun 12 to 3, 7 to 10.30*

BROAD CAMPDEN

Gloucestershire map 5

Bakers Arms

TEL: (01386) 840515

off B4081, 1m SE of Chipping Campden

Landlady Carolyn Perry ensures that a regular stock of around six real ales is a highlight of this wisteria-covered Cotswold pub. The list varies, but expect representatives from Donnington, Stanway, Wickwar and other independents. Families with children are more than welcome; there's a play area in the garden.

Open *Mon to Sat and bank hols 11.30 to 2.30, 6 to 11, Sun and Good Friday 12 to 3, 7 to 10.30*

BROADWAY

Hereford & Worcester map 5

Crown and Trumpet ◆

Church Street

TEL: (01386) 853202

off High Street (A44), on Snowshill road

A genuine, 'comfortable old brown pub' that runs against Broadway's tourist tide. Bar billiards and 'other ancient forms of recreation' – plus live music on Saturday nights – attract the crowds and drinks are kept in tip-top condition: look for Stanway Bitter (brewed near Cheltenham) as well as Wadworth 6X and Flowers Original, and Bulmer's traditional cider. There's Kir in summer, mulled wine in winter. Children are welcome in the eating area of the bar, and accommodation is available. Snowshill Manor and gardens (National Trust) are nearby.

Open *11 to 3, 5 to 11, Sun 12 to 3, 7 to 10.30*

BROCKHAM

Surrey map 3

Royal Oak

Brockham Green
TEL: (01737) 843241
just off A25, 2m E of Dorking

Six real ales from six brewers are one of the attractions in this pub by the village green: Harveys Best, Adnams Bitter, Gale's HSB, Greene King Abbot Ale, Young's Special and Wadworth 6X are the names to look for. Highly popular in summer, when customers bring their own deckchairs and sit outside.

Open *12 (11 Fri to Sun) to 11 (10.30 Sun)*

BROOKLAND

Kent map 3

Woolpack

TEL: (01797) 344321
just off A259, 5m W of New Romney

'An absolute stunner' is one description of this isolated medieval pub on the edge of Romney Marsh. The setting is a crowd-puller, although drinkers who favour Shepherd Neame beers will have plenty to relish in the old-fashioned bar. Children can play in the games room and the garden.

Open *11 to 3, 6 to 11, Sun 12 to 3, 7 to 10.30*

BROOM

Bedfordshire map 6

Cock

23 High Street
TEL: (01767) 314411
on B658, 2m SW of Biggleswade

Locally renowned as 'the pub with no bar': Greene King IPA, Abbot Ale and Rayments Bitter are dispensed direct from the cellar. The pub is a cottage-like building with a maze of little rooms and drinking areas leading off the low-ceilinged corridor; ornaments and curios are everywhere. Children are welcome throughout the place.

Open *12 to 3 (4 Sat), 6 to 11, Sun 12 to 4, 7 to 10.30*

BURCOT

Oxfordshire map 2

Chequers

TEL: (01867) 407771
on A415, 4½m E of Abingdon

Special events are a great draw at this handsome-looking thatched inn: licensees Michael and May Weeks put on everything from Italian nights to 'Valentine's chocolate fondue' evenings – not to mention 'old thyme sing songs'. Ushers, Ruddles and Brakspear ales are on draught and the wine list includes bottles from the local Hendred vineyard. Children are welcome in the eating area and no-smoking gallery.

Open *11 to 2.30, 6 to 11, Sun 12 to 3, 7 to 10.30*

BURGH ISLAND

Devon map 1

Pilchard Inn ◆

TEL: (01548) 810344
island (opposite Bigbury-on-Sea) signposted from A379 Modbury to Kingsbridge road

Must rank as one of England's most curious pubs, largely because of its extraordinary island setting. A 600-year-old smugglers' inn, the Pilchard gets cut off by the tide twice a day: you can either walk across the causeway from Bigbury-on-Sea, or take a trip on the unique 'sea tractor' on stilts when the water is up. Either way, you'll find two hugely atmospheric bars where you can sample Ushers Best, Wadworth 6X, John Smith's and pints of local scrumpy. The pub has a children's room and there are picnic tables by the water's edge.

Open *Summer 11am to 11pm, Sun 12 to 10.30, winter all week 12 to 3, 7 to 10*

BURNHAM THORPE

Norfolk map 6

Lord Nelson ◆

Walsingham Road
TEL: (01328) 738241
off A149/B1155/B1355, 2m S of Burnham Market
Lord Nelson was born in the village in 1758 and had his farewell bash at this historic pub before returning to sea. Inside, the floors are flagstoned and the place is bedecked with books, paintings and memorabilia (some for sale). There's no bar: pints of Greene King IPA, Abbot Ale Mild and – of course – Woodforde's Nelson's Revenge are drawn direct from the cask. 'Nelson's Blood' – a secret rum-based brew – is unique to the pub. Outside is a large garden and children's play area.
Open *11 to 3, 6 to 11, Sun 12 to 3, 7 to 10.30*

BUTTERLEIGH

Devon map 1

Butterleigh Inn

TEL: (01884) 855407
off M5 at Cullompton, right at Midland Bank, follow signs
'Follow the signs carefully' to reach this remote sixteenth-century pub in a tiny village. The atmosphere is one of 'cosy simplicity'; locals and tourists rub shoulders at the bar, and ornithologically named beers like Tawny and Barn Owl from Cotleigh Brewery are on draught. Children are welcome at lunch-time and the pub has two bedrooms.
Open *12 to 2.30, 6 (5 Fri) to 11, Sun 12 to 3, 7 to 10.30*

BYWORTH

West Sussex map 3

Black Horse

TEL: (01798) 342424
just S of Petworth, off A283
A new team took over this Downland village local towards the end of 1996. Re-decoration has made the place 'more snug' and there have been changes in the cellar: local beers from the Hermitage Brewery now appear alongside Youngs, Flowers and guests – perhaps from the Cottage Brewery. Children are welcome and the pub has a big garden with unmissable views.
Open *12 to 3, 6 to 11 (7 to 10.30 Sun)*

CARDINGTON

Shropshire map 5

Royal Oak

TEL: (01694) 771266
off B4371, 4m E of Church Stretton
'Spontaneous' live music occasionally bursts forth over the bustle of conversation in this 500-year-old village pub not far from Wenlock Edge. Bass, Hobsons Bitter and a guest brew provide suitable liquid accompaniment. Children are welcome in the pub at lunch-times.
Open *12 to 2.30 (2.45 Sun), 7 to 11 (10.30 Sun)*

CAREY

Hereford & Worcester map 5

Cottage of Content

TEL: (01432) 840242
between A49 and B4224, 6m SE of Hereford
Five-hundred-year-old whitewashed pub down a tangle of country lanes by a bridge over a stream. Dried hops dangle from the beams, a fire burns in the stone hearth and Hook Norton Bitter is on draught, alongside Weston's Old Rosie cider. Children are welcome and the inn is recommended for its accommodation.
Open *12 to 2.30, 7 to 11 (10.30 Sun)*

CASTLE ACRE

Norfolk map 6

Ostrich Inn

Stocks Green
TEL: (01760) 755398
just off A1065 Swaffham to Fakenham road, 4m N of Swaffham
Claims to be the only inn on the Pedders Way – the ancient footpath that cuts across west Norfolk – and a handy refuelling point for walkers and visitors exploring the ruins of the Cluniac Priory and the ancient castle. The interior embodies classic traditional style; draught beers are

Greene King IPA and Abbot Ale. A family room and accommodation are available.
Open *12 to 3, 7 to 11, Sun 12 to 3, 7 to 10.30*

CAULDON

Staffordshire map 5

Yew Tree Inn ◆

TEL: (01538) 308348
off A523 Leek to Ashbourne road at Waterhouses, 6m NE of Cheadle
One of Britain's most splendidly eccentric hostelries, 'more of a museum than a pub', but absolutely unmissable. For more than 35 years, landlord Alan East has amassed a unique collection of curios, antiques and bizarre artefacts of every description. Pride of place goes to the extraordinary polyphons and other musical devices, but there is fascination wherever you look. As befits a 'proper pub', real ales come first (food, in the landlord's words, is 'secondary'), and you'll find Burton Bridge Bitter, Bass and M&B Mild on handpump. The inn, which is fronted by a yew tree of great age, stands between two quarries on the fringes of the Peak District.
Open *10 to 2.30, 6 to 11, Sun 12 to 3, 7 to 10.30*

CERNE ABBAS

Dorset map 2

New Inn

14 Long Street
TEL: (01300) 341274
on A352, 7m N of Dorchester
Cerne Abbas is synonymous with the rampant 'giant' carved out of the chalk hillside, and sightseers often repair to this sixteenth-century pub after admiring his vital statistics. Beers from Eldridge Pope are kept in 'excellent' condition, and the pub has its own walled fruit garden. Accommodation is available.
Open *11.45 (11 Sat) to 2.30, 6.45 (6.30 Sat) to 11, Sun 12 to 10.30*

CHAPELGATE

Lincolnshire map 6

Old Black Lion

Gedney
TEL: (01406) 363767
just off the A17, 1m W of Long Sutton
Highly popular red-brick hostelry in a Fenland village just off the A17. Reporters praise in particular the appealing family atmosphere, the 'obliging, friendly and courteous' service, and the generosity of the food portions. Bass and a guest ale, such as Batemans, are on handpump. Children are welcome throughout the pub.
Open *12 to 2.30 (3 Sat summer), 7 to 11, Sun 12 to 3, 7 to 10.30*

CHEDDAR

Somerset map 2

Gardeners Arms

Silver Street
TEL: (01934) 742235
Arguably the oldest drinking house in Cheddar and only five minutes from the Gorge in an area of outstanding natural beauty. The pub is four centuries old and vine-clad. Ushers beers are on handpump, and children are welcome in the family room and dining area.
Open *12 to 3, 6 to 11, Sun 12 to 3, 7 to 10.30; closed Mon to Thu L in winter*

CHEDINGTON

Dorset map 2

Winyard's Gap

TEL: (01935) 891244
on A356, between Crewkerne and Dorchester, at Winyard's Gap
The views hereabouts inspired Thomas Hardy to pen 'At Winyard's Gap', and this old-fashioned pub makes the most of its setting in deepest Dorset. Up to four real ales – including Flowers Original and Wadworth 6X – are regularly on handpump along with some acceptable wines. The pub has a family room, and accommodation is in two so-called 'travel lodges'.
Open *11 to 2.30, 7 to 11, Sun 12 to 3, 7 to 10.30*

CHEDWORTH

Gloucestershire map 5

Seven Tuns

TEL: (01285) 720242

off A429, 5m N of Cirencester

'Circa 1690' says the sign over the door of this Cotswold pub not far from the village cricket pitch. Appetising seasonal tipples such as 'cider cup' and 'ginger snap' are an unusual feature in autumn and winter; otherwise George's Bristol Bitter is on draught, as well as guest ales. Children are welcome in the games room and eating area. A short walk will take you to Chedworth Roman Villa (National Trust) and the Coln Valley.

Open *12 to 3, 7 to 11 (10.30 Sun)*

CHIDDINGFOLD

Surrey map 3

Crown Inn ◆

The Green, Petworth Road

TEL: (01428) 682255

on A283, 5m S of Milford

A slice of living history. This gloriously preserved timber-framed building started life in 1285 and, over the centuries, has played host to kings and queens as well as the populace in this part of rural Surrey. What dazzles is the detail: stained-glass windows, moulded beams, curved oak brackets carved with trefoils, not to mention four-poster beds in three of the eight rooms. After soaking up the heritage, you can sample a fine range of beers like Charles Wells Eagle, Wadworth 6X, and Hall & Woodhouse Tanglefoot and Badger Best. Cream teas are served in the lounge or out on the terrace.

Open *all week 11am to 11pm, Sun 12 to 10.30*

CHILHAM

Kent map 3

White Horse

TEL: (01227) 730355

on A252, 6m SW of Canterbury

In a Kentish village used as the setting for a film version of *Moll Flanders* and noted for its ancient church and impressive castle. The pub is half-timbered, the fire-grate is Tudor, and there are real ales from Fremlins, Flowers and Boddingtons. Also look for the local fruit wines. Cheery service. No children.

Open *11am to 11pm, Sun 12 to 10.30*

CHURCH HOUSES

North Yorkshire map 9

Feversham Arms

TEL: (01751) 433206

off A170, 7m N of Kirkbymoorside

The famous walk through acres of wild daffodils is a springtime delight in the Farndale valley; at other times the area brings hordes of tourists and trippers to the area. This simple stone pub at the head of the Dale is a popular haunt at any time; real ales are on draught, the mood is chatty and B&B is available.

Open *12 to 2.30 (11 to 3.30 summer), 7 (6 summer) to 11, Sun 12 to 3, 6.30 to 10.30*

CHURCHILL

N. W. Somerset map 2

Crown Inn

The Batch

TEL: (01934) 852995

off A368, 3m S of Congresbury

'A little cottage on the hill' at the foot of the Mendips. There are good views from the garden and the Wildlife Trust Reserve at Dolebury Warren is close by. More than six real ales are generally on tap, including Batch Bitter (the house beer), Palmers IPA and Bass. Children are welcome in the dining area away from the bar.

Open *11.30 to 3.30, 5.30 to 11, Sun 12 to 10.30*

COCKWOOD

Devon map 1

Anchor

off A379, on W side of River Exe estuary opposite Exmouth

Historic former seamen's mission by the river, with tiny windows, low ceilings, huge communal tables, and a 'strong local atmosphere'. Most come for the beer – Bass, Flowers Original, Boddingtons and Wadworth 6X are on handpump or tapped direct from the

cask. The kitchen specialises in really fresh fish. Children allowed in eating and snug areas.
Open *11am to 11pm, Sun 12 to 10.30*

CONDER GREEN

Lancashire map 8

Stork Hotel

TEL: (01524) 751234
between A6 and A588, 4m S of Lancaster
The name derives from the coat-of-arms of the Starkies of Huntroyde, who acquired the local estate in the 1880s. The Stork is now a favourite stopover for wildlife enthusiasts: the mud flats of the Lune estuary and Glasson Dock are nearby, as is the Lancashire coastal path. Boddingtons, Bentleys and guests like Ramsbottom Strong Ale are on handpump, and the specials menu looks promising. Reports, please.
Open *11am to 11pm, Sun 12 to 10.30*

CONYER QUAY

Kent map 3

Ship

TEL: (01795) 521404
off A2, 4m NW of Faversham, and just N of Teynham
A splendid estuary setting by Conyer Creek (where seals are sometimes seen) and the prospect of good bird-watching on the nearby marshes are two big pluses at this 300-year-old smugglers' pub. Adnams, Boddingtons and others are supplemented by regular guest brews. No children under 14 in the bar.
Open *winter Mon to Fri 12 to 3, 6 to 11, Sat 11am to 11pm, Sun 12 to 3, 7 to 10.30, summer Mon to Sat 11am to 11pm, Sun 12 to 10.30*

COOKHAM

Berkshire map 3

Bel and the Dragon ◆

High Street
TEL: (01628) 521263
on A4094, off A404 just N of Marlow
Fascinating fifteenth-century inn curiously named after one of the books of the Apocrypha. The bar is a 'lovely spot to relax in', and there is still evidence of the past in the heavily beamed ceiling and wattle and daub walls. Brakspear Bitter and Old Ale are drawn direct from the cask and some good ports are on display. Snacks are served in the lounge, but most emphasis is on the restaurant. Children are welcome in the eating areas and the garden. Pay a visit to the Stanley Spencer gallery across the road before leaving the village.
Open *11 to 3, 6 to 11, Sun 12 to 3, 7 to 11*

CORFTON

Shropshire map 5

Sun Inn ◆

TEL: (01584) 861239
on B4368, 4m E of Craven Arms
'Very decent, very unpretentious and extremely friendly,' notes a reporter. This congenial seventeenth-century local takes beer seriously. Up to 20 different brews may appear on bank holidays, but there are regularly as many as six on show; micro-breweries get preference (Burton Bridge Knot Brown Ale, for example). Children are happily accommodated throughout the pub and there's an impressively equipped play area in the garden. Full marks too for the care with which the place has been adapted for the disabled. Handy for a trip to Corfe Castle or Ludlow Races.
Open *11 to 2.30, 6 to 11 (11am to 11pm bank hols), Sun 12 to 3, 7 to 10.30*

CRANBORNE

Dorset map 2

Fleur de Lys

TEL: (01725) 517282
on B3078 in centre of Cranborne
Thomas Hardy stayed here while writing *Tess of the d'Urbervilles* and Rupert Brooke put pen to paper in verses dedicated to both the village and the pub. The building is all old stone and creepers, with panelling and a massive fireplace in the bar. 'Exceptionally friendly' staff, Hall & Woodhouse beers on handpump and popular accommodation.
Open *10 to 3, 6 to 11, Sun 12 to 3, 7 to 10.30*

CRASTER

Northumberland map 10

Jolly Fisherman

TEL: (01665) 576218

off B1339, 6m NE of Alnwick

Convivial harbourside local in a village famous for its fish curing. The menu is limited, but it's worth checking out the local crab and kipper pâté. Thorne Best Bitter and Lorimer's Best Scotch are on draught. Children can sit in the eating area away from the bar. From the quay you can see Dunstanburgh Castle (NT) on a clear day.

Open *summer 11am to 11pm, Sun 12 to 10.30, winter 11 to 3, 6 to 11, Sun 12 to 3, 7 to 10.30*

CROSCOMBE

Somerset map 2

Bull Terrier

TEL: (01749) 343658

on A371, 3m of Wells

Formerly a priory used by the abbots of Glastonbury, now a popular re-fuelling point for travellers exploring the sights of Somerset or heading for the Royal Bath & Wells Show. Good real ales include Bull Terrier Bitter, Butcombe and Courage Directors among others. Children are welcome in the dining-room, and the pub has three bedrooms.

Open *12 to 2.30, 7 to 11, Sun 12 to 2.30, 7 to 10.30*

DENT

Cumbria map 8

Sun ◆

Main Street

TEL: (01539) 625208

in Dentdale, 4m SE of Sedburgh

Great little old-fashioned local that is 'a walker's delight and a real ale fanatic's oasis'. Energetic types appreciate the setting deep in the heart of the Dales National Park, while drinkers go for the splendid beers from the Dent micro-brewery; three – including Dent Brewery Bitter – are generally on handpump. To go with your pint, there's a basic menu of honest home-cooked food. Children are welcome throughout and the pub offers useful B&B.

Open *summer 11am to 11pm, winter Mon to Fri 11 to 2.30, 7 (6 Fri) to 11, Sat 11am to 11pm, Sun 12 to 10.30*

DITCHLING

East Sussex map 3

Bull Hotel

2 High Street

TEL: (01273) 843147

on B2112, midway between Haywards Heath and Brighton

Imposing brick-clad pub first licensed in 1636 and once the courthouse for the 'Society for the Prosecution of Thieves'. These days a less dramatic mood prevails and visitors trekking the North Downs can call in for a pint of Brakspear Bitter, Flowers Original, Marston's Pedigree or Morland Old Speckled Hen. The pub has a family room and *en suite* accommodation.

Open *summer 11am to 11pm, Sun 12 to 10.30, winter Mon to Fri 11 to 3, 5.30 to 11, Sat 11am to 11pm, Sun 12 to 3, 7 to 10.30*

DOCKING

Norfolk map 6

Pilgrims Reach

High Street

TEL: (01485) 518383

on B1153, 11m W of Fakenham

'A pleasant stopover for holidaymakers' doing the sightseeing rounds through west Norfolk: families with children are more than welcome. The pub is a freehouse with East Anglian real ales courtesy of Adnams and Greene King. Bar food is mostly familiar stuff, but good value.

Open *Mon and Wed to Sat 12 to 3, 6.30 to 11, Sun 12 to 2.30, 7 to 10.30*

DONINGTON ON BAIN

Lincolnshire map 9

Black Horse

TEL: (01507) 343640

between A153 and A157, 6m SW of Louth

'A working country pub – walkers, tandem riders on the Viking Way, farmers and their wives out for Sunday lunch' sums up this local in a village 'far from the beaten path'. Drinkers in the low-ceilinged bars can sup Ruddles Best, Courage Directors, John Smith's Bitter and a summertime guest brew. Children are welcome in most parts of the pub and plenty of family accommodation is available.

Open *11.30 to 3, 6.30 to 11 (12 to 2.30, 7 to 11 in winter), Sun 12 to 3, 7 to 10.30*

DREWSTEIGNTON

Devon map 1

Drewe Arms

TEL: (01647) 281224

2m S of A30, 8m W of Exeter

Revered by aficionados for its unimproved charm and for the fact that it had England's longest-serving and oldest landlady. The redoubtable Mabel Mudge retired in 1994, aged 99. This is now a Whitbread pub, with four ales drawn direct from the cask; Tom Grey's local cider is on tap and the menu looks promising. Accommodation is available. Children are welcome in the dining-room.

Open *winter 11 to 3, 6 to 11, Sun 12 to 3, 7 to 10.30, summer 11am to 11pm, Sun 12 to 10.30*

EARL SOHAM

Suffolk map 6

Victoria

TEL: (01728) 685758

on A1120, 3m W of Framlingham

Inauspicious whitewashed pub famous for the home brewery set up by landlord John Bjornson in a converted malt house. Drinkers in the cosy, pine-panelled bar can sample Victoria Bitter, Albert Ale, Gannet Mild and Jolabrugg in winter. Most dishes on the homespun menu come with hunks of bread.

Open *12 to 2.30, 5.30 to 11, Sun 12 to 3, 7 to 10.30*

EASTBRIDGE

Suffolk map 5

Eels Foot

TEL: (01728) 830154

off B1122, 2m N of Leiston

The sign depicts an eel wriggling out of an old boot, and this Suffolk pub lives up to its 'slightly crazy' reputation. Wardens from nearby Minsmere RSPB Reserve rub shoulders with bird-watchers, walkers and holidaymakers. Adnams beers are on draught and musicians play occasionally. Children are most welcome: there are terraces at the front and a meadow behind (complete with a certified caravan/camp site).

Open *June to Sept 11am to 11pm, Sun 12 to 10.30, Oct to May Mon to Sat 11 to 3, Tue to Sat 7 to 11, Sun 12 to 3, 7 to 10.30*

EAST ILSLEY

Berkshire map 2

Crown & Horns

TEL: (01635) 281545 and 281205

just off A34, 9m N of Newbury

Seventeenth-century local in a village once famous for its huge sheep fair. Now the place has strong horse-racing connections, and the pub featured in the TV drama series *Trainer*. Real ales includes Morland Original, Fuller's London Pride and four guest brews. There's a TV room for youngsters, and the pub has bedrooms.

Open *11am to 11pm, Sun 12 to 10.30*

EAST LYNG

Somerset map 2

Rose & Crown

TEL: (01823) 698235

on A361, 5m NE of Taunton

A well-tended flower garden with views of Sedgemoor is one of the scoring points at this civilised, spick-and-span country pub. Service is courteously old-fashioned, classical music plays in the background, and decent real ales such as Butcombe Bitter and brews from Eldridge Pope are on handpump. No children under 14 inside.

Open *11 to 2.30, 6.30 to 11, Sun 12 to 3, 7 to 10.30*

EAST MEON

Hampshire map 2

Ye Olde George Inn

Church Street
TEL: (01730) 823481
2m off A272, 4m W of Petersfield
A charming setting in a downland village close to the River Meon makes this 500-year-old pub a popular rendezvous. In summer you can sit outside, admire the Norman church and sup well-kept ales from Greene King, Bass, Fuller's and Gales; fruit wines are also on show. Children are welcome and the pub provides accommodation.
Open *11am to 11pm, Sun 12 to 10.30*

EAST PRAWLE

Devon map 1

Pig's Nose Inn

TEL: (01548) 511209
off A379, 1m NE of Prawle Point
Devon's most southerly pub lies within sight of Lannacombe Bay. Popular with walkers trekking the coastal path from Start Point to Salcombe and also bird-watchers (the landlord apparently keeps a 'bird log' which customers can add to). Wadworth 6X and Flowers IPA are on draught; children are welcome if eating and the pub has a games room.
Open *11 to 2.30 (3 summer), 5.30 to 11, Sun 12 to 2.30 (3 summer), 7 to 10.30*

EGLINGHAM

Northumberland map 10

Tankerville Arms

TEL: (01665) 578444
on B6346, 6m N of Alnwick
Promising Northumbrian dining pub owned by Phil and Lynn Farmer, who run the Cook & Barker Inn (see main entry, Newton-on-the-Moor). Phil's brother is the licensee. Four regularly changing real ales could include Ruddles, Theakston, Jennings and so forth. Dishes such as warm pigeon and bacon salad, and lemon sole with capers are typical of the menu. Children welcome. Reports, please.
Open *11 to 3, 6 to 11 (closed Mon and Tues 11 to 3 winter), Sun 12 to 3, 7 to 10.30*

ETAL

Northumberland map 10

Black Bull

TEL: (01890) 820200
just off B6354, 8m NW of Wooler
Substantially re-built after a fire in 1979, this 300-year-old inn is – reputedly – Northumberland's only thatched pub. It's also convenient for the Cheviots, Etal Castle, Lady Waterford Hall at Ford and Heatherslaw Corn Mill. Thorne Best Bitter, Lorimer's Best Scotch and others are on draught. Children are welcome throughout the pub. Extensions are planned for 1997.
Open *11am to 11pm, Sun 12 to 10.30 (phone to check opening in winter)*

EXEBRIDGE

Somerset map 1

Anchor Inn

TEL: (01398) 323433
on B3222, 2m NW of Bampton
A glorious setting, with landscaped gardens bordering the River Exe, makes this a delightful spot in summer. Hotel guests have free fishing rights, and the pub has a well-equipped children's play area. Real ales served in the modernised bar include names like Usher's Best, Courage Directors and Ruddles County. Hotel-style accommodation is available.
Open *11 to 3, 6 to 11 (11am to 11pm in summer), Sun 12 to 3, 7 to 10.30*

EXTON

Leicestershire map 6

Fox and Hounds

The Green
TEL: (01572) 812403
2m off A606, between Stamford and Oakham
Creeper-clad 300-year-old inn that looks for all the world like a mature country residence. Samuel Smith Old Brewery Bitter and Ruddles County are on draught, and wines are from Eldridge Pope. Children are welcome, and the pub offers accommodation. Handily placed for a trip to Rutland Water.
Open *11 to 3, 6.30 to 11, Sun 12 to 3, 6.30 to 10.30*

FALSTONE

Northumberland map 10

Blackcock Inn

TEL: (01434) 240200

off B6320, 8m W of Bellingham

'Miles from anywhere, but handy for visitors making the long, scenic trip to Kielder Water,' ran one explorer's report. Refreshment comes in the form of Buchanan Best Bitter, Boddingtons, Castle Eden and Old Hazy cider; food includes Yorkshire puddings and jacket potatoes with all manner of home-made fillings. There's a games room for youngsters and the pub has four bedrooms.

Open *11 to 3, 6.30 to 11, Sun 12 to 3, 7 to 10.30*

FEERING

Essex map 3

Sun Inn

TEL: (01376) 570442

off A12, 5m NE of Witham

Brilliant beers – and not just the output of local favourite Ridleys – are a justifiable reason for seeking out this village free house a few miles from the A12. Casks of Otter Bitter, Lichfield Inspired and Old Hanlons Celtic Gold line up alongside Morland Old Speckled Hen and 'Feering Ferret'. Children are welcome.

Open *11 to 3, 6 to 11, Sun 12 to 3, 6 to 10.30*

FEN DRAYTON

Cambridgeshire map 6

Three Tuns

High Street

TEL: (01954) 230242

off A14, 7m SE of Huntingdon, in centre of village

Neat-and-tidy thatched pub in a Fenland village with wide open spaces and 'big skies' all around. Inside, it suggests 'cottage tea-room', with polished brasses and shelves of china, but Greene King IPA, Abbot Ale and Rayments are on draught thanks to 'proper beer engines'. No children after 8pm.

Open *11 to 2.30, 6.30 to 11, Sun 12 to 2.30, 7 to 10.30*

FERNHAM

Oxfordshire map 2

Woodman Inn

TEL: (01367) 820643

on B4508, 2m S of Faringdon

John Lane recently celebrated 25 years as 'mine host' in this sixteenth-century pub. Curios – including clay pipes for sale – help to give the place its genuine and distinctive atmosphere. Real ales include Morland Original, Tanner's Jack and Boddingtons, among others. Children are welcome. The pub is pleasantly situated in the Vale of the White Horse.

Open *11 to 3, 6.30 to 11, Sun 12 to 3, 7 to 10.30*

FOOLOW

Derbyshire map 8

Bulls Head

TEL: (01433) 630873

off A623 Chapel-en-le-Frith to Chesterfield road, 3m E of Tideswell

New owners the Hall family moved into this Peak District pub opposite the village duck pond in summer 1996. Plus points here are the great views, excellent walking, fishing and sightseeing. Black Sheep Bitter and a guest please the drinkers, and the pub welcomes children. Accommodation is also available.

Open *Tue to Sun 12 to 2.30 (3 summer), 7 (6.30 summer) to 11; open Mon evening 6.30 to 11 summer*

FORDCOMBE

Kent map 3

Chafford Arms

TEL: (01892) 740267

on B2188, off A264 East Grinstead to Tunbridge Wells road, 4m W of Tunbridge Wells

A stunning, tile-hung building 'smothered in flowers': the luxuriant displays have won awards and the exterior is a riot of colour – even at the end of October. Drinkers in the uncluttered bar can enjoy beers from Larkins, Flowers and King & Barnes as well as Chafford cider. Children are welcome in the eating areas. Chafford is midway between Groombridge Place and Penshurst Place.

Open *11 to 3, 6 to 11, Sun 12 to 3.30, 7 to 10.30*

FORTY GREEN

Buckinghamshire map 3

Royal Standard of England ◆

TEL: (01494) 673382

off B474 out of Beaconsfield at Knotty Green

Majestically historic Chiltern pub with some beams and timbers dating back 900 years. Don't miss the showpiece King Charles Room (the pub was given its unique name by Charles II in gratitude for the protection he received while hiding in the rafters during his flight in 1651). The lounge is a treasure trove of swords, pistols, pewter mugs and other antiques; the famous stained-glass is from churches bombed during the Blitz. Owd Roger was first brewed here before the recipe was passed on to Marston's; you can still sample it, alongside other beers such as Vale Brewery Notley Ale and Morland Old Speckled Hen. Food centres around an extensive buffet bar. Children are welcomed in three areas.

Open *11 to 3, 5.30 to 11, Sun 12 to 3, 7 to 10.30; open 25 Dec 12 to 2*

FRAMSDEN

Suffolk map 6

Dobermann Inn

The Street

TEL: (01473) 890461

off A1120, 3m SE of Debenham

Converted from sixteenth-century thatched cottages to a pub in 1794; was called the Greyhound, but the present owners breed Dobermanns. Wines – and some of the draught beers – are supplied by Adnams. Children are not allowed inside, but the pub has a garden with a stream. 'Take a walk to the local churchyard, where rare breeds of sheep may safely graze,' advises a correspondent.

Open *11.30 to 3 (12 to 3.30 Sun), 7 to 11 (10.30 Sun)*

FRIETH

Buckinghamshire map 3

Yew Tree

TEL: (01494) 882330

off B482 Stokenchurch to Marlow road, at Lane End

A useful venue for 'first-class' real ales in a 'truly rural' Chiltern village. Expect brews such as Fuller's London Pride, Brakspear Bitter, as well as Gibbs Mew Bishop's Tipple. Children are welcome in the dining areas and the pub has a games room plus plenty of space outside in the patio.

Open *11 to 3, 6 to 11, Sun 12 to 3, 7 to 10.30*

GARRIGILL

Cumbria map 10

George & Dragon

TEL: (01434) 381293

off B6277, 4m SE of Alston

Cross Fell – the highest peak in the Pennines – is just a hike from this 300-year-old inn. Once a watering-hole for the local zinc and lead-mining community, it now looks after the needs of foot-sloggers and cyclists. Liquid refreshment comes in the form of Theakston beers; the food is sustaining, and there are rooms at the inn. Children are welcome.

Open *12 to 4, 6 to 11, Sun 7 to 10.30*

GESTINGTHORPE

Essex map 3

Pheasant

TEL: (01787) 461196

off B1058, from A131, 4m SW of Sudbury

Restored pinkwashed pub in a tiny Essex village between the River Colne and the Suffolk border. Three bars are nicely laid out, service is friendly and the beer is 'very well kept'. Expect Adnams Bitter and Broadside, Greene King IPA and a guest such as Fuller's London Pride. The family room and garden are a bonus for those with children.

Open *12 to 3, 6 to 11, Sun 12 to 3, 7 to 10.30*

GNOSALL

Staffordshire map 5

Boat Inn

Wharf Road
TEL: (01785) 822208
just off A518, 6m W of Stafford
Cottagey little pub right on the towpath of the Shropshire Union Canal, and a great favourite with narrowboat enthusiasts. This is a Marston's tied house, with Bitter and Pedigree on handpump. Food may be limited to the summer months. Children welcome.
Open *all week 12 to 11*

GODALMING

Surrey map 3

Ram Cider House

Catteshall Lane
TEL: (01483) 421093
take Catteshall Road off A3100 Guildford to Godalming road, then second left after Farncombe boathouse, turn immediately right then left
Around 30 different ciders (cask and keg) and other apple-related brews are the outstanding feature of this fifteenth-century wattle-and-daub building surrounded by 'leafy bridlepaths'. The pub's name refers to a Victorian gravity pump for raising water – not a horned animal. The children's play area is in an old orchard in the grounds.
Open *Mon to Fri 11 to 3.30, 6 to 11 (summer 11am to 11pm), Sat 11am to 11pm, Sun 12 to 10.30*

GRATELEY

Hampshire map 2

Plough Inn

TEL: (01264) 889221
off B3084, 6m SW of Andover
Tip-top children's facilities, including an adventure playground and a family room overlooking the garden, are bonuses for families on the move. This is a Gibbs Mew pub, with Salisbury Best, Overlord and – occasionally – Bishop's Tipple, Deacon Ale and Wake Ale on draught. Occasional theme nights.
Open *11 to 2.30, 6 to 11, Sun 12 to 3, 7 to 10.30*

GREASBY

Merseyside map 7

Irby Mill

Irby Mill Hill
TEL: (0151) 604 0194
off B5139, W of Birkenhead, at Irby Mill crossroads
Diminutive Wirral country pub built on the site of an eighteenth-century post mill that remained in production until 1896. These days, the main business is the provision of North Country beers such as Cains Bitter and Mild, Tetley, Theakston and Jennings, plus two weekly guest brews. There are no facilities for children, although the garden is handy on fine days.
Open *11.30 to 11, Sun 12 to 10.30*

GREAT BARRINGTON

Gloucestershire map 5

Fox Inn

TEL: (01451) 844385
off A40, 3m W of Burford
Pleasant Cotswold pub in an 'area of outstanding natural beauty' close to the banks of the River Windrush. Bird-watchers and anglers congregate and order real ales from the Donnington Brewery, including BB, SBA and Mild. Children are welcome, the pub has a games room and accommodation is available.
Open *11am to 11pm, Sun 12 to 3, 7 to 10.30 (12 to 10.30 summer)*

GREAT LANGDALE

Cumbria map 8

Old Dungeon Ghyll Hotel ◆

TEL: (01539) 437272
on B5343, off A593, 6m from Skelwith Bridge
Originally a farm before becoming an inn, this gloriously remote pub was donated to the National Trust by Professor G. M. Tevelyan at the turn of the century. Its dramatic setting at the foot of the Langdale Pikes makes it a must for walkers and climbers of serious intent. Most of the action takes place in the rough-hewn Hikers Bar, where Jennings, Theakston and Yates beers are on draught beside a guest brew and Weston's Old Rosie cider. Children are welcome in the eating

areas and the garden, and the hotel has plenty of family accommodation.

Open *11am to 11pm, Sun 12 to 10.30*

GREAT OFFLEY

Hertfordshire map 3

Green Man

TEL: (01462) 768256

off A505, midway between Luton and Hitchin

Outstanding views of the Hertfordshire countryside are one of the attributes of this substantial Home Counties pub. To make the most of it all, sit in the huge glass-ceilinged conservatory, which opens on to pleasurable terraces and gardens. Familiar brews such as Boddingtons and Courage Best are on draught.

Open *11am to 11pm, Sun 12 to 3, 7 to 10.30*

GREAT TEW

Oxfordshire map 5

Falkland Arms ◆

TEL: (01608) 683653

off B4022, 5m E of Chipping Norton

'Phenomenal' was a reporter's ecstatic conclusion after a visit to this enduring Cotswold classic. After years dutifully preserving its uniqueness, custodians John and Hazel Milligan departed towards the end of 1996 and a new regime moved in. It would be hard to imagine that anything about the place itself will change – after all, that's why it attracts visitors. Creepers virtually envelope much of the original 500-year-old building, and inside it is a marvel to behold: huge numbers of mugs hang from the ceiling, clay pipes and 50 kinds of snuff are for sale and the choice of drinks is prodigious. Up to eight real ales ranging from Hall & Woodhouse Tanglefoot to Wadworth 6X are on draught, and cider and mead are also available. Children are welcome and accommodation is described as 'delightful'.

Open *Apr to Oct 11.30 to 11, Sun 12 to 10.30, Nov to Mar 12 to 3, 7 to 10.30*

GUITING POWER

Gloucestershire map 5

Ye Olde Inne

Winchcombe Road

TEL: (01451) 850392

off B4068, 6m W of Stow-on-the-Wold

Otherwise known as 'Th' Hollow Bottom', this Cotswold pub makes a useful refuelling point if you are exploring the countryside around the River Windrush. Hook Norton Best, Bass and Goff's Jouster are suitable thirst-quenchers and the wine list includes some promising stuff. Children are welcome. The pub was taken over in June 1996 by a consortium of names from the horse-racing world, including Peter Scudamore and Nigel Twiston-Davies. Accommodation is available.

Open *11.30 to 2.30, 6 to 11, Sun 12 to 3, 7 to 10.30*

HAMBLEDEN

Buckinghamshire map 3

Stag & Huntsman

TEL: (01491) 571227

off A4155, 3m NE of Henley-on-Thames

Well-signed walks in and around the Chiltern beechwoods attract visitors to this attractive village. The pub is a popular re-fuelling point, offering beers from Brakspear and Wadworth, as well as Marlow Rebellion or Mutiny in summer. Gambrinus lager and Luxters Barn Ale are in bottles. Children are welcome in the dining areas and the garden; accommodation is available.

Open *11 to 2.30, 6 to 11, Sun 12 to 3, 7 to 10.30*

HAMPSTHWAITE

North Yorkshire map 8

Joiners Arms

TEL: (01423) 771673

between B6165 and A59, 4m NW of Harrogate

Lovers of horticultural technicolour should be delighted by the spectacular floral displays that brighten up the garden of this cosy beamed pub close by the River Nidd. John Smith's Bitter

is on handpump. Children are welcome in the pub's eating areas.
Open *11.30 to 2.30, 5.30 to 11, Sun 12 to 2.30, 7 to 10.30*

HAPPISBURGH

Norfolk map 6

Hill House

TEL: (01692) 650004
on B1159, 6m E of N Walsham
Scotts Blues and Bloater is a local brew worth checking out at this 400-year-old-pub by the coast. Fans of real ale can also choose from Adnams, Shepherd Neame Spitfire, Fuller's London Pride and others. A takeaway menu is handy for holidaymakers wanting an evening meal. Children are welcome and there's a games room; three bedrooms are also available.
Open *12 to 2.30, 7 to 11 (11am to 11pm summer), Sun 12 to 10.30*

HARBERTON

Devon map 1

Church House Inn

TEL: (01803) 863707
off A381 Totnes to Kingsbridge road, 2½m S of Totnes
One of the oldest pubs in the country, built around 1100 to house the masons working on the nearby church. Some ancient hand-made glass can be still be seen and the family room is separated from the bar by a massive medieval oak screen. Courage Best, Hall & Woodhouse Tanglefoot and Churchwards local farm cider are the favoured tipples. Accommodation available from spring 1997.
Open *12 to 3, 6 to 11, Sun 12 to 3, 7 to 10.30; closed evening 25 and 26 Dec and 1 Jan*

HARTFIELD

East Sussex map 3

Anchor Inn

Church Street
TEL: (01892) 770424
village on junction of B2026 and B2110, 6m SE of East Grinstead
A.A. Milne, creator of *Winnie the Pooh*, lived in Hartfield, and this modernised fifteenth-century pub is firmly on the tourist circuit. Often it's full to bursting with hikers, families and others looking for sustenance. Liquid refreshment comes in the form of Harveys Best, Wadworth 6X, Marston's Pedigree and others. Accommodation is available.
Open *11am to 11pm; closed evening 25 and 26 Dec*

HASELBURY PLUCKNETT

Somerset map 2

Haselbury Inn

TEL: (01460) 72488
off A30, 2m E of Crewkerne
Hugely extended roadside village pub with a good local following and a tempting blackboard of cask beers: expect names like Butcombe Bitter, Otter Ale, Morland Old Speckled Hen, Hook Norton Old Hooky, among others. The landlord is 'a real old-school charmer', confessed one reporter. Children are welcome.
Open *11.45 to 3, 6.45 to 11, Sun 12 to 3, 6.45 to 10.30*

HATHERSAGE

Derbyshire map 9

Hathersage Inn

TEL: (01433) 650259
on A625, 8m N of Bakewell
Quite grand and hotel-like, although the Cricketer's Bar is 'distinctly pubby' with local memorabilia on the walls and three real ales dispensed by handpump. This is a good base camp for trips to Little John's grave (of Robin Hood fame), Kinder Scout, Axe Edge Moor, Haddon Hall and Chatsworth. Dogs are welcome.
Open *all week 11 to 3, 6 to 11*

HEATH

West Yorkshire map 9

Kings Arms

Heath Common
TEL: (01924) 377527
from A638 between Wakefield and Crofton take A655, then turning to Heath and Kirkthorpe
One hundred acres of common grassland provide the setting for this evocative old pub, which has been dispensing hospitality since 1841. Gas

lights glow in the maze of tiny rooms, where you can sample excellent beers from Clark's of Wakefield as well as guests such as Timothy Taylor Landlord. Children are welcome in the conservatory and garden.

Open *11.30 to 3, 5.30 to 11, Sun 12 to 10.30*

HELFORD

Cornwall map 1

Shipwrights Arms

TEL: (01326) 231235

take A3038 from Helston towards Lizard, join B3293 for Coverack, turn left for St Martin's and follow signs for Helford

Go for the setting. This immensely popular thatched hostelry stands by the banks of the Helford River (moorings are available), with terraces sloping down to the water. Inside it is, not surprisingly, nautically inclined. Whitbread Castle Eden Ale and Flowers are on draught. The owners say that theirs is a 'family-oriented pub', and well-behaved children are welcome until around 8pm.

Open *11 to 2.30, 6 to 11, Sun 12 to 2.30, 7 to 10.30 (closed Sun evening winter)*

HELSTON

Cornwall map 1

Blue Anchor

50 Coinagehall Street

TEL: (01326) 562821

off A394, 15m SW of Truro

Five hundred years ago, this tiny thatched building was a resting house for monks, but in recent times it has gained fame as a home-brew pub. Three potent 'Spingo' brews are generally on tap, including Middle, Best and Special. Bar snacks are served lunch-times only Monday to Saturday. Children have their own room.

Open *11am to 11pm, Sun 12 to 10.30*

HEMPSTEAD

Norfolk map 6

Hare & Hounds

TEL: (01263) 713285

from Holt bypass (A148) take road signposted Baconsthorpe, 2m SE of Holt

Homely brick-and-flint pub on the road between Hempstead and Baconsthorpe (noted for its castle ruins). A local atmosphere prevails in the bar, where Hare & Hounds Bitter and other East Anglian real ales such as Woodforde's Wherry are on draught. Children are welcome. The north Norfolk coast is reasonably close.

Open *11 to 3, 5.30 to 11, Sun 12 to 3, 7 to 10.30*

HERMITAGE

West Sussex map 3

Sussex Brewery

36 Main Road

TEL: (01243) 371533

on A259, just out of Emsworth towards Chichester

Not a working brewery, but well worth a visit if you are a fan of real ale. Beers on handpump could include such names as Hall & Woodhouse Tanglefoot, Burts Nobbler, Charles Wells Bombardier and a couple of weekly guests; Weston's cider is also on tap. Over forty kinds of traditionally made sausages dominate the menu. Children are welcome in the eating areas.

Open *11am to 11pm, Sun 12 to 10.30*

HEYTESBURY

Wiltshire map 2

Angel

TEL: (01985) 840330

just off A36, 3m E of Warminster

Worth knowing about if you want a stop-over between London and the West Country. Around five real ales are generally on show – including Ringwood Best, Shepherd Neame Spitfire and Adnams Broadside – alongside Inch's cider and 'rare French rums'. The wine list reads impressively and the menu suggests a deft hand in the kitchen. Children are welcome and

family accommodation is offered. Reports, please.
Open *11.30 to 3, 6.30 to 11, Sun 12 to 3, 7 to 10.30*

HOLBETON

Devon map 1

Mildmay Colours

TEL: (01752) 830248
off A379 Plymouth to Modbury road, 1m after National Shire Horse Centre, signposted Mothecombe and Holbeton
Home-brewed beers are the main attraction at this converted seventeenth-century manor house. Four real ales include Colours Best, SP Ale and Old Horse Whip; locally made Symons cider is also on tap. Children are welcome throughout the pub, and overnight accommodation is available.
Open *11 to 3, 6 to 11, Sun 12 to 3, 6.30 to 10.30*

HOLT

Wiltshire map 2

Old Ham Tree Inn

TEL: (01225) 782581
on B3107, between Bradford-on-Avon and Melksham, 2m N of Trowbridge
Homely eighteenth-century inn conveniently placed if you fancy a trip to nearby National Trust properties such as The Courts or Great Chalfield Manor. Locals tend to use the place for chat and pints of Robinson's Best, Timothy Taylor Landlord, Wadworth 6X or even Thatcher's cider. The pub has a games room and does B&B.
Open *11.15 to 3, 6.30 to 11, Sun 12 to 3, 7 to 10.30*

HOLYPORT

Berkshire map 3

Belgian Arms

TEL: (01628) 34468
off M4, 2m S of Maidenhead
Formerly 'The Eagle', but re-named during World War I after German prisoners held nearby saluted the pub sign as they walked by. This friendly place now serves locals and M4 travellers: the atmosphere is homely, Brakspear ales are on draught, and there's a child-friendly garden.
Open *11 to 3, 5.30 to 11, Sun 12 to 3, 7 to 10.30*

HOLYWELL

Cambridgeshire map 6

Old Ferry Boat Inn ◆

TEL: (01480) 463227
off A1123, 2m E of St Ives
The eerie landscape of the tidal Great Ouse makes the perfect backdrop for this ancient Fenland inn. A building has stood on this site for more than 1,000 years: it's claimed that Hereward the Wake used the ferry during the Norman invasion and boats were still plying the waters up to the 1930s. The roof is thatched, the windows are tiny and the beams are thick. A granite slab in the bar marks the grave of Juliet Tewsley, a young girl who died for love centuries ago and whose ghost is said to rise on 17 March each year. If things become too spooky, order a calming pint of Nethergate IPA, one of the guest ales or Inch's cider. Children are welcome and the pub has several bedrooms.
Open *11 to 3, 6 to 11, Sun 12 to 3.30, 7 to 10.30*

HOOK NORTON

Oxfordshire map 5

Pear Tree Inn

Scotland End
TEL: (01608) 737482
off A361, 5m NE of Chipping Norton
Great if you have visited Hook Norton Brewery and want to sample the beers in the setting of a genuine Oxfordshire village pub. The line-up is likely to include standards like Mild, Bitter and Old Hooky, as well as seasonal Twelve Days and Haymaker. Children are welcome and the pub has one double bedroom for anyone who wants to sleep off the after-effects.
Open *12 to 2.30 (3 Sat), 6 to 11, Sun 12 to 3, 7 to 10.30*

HOPE

Derbyshire map 8

Poachers Arms

Castleton Road
TEL: (01433) 620380
on A625, between Chapel-en-le-Frith and Hathersage
The Blue John Cavern at Castleton is one nearby attraction within striking distance of this pub in the tourist-trap High Peaks. John Smith's, Courage Directors and Marston's Pedigree should satisfy the thirst. Children are welcome in the eating areas and the garden; the pub also provides accommodation, if you don't fancy camping.
Open *all week 12 to 3, 6 to 11*

HORN'S CROSS

Devon map 1

Hoops Inn

TEL: (01237) 451222
on A39, 5m SW of Bideford
Classic thirteenth-century thatched inn, with four-posters in some of its bedrooms and a reputation for good drink. The landlord stages a yearly beer festival and always has at least four real ales on draught, as well as 'real scrumpy'. Wines – and champagne – are served by the glass, and the menu looks promising. Reports, please.
Open *11am to 11pm, Sun 12 to 10.30*

HORSEBRIDGE

Devon map 1

Royal Inn

TEL: (01822) 870214
off A384, 5m W of Tavistock
The Horsebridge Brewery has its home at this 500-year-old village pub. Four ales – including Best, Tamar, Right Royal and high-strength Heller – are normally on draught. Local cider is also available during the summer. Children are welcome inside the pub at lunch-time, and there is a one-acre garden and patio where they can play.
Open *winter all week 12 to 3, 7 to 11 (10.30 Sun), summer and bank hols 12 to 11 (10.30 Sun)*

HORSEY

Norfolk map 6

Nelson Head

Beach Road
TEL: (01493) 393378
off B1159, 9m NE of Acle
Brick-built 400-year-old pub down a dead-end lane (look for signs 'to the sea') on the fringes of Hickling Broad. Also perfectly placed for a wildlife trip to Horsey Mere or a visit to Horsey Mill (National Trust). Genuine atmosphere, friendly Austrian landlord, and well-kept Woodforde's beers. Family room and garden.
Open *11 to 2.30, 7 (6 summer) to 11, Sun 12 to 3, 7 to 10.30*

HUNDON

Suffolk map 6

Plough Inn

TEL: (01440) 786789
off A143, 2m N of Haverhill, take right turn to Kedington, then 1m towards Hundon
Set in five acres of grounds with views of the Stour Valley, the Plough now functions as local pub, restaurant and hotel with conference facilities. One local brew and two guests are generally on draught and the wine list has some good bottles from Adnams and Lay & Wheeler. Children are welcome in the dining-room and garden.
Open *12 to 2.30, 6 to 11 (11am to 11pm summer), Sun 12 to 3, 7 to 11*

HURLEY

Berkshire map 2

Dew Drop

Batts Green
TEL: (01628) 824327
take Honey Lane off A423, just outside Hurley between Maidenhead and Henley-on-Thames, continue past council houses and through farm until wood, at T-junction take right turn on to smaller lane, inn is a few hundred yds on right
Devilishly hard to track down, but a delightful little place hidden away in woods outside the village. Walkers on the Knowl Hill footpath pass right by the door, although they might be

tempted to nip inside for a pint of Brakspear. Children can use the snug; otherwise the pub is surrounded by more than an acre of grounds.
Open *Summer Mon to Fri 11 to 3, 6 to 11, Sat 11am to 11pm, Sun 12 to 10.30, winter 11.30 to 3, 6 to 11, Sun 12 to 3, 6 to 10.30*

ICKLESHAM

East Sussex map 3

Queens Head

Parsonage Lane
TEL: (01424) 814552
just off A259 Hastings to Rye road, 2m W of Winchelsea
The name is emblazoned on the tiled roof of this seventeenth-century village pub, which also boasts 'one of the finest views in East Sussex'. Real ale gets top billing in the bar, with a great choice including Pett Progress, Harveys Old Ale, and Ringwood Old Thumper, among others; Biddenden cider is also available. No children under 14 after 9pm.
Open *11am to 11pm, Sun 12 to 5, 7 to 10.30*

ILMINGTON

Warwickshire map 5

Howard Arms

Lower Green
TEL: (01608) 682226
off A3400, 4m NW of Shipston on Stour
Civilised 300-year-old inn in a pleasant setting overlooking the village green. Beers such as Everards Tiger and Marston's Pedigree are on draught, and accommodation is still provided. Children are welcome and the pub has a pretty back garden. New owners arrived in autumn 1996 and tell us that food may be limited in winter. Reports please.
Open *11 to 2.30, 6 to 11, Sun 12 to 3, 7 to 10.30*

INGLEBY

Derbyshire map 5

John Thompson

TEL: (01332) 862469
off A514, 3m NW of Melbourne
John Thompson converted his ancient farmhouse into a pub in 1969 and started brewing beer in 1977 (to commemorate the Queen's Jubilee). In a setting of oak furniture, paintings and antiques, visitors can sup JTS Bitter and Porter, alongside Bass. Snacks are served at lunch-time (although the choice is limited on Sundays). The pub garden runs down to the banks of the Trent, and Calke Abbey is a short drive away.
Open *10.30 to 2.30, 7 to 11, Sun 12 to 2.30, 7 to 10.30*

INGS

Cumbria map 8

Watermill

TEL: (01539) 821309
just off A591, 2m E of Windermere
Originally a woodmill, later a B&B and more recently a family-run pub with a resounding reputation for its real ales. Up to 14 are often on handpump, and if you are fond of diversity, this is the place to come: big names like Theakston and Jennings share the billing with beers from Dent and Coniston. Children are welcome in the 'top bar', there are tables by the River Gowan, and the pub has six bedrooms.
Open *12 to 2.30, 6 to 11, Sun 12 to 3, 6 to 10.30*

INKBERROW

Hereford & Worcester map 5

Old Bull

TEL: (01386) 792428
on A422 Worcester to Stratford-upon-Avon road, 5m W of Alcester
This photogenic Tudor pub is known to millions of devoted listeners as 'The Bull' in the radio saga *The Archers*. It looks the part, with its wonky half-timbered façade, tall chimneys and seriously pitched roof. Customers occasionally rub shoulders with stars of the show in the bar, where three real ales are on draught. Children are allowed inside.
Open *12 to 3, 6 to 11, Sun 12 to 10.30*

INKPEN

Berkshire map 2

Swan Inn

Lower Inkpen
TEL: (01488) 668326
off A388, 4m SE of Hungerford
This seventeenth-century farmhouse pub close to the Wayfarers Walk was about to enter a new era as we went to press. The place is now run by Chris Butt and friend – founders of Butts micro-brewery – and their beers appear on handpump alongside Adnams. Plans are afoot to open a restaurant and possibly a farm shop stocking organic produce in 1997. Progress reports, please.
Open *Tue to Sat 12 to 2.30, 6.30 to 11, Sun 12 to 2.30, 7 to 10.30*

KELD

North Yorkshire map 8

Tan Hill Inn

TEL: (01833) 628246
off B6270 at Keld, then 4m N
England's 'highest pub' stands in a remote spot, more than 1,700 feet above sea level. Open fires help to keep out the Pennine chills, a dram or two of malt whisky helps the mood along; otherwise order a pint of Theakston or Black Sheep Bitter. If the weather closes in, there are rooms where you can stay the night.
Open *all week 11am to11pm*

KERSEY

Suffolk map 6

Bell Inn ◆

The Street
TEL: (01473) 823229
1m W of A1141, 2m NW of Hadleigh
Much-photographed half-timbered medieval pub in a village that has had more than its share of TV coverage – the 'water splash' across the high street has featured in numerous programmes. New owners have polished up the interior, which now boasts re-varnished wood, horse brasses and dried flower arrangements. Draught beers such as Theakston XB and Courage Directors appear alongside superbly kept guests including perhaps Bateman's Valiant; the wine list is wide-ranging. Children are welcome in the eating areas and outside.
Open *11 to 3, 6.30 to 11 (11am to 11pm summer), Sun 12 to 10.30*

KILNSEA

Humberside map 9

Crown and Anchor

Main Road
TEL: (01964) 650276
off B1445, at N end of spit of land on N side of mouth of River Humber
Eighteenth-century whitewashed pub on far reaches of the Spurn Peninsula with superb views over Spurn Point (a hot-spot for bird-watchers). You can watch the goings-on from its large window while sampling a pint of Bass or Tetley Bitter. There's space for children inside and out, and the pub has four bedrooms.
Open *11am to 11pm, Sun 12 to 10.30*

KINGSAND

Cornwall map 1

Halfway House Inn

Fore Street
TEL: (01752) 822279
just off B3247 at Cawsand Bay, 1m SE of Millbrook
So called because a stream in the garden once marked the border between Cornwall and Devon. This is an excellent child-friendly venue with family accommodation, plenty of seafood on the menu and several real ales on draught. Recommended for superb walks along the coastal path to Rames Head and Mount Edgecumbe House and Gardens.
Open *winter 12 to 3.30, 7 to 11 (10.30 Sun), summer 12 to 4, 6.30 to 11 (10.30 Sun)*

KINGSBRIDGE

Devon map 1

Crabshell Inn

Embankment Road
TEL: (01548) 852345
off A381, 8m SW of Totnes
Originally a watering-hole for sailors off the barges, this 300-year-old inn right by the quayside is now a popular,

child-friendly venue. A waterside garden fronts the estuary, which is great for bird-watching at low tide. Drinkers do well with Bass, Boddingtons, Flowers IPA and organic ciders. Monster seafood platters are the stars on the menu.

Open *11am to 11pm, Sun 12 to 10.30*

KNIPTON

Leicestershire map 5

Red House

Croxton Road
TEL: (01476) 870352
off A607, 6m SW of Grantham

'A great place,' enthused one visitor to this 250-year-old converted hunting lodge in two acres of grounds. Much attention focuses on Hornbeams Restaurant, but the bar feels domestically civilised and there's occasional live jazz in winter. Marston's Pedigree and Tetley Bitter are bolstered by a guest ale. Children are welcome and accommodation is available. Belvoir Castle is close by.

Open *11 to 3, 6 to 11, Sun 12 to 4, 7 to 10.30*

LAND'S END

Cornwall map 1

Trenwith Arms

Land's End Hotel
TEL: (01736) 871844
at end of A30, 10m SW of Penzance

The pub attached to the nineteenth-century Land's End Hotel is a favourite with walkers doing the Coastal Path, and its terraces are perfect for watching birds or scanning the water for grey seals or basking sharks. St Austell beers are on draught, along with Boston Bitter and Lioness Bitter. Children are welcome.

Open *all week 11am to 11pm*

LANGLEY MARSH

Somerset map 2

Three Horseshoes

TEL: (01984) 623763
off B3227 or B3188, 1m N of Wiveliscombe

Palmers IPA, Otter Best, Ringwood Best and Perry's farmhouse cider are tapped direct from the cask in this sandstone roadside pub. The landlord's wife does her cooking on an Aga. There's a games room inside and a beer garden with a 'log play area' for the youngsters.

Open *12 to 2.30, 7 to 11 (10.30 Sun)*

LANREATH

Cornwall map 1

Punch Bowl Inn

TEL: (01503) 220218
off B3359, 5m NW of Looe

New licensee James Brown took the helm of this ancient Cornish hostelry in 1996. The pub was once a courthouse and later a smugglers' haunt; some of the old atmosphere still prevails. It claims to be the only inn in Britain where the licensed bars are called 'kitchens'. Children are welcome 'everywhere except the public bar'. Four-posters and half-testers are available for overnight guests.

Open *11 to 3, 6 to 11 (11am to 11pm summer), Sun 12 to 3, 7 to 10.30 (12 to 10.30 summer)*

LEY HILL

Buckinghamshire map 3

Swan Inn

TEL: (01494) 783075
off B4505, 2m E of Chesham

This sixteenth-century cottage pub looks delightfully enticing with its terraces full of flowers and views across the common and the cricket pitch. The rustic, low-beamed interior doesn't disappoint either. Regular live jazz sessions attract the fans, and there are well-kept beers to go with the music. Children are welcome in the restaurant and games room.

Open *11 to 2.30, 5.30 to 11, Sat 11 to 11, Sun 12 to 10.30*

LICKFOLD

West Sussex map 3

Lickfold Inn

TEL: (01798) 861285

off A272 Midhurst to Petworth road, signposted Lodsworth, 4m NE of Midhurst

Beautifully restored 400-year-old inn with splendid herringbone brickwork, a charming terraced garden and a superb selection of real ales ranging from award-winners to esoteric curiosities from micro-breweries. No children under 14. There was a change of ownership as went to press.

Open *11 to 2.30, 6 to 11, Sun 12 to 3, 7 to 10.30*

LINWOOD

Hampshire map 2

High Corner Inn

TEL: (01425) 473973

off A338/A31, 7m NE of Ringwood

Conference facilities, a squash court, accommodation and a woodland garden with an adventure playground are unexpected additions to this 250-year-old thatched pub deep in the New Forest. Children can amuse themselves in the 'Lego' games room; adults can sample King Alfred Bitter, Flowers IPA and Wadworth 6X.

Open *11.30 to 2.30, 7 to 10.30 (11 to 3, 6 to 11 summer), Sat 11am to 11pm, Sun 12 to 10.30*

LITTLE HADHAM

Hertfordshire map 3

Nags Head

The Ford

TEL: (01279) 771555

off A120 at traffic lights towards Much Hadham

Three members of the Robinson family are at the helm of this 400-year-old pub in a quiet Hertfordshire village. The full range of Greene King beers – including seasonal Mad Judge and Royal Raven – are available, and the kitchen specialises in fish. Children welcome if eating.

Open *11 to 2.30, 6 to 11, Sun 12 to 3, 7 to 10.30*

LITTLEHEMPSTON

Devon map 1

Tally Ho!

TEL: (01803) 862316

off A381, 2m NE of Totnes

Open fires in winter and a flower-filled patio in summer are seasonal draws at this 600-year-old inn by the local church. Liquid nourishment comes in the form of Devon brews such as Dartmoor Best, Teignworthy 'Reel' Ale and Tally Ho Strong Ale. Children are welcome in the eating area of the bar.

Open *12 to 2.30, 6 to 11, Sun 12 to 3, 7 to 10.30*

LITTLE LONGSTONE

Derbyshire map 8

Packhorse Inn

TEL: (01629) 640471

off B6465, 2m NW of Bakewell

New licensees are finding their feet at this unspoilt moorland local – originally a miner's cottage, but now popular with Peak District hikers and tourists. The bars are done out in rustic style, there is live folk music every Wednesday, and Marston's beers are on draught. Children are welcome.

Open *11 to 3, 5 to 11, Sun 12 to 3, 7 to 10.30*

LITTLE STRETTON

Shropshire map 5

Ragleth Inn

Ludlow Road

TEL: (01694) 722711

on B4370, off A49, just S of Church Stretton

Dating from 1663 and still going strong. The setting – in Shropshire countryside within trekking distance of the Long Mynd – makes it a popular pit-stop for walking types. Others call in simply for a pint of Marston's Pedigree, Morland Old Speckled Hen or Bateman's Mild. Children are welcome and the pub offers B&B.

Open *12 to 2.30, 6 to 11, Sun 12 to 10.30*

LLANYBLODWEL

Shropshire map 5

Horseshoe

TEL: (01691) 828969

just off B4396, 5m SW of Oswestry

Only just in Shropshire, according to the map, in an 'undiscovered' hamlet by a tributary of the Severn. The building is 'gorgeous fifteenth-century', while 'all-round charm' sums up the tiny, dimly lit bar with its genuine local atmosphere, black ceiling beams and bare wooden floor. Real ales and ciders are on tap. Children are welcome.

Open *11.30 to 3, 6.30 to 11, Sun 12 to 3, 7 to 10.30; closed Mon L in winter*

LONG PRESTON

North Yorkshire map 8

Maypole Inn

TEL: (01729) 840219

on A65 Skipton to Settle road

Oakmoor Yorkshire cider is an unexpected tipple in this three-centuries-old pub in the Dales National Park. Drinkers can also sup North Country brews such as Alesman from the Worth Brewery and Timothy Taylor Landlord. Children are welcome until 9pm and the pub has useful family accommodation. The Settle–Carlisle Railway is not far away.

Open *11 to 3, 6 to 11, Sat 11am to 11pm, Sun 12 to 10.30*

LOW CATTON

East Riding of Yorkshire map 9

Gold Cup Inn

TEL: (01759) 371354

off A166, just S of Stamford Bridge

In walking country a short detour from the Wolds Way near Thixendale, this family-run village pub also draws custom from city dwellers out from York. Tetley Bitter and John Smith's are on handpump. Children are welcome if eating; the pub has a games room, as well as an outdoor play area and paddock in the garden running down to the banks of the River Derwent.

Open *Mon 7 to 11, Tue to Fri 12 to 3, 7 to 11, Sat 12 to 11, Sun 12 to 10.30*

LOWER ASHTON

Devon map 1

Manor Inn

TEL: (01647) 252304

from A38 S of Exeter take B3193 towards Christow, signposted on right after 5m

First and foremost 'a no-frills drinking pub' that has put on close to 1,000 guest beers to date: Teignworthy Reel Ale, Adnams Extra, Wadworth 6X, Goff's Sleepless Night and others are tapped from the cask. Also look for local Green Valley cider. Children can use the garden, which is a delightful spot in summer.

Open *Tue to Sat 12 to 2.30, 7 (6 Sat) to 11, Sun 12 to 2.30, 7 to 10.30*

LOWER PEOVER

Cheshire map 7

Bells of Peover ◆

The Cobbles

TEL: (01565) 722269

on B5081, 6m E of Northwich

At the end of a cobbled lane that also leads to the beautiful medieval church of St Oswald (complete with a sandstone tower): 'the whole set-up must be ideal for weddings,' noted one visitor. Inside, it's a treasure, with oak furniture, huge fires a-blazing and a noteworthy collection of Toby jugs dotted around. Children aren't allowed in the bar, but there is a pleasant garden outside. The pub was acquired by Greenalls Brewery towards the end of 1996. Reports, please.

Open *11.30 to 3, 5.30 to 11, Sun 12 to 3, 7 to 10.30*

LOWSONFORD

Warwickshire map 5

Fleur de Lys

Larworth Street

TEL: (01564) 782431

off B4095, 3m NE of Henley-in-Arden

This attractive seventeenth-century cottage pub is particularly appealing in summer, when families take advantage of the gardens sweeping down to the Stratford-upon-Avon Canal. At other times, there might be up to six fires blazing in the genuine beamed bars.

Wadworth 6X, Flowers Original and Marston's Pedigree are on draught.
Open *11am to 11pm, Sun 12 to 10.30*

LYNMOUTH

Devon map 1

Rising Sun Hotel

Harbourside
TEL: (01598) 753223
on A39, 9m W of Porlock
A seductive harbourside setting is one of the joys at this beguiling 600-year-old inn overlooking the East Lyn River. Excellent walks along the coast to Countisbury cliffs and inland are an added attraction. Exmoor ales, decent wines and first-rate service. Note that the hotel is not suitable for children.
Open *11 to 3, 5.30 (7 winter) to 11, Sun 12 to 2.30, 6.30 to 10.30*

MALHAM

North Yorkshire map 8

Buck Inn

TEL: (01729) 830317
off A65, 5m E of Settle
Enticing stone-built Dales inn popular with Pennine walkers and those interested in natural history. Malham Tarn Reserve is close by, as are the extraordinary 'geological phenomena' of Gordale Scar and Malham Cove's 'natural amphitheatre'. Beers from Theakston and Black Sheep make ideal thirst quenchers. Children are welcome, and ample family accommodation is offered.
Open *11 to 3, 7 to 11 (11am to 11pm July to Sept), Sat 11am to 11pm, Sun 12 to 10.30*

MARSWORTH

Buckinghamshire map 3

Red Lion

90 Vicarage Road
TEL: (01296) 668366
off B489, 2m N of Tring
Seventeenth-century brick pub in the village centre by Bridge 130 of the Grand Union Canal. Popular with narrowboat enthusiasts, towpath walkers, bird-watchers and anglers (Tring Reservoirs are not far away). Bass, London Pride and others are on handpump; a cask of Weston's cider is also on the bar. Children can use the games room.
Open *11 to 3, 6 to 11 (11am to 11pm Sat summer), Sun 12 to 3, 7 to 10.30 (12 to 10.30 summer)*

MARTYR'S GREEN

Surrey map 3

Black Swan

Old Lane
TEL: (01932) 862364
off M25 and A3, 2m SW of Cobham
No fewer than 14 real ales are regularly on show throughout the year in this much-favoured family pub within easy reach of the Royal Horticultural Society gardens at Wisley. Children are welcome throughout the pub, although the playground at the back is a great inducement when the weather allows.
Open *11am to 11pm, Sun 12 to 10.30*

MATFEN

Northumberland map 10

Black Bull

TEL: (01661) 886330
off A68 or B3618, 5m NE of Corbridge
Fabulous floral displays and hanging baskets festoon the front of this 200-year-old stone pub in summer. Attractions within include Black Bull Bitter, Morland Old Speckled Hen and guests such as Everards Tiger Best. Children are welcome, and the pub has family accommodation. The pub is convenient for Hadrian's Wall, Chesters Fort and George Stephenson's birthplace (NT).
Open *11 to 3, 6 to 11 (summer 11am to 11pm)*

MAYFIELD

East Sussex map 3

Rose & Crown Inn ◆

Fletching Street
TEL: (01435) 872200
off A267, ¼m E of village centre, 8m S of Tunbridge Wells
Fifteenth-century weatherboarded pub opposite the green in a spectacularly pretty Sussex village. The interior is fascinatingly laid out on different

levels, with large open fires and stoves providing warmth, and a clutter of rural memorabilia adding distraction. Harveys Sussex Best, Greene King Abbot Ale and Gale's HSB are on handpump and the wine list is extensive. Children are welcome throughout, and the pub has four bedrooms. There was a change of licensee as we went to press. Reports, please.

Open *11 to 3.30, 5.30 to 11, Sat 11am to 11pm, Sun 12 to 10*

MEAVY

Devon map 1

Royal Oak Inn

TEL: (01822) 852944

off A386/B3212 at Yelverton, SW of Burrator Reservoir

Pub buildings owned by the local parish council are few and far between, so this old thatched pub on the village green has a special claim to fame. Excellent real ales are Eldridge Pope Royal Oak, Otter Bitter and Courage Best; Luscombe farm cider is also on tap. No children.

Open *11.30 to 3, 6.30 to 11, Sun 12 to 3, 7 to 10.30*

MENITHWOOD

Hereford & Worcester map 5

Cross Keys

TEL: (01584) 881425

between A443 Tenbury Wells to Worcester road and B4202 Clows Top to Abberley road

Top-drawer real ales including Marston's Bitter and Pedigree, Wye Valley, Hobsons and many more are the prime reasons for visiting this genuine village local. Food includes sandwiches of great renown, plus occasional balti dishes, which can be ordered as takeaways. Children are welcome away from the bar.

Open *Mon to Wed and Fri 11 to 3, 6 to 11, Thur and Sat 11am to 11pm, Sun 12 to 3, 7 to 10.30*

MICHELDEVER

Hampshire map 2

Dever Arms

Winchester Road

TEL: (01962) 774339

off A33, 6m N of Winchester

A new licensee had just moved into this village pub by the local cricket ground as we went to press. The place seems to be maintaining its reputation for decent real ales, although most are now from Marston's; the house wine is also reckoned to be 'outstandingly good'. Friendliness prevails and there's a games room for the youngsters.

Open *12 to 3, 6 to 11, Sun 12 to 3, 7 to 10.30*

NEAR SAWREY

Cumbria map 8

Tower Bank Arms

TEL: (015394) 36334

on B5285, 2m SE of Hawkshead

Hilltop – Beatrix Potter's cottage – stands next door to this delightful little pub: readers of her bedtime stories will recognise the Tower Bank as 'the small country inn' mentioned in *The Tale of Jemima Puddleduck*. Theakston beers are on draught; also look for the stock of Belgian and other imported bottled beers. Children are welcome at lunch-time and in the dining-room in the evening. Accommodation is available.

Open *11 to 3, 6 (5.30 summer) to 11, Sun 12 to 3, 6 to 10.30 (12 to 10.30 summer)*

NESSCLIFFE

Shropshire map 7

Old Three Pigeons

TEL: (01743) 741279

on A5, 8m NW of Shrewsbury

Real ales are changed daily in this ancient low-beamed pub dating from 1405. Menus are dominated by a vast selection of fresh fish. Children are welcome where food is served, and the pub has a sizeable garden.

Open *all week 12 to 3, 7 to 11 (10.30 Sun)*

NETHER HEAGE

Derbyshire map 5

Spanker Inn

20 Spanker Lane
TEL: (01773) 853222
off A6, 3m W of Ripley
Handily placed for fishing on the Derwent or walks in the Amber Valley. Real ales include Vaux Samson as well as Mansfield Bitter and Mild; food is limited to lunch-times – apart from Wednesday night, when steaks are the thing. Children are welcome, and the pub has a games room.
Open *11 to 3, 7 (6 Wed) to 11, Sun 12 to 3, 7 to 10.30*

NEWTON

Cambridgeshire map 6

Queens Head ◆

TEL: (01223) 870436
off A10 at Harston, on B1368, 6m S of Cambridge
David Short and family continue to run this quirky gem of a place in perfect style and with no concessions to fashion. The extraordinary building, with its precariously tall chimney, looks wonderfully weathered, and the interior is splendidly unimproved, with its crooked beams and rickety furniture. Adnams Bitter and Broadside, plus seasonal brews, are drawn direct from the cask, while cider buffs have a choice of Cassells or Crones. Food is exactly what you might expect: mugs of soup, dripping on toast, Aga-baked potatoes. Children are welcome 'if under control' and there are seats outside.
Open *11.30 to 2.30, 6 to 11, Sun 12 to 2.30, 7 to 10.30*

NORTH NIBLEY

Gloucestershire map 2

New Inn

Waterley Bottom
TEL: (01453) 543659
off B4060, 2m SW of Dursley and just E of North Nibley
A useful destination for walkers rambling through the nearby beechwoods and valleys – especially those with a taste for real ale. Cotleigh WB and Tawny, Smiles Best and Exhibition, Theakston Old Peculier and Greene King Abbot Ale are dispensed from 'antique beer engines'. Inch's cider is also on tap. Children can use the garden, and the pub offers accommodation.
Open *12 to 2.30, 7 to 11, Sun 12 to 3, 7 to 10.30*

NORTH WOOTTON

Dorset map 2

Three Elms

TEL: (01935) 812881
on A3030 Sherborne to Sturminster Newton road, 2m SE of Sherborne
'A true free house' with a dazzling selection of up to nine beers on draught, including Three Elms Traditional (brewed by Smiles), Butcombe Bitter and East Street Cream; also note the Burrow Hill cider. More than 1,000 'classic American car models' are displayed in cases around the bar. Children are welcome in the eating area, and the pub offers accommodation.
Open *11 to 2.30, 6.30 (6 Fri and Sat) to 11, Sun 12 to 3, 7 to 10.30*

NUNNEY

Somerset map 2

George

11 Church Street
TEL: (01373) 836458
off A361, 2m SW of Frome
Seventeenth-century coaching-inn directly opposite the impressive ruins of Nunney's medieval castle in a 'conservation area' of historic cottages. Over 100 whiskies provide the back-up for Wadworth 6X, Bass and Exmoor Ale. The pub has a family room, a big garden and 14 bedrooms. Longleat and Wookey Hole are within easy reach.
Open *12 to 3, 6.30 to 11 (10.30 Sun)*

OLDBURY-ON-SEVERN

South Gloucestershire map 2

Anchor Inn

Church Road
TEL: (01454) 413331
off B4061, 2m NW of Thornbury
Built on the site of a seventeenth-century mill house and once used as a mooring point for barges heading up the Severn. The views and the setting attract, as does the prospect of sampling Bass 'from the barrel', Black Sheep or Theakston Old Peculier. Games of boules are played in the 'streamside' garden.
Open *11.30 to 2.30, 6.30 to 11, Sat 11.30 to 11, Sun 12 to 3, 7 to 10.30*

OLD WARDEN

Bedfordshire map 6

Hare and Hounds

TEL: (01767) 627225
off A1/A600, 4m W of Biggleswade
Friendly thatched pub in a fascinating showpiece estate village remodelled in 'Victorian rustic' style. Grown-ups can enjoy pints of Charles Wells Eagle, Mansfield Bitter and Adnams Broadside, while children have a play area. The landscaped Swiss Garden and the Shuttleworth Collection of vintage aircraft are prime local attractions.
Open *11 to 3, 6 to 11, Sun 12 to 3, 7 to 10.30*

OMBERSLEY

Hereford & Worcester map 5

Crown & Sandys Arms

TEL: (01905) 620252
off A449 Worcester to Kidderminster road, 4m W of Droitwich
The name refers to connections between King Charles and the Sandys family during the Civil War, and this re-modelled inn still plays its historical trump card effectively. The mood is civilised, real ales from Hook Norton, Hobsons and others are in good order, and the inn provides decent accommodation. No children.
Open *11 to 3, 6 to 11, Sun 12 to 3, 7 to 10.30*

ONECOTE

Staffordshire map 5

Jervis Arms

TEL: (01538) 304206
on B5053, 1m off A523 Leek to Ashbourne road, 4m E of Leek
New licensee Ronald Foster took over in summer 1996, but this pub by a stream seems likely to remain a popular choice with tourists and holidaymakers – particularly those with children and devotees of well-kept real ales. Onecote is in the heart of the Peak District National Park; nearby Brindley Mill is worth visiting.
Open *11 to 3, 7 to 11, Sun 12 to 10.30*

ORFORD

Suffolk map 6

Jolly Sailor

Quay Street
TEL: (01394) 450243
on B1084, 9m E of Woodbridge
Splendid former smugglers' haunt on the edge of the village heading towards the quay. Seasonally changing brews such as Adnams Mild, Old, Bitter and Broadside can be sampled in the genuine old-timbered bar, and the pub offers useful B&B. Children are not allowed inside, but the garden is handy, weather permitting. Orford's Norman castle keep and ancient church are worth a look.
Open *11.30 to 2.30, 7 to 11, Sun 12 to 2.45, 7 to 10.30*

OSWALDKIRK

North Yorkshire map 9

Malt Shovel

TEL: (01439) 788461
on B1363, 4m S of Helmsley
Grade-II listed manor house turned coaching-inn, set on the edge of the Yorkshire Moors and Hambleton Hills, close to Ampleforth College. No fewer than four fires often blaze in the comfortable, heavily beamed bars. Samuel Smith Old Brewery Bitter is on handpump. The pub has a family room and a pleasant beer garden.
Open *11.30 to 3, 6.30 to 11 (11am to 11pm Sat summer), Sun 12 to 3, 7 to 10.30*

OVING

West Sussex map 3

Gribble Inn

Gribble Lane
TEL: (01243) 786793
off A259, 4m E of Chichester
Home-brewed beer is the thing in this pretty little thatched pub. The brewery produces up to seven ales with names like Ewe Brew, Plucking Pheasant, Pig's Ear and Wobbler, and they can be sampled in the bar, along with Hall & Woodhouse Dorset Best. The inn has a family room and a popular skittle alley.
Open *11 to 2.30, 6 to 11, Sun 12 to 3, 7 to 10.30*

OWSLEBURY

Hampshire map 2

Ship Inn

TEL: (01962) 777358
off A33/A272, 4m S of Winchester
Seventeenth-century hilltop local which is exceedingly popular with families visiting nearby Marwell Zoological Park. The 'perfect summer garden' has tip-top children's facilities, including a play area, aviary and rabbits, while jazz evenings attract the adults. Marston's beers are kept in good condition.
Open *Mon to Sat 11 to 3, 6 to 11, Sun 2 to 10.30*

PAGLESHAM

Essex map 3

Plough & Sail

East End
TEL: (01702) 258242
off B1013, 4m E of Rochford
The Plough & Snail has been in the capable hands of the Oliver family for the last 30 of its 400 years. A short walk away, you'll find the historic oyster beds which date back to Roman times – fans of the famous bivalves will be pleased to know that trade is once again thriving. In the pub's garden there's a children's play area with an aviary, and Marston's Pedigree is among the real ales on tap at the bar.
Open *11.30 to 2.30, 7 to 11, Sun 12 to 3, 7 to 10.30*

PEACEMARSH

Dorset map 2

Dolphin Inn

TEL: (01747) 822758
on B3092, N of Gillingham
Creeper-clad converted farmhouse that now does well from tourists exploring the countryside of north Dorset and the Stour Valley. Hall & Woodhouse Dorset Best Bitter and Tanglefoot and Inch's cider are the favoured tipples. Children are welcome in the eating area of the bar and the garden.
Open *11 to 2.30, 6 to 11, Sun 12 to 10.30*

PELDON

Essex map 3

Peldon Rose

Mersea Road
TEL: (01206) 735248
off B1025, 5m S of Colchester
From the garden of this fourteenth-century pinkwashed inn, there are great views of the Pyefleet Channel and the Essex saltmarshes. Its location is also handy if you are visiting Abberton Reservoir or Fingringhoe Wick Nature Reserve. Flowers IPA and Boddingtons are on handpump, and the pub serves afternoon cream teas in summer. Children are welcome and the pub provides accommodation.
Open *winter 11 to 3, 5.30 to 11, Sun 12 to 3, 7 to 10.30, summer 11am to 11pm, Sun 12 to 10.30*

PELYNT

Cornwall map 1

Jubilee Inn

TEL: (01503) 220312
on B3359, 3m NW of Looe
Family run, 400-year-old inn re-named in honour of Queen Victoria's jubilee and bedecked with all manner of 'royal reminders'. Bass and St Austell Trelawny's Pride are on draught in the oak-beamed bar, and the wine list is extensive. Children are welcome, and the inn has commendable family accommodation.
Open *Mon to Fri 11 to 3 (3.30 summer), 6 to 11, Sat 11am to 11pm, Sun 12 to 10.30*

PENELWEY

Cornwall map 1

Punch Bowl & Ladle

TEL: (01872) 862237

off A39 at Playing Place, on to B3249 Feock road, 3m S of Truro

Greatly extended 500-year-old thatched pub much favoured by families and tourists heading for the King Harry Ferry and the National Trust gardens at Trelissick. Inside, it is cosy, with 'overstuffed sofas', books piled on window sills and lots of knick-knacks around. Bass, Flowers Original and Courage are on draught. The pub welcomes children.

Open *11 to 3, 5.30 to 11 (11am to 11pm summer), Sun 12 to 3, 6.30 to 10.30*

PHILLACK

Cornwall map 1

Bucket of Blood Inn

TEL: (01736) 752378

off A30, across the canal, N of Hayle

The name refers to a gory incident relating to blood being drawn from the local well. On a brighter note, this 400-year-old pub stocks the full range of draught beers from the St Austell brewery, as well as Old Hazy cider. The pub is handy for bird-watching on the Hayle estuary and walks on 'the Towans' – an area of prime dune-land.

Open *11 to 2.30 (3 Sat and summer), 6 (5.30 summer) to 11, Sun 12 to 4, 7 (6 summer) to 10.30*

PIERCEBRIDGE

Co Durham map 10

George Hotel

TEL: (01325) 374576

just off A67, 5m W of Darlington

The riverside setting by a bridge over the River Tees is a good reason for visiting this 300-year-old coaching-inn. Black Sheep Bitter and Webster's Bitter are on handpump, and the wine list runs to 40 bins. Children are welcome in eating areas and there's a delightful riverside garden for fine days. Accommodation is available.

Open *11am to 11pm, Sun 12 to 10.30*

PILLATON

Cornwall map 1

Weary Friar

TEL: (01579) 350238

2m W of A38, between Saltash and Callington

Dating from the twelfth century and once a 'rest-house inn' for artisans working on the nearby Church of St Odolphus. Ancient and modern blend inside, where Dartmoor Best and Legend, Plymouth Pride, Ediston Light, guest beers and local ciders are on draught, and there is local mead too. Children are welcome, and the pub has up-to-date accommodation. St Mellion Golf & Country Club is almost next door.

Open *11.30 to 3.30, 6.30 to 11, Sun 12 to 3, 7.30 to 10.30*

PIN MILL

Suffolk map 6

Butt & Oyster ◆

TEL: (01473) 780764

off B1456, 5m SE of Ipswich

A real crowd-puller that attracts all comers because of its glorious views of the Orwell estuary. From the big bow window you can watch the yachts, barges and dinghies. The main bar is all flagstones and high-backed settles, with model ships and maritime photos dotted around. Tolly Cobbold beers are dispensed from handpumps on the polished counter; other brews are tapped from the cask. Two rooms away from the bar are intended for families.

Open *summer 11am to 11pm, Sun 12 to 10.30, winter Mon to Fri 11 to 3, 7 to 11, Sat 11am to 11pm, Sun 12 to 10.30*

PITTINGTON

Co Durham map 10

Blacksmiths Arms

TEL: (0191) 372 0287

off A1(M)/A690, 4m E of Durham

In stunning countryside at the foot of Pittington Hill (a site of special scientific interest) and a good place to mull over the day's sightings and floral discoveries. Vaux Samson, a guest ale, and Bulmer's Original cider are on

draught. Children are more than welcome, and 'The Travellers entertain on Wednesday evenings.'
Open *12 to 11, Sun 12 to 3.30, 7 to 10.30*

PLUMLEY

Cheshire map 7

Smoker

TEL: (01565) 722338
off A566, 3m SW of Knutsford
Five centuries old and still thriving, this 'civilised' thatched pub is a popular staging-post for visitors to Tatton Park (National Trust) with its mansion and wonderful grounds. Beams and real flowers set the tone, Robinson's beers are on handpump. Children are welcome, and the pub has a pleasant garden.
Open *11 to 3, 5.30 to 11, Sun 12 to 10.30*

POLPERRO

Cornwall map 1

Blue Peter

The Quay
TEL: (01503) 272743
on A387, 3m SW of Looe
Invitingly situated at the end of the fish quay in a popular Cornish village. Locals play games in the bar, five handpumps dispense local Sharps Doom Bar and St Austell HSD, as well as farm cider. There's a children's room upstairs. The pub doesn't serve food, but 'people can bring in their own sandwiches'.
Open *11am to 11pm , Sun 12 to 10.30*

POSTBRIDGE

Devon map 1

Warren House Inn

TEL: (01822) 880208
on B3212, between Postbridge and Moretonhampstead
Stunning Dartmoor views and splendid real ales are the twin attributes of this unpretentious inn. Gibbs Mew Bishops Tipple, Hall & Woodhouse Tanglefoot and Butcombe Bitter are supplemented by a monthly guest ale; in addition there are local fruit wines, farm scrumpy and imported Chimay beer. The pub has a family room.
Open *10.30 to 2, 5.30 to 11 (11am to 11pm summer), Sun 5.30 (12 summer) to 10.30*

RAITHBY

Lincolnshire map 6

Red Lion Inn

Main Street
TEL: (01790) 753727
off A115, 2m W of Spilsby
As we went to press landlord Roger Smith was in the process of setting up his own micro-brewery to supplement superbly kept beers such as Highwood Tom Wood Harvest Bitter and Ind Coope Burton Ale. Pizzas and trattoria dishes are main attractions on the food front. Children are welcome before 9pm (note that the pub is closed weekday lunch-times). Accommodation is available.
Open *Sat 12 to 3, all week 7 to 11 (10.30 Sun)*

RAVENGLASS

Cumbria map 8

Ratty Arms

TEL: (01229) 717676
on A595, 4m S of Seascale
Originally the old Furness railway station, now a popular family pub at the starting point of the miniature Ravenglass & Eskdale railway. Cumbrian beers from Jennings, Cartmel and others are on handpump. The exquisite Esk estuary and the Owl Centre at Muncaster Castle are nearby wildlife attractions.
Open *11 to 3, 6 to 11 (11am to 11pm summer), Sun 12 to 3, 7 to 10.30 (12 to 10.30 summer)*

REEDHAM

Norfolk map 6

Reedham Ferry Inn

TEL: (01493) 700429
off B1140, 6m S of Acle
Immensely popular Broadlands holiday pub run for close to 50 years by the Archer family. The seventeenth-century building stands alongside the 'chain

ferry' over the River Yare and has its own slipway. East Anglian brews such as Woodforde's Wherry Bitter and Adnams Broadside are on draught. The nearby RSPB Sanctuary at Strumpshaw and the Steam Engine Collection are both worth a visit.

Open *winter 11 to 2.30, 7 to 11, Sun 12 to 3, 7 to 10.30 , summer 11 to 3, 6.30 to 11, Sun 12 to 10.30*

REIGATE HEATH

Surrey map 3

Skimmington Castle

Bonny's Road
TEL: (01737) 243100
off A25, nr Reigate

'Westerham ales from the wood' were once sold at this 400-year-old pub high on a leafy mound in the middle of nowhere. These days, thirsty walkers and horse-riders refresh themselves with Allied-related brews such as Ind Coope Burton Ale, Ansells and Aylesbury Duck. Children are welcome in the family room and dining-room.

Open *Mon to Fri 11 to 2.30, 5.30 to 11, Sat 11 to 3, 6 to 11, Sun 12 to 4, 7 to 10.30*

RIBCHESTER

Lancashire map 8

White Bull

Church Street
TEL: (01254) 878303
on B6245, 5m N of Blackburn

Tuscan columns (retrieved from a local site) grace the front of this early-eighteenth-century pub in the heart of the Ribble Valley: don't miss the Roman museum or the ancient Bath House while in the village. Beers are familiar names like Boddingtons, Flowers IPA and Theakston. Children are welcome.

Open *11.30 to 3, 6.30 to 11, Sun and bank hols 12 to 10.30*

RINGMER

East Sussex map 3

Cock Inn

Uckfield Road
Tel: (01273) 812040
just off A26, 2m NE of Lewes

'A round-trip of 84 miles' is no deterrent for one couple who regularly drive out to this unpretentious country pub. Inside is comfortable, service comes 'with a smile' and there are well-kept ales in the shape of Harveys Best, Morland Old Speckled Hen and Ruddles. From the garden you can see the South Downs, and Glyndebourne is close by.

Open *11 to 3, 6 to 11, Sun 12 to 3, 7 to 11*

RINGSTEAD

Norfolk map 6

Gin Trap Inn

High Street
TEL: (01485) 525264
off A149, 2m E of Hunstanton

Three-centuries-old village pub much favoured by Norfolk holidaymakers and hikers trudging the Peddars Way; also convenient for the Lavender fields of Heacham. 'Deadly traps', bottles and farming tools hang from the beams and walls, and good East Anglian beers from Woodforde's, Adnams and Greene King are on handpump. 'Well-behaved' children are welcome.

Open *11.30 to 2.30 (3 summer), 7 (6.30 summer) to 11, Sun 12 to 2.30, 7 to 10.30*

ROBIN HOOD'S BAY

North Yorkshire map 9

Laurel Inn

The Bank
TEL: (01947) 880400
at end of B1447 (off A171), 5m SE of Whitby

Tiny pub in a much-favoured cliffside village famed for its breathtaking seascapes. Inside is traditional to T;

Theakston Old Peculier is always on draught beside Black Bull, Ruddles Best and others. Families can use the 'snug', and the new licensee is planning food and accommodation.

Open *all week 12 to 11 (10.30 Sun)*

ROMALDKIRK

Co Durham map 10

Kirk Inn

TEL: (01833) 650260

Tiny one-room pub – also the village post office – specialising in beers from independent North Country breweries. Butterknowle, Hambleton, Rudgate, Black Sheep and Teesdale Bitter from the High Foss Brewery are names to look for. The ale and the atmosphere make it popular with Pennine walkers. There's a toy box for children and a play area outside.

Open *12 to 2.30, 6 to 11, Sun 12 to 3, 7 to 10.30*

RUDGE

Somerset map 2

Full Moon

TEL: (01373) 830936

off A36/A361, 3m W of Westbury

'What a pity we had only one night to spare at this rare old English commodity: value for money with a smile on its face,' concludes one report. This 300-year-old cider house is exactly 'what an English pub should be'. The core of the place still has a great local atmosphere and you can sample brews from Bass, Wadworth and Butcombe as well as Thatcher's cider. There's a play area in the garden.

Open *all week 12 to 3, 6 to 11 (10.30 Sun)*

RYE

East Sussex map 3

Mermaid Inn ◆

Mermaid Street

TEL: (01797) 223065

Built in 1156 and resurrected in 1420 after French raiders had reduced the place to ruins, the Mermaid is majestically atmospheric. The setting is a narrow cobbled hill, and the interior breathes antiquity (ornately carved four-posters grace some of the bedrooms). Smuggling was once the name of the game hereabouts, but today's visitors come for the feel of the place. Real ales and wines provide adequate refreshment – which might be needed if you chance upon one of the inn's five resident ghosts.

Open *all week 11am to 11pm*

ST AGNES

Isles of Scilly map 1

Turk's Head ◆

TEL: (01720) 422434

take a boat or helicopter from Penzance to St Mary's, then a boat to St Agnes

Overlooking the jetty at St Agnes, 'The Turk' is a nineteenth-century slate-roofed cottage bedecked with nautical memorabilia. It's a mecca for serious bird-watchers and wildlife buffs, who come for the seals, seabirds and rare migrations. Giant pasties have a legendary reputation, beers include Ind Coope Burton Ale and Dartmoor Best, while the house special is hot chocolate laced with St Agnes brandy. Children are welcome, and the pub has one bedroom for overnight visitors.

Open *Easter to end Oct 11am to 11pm, Sun 12 to 10.30 (opening times limited Nov to Mar)*

ST BREWARD

Cornwall map 1

Old Inn

TEL: (01208) 850711

off B3266, 4m S of Camelford

The drive to this tiny 900-year-old granite pub is 'spectacular', and the building lays claim to being 'the highest inn in Cornwall'. This is a 'real local' with no frills, slate floors and two rooms – one above the other. Drinkers can quaff Sharp's Doom Bar, Bass or John Smith's, 80 malts are on display, and the wine list is worth considering. Children are welcome if eating.

Open *12 to 3, 6 to 11, Sun 12 to 3, 7 to 10.30*

ST EWE

Cornwall map 1

Crown Inn

TEL: (01726) 843322

between B3287 and B3273, 5m SW of St Austell

Long-serving licensees, Norman and Ruth Jeffrey, have been at the tiller of this 400-year-old whitewashed pub for more than four decades and have made it a fixture of the local scene. Beers from the St Austell brewery are on draught. Overnight accommodation is offered and the beach is only three miles away.

Open *11 to 3 (2.30 in winter), 6 to 11, Sun 12 to 3, 7 to 10.30*

ST JUST

Cornwall map 1

Star Inn

Fore Street

TEL: (01736) 788767

on A3071/B3306, 4m N of Land's End

Genuine Cornish watering-hole with nautical echoes. Drinkers have the full range of beers from the St Austell brewery; in addition there's strong scrumpy in summer and mulled wine in winter. Also note the home-made lemonade. Children are welcome in the toy-filled snug and the garden. Accommodation is available.

Open *summer 11am to 11pm, Sun 12 to 10.30; closed afternoons 3 to 6 Mon to Thur winter*

SAPPERTON

Gloucestershire map 2

Daneway Inn

TEL: (01285) 760297

off A419, 5m W of Cirencester

West Berkshire Skiff, Archers Best and Daneway Bitter – plus guest brews – are regularly on handpump in this quiet country pub not far from the defunct Thames & Severn Canal. A no-smoking family room is a bonus for children; otherwise the pub garden is handy if the weather allows.

Open *11 to 2.30 (3 Sat), 6.30 to 11, Sun 12 to 3, 7 to 10.30*

SCAWTON

North Yorkshire map 9

Hare Inn

TEL: (01845) 597289

off A170, 4m W of Helmsley

Richard III, Cromwell, Wordsworth and Turner all stayed at this twelfth-century stone inn, says the brochure; and the monks of Rievaulx Abbey once brewed their mead here. Today, alcoholic refreshment comes in the shape of Theakston beers, guest ales and some good-value bin-end wines. The kitchen specialises in curries. Children are welcome in the eating areas, games room and large garden.

Open *Tue to Sun 12 to 2.30 (3 summer), all week 7 (6.30 Fri and Sat) to 11 (10.30 Sun)*

SCOLE

Norfolk map 6

Scole Inn

Norwich Road,

TEL: (01379) 740481

on A140, 2m E of Diss

Recommended for its architecture and history: the building, which dates from 1655, is Grade-I listed, with wonderful Dutch gables to front and rear. Adnams Bitter and others are on handpump. A splendid oak staircase leads to the bedrooms, although extensive refurbishment and improvements are under way.

Open *11am to 11pm, Sun 12 to 10.30*

SHALFLEET

Isle of Wight map 2

New Inn

TEL: (01983) 531314

This 200-year-old pub stands on the site of an ancient church house that was apparently mentioned in the Domesday Book. The flagstones date back to the eleventh century; other fixtures and fittings are from a more modern era. Flowers, Bass and Boddingtons please drinkers and wildlife types *en route* to the nature reserve near Newtown Creek. Children are welcome.

Open *summer 11am to 11pm, Sun 12 to 10.30, winter 11 to 3, 6 to 11, Sun 12 to 3, 7 to 10.30*

SHARDLOW

Derbyshire map 5

Malt Shovel

The Wharf
TEL: (01332) 799763
off A6, 6m SE of Derby
A ghost named Humphrey reputedly causes mischief at this coverted malthouse alongside the Trent & Mersey Canal. Real-life visitors include summertime Morris dancers and a canal theatre company; jazz musicians entertain the crowds of boaters, cyclists and walkers once a month. Marston's beers are on handpump. No children.
Open *11am to 11pm, Sun 12 to 3, 7 to 10.30 (12 to 10.30 summer)*

SHAVE CROSS

Dorset map 2

Shave Cross Inn

TEL: (01308) 868358
off B3165, in Marshwood Vale, 5m NW of Bridport
Medieval monks once used this fourteenth-century thatched inn as a lodging house and took the opportunity of having their tonsures shaved while they were in residence – hence the name. Bass, Eldridge Pope Royal Oak and Hall & Woodhouse Dorset Best are on handpump. Outside is a family garden with a 'unique mural challenge' in the children's playground; further afield is Pilson Pen hill-fort.
Open *Tue to Sun and bank hols 12 to 2.30, 7 to 11 (10.30 Sun)*

SHEEPSCOMBE

Gloucestershire map 2

Butchers Arms

TEL: (01452) 812113
off A46 Cheltenham to Stroud road, 2m E of Painswick
The sign showing a butcher with a pig tied to his leg and holding a pint is nationally renowned. Originally a butchery for Henry VIII's deer hunters, this enchanting stone inn also boasts glorious views over the Painswick Valley. Uley Old Spot Prize Ale, Hook Norton Bitter and Fuller's London Pride are bolstered by Bulmer's Traditional cider. Children are welcome in the eating areas.
Open *winter Mon to Sat 11.30 to 2.30, 6.30 to 11, Sun 12 to 3.30, 7 to 10.30, summer Mon to Sat 11 to 3.30, 6 to 11, Sun 12 to 10.30*

SHIPTON-UNDER-WYCHWOOD

Oxfordshire map 5

Shaven Crown Hotel ◆

High Street
TEL: (01993) 830330
on A361, 4m NE of Burford
Historic fourteenth-century stone inn – once the hospice to Bruern Abbey – that still retains its courtyard and ancient arched gateway; the tiny bar occupies converted stables, while the lounge is the medieval hall with its double-collar braced roof. Some interesting wines are listed on the blackboard, and beer drinkers have a choice of Hook Norton Bitter or one of the guest brews; Inch's cider is also on draught. Children are welcome, and the pub offers accommodation. The Oxfordshire Way runs through the village, the River Evenlode alongside it.
Open *11 to 2.30, 6 to 11, Sun 12 to 2.30, 7 to 10 (12 to 10.30 summer); closed 25 Dec eve*

SHRALEYBROOK

Staffordshire map 5

Rising Sun

Knowle Bank Road
TEL: (01782) 720600
on B5367, 1m S of M6 Jct. 16
Alcoholic tipples of every description bring imbibers to this whitewashed village pub. Three real ales are brewed on the premises, others (such as Hadrian and Burton Bridge) are well chosen. Added to this you will find 126 malt whiskies, Belgian bottled beers, Dunkertons perry and plenty of wines (although France is notable by its absence). Children are welcome.
Open *Mon to Thur 11.30 to 3.30, 6.30 to 11, Fri and Sat 11.30 to 11, Sun 11.30 to 10.30*

SHUSTOKE

Warwickshire map 5

Griffin

TEL: (01675) 481205

on B4114, 2½m E of Coleshill

The Church End Brewery does its stuff in this seventeenth-century village pub a few miles from the outskirts of Birmingham. Other brews on offer might include Marston's Pedigree, M&B Mild, Adnams and Burton Bridge XL. Children are welcome in the conservatory.

Open *12 to 2.30, 7 to 11 (10.30 Sun)*

SMARDEN

Kent map 3

Chequers Inn

TEL: (01233) 770217

off A28/A274, 7m SW of Charing

Lovely 600-year-old pub in one of Kent's prettiest villages. Outside is clapboard and brick, inside are tiny doors, ancient beams and a log fire. Staff are on the ball. Bass, Morland Old Speckled Hen and Young's Special please the real ale brigade. Children are welcome in the eating areas, and accommodation is available.

Open *11 to 3, 6 to 11, Sun 12 to 3, 7 to 10.30*

SNAPE

Suffolk map 6

Golden Key

Priory Road

TEL: (01728) 688510

just off B1069, 3m S of Saxmundham

A favourite desination at Aldeburgh Festival time, but far enough away for those who want a break from the action. The cooking is homespun and nourishing, and the full range of Adnams beers – including seasonal brews – is kept in good order. Wines are also from Adnams. Children are welcome in the dining-room, and the pub has a couple of bedrooms.

Open *11 to 3, 6 to 11, Sun 12 to 3, 7 to 10.30*

SOUTH DALTON

East Riding of Yorkshire map 9

Pipe and Glass Inn

TEL: (01430) 810246

off A1079/A164, 6m E of Market Weighton

A 500-year-old yew tree holds pride of place in the garden of this white-painted cottage pub close to the entrance of Dalton Park. Drinkers can sup Theakston, Younger IPA and Morland Old Speckled Hen, children are welcome, and the pub has three bedrooms. It is convenient for exploring the Wolds.

Open *12 to 2.30, 7 to 11, Sun 12 to 3, 7 to 10.30*

SOUTH WOODCHESTER

Gloucestershire map 2

Ram Inn

Station Road

TEL: (01453) 873329

off A46, 2m S of Stroud

Likeable Cotswold village pub famed for its stock of draught beers. Up to eight might be on show at any time, including Archers Best, Uley Old Spot, Buchanan's Best, Woodforde's Wherry and three rotating guest beers; bottles of Czech Budvar are also available. Children are welcome in the eating areas, and an Irish band plays occasionally.

Open *11 to 3, 5.30 to 11, Sat 11am to 11pm, Sun 12 to 3, 7 to 10.30*

SPARK BRIDGE

Cumbria map 8

Royal Oak

TEL: (01229) 861170

off A5092, 5m N of Ulverston

Nicely appointed pub in a former mill village just off the Whitehaven to Broughton road. Licensees Jackie and Johnathan Stoker are 'putting their "all"' into the place, according to reporters. Beers include Boddingtons, Flowers Original and Wadworth 6X, and fish is apparently from Fleetwood.

Open *11 to 3, 5.30 to 11 (all day mid July to mid Sept), Sun 12 to 10.30*

SPELDHURST

Kent map 3

George & Dragon

TEL: (01892) 863125

between A26 and A264, 2m NW of Tunbridge Wells

Never mind the crowds, it's worth making the trip just to admire the features of this ancient pub built around a medieval Wealden Hall. This is one of the oldest pubs in southern England – and it shows in the massive log-burning inglenook, great flagstone floors, mighty beams and rough plastered walls. Harveys beers, Bass and guests are on handpump. Children are welcome if eating.

Open *11am to 11pm, Sun 12 to 10.30*

SPREYTON

Devon map 1

Tom Cobley Tavern

TEL: (01647) 231314

off B3219 (from A30), 7m E of Okehampton

Its name and setting on the northern fringes of Dartmoor explain why sightseers descend on this 400-year-old music-free pub. West Country tipples such as Cotleigh Tawny and Butcombe Bitter, and Luscombe farm cider also attract the drinkers. Children can use the games room and dining-room; the pub also has four bedrooms.

Open *Mon 7 to 11, Tue to Sat 12 to 2.30, 6 to 11, Sun 12 to 3, 7 to 10.30; open bank hols*

SPROTBROUGH

South Yorkshire map 9

Boat

Nursery Lane

TEL: (01302) 857188

just off A1(M), 3m W of Doncaster

Recommended for its location in the Don Valley, right by the river: there are good walks upstream to a nature reserve, and Conisbrough Castle is a short drive away. The building started life as a farmhouse, and Sir Walter Scott later used it as a bolt-hole while writing *Ivanhoe*. Inside is chattily convivial, and there's a sheltered courtyard for summer imbibing (Courage-related ales are on draught). Good for families.

Open *11 to 3, 6 to 11, Sun 12 to 3, 7 to 10.30*

STAMFORDHAM

Northumberland map 10

Bay Horse Inn

TEL: (01661) 886244

on B6309, 6m N of Prudhoe

Family-run stone-built pub in Northumbrian countryside, but only 15 minutes' drive from Newcastle. Traditional games are taken seriously, and contestants – and others – quench their thirsts with Butterknowle Banner, Boddingtons and Castle Eden Ale. The inn has six *en suite* bedrooms.

Open *11.30 to 3, 6.30 to 11, Sun 12 to 3, 7 to 10.30*

STEYNING

West Sussex map 3

Star Inn

130 High Street

TEL: (01903) 813078

just off A283, 5m NW of Shoreham-by-Sea

Once a farmers' watering-hole, now a good venue for families, the pub has a well-stocked games room, as well as two gardens (one with children's play equipment). For adults, there's a choice of Boddingtons, Wadworth 6X, Fuller's London Pride and other real ales.

Open *Mon to Fri 11 to 2.30 (3 Fri), 5.30 to 11.30, Sat 11am to 11pm, Sun 12 to 3, 7 to 10.30*

STOKE BRUERNE

Northamptonshire map 5

Boat

TEL: (01604) 862428

just W of A508, 4m E of Towcester

Famous in narrowboat circles, as it stands beside the Grand Union Canal, opposite the Canal Museum. The Woodward family (who have been in residence since 1877) have turned the pub from modest lock-side watering-hole to a fully fledged family venue complete with a bistro and plenty of outdoor seating. At least six real ales are on show, including Marston's Pedigree, Banks's Mild, Wadworth 6X and others.

Open *11 to 4, 6 to 11, Sun 12 to 10.30*

STOKE FLEMING

Devon map 1

Green Dragon

Church Street

TEL: (01803) 770238

off A379, 2m S of Dartmouth

Nautically inclined pub much used by travellers visiting the South Hams coast. Sit in the 'The Mess Deck' dining area (where children are welcome) and you will be surrounded by ensigns and other maritime memorabilia. Several real ales such as Bass, Flowers Original and Eldridge Pope Royal Oak are useful thirst-quenchers.

Open *11 to 2.30, 5.30 to 11, Sun 12 to 3, 7 (6.30 summer) to 10.30*

STOKENHAM

Devon map 1

Tradesmans Arms

TEL: (01548) 580313

off A379 Kingsbridge to Dartmouth road, 5m E of Kingsbridge

The tradesmen in question were artisans who once trekked the coastal path from Dartmouth; these days the customers are likely to be tourists on their way to Slapton Sands and Torcross. Drinking is serious business here: choose from Adnams Bitter, Hook Norton, Shepherd Neame Master Brew, or ciders including Luscombe. 'Older minors' are welcome in the dining-room and garden.

Open *12 to 3, 7 (5 summer) to 11*

STOKESBY

Norfolk map 6

Ferry Inn

TEL: (01493) 751096

off A1064, 2m E of Acle

Just the spot for 'car-bound travellers' wanting a relaxed summer drink beside the River Bure, for Broadland boating people and for visitors to the nearby Conservation Centre. Draught beers are from Adnams. Children are welcome in the family room, where there are games and a video.

Open *11 to 3, 6 to 11, Sun 12 to 3, 7 to 10.30*

STONE STREET

Kent map 3

Padwell Arms

TEL: (01732) 761532

off A25, 3m E of Sevenoaks

A genuine country 'alehouse' with seven brews regularly on tap throughout the year: expect names such as Hook Norton Old Hooky, Harveys Best and Hall & Woodhouse Badger Best, among others. The atmosphere is friendly, dogs are welcome and although children are not allowed in the pub there is a garden they can use in fine weather.

Open *12 to 3, 6 to 11, Sun 12 to 3, 7 to 10.30*

SUSWORTH

Lincolnshire map 9

Jenny Wren

Main Street

TEL: (01724) 784000

off A519, 3m W of Scotter

Built in 1712 on the east bank of the Trent and formerly both church and courthouse, this is now a country pub with aspirations. A host of real ales (both session beers and guests) might include anything from local Tom Woods to Jennings Sneck Lifter, while the kitchen works to an eclectic menu. No-smoking family room. Reports, please.

Open *summer 12 to 11 (10.30 Sun), winter 12 to 3 (3.30 Sun), 5.30 (6.30 Sun) to 11*

TENTERDEN

Kent map 3

William Caxton

Westcross, High Street

TEL: (01580) 763142

on A28, 10m SW of Ashford

'A real Kentish pub with real Kentish ale and hops around the bar.' Shepherd Neame provides the beer, and warmth comes from inglenook fireplaces. Children are welcome and there are summer barbecues in the garden. Accommodation is available. The inn is on the edge of town, within reach of Leeds Castle and Battle.

Open *11am to 11pm, Sun 12 to 10.30*

THOMPSON

Norfolk map 6

Chequers Inn

Griston Road
TEL: (01953) 483360
1m off A1075, 3m S of Watton

Splendid-looking Norfolk hostelry, with an eye-catching thatched roof, tall brick chimneys and old iron street lamps in the garden. Adnams, Tetley Bitter, Highgate IPA and Fuller's London Pride are on handpump; Kingfisher farm cider is a fruity alternative. Children are welcome throughout the pub.

Open *11 to 3, 6 to 11, Sun 12 to 3, 7 to 10.30*

THORNDON

Suffolk map 6

Black Horse Inn

The Street
TEL: (01379) 678523
between A140 and B1077, 3m S of Eye

Extended 500-year-old pub that looks like a row of cottages, painted white. Inside, it is all old beams and standing timbers, with a brick fireplace at one end. Greene King IPA and Abbot Ale are on draught alongside Woodforde's Wherry Bitter. The pub has a games room and children are welcome.

Open *11.30 to 2.30, 6.30 to 11, Sun 12 to 3, 7 to 10.30*

THORNHAM MAGNA

Suffolk map 6

Four Horseshoes Country Inn

TEL: (01379) 678777
just W of A140, 3m SW of Eye

A spectacular thatched roof is the crowning glory of this twelfth-century pub. This is a venue for walkers and families, as it's not far from Thornham Country Park with its miles of footpaths and numerous other attractions. Adnams and Courage Directors are resident brews, alongside guests such as Shepherd Neame Spitfire. The pub has eight bedrooms.

Open *12 to 2.30, 7 to 11, Sun 12 to 3, 7 to 10.30*

THURGARTON

Nottinghamshire map 5

Red Lion

Southwell Road
TEL: (01636) 830351
on A612, 3m S of Southwell

Busy roadside pub dating back to the sixteenth century and once frequented by the monks of nearby Thurgarton Priory. Ruddles Best, Courage Directors and Younger Best are on handpump. Children are welcome throughout the pub, which is a useful pit-stop on route to Southwell and its famous Minster.

Open *Mon to Fri 11.30 to 2.30, 6.30 to 11, Sat 11.30 to 11, Sun 12 to 10.30*

TOLLARD ROYAL

Wiltshire map 2

King John Hotel

TEL: (01725) 516207
on B3081 (off A354), 14m SW of Salisbury

King John held court here and used it as one of his hunting lodges, so we are told. The pub, which is in good walking country, is known for its local real ales: expect Pigswill from Bunces in Netheravon, and various brews from Tisbury and Smiles. Somerset cider and cider brandy are also stocked. Home-cooked hams and local cheeses feature on the menu. Accommodation is available.

Open *all week 12 to 2.30, 6.30 to 11; closed Tue L Jan to Mar*

TOOT HILL

Essex map 3

Green Man

TEL: (01992) 522255
off A414, between North Weald and Chipping Ongar

A spectacular 100-strong wine list and a fine range of real ales are the main attractions at this re-vamped Victorian

pub. The cellar has clarets dating back to 1978, while several handpumps dispense brews such as Crouch Vale Best, Young's Bitter, Adnams and Marston's Pedigree. Children over ten are welcome in the dining area.
Open *11 to 3, 6 to 11, Sun 12 to 3, 7 to 10.30*

TOPSHAM

Devon map 1

Bridge ◆

Bridge Hill
TEL: (01392) 873862
2¼m from M5 Jct. 30; in Topsham follow signs to Exmouth
The Cheffers family have clocked up a century as owners of this popular venue overlooking the River Clyst. In former times it was famous for its home-brewed beer; these days a spectacular selection of real ales is procured from far and wide. Gibbs Mew Bishop's Tipple, T'Owd Tup from the Dent brewery in Cumbria, and Exe Valley Autumn Glory are typical; go in summer and you can also sample traditional cask lager from the Harviestoun brewery in Scotland. Snacks are served at lunch-time: note the ploughman's with unusual home-made pickles such as gooseberry and elderflower. Children are welcome in a separate room.
Open *all week 12 to 2, 6 to 10.30 (11 Fri and Sat)*

TRESCO

Isles of Scilly map 1

New Inn

TEL: (01720) 422844
take the ferry or helicopter from Penzance
Excellent destination for families holidaying on the island. Children are well accommodated, and thirsty grown-ups have a decent choice of real ales, including Castle Eden, Fuggles Imperial IPA and St Austell Trelawny's Pride. Fish is the kitchen's strong point – with everything from monkfish in mustard sauce to a 'magnificent sandwich lunch' of home-made bread packed with heaps of sea-tasting Bryher crab interleaved with smoked salmon. More reports, please.
Open *10.30am to 11.30pm, Sun 12 to 10.30*

TROUTBECK

Cumbria map 10

Mortal Man Hotel

TEL: (01539) 433193
at start of Kirkstone Pass, 2½m from junction of A591 and A592
Dating back to 1689 and recommended as a slightly grand, but very civilised, bolt-hole with staggeringly fine views of Windermere and mountainous horizons in the distance. John Smith's and Theakston Bitter are on handpump. Children are welcome and the inn is well known for its accommodation.
Open *all week 12 to 2.30, 5.30 to 11 (10.30 Sun); closed mid-Nov to mid-Feb*

TRUDOXHILL

Somerset map 2

White Hart

TEL: (01373) 836324
1m off A361 Frome to Shepton Mallet road
'The only pub in Somerset to brew its own beer,' says landlord Robert Viney. The Ash Vine micro-brewery operates behind this 300-year-old coaching-inn, and you can sample its output in the stone-walled bar. Bitter, Challenger and Hop & Glory are regulars; also look for bottles of Penguin Porter, Thatcher's cider and the range of Gales fruit wines. Brewery tours can be arranged. Children are welcome.
Open *12 to 3, 7 (6.30 Fri and Sat) to 11 (10.30 Sun)*

TYTTENHANGER

Hertfordshire map 3

Barley Mow

Barley Mow Lane
TEL: (01727) 827777
2m SE of St Albans
Legendary Home Counties' watering-hole 'now restored back to its former glory'. Its reputation hinges on a prodigious line-up of real ales, all advertised on a chalk board: names such as Courage Directors, Fuller's ESB, Adnams, and locally brewed McMullen Gladstone are typical. Children, dogs and horses are welcome.
Open *all week 11am to 11pm (10.30 Sun)*

UPTON GREY

Hampshire map 2

Hoddington Arms

TEL: (01256) 862371

off B3349, 4m SE of Basingstoke

Handy 'if you're taking the kids to Odiham Castle or The Vyne (National Trust)' noted one reporter. New licensees are sustaining the pub's child-friendly image and amenities, service is prompt and friendly, and there are Morland beers on handpump.

Open *11.30 to 2.30, 6 to 11, Sun 12 to 2.30, 7 to 10.30*

VENTNOR

Isle of Wight map 2

Spyglass Inn

The Esplanade

TEL: (01983) 855338

'Sprawling' Victorian pub with superb views of the Channel from its terraces. The interior with its seafaring memorabilia is also worth admiring. Beers include Dorset Best Bitter, Dempsey's and Worthington Dark Mild; otherwise ask to see the full wine list; also note local White Monk apple wine. 'Children, well-behaved dogs and muddy boots welcome,' says a note on the menu. There's live entertainment most evenings, and the pub has three bedrooms.

Open *10.30 to 3, 7 to 11, Sun 12 to 10.30*

WARBLETON

East Sussex map 3

War-Bill-in-Tun

TEL: (01435) 830636

off B2096, 4m S of Heathfield, opposite village church

The name may be a play on 'Warbleton'; a more colourful explanation relates to an incident during the Civil War when marauding soldiers tapped a barrel (or 'tun') using an axe. Today's brews are likely to be Warbill Special Bitter, Harveys and Courage Directors. Children are welcome in the eating areas, and the pub has a pleasant garden.

Open *11 to 3, 7 to 11, Sun 12 to 3, 7 to 10.30*

WASDALE HEAD

Cumbria map 8

Wasdale Head Inn

TEL: (01946) 726229

off A595, between Gosforth and Holmrook; follow signs for 8m

One of the most remote pubs in the Lakes in a challenging valley where British rock-climbing was born. The pub is a welcome base camp for hikers who congregate in Ritson's Bar – named after the inn's first landlord whose prowess as a liar gave birth to annual competitions. Own-brew Wast Ale lines up beside Yates, Jennings, Theakston and others. The pub has a children's room and accommodation.

Open *11am to 11pm, Sun 12 to 10.30*

WATLINGTON

Oxfordshire map 2

Chequers

Love Lane

TEL: (01491) 612874

take B4009 from M40 Jct. 6, turn right down Love Lane just before Watlington, signposted Icknield School

Useful stopover if you are visiting the town or are *en route* to Stonor Park or the Chiltern beechwoods. The neatly furnished bar has a cosy atmosphere, while the garden and vine-covered conservatory (where children can go) are great in summer. This is a Brakspear pub, with the full range on draught.

Open *11.30 to 2.30, 6 to 11, Sun 12 to 3, 7 to 10.30*

WEST ILSLEY

Berkshire map 2

Harrow

TEL: (01635) 281260

1½m off A34, 10m N of Newbury

Archetypal village pub opposite the cricket pitch and the duck pond, and within hiking distance of the Ridge Way path. A new team took over shortly before we went to press, but the famed speciality – pies of every description – seems likely to continue. Morland beers are on draught. Children welcome.

Open *11 to 3, 6 to 11, Sun 11 to 3, 7 to 10.30*

WEST TANFIELD

North Yorkshire map 9

Bull Inn

Church Street
TEL: (01677) 470678
on A6108 Ripon to Masham road
'On the tourist trail to Lightwater Valley theme park' and with a picturesque garden by the banks of the River Ure. This is a useful family venue with 'good beer', including Theakston Best, Black Sheep Bitter and Riggwelter, and a reputation for giant Yorkshire puddings with onion gravy. Accommodation is available.
Open *11am to 11pm, Sun 12 to 10.30*

WEST WITTON

North Yorkshire map 9

Wensleydale Heifer

TEL: (01969) 622322
on A684 Leyburn to Hawes road
Civilised seventeenth-century inn much favoured by devotees of *All Creatures Great and Small*, and a comfortable base from which to explore the Dales. Real ales include Theakston Best and Old Peculier, and John Smith's. Children are welcome throughout the pub and there are four-poster beds in a few of the bedrooms.
Open *all week 11am to 11pm*

WHERWELL

Hampshire map 2

White Lion

Fullerton Road
TEL: (01264) 860317
on B4320, 3m SE of Andover
Much sought after because of its village setting close to the River Test. A bustling, extrovert mood prevails as locals mingle with tourists. Flowers Original, Boddingtons and Castle Eden Ale are on draught and house wines come by the generous glass. Children are welcome in the dining-room and the pub has bedrooms.
Open *10 to 2.30, 6 (7 Sun to Tue) to 11, Sun 12 to 3, 7 to 10.30; closed evening 25 Dec*

WIDDOP

West Yorkshire map 8

Pack Horse Inn

TEL: (01422) 842803
on the Hebden Bridge to Colne road, 1½m SE of Widdop Reservoir
This centuries-old pub is high up on the crest of a hill in wild moorland, almost 1,000 feet above sea level. The journey up can be tortuous, whatever the weather, whatever your mode of transport; even so, walkers and escapees from the conurbations regularly make the trip. Refreshment comes in the form of Thwaites and Theakston beers, and a decent-sized list of mostly New World wines. The pub now has accommodation.
Open *12 to 2.30, 7 to 11, Sun 12 to 3, 7 to 10.30*

WIDECOMBE IN THE MOOR

Devon map 1

Rugglestone Inn

TEL: (01364) 621327
off A38, 5m NW of Ashburton
Named after a huge granite stone that rests precariously on the nearby moors, this cosy little pub is notable because of the annual Widecombe Fair. Real ales such as Butcombe Bitter are drawn straight from the barrel and local farm cider is on tap. Children aren't allowed inside the pub, but there's an enclosed garden by a stream for fine days.
Open *11 to 2.30 (3 Sat), 6 (7 Mon to Fri winter) to 11, Sun 12 to 3, 6 (7 winter) to 10.30*

WILDBOARCLOUGH

Cheshire map 8

Crag Inn

TEL: (01260) 227239
off A54, 5m SE of Macclesfield
Peak District walkers' pub on a hillside near the point where three counties meet (Cheshire, Staffs and Derbyshire). The patio is popular with muddy-booted hikers, who refuel with Bass, Black Sheep Bitter and Morland Old Speckled Hen. The pub's history – from 1629 onwards – is documented on the menu. Children welcome.
Open *summer 11am to 11pm, Sun 12 to 10.30, winter 12 to 3, 7 to 11 (10.30 Sun)*

WINEHAM

West Sussex map 3

Royal Oak

Wineham Lane
TEL: (01444) 881252
1½m W of A23, between A272 and B2116
'Amazing' black and white pub in a village just off the Brighton road. The place is renowned for its pub games and also its draught beers: Marston's Pedigree, Harveys Sussex Best Bitter and Flowers Original are on handpump. Food is limited to sandwiches and ploughman's, plus soup in winter. Children are welcome in the garden.
Open *11 to 2.30, 5.30 (6 Sat) to 11, Sun 12 to 3, 7 to 10.30*

WISTANSTOW

Shropshire map 5

Plough

TEL: (01588) 673251
off A49 Church Stretton to Ludlow road, 2m N of Craven Arms
If you want to sample the excellent output of the Wood Brewery on its home patch, this is the place to go: the brewery stands right next to the pub, and tours can be arranged. All-year fixtures are Parish Bitter, Special and Shropshire Lad; seasonal offerings include Christmas Cracker, a 'honey beer' and others. Children welcome.
Open all week *12 to 3, 7 to 11*

WIVENHOE

Essex map 3

Black Buoy

Black Buoy Hill
TEL: (01206) 822425
take B1028 (off A133 1½m E of Colchester); in Wivenhoe turn left at church into East St, pub is 200 yds on right
A great location less than 100 yards from the River Colne is one of the reasons for tracking down this 400-year-old pub. Beams, nooks and crannies set the mood in the bar and the atmosphere is jovial. Seasonal Tolly Cobbold Old Strong, plus beers from Flowers and Greene King are on handpump, and there's mulled wine in winter. Wivenhoe is in a conservation area much favoured by the wildlife fraternity.
Open *11.30 to 3, 6.30 to 11, Sun 12 to 3, 7 to 10.30*

WOODBASTWICK

Norfolk map 6

Fur & Feather Inn ◆

Slad Lane
TEL: (01603) 720003
1½m N of B1140, 8m NE of Norwich
Converted from a row of thatched cottages in 1992 and now the brewery tap for Woodforde's – who produce their beers in buildings at the back. The full range – with names such as Great Eastern, Broadsman, Nelson's Revenge and Norfolk Nog – can be sampled in the tile-floored bar; otherwise take a tour of the brewery to see how it's done. Children are welcome in the pub dining-room and the front garden. Woodbastwick is an attractive estate village convenient for the Broads, Broadland Conservation Centre and Fairhaven Gardens.
Open *12 to 2.30, 6 to 11, Sun 12 to 3, 7 to 10.30*

WRENINGHAM

Norfolk map 6

Bird in Hand

Church Road
TEL: (01508) 489438
off B1113, 5m S of Norwich
Red-brick village pub that is back in business after a while as a private residence. Locals support the place for its friendly atmosphere, food and decent range of real ales, including Adnams Bitter, Marston's Pedigree, Fuller's London Pride and seasonal Snowman's Revenge. Children are welcome throughout the pub.
Open *11.30 to 3, 6.30 to 11, Sun 12 to 3, 7 to 10.30*

YARPOLE

Hereford & Worcester map 5

Bell

TEL: (01568) 780359
off B4361, 4m N of Leominster
Irish landlord Billy McAuley tells us he used to own a restaurant in Los Angeles.

He now runs this attractive, half-timbered, rural pub with his Japanese wife, Mari. Naturally, the bar menu is an international affair, specialising in Oriental cuisine. Added attractions are live music four nights every week – from traditional Irish folk to jazz and blues – and real ales including Marston's Pedigree and Wood Shropshire Lad. More reports please.

Open *11.30 to 3, 6.30 to 11, Sun 12 to 3, 7 to 10.30*

SCOTLAND

ARDVASAR

Highland map 11

Ardvasar Hotel

Isle of Skye
TEL: (01471) 844223
1½m from Armadale ferry (from Mallaig)

Gloriously situated eighteenth-century inn at the south end of the Sleat Peninsula – an exquisite wildlife paradise. Stand outside and you can also gaze out towards the mountainous wilderness of Knoydart and the white sands of Morar. Reputable Scottish ales are on draught. Children are happily accommodated.

Open *winter 12 (12.30 Sun) to 2.30, 5 to 11, summer 12 (12.30 Sun) to 11*

BRIDGE OF CALLY

Perthshire & Kinross map 11

Bridge of Cally Hotel

TEL: (01250) 886231
on A93, 6m N of Blairgowrie

'They run a good ship' here, notes a reporter. This is a countryman's pub with a vengeance: the bar is much favoured by dog walkers, anglers and anyone with wellies – not to mention skiers looking for some warming sustenance. Landlord William McCosh tells us his cellar is 'too small and too hot' for real ale, but he stocks some interesting bottled beers. Children are welcome and accommodation is available. Note that the 'car park' extends to 'two-and-a-half thousand acres'.

Open *all week 11am (12 Sun) to 11pm*

BROUGHTY FERRY

Dundee map 11

Fisherman's Tavern ◆

10–14 Fort Street
TEL: (01382) 775941
off A930 Dundee to Monfieth road

A real cracker situated by the lifeboat sheds on the shores of the Tay estuary. Top-drawer real ales, such as Maclay 80/-, Belhaven St Andrew's and guests are on draught; Fraoch heather ale and Scottish fruit wines constitute a formidable back-up. This is an excellent family venue with good facilities and an open-minded attitude towards children. Affordable accommodation is yet another plus point.

Open *11am to midnight (1am Thu to Sat), Sun 12.30 to 12*

CLOVENFORDS

Borders map 10

Clovenfords Hotel

1 Vine Street
TEL: (01896) 850203
on A72, 3m W of Galashiels

Forest walks to Cardrona and Glentress, plus fishing on the Tweed, are nearby inducements within reach of this Borders village inn. There are decent facilities for children throughout the pub, while grown-ups can appreciate Scottish ales such as Caledonian 80/- and Calder's 60/- and IPA. Accommodation is available. New owners took over shortly before we went to press. Reports, please.

Open *11am (noon Sun) to midnight*

DERVAIG

Argyll & Bute map 11

Bellachroy Hotel

Isle of Mull
TEL: (01688) 400314
on B8073, 8m W of Tobermory

Enticingly situated at the head of one of the most delightful villages on Mull, this country inn is a greaty favourite with bird-watchers, sea anglers and lovers of dramatic scenery. Beers are mostly keg, but Fraoch Heather Ale is in bottles and the pub stocks a 'huge selection' of malts. Children are

welcome and accommodation is geared to families.
Open *all week 11am (12 Sun) to 1am*

FINDHORN

Moray map 11

Kimberley Inn

TEL: (01309) 690492
on B9011, N of Forres
Constructed as a sailmaker's cottage in 1796, this is a Scottish pub with an affection for English real ales. On draught you might find Adnams Broadside, Morland Old Speckled Hen and Triple Diamond in addition to Calder's 80/-. Children are welcome and the pub has a patio with views across Findhorn Bay – seals, boats and all.
Open *11am to 11pm (11.45 Thu, 12.30 Fri and Sat), Sun 12.30 to 11.45*

GLENCOE

Highland map 11

Clachaig Inn

TEL: (01855) 811252
just off A82, Crianlarich to Fort William road
Modernised over the years, but still a thoroughly genuine Scottish country pub. It stands in the heart of Glencoe, against a majestic mountainous backdrop with Loch Leven not far away. Outdoor types can hire mountain bikes, attend courses and listen to live folk music. Beer buffs also have a field day with Arrol's 80/-, Tetley Bitter, Ind Coope Burton Ale and Fraoch Heather Ale; 120 malts are an added alcoholic distraction. Accommodation extends to self-catering chalets.
Open *11am to 11pm, Sun 12.30 to 11*

HALBEATH

Fife map 11

Hideaway

Kingseat Road
TEL: (01383) 725474
on A907, 2m E of Dunfermline
Tip-top facilities for families with children (including free baby food and nappies) are a major plus at this cavernous pub overlooking fields on the outskirts of Dunfermline. Real ales could include Morland Old Speckled Hen and Calder's Cream Ale.
Open *11 to 2.30, 5 to 1am, Sun 12.30 to 11*

ISLE OF WHITHORN

Dumfries & Galloway map 11

Steam Packet

Harbour Row
TEL: (01988) 500334
off A750, 12m S of Wigtown
Harbourside inn that takes its name from the paddle steamer which once plied between the Galloway coast and Liverpool during Victorian times. Thirty malt whiskies line up alongside Theakston XB and Boddingtons. Children are welcome and the pub offers accommodation.
Open *summer 11am to 11pm (11.30 Fri and Sat), Sun 12 to 11, winter 11 to 2.30, 6 to 11*

ISLE ORNSAY

Highland map 11

Hotel Eilean Iarmain

Sleat, Isle of Skye
TEL: (01471) 833332
off A851, Broadfoot to Ardvasar road
In 1976 hotel owner Sir Iain Noble set up the Gaelic Whisky distillery on this outpost of the Hebrides, and you can take a dram or two in the bar. Other inducements for visiting the place are its seductively peaceful setting and the prospect of shooting, fishing or taking in one of the artistic exhibitions in nearby Talla Dearg. Children welcome.
Open *winter 12 to 2.30, 5 to 12, summer 12 to 12, all year Sun 12.30 to 2.30, 6.30 to 11*

KIPPFORD

Dumfries & Galloway map 11

Anchor Hotel

TEL: (01556) 620205
off A710, 4m S of Dalbeattie
Aptly named harbourside pub in a pretty waterside village overlooking the yachting marina and the estuary: the beach is a short drive away. Grown-ups can sup Theakston Best, Boddingtons and Younger No. 3 Ale in the bar; children have plenty to amuse them in

the games room. Accommodation is available.
Open *all week 11am (12 Sun) to midnight (11pm in winter)*

KIRKTON OF GLENISLA

Angus map 11

Glenisla Hotel

TEL: (01575) 582223
from Alyth head N on B954, turn left on to B951, follow signs
Dubbed 'the Inn on the Glen' (the Angus Glens, to be precise), this 300-year-old white-painted hostelry is highly praised for its comfort and friendliness. Fans of real ale have a choice of three in the bar – including Theakston Best, Boddingtons and McEwan's 80/-; the hotel has its own blended Scotch whisky. Children are welcome and hotel asccommodation is available.
Open *Mon to Fri 11.30 to 2.30, Sat and Sun 11am to midnight*

LINLITHGOW

West Lothian map 11

Bridge Inn

Linlithgow Bridge
TEL: (01506) 842777
on A803, 16m W of Edinburgh
By the bridge over Scotland's River Avon, this hostelry is now a highly popular pub catering admirably for families (note that food is served throughout the day on Sundays). To refresh the palate there are beers such as Orkney Dark Mild and Tennents 70/-, and the inn has a shelf of 60 malt whiskies.
Open *12 to 2.30, 5 to 10, Sun 12 to 10*

Four Marys

65 High Street
TEL: (01506) 842171
Arguably the first choice for real ale in Linlithgow. The current line-up includes Belhaven 80/-, Deuchars IPA, Harviestoun Ptarmigan, Timothy Taylor Landlord and others. One hundred malts provide a spirited challenge. Linlithgow Palace – the birthplace of one of the 'Marys' – is across the road.
Open *12 to 2.30, 5 to 11, Sun 12.30 to 2.30, 7 to 11*

LOCH ECK

Argyll & Bute map 11

Coylet Inn

TEL: (01369) 840426
on A815, 9m N of Dunoon, at S end of loch
The setting – only yards from the stupendous expanses of Loch Eck – is a major draw for visitors to this pub surrounded by swathes of woodland. After taking the views, head for the bar, where McEwans 80/-, Younger No. 3 Ale and Deuchars IPA are on handpump. Children are welcome in the lounge and the inn provides accommodation.
Open *11 to 2.30, 5 to 11 (12 Fri and Sat), Sun 11 to 2.30, 6.30 to 11*

PENNAN

Aberdeenshire map 11

Pennan Inn

TEL: (01346) 561201
on B9031, between Banff and Fraserburgh
Pennan gained a high profile after film-makers used it as the setting for *Local Hero*: the village telephone box has since been designated 'a listed building'. The 200-year-old inn is ideal for sightseers, birdwatchers and those who enjoy clifftop walks or simply relaxing on the shingle beach. A short drive away are the sea caves of Aberdour Bay, Fyvie Castle and the Malt Whisky Trail. Families can use the lounge and the inn has six bedrooms.
Open *all week 11am to midnight (11pm Sun)*

ST MARY'S LOCH

Borders map 10

Tibbie Shiels Inn

TEL: (01750) 42231
100yds off A708, 13m W of Selkirk
Named after a certain Isabella (Tibbie) Shiels – forward-looking innkeeper who converted her cottage into a hostelry much frequented by nineteenth-century poets. Today, the place is recommended for its lochside setting, which attracts everyone from walkers to windsurfers. Scottish real ales are on draught and in bottles (look

for Black Douglas and Fraoch Heather Ale). Children are welcome and accommodation is available.

Open *11.30 to 11 (midnight Fri an Sat), Sun 12.30 to 11*

SHIELDAIG

Highland map 11

Shieldaig

Tigh an Eilean Hotel

TEL: (01520) 755251

on A896, midway between Kinlochewe and Strathcarron

The setting is unbeatable: Tigh an Eilean stands dramatically by the sea's edge deep in the ancient Torridon Hills. No wonder it attracts sightseers and serious hill walkers – not to mention fishermen. Wine and whisky are probably the best options for tipplers in the Shieldaig pub attached to the hotel; otherwise Tennents 80/- is available.

Open *summer 11am to 11pm, Sun 12.30 to 2.30, winter 11 to 2.30, 5 to 11 (closed Sun)*

SOUTH QUEENSFERRY

Edinburgh map 11

Hawes Inn

Newhalls Road

TEL: (0131) 331 1990

on A904, off M9, S side of Forth Road Bridge

Ancient stone-walled coaching-inn famous as the starting point for Robert Louis Stevenson's *Kidnapped*. The setting – by the Forth railway bridge overlooking the sea – comes complete with bracing winds, even in summer. Scottish brews such as Arrols 80/-, Calder's 70/- and 'Auld Reekie' are appropriate. Children are welcome where food is served, and the inn has rooms.

Open *11am to 11pm (midnight Fri and Sat), Sun 12 to 11*

STROMNESS

Orkney map 11

Ferry Inn

John Street

TEL: (01856) 850280

take the ferry from Aberdeen or Scrabster

If you are waiting for the ferry or simply want to explore the island, this modernised inn by the terminal and the harbour is just the job. A nautical theme runs through the bar, which has been designed to look like the interior of a schooner. Real ales are from the local Orkney Brewery at Quoyloo; there are also plenty of island malts. Children are welcome.

Open *11am to midnight (1am Thu to Sat), Sun 11.30am (12.30 nov to Mar) to 11.30pm*

WALES

BLAENAU FFESTINIOG

Gwynedd map 7

Miners Arms

Llechwedd Slate Caverns

TEL: (01766) 830306

off A470 at Blaenau Ffestiniog, and follow signs to Llechwedd Slate Caverns

Llechwedd Slate Caverns are an evocative reconstruction of the world of the Victorian slate miner. The aptly named pub is part of the tourist complex. Floors are stone-flagged, staff wear traditional costumes, re-minted coins change hands, and Whitbread Welsh Bitter is on handpump. Note the daytime licensing hours.

Open *11 to 5.30, Sun 12 to 5.30*

BODFARI

Denbighshire map 7

Dinorben Arms

TEL: (01745) 710309

off A55, 4m NE of Denbigh

A staggering collection of more than 200 whiskies, not to mention rare cognacs and a private cellar, are imbibers' delights in this seventeenth-century free house. There are also decent real ales such as Shipstone's. Children are welcome throughout, and the gardens are delightful.

Open *12 to 3.30, 6 to 11, Sun 12 to 10.30*

CADOLE

Flintshire map 7

We Three Loggerheads

TEL: (01352) 810337

on A494 Ruthin road, 2m SW of Mold

Directly opposite Loggerheads Country Park, and extremely popular with families on a day out – as well as walkers and tourists. The pub, which dates from 1750, stocks Bass and Worthington Best Bitter. Children are welcome in the eating area of the bar and in the garden.

Open *Mon to Fri 12 to 3, 6.30 to 11.30, Sat 12 to 11.30, Sun 12 to 10.30*

CILGERRAN

Pembrokeshire map 4

Pendre Inn

High Street

TEL: (01239) 614223

off A478, 3m S of Cardigan

Tiny fourteenth-century stone inn with a minuscule bar that 'oozes low-key atmosphere'. Popular with visitors to the nearby Welsh Wildlife Centre and the Norman castle – as well as sightseers watching coracle fishing on the River Teifi. Bass, Reverend James and Worthington Best are on draught. Children are welcome throughout the pub.

Open *11 to 3.30, 6 to 11, Sun 12 to 3, 7 to 10.30 (summer 11am to 11pm)*

COYCHURCH

Vale of Glamorgan map 4

White Horse

Main Road

TEL: (01656) 652583

off M4 Jct. 35 and A48, 2m E of Bridgend

Jeff Johnston has been in residence at this friendly village pub for more than 15 years and maintains a good cellar, with Brains Bitter and SA regularly on handpump. The pub is convenient for the M4 and is within easy reach of Coity Castle. Children welcome.

Open *Mon to Thu 11 to 4, 5.30 to 11, Fri and Sat 11am to 11pm, Sun 12 to 3.30, 7 to 10.30*

DREENHILL

Pembrokeshire map 4

Denant Mill Inn

TEL: (01437) 766569

just off B4327, 1m SW of Haverfordwest

Four regularly changing real ales draw the faithful to this pub in a converted 400-year-old corn mill. Devotees can expect such delights as Hop Back Summer Lightning and Exmoor Gold, among others. Children are welcome and there's a play area in the garden; beyond are woods and a stream. The pub provides accommodation.

Open *Mon to Fri summer 11am to 11pm, winter 12 to 3, 5.30 to 11, all year Sat 11am to 11pm, Sun 12 to 3, 7 to 10.30*

HOWEY

Powys map 4

Drovers Arms

TEL: (01597) 822508

off A483, 1m S of Llandrindod Wells

Amicably run pub in a red-brick Victorian building that might be mistaken for a private residence. Drinkers head for the bar, where Drovers Ale and guest Welsh brews from Brains, Felinfoel and Tomos Watkin are on draught. Those wanting food populate the lounge. The pub has two bedrooms for overnight visitors.

Open *Wed to Mon 12 to 2.30, all week 7 to 11 (10.30 Sun)*

HUNDLETON

Pembrokeshire map 4

Speculation Inn

TEL: (01646) 661306

at junction of B4320/B4319 at Pembroke, follow Texaco and power station signs

Known to just about everybody in the area as 'The Spec', this unassuming village local has been in the Nelson family since 1915. It attracts a varied crowd, from anglers to beer buffs, who appreciate pints of Felinfoel Bitter and Double Dragon, as well as Worthington Best. Food is limited to simple snacks. Children welcome.

Open *all week 12 to 3, 6 (7 Sun) to 11*

LIBANUS

Powys map 4

Tai'r Bull

TEL: (01874) 625849

on A470, 3m SW of Brecon

A godsend for walkers and hill-climbers, conveniently close to the Brecon Breacons Mountain Centre with superb views of that great peak Pen-y-Fan. The setting is a refurbished stone building with a friendly atmosphere, geared to the needs of outdoor types and travellers on the A470.

Open *Mon 6 to 11, Tue to Sun 12 to 11 (phone to check opening in winter)*

LLANDDAROG

Carmarthenshire map 4

Butchers Arms

TEL: (01267) 275330

off A48, 5m E of Carmarthen

Impeccably maintained Victorian cottage – and former butcher's shop – in a 'nucleated hamlet on a hill'. The place clings to its local Welsh roots, and friendly licensees provide 'the personal touch'. On draught are suitably patriotic brews such as Felinfoel Bitter and Double Dragon. The dining areas are fine for children and there are tables outside.

Open *11 to 3, 5.30 to 11, Sun 7 to 10.30*

LLANTHONY

Monmouthshire map 4

Abbey Hotel ◆

TEL: (01873) 890487

signposted from A465 Abergavenny to Hereford road

'The setting is like no other I have ever seen,' commented a reporter. Beyond green lawns, broken stone pillars and arches of the ruins of the twelfth-century Augustine Priory is 'the hotel' (once the prior's house). The bar is down some steps in the vaulted crypt, where crowds of backpackers, hikers and farmers sit at wooden settles and sup pints of Ruddles County and Flowers Original. Food is, appropriately, honest, cheap and cheerful. Children are not allowed inside, but the cloisters/gardens make amends.

Open *all week 11 to 3, 6 to 11; closed Mon to Fri Nov to Mar*

LLOWES

Powys map 4

Radnor Arms

TEL: (01497) 847460

on A438 between Glasbury and Clyro, 2m W of Hay-on-Wye

There are delightful views of the Wye Valley from the neat and tidy gardens of this roadside pub. Owners Tina and Brian Gorringe care for the place lovingly: take a look at the splendid beamed room open to the gable roof. Felinfoel Bitter is on draught and the wine list is worth more than a passing glance (note the French country wines). 'Well-behaved' children are welcome.

Open *Tue to Sat 11 to 2.30, 6.30 to 11, Sun 11 to 2.30 (open bank hol Mons)*

LLWYNDAFYDD

Ceredigion map 4

Crown

TEL: (01545) 560396

off A487 at Synod Inn, take A486 signposted for New Quay, turn left at Cross Inn

Go for the setting. The pub – a modernised 200-year-old building with pretty gardens – is hidden away in a wooded valley on the 'fascinating' Cove of Cwmtudu. Just up the coast are the National Trust cliffs near New Quay. Four real ales are on tap. Children are welcome where food is served and there's a play area outside.

Open *12 to 3, 6 to 11, Sun 12 to 3, 6 to 10.30*

MARLOES

Pembrokeshire map 4

Lobster Pot

TEL: (01646) 636233

off B4327, 6m W of Milford Haven

'Absolutely fantastic value and very accommodating,' noted one reporter about this friendly pub – the most westerly in Wales. This is a good family destination, Worthington Best is on

draught, and there are six bedrooms as well. Beyond Marloes are the islands of Skomer and Skokholm (renowned for the birds).
Open *11am to 11pm, Sun 12 to 10.30*

MILTON

Pembrokeshire map 4

Milton Brewery Inn

TEL: (01646) 651202
on A477, 4m E of Pembroke
No longer a working brewery, but still a decent venue for those who want a taste of Bass, Worthington Best or – in summer – locally produced Main Street Bitter from the Pembroke Brewery. Chinese dishes – and banquets – are an unexpected feature on the food front. The pub has a family room and the village play area is close by.
Open *11am to 11pm, Sun 12 to 10.30*

MONTGOMERY

Powys map 4

Dragon

TEL: (01686) 668359
on B4385, 3m E of A483 Newtown to Welshpool road
Impressive half-timbered coaching-inn/hotel, parts of which date back to the 1600s. Some beams and masonry in the bar reputedly came from the nearby castle after its destruction by Oliver Cromwell; the pub also has an unusual enclosed patio. Drinkers have a choice of Wood Special or two guest beers. Montgomery stands on Offa's Dyke Path, and Powis Castle is within reach.
Open *11am to 11pm, Sun 12 to 10.30*

NEVERN

Pembrokeshire map 4

Trewern Arms

TEL: (01239) 820395
on B4582, 2m E of Newport
History buffs have plenty of distractions hereabouts: the ancient local church is renowned for its Celtic crosses, and it's worth taking a look at the medieval bridge over the River Nyfer. In the 200-year-old pub you will find Flowers Original and Castle Eden Ale on handpump, plus a guest in summer. Three family rooms are listed among the accommodation.
Open *11 to 3, 6 to 11, Sun 12 to 3, 7 to 10.30*

OLD RADNOR

Powys map 4

Harp Inn

TEL: (01544) 350655
off A44, between New Radnor and Kington
Explore the Welsh Marches, Radnor Forest or Offa's Dyke, or simply wander across the road from this 500-year-old inn to the magnificent local church. Interesting brews are Wood Special Bitter and Hanby Drawell, plus Owen's Radnorshire cider to drink. Children are welcome where food is served. Accommodation is available.
Open *11.30 to 11, Sun 12 to 3, 7.30 to 10.30*

OLDWALLS

Swansea map 4

Greyhound

TEL: (01792) 391027 and 390146
off B4295/B4271, just W of Llanrhidian
A great location, with garden views across the hill to Cefyn Bryn (the highest hill in Gower) and Arthur's Stone, is a big plus at this Gower pub. Another bonus is the stock of real ales, which might include such names as Marston's Pedigree, Bullmastiff Gold Brew, Bass and Wadworth 6X. The pub has excellent facilities for children.
Open *11am to 11pm, Sun 12 to 10.30*

REYNOLDSTON

Swansea map 4

King Arthur

TEL: (01792) 390775
Slate-roofed hostelry at the base of Cefn Bryn, with Penrice woods to the south. The bar has been 'hacked back to the stone', with much stable timber adding to the bucolic effect. Worthington beers are on draught, and local seafood is the kitchen's speciality. There is a games room where children are welcome, and the pub offers accommodation.
Open *noon (11am summer) to 11pm*

ST DOGMAELS

Pembrokeshire map 4

Ferry Inn

TEL: (01239) 615172

on B4546, 1m W of Cardigan

Popular family pub (children are welcome throughout) by the old ferry across the water to Cardigan. Welsh brews such as Brains SA and Felinfoel Double Dragon are bolstered by Wadworth 6X, and around nine wines are served by the glass. Welsh ingredients also show up well on the specials menu.

Open *12 to 3, 7 (5.30 summer) to 11*

TALYBONT

Powys map 4

Star

TEL: (01874) 676635

½m off A40, 6m SE of Brecon

Eighteenth-century stone inn, once a 'gin cutting house', now a purveyor of top-notch real ales. A dozen regularly changing brews might include Theakston Old Peculier, Felinfoel Double Dragon, Freeminer and Bullmastiff among others. Children are welcome, two bedrooms are available for overnighters. A leisurely stroll along the towpath of the Monmouthshire & Brecon Canal is recommended.

Open *11 to 3, 6 to 11, Sat 11am to 11pm, Sun 12 to 10.30*

TREMEIRCHION

Denbighshire map 7

Salusbury Arms

TEL: (01745) 710262

off A55 at Rhualt, on B5429, 5m N of Denbigh

Walkers exploring the Vale of Clwyd often converge on this white-painted, slate-roofed pub, particularly if good beer is required. The line-up on the bar includes Theakston Best and XB, Black Bull Bitter and others. Children can use the games room and the outdoor areas. Note the late licensing hours.

Open *12 to 3, 7 to 11 (12.30 Tue, Fri and Sat, 10.30 Sun)*

ISLE OF MAN

GLENMAYE

Isle of Man map 8

Waterfall

TEL: (01624) 844310

3m S of Peel

One-time smugglers' den, now a 'community pub' at the head of Glen Maye – a short walk from the eponymous waterfall and the beach (on a clear day you can see the Mountains of Mourne). Local tipples include Okells Mild and Bitter, as well as Glen Maye whisky. Children are welcome in the lounge bar/dining area until 7.30pm.

Open *11.30 to 11, Sun 12 to 2.30, 7.30 to 10.30*

INDEX OF ENTRIES

Abbey Bridge, Lanercost, Cumbria 238
Abbey Hotel, Llanthony, Monmouthshire 564
Abbey Inn, Byland Abbey, North Yorkshire 90
Abingdon Arms, Beckley, Oxfordshire 53
Ailean Chraggan, Weem, Perthshire & Kinross 464
Albion, Faversham, Kent 163
Altisidora, Bishop Burton, East Riding of Yorkshire 515
Alvanley Arms, Cotebrook, Cheshire 125
Anchor, Cockwood, Devon 522
Anchor, Runsell Green, Essex 331
Anchor Hotel, Kippford, Dumfries & Galloway 560
Anchor Inn, Beer, Devon 54
Anchor Inn, Exebridge, Somerset 526
Anchor Inn, Hartfield, East Sussex 531
Anchor Inn, Oldbury-on-Severn, South Gloucestershire 543
Anchor Inn, Sutton Gault, Cambridgeshire 377
Anchor Inn, Wyre Piddle, Hereford & Worcester 432
Angel, Heytesbury, Wiltshire 532
Angel, Lavenham, Suffolk 242
Angel Inn, Corbridge, Northumberland 124
Angel Inn, Hetton, North Yorkshire 207
Angel Inn, Long Crendon, Buckinghamshire 254
Angel Inn, Stoke-by-Nayland, Suffolk 368
Annie Bailey's, Cuddington, Buckinghamshire 133
Applecross Inn, Applecross, Highland 437
Ardvasar Hotel, Ardvasar, Highland 559
Armstrong Arms, Stackpole, Pembrokeshire 502
Arundell Arms, Lifton, Devon 245
Ashtree Inn, Ashburnham, East Sussex 513
Assheton Arms, Downham, Lancashire 144
Axe and Compasses, Arkesden, Essex 34
Bagot Arms, Abbots Bromley, Staffordshire 511
Bakers Arms, Broad Campden, Gloucestershire 518
Barbon Inn, Barbon, Cumbria 513
Barge Inn, Seend Cleeve, Wiltshire 338
Barley Mow, Tyttenhanger, Hertfordshire 555
Batcombe Inn, Batcombe, Somerset 52
Bateman Arms, Shobdon, Hereford & Worcester 344
Bay Horse Inn, Stamfordham, Northumberland 552
Bay Horse Inn, Ulverston, Cumbria 395
Bear & Ragged Staff, Cumnor, Oxfordshire 134
Bear Hotel, Crickhowell, Powys 479
Bear Inn, Berkswell, West Midlands 514
Beehive, Horringer, Suffolk 217
Bein Inn, Glenfarg, Perthshire & Kinross 450
Bel and the Dragon, Cookham, Berkshire 523
Belgian Arms, Holyport, Berkshire 533
Bell, Alderminster, Warwickshire 26
Bell, Castle Hedingham, Essex 96
Bell, Little Addington, Northamptonshire 246
Bell, Odell, Bedfordshire 300
Bell, Ramsbury, Wiltshire 317
Bell, Smarden, Kent 349
Bell, Standlake, Oxfordshire 359
Bell, Yarpole, Hereford & Worcester 558
Bellachroy Hotel, Dervaig, Argyll & Bute 559
Bell Hotel, Walberswick, Suffolk 399
Bell Inn, Aldworth, Berkshire 27
Bell Inn, Buckland Dinham, Somerset 84
Bell Inn, Kersey, Suffolk 536
Bell Inn, Llanyre, Powys 491
Bell Inn, Shenington, Oxfordshire 341
Bell Inn, Stilton, Cambridgeshire 366
Bell Inn, Horndon on the Hill, Essex 215
Bells of Peover, Lower Peover, Cheshire 539
Bernard Arms, Great Kimble, Buckinghamshire 186

Best Beech Inn, Best Beech, East Sussex 57
Bewicke Arms, Hallaton, Leicestershire 193
Birch Hall, Beck Hole, North Yorkshire 514
Bird in Hand, Hailey, Oxfordshire 192
Bird in Hand, Knowl Hill, Berkshire 236
Bird in Hand, Wreningham, Norfolk 558
Blackboys Inn, Blackboys, East Sussex 61
Black Bull, Boroughbridge, North Yorkshire 71
Black Bull, Cliffe, Kent 114
Black Bull, Etal, Northumberland 526
Black Bull, Market Overton, Leicestershire 269
Black Bull, Matfen, Northumberland 540
Black Bull Inn, Moulton, North Yorkshire 283
Black Buoy Inn, Wivenhoe, Essex 558
Blackcock Inn, Falstone, Northumberland 527
Black Horse, Byworth, West Sussex 520
Black Horse, Donington on Bain, Lincolnshire 524
Black Horse, Naunton, Gloucestershire 288
Black Horse, Walcote, Leicestershire 400
Black Horse Inn, Chesham, Buckinghamshire 103
Black Horse Inn, Thorndon, Suffolk 554
Black Lion, Abergorlech, Carmarthenshire 469
Black Lion Inn, Butterton, Staffordshire 90
Blacksmith's Arms, Offham, East Sussex 301
Blacksmiths Arms, Pittington, Co Durham 545
Black Swan, Martyr's Green, Surrey 540
Blewbury Inn, Blewbury, Oxfordshire 66
Blue Anchor, Helston, Cornwall 532
Blue Anchor Inn, East Aberthaw, Vale of Glamorgan 481
Blue Ball Inn, Braunston, Leicestershire 75
Blue Boar, Temple Grafton, Warwickshire 380
Blue Boar Inn, Longworth, Oxfordshire 256
Blue Lion, East Witton, North Yorkshire 151
Blue Peter, Polperro, Cornwall 546
Boar's Head, Ardington, Oxfordshire 33
Boat, Sprotbrough, South Yorkshire 552
Boat Inn, Ashleworth, Gloucestershire 513
Boat Inn, Erbistock, Wrexham 481
Boat Inn, Gnosall, Staffordshire 529
Boat Inn, Penallt, Monmouthshire 495
Boat Inn, Stoke Bruerne, Northamptonshire 552
Bonchurch Inn, Bonchurch, Isle of Wight 69
Boot Inn, Barnard Gate, Oxfordshire 49
Boot Inn, Boothsdale, Cheshire 70
Bottle and Glass, Gibraltar, Buckinghamshire 181
Bottle House Inn, Smart's Hill, Kent 349
Bowl Inn, Almondsbury, South Gloucestershire 511
Brace of Pheasants, Plush, Dorset 313
Bradford Arms, Llanymynech, Shropshire 252
Brewers Arms, Rattlesden, Suffolk 319
Brickmakers Arms, Windlesham, Surrey 420
Bridge, Topsham, Devon 555
Bridge Hotel, Buttermere, Cumbria 89
Bridge Inn, Linlithgow, West Lothian 561
Bridge Inn, Ratho, Edinburgh 461
Bridge of Cally Hotel, Bridge of Cally, Perthshire & Kinross 559
Brisley Bell, Brisley, Norfolk 79
Britannia Inn, Elterwater, Cumbria 158
Brocket Arms, Ayot St Lawrence, Hertfordshire 513
Bryn Tyrch Hotel, Capel Curig, Gwynedd 475

Bucket of Blood Inn, Phillack, Cornwall 545
Buckinghamshire Arms, Blickling, Norfolk 516
Buck Inn, Buckden, North Yorkshire 82
Buck Inn, Malham, North Yorkshire 540
Buck Inn, Thornton Watlass, North Yorkshire 383
Bull, Bellingdon, Buckinghamshire 55
Bull, Cottered, Hertfordshire 128
Bull, Three Legged Cross, East Sussex 384
Bull and Butcher, Turville, Buckinghamshire 393
Bull Hotel, Ditchling, East Sussex 524
Bull Inn, Blackmore End, Essex 62
Bull Inn, West Tanfield, North Yorkshire 557
Bulls Head, Foolow, Derbyshire 527
Bull Terrier, Croscombe, Somerset 524
Burts Hotel, Melrose, Borders 458
Bushell's Arms, Goosnargh, Lancashire 183
Bush Inn, Morwenstow, Cornwall 282
Bush Inn, Ovington, Hampshire 305
Bush Inn, St Hilary, Vale of Glamorgan 500
Butchers Arms, Alltwen, Neath Port Talbot 471
Butchers Arms, Hepworth, West Yorkshire 206
Butchers Arms, Llandarog, Carmarthenshire 564
Butchers Arms, Sheepscombe, Gloucestershire 550
Butchers Arms, Woolhope, Hereford & Worcester 428
Butt & Oyster, Pin Mill, Suffolk 545
Butterleigh Inn, Butterleigh, Devon 520
Byre Inn, Brig o'Turk, Stirling 441
Caesar's Arms, Creigiau, Cardiff 478
Cambrian Inn, Solva, Pembrokeshire 501
Cap & Feathers, Tillingham, Essex 385
Carew Inn, Carew, Pembrokeshire 476
Carpenters Arms, Shirenewton, Monmouthshire 501
Carpenters Arms, Slapton, Buckinghamshire 347
Carpenters Arms, Stanton Wick, Bath & N.E. Somerset 361
Carrington Arms, Moulsoe, Buckinghamshire 283
Castle Inn, Chiddingstone, Kent 105
Castle Inn, Lydford, Devon 265
Cavendish Arms, Brindle, Lancashire 518
Chafford Arms, Fordcombe, Kent 527
Chequers, Burcot, Oxfordshire 519
Chequers, Fowlmere, Cambridgeshire 176
Chequers, Gedney Dyke, Lincolnshire 180
Chequers, Watlington, Oxfordshire 556
Chequers Inn, Calver, Derbyshire 92
Chequers Inn, Fingest, Buckinghamshire 167
Chequers Inn, Smarden, Kent 551
Chequers Inn, Thompson, Norfolk 554
Chequers Inn, Well, Hampshire 406
Chequers Inn, Weston Turville, Buckinghamshire 413
Chequers Inn, Wooburn Common, Buckinghamshire 427
Cholmondeley Arms, Cholmondeley, Cheshire 108
Church House Inn, Harberton, Devon 531
Church House Inn, Holne, Devon 213
Church House Inn, Rattery, Devon 319
Clachaig Inn, Glencoe, Highland 560
Clachan Inn, Drymen, Stirling 446
Clanfield Tavern, Clanfield, Oxfordshire 111
Claycutters Arms, Chudleigh Knighton, Devon 109
Cleave, Lustleigh, Devon 263
Cliffe Tavern, St Margaret's at Cliffe, Kent 332
Clovenfords Hotel, Clovenfords, Borders 559

Cluanie Inn, Loch Cluanie, Highland 457
Clytha Arms, Clytha, Monmouthshire 477
Coach & Horses, Danehill, East Sussex 137
Coach and Horses, Rotherwick, Hampshire 328
Cock, Broom, Bedfordshire 519
Cock Inn, Ringmer, East Sussex 547
Compasses Inn, Chicksgrove, Wiltshire 103
Compasses Inn, Pattiswick, Essex 306
Cook and Barker Inn, Newton-on-the-Moor, Northumberland 292
Cotley Inn, Wambrook, Somerset 400
Cottage of Content, Barton, Warwickshire 514
Cottage of Content, Carey, Hereford & Worcester 520
Cott Inn, Dartington, Devon 137
Courtyard, Eaglesfield, Dumfries & Galloway 447
Coylet Inn, Loch Eck, Argyll & Bute 561
Crab & Lobster, Asenby, North Yorkshire 36
Crabshell Inn, Kingsbridge, Devon 536
Crabtree, Lower Beeding, West Sussex 258
Crag Inn, Wildboarclough, Cheshire 557
Craw Inn, Auchencrow, Borders 439
Creebridge House Hotel, Minnigaff, Dumfries & Galloway 459
Creek Inn, Peel, Isle of Man 507
Creggans Inn, Strachur, Argyll & Bute 461
Cricketers, Clavering, Essex 112
Cricketers, Duncton, West Sussex 144
Cricketers Arms, Berwick, East Sussex 57
Cricketers Arms, Rickling Green, Essex 322
Cridford Inn, Trusham, Devon 392
Crooked Billet, Stoke Row, Oxfordshire 370
Cross Keys, Kippen, Stirling 455
Cross Keys, Menithwood, Hereford & Worcester 541
Cross Keys, Upton, Nottinghamshire 396
Crossways Inn, West Huntspill, Somerset 411
Crown, Bildeston, Suffolk 515
Crown, Lanlivery, Cornwall 241
Crown, Llwyndafydd, Ceredigion 564
Crown, Munslow, Shropshire 286
Crown, Portpatrick, Dumfries & Galloway 460
Crown, Wentnor, Shropshire 406
Crown, Westleton, Suffolk 411
Crown and Anchor, Kilnsea, East Riding of Yorkshire 536
Crown & Anchor, Lugwardine, Hereford & Worcester 262
Crown & Horns, East Ilsley, Berkshire 525
Crown & Sandys Arms, Ombersley, Hereford & Worcester 543
Crown and Sceptre, Newton St Cyres, Devon 293
Crown and Trumpet, Broadway, Hereford & Worcester 518
Crown Hotel, Exford, Somerset 159
Crown Inn, Blockley, Gloucestershire 67
Crown Inn, Chiddingfold, Surrey 522
Crown Inn, Churchill, N.W. Somerset 522
Crown Inn, Hopton Wafers, Shropshire 214
Crown Inn, Old Dalby, Leicestershire 301
Crown Inn, St Ewe, Cornwall 549
Crown Inn, Snape, Suffolk 351
Crown Inn, Woolhope, Hereford & Worcester 429
Cuilfail Hotel, Kilmelford, Argyll & Bute 454
Cwellyn Arms, Rhyd-Ddu, Gwynedd 498
Daneway Inn, Sapperton, Gloucestershire 549
Deil's Cauldron, Comrie, Perthshire & Kinross 444
Denant Mill Inn, Dreenhill, Pembrokeshire 563
Dering Arms, Pluckley, Kent 313
Dever Arms, Micheldever, Hampshire 541
Devonport Hotel, Middleton One Row, Co Durham 277

Devonshire Arms, Mellor, Greater Manchester 272
Dew Drop, Hurley, Berkshire 534
Dial Inn, Lamphey, Pembrokeshire 484
Dinorben Arms, Bodfari, Denbighshire 562
Dinton Hermit, Ford, Buckinghamshire 171
Dipton Mill, Hexham, Northumberland 209
Dobermann Inn, Framsden, Suffolk 528
Dog Inn, Over Peover, Cheshire 304
Dolphin, Betchworth, Surrey 514
Dolphin Inn, Peacemarsh, Dorset 544
Dorset Arms, Withyham, East Sussex 425
Dragon, Montgomery, Powys 565
Drewe Arms, Broadhembury, Devon 80
Drewe Arms, Drewsteignton, Devon 525
Drovers Arms, Howey, Powys 563
Druid Inn, Birchover, Derbyshire 59
Drunken Duck Inn, Ambleside, Cumbria 28
Duke of York, Berrow, Hereford & Worcester 56
Duke of York, Fir Tree, Co Durham 169
Dukes Head, Armathwaite, Cumbria 35
Dundas Arms, Kintbury, Berkshire 229
Durant Arms, Ashprington, Devon 38
Earl of St Vincent, Egloshayle, Cornwall 153
Eels Foot, Eastbridge, Suffolk 525
Elephant's Nest, Horndon, Devon 215
Eliot Arms, Tregadillet, Cornwall 389
Elm Tree, Langton Herring, Dorset 240
Elsted Inn, Elsted Marsh, West Sussex 157
Engine & Tender, Broome, Shropshire 82
Eyre Arms, Hassop, Derbyshire 199
Falcon, Arncliffe, North Yorkshire 512
Falcon Inn, Fotheringhay, Northamptonshire 175
Falkland Arms, Great Tew, Oxfordshire 530
Farmer's Arms, Apperley, Gloucestershire 30
Fauconberg Arms, Coxwold, North Yorkshire 129
Feathers, Brockton, Shropshire 81
Ferry Inn, Alveston, Warwickshire 512
Ferry Inn, Pembroke Ferry, Pembrokeshire 494
Ferry Inn, St Dogmaels, Pembrokeshire 566
Ferry Inn, Stokesby, Norfolk 553
Ferry Inn, Stromness, Orkney 562
Feversham Arms, Church Houses, North Yorkshire 522
Fish, Bray, Berkshire 76
Fishermans Return, Winterton-on-Sea, Norfolk 423
Fisherman's Tavern, Broughty Ferry, Dundee 559
Fitzhead Inn, Fitzhead, Somerset 170
Five Arrows Hotel, Waddesdon, Buckinghamshire 397
Five Bells, Buriton, Hampshire 86
Five Bells, West Chiltington, West Sussex 410
Five Horseshoes, Maidensgrove, Oxfordshire 268
Fleece Inn, Bretforton, Hereford & Worcester 518
Fleur de Lys, Cranborne, Dorset 523
Fleur de Lys, Lowsonford, Warwickshire 539
Fleur de Lys, Pilley, Hampshire 310
Flower Pots Inn, Cheriton, Hampshire 101
Fordwich Arms, Fordwich, Kent 174
Foresters Arms, Carlton, North Yorkshire 92
Fountain Inn, Ingbirchworth, South Yorkshire 222
Four Horseshoes Country Inn, Thornham Magna, Suffolk 554
Four Marys, Linlithgow, West Lothian 561
Fox & Hounds, Barley, Hertfordshire 48
Fox & Hounds, Barnston, Merseyside 50

Fox and Hounds, Carthorpe, North Yorkshire 94
Fox and Hounds, Cotherstone, Co Durham 126
Fox and Hounds, Exton, Leicestershire 526
Fox & Hounds, Great Wolford, Warwickshire 188
Fox and Hounds, South Godstone, Surrey 352
Fox & Hounds, Starbotton, North Yorkshire 362
Fox Inn, Bramdean, Hampshire 73
Fox Inn, Corscombe, Dorset 124
Fox Inn, Great Barrington, Gloucestershire 529
Fox Inn, Lower Oddington, Gloucestershire 259
Fox Inn, Tangley, Hampshire 379
Freemasons Arms, Wiswell, Lancashire 424
Full Moon, Rudge, Somerset 548
Fur & Feather Inn, Woodbastwick, Norfolk 558
Galley of Lorne, Ardfern, Argyll & Bute 438
Gardeners Arms, Alderton, Gloucestershire 27
Gardeners Arms, Cheddar, Somerset 521
Gatehangers Inn, Ashendon, Buckinghamshire 513
Gate Inn, Marshside, Kent 272
General Havelock Inn, Haydon Bridge, Northumberland 202
General Tarleton, Ferrensby, North Yorkshire 166
George, Norton St Philip, Somerset 298
George, Nunney, Somerset 542
George and Dragon, Burpham, West Sussex 88
George & Dragon, Garrigill, Cumbria 528
George & Dragon, Kirkbymoorside, North Yorkshire 231
George & Dragon, Much Wenlock, Shropshire 284
George & Dragon, Rowde, Wiltshire 329
George & Dragon, Speldhurst, Kent 552
George & Dragon, Watton-at-Stone, Hertfordshire 405
George and Dragon, West Wycombe, Buckinghamshire 414
George & Dragon Hotel, Cley Next the Sea, Norfolk 113
George Hotel, Brecon, Powys 473
George Hotel, Dorchester on Thames, Oxfordshire 142
George Hotel, Piercebridge, Co Durham 545
George Inn, Hubberholme, North Yorkshire 219
George Inn, Newnham, Kent 292
George Inn, St Mary Bourne, Hampshire 333
George III Hotel, Penmaenpool, Gwynedd 496
Gin Trap Inn, Ringstead, Norfolk 547
Glenelg Inn, Glenelg, Highland 450
Glenisla Hotel, Kirkton of Glenisla, Angus 561
Globe Inn, Appley, Somerset 32
Globe Inn, Lostwithiel, Cornwall 257
Gold Cup Inn, Low Catton, East Riding of Yorkshire 539
Golden Eagle, Burham, Kent 85
Golden Key, Snape, Suffolk 551
Grapes Hotel, Maentwrog, Gwynedd 493
Green Dragon, Stoke Fleming, Devon 553
Green Man, Gosfield, Essex 183
Green Man, Great Offley, Hertfordshire 530
Green Man, Toot Hill, Essex 554
Green Man Inn, Fownhope, Hereford & Worcester 177
Greyhound, Oldwalls, Swansea 565
Greyhound Inn, Marsh Gibbon, Buckinghamshire 271
Greyhound Inn, Staple Fitzpaine, Somerset 362
Greyhound Inn, Warslow, Staffordshire 402
Gribble Inn, Oving, West Sussex 544
Griffin, Shustoke, Warwickshire 551
Griffin Inn, Fletching, East Sussex 170
Griffin Inn, Llyswen, Powys 492
Half Moon Inn, Kirdford, West Sussex 230
Half Moon Inn, Sheepwash, Devon 340
Halfway Bridge Inn, Halfway Bridge, West Sussex 193

Halfway House, Bontddu, Gwynedd 473
Halfway House Inn, Kingsand, Cornwall 536
Halzephron Inn, Gunwalloe, Cornwall 191
Hambro Arms, Milton Abbas, Dorset 278
Hamilton Arms, Stedham, West Sussex 364
Hampden Arms, Great Hampden, Buckinghamshire 185
Harbour Inn, Bowmore, Argyll & Bute 440
Harcourt Arms, Stanton Harcourt, Oxfordshire 360
Hare, Langton Green, Kent 240
Hare and Hounds, Foss Cross, Gloucestershire 175
Hare and Hounds, Hebden Bridge, West Yorkshire 204
Hare & Hounds, Hempstead, Norfolk 532
Hare and Hounds, Old Warden, Bedfordshire 543
Hare & Hounds, Stoughton, West Sussex 372
Hare & Hounds Inn, Bowland Bridge, Cumbria 517
Hare Arms, Docking, Norfolk 140
Hare Arms, Stow Bardolph, Norfolk 372
Hare Inn, Scawton, North Yorkshire 549
Hark to Bounty, Slaidburn, Lancashire 347
Harp Inn, Llandwrog, Gwynedd 486
Harp Inn, Old Radnor, Powys 565
Harrow, West Ilsley, Berkshire 556
Harrow Inn, Compton, Surrey 121
Harrow Inn, Ightham, Kent 221
Harrow Inn, Little Bedwyn, Wiltshire 247
Haselbury Inn, Haselbury Plucknett, Somerset 531
Hathersage Inn, Hathersage, Derbyshire 531
Hawes Inn, South Queensferry, Edinburgh 562
Hideaway, Halbeath, Fife 560
High Corner Inn, Linwood, Hampshire 538
Highwayman, Exlade Street, Oxfordshire 160
Hill House, Happisburgh, Norfolk 531
Hoddington Arms, Upton Grey, Hampshire 556
Home Sweet Home, Roke, Oxfordshire 326
Hood Arms, Kilve, Somerset 226
Hoops Inn, Horn's Cross, Devon 534
Hope & Anchor Inn, Midford, Bath & N.E. Somerset 277
Horns, Crazies Hill, Berkshire 130
Horse and Groom, Charlton, Wiltshire 99
Horse & Groom, East Woodlands, Somerset 152
Horse Guards Inn, Tillington, West Sussex 386
Horseshoe, Llanyblodwel, Shropshire 539
Horseshoe Inn, Eddleston, Borders 448
Hoste Arms, Burnham Market, Norfolk 87
Hotel Eilean Iarmain, Isle Ornsay, Highland 560
Howard Arms, Ilmington, Warwickshire 535
Hundred House Hotel, Norton, Shropshire 296
Ilchester Arms, Abbotsbury, Dorset 511
Inn at Freshford, Freshford, Bath & N.E. Somerset 177
Inn at Whitewell, Whitewell, Lancashire 416
Inn on the Green, Cookham Dean, Berkshire 122
Irby Mill, Greasby, Merseyside 529
Isle of Colonsay Hotel, Colonsay, Argyll & Bute 443
Jack in the Green, Rockbeare, Devon 324
Jenny Wren, Susworth, Lincolnshire 553
Jervis Arms, Onecote, Staffordshire 543
John of Gaunt, Horsebridge, Hampshire 218
John Thompson, Ingleby, Derbyshire 535
Joiners Arms, Hampsthwaite, North Yorkshire 530
Jolly Farmer, Cookham Dean, Berkshire 123
Jolly Fisherman, Craster, Northumberland 524
Jolly Sailor, Orford, Suffolk 543

Jolly Sailors, Brancaster Staithe, Norfolk 518
Jolly Waggoner, Ardeley, Hertfordshire 32
Jubilee Inn, Pelynt, Cornwall 544
Juggs, Kingston Near Lewes, East Sussex 228
Kaye Arms, Grange Moor, West Yorkshire 184
Kilberry Inn, Kilberry, Argyll & Bute 452
Kimberley Inn, Findhorn, Moray 560
King Arthur, Reynoldston, Swansea 565
King John Hotel, Tollard Royal, Wiltshire 554
The Kings, Reach, Cambridgeshire 320
Kings Arms, Amersham, Buckinghamshire 29
King's Arms, Blakeney, Norfolk 516
Kings Arms, Heath, West Yorkshire 531
Kings Arms, Ombersley, Hereford & Worcester 303
King's Arms, Wing, Leicestershire 422
King's Arms Hotel, Askrigg, North Yorkshire 40
Kings Arms Inn, Montacute, Somerset 281
Kings Arms Inn, Stockland, Devon 367
Kings Head, Bledington, Gloucestershire 65
King's Head, Laxfield, Suffolk 242
King's Head, Newton under Roseberry, Redcar 294
King's Head, Wadenhoe, Northamptonshire 398
Kings Head, Wootton, Oxfordshire 430
King William IV, Fenstanton, Cambridgeshire 165
King William IV, Mickleham, Surrey 276
King William IV, Speen, Buckinghamshire 357
Kirk Inn, Romaldkirk, Co Durham 548
Kirkstone Pass Inn, Ambleside, Cumbria 512
Knife & Cleaver, Houghton Conquest, Bedfordshire 218
Kylesku Hotel, Kylesku, Highland 456
Lade Inn, Kilmahog, Stirling 453
Lairhillock Inn, Netherley, Aberdeenshire 459
Lamb at Hindon, Hindon, Wiltshire 212
Lamb Inn, Buckland, Oxfordshire 83
Lamb Inn, Burford, Oxfordshire 85
Lamb Inn, Shipton-under-Wychwood, Oxfordshire 343
Langton Arms, Tarrant Monkton, Dorset 380
Laurel Inn, Robin Hood's Bay, North Yorkshire 547
Leather's Smithy, Langley, Cheshire 239
Lickfold Inn, Lickfold, West Sussex 538
Lions of Bledlow, Bledlow, Buckinghamshire 65
Little Brown Jug, Chiddingstone Causeway, Kent 105
Little Packhorse, Bewdley, Hereford & Worcester 514
Lobster Pot, Marloes, Pembrokeshire 564
Loch Melfort Hotel, Arduaine, Argyll & Bute 438
Loders Arms, Loders, Dorset 253
Lomond Country Inn, Kinnesswood, Perthshire & Kinross 455
Lord Nelson, Burnham Thorpe, Norfolk 520
Lough Pool Inn, Sellack, Hereford & Worcester 338
Lytton Arms, Knebworth, Hertfordshire 234
Malt Shovel, Brearton, North Yorkshire 76
Malt Shovel, Eynsford, Kent 162
Malt Shovel, Oswaldkirk, North Yorkshire 543
Malt Shovel, Shardlow, Derbyshire 550
Maltsters Arms, Chapel Amble, Cornwall 98
Manor Hotel, West Bexington, Dorset 408
Manor House Inn, Carterway Heads, Northumberland 93
Manor Inn, Lower Ashton, Devon 539
Marquis of Lorne, Nettlecombe, Dorset 290
Martins Arms, Colston Bassett, Nottinghamshire 119
Mason Arms, South Leigh, Oxfordshire 353

Masons Arms, Branscombe, Devon 73
Masons Arms, Cartmel Fell, Cumbria 95
Masons Arms, Meysey Hampton, Gloucestershire 275
Masons Arms Inn, Knowstone, Devon 237
Mayfly, Testcombe, Hampshire 381
Maypole Inn, Long Preston, North Yorkshire 539
Mermaid Inn, Rye, East Sussex 548
Merrie Harriers, Cowbeech, East Sussex 128
Merry Miller, Cothill, Oxfordshire 127
Mexico Inn, Longrock, Cornwall 255
Mildmay Colours, Holbeton, Devon 533
Millbrook Inn, South Pool, Devon 354
Millstone, Mellor, Lancashire 273
Milton Brewery Inn, Milton, Pembrokeshire 565
Miners Arms, Blaenau Ffestiniog, Gwynedd 562
Miners Arms, Eyam, Derbyshire 161
Miners Arms, Mithian, Cornwall 280
Mole & Chicken, Easington, Buckinghamshire 147
Moody Cow, Upton Bishop, Hereford & Worcester 396
Moorcock Inn, Blacko, Lancashire 63
Morritt Arms, Greta Bridge, Co Durham 190
Mortal Man Hotel, Troutbeck, Cumbria 555
Museum Hotel, Farnham, Dorset 162
Nags Head, Heckington, Lincolnshire 205
Nags Head, Little Hadham, Hertfordshire 538
Nags Head, Pickhill, North Yorkshire 310
Nags Head Inn, Hill Top, Leicestershire 211
Nantyffin Cider Mill Inn, Crickhowell, Powys 479
Navigation Inn, Dobcross, Greater Manchester 139
Nelson Head, Horsey, Norfolk 534
New Crown, Ainstable, Cumbria 511
New Inn, Cerne Abbas, Dorset 521
New Inn, Church Knowle, Dorset 110
New Inn, Coleford, Devon 116
New Inn, Coln St Aldwyns, Gloucestershire 118
New Inn, North Nibley, Gloucestershire 542
New Inn, Pembridge, Hereford & Worcester 307
New Inn, Shalfleet, Isle of Wight 549
New Inn, Tresco, Isles of Scilly 555
New Inn, Yealand Conyers, Lancashire 434
Nickerson Arms, Rothwell, Lincolnshire 329
Nobody Inn, Doddiscombsleigh, Devon 140
Noel Arms, Whitwell, Leicestershire 418
Normandy Arms, Blackawton, Devon 515
Notley Arms, Monksilver, Somerset 280
Old Barn Inn, Glooston, Leicestershire 181
Old Beams Inn, Ibsley, Hampshire 220
Old Black Lion, Chapelgate, Lincolnshire 521
Old Black Lion, Hay-on-Wye, Powys 483
Old Boot Inn, Stanford Dingley, Berkshire 360
Old Bridge Inn, Ripponden, West Yorkshire 324
Old Bull, Inkberrow, Hereford & Worcester 535
Old Chequers, Friston, Suffolk 179
Old Crown, Skirmett, Buckinghamshire 346
Old Dungeon Ghyll Hotel, Great Langdale, Cumbria 529
Ye Olde Anchor, Ruthin, Denbighshire 499
Ye Olde Bulls Head Inn, Beaumaris, Isle of Anglesey 471
Olde Coach House Inn, Ashby St Ledgers, Northamptonshire 37
Ye Olde Cross Keys Inn, Aldeburgh, Suffolk 511
Olde Dog & Partridge, Tutbury, Staffordshire 394

Ye Olde Gate Inn, Brassington, Derbyshire 74
Ye Olde George Inn, East Meon, Hampshire 526
Ye Olde Globe, Berrynarbor, Devon 514
Ye Olde Inne, Guiting Power, Gloucestershire 530
Ye Olde Salutation Inn, Weobley, Hereford & Worcester 407
Olde Ship Hotel, Seahouses, Northumberland 336
Old Ferry Boat Inn, Holywell, Cambridgeshire 533
Old Hall Inn, Threshfield, North Yorkshire 385
Old Ham Tree Inn, Holt, Wiltshire 533
Old House, Llangynwyd, Bridgend 489
Old Inn, St Breward, Cornwall 548
Old Inn, Widecombe in the Moor, Devon 419
Old Oak, Arlington, East Sussex 35
Old Rectory, Dysart, Fife 446
Old Rydon Inn, Kingsteignton, Devon 227
Old Swan Inn, Gargrave, North Yorkshire 179
Old Swan, Swan Bottom, Buckinghamshire 378
Old Thatch Inn, Cheriton Bishop, Devon 102
Old Thistle Inn, Westruther, Borders 464
Old Three Pigeons, Nesscliffe, Shropshire 541
Old White Hart, Lyddington, Leicestershire 264
Olive Branch, Marsden, West Yorkshire 269
Ostrich Inn, Castle Acre, Norfolk 520
Ostrich Inn, Newland, Gloucestershire 291
Otter Inn, Weston, Devon 413
Oxenham Arms, South Zeal, Devon 356
Oyster Inn, Butley, Suffolk 88
Packhorse Inn, Little Longstone, Derbyshire 538
Pack Horse Inn, Widdop, West Yorkshire 557
Padwell Arms, Stone Street, Kent 553
Pandora Inn, Mylor Bridge, Cornwall 286
Pandy Inn, Dorstone, Hereford & Worcester 143
Pant yr Ochain, Gresford, Wrexham 483
Peacock, Bolter End, Buckinghamshire 69
Peacock, Boraston, Shropshire 70
Peacock, Shortbridge, East Sussex 344
Peacock Inn, Chelsworth, Suffolk 100
Peacock Inn, Redmile, Leicestershire 321
Pear Tree, Hildersham, Cambridgeshire 210
Pear Tree Inn, Hook Norton, Oxfordshire 533
Peat Spade Inn, Longstock, Hampshire 255
Peldon Rose, Peldon, Essex 544
Pendre Inn, Cilgerran, Pembrokeshire 563
Penhelig Arms Hotel, Aberdovey, Gwynedd 469
Pennan Inn, Pennan, Aberdeenshire 561
Penny Farthing, Aston Crews, Hereford & Worcester 513
Perch, Binsey, Oxfordshire 515
Perch & Pike Inn, South Stoke, Oxfordshire 355
Peter Tavy Inn, Peter Tavy, Devon 307
Pheasant, Ballinger Common, Buckinghamshire 45
Pheasant, Gestingthorpe, Essex 528
Pheasant, Worth, Somerset 431
Pheasant Inn, Bassenthwaite Lake, Cumbria 51
Pheasant Inn, Casterton, Cumbria 96
Pheasant Inn, Higher Burwardsley, Cheshire 209
Pheasant Inn, Keyston, Cambridgeshire 225
Picton Inn, Clarbeston Road, Pembrokeshire 476
Pig's Nose Inn, East Prawle, Devon 526
Pilchard Inn, Burgh Island, Devon 519
Pilgrims Reach, Docking, Norfolk 524
Pipe and Glass Inn, South Dalton, East Riding of Yorkshire 551
Plough, Blackbrook, Surrey 62
Plough, Bodicote, Oxfordshire 516

Plough, East Hendred, Oxfordshire 150
Plough, Effingham, Surrey 153
Plough, Finstock, Oxfordshire 168
Plough, Rede, Suffolk 321
Plough, Sparsholt, Hampshire 356
Plough, Stalisfield Green, Kent 358
Plough, Trottiscliffe, Kent 390
Plough, Wistanstow, Shropshire 558
Plough and Fleece, Horningsea, Cambridgeshire 216
Plough & Sail, Paglesham, Essex 544
Plough Inn, Clifton Hampden, Oxfordshire 115
Plough Inn, Coldharbour, Surrey 116
Plough Inn, Ford, Gloucestershire 172
Plough Inn, Grateley, Hampshire 529
Plough Inn, Henfield, West Sussex 205
Plough Inn, Hundon, Suffolk 534
Plough Inn, Saxton, North Yorkshire 335
Plume of Feathers, Crondall, Hampshire 131
Poachers Arms, Hope, Derbyshire 534
Polecat Inn, Prestwood, Buckinghamshire 316
Pot Kiln, Frilsham, Berkshire 178
Punch Bowl & Ladle, Penelwey, Cornwall 545
Punch Bowl Inn, Crosthwaite, Cumbria 132
Punch Bowl Inn, Lanreath, Cornwall 537
Punch Bowl Inn, Oakwood Hill, Surrey 299
Pwll Gwyn Hotel, Afon-Wen, Flintshire 470
Pykkerell, Ixworth, Suffolk 224
Quarry House Inn, Haworth, West Yorkshire 201
Queen's Head, Glanwydden, Conwy 482
Queens Head, Icklesham, East Sussex 535
Queen's Head, Kirtling, Cambridgeshire 232
Queens Head, Newton, Cambridgeshire 542
Queens Head, Stow on the Wold, Gloucestershire 373
Queens Head, Sutton Bassett, Northamptonshire 376
Queens Head, Tirril, Cumbria 387
Queen's Head Hotel, Hawkshead, Cumbria 200
Queens Head Hotel, Troutbeck, Cumbria 391
Queen's Head Inn, Blyford, Suffolk 68
Queens Head Inn, Great Whittington, Northumberland 187
Queens Head Inn, Littlebury, Essex 249
Raby Hunt Inn, Summerhouse, Co Durham 375
Radnor Arms, Llowes, Powys 564
Ragleth Inn, Little Stretton, Shropshire 538
Ram Cider House, Godalming, Surrey 529
Ram Inn, Firle, East Sussex 168
Ram Inn, South Woodchester, Gloucestershire 551
Rams Head Inn, Denshaw, Greater Manchester 138
Ramsholt Arms, Ramsholt, Suffolk 318
Ratcatchers Inn, Eastgate, Norfolk 148
Rat Inn, Anick, Northumberland 512
Ratty Arms, Ravenglass, Cumbria 546
Red Hart, Llanvapley, Monmouthshire 490
Red Hart Inn, Awre, Gloucestershire 41
Red House, Knipton, Leicestershire 537
Red House, Whitchurch, Hampshire 415
Red Lion, Axford, Wiltshire 42
Red Lion, Chenies, Buckinghamshire 101
Red Lion, Coleshill, Buckinghamshire 117
Red Lion, Great Kingshill, Buckinghamshire 187
Red Lion, Icklingham, Suffolk 221
Red Lion, Kirtling, Cambridgeshire 233
Red Lion, Lacock, Wiltshire 238
Red Lion, Little Compton, Warwickshire 249
Red Lion, Llanfair Waterdine, Shropshire 252

Red Lion, Marsworth, Buckinghamshire 540
Red Lion, Steeple Aston, Oxfordshire 365
Red Lion, Stiffkey, Norfolk 365
Red Lion, Thurgarton, Nottinghamshire 554
Red Lion Hotel, East Haddon, Northamptonshire 149
Red Lion Inn, Boldre, Hampshire 516
Red Lion Inn, Llanfihangel nant Melan, Powys 487
Red Lion Inn, Raithby, Lincolnshire 546
Red Lion Inn, Shamley Green, Surrey 340
Reedham Ferry Inn, Reedham, Norfolk 546
Rhydspence Inn, Whitney, Hereford & Worcester 417
Ringlestone Inn, Harrietsham, Kent 197
Ring O'Bells, Compton Martin, Bath & N.E. Somerset 122
Ring O'Bells, Thornton, West Yorkshire 382
Rising Sun, Gunnislake, Cornwall 190
Rising Sun, Knapp, Somerset 234
Rising Sun, Little Hampden, Buckinghamshire 251
Rising Sun, Shraleybrook, Staffordshire 550
Rising Sun Hotel, Lynmouth, Devon 540
Riverside Inn, Aymestrey, Hereford & Worcester 43
Riverside Inn, Canonbie, Dumfries & Galloway 442
Robin Hood Inn, Elkesley, Nottinghamshire 154
Rock Inn, Haytor Vale, Devon 203
Roebuck, Brimfield, Hereford & Worcester 77
Roebuck, Sixpenny Handley, Dorset 345
Roebuck Inn, North Newington, Oxfordshire 295
Roebuck Inn, Strinesdale, Greater Manchester 374
Rose & Crown, East Lyng, Somerset 525
Rose & Crown, Hawridge Common, Buckinghamshire 201
Rose & Crown, Playley Green, Gloucestershire 312
Rose and Crown, Romaldkirk, Co Durham 326
Rose & Crown, Snettisham, Norfolk 351
Rose and Crown, Woodhill, Somerset 427
Rose & Crown Hotel, Bainbridge, North Yorkshire 45
Rose & Crown Inn, Mayfield, East Sussex 540
Rose & Crown Inn, Sutton-on-the-Forest, North Yorkshire 378
Rose & Thistle, Rockbourne, Hampshire 325
Rose Cottage, Alciston, East Sussex 25
Roseland Inn, Philleigh, Cornwall 308
Royal and Ancient, Colne Bridge, West Yorkshire 118
Royal Hotel, Cromarty, Highland 445
Royal Inn, Horsebridge, Devon 534
Royal Oak, Brockham, Surrey 519
Royal Oak, Cardington, Shropshire 520
Royal Oak, Lostwithiel, Cornwall 257
Royal Oak, Nunnington, North Yorkshire 298
Royal Oak, Over Stratton, Somerset 305
Royal Oak, Spark Bridge, Cumbria 551
Royal Oak, Wineham, West Sussex 558
Royal Oak, Wootton Rivers, Wiltshire 431
Royal Oak, Yattendon, Berkshire 433
Royal Oak Inn, Appleby, Cumbria 31
Royal Oak Inn, Meavy, Devon 541
Royal Oak Inn, Winsford, Somerset 423
Royal Oak Inn, Withypool, Somerset 425
Royal Oak of Luxborough, Luxborough, Somerset 263
Royal Standard Of England, Forty Green, Buckinghamshire 528
Rugglestone Inn, Widecombe in the Moor, Devon 557
Salisbury Arms, Halstead, Leicestershire 194
Salusbury Arms, Tremeirchion, Denbighshire 566

Sands House, Crosland Hill, West Yorkshire 132
Saracen's Head, Wolterton, Norfolk 426
Sawley Arms, Sawley, North Yorkshire 334
Scole Inn, Scole, Norfolk 549
Sea Trout, Staverton, Devon 363
Seaview Hotel, Seaview, Isle of Wight 337
Seland Newydd, Pwllgloyw, Powys 496
Seven Tuns, Chedworth, Gloucestershire 522
Shave Cross Inn, Shave Cross, Dorset 550
Shaven Crown Hotel, Shipton-under-Wychwood, Oxfordshire 550
Shepherds Inn, Melmerby, Cumbria 275
Shieldaig, Shieldaig, Highland 562
Ship, Conyer Quay, Kent 523
Ship, Levington, Suffolk 243
Ship, Low Newton-by-the-Sea, Northumberland 261
Ship Inn, Barnoldby le Beck, N. E. Lincolnshire 50
Ship Inn, Dunwich, Suffolk 146
Ship Inn, Elie, Fife 448
Ship Inn, Limekilns, Fife 457
Ship Inn, Owslebury, Hampshire 544
Ship Inn, Porthleven, Cornwall 314
Ship Inn, Red Wharf Bay, Isle of Anglesey 497
Ship Inn, Wincle, Cheshire 420
Shipwrights Arms, Helford, Cornwall 532
Shipwrights Arms, Oare, Kent 299
Shoulder of Mutton, Appleton Roebuck, North Yorkshire 512
Silver Fox, Hertford Heath, Hertfordshire 207
Silver Plough, Pitton, Wiltshire 311
Sir Charles Napier Inn, Chinnor, Oxfordshire 107
Six Bells, Bardwell, Suffolk 47
Six Bells, Chiddingly, East Sussex 104
Six Bells, Felsham, Suffolk 164
Skimmington Castle, Reigate Heath, Surrey 547
Skirrid Mountain Inn, Llanvihangel Crucorney, Monmouthshire 491
Sloop Inn, Bantham, Devon 46
Smith's Arms, Godmanstone, Dorset 182
Smoker, Plumley, Cheshire 546
Snooty Fox, Kirkby Lonsdale, Cumbria 230
Snooty Fox, Lowick, Northamptonshire 261
Sorrel Horse, Barham, Suffolk 48
Spanker Inn, Nether Heage, Derbyshire 542
Speculation Inn, Hundleton, Pembrokeshire 563
Sportsman, Hayfield, Derbyshire 203
Sportsman's Arms, Wath-in-Nidderdale, North Yorkshire 404
Spotted Dog Inn, Smart's Hill, Kent 350
Springer Spaniel, Treburley, Cornwall 388
Spyglass Inn, Ventnor, Isle of Wight 556
Spyway Inn, Askerswell, Dorset 39
Stag & Huntsman, Hambleden, Buckinghamshire 530
Stanley Arms, Bottom-of-the-Oven, Cheshire 517
Star, Old Heathfield, East Sussex 302
Star, Talybont, Powys 566
Star Inn, Harome, North Yorkshire 195
Star Inn, Lidgate, Suffolk 244
Star Inn, St Just, Cornwall 549
Star Inn, Steyning, West Sussex 552
Start Bay Inn, Torcross, Devon 388
Steam Packet, Isle of Whithorn, Dumfries & Galloway 560
Stockton Cross Inn, Kimbolton, Hereford & Worcester 226
Stork Hotel, Conder Green, Lancashire 523
Strines Inn, Bradfield, South Yorkshire 517
Strode Arms, Cranmore, Somerset 130
Stumble Inn, Bwlch-y-Cibau, Powys 474
Sun, Bentworth, Hampshire 55
Sun, Dent, Cumbria 524
Sun Inn, Corfton, Shropshire 523
Sun Inn, Dunsfold, Surrey 145
Sun Inn, Feering, Essex 527
Sun Inn, Winforton, Hereford & Worcester 421
Sussex Brewery, Hermitage, West Sussex 532

Sussex Ox, Milton Street, East Sussex 279
Sutton Hall, Sutton, Cheshire 375
Swan Inn, Inkpen, Berkshire 536
Swan Inn, Ley Hill, Buckinghamshire 537
Swan Inn, Little Haven, Pembrokeshire 485
Swan Inn, Southrop, Gloucestershire 354
Swan with Two Nicks, Little Bollington, Cheshire 248
Tafarn Newydd, Rosebush, Pembrokeshire 498
Tai'r Bull, Libanus, Powys 564
Talbot Hotel, Knightwick, Hereford & Worcester 235
Talbot Inn, Mells, Somerset 274
Talbot Inn, Much Wenlock, Shropshire 285
Tally Ho, Hatherleigh, Devon 199
Tally Ho!, Littlehempston, Devon 538
Tally Ho Inn, Aswarby, Lincolnshire 40
Tan Hill Inn, Keld, North Yorkshire 536
Tankerville Arms, Eglingham, Northumberland 526
Tayvallich Inn, Tayvallich, Argyll & Bute 463
Tempest Arms, Elslack, North Yorkshire 155
Thelbridge Cross Inn, Thelbridge, Devon 382
Three Acres Inn, Roydhouse, West Yorkshire 330
Three Chimneys, Biddenden, Kent 58
Three Cranes, Turvey, Bedfordshire 393
Three Crowns, Brinkworth, Wiltshire 78
Three Elms, North Wootton, Dorset 542
Three Hares, Bilbrough, North Yorkshire 59
Three Horseshoes, Elsted, West Sussex 156
Three Horseshoes, Langley Marsh, Somerset 537
Three Horseshoes, Little Cowarne, Hereford & Worcester 250
Three Horseshoes, Madingley, Cambridgeshire 267
Three Horseshoes, Powerstock, Dorset 315
Three Horseshoes, Warham All Saints, Norfolk 402
Three Stags Heads, Wardlow Mires, Derbyshire 401
Three Tuns, Bishop's Castle, Shropshire 515
Three Tuns, Fen Drayton, Cambridgeshire 527
Three Tuns Inn, Osmotherly, North Yorkshire 303
Tibbie Shiels Inn, St Mary's Loch, Borders 561
Tickell Arms, Whittlesford, Cambridgeshire 418
Tiger Inn, East Dean, East Sussex 148
Tigh an Truish, Clachan, Argyll & Bute 443
Tite Inn, Chadlington, Oxfordshire 97
Tom Cobley Tavern, Spreyton, Devon 552
Tormaukin Hotel, Glendevon, Perthshire & Kinross 449
Tower Bank Arms, Near Sawrey, Cumbria 541
Tower Inn, Slapton, Devon 348
Towie Tavern, Auchterless, Aberdeenshire 440
Tradesmans Arms, Stokenham, Devon 553
Traquair Arms, Innerleithen, Borders 452
Travellers Rest, Grasmere, Cumbria 185
Trengilly Wartha Inn, Nancenoy, Cornwall 287
Trenwith Arms, Land's End, Cornwall 537
Trevor Arms Hotel, Marford, Wrexham 494
Trewern Arms, Nevern, Pembrokeshire 565
Trout, Itchen Abbas, Hampshire 223
Tuckers Arms, Dalwood, Devon 136
Turk's Head, St Agnes, Isles of Scilly 548
Turk's Head Inn, Alston, Cumbria 511
Ty Gwyn Hotel, Betws-y-Coed, Conwy 472
Union Inn, Dolton, Devon 141
Valiant Trooper, Aldbury, Hertfordshire 25
Victoria Inn, Earl Soham, Suffolk 525

Victoria Inn, West Marden, West Sussex 412
Village Green, Trellech, Monmouthshire 503
Vine Inn, Cumnor, Oxfordshire 135
Vine Tree Inn, Llangattock, Powys 488
Walnut Tree, Fawley, Buckinghamshire 164
Walnut Tree, West Camel, Somerset 409
Walpole Arms, Itteringham, Norfolk 223
Waltzing Weasel, Birch Vale, Derbyshire 60
War-Bill-in-Tun, Warbleton, East Sussex 556
Warren House Inn, Postbridge, Devon 546
Wasdale Head Inn, Wasdale Head, Cumbria 556
Waterfall, Glenmaye, Isle of Man 566
Waterman's Arms, Ashprington, Devon 38
Watermill, Ings, Cumbria 535
Water Rat, Marsh Benham, Berkshire 270
Waterside, Haddington, East Lothian 451
Weary Friar, Pillaton, Cornwall 545
Weighbridge Inn, Minchinhampton, Gloucestershire 279
Wenlock Edge Inn, Hilltop, Shropshire 212
Wensleydale Heifer, West Witton, North Yorkshire 557
West Arms Hotel, Llanarmon Dyffryn Ceiriog, Wrexham 485
Westbury Inn, Westbury-sub-Mendip, Somerset 409
We Three Loggerheads, Cadole, Flintshire 563
Wheatsheaf, Combe Hay, Bath & N.E. Somerset 120
Wheatsheaf Hotel, Swinton, Borders 462
White Bear, Shipston on Stour, Warwickshire 342
White Bull, Ribchester, Lancashire 547
White Hart, Boxford, Suffolk 72
White Hart, Bythorn, Cambridgeshire 91
White Hart, Ford, Wiltshire 173
White Hart, Great Yeldham, Essex 189
White Hart, Hamstead Marshall, Berkshire 195
White Hart, Llangybi, Monmouthshire 488
White Hart, Lydgate, Greater Manchester 266
White Hart, Nayland, Suffolk 289
White Hart, Stopham, West Sussex 371
White Hart, Trudoxhill, Somerset 555
White Hart Inn, Blythburgh, Suffolk 516
White Hart Inn, Bouth, Cumbria 517
White Horse, Chilham, Kent 522
White Horse, Coychurch, Vale of Glamorgan 563
White Horse, Easebourne, West Sussex 146
White Horse, Easton, Suffolk 151
White Horse, Empingham, Leicestershire 159
White Horse, Hascombe, Surrey 198
White Horse, Norton Heath, Essex 297
White Horse, Ridgewell, Essex 323
White Horse, Shere, Surrey 342
White Horse, Stogumber, Somerset 367
White Horse, Whepstead, Suffolk 415
White Horse Farm Hotel, Rosedale Abbey, North Yorkshire 327
White Horse Hotel Blakeney, Norfolk 64
White Horse Inn, Bradford-on-Tone, Somerset 517
White Horse Inn, Chilgrove, West Sussex 106
White Horse Inn, Priors Dean, Hampshire 316
White Horse Inn, Scales, Cumbria 336
White Horse Inn, Woolley Moor, Derbyshire 429
White Lion, Selling, Kent 339
White Lion, Wherwell, Hampshire 557
White Lion Inn, Bourton, Dorset 517
White Pheasant, Fordham, Cambridgeshire 173
White Swan, Ampleforth, North Yorkshire 30
White Swan, Harringworth, Northamptonshire 197

White Swan, Pickering, North Yorkshire 309
Wight Mouse Inn, Chale, Isle of Wight 98
Wildebeest Arms, Stoke Holy Cross, Norfolk 369
William Caxton, Tenterden, Kent 553
William IV, Bletchingley, Surrey 516
Windmill, Badby, Northamptonshire 44
Windmill Inn, Linton, West Yorkshire 246
Winyard's Gap, Chedington, Dorset 521
Wombwell Arms, Wass, North Yorkshire 403
Woodbridge Inn, North Newnton, Wiltshire 295
Woodman Inn, Fernham, Oxfordshire 527
Woolpack Beckington, Somerset 52
Woolpack, Brookland, Kent 519
Woolpack, Elstead, Surrey 156
Wyndham Arms, Clearwell, Gloucestershire 113
Ye Olde Anchor, Ruthin, Denbighshire 499
Ye Olde Bulls Head Inn, Beaumaris, Isle of Anglesey 471
Ye Olde Cross Keys Inn, Aldeburgh, Suffolk 511
Ye Olde Gate Inn, Brassington, Derbyshire 74
Ye Olde George Inn, East Meon, Hampshire 526
Ye Olde Globe, Berrynarbor, Devon 514
Ye Olde Inne, Guiting Power, Gloucestershire 530
Ye Olde Salutation Inn, Weobley, Hereford & Worcester 407
Yew Tree Inn, Cauldon, Staffordshire 521
Yew Tree, Frieth, Buckinghamshire 528
Yew Tree Inn, Lower Wield, Hampshire 260
York Inn, Churchinford, Somerset 109
Ypres Inn, Rye, East Sussex 332

Report form

Pub 3

To *The Which? Guide to Country Pubs,*
FREEPOST, 2 Marylebone Road, London NW1 1YN

PUB NAME ____

Address ____

______________________________ Telephone ____________

Date of visit ____

From my personal experience this establishment should be
(please tick)

main entry ❑ 'Out and about' entry ❑ excluded ❑

Please describe what you ate and drank (with prices, if known), and give details of location, service, atmosphere etc.

Please turn over

My meal for ___ people cost £____ Value for money? yes ❑ no ❑

I am not connected in any way with the management or proprietors.

Name and address (BLOCK CAPITALS) ______________________________

____

____

____

Report form

Pub 3

To *The Which? Guide to Country Pubs,*
FREEPOST, 2 Marylebone Road, London NW1 1YN

PUB NAME ____________________

Address ____________________

____________________ Telephone ____________________

Date of visit ____________________

From my personal experience this establishment should be (please tick)

main entry ☐ 'Out and about' entry ☐ excluded ☐

Please describe what you ate and drank (with prices, if known), and give details of location, service, atmosphere etc.

Please turn over

My meal for ___ people cost £____ Value for money? yes ❑ no ❑

I am not connected in any way with the management or proprietors.

Name and address (BLOCK CAPITALS) ______________________________

____

____

____

Report form

Pub 3

To *The Which? Guide to Country Pubs,*
FREEPOST, 2 Marylebone Road, London NW1 1YN

PUB NAME ______________________________

Address ______________________________

______________________________ Telephone ______________

Date of visit ______________________________

From my personal experience this establishment should be (please tick)

main entry ❑ 'Out and about' entry ❑ excluded ❑

Please describe what you ate and drank (with prices, if known), and give details of location, service, atmosphere etc.

Please turn over

My meal for ___ people cost £____ Value for money? yes ❑ no ❑

I am not connected in any way with the management or proprietors.

Name and address (BLOCK CAPITALS) ______________________________

____

____

____

Report form

Pub 3

To *The Which? Guide to Country Pubs,*
FREEPOST, 2 Marylebone Road, London NW1 1YN

PUB NAME ______________________________

Address ______________________________

______________________________ Telephone ______________

Date of visit ______________________________

From my personal experience this establishment should be (please tick)

main entry ❑ 'Out and about' entry ❑ excluded ❑

Please describe what you ate and drank (with prices, if known), and give details of location, service, atmosphere etc.

Please turn over

My meal for ___ people cost £____ Value for money? yes ❑ no ❑

I am not connected in any way with the management or proprietors.

Name and address (BLOCK CAPITALS) ____________________

____

____

____

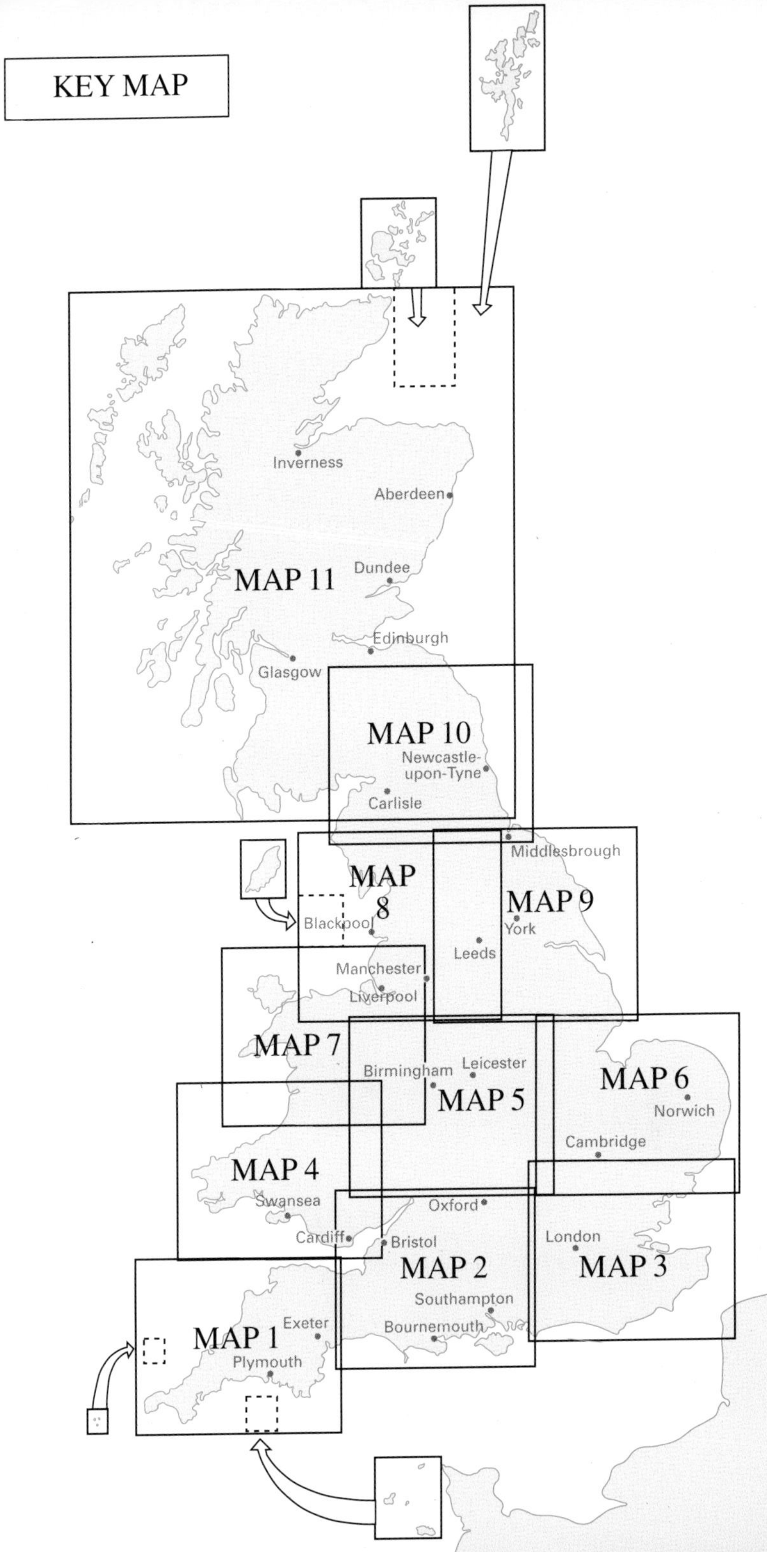
KEY MAP
Inverness
Aberdeen
Dundee
MAP 11
Edinburgh
Glasgow
MAP 10
Newcastle-
upon-Tyne
Carlisle
Middlesbrough
MAP
8
MAP 9
York
Blackpool
Leeds
Manchester
Liverpool
MAP 7
Birmingham
Leicester
MAP 5
MAP 6
Norwich
Cambridge
MAP 4
Swansea
Oxford
Cardiff
Bristol
London
MAP 2
MAP 3
Southampton
Exeter
MAP 1
Bournemouth
Plymouth

MAP 1

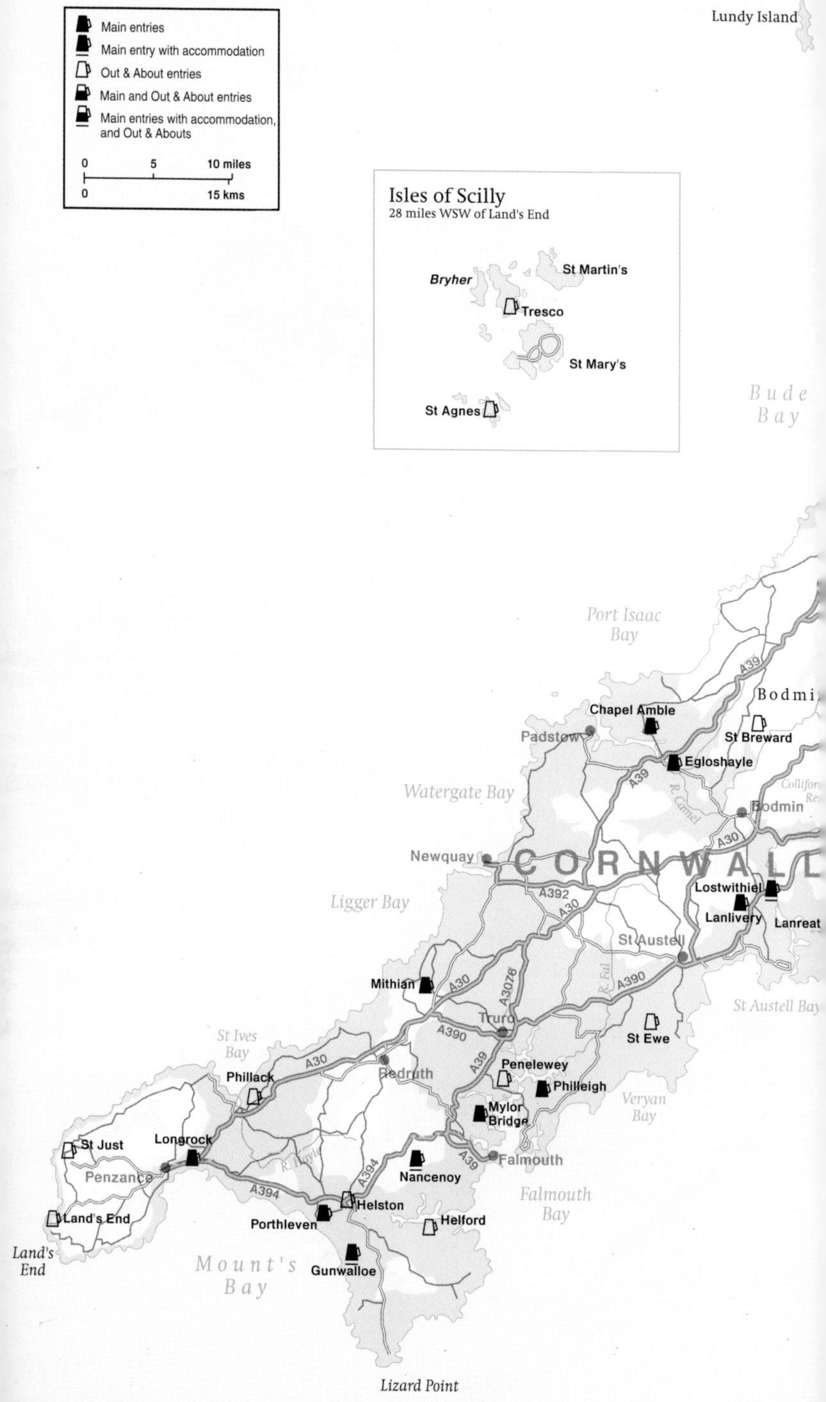

4

Main entries
Main entry with accommodation
Out & About entries
Main and Out & About entries
Main entries with accommodation, and Out & Abouts

0 5 10 miles
0 15 kms

Lundy Island

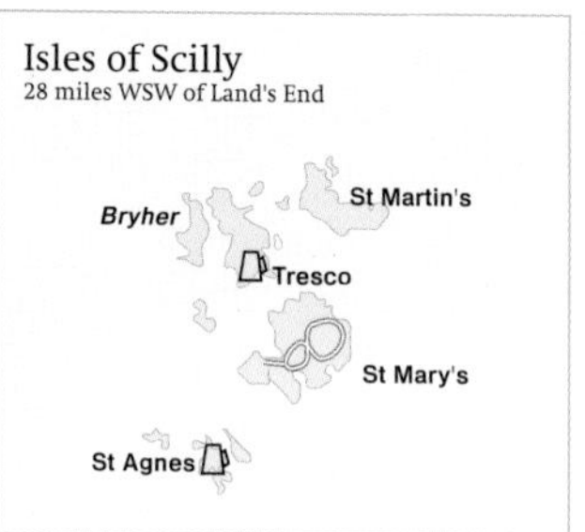

Bude Bay
Port Isaac Bay
Bodmin
Chapel Amble
Padstow
St Breward
Egloshayle
A39
Watergate Bay
R. Camel
Colliford Res.
Bodmin
A30
Newquay
CORNWALL
A392
Lostwithiel
Lanlivery
Lanreath
Ligger Bay
A30
St Austell
A3076
R. Fal
A390
Mithian
A30
St Austell Bay
Truro
St Ewe
St Ives Bay
A390
A30
Redruth
A39
Penelewey
Phillack
Philleigh
Veryan Bay
Mylor Bridge
St Just
Longrock
R. Hayle
A394
A39
Falmouth
Penzance
Nancenoy
A394
Falmouth Bay
Helston
Land's End
Porthleven
Helford
Land's End
Mount's Bay
Gunwalloe
Lizard Point

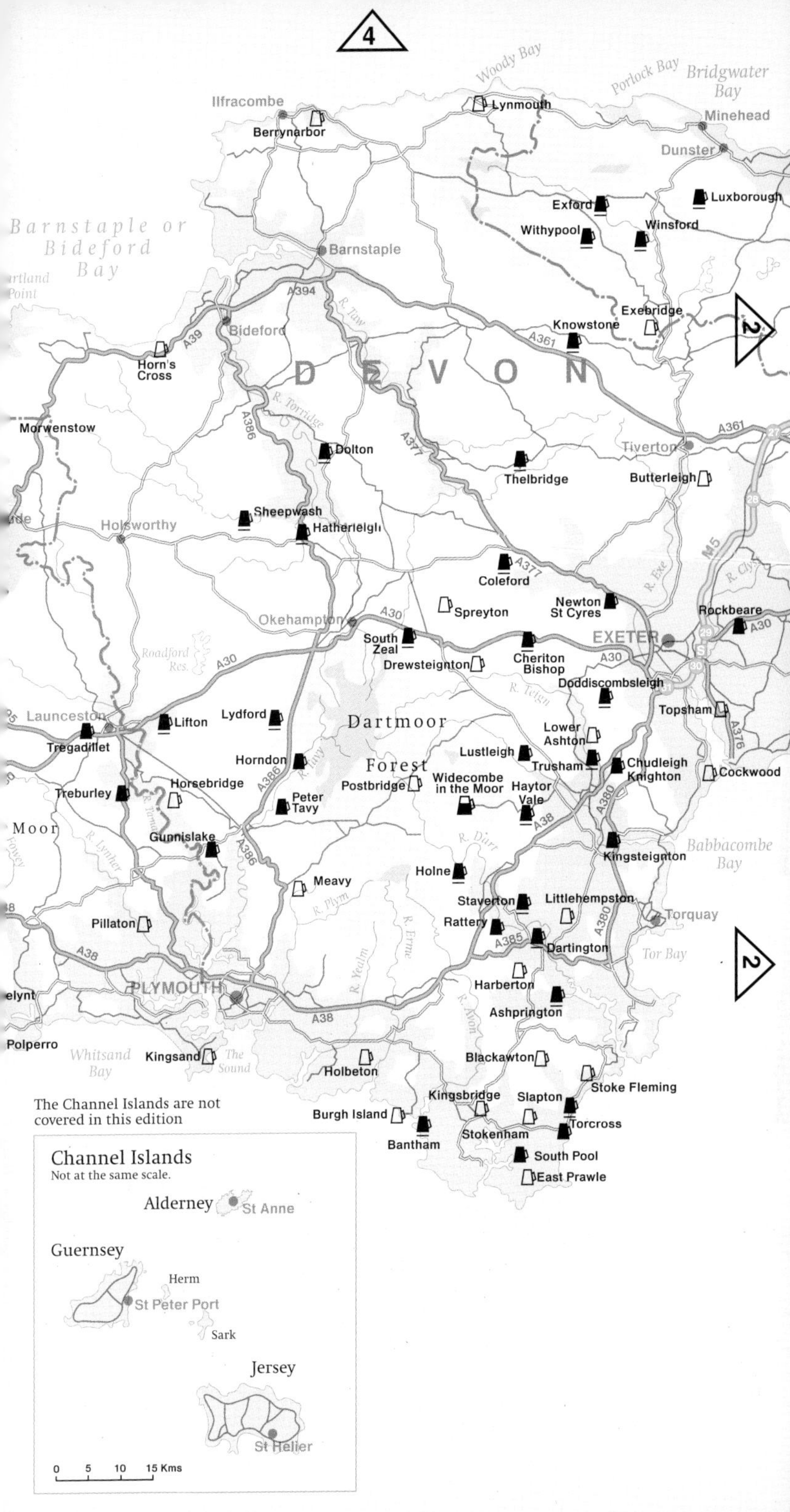
4
Woody Bay
Porlock Bay
Bridgwater Bay
Ilfracombe
Lynmouth
Minehead
Berrynarbor
Dunster
Luxborough
Exford
Winsford
Withypool
Barnstaple or Bideford Bay
Barnstaple
Hartland Point
A394
R. Taw
Exebridge
Knowstone
2
Bideford
A39
A361
Horn's Cross
DEVON
R. Torridge
A386
A377
Morwenstow
Dolton
Tiverton
A361
Thelbridge
Butterleigh
Sheepwash
Holsworthy
Hatherleigh
M5
R. Exe
Coleford
A377
Newton St Cyres
Spreyton
Rockbeare
Okehampton
A30
EXETER
A30
South Zeal
Cheriton Bishop
Roadford Res.
A30
Drewsteignton
A30
R. Teign
Doddiscombsleigh
Launceston
Lydford
Lifton
Dartmoor
Topsham
Tregadillet
Lower Ashton
Lustleigh
Horndon
Forest
Trusham
Chudleigh Knighton
Cockwood
Horsebridge
Treburley
R. Tavy
Postbridge
Widecombe in the Moor
Haytor Vale
Peter Tavy
A386
A380
A38
A376
Moor
R. Dart
Kingsteignton
Babbacombe Bay
Gunnislake
R. Lynher
A386
Holne
Meavy
R. Plym
Staverton
Littlehempston
Torquay
Pillaton
Rattery
R. Erme
A385
Dartington
A380
Tor Bay
2
A38
R. Yealm
Harberton
PLYMOUTH
Ashprington
R. Avon
A38
Polperro
Whitsand Bay
Kingsand
The Sound
Holbeton
Blackawton
Stoke Fleming
The Channel Islands are not covered in this edition
Kingsbridge
Slapton
Burgh Island
Torcross
Bantham
Stokenham
South Pool
East Prawle
Channel Islands
Not at the same scale.
Alderney
St Anne
Guernsey
Herm
St Peter Port
Sark
Jersey
St Helier
0 5 10 15 Kms

Main entries
Main entry with accommodation
Out & About entries
Main and Out & About entries
Main entries with accommodation, and Out & Abouts
0 5 10 miles
0 15 kms
GLOUCESTERSHIRE
MONMOUTHSHIRE
CAERPHILLY
TORFAEN
BLAENAU GWENT
NEWPORT
CARDIFF
VALE OF GLAMORGAN
SOUTH GLOUCESTERSHIRE
BRISTOL
N.W. SOMERSET
BATH & N.E. SOMERSET
SOMERSET
DORSET
Cotswolds
Mouth of the Severn
Mendip Hills
N. Dorset Downs
Bridgwater Bay
Lyme Bay
Babbacombe Bay
Weymouth Bay
Bill of Portland
Crickhowell
Llangattock
Llanvapley
Abergavenny
Ebbw Vale
Merthyr Tydfil
Clytha
Penallt
Newland
Awre
Sheepscombe
Clearwell
Trellech
Llangybi
Cwmbran
Shirenewton
South Woodchester
Minchinhampton
North Nibley
Oldbury-on-Severn
Creigiau
New Severn Crossing
Almondsbury
Portishead
Ford
East Aberthaw
Stanton Wick
Midford
Freshford
Holt
Weston-super-Mare
Churchill
Combe Hay
Compton Martin
Norton St Philip
Cheddar
Beckington
Burnham-on-Sea
Westbury-sub-Mendip
Mells
Buckland Dinham
Frome
Worth
West Huntspill
Kilve
Croscombe
Nunney
East Woodlands
Cranmore
Trudoxhill
Monksilver
Stogumber
Glastonbury
Batcombe
Bridgwater
Langley Marsh
Bourton
Fitzhead
Taunton
East Lyng
Woodhill
Peacemarsh
Knapp
Bradford-on-Tone
West Camel
Appley
Over Stratton
Staple Fitzpaine
Montacute
Yeovil
North Wootton
Churchinford
Haselbury Plucknett
Wambrook
Chard
Broadhembury
Stockland
Corscombe
Chedington
Blandford Forum
Weston
Honiton
Dalwood
Cerne Abbas
Plush
Milton Abbas
Shave Cross
Powerstock
Loders
Nettlecombe
Godmanstone
Askerswell
Beer
Branscombe
Dorchester
West Bexington
Abbotsbury
Langton Herring
Weymouth

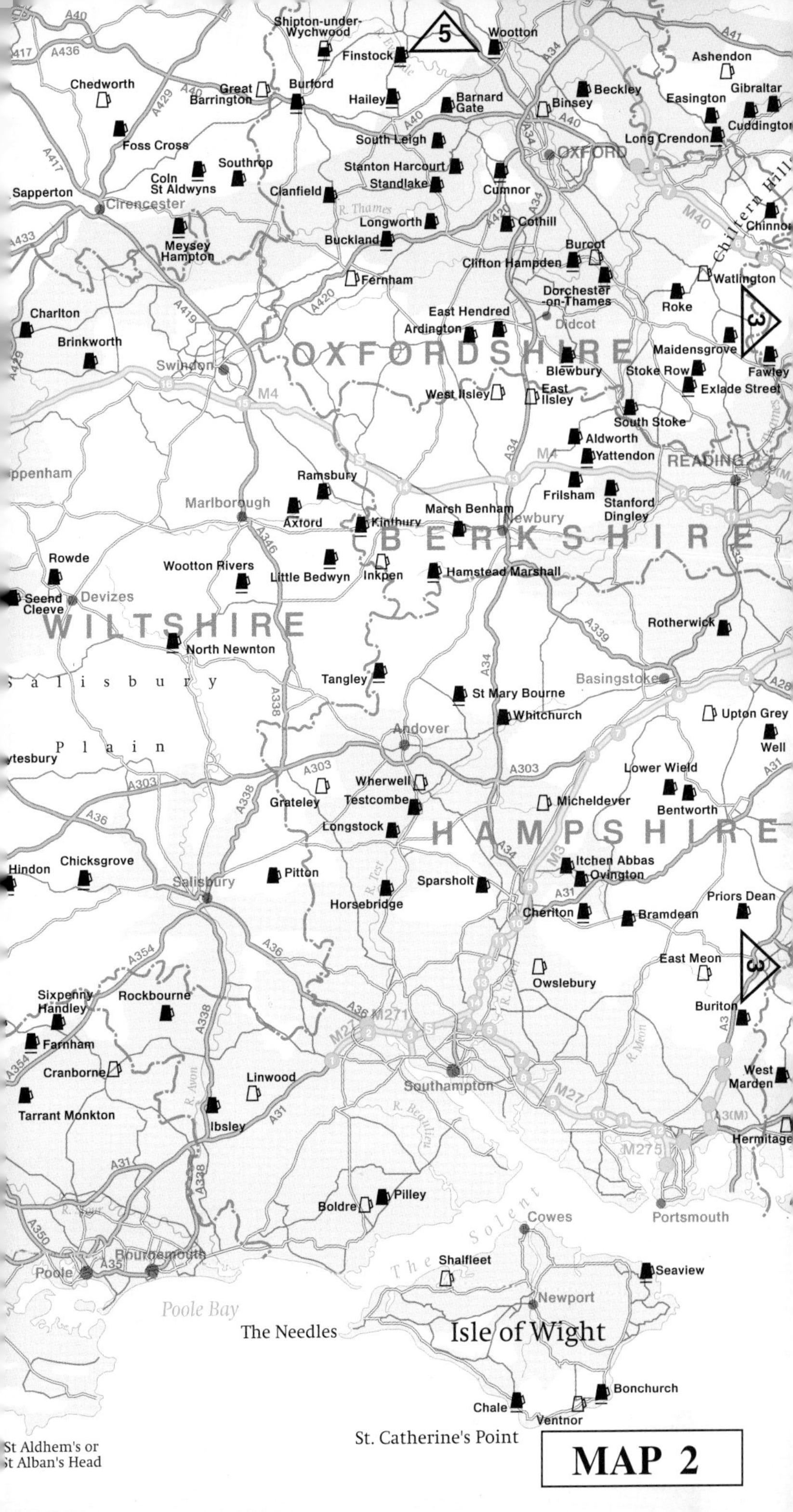

Shipton-under-Wychwood
Finstock
5
Wootton
Ashendon
Chedworth
Great Barrington
Burford
Hailey
Barnard Gate
Beckley
Binsey
Easington
Gibraltar
Cuddington
Foss Cross
South Leigh
Long Crendon
OXFORD
Southrop
Coln St Aldwyns
Stanton Harcourt
Standlake
Clanfield
Cumnor
Sapperton
Cirencester
R. Thames
Longworth
Cothill
Chiltern Hills
Chinnor
Meysey Hampton
Buckland
Burcot
Clifton Hampden
Watlington
Fernham
Dorchester-on-Thames
Roke
Charlton
East Hendred
Ardington
Didcot
3
Brinkworth
OXFORDSHIRE
Maidensgrove
Blewbury
Stoke Row
Fawley
Swindon
Exlade Street
West Ilsley
East Ilsley
M4
South Stoke
Aldworth
Yattendon
READING
Ramsbury
Frilsham
Stanford Dingley
Marlborough
Marsh Benham
Newbury
Axford
Kintbury
BERKSHIRE
Rowde
Wootton Rivers
Little Bedwyn
Inkpen
Hamstead Marshall
Seend Cleeve
Devizes
WILTSHIRE
Rotherwick
North Newnton
Salisbury
Plain
Tangley
Basingstoke
St Mary Bourne
Whitchurch
Upton Grey
Andover
Well
A303
Lower Wield
Wherwell
Grateley
Testcombe
Micheldever
Bentworth
Longstock
HAMPSHIRE
Itchen Abbas
Ovington
Chicksgrove
Hindon
Pitton
Salisbury
Sparsholt
Horsebridge
Cheriton
Bramdean
Priors Dean
East Meon
Owslebury
Sixpenny Handley
Rockbourne
Buriton
Farnham
Cranborne
Linwood
Southampton
West Marden
Tarrant Monkton
Ibsley
Hermitage
Pilley
Boldre
Cowes
Portsmouth
The Solent
Shalfleet
Seaview
Poole
Bournemouth
Newport
Poole Bay
The Needles
Isle of Wight
Bonchurch
Chale
Ventnor
St. Catherine's Point
St Aldhem's or St Alban's Head
MAP 2

6
2
Arkesden
Cottered
Clavering
Rickling Green
Ardeley
Great Offley
Little Hadham
LUTON
Stevenage
A120
Waddesdon
Slapton
Knebworth
Watton-at-Stone
Ayot St Lawrence
Marsworth
Aylesbury
Aldbury
Weston Turville
HERTFORDSHIRE
Hertford Heath
Ford
Swan Bottom
St Albans
A414
Great Kimble
Great Hampden
Hawridge Common
Norton Heath
Bledlow
Ballinger Common
Tyttenhanger
Little Hampden
Ley Hill
Toot Hill
Speen
Bellingdon
Prestwood
Chesham
M25
Great Kingshill
Chenies
West Wycombe
High Wycombe
Amersham
Watford
Turville
Coleshill
Fingest
Bolter End
Forty Green
Beaconsfield
Freith
BUCKINGHAM-
Skirmett
Wooburn Common
Cookham Dean
Hambleden
GREATER
Cookham
SHIRE
Hurley
Henley-
Crazies Hill
Bray
Maidenhead
SLOUGH
Thames
Knowl Hill
Holyport
LONDON
Windsor
BERK-
SHIRE
M3
A322
Windlesham
Weybridge
Eynsford
M26
Martyr's Green
Ightham
HAMP-
SURREY
Stone Street
Mickleham
Sevenoaks
SHIRE
Aldershot
Effingham
Betchworth
Bletchingley
Guildford
Brockham
Reigate
Crondall
Shere
Reigate Heath
Chiddingstone Causeway
Well
Compton
Shamley Green
South Godstone
Blackbrook
Chiddingstone
Elstead
Coldharbour
Godalming
Smart's Hill
Speldhurst
Hascombe
Langton Green
East Grinstead
Fordcombe
Royal Tunbridge Wells
Oakwood Hill
Chiddingfold
Dunsfold
Crawley
Hartfield
Withyham
Horsham
Kirdford
Lower Beeding
Ardingly Res.
Danehill
Lickfold
WEST
Mayfield
A272
EAST
Halfway Bridge
Easebourne
Fletching
Old Heathfield
Stedham
Byworth
Blackboys
Elsted Marsh
Stopham
Wineham
Shortbridge
Tillington
West Chiltington
Elsted
Duncton
Henfield
SUSSEX
Warbleton
SUSSEX
Cowbeech
South Downs
Chilgrove
Ditchling
West Marden
Offham
Chiddingly
Lewes
Steyning
Ringmer
Stoughton
Burpham
Alciston
Kingston near Lewes
Firle
Arlington
Berwick
Hermitage
BRIGHTON
Chichester
Oving
Milton Street
Worthing
Eastbourne
East Dean

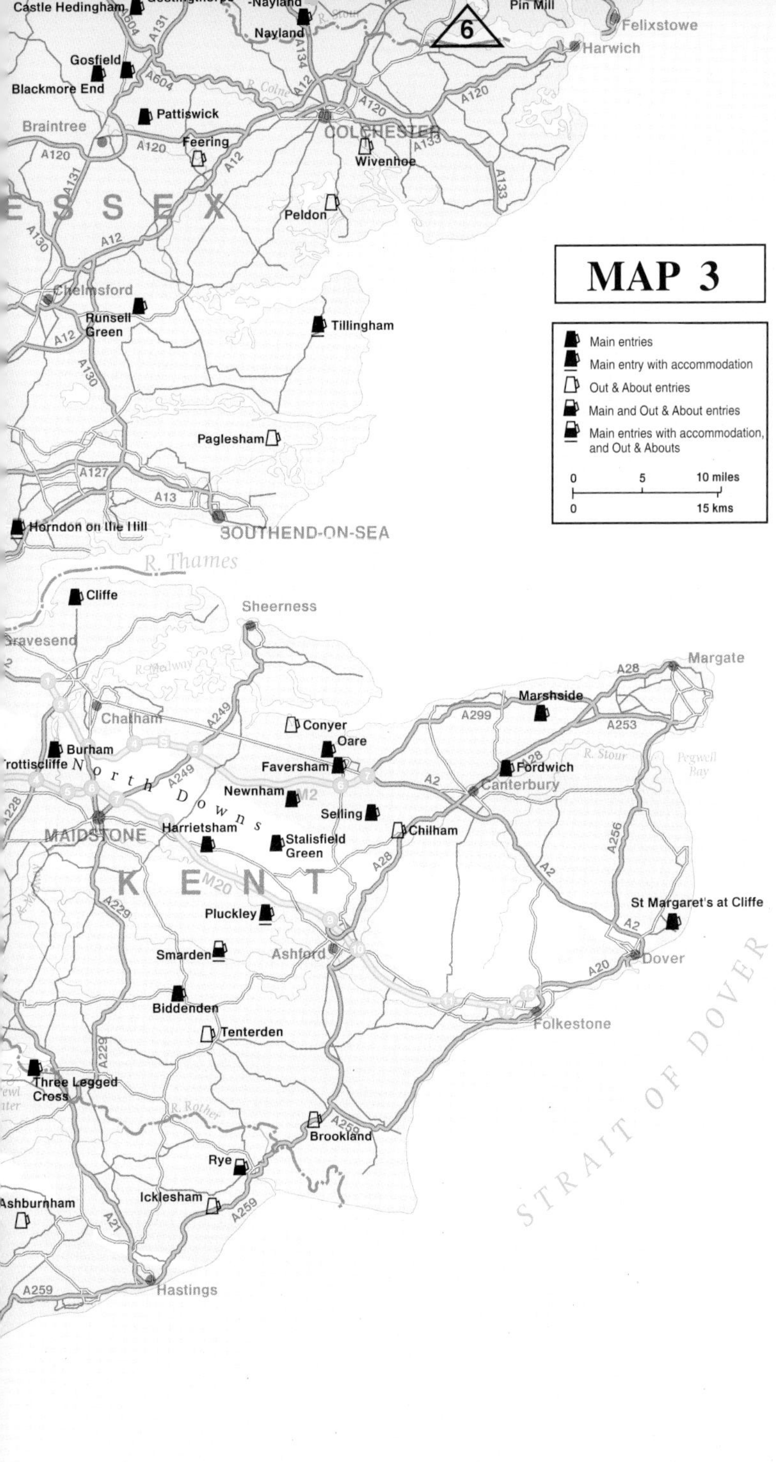
MAP 3
Main entries
Main entry with accommodation
Out & About entries
Main and Out & About entries
Main entries with accommodation, and Out & Abouts
0
5
10 miles
0
15 kms
6
Castle Hedingham
Nayland
Pin Mill
Felixstowe
Harwich
Gosfield
Blackmore End
Pattiswick
Braintree
Feering
COLCHESTER
Wivenhoe
ESSEX
Peldon
Chelmsford
Runsell Green
Tillingham
Paglesham
Horndon on the Hill
SOUTHEND-ON-SEA
R. Thames
Cliffe
Sheerness
Gravesend
Margate
Marshside
Chatham
Conyer
Oare
Burham
Trottiscliffe
North Downs
Faversham
Fordwich
Canterbury
Pegwell Bay
R. Stour
Newnham
Selling
Chilham
MAIDSTONE
Harrietsham
Stalisfield Green
KENT
Pluckley
St Margaret's at Cliffe
Smarden
Ashford
Dover
Biddenden
Folkestone
Tenterden
Three Legged Cross
R. Rother
Brookland
Rye
Icklesham
Ashburnham
Hastings
STRAIT OF DOVER
A120
A12
A131
A604
A134
A133
A130
A127
A13
A249
A229
A228
A28
A299
A253
A2
A256
A20
A259
A21
M2
M20

MAP 4

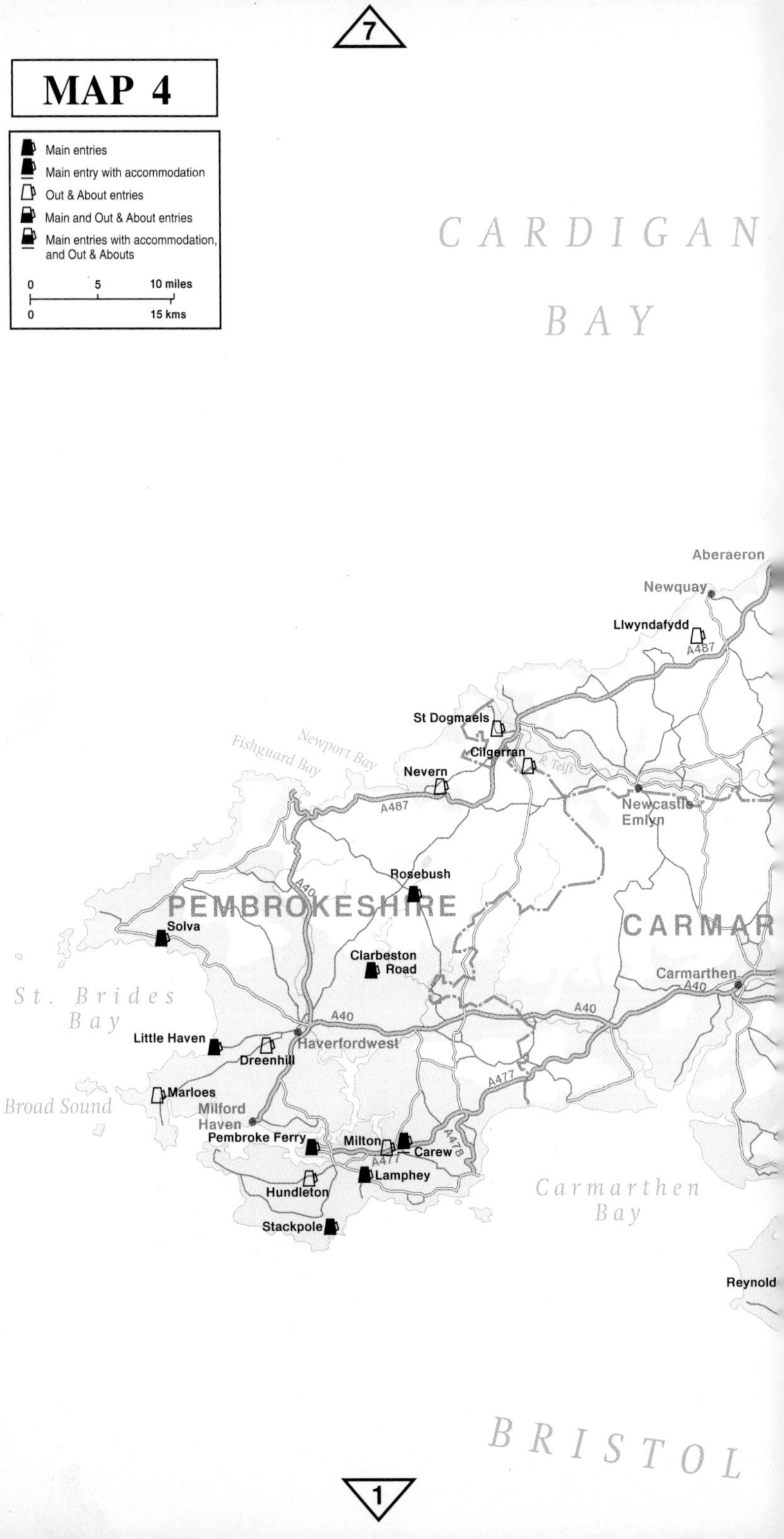

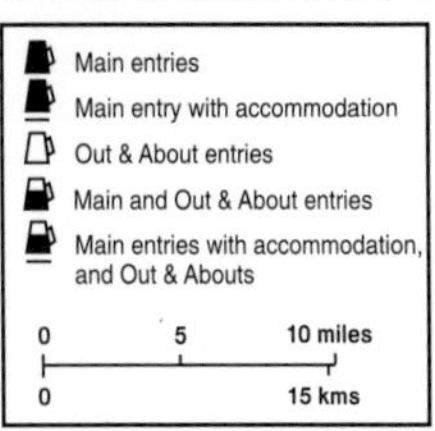

CARDIGAN BAY

Aberaeron
Newquay
Llwyndafydd
A487
St Dogmaels
Cilgerran
R. Teifi
Newport Bay
Fishguard Bay
Nevern
A487
Newcastle Emlyn
Rosebush
A40
PEMBROKESHIRE
CARMAR
Solva
Clarbeston Road
Carmarthen
A40
St. Brides Bay
A40
A40
Little Haven
Dreenhill
Haverfordwest
A477
Marloes
Broad Sound
Milford Haven
Pembroke Ferry
Milton
Carew
A478
A477
Lamphey
Hundleton
Stackpole
Carmarthen Bay
Reynold

BRISTOL

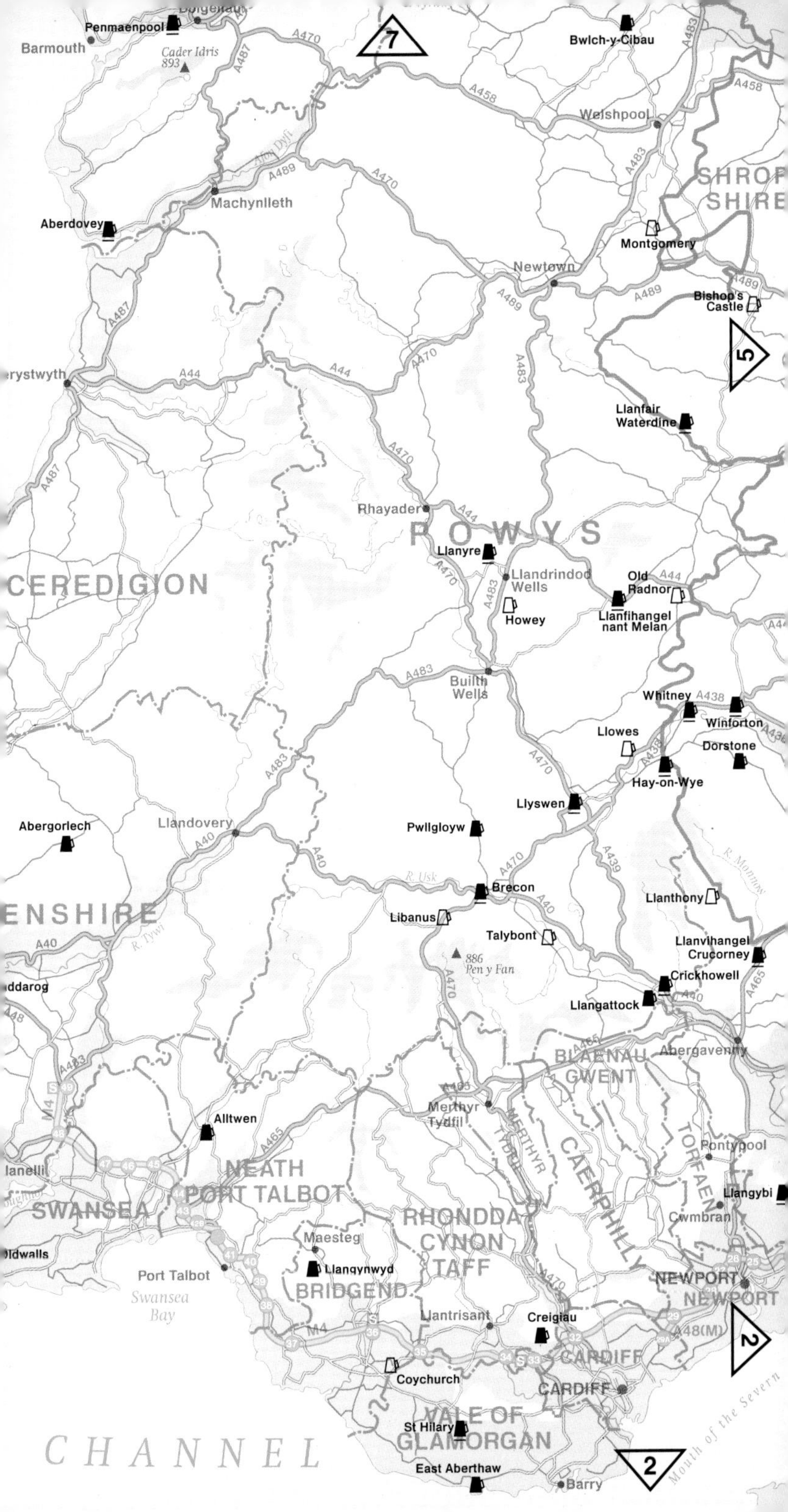
Penmaenpool
Barmouth
Cader Idris
893
A470
7
Bwlch-y-Cibau
A483
A487
A458
Welshpool
Afon Dyfi
A489
A470
SHROPSHIRE
Machynlleth
Aberdovey
Montgomery
Newtown
A489
Bishop's Castle
A487
A489
5
A44
A44
A470
A483
Llanfair Waterdine
A470
A487
Rhayader
A44
POWYS
Llanyre
CEREDIGION
Llandrindod Wells
Old Radnor
A44
A470
A483
Howey
Llanfihangel nant Melan
A483
Builth Wells
Whitney
A438
Winforton
Llowes
Dorstone
A483
A470
Hay-on-Wye
Llyswen
Abergorlech
Llandovery
Pwllgloyw
A40
A40
A470
A439
R. Usk
Brecon
R. Monnow
Llanthony
ENSHIRE
Libanus
A40
A40
R. Tywi
Talybont
Llanvihangel Crucorney
886
Pen y Fan
A470
Crickhowell
A465
Llangattock
A40
A465
BLAENAU GWENT
Abergavenny
A483
M4
Merthyr Tydfil
Alltwen
MERTHYR TYDFIL
A465
CAERPHILLY
TORFAEN
Pontypool
NEATH PORT TALBOT
Llangybi
SWANSEA
RHONDDA CYNON TAFF
Cwmbran
Maesteg
Llangynwyd
NEWPORT
NEWPORT
Port Talbot
A470
Swansea Bay
BRIDGEND
Llantrisant
Creigiau
M4
A48(M)
2
CARDIFF
Coychurch
CARDIFF
VALE OF GLAMORGAN
St Hilary
CHANNEL
East Aberthaw
2
Barry
Mouth of the Severn

MAP 5
WREXHAM
STAFFORDSHIRE
SHROPSHIRE
POWYS
HEREFORD AND WORCESTER
GLOUCESTERSHIRE
MONMOUTHSHIRE
Marford
Gresford
Wrexham
Higher Burwardsley
Cholmondeley
Crewe
Shraleybrook
Newcastle-under-Lyme
STOKE-ON-TRENT
Erbistock
Oswestry
Llanyblodwel
Llanymynech
Nesscliffe
Gnosall
Stafford
Shrewsbury
TELFORD
Welshpool
Much Wenlock
Norton
WOLVERHAMPTON
Montgomery
Wentnor
Hilltop
Cardington
Brockton
Bridgnorth
Little Stretton
Bishop's Castle
Munslow
Wistanstow
Corfton
Broome
Hopton Wafers
Llanfair Waterdine
Kidderminster
Bewdley
Boraston
Menithwood
Brimfield
Ombersley
Aymestrey
Shobdon
Yarpole
Kimbolton
Old Radnor
Pembridge
Leominster
Llanfihangel nant Melan
Inkberrow
Little Cowarne
Knightwick
Worcester
Weobley
Whitney
Winforton
Wyre Piddle
Lugwardine
Hay-on-Wye
Dorstone
Hereford
Berrow
Woolhope
Fownhope
Tewkesbury
Carey
Llanthony
Sellack
Upton Bishop
Playley Green
Ashleworth
Apperley
Aston Crews
Llanvihangel Crucorney
Crickhowell
Llangattock
Gloucester
Cheltenham
Minsterworth
Llanvapley
Monmouth
Clytha
Penallt
Newland
Awre
Sheepscombe
Stroud
R. Severn
R. Wye
R. Monnow
R. Dee

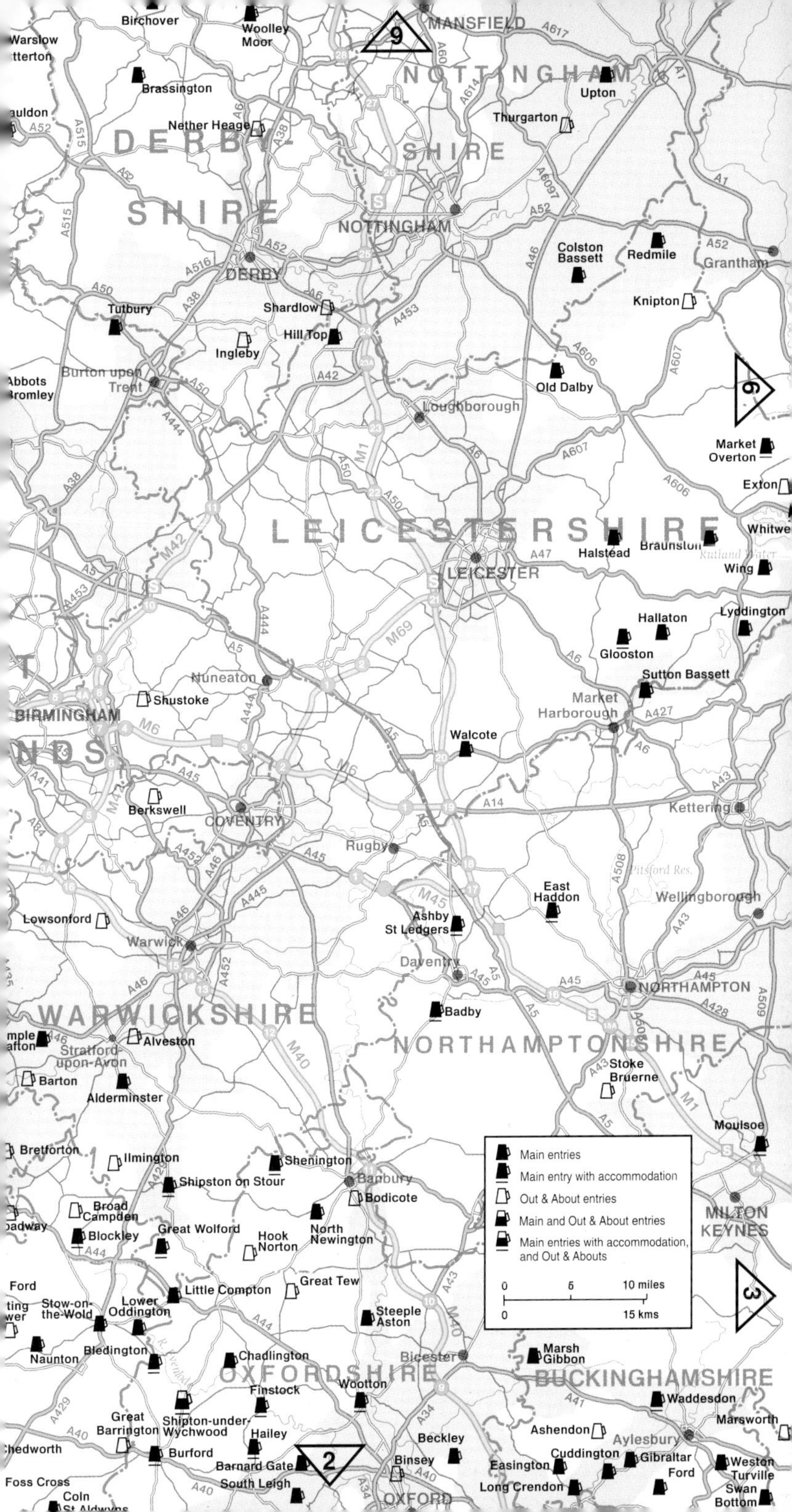

Main entries
Main entry with accommodation
Out & About entries
Main and Out & About entries
Main entries with accommodation, and Out & Abouts
0 5 10 miles
0 15 kms

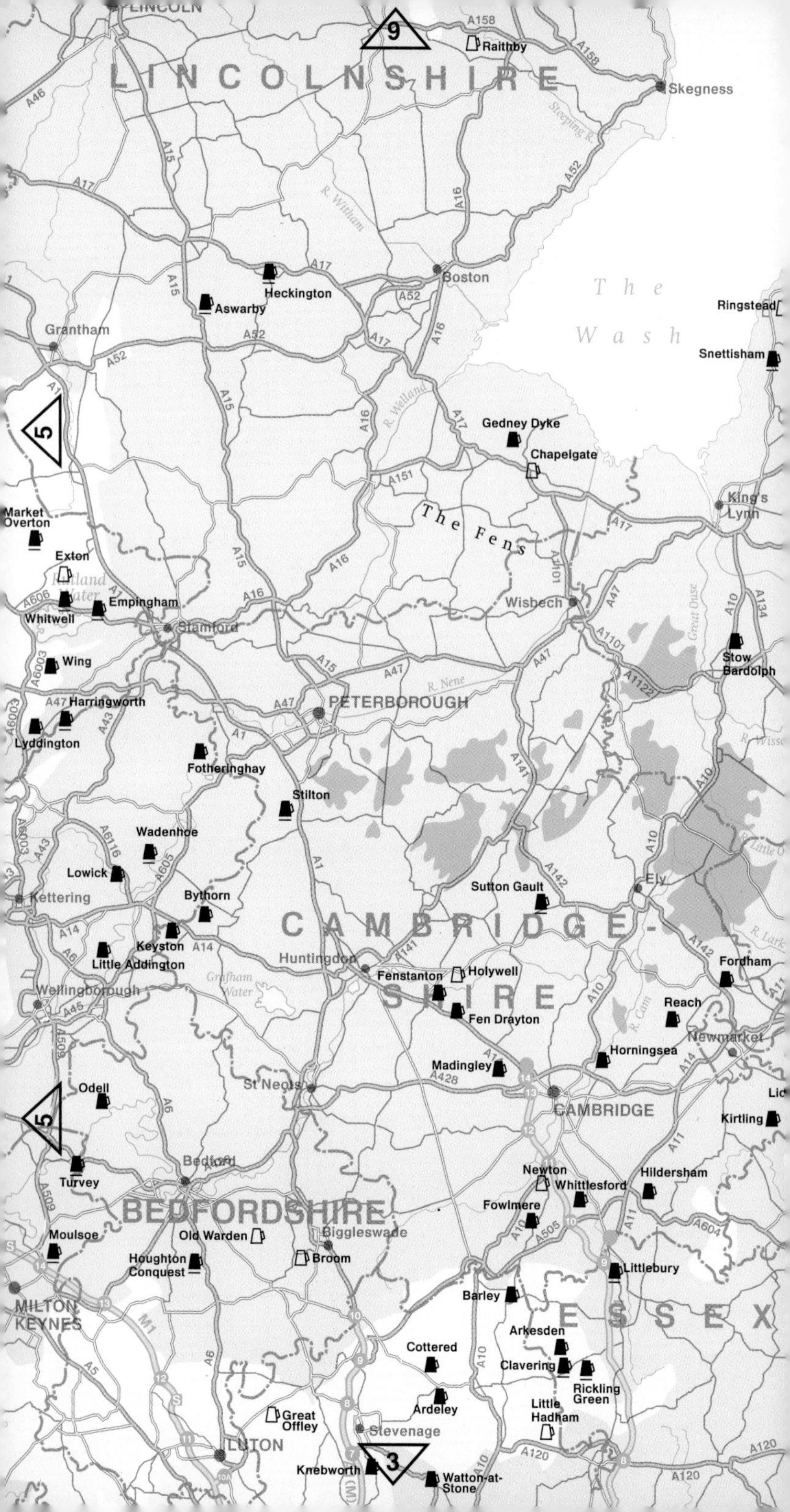

LINCOLN
9
Raithby
LINCOLNSHIRE
Skegness
Steeping R.
R. Witham
Heckington
Boston
Aswarby
The Wash
Ringstead
Snettisham
Grantham
5
Gedney Dyke
Chapelgate
King's Lynn
The Fens
Market Overton
Exton
Rutland Water
Empingham
Whitwell
Stamford
Wisbech
Great Ouse
Wing
Stow Bardolph
Harringworth
PETERBOROUGH
R. Nene
Lyddington
Fotheringhay
Stilton
Wadenhoe
Lowick
Bythorn
Kettering
Sutton Gault
Ely
R. Lark
Keyston
Little Addington
CAMBRIDGESHIRE
Huntingdon
Fenstanton
Holywell
Fen Drayton
Fordham
Grafham Water
Wellingborough
Reach
R. Cam
Newmarket
Horningsea
Madingley
St Neots
CAMBRIDGE
Odell
Kirtling
5
Turvey
Bedford
Newton
Whittlesford
Hildersham
BEDFORDSHIRE
Fowlmere
Moulsoe
Old Warden
Biggleswade
Houghton Conquest
Broom
Littlebury
Barley
MILTON KEYNES
ESSEX
Arkesden
Cottered
Clavering
Rickling Green
Ardeley
Little Hadham
Great Offley
Stevenage
LUTON
Knebworth
3
Watton-at-Stone

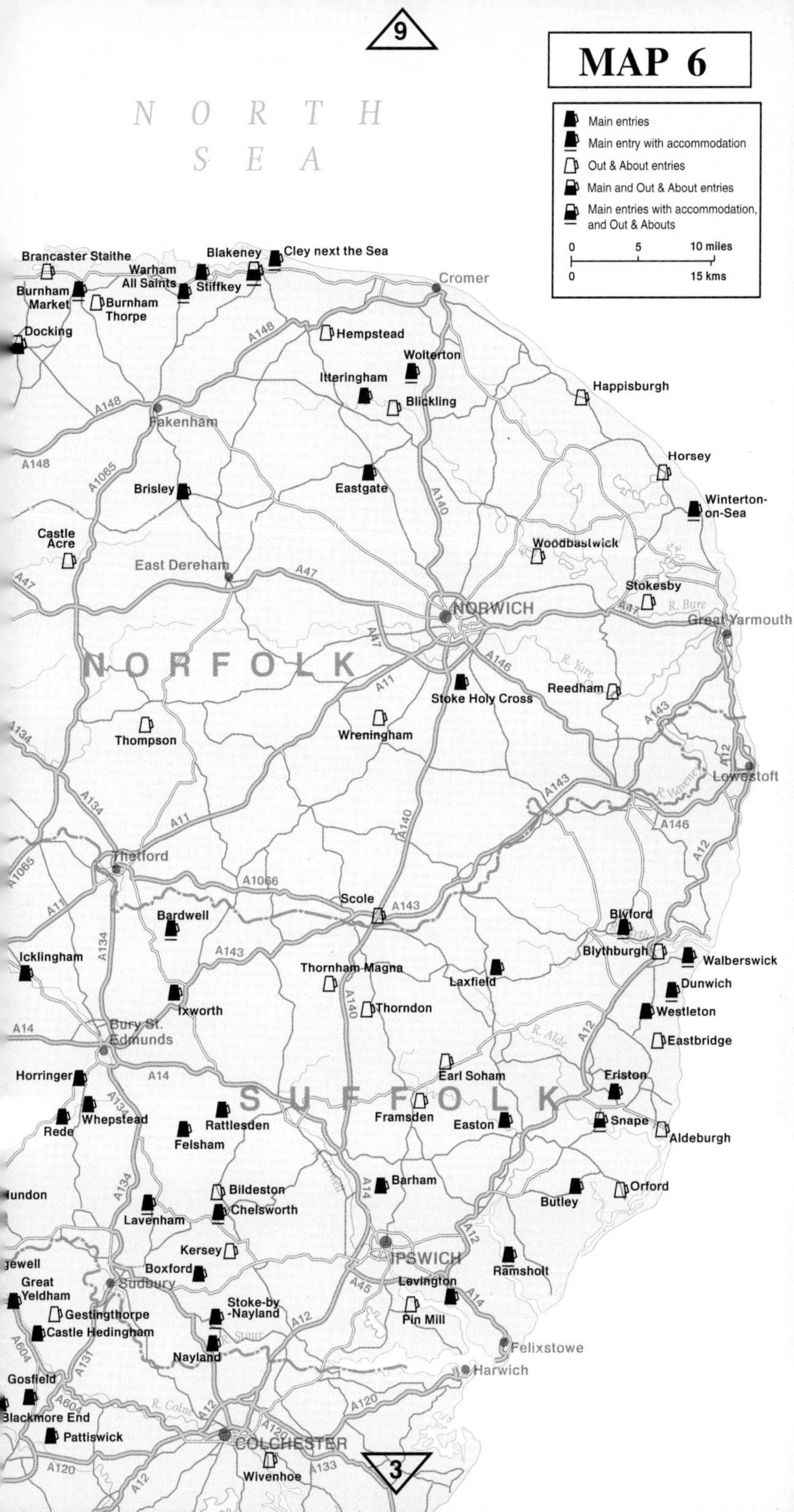

9
MAP 6
Main entries
Main entry with accommodation
Out & About entries
Main and Out & About entries
Main entries with accommodation, and Out & Abouts
0 5 10 miles
0 15 kms
NORTH SEA
Brancaster Staithe
Blakeney
Cley next the Sea
Warham All Saints
Stiffkey
Burnham Market
Burnham Thorpe
Cromer
Docking
Hempstead
Wolterton
Itteringham
Blickling
Happisburgh
Fakenham
Horsey
Brisley
Eastgate
Winterton-on-Sea
Castle Acre
Woodbastwick
East Dereham
Stokesby
NORWICH
Great Yarmouth
R. Bure
NORFOLK
R. Yare
Reedham
Stoke Holy Cross
Thompson
Wreningham
Lowestoft
R. Waveney
Thetford
Scole
Bardwell
Blyford
Blythburgh
Walberswick
Icklingham
Thornham Magna
Laxfield
Dunwich
Ixworth
Thorndon
Westleton
Bury St. Edmunds
Eastbridge
R. Alde
Earl Soham
Horringer
Friston
Whepstead
SUFFOLK
Rede
Framsden
Easton
Snape
Aldeburgh
Rattlesden
Felsham
Barham
Butley
Orford
Bildeston
Chelsworth
Lavenham
Kersey
IPSWICH
Ramsholt
Boxford
Great Yeldham
Sudbury
Levington
Gestingthorpe
Stoke-by-Nayland
Pin Mill
Castle Hedingham
R. Stour
Nayland
Felixstowe
Harwich
Gosfield
Blackmore End
R. Colne
Pattiswick
COLCHESTER
Wivenhoe
3
A148
A1065
A47
A140
A11
A146
A143
A12
A134
A1066
A14
A45
A604
A131
A120
A133

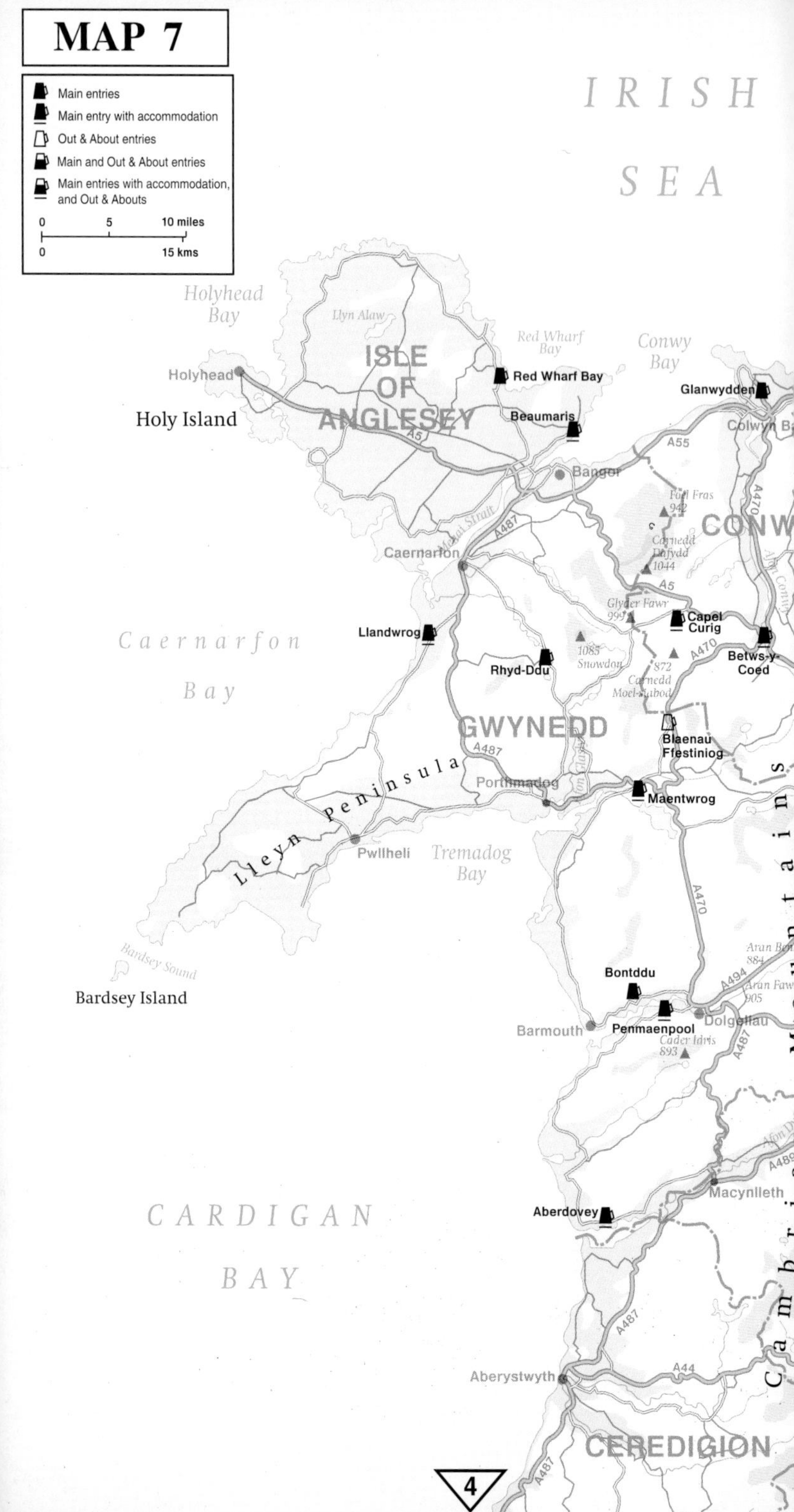

MAP 7
Main entries
Main entry with accommodation
Out & About entries
Main and Out & About entries
Main entries with accommodation, and Out & Abouts
0
5
10 miles
0
15 kms
IRISH
SEA
Holyhead Bay
Llyn Alaw
ISLE OF ANGLESEY
Red Wharf Bay
Conwy Bay
Holyhead
Red Wharf Bay
Glanwydden
Holy Island
Beaumaris
A5
A55
Bangor
Menai Strait
A487
Caernarfon
A5
Glyder Fawr 999
Capel Curig
Llandwrog
Caernarfon
Bay
Rhyd-Ddu
1085 Snowdon
872
A470
Betws-y-Coed
Carnedd Moel-siabod
GWYNEDD
A487
Blaenau Ffestiniog
Lleyn Peninsula
Porthmadog
Maentwrog
Pwllheli
Tremadog Bay
A470
Bardsey Sound
Bardsey Island
Bontddu
A494
Barmouth
Penmaenpool
Dolgellau
Cader Idris 893
A487
A489
Macynlleth
Aberdovey
CARDIGAN
BAY
Cambrian Mountains
A487
A44
Aberystwyth
CEREDIGION
A487
4

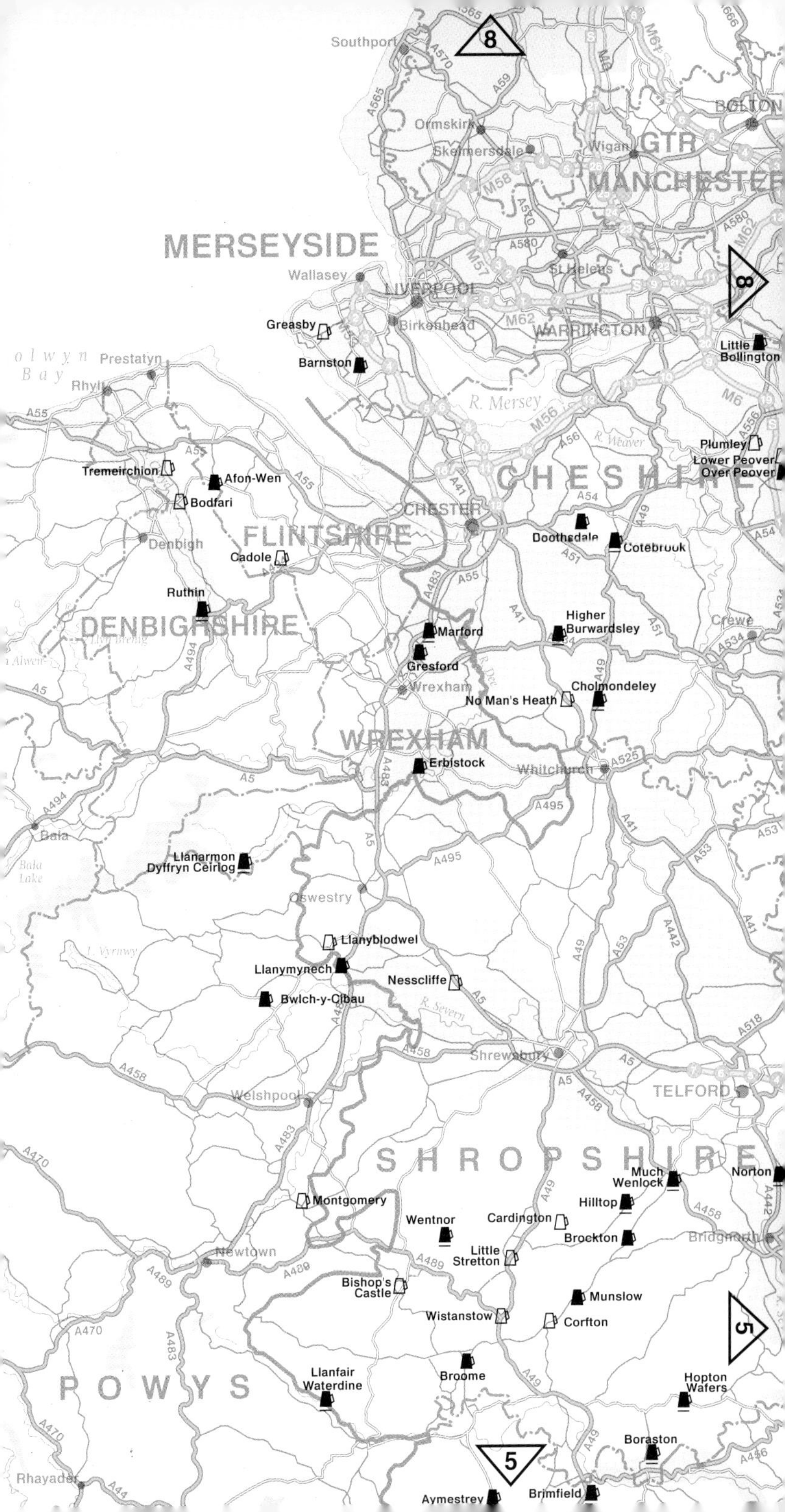

8
Southport
Ormskirk
Skelmersdale
Wigan
GTR MANCHESTER
BOLTON
MERSEYSIDE
Wallasey
LIVERPOOL
Birkenhead
St Helens
WARRINGTON
8
Greasby
Barnston
Little Bollington
Prestatyn
Rhyl
R. Mersey
Plumley
Lower Peover
Over Peover
Tremeirchion
Afon-Wen
Bodfari
CHESHIRE
CHESTER
Denbigh
FLINTSHIRE
Doothsdale
Cotebrook
Cadole
Ruthin
DENBIGHSHIRE
Marford
Higher Burwardsley
Crewe
Gresford
Wrexham
Cholmondeley
No Man's Heath
WREXHAM
Erbistock
Whitchurch
Bala
Bala Lake
Llanarmon Dyffryn Ceirlog
Oswestry
Llanyblodwel
Llanymynech
Nesscliffe
Bwlch-y-Cibau
R. Severn
Shrewsbury
TELFORD
Welshpool
SHROPSHIRE
Much Wenlock
Norton
Hilltop
Montgomery
Wentnor
Cardington
Brockton
Bridgnorth
Little Stretton
Newtown
Bishop's Castle
Munslow
Wistanstow
Corfton
5
Broome
Llanfair Waterdine
POWYS
Hopton Wafers
Boraston
5
Rhayader
Aymestrey
Brimfield

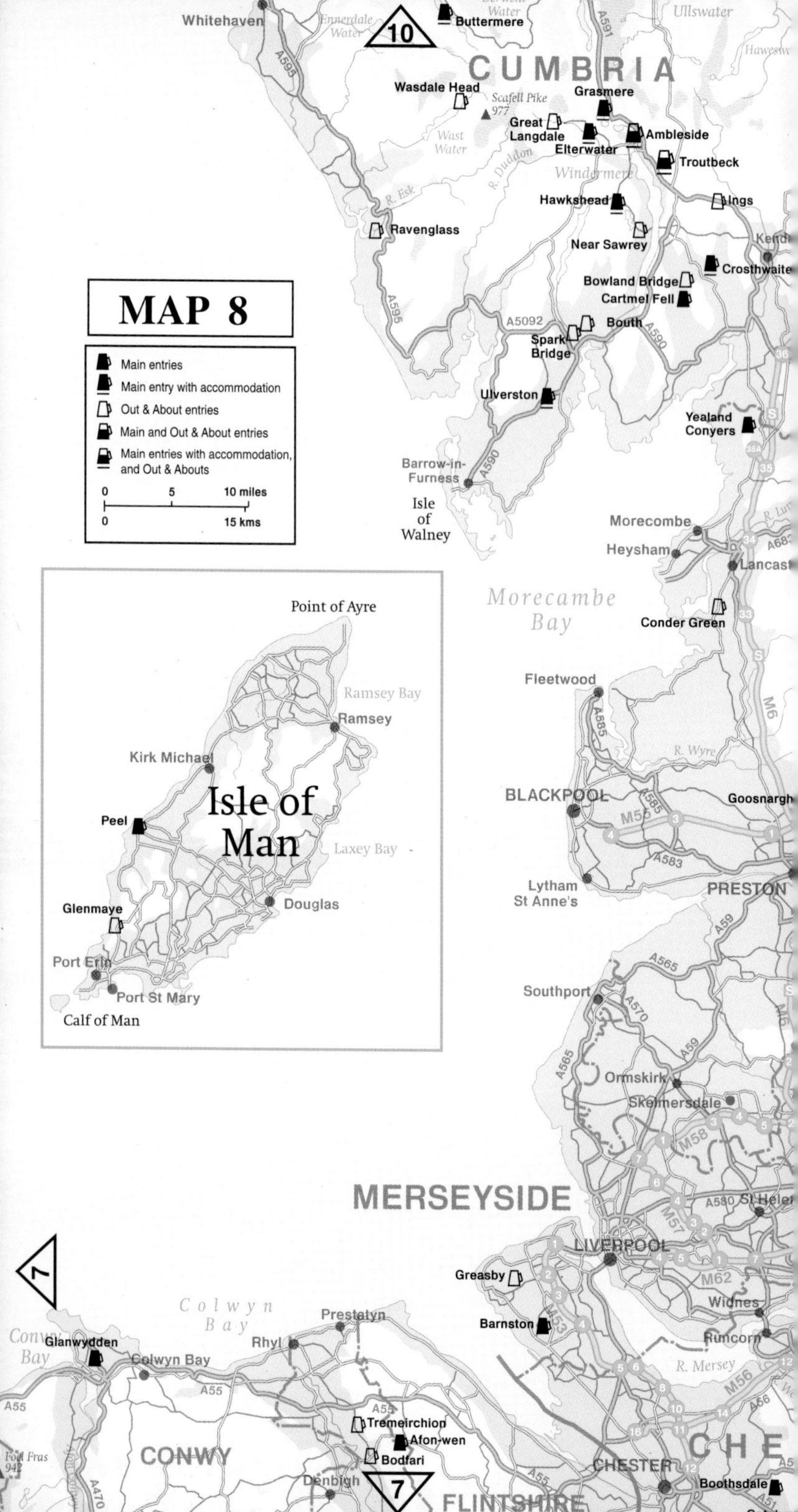

MAP 8
Main entries
Main entry with accommodation
Out & About entries
Main and Out & About entries
Main entries with accommodation, and Out & Abouts
0 5 10 miles
0 15 kms
CUMBRIA
Whitehaven
Buttermere
Ullswater
Wasdale Head
Scafell Pike 977
Grasmere
Great Langdale
Elterwater
Ambleside
Troutbeck
Windermere
Hawkshead
Ings
Ravenglass
Near Sawrey
Crosthwaite
Bowland Bridge
Cartmel Fell
Bouth
Spark Bridge
Ulverston
Yealand Conyers
Barrow-in-Furness
Isle of Walney
Morecambe
Heysham
Morecambe Bay
Conder Green
Fleetwood
BLACKPOOL
Goosnargh
Lytham St Anne's
PRESTON
Southport
Ormskirk
Skelmersdale
MERSEYSIDE
LIVERPOOL
Greasby
Barnston
Widnes
Runcorn
R. Mersey
Colwyn Bay
Conwy Bay
Glanwydden
Prestatyn
Rhyl
Tremeirchion
Afon-wen
Bodfari
CONWY
Denbigh
FLINTSHIRE
CHESTER
Boothsdale
Isle of Man
Point of Ayre
Ramsey Bay
Ramsey
Kirk Michael
Peel
Laxey Bay
Douglas
Glenmaye
Port Erin
Port St Mary
Calf of Man

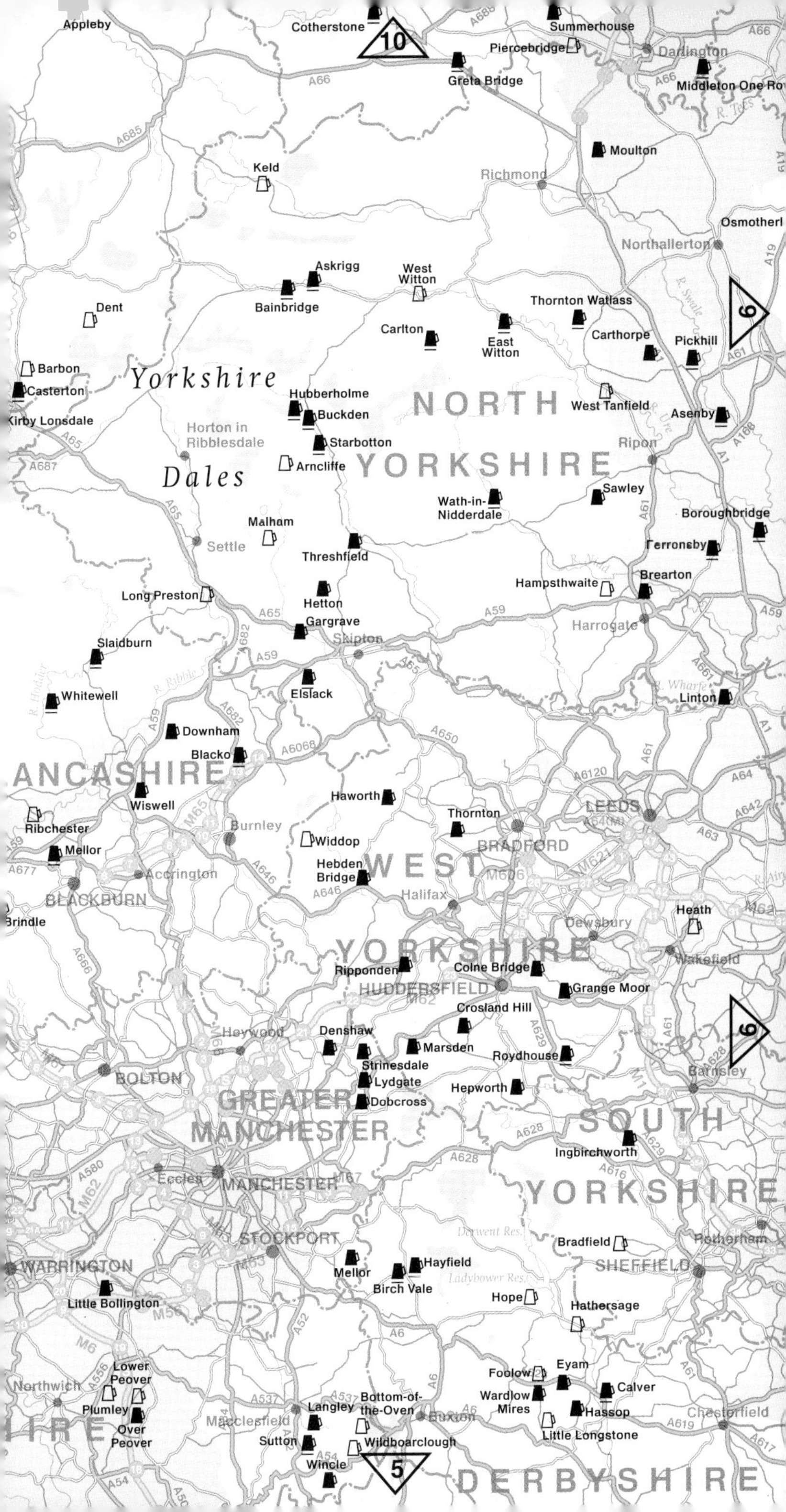
Appleby
Cotherstone
10
Summerhouse
Piercebridge
Darlington
Greta Bridge
Middleton One Row
Keld
Moulton
Richmond
Osmotherley
Northallerton
Askrigg
West Witton
Bainbridge
Dent
Thornton Watlass
Carlton
East Witton
Carthorpe
Pickhill
6
Barbon
Casterton
Kirby Lonsdale
Yorkshire
Hubberholme
Buckden
Starbotton
NORTH
YORKSHIRE
West Tanfield
Asenby
Ripon
Horton in Ribblesdale
Dales
Arncliffe
Wath-in-Nidderdale
Sawley
Malham
Boroughbridge
Settle
Threshfield
Ferrensby
Brearton
Hampsthwaite
Long Preston
Hetton
Gargrave
Harrogate
Skipton
Slaidburn
Whitewell
Elslack
Linton
Downham
Blacko
ANCASHIRE
Wiswell
Haworth
Ribchester
Thornton
LEEDS
Burnley
Widdop
BRADFORD
Mellor
Hebden Bridge
WEST
Accrington
BLACKBURN
Halifax
Brindle
Heath
Dewsbury
YORKSHIRE
Wakefield
Ripponden
Colne Bridge
HUDDERSFIELD
Grange Moor
Crosland Hill
Heywood
Denshaw
Marsden
Roydhouse
6
BOLTON
Strinesdale
Lydgate
Barnsley
GREATER
Hepworth
Dobcross
MANCHESTER
SOUTH
Ingbirchworth
Eccles
MANCHESTER
YORKSHIRE
STOCKPORT
Bradfield
Rotherham
WARRINGTON
Mellor
Hayfield
SHEFFIELD
Birch Vale
Little Bollington
Hope
Hathersage
Lower Peover
Eyam
Foolow
Northwich
Wardlow Mires
Calver
Plumley
Langley
Bottom-of-the-Oven
Hassop
Over Peover
Macclesfield
Buxton
Chesterfield
Sutton
Wildboarclough
Little Longstone
Wincle
5
DERBYSHIRE

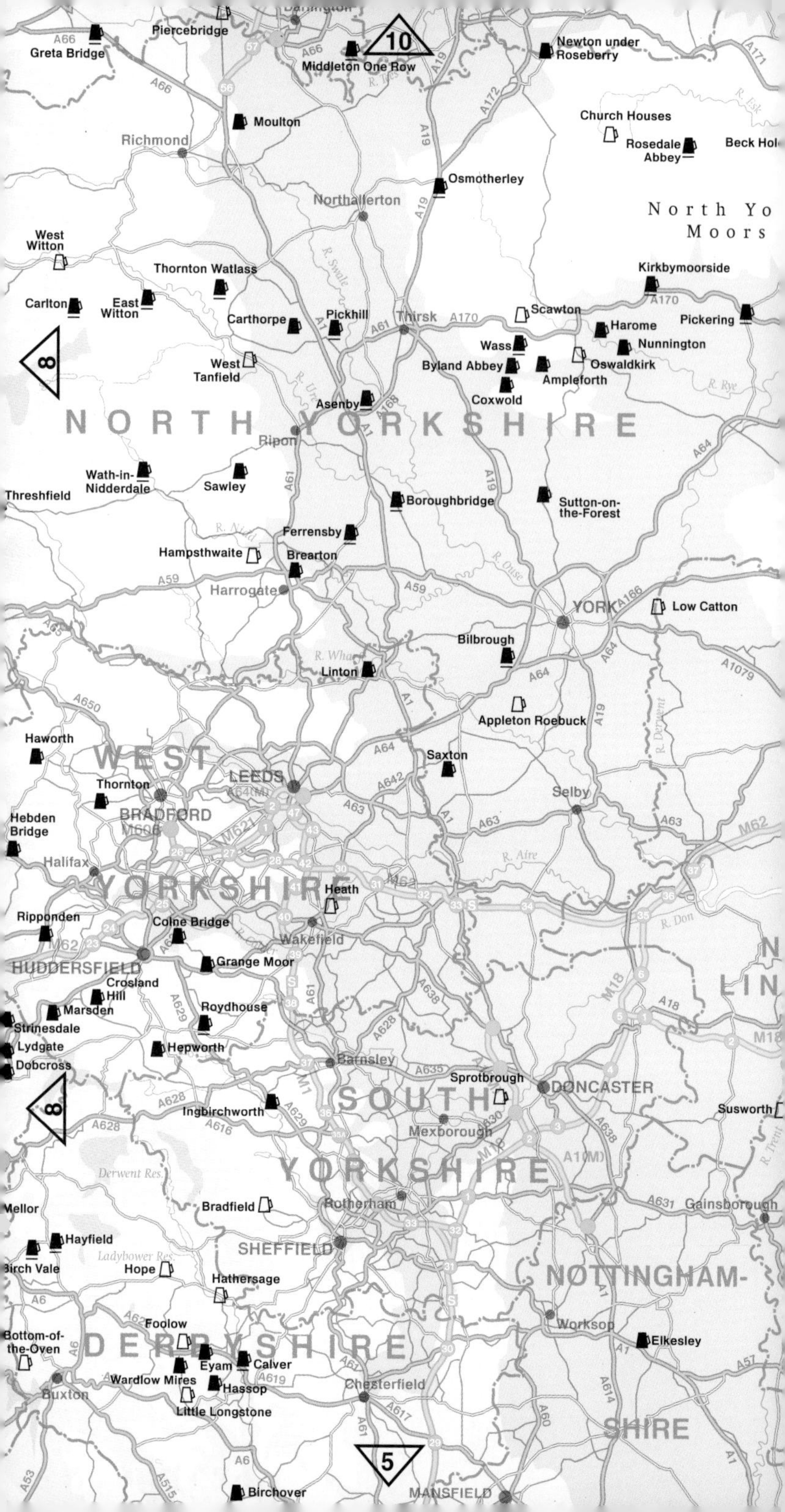

10
Piercebridge
Greta Bridge
Middleton One Row
Newton under Roseberry
Moulton
Richmond
Church Houses
Rosedale Abbey
Beck Hole
Osmotherley
Northallerton
North York Moors
West Witton
Thornton Watlass
Kirkbymoorside
Carlton
East Witton
Carthorpe
Pickhill
Thirsk
Scawton
Harome
Pickering
Wass
Nunnington
Byland Abbey
Oswaldkirk
Ampleforth
West Tanfield
Asenby
Coxwold
8
NORTH YORKSHIRE
Ripon
Wath-in-Nidderdale
Sawley
Threshfield
Boroughbridge
Sutton-on-the-Forest
Ferrensby
Hampsthwaite
Brearton
Harrogate
YORK
Low Catton
Bilbrough
Linton
Appleton Roebuck
Haworth
WEST
Saxton
Thornton
LEEDS
BRADFORD
Selby
Hebden Bridge
Halifax
YORKSHIRE
Heath
Ripponden
Colne Bridge
Wakefield
HUDDERSFIELD
Grange Moor
Crosland Hill
Marsden
Roydhouse
Strinesdale
Lydgate
Hepworth
Dobcross
Barnsley
Sprotbrough
DONCASTER
8
SOUTH
Ingbirchworth
Susworth
Mexborough
YORKSHIRE
Bradfield
Rotherham
Gainsborough
Mellor
Hayfield
SHEFFIELD
Birch Vale
Hope
NOTTINGHAM-
Hathersage
Foolow
Worksop
Bottom-of-the-Oven
DERBYSHIRE
Elkesley
Eyam
Calver
Wardlow Mires
Hassop
Buxton
Chesterfield
Little Longstone
SHIRE
5
Birchover
MANSFIELD

10
MAP 9
Main entries
Main entry with accommodation
Out & About entries
Main and Out & About entries
Main entries with accommodation, and Out & Abouts
0
5
10 miles
0
15 kms
Whitby
Robin Hood's Bay
A171
Scarborough
A170
A64
A165
Flamborough Head
Bridlington
A166
Bridlington Bay
Yorkshire Wolds
A165
EAST RIDING OF YORKSHIRE
South Dalton
A1035
A1079
Bishop Burton
A165
R. Hull
KINGSTON UPON HULL
KINGSTON UPON HULL
R. Humber
Barton-upon-Humber
Kilnsea
A15
A160
Scunthorpe
A18
M180
Grimsby
Spurn Head
Cleethorpes
A46
N.E. LINCOLNSHIRE
A173
Barnoldby le Beck
Rothwell
A18
A16
A15
A46
A1103
A631
Market Rasen
A15
Louth
Mablethorpe
The Wolds
Donington on Bain
A46
A16
A158
A158
A57
LINCOLN
LINCOLNSHIRE
A158
Raithby
A158
6
Skegness

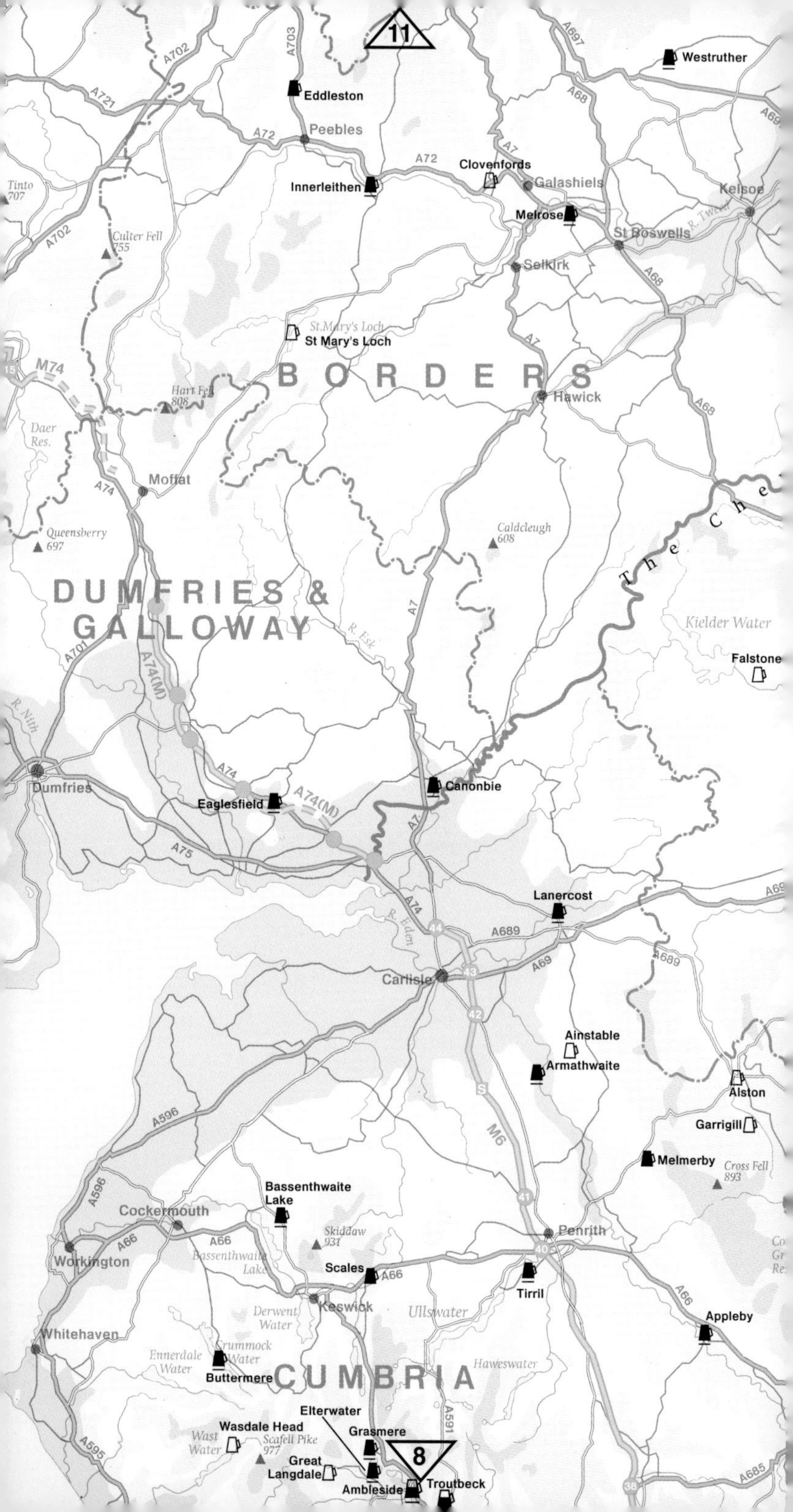

11
Westruther
Eddleston
Peebles
Innerleithen
Clovenfords
Galashiels
Melrose
Kelsoe
St Boswells
Selkirk
Tinto 707
Culter Fell 755
St.Mary's Loch
St Mary's Loch
BORDERS
Hawick
M74
Hart Fell 808
Daer Res.
Moffat
Queensberry 697
Caldcleugh 608
The Cheviots
DUMFRIES & GALLOWAY
R. Esk
Kielder Water
Falstone
R. Nith
Dumfries
Eaglesfield
Canonbie
Lanercost
R. Eden
Carlisle
Ainstable
Armathwaite
Alston
Garrigill
Melmerby
Cross Fell 893
Bassenthwaite Lake
Cockermouth
Skiddaw 931
Workington
Bassenthwaite Lake
Scales
Penrith
Tirril
Keswick
Derwent Water
Ullswater
Appleby
Whitehaven
Ennerdale Water
Crummock Water
Buttermere
CUMBRIA
Haweswater
Elterwater
Wasdale Head
Grasmere
Wast Water
Scafell Pike 977
8
Great Langdale
Ambleside
Troutbeck

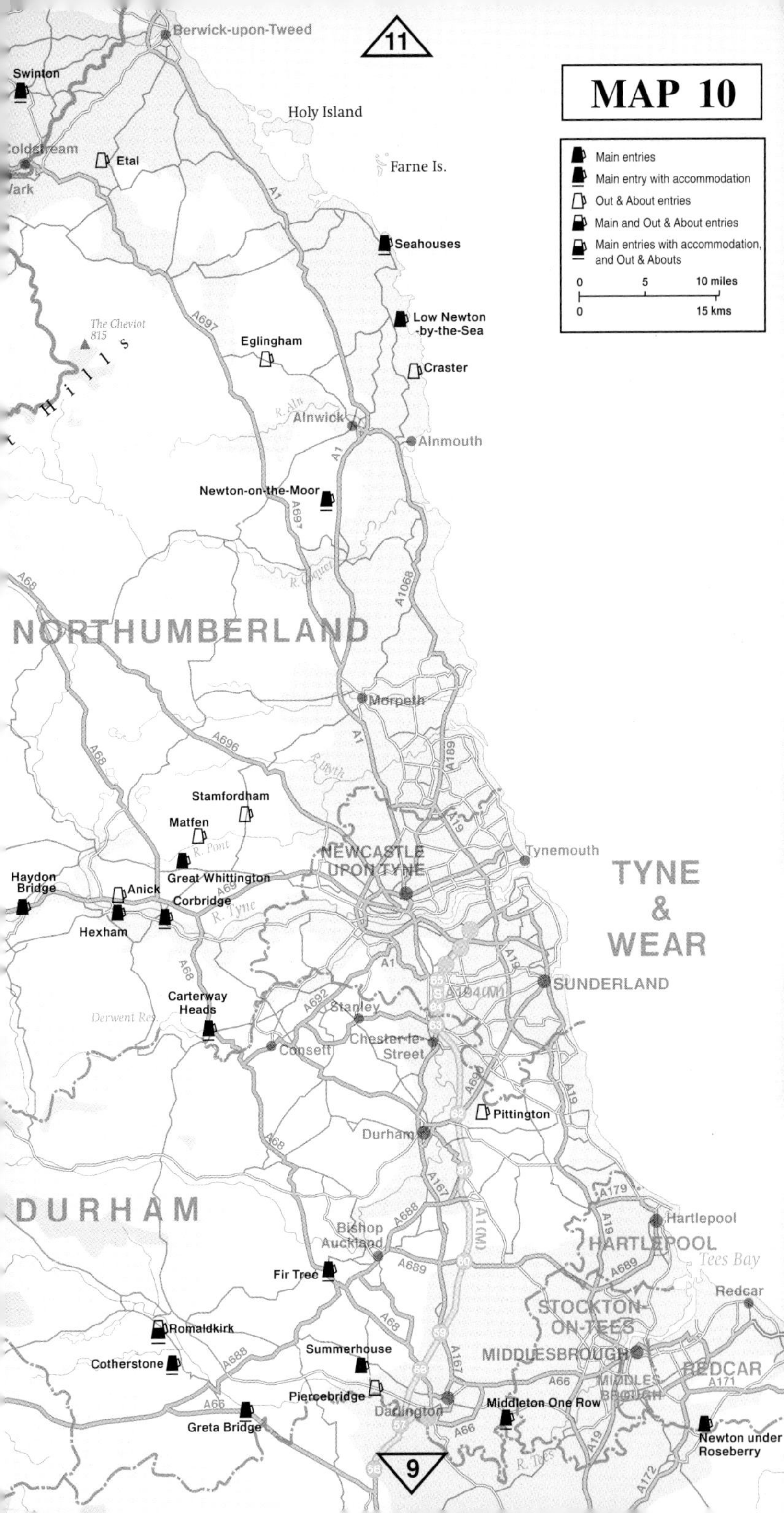

MAP 10
11
9
Main entries
Main entry with accommodation
Out & About entries
Main and Out & About entries
Main entries with accommodation, and Out & Abouts
0
5
10 miles
0
15 kms
Berwick-upon-Tweed
Swinton
Holy Island
Farne Is.
Coldstream
Etal
Wark
Seahouses
Low Newton -by-the-Sea
Craster
The Cheviot 815
Eglingham
Alnwick
Alnmouth
Newton-on-the-Moor
NORTHUMBERLAND
Morpeth
Stamfordham
Matfen
NEWCASTLE UPON TYNE
Tynemouth
TYNE & WEAR
Haydon Bridge
Anick
Great Whittington
Corbridge
Hexham
SUNDERLAND
Carterway Heads
Derwent Res.
Stanley
Consett
Chester-le-Street
Pittington
Durham
DURHAM
Bishop Auckland
Hartlepool
HARTLEPOOL
Tees Bay
Fir Tree
Redcar
STOCKTON-ON-TEES
Romaldkirk
MIDDLESBROUGH
Summerhouse
Cotherstone
REDCAR
Piercebridge
Darlington
Middleton One Row
Greta Bridge
Newton under Roseberry

MAP 11

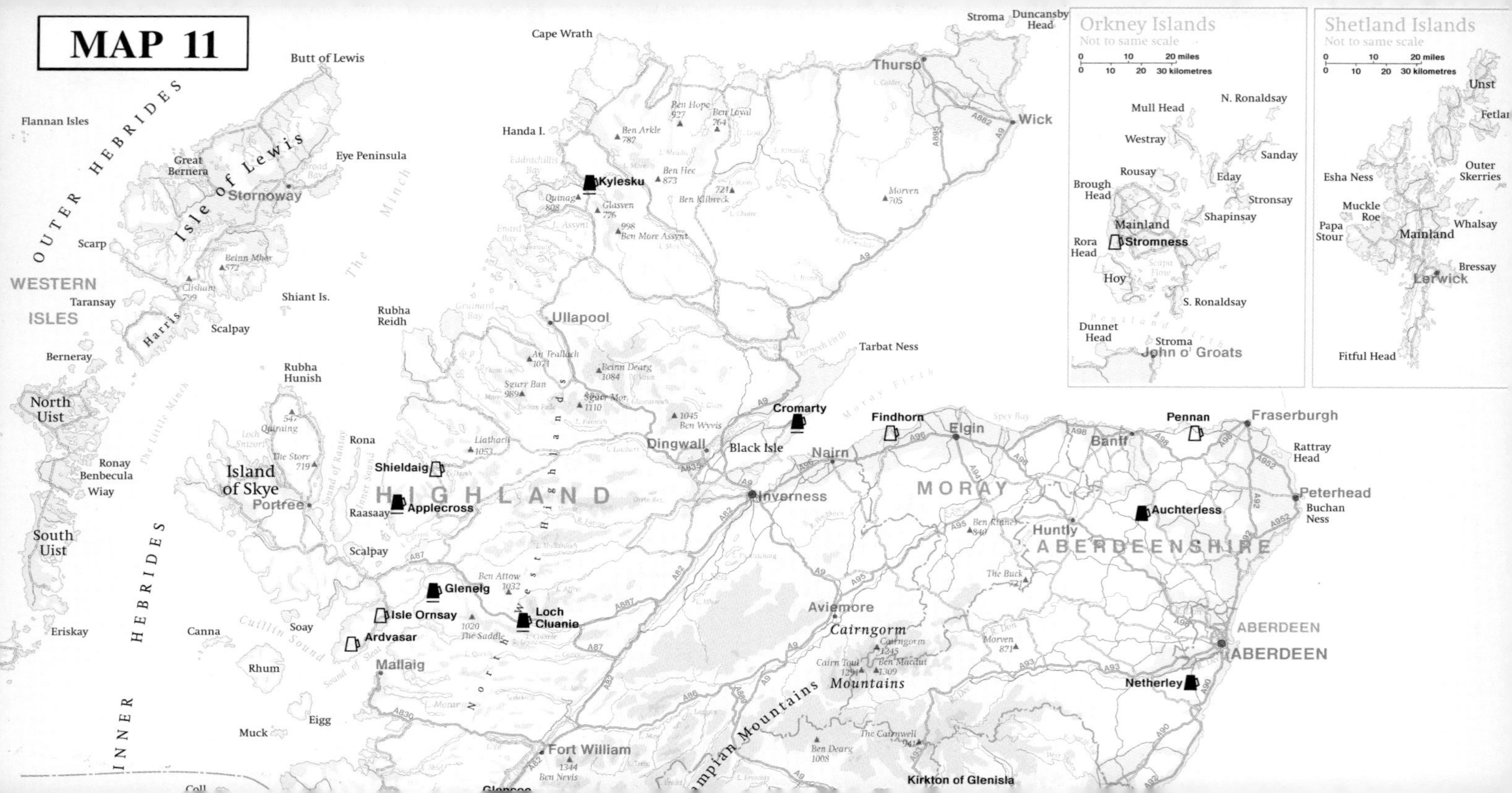

Orkney Islands
Not to same scale
0 10 20 miles
0 10 20 30 kilometres
Mull Head
N. Ronaldsay
Westray
Sanday
Rousay
Eday
Brough Head
Stronsay
Shapinsay
Mainland
Stromness
Rora Head
Hoy
S. Ronaldsay
Dunnet Head
Stroma
John o' Groats
Shetland Islands
Not to same scale
0 10 20 miles
0 10 20 30 kilometres
Unst
Fetlar
Esha Ness
Outer Skerries
Muckle Roe
Papa Stour
Mainland
Whalsay
Bressay
Lerwick
Fitful Head
Butt of Lewis
Flannan Isles
OUTER HEBRIDES
Isle of Lewis
Great Bernera
Eye Peninsula
Stornoway
Scarp
Beinn Mhor 572
Clisham 799
WESTERN ISLES
Taransay
Harris
Scalpay
Shiant Is.
Berneray
North Uist
Ronay
Benbecula
Wiay
South Uist
Eriskay
The Minch
The Little Minch
Rubha Reidh
Rubha Hunish
Rona
Quiraing
547
The Storr 719
Island of Skye
Portree
Raasaay
Scalpay
Soay
Canna
Cuillin Sound
Rhum
Eigg
Muck
Coll
INNER HEBRIDES
Cape Wrath
Handa I.
Kylesku
Quinag 808
Glasven 776
Ben More Assynt 998
Ben Arkle 787
Ben Hope 927
Ben Loyal 764
Ben Hee 873
Ben Klibreck 721
Ullapool
An Teallach 1071
Sgurr Ban 989
Beinn Dearg 1084
Sgurr Mor 1110
Ben Wyvis 1045
Liathach 1053
Shieldaig
Applecross
HIGHLAND
North West Highlands
Ben Attow 1032
Glenelg
Isle Ornsay
Ardvasar
The Saddle 1020
Loch Cluanie
Mallaig
Fort William
Ben Nevis 1344
Glencoe
Stroma
Duncansby Head
Thurso
Wick
Morven 705
Tarbat Ness
Moray Firth
Cromarty
Dingwall
Black Isle
Inverness
Nairn
Findhorn
Elgin
Spey Bay
MORAY
Banff
Pennan
Fraserburgh
Rattray Head
Peterhead
Buchan Ness
Auchterless
Huntly
ABERDEENSHIRE
Ben Rinnes 840
The Buck 721
Aviemore
Cairngorm
Cairngorm 1245
Cairn Toul 1291
Ben Macdui 1309
Mountains
Grampian Mountains
Morven 871
ABERDEEN
Netherley
The Cairnwell 941
Ben Dearg 1008
Kirkton of Glenisla
A9
A82
A87
A830
A835
A86
A887
A95
A96
A98
A93
A90
A92
A952
A941
A882
A895

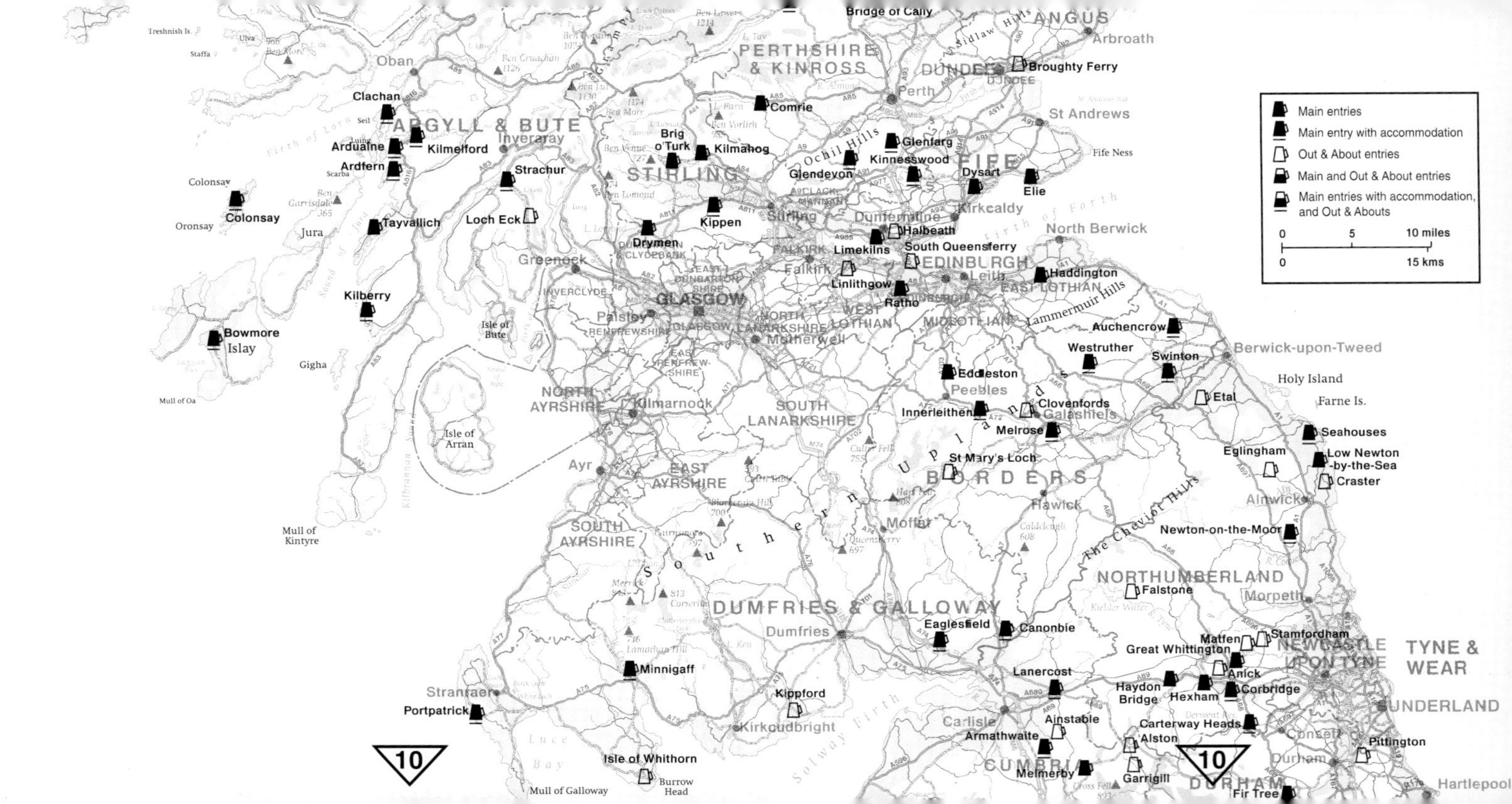

Main entries
Main entry with accommodation
Out & About entries
Main and Out & About entries
Main entries with accommodation, and Out & Abouts
0 5 10 miles
0 15 kms
10
Clachan
Arduaine
Kilmelford
Ardfern
Colonsay
Tayvallich
Kilberry
Bowmore
Islay
Strachur
Loch Eck
Brig o'Turk
Kilmahog
Comrie
Drymen
Kippen
Glendevon
Kinnesswood
Glenfarg
Dysart
Elie
Broughty Ferry
Halbeath
Limekilns
South Queensferry
Linlithgow
Ratho
Haddington
Auchencrow
Westruther
Swinton
Eddleston
Clovenfords
Innerleithen
Melrose
St Mary's Loch
Etal
Seahouses
Eglingham
Low Newton -by-the-Sea
Craster
Newton-on-the-Moor
Falstone
Eaglesfield
Canonbie
Minnigaff
Kippford
Portpatrick
Isle of Whithorn
Lanercost
Ainstable
Armathwaite
Melmerby
Alston
Garrigill
Carterway Heads
Haydon Bridge
Hexham
Corbridge
Great Whittington
Anick
Matfen
Stamfordham
Pittington
Fir Tree
Bridge of Cally
ANGUS
Arbroath
PERTHSHIRE & KINROSS
DUNDEE
Perth
St Andrews
Fife Ness
FIFE
ARGYLL & BUTE
Inveraray
Oban
STIRLING
Ochil Hills
Kirkcaldy
North Berwick
EDINBURGH
Leith
EAST LOTHIAN
Lammermuir Hills
Stirling
Falkirk
Greenock
GLASGOW
Paisley
Motherwell
WEST LOTHIAN
MIDLOTHIAN
NORTH LANARKSHIRE
SOUTH LANARKSHIRE
INVERCLYDE
EAST RENFREW-SHIRE
NORTH AYRSHIRE
Kilmarnock
Ayr
EAST AYRSHIRE
SOUTH AYRSHIRE
Isle of Bute
Isle of Arran
Mull of Kintyre
Gigha
Jura
Oronsay
Mull of Oa
Treshnish Is.
Staffa
Ulva
Peebles
Galashiels
Southern Uplands
BORDERS
Hawick
Moffat
The Cheviot Hills
Berwick-upon-Tweed
Holy Island
Farne Is.
Alnwick
NORTHUMBERLAND
Morpeth
NEWCASTLE UPON TYNE
TYNE & WEAR
SUNDERLAND
Hartlepool
Durham
DURHAM
Consett
DUMFRIES & GALLOWAY
Dumfries
Kirkcudbright
Stranraer
Luce Bay
Mull of Galloway
Burrow Head
Carlisle
CUMBRIA
Solway Firth
Firth of Forth

Report form

Pub 3

To *The Which? Guide to Country Pubs,*
FREEPOST, 2 Marylebone Road, London NW1 1YN

PUB NAME ______________________________

Address ______________________________

______________________________ Telephone ______________

Date of visit ______________________________

From my personal experience this establishment should be (please tick)

main entry ☐ 'Out and about' entry ☐ excluded ☐

Please describe what you ate and drank (with prices, if known), and give details of location, service, atmosphere etc.

Please turn over

My meal for ___ people cost £____ Value for money? yes ❑ no ❑

I am not connected in any way with the management or proprietors.

Name and address (BLOCK CAPITALS) ______________________________

Report form

Pub 3

To *The Which? Guide to Country Pubs*,
FREEPOST, 2 Marylebone Road, London NW1 1YN

PUB NAME ______________________________

Address ______________________________

______________________________ Telephone ______________

Date of visit ______________________________

From my personal experience this establishment should be (please tick)

main entry ❑ 'Out and about' entry ❑ excluded ❑

Please describe what you ate and drank (with prices, if known), and give details of location, service, atmosphere etc.

Please turn over

My meal for ___ people cost £____ Value for money? yes ❑ no ❑

I am not connected in any way with the management or proprietors.

Name and address (BLOCK CAPITALS) ________________________________

____

____

____

Report form

Pub 3

To *The Which? Guide to Country Pubs,*
FREEPOST, 2 Marylebone Road, London NW1 1YN

PUB NAME ______________________________

Address ______________________________

______________________________ Telephone ______________

Date of visit ______________________________

From my personal experience this establishment should be (please tick)

main entry ☐ 'Out and about' entry ☐ excluded ☐

Please describe what you ate and drank (with prices, if known), and give details of location, service, atmosphere etc.

Please turn over

My meal for ___ people cost £____ Value for money? yes ❑ no ❑

I am not connected in any way with the management or proprietors.

Name and address (BLOCK CAPITALS) ______________________________

____

____

____